T0211553

Lecture Notes in Artificial Intelligence   10400

Subseries of Lecture Notes in Computer Science

More information about this series at http://www.springer.com/series/1244

Wei Peng · Damminda Alahakoon
Xiaodong Li (Eds.)

AI 2017: Advances in Artificial Intelligence

30th Australasian Joint Conference
Melbourne, VIC, Australia, August 19–20, 2017
Proceedings

 Springer

Editors
Wei Peng
La Trobe University
Melbourne
Australia

Xiaodong Li
RMIT University
Melbourne
Australia

Damminda Alahakoon
La Trobe University
Melbourne
Australia

ISSN 0302-9743   ISSN 1611-3349   (electronic)
Lecture Notes in Artificial Intelligence
ISBN 978-3-319-63003-8   ISBN 978-3-319-63004-5   (eBook)
DOI 10.1007/978-3-319-63004-5

Library of Congress Control Number: 2017946064

LNCS Sublibrary: SL7 – Artificial Intelligence

Printed on acid-free paper

This Springer imprint is published by Springer Nature
The registered company is Springer International Publishing AG
The registered company address is: Gewerbestrasse 11, 6330 Cham, Switzerland

Preface

This volume encompasses the papers presented at the 30th Australasian Joint Conference on Artificial Intelligence 2017 (AI 2017), which was held during August 19–20, 2017, in Melbourne, Australia. The Australasian Joint Conference on Artificial Intelligence is an annual conference that has been dedicated to fostering research communications and collaborations among researchers in the AI community since its inception.

AI 2017 was co-hosted by RMIT University and La Trobe University and co-located with the International Joint Conference on Artificial Intelligence (IJCAI 2017). This volume covers a wide spectrum of research streams in artificial intelligence ranging from machine learning, optimization, to big data science and their practical applications. Out of 58 submissions from authors in 19 countries, there were 29 manuscripts accepted for oral presentation at AI 2017. All submissions were peer-reviewed each by three or more international Program Committee members and reviewers.

We would like to thank our international Program Committee members and reviewers for their support and contributions to AI 2017. We also acknowledge the support from RMIT University and La Trobe University for hosting this conference. The assistance and sponsorship from Springer were essential for this volume to be published in the *Lecture Notes in Artificial Intelligence* series, and we are very grateful for that.

June 2017

Wei Peng
Damminda Alahakoon
Xiaodong Li

Organization

Conference Chairs

Xiaodong Li
  (General Chair)
RMIT University, Australia

Damminda Alahakoon
  (Program Co-chair)
La Trobe University, Australia

Wei Peng
  (Program Co-chair)
La Trobe University, Australia

Best Paper Award Chair

Vic Ciesielski
RMIT University, Australia

Publicity Chairs

Kai Qin
Swinburne University of Technology, Australia

Yutao Qi
Xidian University, China

Local Organizing Committee

Yujie Wang
La Trobe University, Australia

Tharindu Bandaragoda
La Trobe University, Australia

Angus Kenny
RMIT University, Australia

Behrooz
Ghasemishabankareh
RMIT University, Australia

Webmaster

Indika Kumara
La Trobe University, Australia

Senior Program Committee

Chengqi Zhang	University of Technology, Sydney, Australia
Dianhui Wang	La Trobe University, Australia
Dongmo Zhang	University of Western Sydney, Australia
Ian Watson	University of Auckland, New Zealand
Hepu Deng	RMIT University, Australia
Jimmy Lee	The Chinese University of Hong Kong, SAR China
John Gero	University of North Carolina at Charlotte, USA
Jussi Rintanen	Aalto University, Finland
Michael Maher	University of New South Wales, Australia

Michael Sheng	Macquarie University, Australia
Reinhard Klette	Auckland University of Technology, New Zealand
Stephen Cranefield	University of Otago, New Zealand
Thomas Meyer	Centre for Artificial Intelligence Research, UKZN and CSIR Meraka, South Africa
Wray Buntine	Monash University, Australia
Naveen Chilamkurti	La Trobe University, Australia
Zhen He	La Trobe University, Australia

Program Committee

Ajendra Dwivedi	RMIT University, Australia
Andy Chun	City University of Hong Kong, SAR China
Andy Song	RMIT University, Australia
Bing Xue	Victoria University of Wellington, New Zealand
C. Maria Keet	University of Cape Town, South Africa
Chao Chen	Deakin University, Australia
Damminda Alahakoon	La Trobe University, Australia
Danchi Jiang	University of Tasmania, Australia
Daniel Schmidt	University of Melbourne, Australia
Fei Liu	La Trobe University, Australia
Fei Zheng	AUSTRAC, Australia
Haohui Chen	DATA61, Australia
Hui Ma	Victoria University of Wellington, New Zealand
Ivan Varzinczak	CNRS - Université d'Artois, France
Jie Yin	DATA61, Australia
Junfu Yin	University of Technology, Sydney, Australia
Kathryn Merrick	University of New South Wales, Australia
Ke Deng	RMIT University, Australia
Kok-Leong Ong	La Trobe University, Australia
Maolin Tang	Queensland University of Technology, Australia
Markus Wagner	The University of Adelaide, Australia
Michael Cree	University of Waikato, New Zealand
Mohamed Gaber	Birmingham City University, UK
Mohammad Nabi Omidvar	University of Birmingham, UK
Nilupulee Nathawitharana	La Trobe University, Australia
Nina Narodytska	Samsung Research, USA
Nung Kion Lee	Universiti Malaysia Sarawak, Malaysia
Partha Bhowmick	Indian Institute of Technology, Kharagpur, India
Qing Liu	DATA61, Australia
Rafal Rzepka	Hokkaido University, Japan
Ricardo Sosa	Auckland University of Technology, New Zealand
Seyedali Mirjalili	Universiti Teknologi, Malaysia
Su Nguyen	La Trobe University, Australia
Sung-Bae Cho	Yonsei University, Japan
Terence Chen	Telstra, Australia

Tharindu Bandaragoda	La Trobe University, Australia
Wei Peng	La Trobe University, Australia
Xiaodong Li	RMIT University, Australia
Yanchang Zhao	IBM, Australia
Yi Mei	Victoria University of Wellington, New Zealand
Yujie Wang	La Trobe University, Australia
Zhi-Hua Zhou	Nanjing University, China

Additional Reviewers

Achini Adikari	Mario Benevides
Addi Ait-Mlouk	Patrycja Swieczkowska
Behrooz Ghasemishabankareh	Rashmika Nawaratne
Chao Qian	Safwan Shatnawi
Daokun Zhang	Sylwia Polberg
Dinithi Nallaperuma	Wei Emma Zhang
Gang Chen	Xianzhi Wang
Hossein Ghomeshi	Xiu Susie Fang
Madhura Jayaratne	Xiuzhen Zhang
Mariam Adedoyin-Olowe	Yiming Peng

Contents

Machine Learning

Optimization

Swarm Intelligence and Evolutionary Computing

Text Mining and Linguistic Analysis

Vision and Image

Other Areas in Artificial Intelligence

Machine Learning

Context-Aware Recommender Systems Based on Item-Grain Context Clustering

Yilong Shi[✉], Hong Lin, and Yuqiang Li

School of Computer Science and Technology, Wuhan University of Technology,
Wuhan 430061, China
798266215@qq.com

Abstract. Context-aware recommender systems (CARS), aiming to further improve recommendation accuracy and user satisfaction by taking context information into account, has become the hottest research topic in the field of recommendation. Integrating context information into recommendation frameworks is challenging, owing to the high dimensionality of context information and the sparsity of the observations, which state-of-the-art methods do not handle well. We suggest a novel approach for context-aware recommendation based on Item-grain context clustering (named IC-CARS), which first extracts context clusters for each item based on K-means method, then incorporates context clusters into Matrix Factorization model, and thus helps to overcome the often encountered problem of data sparsity, scalability and prediction quality. Experiments on two real-world datasets and the complexity analysis show that IC-CARS is scalable and outperforms several state-of-the-art methods for recommending.

Keywords: Recommender systems · Context clustering · Matrix Factorization · K-means

1 Introduction

With the rapid development of information technology, it is more and more difficult for people immersed in the ocean of information to obtain information they need in time, and so the problem of "Information Overload" is raised [1]. Search engines (such as *Google*, *Baidu*, etc.) are the most common tools to help people get information, but still can't meet the personalized information needs in different backgrounds, different purposes and different periods, and thus cannot effectively solve the problem [2]. As an important research branch in the field of personalized service, recommendation system, which helps users find interest items (online goods, music, movies, services, etc.) from large amounts of data by mining the relationship between users and items, can effectively solve the problem. Among the domain of recommendation systems, context-aware recommender systems (CARS) fully utilizing contextual information to further improve recommendation accuracy and user satisfaction, have become one of the hottest topics recently [3].

Under the assumption that each rating of an item must relate to a typical context, the training process of contextual modeling is associated with the each quadruple of <user, item, context, rating>. Since the observation is sparse and the additional environmental contexts have various types resulting in a large dimensionality, the serious

© Springer International Publishing AG 2017
W. Peng et al. (Eds.): AI 2017, LNAI 10400, pp. 3–13, 2017.
DOI: 10.1007/978-3-319-63004-5_1

sparsity problem is further intensified. In recent years, many scholars [2, 4–6] have put forward a lot of approaches to solve this problem, which can be roughly divided into two categories: explicit specific contexts reduction and dimensional compression. The first requires the identification of the contextual data segments which is expensive to be determined, and the dimensionality of the explicit contexts is still large enough to present a sparsity challenge [2, 5]. While the other uses traditional dimension compression methods, such as Principal Component Analysis (PCA) and Auto-Encoder, to mine latent context factors [6] which is highly reduced relative to explicit contexts. Although the dimensional compression method can deal with the sparsity problem to a certain extent, the compression rate cannot be small enough and thus it still suffers from sparsity problem.

In order to overcome the sparsity problem, underlying the idea that the impact of contexts on item has its inner patterns, e.g., sweaters are popular in winter, but not in summer; most of the people who go to the Great Wall come from China, but a few from India, we propose to cluster context information in item-grain to abstract item-wise context clusters firstly, then incorporate them into Matrix Factorization model. In our proposed method, the item-wise context clusters are of high quality, and thus have little opportunity to intensity the sparsity problem. Additionally, on the basis of IC-CARS model, we further propose a hybrid model which integrates explicit context factors with IC-CARS, and we fortunately find that the hybrid model outperforms IC-CARS when applied some distinguishing explicit context factors. The extensive experiments show that our proposed has outstanding performance in solving data sparsity problem, and outperforms several state-of-the-art methods for recommending. Besides, complexity analysis proves the scalability, so that it can be applied to large datasets efficiently.

The remainder of the paper is organized as follows. In the next section we describe the related work. The proposed model and complexity analysis are presented in Sect. 3. Section 4 displays and analyzes the experimentresults. Finally the conclusion and future work are shown in Sect. 5.

2 Related Work

The area of CARS deals with modeling user preference and tastes by incorporating available contextual information into recommendation process. As Adomavicius et al. [7, 8] suggested, there are three main approaches to recommend items while considering context: pre-filtering, post-filtering, contextual modeling. The pre- and post-methods filter recommendation using contextual restrictions before or after the recommendation list is generated, while the contextual modeling method incorporates context into recommender framework directly. Among the three main methods, contextual modeling generally performs best [8].

In these years, the research on CARS has made a lot of progress. Chen [9] studied it earlier, behind the idea that similarity calculation should consider the context conditions, he proposed to integrate context information which is represented as a multidimensional vector model, item-grain context correlation coefficient and user-grain context similarity into collaborative filtering technology, and the proposed achieved a good result. Wang [10] and Shi [11] integrated context information into user vector and item vector, and studied CARS from the perspective of user context similarity and item context similarity. From the perspective of context similarity, Shin [12] firstly measured the similarity between the user's current context and historical context using cosine similarity, and then combined the historical context of user preferences to predict the user's preference in the current context. Adomavicius et al. [7] suggested a multi-dimensional context of user preference similarity model, which is based on the calculation of each "user-item-context" preference value to find the nearest neighbor distance from high-dimensional context data, and predict the potential context of the user preferences. Although it performs poorly in terms of computational efficiency and real-time performance, it has the advantages of recommendation accuracy and diversity.

The above research work mainly focus on the context modeling accuracy, while ignoring the sparsity problem leaded by the high dimension of context information. Recent researches have drawn increasing attention to the sparsity problem. In Baltrunas' proposed [5], circumstances and situations are modeled as explicit context factors in three difference granularity, namely item-grain, category-grain and global-grain. Although explicit context can be better explained by users and human experts, its dimension is still large enough to trigger the sparsity problem. In order to overcome the defects, Unger et al. [6] suggested to use latent context which can be automatically acquired by dimension reduction method, and they further described a novel recommendation technique that uses latent context and improves the recommendation accuracy. In their experiment, the initial size of context dimensionality is approximately 520, after the dimension reduction, the dimensionality had reduced dramatically and the final recommendation accuracy increased by nearly 20%. Although their experiment result is applausive, the compression rate cannot be small enough and thus their method still suffers from sparsity problem.

Although explicit context and latent context can reduce the dimension of context to some degree, they still cannot solve the sparsity problem well. In our research, we firstly cluster context information for each item to abstract item-wise context clusters which can express as the inner patterns within the impact of context on item, then incorporate it into recommendation framework using Matrix Factorization method. In the context clustering method, we apply elastic inner-distance and maximum cluster number on K-means algorithm, which have a great effect on the recommendation results, and due to the high quality and tiny number of item-wise context clusters, the sparsity problem is effectively solved.

3 Method

In this section, we first introduce the item-grain context clustering model based on K-means method. After that, the context-aware recommendation framework based on MF is detailly demonstrated. Finally we show the complexity analysis.

3.1 Item-Grain Context Clustering

The contextual modeling approach is known to be challenging due to the additional variety type of contextual information resulting in the expansion of its dimensionality, which further intensifies the sparsity problem. We suggest to extract context clusters for each item using K-means methods, and then assign a contextual factor parameter to each item-wise context cluster in MF based recommendation framework, in which, the contextual factor parameter promotes no opportunity for sparsity problem because the number of context clusters is very small.

To simplify modeling, we assume that the context is non-hierarchical in this paper (additionally, our model is fit for hierarchical context which is more in line with the actual needs when using hierarchical clustering methods), and we choose Euclidean Distance [13] as the distance measure function $Dis(C_e, C_f)$ describing the distance between context vector C_e and C_f. The item-grain context clustering model first extracts context training set $S_j = \{C_1, C_2, C_3, ..\}$ for each item j, and then mines context clusters for each item j. To control the quality of context clusters, we suggest some restrictions on the clustering process. Specifically, for each item j, we define P as the maximum number of context clusters, and the minimum size of cluster is defined as T_j, where $T_j = |S_j|/(2P)$, additionally, the maximum cluster intra-distance d_j is defined as the $\delta * |S_j| * (|S_j| - 1)$ ordinal number of $\{Dis(C_e, C_f)|C_e, C_f \in S_j$ and $e \neq f\}$ where $\delta \in (0, 1)$. However, to improve calculation efficiency, d_j is generally obtained by sampling. In these definitions, only P and δ are the model parameters, which are the trade-off parameters having an important influence on the quality of context clusters. Algorithm 1 describes the item-grain context clustering model based on K-means method.

Algorithm 1. Item-grain context clustering model based on K-means method.

Input: Training set S, model parameters P and ∂
Output: Context clusters O helping to form the clustering function $K_j(\ )$ for each
      item j.

1.   Extract $\{S_j \mid j = 1, 2, ..M\}$ from S

2.   **For** each S_j **do**

3.   Compute T_j and d_j

4.   **For** cluster number K from 1 to P **do**

5.   Item-wise context clusters $O_j \leftarrow$ Using K-means method on S_j

6.   Check each cluster in O_j: if all or at least T_j points in the cluster meet
    the maximum cluster intra-distance restriction.

7.   If all clusters in O_j meet the restriction in line 6, **jump to** line 9.

8.   **End For**

9. $O = O \ \ O_j$

10. **End For**

11. **Return** O

3.2 Rating Model

In this subsection, we first recall the classical Matrix Factorization (MF) model, based on which our context-aware rating model IC-CARS incorporates item-wise context clusters, and assign each context cluster a contextual factor. In [5], it is shown that modeling parameters not useful to capture the dependency of the ratings can reduce the rating accuracy. So a contextual factor plays a role of noise when it has no influence on the rating. IC-CARS has a greater opportunity to solve the problem due to that IC-CARS has a very fewer number of contextual factors than classical MF based CARS. In general, a more complex model, with more parameters, can perform better in large training set. Considering the trade-off between the amount of available training data and the model complexity, we further suggest a hybrid model adding explicit context factors to IC-CARS.

As the baseline rating model, MF only takes rating information into account. The inner idea of MF is that there are D latent factors which determine the user's preference of items. Recent researches show that MF which also considers the overall preference of users and the overall popularity of items outperforms the original MF [1]. In this paper, we choose the modified MF as the basic model, the prediction rule of MF is shown in Eq. 1

$$R_{i,j}^{\wedge} = b_i + q_j + U_i^T V_j \tag{1}$$

Where $R_{i,j,C}^{\wedge}$ represents the predictive rating value of user i for item j, b_i which is the baseline estimator of user i captures the overall preference of user i, q_j is the baseline estimator of item j, and the parameter indicates the overall popularity of item j. and D-dimensional column vectors U_i and V_j representing user-specific and item-specific latent feature vectors respectively.

Based on the prediction rule in Eq. 1, IC-CARS adds a new component to provide context-aware recommendation. It is presented in Eq. 2.

$$R_{i,j,C}^{\wedge} = b_i + q_j + U_i^T V_j + W_{j,K_j(C)} Q_{j,K_j(C)} \tag{2}$$

Where $R_{i,j,C}^{\wedge}$ represents the predicted rating of user i for item j on the condition of context C which is a t dimensional context vector $(c_1, c_2, .., c_t)^T$ expressing time, location, price factors and so on. $K_j(\bullet)$ obtained by item-grain context clustering method is the clustering function of item j, W_j is the weight vector of item j, with elements $W_{j,k}$ representing the proportion of the k-th context cluster of item j. $Q_{j,k}$ is the rating bias of the k-th context cluster for a given item j, which captures the contextual effect.

IC-CARS can handle the data sparsity problem well, while it cannot performs well when there are some context factors very sensitive to recommendation results, because IC-CARS originally is fair to every context factors. However, some context factors may have a distinguishing influence on recommendation results. For example, the influence of seasonal factor on sweater sales is much larger than the location factor. So we further suggest a hybrid model adding explicit context factors to IC-CARS. The prediction rule of the hybrid rating model is presented in Eq. 3.

$$R^{\wedge}_{i,j,C,e_1,\dots,e_d,} = b_i + q_j + U_i^T V_j + W_{j,K_j(C)} Q_{j,K_j(C)} + \sum_{l=1}^{d} E_{j,e_l} \qquad (3)$$

Where vector $(e_1,\dots,e_d)$ denotes the explicit context factors which may be very sensitive to recommendation results and can be chosen by human experts, typically, when $d = 0$, the hybrid rating model is equal to IC-CARS which not takes explicit context factors into account. E_{j,e_l} is the rating bias of a given item j under the explicit context condition e_l, e.g., if a sweater is more popular with the explicit context e_{season} = "winter", a bias value may be higher. However, in scenarios where the explicit context is missing, the bias causes no effect on the predicted rating.

In order to provide rating predictions, the variables of the models must be learned. As is shown in Eq. 4, we define an optimization problem aiming to minimize the square error between the actual rating and the predicted rating according to the prediction rule. However, to counter over-fitting problem, we add a regularization component which is controlled by the parameter λ. And to solve the optimization problem, we apply the stochastic gradient descent learning algorithm.

$$\min_{b*,q*,U*,V*,Q*,E*} \sum_{R_{i,j,C,e_1,\dots,e_d} \in R} (R_{i,j,C,e_1,\dots,e_d} - R^{\wedge}_{i,j,C,e_1,\dots,e_d})^2$$
$$+ \lambda(\|b\|^2 + \|q\|^2 + \|U\|^2 + \|V\|^2 + \|Q\|^2 + \|E\|^2) \qquad (4)$$

Where R is the training set, and $\|\bullet\|^2$ is the Frobenius Norm.

3.3 Complexity Analysis

The IC-CARS model contains two phases: the item-grain context clustering phase and the phase of incorporating item-wise context clusters and explicit context factors into MF model. The first phase is based on K-means method, whose time complexity and space complexity are $O(I * n * k * m)$ and $O(n * m)$ respectively, where n is the sample size, m is the sample dimension, and I is the number of iterations. In general, m, I, k is relatively small compared to n, so the time complexity and space complexity of K-means are all $O(n)$. As for the IC-CARS model, suppose we have L observations, N users, M items, the average number of ratings for each items is L/M, so the time complexity and space complexity of item-grain context clustering phase are all $O(L/M)$. The second phase is similar to MF model which scales linearly with the observations. Specifically, the space complexity is determined by the number of learned parameters. In Eq. 4, the number of parameters in b, q, Q, E is relatively small compared to that in U, V, so the space complexity is $O(D * (N + M))$. The time complexity of each iteration is determined by the number of observations, and in each iteration, all parameters need to be updated, so the time complexity is $O(D * (N + M) * L)$, in which D, N, M is relatively small compared to L. This complexity analysis demonstrates that our proposed model scales linearly with the observations and can be applied efficiently in large datasets.

4 Experimental Evaluation

In this section, we firstly describe the experimental datasets, and then we show the effectiveness comparison with other state-of-the-art approaches. After that, we analyze the impact of trade-off parameters in item-grain context clustering. Finally, the experiment of exploiting the effect of explicit context factors is presented.

4.1 Experimental Datasets

We evaluate our proposed model on two real-world datasets. The first dataset is *TencentWeibo* dataset, which is provided by *Tencent*Weibo and released in 2012 KDD Cup. The dataset contains almost 2 million active users, 6000 items and 300 million historical records, and also includes a wealth of social networks, user labels, item categories, item tags and other rich contextual information. Additionally, we also apply some derived attributes, such as time of week (weekend or weekday), time of day (day or night), time of year (holidays or non-holidays). However, such a large data set has far exceeded the laboratory's computing power. After data cleaning and extraction, we get a smaller dataset. The second dataset we use is *MBookCrossing*, which is firstly used in [14] and derived from real-world dataset *BookCrossing*. Apart from 1149780 valid ratings from 278858 users on 271379 books, we obtain abundant contextual information, e.g., time factors similar to the derived attributes of the first dataset, location (office, home, school, or restaurant), surrounding environment (e.g., visual environment, sound environment and space environment), status information (recreation, work, or study), etc. The summary of the datasets is shown in Table 1.

Table 1. The summary of the datasets

Dataset	Ratings	Users	Items	Contextual factors
TencentWeibo	391283	12574	3724	12
MBookCrossing	1149780	278858	271379	8

4.2 Effectiveness Comparison

In order to evaluate the effectiveness of our proposed, we compare the following state-of-the-art models:

1. MF: regular Matrix Factorization model without fusing context information.
2. CAMF-C [5]: A matrix factorization technique for context aware recommendation in global-grain, which assume that each contextual condition has a global influence on all ratings.
3. CAMF-CC [5]: Similar to CAMF-C, while the contextual influence is category-wise.
4. CAMF-CI [5]: Similar to CAMF-C, while the contextual influence is item-wise.
5. LCMF [6]: A latent matrix factorization context-aware recommendation model based on PCA.
6. IC-CARS: our proposed model based on item-grain context clustering.

In the comparison experiment, we use 80:20 split ratio for training and testing, and repeat each split 5 times. We use cross-validation for calibration, the learning ratio we set is 0.001, the regularization parameter λ is selected from {0.0005, 0.01, 0.05, 0.1, 0.2, 0.4, 0.8, 1.2}, the maximum number of context clusters P is selected from {5, 10, 15, 20, 25, 30, 35}, the elastic parameter δ is selected form {0.1, 0.2, 0.3, 0.4, 0.5, 0.6, 0.7, 0.8, 0.9}. We employ RMSE for assessing the quality of the recommendation in the case of $D = 10$, $D = 15$ and $D = 20$, and Table 2 displays the comparison results.

Table 2. RMSE of the compared models

Models	TencentWeibo			MBookCrossing		
	10	15	20	10	15	20
MF	0.2681	0.2675	0.2683	0.9121	0.9115	0.9123
CAMF-C	0.2313	0.2315	0.2327	0.8818	0.8809	0.8827
CAMF-CC	0.2378	0.2389	0.2387	0.8849	0.8861	0.8871
CAMF-CI	0.2427	0.2421	0.2431	0.8751	0.8755	0.8767
LCMF	0.2307	0.2302	0.2305	0.8747	0.8742	0.8745
IC-CARS	**0.2156**	**0.2155**	**0.2159**	**0.8626**	**0.8625**	**0.8629**

From Table 2, we can observe that the above MF based context-aware recommendation models significantly outperform the regular MF model without fusing context information, which further prove the effectiveness of incorporating context information in MF model. As for the three homogeneous context-aware recommendation models, CAMF-C, CAMF-CC and CAMF-CI, which fuse explicit context factors in different granularities, behave differently on different datasets. Specifically, CAMF-C which is coarsest and assume that each contextual condition has a global influence on all ratings, performs best on *TencentWeibo* dataset, while CAMF-CI, the most grained, performs best on *MBookCrossing* dataset. Compared with the three explicit context factors fusing models, LCMF performs better, indicating that using latent contexts can improve the accuracy to some extent, which mainly because latent contexts can reduce the opportunity for data sparsity problem. Fortunately, we discover that IC-CARS performs best within the compared models. The significant performance demonstrates that item-wise inner context clusters hidden in contextual information has a good effect on recommendation results, and it further show the effectiveness of IC-CARS.

4.3   Impact of Trade-off Parameters P and δ

In IC-CARS model, trade-off parameters P and δ play an important role in controlling the quality the item-wise context clusters. Specifically, P controls the maximum number of context clusters for each item, δ controls the maximum cluster intra-distance. In general, the smaller P and δ, the more grained the model. However, there is a trade-off between model granularity and sample sparsity. In this experiment, we probe the impact of trade-off parameters P and δ. The experiment setting remains

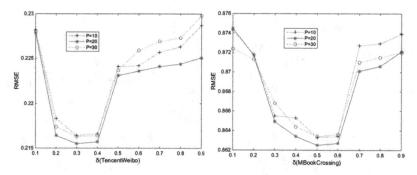

Fig. 1. Impact of trade-off parameters P and δ

the same as the comparison experiment in the last subsection, except that we fix the regularization parameter λ equal to 0.01, set $D = 15$ and select P from $\{10, 20, 30\}$. Figure 1 show the experiment results.

Form Fig. 1, we can discovery that when δ increases with the initial value 0.1, RMSE gradually decrease (the lower the better), however, when it reach a certain threshold (specifically, 0.3 for *TencentWeibo* and 0.5 for *MBookCrossing* observed from Fig. 1), RMSE starts to increase, which mainly because that a lower value for δ make the model more grained, while a higher value make the model coarser. However, there is a trade-off between the model granularity and the sample sparsity. Additionally, Fig. 1 tells us that P is also a trade-off parameter, while is more stable than δ. Specifically, $P = 20$ is most suitable both on *TencentWeibo* and on *MBookCrossing*, and the performance difference caused by P is much smaller than δ.

4.4   The Effect of Explicit Context Factors

In order to probe the effectiveness of the hybrid model which fuses explicit context factors with IC-CARS, we select some context factors, such as *Time of week*, *Time of day*, *Time of year*, and *Location*, as explicit context factors, additionally, for *TencentWeibo* dataset, we also treat *Social relation* as an explicit context factor, while for *MBookCrossing* dataset, *Status* factor is also selected. In the experiment, we compare the RMSE performance for the hybrid model when using different single explicit context factor, and we also compare the hybrid model with IC-CARS which is denoted as *None*. To simply the complexity, we set D = 15, λ = 0.01, and the rest experimental configuration remains the same as the experiment in Subsect. 4.2.

The experimentresults are shown in Fig. 2, from which we can observe that explicit context factors have a significant impact on recommendation results. For *TencentWeibo* dataset, when using *Social relation* as explicit context factor, the RMSE of the hybrid model is lowest (the lower the better). While for *MBookCrossing* dataset, *Status* factor is most suitable. However, when using some other explicit context factors, such as *Time of day*, *Location* for *TencentWeibo*, and *Time of year* for *MBookCrossing*, the performance of the hybrid model is reduced a lot, which mainly because that mean-ingless explicit context factors may trigger the problem of sparsity. What's more, the

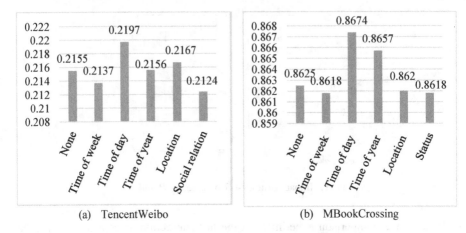

(a) TencentWeibo   (b) MBookCrossing

Fig. 2. RMSE performance for the hybrid model

huge difference hidden in Fig. 2 tell us that when we apply some distinguishing explicit context factors in the hybrid model, the performance improvement may be great, while meaningless explicit context factors can also reduce the performance.

5 Conclusion and Future Work

In this paper, based on the intuition that the impact of context on item has its inner patterns affecting the behavior of users to items, we firstly present a novel item-grain context clustering method which mines context clusters for each item, and then we incorporate context clusters into Matrix Factorization model to provide context-aware recommendation. The experiment results show that our proposed outperforms the state-of-the-art baseline models, and the complexity analysis indicates that it is scalable to large datasets. Additionally, in view of the fact that our proposed cannot handle distinguished explicit context factors well, we further propose a hybrid model adding explicit context factors to IC-CARS, and the relevant experimentresults show that the hybrid model outperforms IC-CARS when applied some distinguished explicit context factors. However, how to select and recognize distinguished explicit factors is still a problem to be solved, which is worthy of further study and will be the focus of our next research.

References

1. Ricci, F., Rokach, L., Shapira, B.: Recommender Systems Handbook. Springer, New York (2011)
2. Wang, L.C., Meng, X.W., Zhang, Y.J.: Context-aware recommender systems. J. Softw. **23**, 1–20 (2012)

3. Natarajasivan, D., Govindarajan, M.: Location based context aware user interface recommendation system. In: International Conference on Informatics and Analytics, Pondicherry, pp. 78–83. ACM (2016)
4. Karatzoglou, A., Amatriain, X., Baltrunas, L.: Multiverse recommendation: n-dimensional tensor factorization for context-aware collaborative filtering. In: ACM Conference on Recommender Systems, Barcelona, pp. 79–86. ACM (2010)
5. Baltrunas, L., Ludwig, B., Ricci, F.: Matrix factorization techniques for context aware recommendation. In: ACM Conference on Recommender Systems, Chicago, pp. 301–304. ACM (2011)
6. Unger, M., Bar, A., Shapira, B.: Towards latent context-aware recommendation systerms. J. Knowl.-Based Syst. **104**, 165–178 (2016)
7. Adomavicius, G., Sankaranarayanan, R., Sen, S.: Incorporating contextual information in recommender systems using a multidimensional approach. J. ACM Trans. Inf. Syst. **23**, 103–145 (2005)
8. Adomavicius, G., Tuzhilin, A.: Context-aware recommender systems. In: ACM Conference on Recommender Systems, Lausanne, pp. 335–336. ACM (2010)
9. Chen, A.: Context-aware collaborative filtering system: predicting the user's preference in the ubiquitous computing environment. In: Strang, T., Linnhoff-Popien, C. (eds.) LoCA 2005. LNCS, vol. 3479, pp. 244–253. Springer, Heidelberg (2005). doi:10.1007/11426646_23
10. Wang, L.C., Meng, X.W., Zhang, Y.J., Shi, Y.C.: New approaches to mood-based hybrid collaborative filtering. In: 2010 Workshop on CAMRa 2010, pp. 28–33. ACM, New York (2010)
11. Shi, Y., Larson, M., Hanjalic, A.: Mining mood-specific movie similarity with matrix factorization for context-aware recommendation. In: Proceedings of the CAMRa 2010, pp. 34–40. ACM, New York (2010)
12. Shin, D., Lee, J.W., Yeon, J., Lee, S.G.: Context-aware recommendation by aggregating user context. In: Proceedings of the CEC 2009, pp. 423–430. IEEE, Washington (2009)
13. Kuzelewska, U.: Clustering algorithms in hybrid recommender system on MovieLens data. J. Stud. Logic Gramm. Rhetor. **37**, 125–139 (2014)
14. Gao, Q.L., Ling, G., Yang, J.F.: A preference elicitation method based on users' cognitive behavior for context-aware recommender system. J. Chin. J. Comput. **9**, 1767–1776 (2015)

Competitive Reinforcement Learning in Atari Games

Mark McKenzie[1]([✉]), Peter Loxley[2], William Billingsley[2],
and Sebastien Wong[1]

[1] Defence Science and Technology Group, Adelaide, SA, Australia
mark.colin.mckenzie@gmail.com
[2] University of New England, Armidale, NSW, Australia

Abstract. This research describes a study into the ability of a state
of the art reinforcement learning algorithm to learn to perform multiple tasks. We demonstrate that the limitation of learning to performing
two tasks can be mitigated with a competitive training method. We show
that this approach results in improved generalization of the system when
performing unforeseen tasks. The learning agent assessed is an altered
version of the *DeepMind* deep Q–learner network (DQN), which has been
demonstrated to outperform human players for a number of Atari 2600
games. The key findings of this paper is that there were significant degra-
dations in performance when learning more than one game, and how this
varies depends on both similarity and the comparative complexity of the
two games.

Keywords: Reinforcement learning · DQN · Atari

1   Introduction

Reinforcement Learning is a distinct area within the broader fields of machine
learning and artificial intelligence, utilising learning through action principles
against its understanding of the environment, in order to choose the best course
of action given some interpreted state, to achieve maximum long term reward
[11]. Iteratively the reinforcement learning approach investigates its available
actions and after some period of searching, refines a course of actions to achieve
its objective. Recent progress in the application of reinforcement learning with
deep networks has led to the *DeepMind* deep Q–learner network (DQN) [8],
which can autonomously learn to play Atari video games [1,7] at or above the
level of expert humans [10]. This system was able to consistently and con-
temptibly outperform a skilled human player across a variety of games with
different game objectives, and was shown to learn the same high level strategies
adopted by expert human players. As a result the DQN is considered to be the
state of the art approach for reinforcement learning.

While DQNs were demonstrated to outperform human players at Atari
games, one limitation is that the DQN agents received specialist training on

© Springer International Publishing AG 2017
W. Peng et al. (Eds.): AI 2017, LNAI 10400, pp. 14–26, 2017.
DOI: 10.1007/978-3-319-63004-5_2

a single game. Whereas human agents are able learn and play multiple games. The problem of interest in our research is the ability of a DQN agent to perform multiple tasks, which we will assess through its ability to learn multiple Atari games.

Previous research into reinforcement learning agents performing multiple tasks has created the technique known as *distilling*, which was first presented by [2] and later adapted by [3] for neural networks. Using this approach DQN agents are first trained on individual games and then fused together to form one agent which applies to both games [9].

Recent work has demonstrated that when learning two tasks sequentially a DQN will suffer from catastrophic forgetting [4]. Where the process of learning a second task will destroy the network weights associated with the first task. This issue with sequential learning can be mitigated using elastic weight consolidation, where weights that are important for performing the first task are protected from large alterations when learning the second task [4].

The training method we propose is to simultaneously learn two games, effectively 'competing' for representational space within the neural network. This differs from the original *DeepMind* DQN [8] where the entire representational space of the neural network was *specialized* for a single game.

An interesting research question is how the representational space of the neural network will be allocated in a competitive learning environment; will the representational space be shared or segregated for the two tasks? An example of this being how well can the DQN agent perform at both Breakout, and Space Invaders; where one game is required to avoid falling objects, and another is required to hit and return falling objects. Our hypothesis is that the DQN will suffer significantly when learning competing tasks. The full extent of this detriment to performance being a function of the differences in the tasks at hand. A corollary supposition being that the architecture will increasingly segregate expressive power across the network for the alternate tasks as a function of the perceived differences in action for reward. This supposition is corroborated by success of the *distilling* approach [9] where a fuzed network is formed from two individual networks.

Another hypothesis is that a DQN agent that is trained in a competitive environment will generalise to new unforeseen tasks better than a specialist DQN agent that is trained on a single task.

Our contribution is an evaluation of one DQN agent acting on two environments, and this differs from [9] where two agents learning on separate environments are combined, and [4] where one agent acts and learns on a sequence of environments.

2   Methodology and Experimentation

The data used for training and testing was presented in [7,8] in which Atari 2600 games are used for DQN performance evaluation. For the purposes of this research pairs of games were selected according to different concepts of which

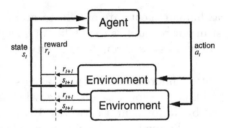

Fig. 1. The competitive reinforcement learning paradigm of interpreting the optimal action to receive reward for the current state, adapted from [11]

two are shown here; a pair of similar games i.e. functionally similar objectives and reward schemes, and a pair of high performing games i.e. those which the original code base easily converged on a suitable reward strategy. A common learning agent was then expected to learn both environment pairs competitively as depicted in Fig. 1. A baseline of performance was completed to ensure that the changes made to the code to assess multiple games did not alter its ability to converge to a similar performance as per the original research.

2.1   Alterations to the Deep Q-Learner Code

Due to the fundamental requirement to maintain similarity in learning approach with the original code base, a large portion of the code was necessarily kept identical to that provided [5]. However, some code alterations were made to functions responsible for training and testing of the architectures, and in some cases significant code changes were required to allow dual game learning. Fundamentally, the code base initialises two game environments and then alternates between their episodes to build the training database with equal weighting. The issue then arises where the two games selected do not necessarily have the same scoring range.

During the evaluation of performance for the delayed reward phase of learning, each competitive game is processed equally as was done in the original code. The total reward of each game is then normalized by the maximum score respectively observed as to remove bias on games with higher possible scores and accumulated for the decision as to improvement in the agent. This allows relative improvement of one game to supersede a smaller relative decrease in performance of another.

3   Experimental Results

The following section details the analysis results for the two presented scenarios consisting of a pair of similar games, and a pair of high performing games. The results presented show the relative performance decrease caused by competing environment learning as well as how well the learnt competitive agent then performed against unseen games. All comparisons are made relative to the performance measured by the original research presented by Mnih et al. [8].

3.1   Similar Games

Initially we will discuss the competitive training of two similar games within a common DQN architecture. It is noted that a neural network architecture is required to express a high level functional description of a task within the sequence of neurons of the network, and the success or otherwise in terms of performance lies in its ability to capture that high level function. Within this research, the fundamental question is how competing tasks affect that ability. As such, the first scenario to be applied in this competitive sense is the simultaneous learning of the classic game *Space Invaders* and a very similar game called *Demon Attack*. Both games require the player at the bottom of the screen to fire upwards to destroy descending targets, whilst avoiding being hit by return fire coming down the screen from only a subset of those targets. The motion of the targets and the absence of shields in *Demon Attack* are the only discernable differences between the games.

Under this applied competitive scenario it is hypothesised that there will be only a minor decrease in performance overall, due to the fact that the network is only required to represent some small high level differences between the games within the nodes of the network. The original code base was able to get a score of 121.5% that of human level performance for *Space Invaders*, and 294.2% for *Demon Attack*.

The scenario consisting of competitively playing the similar games of *Space Invaders* and *Demon Attack* within a single DQN architecture has been run, and the resulting performance against these two games is shown below in Figs. 2 and 3 respectively, at discrete stages of the learning process.

The network was able to achieve a mean score of 846.3 in the game *Space Invaders* whilst also achieving an average score of 4684.3 at *Demon Attack*. This is a reduction of approximately half for both games, 42.8% and 48.2% of the original scores respectively. Additionally the DQN agent was still able to beat the human score in *Demon Attack* by a reasonable margin (138%); however the agent was not able to beat the score of a human player in the game *Space Invaders*, only managing to achieve 51% that of the human. Despite this reduction in performance for these specific games, it is expected that the ability to generalise the solution to other games is improved given more diverse sampling of inputs.

A comparison against other games which are compatible with the network are provided in Table 1. Here we are interested in the *generalisability* of an agent to perform an unforeseen task; the ability to receive reward on games that it was not trained on. Table 1 shows the generalisability of the competitive DQN agent (trained on *Space Invaders* and *Demon Attack*) has increased from the original specialist DQN agent (trained on *Space Invaders*). In many cases dramatic increases were observed, the largest was over 15000 times better performance. The remaining games also displayed significant improvement due to the competitive training method, at the expense of performance on the game of *Space*

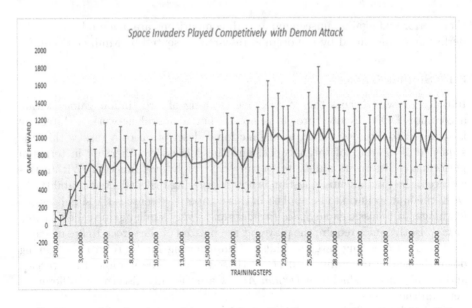

Fig. 2. Measured performance of the game Space Invaders across the competitive Reinforcement Learning process of Space Invaders and Demon Attack

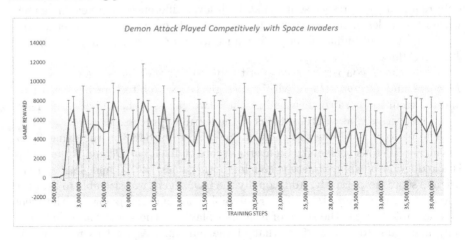

Fig. 3. Measured performance of the game Demon Attack across the competitive Reinforcement Learning process of Space Invaders and Demon Attack

Invaders. Hence, by sacrificing some performance, in this case approximately half, the overall ability to play many games is substantially improved. The only exceptions to this being the games *Breakout* and *Freeway*, which showed no ability to play the game by either network. As such the primary hypothesis of this research has been shown through this example, that competitive training of a DQN agent would result in better general performance at unseen tasks, at the expense of specific ability at a single trained task. Further to this, it is noted the

Table 1. Comparison of game scores obtained by different agents for several Atari games. The first column is a expert human agent. The second column is original specialist DQN agent when applied to the game it specializes in. The third column is a specialist Space Invaders DQN agent when applied to unforeseen games. The forth column is a competitive DQN agent (trained on Space Invaders and Demon Attack) when applied to other games. The fifth column is the performance of the competitive DQN compared to the original DQN. The sixth column is improvement of the competitive DQN over the specialist DQN in being able to generalise to unforeseen games.

Game	Human	Original DQN ($\pm\sigma$)	Specialist DQN ($\pm\sigma$)	Competitive DQN ($\pm\sigma$)	Performance (% Original)	Generalisability (% Increase)
Asteroids	13157	1629 ($\pm$542)	0.0 ($\pm$0.0)	188.7 ($\pm$255.6)	11.6%	100.0%
Atlantis	29028	85641 ($\pm$17600)	4050.0 ($\pm$1234.8)	5066.7 ($\pm$1411.1)	5.9%	25.1%
Bowling	154.8	42.4 ($\pm$88)	23.9 ($\pm$8.7)	29.9 ($\pm$0.6)	70.5%	24.9%
Breakout	31.8	401.2 ($\pm$26.9)	0.0 ($\pm$0.4)	0.0 ($\pm$0.2)	0.0%	0.0%
Demon attack	3401	9711 ($\pm$2406)	103.0 ($\pm$54.3)	4684.3 ($\pm$2547.3)	48.2%	4447.9%
Freeway	29.6	30.3 ($\pm$0.7)	0.0 ($\pm$0.0)	0.0 ($\pm$0.0)	0.0%	0.0%
Name this game	4076	7257 ($\pm$547)	287.0 ($\pm$269.9)	718.7 ($\pm$390.6)	9.9%	150.4%
Q'bert	13455	10596 ($\pm$3294)	1.7 ($\pm$9.1)	260.8 ($\pm$47.7)	2.5%	15549.8%
Space invaders	1652	1976 ($\pm$893)	1785.0 ($\pm$607.6)	846.3 ($\pm$279.7)	42.8%	−52.6%
Up'n down	9082	8456 ($\pm$3162)	1239.3 ($\pm$745.2)	2039.0 ($\pm$763.8)	24.1%	64.5%

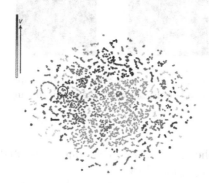

Fig. 4. Network analysis of estimated game reward using the t-SNE technique for the Neural Network trained competitively for the games Space Invaders and Demon Attack

increased ability at some of these games could be due to some small similarity in game play to both *Space Invaders* and *Demon Attack*. For example *Atlantis*; but other games such as *Bowling or Q'bert* which have no similarity to either game showed significant improvement due to competitive learning.

A corollary hypothesis specific to this example of *Similar Games* was that the representative space of the network was capable of capturing the required information to play each game due to the similarity of the games. Figure 4 shows that the network has in fact retained the ability to predict high reward states of the game, where the state information contained within the screen has been clustered by similarities, and predictive of reward according to the clustered region. This corresponds to the findings of the original *DQN* network, except what is also shown is that the network representation has also segregated between the two games, as seen in Fig. 5, where the graphical representations shown have

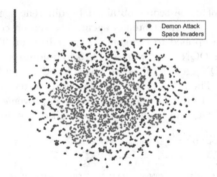

Fig. 5. Network analysis of game type using the t-SNE technique for the Neural Network trained competitively for the games Space Invaders and Demon Attack

Fig. 6. High reward states for the games Space Invaders and Demon Attack trained under competitive DQN conditions, showing the similarity in game state for the high predicted reward

been generated using the visualization techniques presented by Van der Maaten and Hinton [6] as per the original research.

The final observation to note from the analysis of the competitive training of similar games is that qualitative similarities between the games has also been clustered, shown in Fig. 4 by the blue circle, according to similar predictions of reward as shown in Fig. 6, where the network has determined a game strategy of clearing an area on the left of screen and attacking from one side to minimise the chance of being hit by return fire. Given this similar strategy being applicable to both games, it is not surprising that the network was able to perform relatively well in both cases.

3.2   High Performing Games

Consider the case of two high performing games; games in which the original DQN easily learnt an optimal strategy and dramatically beat the scores of a human player. These games are performing at this high standard due to the inherent simplistic state-action relationship. Two such games being *Boxing* and *Robotank*, where the original code base was able to get a score of 1707.9% that of human level performance for *Boxing*, and 509.0% for *Robotank*. Under this condition of competitive training for the games *Boxing* and *Robotank* it is hypothesised that after competitive training a moderate decrease in performance will be observed, as there is still considerable space within the architecture to represent and interpret the state of the two games. However their actions space is significantly different as are the input signals, for example the game *Boxing* requires the DQN to position the player at a distance to the opponent by moving along two axes, and strike at an opportune moment to minimise the number of hits taken and maximise hits landed. The response has translational invariance, i.e. indifferent to where on the image the players may be, with the exception of being near the edge which restricts movement. In contrast, the game *Robotank* pans left and right in order to find the enemy based on a radar guidance of enemy locations, and fire upon them without being destroyed, i.e. quickly lining up the target with the crosshairs. These are very different game objectives, particularly when considering the previous scenario discussed. Given this, the hypothesis is that the network will be required to prioritise areas of the architecture towards specific tasks, effectively dividing up the expressive power of the network, and as a result, the performance of each game and the rate of convergence to an optimal solution will suffer.

Again the scenario consisting of competitively playing the games *Boxing* and *Robotank* within a single DQN architecture has been run, and the resulting performance against these two games are shown below in Figs. 7 and 8.

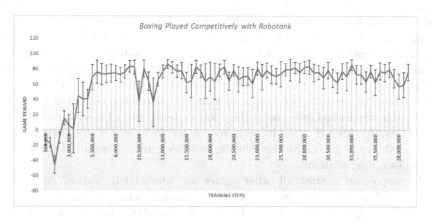

Fig. 7. Measured performance of the game Boxing across the competitive Reinforcement Learning process of Robotank and Boxing

The network was able to achieve a score of 73.7 in the game *Boxing* whilst also achieving a score of 1.4 at *Robotank*. What is of interest here is that the score achieved for *Boxing* is actually higher than what was reported by the original research, suggesting that the competitive training has actually improved the network at its ability to play *Boxing*. However the difference in score is within the confidence interval and hence is not a statistically significant difference. In

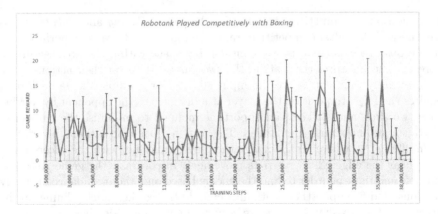

Fig. 8. Measured performance of the game Robotank across the competitive Reinforcement Learning process of Robotank and Boxing

contrast to this, the score achieved at the game *Robotank* has suffered considerably; an approximate reduction of 97%. As was seen in previous analysis, the ability to determine a strategy is critical to overall reward obtained by the network. Comparing the game play of this competitively trained network against *Robotank* and *Boxing* has shown that the same optimal strategy of pushing the opponent into a corner for *Boxing* is found, and hence the high reward obtained. However, this has resulted in a strategy for *Robotank* of simply going around in circles and firing repeatedly, with no attempts to line up a target, with the opponents eventually landing a hit. This is a poor strategy and results in the exceedingly low score. What this suggests is that the network has been unable to learn different strategies for these games, and perhaps that it is unable to differentiate between the two states, or that the short term reward of the game *Boxing* has dominated over the slightly longer term reward mechanism of *Robotank*. Despite this reduction in performance for *Robotank*, it is again expected that the ability to generalise the solution to other games is improved given more diverse sampling of inputs.

A comparison against all other games are provided in Table 2. What the analysis of the remaining games, not seen during training for the competitive case of the high performing games *Boxing* and *Robotank*, has shown is a highly polarized generalisability. In many cases, a dramatic improvement in the ability of the network to gain reward was found; for example the games *Atlantis, Battle Zone, Bowling, Crazy Climber, Gravitar, James Bond, Private Eye, Tutankham* and *Wizard of Wor*. In contrast, the games *Beam Rider, Centipede, Double Dunk, Frostbite, H.E.R.O., Kung Fu Master, Name This Game, Q'Bert* and *Seaquest* all showed solid decreases in generalisability, with the remaining games showing minor change to generalisability. What is immediately noticed from this list is the fact that these games are fundamentally different, neither the improved or detrimental generalisability cases follow a pattern, simply that the learnt strategy of pushing to one side of the screen and pushing the fire button either applies

Table 2. Comparison of game scores obtained by the competitively learnt agent against Boxing and Robotank with the original single game learning scenario of Boxing

Game	Human	Original DQN ($\pm\sigma$)	Specialist DQN ($\pm\sigma$)	Competitive DQN ($\pm\sigma$)	Performance (% Original)	Generalisability (% Increase)
Alien	6875	3069 ($\pm$1093)	140.0 ($\pm$0)	130.0 ($\pm$23.3)	4.2 %	−7.1 %
Amidar	1676	739.5 ($\pm$3024)	34.8 ($\pm$7.5)	2.1 ($\pm$0.3)	0.3 %	−94.0 %
Asteroids	13157	1629 ($\pm$542)	0.0 ($\pm$0)	0.0 ($\pm$0.0)	0.0 %	-
Atlantis	29028	85641 ($\pm$17600)	1793.3 ($\pm$488.4)	2786.7 ($\pm$1096.9)	3.3 %	55.4 %
Bank heist	734.4	429.7 ($\pm$650)	0.0 ($\pm$0)	0.7 ($\pm$2.5)	0.2 %	100.0 %
Battle zone	37800	26300 ($\pm$7725)	3666.7 ($\pm$3507)	6666.7 ($\pm$3526.6)	25.3 %	81.8 %
Beam rider	5775	6846 ($\pm$1619)	748.3 ($\pm$123.2)	452.3 ($\pm$176.5)	6.6 %	−39.6 %
Bowling	154.8	42.4 ($\pm$88)	0.8 ($\pm$1.6)	5.6 ($\pm$1.9)	13.1 %	595.8 %
Boxing	4.3	71.8 ($\pm$8.4)	78.7 ($\pm$15.8)	73.7 ($\pm$9.7)	102.6 %	−6.4 %
Breakout	31.8	401.2 ($\pm$26.9)	0.4 ($\pm$0.9)	0.2 ($\pm$0.6)	0.0 %	−53.8 %
Centipede	11963	8309 ($\pm$5237)	8388.2 ($\pm$3484.6)	3874.9 ($\pm$1941.6)	46.6 %	−53.8 %
Chopper command	9882	6687 ($\pm$2916)	666.7 ($\pm$260.4)	526.7 ($\pm$216.4)	7.9 %	−21.0 %
Crazy climber	35411	114103 ($\pm$22797)	3.3 ($\pm$18.3)	2123.3 ($\pm$750.9)	1.9 %	63600.0 %
Demon attack	3401	9711 ($\pm$2406)	111.3 ($\pm$37.8)	66.7 ($\pm$17.1)	0.7 %	−40.1 %
Double dunk	−15.5	−18.1 ($\pm$ − 2.6)	−23.5 ($\pm$1)	−21.4 ($\pm$1.5)	−18.2 %	8.8 %
Enduro	301.6	301.8 ($\pm$24.6)	0.0 ($\pm$0)	0.3 ($\pm$1.6)	0.1 %	100.0
Fishing derby	5.5	−0.8 ($\pm$19)	−99.0 ($\pm$0)	−98.4 ($\pm$0.9)	−12200.0 %	0.6 %
Freeway	29.6	30.3 ($\pm$0.7)	0.0 ($\pm$0)	0.0 ($\pm$0.0)	0.0 %	-
Frostbite	4335	328.3 ($\pm$250.5)	83.0 ($\pm$13.2)	0.0 ($\pm$0.0)	0.0 %	−100.0 %
Gopher	2321	8520 ($\pm$3279)	16.7 ($\pm$37.9)	16.7 ($\pm$34.9)	0.2 %	0.0 %
Gravitar	2672	306.7 ($\pm$223.9)	6.7 ($\pm$36.5)	55.0 ($\pm$115.5)	17.9 %	725.0 %
H.E.R.O	25763	19950 ($\pm$158)	92.5 ($\pm$47)	0.0 ($\pm$0.0)	0.0 %	−100.0 %
Ice hockey	0.9	−1.6 ($\pm$2.5)	−21.2 ($\pm$3.5)	−22.4 ($\pm$2.4)	−1302.1 %	−5.8 %
Jamesbond	406.7	576.7 ($\pm$175.5)	6.7 ($\pm$17.3)	35.0 ($\pm$37.5)	6.1 %	425.0 %
Kangaroo	3035	6740 ($\pm$2959)	0.0 ($\pm$0)	0.0 ($\pm$0.0)	0.0 %	-
Krull	2395	3805 ($\pm$1033)	622.3 ($\pm$227.2)	549.3 ($\pm$304.7)	14.4 %	−11.7 %
Kung fu master	22736	23270 ($\pm$5955)	126.7 ($\pm$161.7)	13.3 ($\pm$50.7)	0.1 %	−89.5 %
Montezuma's R	4367	0 ($\pm$0)	0.0 ($\pm$0)	0.0 ($\pm$0.0)	-	-
Ms Pacman	15693	2311 ($\pm$525)	374.3 ($\pm$212.8)	328.7 ($\pm$309.1)	14.2 %	−12.2 %
Name this game	4076	7257 ($\pm$547)	1789.3 ($\pm$658.1)	333.0 ($\pm$212.1)	4.6 %	−81.4 %
Private eye	69571	1788 ($\pm$5473)	−599.3 ($\pm$308.7)	6.7 ($\pm$25.4)	0.4 %	101.1 %
Q'bert	13455	10596 ($\pm$3294)	136.7 ($\pm$32.7)	2.5 ($\pm$7.6)	0.0 %	−98.2 %
River raid	13513	8316 ($\pm$1049)	402.7 ($\pm$54.5)	244.0 ($\pm$50.9)	2.9 %	−39.4 %
Road runner	7845	18257 ($\pm$4268)	0.0 ($\pm$0)	823.3 ($\pm$135.7)	4.5 %	100.0
Robotank	11.9	51.6 ($\pm$4.7)	10.9 ($\pm$3.5)	1.4 ($\pm$1.8)	−97.2 %	−86.8 %
Seaquest	20182	5286 ($\pm$1310)	125.3 ($\pm$35.2)	12.0 ($\pm$12.4)	0.2 %	−90.4 %
Space invaders	1652	1976 ($\pm$893)	180.0 ($\pm$15.3)	155.7 ($\pm$68.7)	7.9 %	−13.5 %
Tennis	−8.9	−2.5 ($\pm$1.9)	−24.0 ($\pm$0)	−16.8 ($\pm$2.4)	−572.0 %	30.0 %
Time pilot	5925	5947 ($\pm$1600)	733.3 ($\pm$590.9)	1066.7 ($\pm$1166.3)	17.9 %	45.5 %
Tutankham	167.6	186.7 ($\pm$41.9)	0.1 ($\pm$0.4)	15.9 ($\pm$9.2)	8.5 %	23799.9 %
Up'n down	9082	8456 ($\pm$3162)	623.3 ($\pm$268.5)	670.0 ($\pm$548.7)	7.9 %	7.5 %
Venture	9083	8457 ($\pm$3163)	0.0 ($\pm$0)	0.0 ($\pm$0.0)	0.0 %	-
Video pinball	9084	8458 ($\pm$3164)	0.0 ($\pm$0)	8166.3 ($\pm$8100.1)	96.6 %	100.0
Wizard of wor	9085	8459 ($\pm$3165)	273.3 ($\pm$267.7)	483.3 ($\pm$136.7)	5.7 %	76.8 %
Zaxxon	9086	8460 ($\pm$3166)	0.0 ($\pm$0)	0.0 ($\pm$0.0)	0.0 %	-

to the specific game to some extent, or it does not. To further analyse what the competitive training of two dissimilar, but high performing games, consider the visualisation of the network as shown in Figs. 9 and 10 for displaying the estimated reward for the given game state, and the game itself respectively.

Comparing the high reward states in Fig. 9 with the network differentiation of the respective games in Fig. 10, the reason for the disparate performance

Fig. 9. Network analysis of estimated game reward using the t-SNE technique for the Neural Network trained competitively for the games Boxing and Robotank

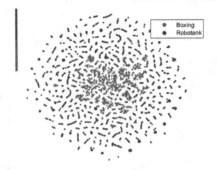

Fig. 10. Network analysis of game type using the t-SNE technique for the Neural Network trained competitively for the games Boxing and Robotank

becomes clear. The node activations for *Boxing* show disparate levels of reward respective of different states of the game. The game *Robotank* does not display this, all game states are representing mid to low reward levels. This is a critical component of the networks ability to play any game, the ability to actively pursue high reward states over low reward states; without this, the game is essentially playing with random actions.

4   Conclusions

We have adapted the original state-of-the-art DQN [8] to simultaneously learn two competing tasks. Considering the case of learning two similar games, it was found that the network could learn to gain reward at both tasks, however this ability rapidly diminished for dissimilar games, even simple ones. The ability to learn multiple examples was completely eroded when considering difficult tasks. Further to this, it was found that a fundamental limitation of this approach was the nature of the game, where the performance of the network relied on the ability to determine a strategy, and strategies which were not conducive to both games resulted in weaker performance.

A major aspect of this research is related to the ability of a reinforcement learning agent to perform multiple tasks well. We have demonstrated that, despite how well a specialist DQN agent performs at a singular specific task, it shows limited ability to generalize to unforeseen tasks. This ability to generalize learning to unforeseen tasks can be improved by competitively training the DQN agent on two tasks simultaneously.

What was largely seen through the analysis of the ability to generalise to unseen tasks, was that training against multiple objectives resulted in improved performance at those unseen tasks, at the expense of performance against specifically trained tasks. In each case of game scenarios applied to the network, be it *Similar, High Performing* games, the network segmented its representational space between the games. Further to this, that segmentation became more pronounced as the difficulty of the training scenario increased, with an increased partitioning clearly observed. What this shows is that the network is devoting representative power to each task, and as hypothesised, that representative power is being saturated as the difficulty increases.

References

1. Bellemare, M.G., Naddaf, Y., Veness, J., Bowling, M.: The arcade learning environment: an evaluation platform for general agents. arXiv preprint arXiv:1207.4708 (2012)
2. Bucila, C., Caruana, R., Niculescu-Mizil, A.: Model compression. In: Proceedings of the 12th ACM SIGKDD International Conference on Knowledge Discovery and Data Mining, pp. 535–541. ACM (2006)
3. Hinton, G., Vinyals, O., Dean, J.: Distilling the knowledge in a neural network. arXiv preprint arXiv:1503.02531 (2015)
4. Kirkpatrick, J., Pascanu, R., Rabinowitz, N., Veness, J., Desjardins, G., Rusu, A.A., Milan, K., Quan, J., Ramalho, T., Grabska-Barwinska, A., et al.: Overcoming catastrophic forgetting in neural networks. arXiv preprint arXiv:1612.00796 (2016)
5. Kuzovkin, I.: Deepmind-atari-deep-q-learner (2015). https://www.github.com/kuz/DeepMind-Atari-Deep-Q-Learner.git
6. Van der Maaten, L., Hinton, G.: Visualizing data using t-SNE. J. Mach. Learn. Res. **9**, 2579–2605 (2008)
7. Mnih, V., Kavukcuoglu, K., Silver, D., Graves, A., Antonoglou, I., Wierstra, D., Riedmiller, M.: Playing Atari with deep reinforcement learning. arXiv preprint arXiv:1312.5602 (2013)
8. Mnih, V., Kavukcuoglu, K., Silver, D., Rusu, A.A., Veness, J., Bellemare, M.G., Graves, A., Riedmiller, M., Fidjeland, A.K., Ostrovski, G., et al.: Human-level control through deep reinforcement learning. Nature **518**(7540), 529–533 (2015)
9. Rusu, A.A., Colmenarejo, S.G., Gulcehre, C., Desjardins, G., Kirkpatrick, J., Pascanu, R., Mnih, V., Kavukcuoglu, K., Hadsell, R.: Policy distillation. arXiv preprint arXiv:1511.06295 (2015)

10. Silver, D., Huang, A., Maddison, C.J., Guez, A., Sifre, L., Van Den Driessche, G., Schrittwieser, J., Antonoglou, I., Panneershelvam, V., Lanctot, M., et al.: Mastering the game of go with deep neural networks and tree search. Nature **529**(7587), 484–489 (2016)
11. Sutton, R.S., Barto, A.G.: Reinforcement Learning: An Introduction, vol. 1. MIT Press, Cambridge (1998)

Density-Based Multiscale Analysis
for Clustering in Strong Noise Settings

Tiantian Zhang and Bo Yuan[(✉)]

Intelligent Computing Lab, Division of Informatics,
Graduate School at Shenzhen, Tsinghua University,
Shenzhen 518055, People's Republic of China
2573546543@qq.com, yuanb@sz.tsinghua.edu.cn

Abstract. Finding clustering patterns in data is challenging when clusters can be of arbitrary shapes and the data contains high percentage (e.g., 80%) of noise. This paper presents a novel technique named density-based multiscale analysis for clustering (DBMAC) that can conduct noise-robust clustering without any strict assumption on the shapes of clusters. Firstly, DBMAC calculates the r-neighborhood statistics with different r (radius) values. Next, instead of trying to find a single optimal r value, a set of radius values appropriate for separating "clustered" objects and "noisy" objects is identified, using a formal statistical method for multimodality test. Finally, the classical DBSCAN is employed to perform clustering on the subset of data with significantly less amount of noise. Experiment results confirm that DBMAC is superior to classical DBSCAN in strong noise settings and also outperforms the latest technique SkinnyDip when the data contains arbitrarily shaped clusters.

Keywords: Multiscale analysis · Density-based clustering · Statistical test

1 Introduction

Clustering has been an active research area in data mining and machine learning in the past decades with fruitful achievements in both academia and industries. Many existing clustering algorithms can produce competitive results when there is only a small percentage of noise. However, in practice, due to various factors such as the inherent randomness in measurements, it is not uncommon that datasets may contain considerably more "noisy" objects than "clustered" or useful objects. Such a large amount of noise will inevitably deteriorate the quality of clustering and make it difficult to correctly detect the cluster structure. This is a challenge that has received relatively less attention from the community as most clustering algorithms are not specifically designed with high percentage of noise in mind.

Many clustering methods such as centroid-based approaches (k-means [1]), model-based approaches (EM [2]) and spectral clustering [3] are generally not suitable for handling noise as they produce a partition of the raw input set, completely ignoring the existence of noise [4]. For low level noise, Murtagh and Raftery [5] introduced a clustering method based on a mixture model where clusters are represented by highly linear multivariate normal densities and clutter is represented by a spatial Poisson

W. Peng et al. (Eds.): AI 2017, LNAI 10400, pp. 27–38, 2017.
DOI: 10.1007/978-3-319-63004-5_3

process. Banfield and Raftery [6] extended this work to high dimensional data with noise. However, it requires the information of the shape of clusters and the number of clusters cannot be properly estimated when the clutter accounts for a majority of the data. Dave [7] introduced the concept of "noise cluster" in a fuzzy centroid-based setting by defining a noise-prototype that is equidistant from all "clustered" points. Cuesta-Albertos et al. [8] proposed the idea of trimming: searching for a subset of the input data of a predetermined size whose removal leads to the maximum improvement of the clustering quality. As a classical example of density-based clusteringtechniques, DBSCAN [9] regards points from the sparse regions as noise. Unfortunately, DBSCAN and other noise-robust algorithms such as SNN [10], SYNC [11], FOSSCLU [12] still suffer from limitations in high-noise settings.

There has also been some development in clustering methods for datasets with strong noise. Dasgupta and Raftery [13] further improved the method of Banfield and Raftery [6] by refining the final partition using the EM algorithm and using approximate Bayes factors to choose the number of clusters. Their method was evaluated on the tasks of detecting minefield and seismic faults from "cluttered" data, which were restricted to the 2D space. Wong and Moore [14] proposed an alternative implementation of the CFF algorithm [15] by addressing the computational issue in both the density estimation and the agglomeration steps, which was also only verified on problems with low dimensionality (up to $d = 5$). In the area of projected clustering, Li et al. [16] presented a divisive projected clustering (DPCLUS) algorithm for detecting correlation clusters in highly noisy data by partitioning the dataset into clusters in a top-down manner to find a suitable criterion for data partition. Most recently, a novel clustering method SkinnyDip [17] was presented in KDD 2016, which is based on Hartigan's dip test of unimodality [18]. It is capable of handling extremely noisy data under the assumption that each cluster coincides with the mode of its multivariate distribution but may not work well on clusters with arbitrary shapes.

In this paper, we propose to remove the noisy objects from possibly highly noisy datasets and then apply density-based clustering to obtain arbitrarily shaped clusters. In the proposed DBMAC (Density-Based Multiscale Analysis for Clustering), multiscale analysis is used to reliably separate "noisy" objects from "clustered" objects and is applicable to clusters of arbitrary shapes. Section 2 introduces DBSCAN and SkinnyDip with some preliminary experiment results to demonstrate their limitations. In Sect. 3, we present the details of multiscale analysis and DBMAC for discovering arbitrarily shaped clusters from noisy datasets. Section 4 contains systematic experimental studies on the effectiveness of DBMAC in various settings. This paper is concluded in Sect. 5 with some analysis and directions for future research.

2 Related Work

2.1 DBSCAN

DBSCAN is one of the most popular clustering algorithms, which can find clusters of arbitrary shapes and has a clear definition of noise. In DBSCAN, the density of a point is obtained by counting the number of points with in a specific distance (radius), *Eps*, from the point. Points with density above the threshold, *MinPts*, are classified as core points, while noisy points are defined as non-core points that do not have a core point within the specific radius.

An effective heuristic for determining the parameter values of *Eps* and *MinPts* is *sorted k-dist graph*. The idea is to calculate the average distance of each point to its *k* nearest neighbors, where the value of *k* (corresponding to *MinPts*) is specified by user, which is usually set to data dimensionality plus one. In *sorted k-dist graph*, the position where a sharp change occurs is chosen as the optimal *Eps* value. This estimation is generally reasonable when the amount of noise is small but can be problematic when the percentage of noise is high. In Fig. 1(a), when the dataset contains 20% noise, the estimated *Eps* can result in a good separation of clusters and noise. By contrast, when the percentage of noise increases to 80%, it becomes very tricky to choose a meaningful single threshold value without detailed information about the dataset itself, as the density of noise is also very high, leading to a poor clustering result, as shown in Fig. 1(b).

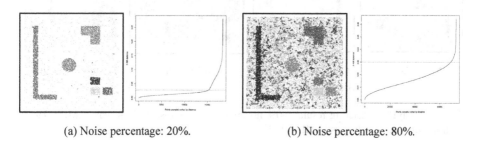

(a) Noise percentage: 20%.   (b) Noise percentage: 80%.

Fig. 1. Clustering results of DBSCAN with different levels of noise: (a) low level of noise, Eps = 0.028, MinPts = 3, AMI = 0.950; (b) high level of noise, Eps = 0.030, MinPts = 3, AMI = 0.377.

2.2 SkinnyDip

SkinnyDip is explicitly proposed as a clustering algorithm for datasets with strong noise. It is claimed to be highly noise-robust, practically parameter-free and completely deterministic. A recursive heuristics based on the formal statistical dip test of unimodality is used to extract clusters in noisy datasets, assuming that each cluster admits a unimodal shape. The *dip* value is defined as the distance of empirical cumulative distribution functions to the class of unimodal distribution functions in terms of the maximum norm. Hartigan proposed an algorithm to compute the values of *dip*, *p-value* and the *modal interval* $[x_L, x_U]$ in which the main modes exist (see Fig. 2). According to the *p-value*, one can reject or favor H_0 (null hypothesis: "*F* is unimodal").

In Fig. 2, for the horizontally projected univariate data, dip test is initially executed on all samples $x_1 \leq x_2 \leq \ldots \leq x_n$, and the identified modal interval spans three modes C, D, E (the gray region). Then, according to the location of the modal interval $[x_L, x_U]$, the algorithm works within this interval recursively to extract inner individual modal intervals $[x_{L_C}, x_{U_C}]$, $[x_{L_D}, x_{U_D}]$, and $[x_{L_E}, x_{U_E}]$. Next, the search range turns to the left and right sides of $[x_L, x_U]$ respectively, until all modes are found. This process (UNIDIP) is the core part of SkinnyDip, suitable for univariate clustering.

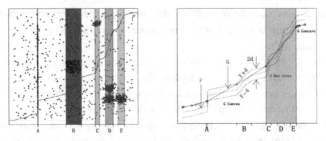

Fig. 2. Dip solution (right) for the horizontal-axis projection of the dataset (left, 30% noise).

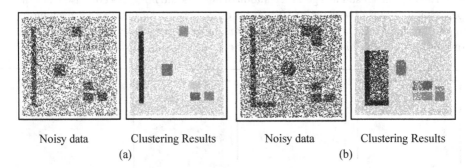

Noisy data   Clustering Results   Noisy data   Clustering Results
                         (a)   (b)

Fig. 3. SkinnyDip clustering results (80% noise): (a) rectangle-shaped clusters, AMI = 0.915; (b) arbitrarily shaped clusters, AMI = 0.616.

Based on UNIDIP, a recursive procedure over the dimensions of the data space is used to generalize to multivariate cases. For real-world data, SkinnyDip incorporates the idea of multimodal project pursuit to find an appropriate basis for clustering. It utilizes the continuity properties of the dip and gradient ascent to find the directions that maximize the dip value as the maximal-multimodal directions.

As shown in Fig. 3(a), SkinnyDip can detect clusters from highly noisy data where each cluster takes a unimodal form along each coordinate. However, when clusters are of irregular shapes or their projections overlap, the limitation of this type of projected clustering is also evident. Figure 3(b) shows that SkinnyDip can only output rectangle-shaped clusters in 2D spaces, regardless of the real shapes of clusters. Meanwhile, some part of a cluster may not be detected due to the heterogeneous density of the cluster along the projection direction.

3 Methodology

3.1 Problem Definitions

The motivation of our work is to develop a competent clustering technique that can reliably identify clustering patterns of arbitrary shapes in extremely noisy settings. The main idea is to design a robust density-based criterion to filter out the noiseand then apply existing clustering algorithms such as DBSCAN to do the clustering.

Problem Description: Formally, let $\mathcal{X}$ be a dataset of n data objects (row vectors) being treated as d-dimensional feature (column) vectors. $x_i \in \mathcal{X}$ stands for the ith object in $\mathcal{X}$ where $x_i = (x_{i1}, x_{i2}, \ldots, x_{id})$. In order to make the problem easier, we assume that all clusters are homogeneous, and the set of noisy objects coincides with a uniform distribution. For this noisy data, the function of DBMAC is as follows:

- **Input:** Data $\mathcal{X} \in R^{n \times d}$, $\mathcal{X} = \{x_1, x_2, \ldots, x_n\}$.
- **Output:** $\{C_1, C_2, \ldots, C_k, \Phi\}$ $(k > 1)$, a partition of $\mathcal{X}$ where Φ represents the "noise cluster" and $C = \{C_1, C_2, \ldots, C_k\}$ represents the set of k normal clusters.

Definition 1 (r-neighborhood statistics): The *r-neighborhood* of a point x_i, denoted by $s_r(x_i)$, is defined as $s_r(x_i) = \{x_j \in X \,|\, dist(x_i, x_j) \leq r\}$. The *r-neighborhood statistics* of point x_i is denoted by $n_r(x_i) = card(s_r(x_i))$.

Definition 2 (multiscale-neighborhood statistics): The *multiscale-neighborhood* of x_i, denoted by $S_R(x_i)$, is defined as $S_R(x_i) = \{s_{r_1}(x_i), s_{r_2}(x_i), \ldots, s_{r_m}(x_i)\}$ where $R = \{r_1, r_2, \ldots, r_m\}$ is the set of radius values that forms an arithmetic sequence: $R = \{minr, minr + \Delta, minr + 2\Delta, \ldots, maxr\}$. Consequently, for each x_i, its *multiscale-neighborhood statistics* is denoted by $N_R(x_i) = \{n_{r_1}(x_i), n_{r_2}(x_i), \ldots, n_{r_m}(x_i)\}$.

3.2 Multiscale Analysis

In strong noise settings, the difference in density between noise and clusters can be much smaller compared to low-level noise situations. In this paper, we propose to use multiscale analysis to find characteristic differentials to divide clusters and noise.

In this paper, all datasets were normalized using the *Z-score normalization* so that consistent algorithm parameter values can be used:

$$Norm(x_{ij}) = \frac{x_{ij} - \mu}{\sigma} \tag{1}$$

In multiscale analysis, for each x_i in $\mathcal{X}$, we compute its *r-neighborhood statistics* $n_r(x_i)$ with various radius values $\{r_1, r_2, \ldots, r_m\}$. The typical neighbor patterns of "clustered" objects and "noisy" objects are shown in Fig. 4(a) and (b), from which it is intuitively to hypothesize that as r increases from a very small value: (i) for "clustered" objects, the *r-neighborhood statistics* increases rapidly and then slow down (more and more noisy points are included); (ii) for "noisy" objects, this statistics should grow slowly initially and then speed up (more and more points from clusters are included). Figure 4(c) shows an illustration of the contrasting patterns of *r-neighborhood statistics* for the two classes of points. As a result, it is plausible to exploit this feature to distinguish "clustered" objects and "noisy" objects.

Note that, although there may exist a single r value that can be used to get satisfactory partition results fora specific raw dataset, in practice, it is likely to be very challenging to obtain such an optimal r. Furthermore, the density of both clusters and noise is often not completely homogeneous for real-world problems and a fixed r value is not expected to work well in such situations. Instead, we choose to use a set of r values, performing multiscale analysis of the raw data.

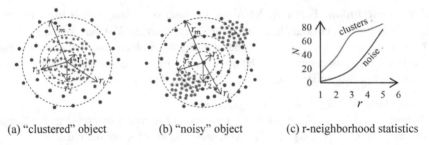

(a) "clustered" object   (b) "noisy" object   (c) r-neighborhood statistics

Fig. 4. Multiscale-neighborhood statistics of a point: the red points represent clustered objects; the blue points represent noisy objects. (Color figure online)

Given a certain r value, the distribution of *r-neighborhood statistics* can be plotted as shown in Fig. 5. Since the objective is to separate "clustered" objects from "noisy" objects, r values that produce distributions with two modes are likely to be useful in terms of discriminatory power. Under the assumption that clusters are of higher density than noise, if there are two modes in the density curve, the dataset can be reasonably divided into two parts, corresponding to two levels of density. From Fig. 5, we can see that when r is small, there are many modes in the density curve and when the r is too large, only one major mode is available. By contrast, within a certain interval of r values, the density curves do present the desired bimodal pattern.

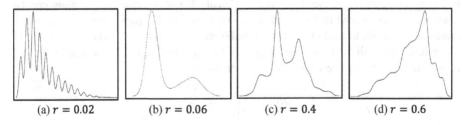

(a) $r = 0.02$ (b) $r = 0.06$ (c) $r = 0.4$ (d) $r = 0.6$

Fig. 5. The density curves of r-neighborhood statistics with different r values.

In order to identify the appropriate interval of radius values that can produce two major modes, the UNIDIP algorithm (see Sect. 2.2) based on the dip test statistics is employed. The results of *multiscale-neighborhood statistics* are as follows where each column represents the results of n data points for a given r value:

$$N = \begin{pmatrix} n_{1,r_1}(x_i) & \cdots & n_{1,r_m}(x_i) \\ \vdots & \ddots & \vdots \\ n_{n,r_1}(x_i) & \cdots & n_{n,r_m}(x_i) \end{pmatrix} \tag{2}$$

The UNIDIP algorithm is applied on each column and identifies the number of modes contained in the corresponding density curves. Only columns/r values that produce two modes are selected as features. Finally, the k-means algorithm with $k = 2$ is applied to group the raw data into two groups corresponding to clusters and noise. An example is shown in Fig. 6 to demonstrate the effectiveness of noise removal.

  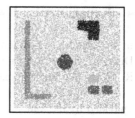

Fig. 6. The result of multiscale analysis: noise part (left) and clusters part (right).

Fig. 7. Clustering result of DBMAC, AMI = 0.886.

3.3 DBMAC: Density-Based Multiscale Analysis for Clustering

In this section, we present the details of DBMAC (Density-Based Multiscale Analysis for Clustering), which is purposefully targeted at discovering clustering patterns in highly noisy data. After multiscale analysis, the raw dataset is transformed into a new subset containing vast majority of the original "clustered" objects with possibly only a small amount of noise. Next, any common clustering algorithm that is weak noise robust and can detect arbitrarily shaped clusters can be used to discover the true clusters. Figure 7 is the clustering result of DBMAC using DBSCAN in the final clustering. Compared to the results of DBSCAN in Fig. 1 and SkinnyDip in Fig. 3, it is evident that DBMAC is clearly superior in strong noise settings with arbitrarily shaped clusters. The pseudo code of DBMAC is listed below.

Algorithm: DBMAC

input : Data $X \in \mathbb{R}^{n \times d}$, $X = \{x_1, x_2, ..., x_n\}$, $minr, maxr, \Delta$

output: Clusters set $C = \{C_1, C_2, ..., C_k\}$

1: $X \leftarrow normalize(X)$, $\mathcal{R} \leftarrow \{minr, minr + \Delta, ..., maxr\}$, $\overrightarrow{N_r} \leftarrow \emptyset, \overrightarrow{N_R} \leftarrow \emptyset$;

    /* Multiscale analysis */

2: **for** $r \in \mathcal{R}$ **do**

      /* r-neighborhood statistics for all data points */

3:     **for** $x_i \in X$ **do**

4:       $\overrightarrow{N_r}.push(card(\{x_j \in X | dist(x_i, x_j) \leq r\}))$;

5:     **end**

      /* select appropriate radius values whose density curve presents bi-modal pattern */

6:     $\overrightarrow{N_r}' \leftarrow sort(\overrightarrow{N_r})$;   /* ascending sort */

7:     $\mathcal{M} \leftarrow UNIDIP(\overrightarrow{N_r}')$;

8:     $\mathcal{N} \leftarrow length(M)$;

9:     **if** $\mathcal{N} == 2$ **then** $\overrightarrow{N_R}.push(\overrightarrow{N_r})$;

10: **end**

11: $[clusteredObjects, noisyObjects] \leftarrow kmeans(\overrightarrow{N_R}, 2)$;

12: $\{C_1, C_2, ..., C_k\} \leftarrow dbscan(clusteredObjects, eps, minPts)$;

13: **return** $\{C_1, C_2, ..., C_k\}$;

4 Experimental Evaluation

In this section, experimental studies were conducted to demonstrate the competence of DBMAC, in comparison with DBSCAN and SkinnyDip. DBMAC was implemented in R. To make a fair comparison, the standard DBSCAN implementation in R was used and the source code of SkinnyDip implemented in R was retrieved from *GitHub* uploaded by its author.

4.1 Clustering Quality

In clusters of highly irregular shapes, two data points in the same cluster may be distant from each other in terms of Euclidean distance. Traditional clustering metrics such as cluster diameter, sum of squared errors and compactness are generally no longer appropriate. Since all benchmark datasets used in the experiments were synthetic and the true clustering patterns were known *apriori*, information theoretic measures such as NMI (Normalized Mutual Information) [19] and AMI (Adjusted Mutual Information) [20] can be employed. Here, we used AMI as the metric of choice due to its correction for chance.

For a dataset $\mathcal{X}$ of n elements, $\mathcal{X} = \{x_1, x_2, \ldots, x_n\}$, given the true set of clusters $U = \{U_1, U_2, \ldots, U_R\}$ and the clusters obtained from some clustering algorithm $V = \{V_1, V_2, \ldots, V_C\}$, AMI is defined as follows:

$$AMI(U, V) = \frac{MI(U, V) - E\{MI(U, V)\}}{\max\{H(U), H(V)\} - E\{MI(U, V)\}} \tag{3}$$

where, $MI(U, V)$ is the mutual information (MI) between two partitions:

$$MI(U, V) = \sum_{i=1}^{R} \sum_{j=1}^{C} P(i, j) \log \frac{P(i, j)}{P(i) P'(j)} \tag{4}$$

$P(i) = \frac{|U_i|}{n}$, $P'(j) = \frac{|V_j|}{n}$, $P(i, j) = \frac{|U_i \cap V_j|}{n}$; $E\{MI(U, V)\}$ is the expected mutual information between two random clusterings:

$$E\{MI(U, V)\} = \sum_{i=1}^{R} \sum_{j=1}^{C} \sum_{n_{ij}=(a_i+b_j-n)^+}^{min(a_i, b_j)} \frac{n_{ij}}{n} \log\left(\frac{n \cdot n_{ij}}{a_i b_j}\right)$$
$$\times \frac{a_i! b_j! (n - a_i)! (n - b_j)!}{n! n_{ij}! (a_i - n_{ij})! (b_j - n_{ij})! (n - a_i - b_j + n_{ij})!} \tag{5}$$

a_i and b_j are partial sums of the contingency table, $a_i = \sum_{j=1}^{C} n_{ij}$, $b_j = \sum_{i=1}^{R} n_{ij}$, $(a_i + b_j - n)^+ = max(1, a_i + b_j - n)$; the entropy $H(U)$. $H(V) = -\sum_{j=1}^{C} P'(j) \log P'(j)$. AMI lies in the range of $[-1, 1]$, with a perfect clustering corresponding to AMI value of 1.

4.2   2D Synthetic Datasets

All 2D synthetic datasets were from *GitHub clustering benchmarks* with extra uniform noise. These datasets consist of 6 to 15 irregular clusters and have been used frequently in clustering research, including CURE [21], and SPARCL [22]. D1–D5, shown in the first column of Fig. 8, each contained 80% noise. The following three columns are clustering results of DBSCAN, SkinnyDip and DBMAC, respectively. The parameter values were chosen as: *Eps* = 0.027 and *MinPts* = 3 for all datasets and for both DBSCAN and DBMAC, as recommended by *sorted k-dist graph*.

To summarize, DBSCAN detected almost all "clustered" objects inthese noisy datasets and has the ability to detect arbitrarily shaped clusters. However, it also made many mistakes by assigning "noisy" objects tosmall clusters, leading to very messy results. SkinnyDip successfullyfiltered out most of the noise but due to the limitation of projected clustering, it cannotcorrectly identify irregular clusters. In fact, the cluster regions produced by SkinnyDip were all horizontal or vertical to the projected directions, which were significantly different from the true clusters. Meanwhile, some clusters located in the area of relatively low density along the projected direction were mistaken for noise. By contrast, despite of a few flaws along the edges of clusters, it is clear that DBMAC not only perfectly filtered outmost of noisy objects but also correctly identified arbitrarily shaped clusters in these highly noisy datasets.

4.3   Multi-dimensional Synthetic Datasets

For multi-dimensional cases, we created synthetic datasets using Gaussian distributions. The number of objects in each cluster was 200 and the standard deviation of Gaussian distribution was 0.02 in each dimension. The centers of Gaussians were generated randomly within $[0.1, 0.9]^d$ and the distance between any two centers was greater than 6σ to minimize the chance of overlapping. Noise was randomly generated within $[0, 1]^d$. Note that all original datasets were further normalized using Eq. (1). Dataset parameters varied in the experiments were dimensionality d, the number of clusters k, and noise percentage η.

Figure 9 shows the results of DBMAC, DBSCAN, and SkinnyDip with different parameter combinations where the vertical axis indicates the AMI value. In Fig. 9 (left), the dimensionality was varied from 2 to 8 with $k = 15$, $\eta = 80\%$. In Fig. 9 (middle), the number of clusters was varied from 5 to 15 with $d = 3$, $\eta = 80\%$. In Fig. 9 (right), the noise percentage was varied from 20% to 90% with $k = 15, d = 3$. In summary, DBMAC shows superior robustness against dimensionality, number of clusters, and noise percentage, compared to other two methods. Note that the performance of DBSCAN was largely dominated by the relative density of clusters compared to noise. For example, as the dimensionality increases, the proportion of space occupied by clusters will shrink dramatically, increasing the difference in density and leading to better performance of DBSCAN. By contrast, as the number of clusters increases (more "clustered" objects), more noise will be generated to maintain the same

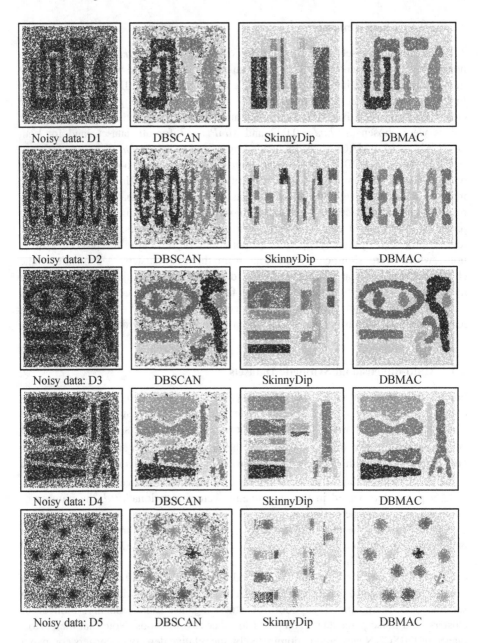

Fig. 8. Clustering results of four 2D synthetic datasets with 80% noise: DBSCAN, SkinnyDip and DBMAC (left to right). It is clear that DBMAC can correctly identify highly irregular clusters from extremely noisy datasets.

noise percentage, leading to higher noise density and deteriorating performance. Similarly, higher noise percentage will result in higher noise density and worse performance.

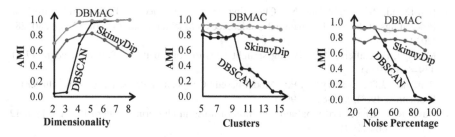

Fig. 9. Experiment results on high-dimensional synthetic datasets: DBMAC (red), DBSCAN (black), and SkinnyDip (blue). It is evident that the performance DBMAC is robust against various problem factors, compared to DBSCAN and SkinnyDip. (Color figure online)

5 Conclusion

The major motivation of our work is to develop a competent clustering algorithm that can effectively handle datasets with strong noise and highly irregular clusters. In the proposed DBMAC algorithm, instead of using a single radius value to distinguish "noisy" objects and "clustered" objects, a set of radius values with good discriminatory power is selected based a principled statistical test to conduct multiscale analysis. The numbers of data points in the corresponding neighborhoods are used as the feature set of each data point. Then, the k-means algorithm with $k = 2$ is used to partition all data points into two groups, representing "noisy" objects and "clustered" objects, respectively. In this way, most of the noise can be effectively removed and the new dataset usually only contains a very small amount of noise. As a result, any existing clustering algorithm such as DBSCAN that can properly handle weak noise and irregular clusters can be employed to do the final clustering.

We conducted systematic empirical studies on a wide range of challenging benchmark datasets with up to 90% noise. Experimental results show that DBMAC features superior effectiveness and robustness in finding arbitrarily shaped clusters from datasets with high level of noise, compared to the classical DBSCAN and the latest technique SkinnyDip. As to future work, we will conduct formal analysis of DBMAC about its time complexity and the impact of parameter settings. It is also an important issue to investigate its performance when the density of noise and/or the densities of clusters are not homogeneous.

References

1. Jain, A.K., Dubes, R.C.: Algorithms for Clustering Data. Prentice Hall Advanced Reference Series: Computer Science. Prentice Hall College Div (1988)
2. Do, C.B., Batzoglou, S.: What is the expectation maximization algorithm. Nat. Biotechnol. **26**(8), 897–899 (2008)
3. Zelnik-Manor, L., Perona, P.: Self-tuning spectral clustering. Adv. Neural. Inf. Process. Syst. **17**, 1601–1608 (2004)

4. Ben-David, S., Haghtalab, N.: Clustering in the presence of background noise. In: Proceedings of the 31st International Conference on Machine Learning, vol. 32, pp. 280–288 (2014)
5. Murtagh, F., Raftery, A.E.: Fitting straight lines to point patterns. Pattern Recogn. **17**(5), 479–483 (1984)
6. Banfield, J.D., Raftery, A.E.: Model-based Gaussian and non-Gaussian clustering. Biometrics **49**(3), 803–821 (1993)
7. Dave, R.N.: Characterization and detection of noise in clustering. Pattern Recogn. Lett. **12** (11), 657–664 (1991)
8. Cuesta-Albertos, J.A., Gordaliza, A., Matran, C.: Trimmed k-means: an attempt to robustifyquantizers. Ann. Stat. **25**(2), 553–576 (1997)
9. Ester, M., Kriegel, H.P., Sander, J., Xu, X.: A density-based algorithm for discovering clusters in large spatial databases with noise. In: Proceedings of the 2nd International Conference on Knowledge Discovery and Data Mining, vol. 96, no. 34, pp. 226–231 (1996)
10. Ertöz, L., Steinbach, M., Kumar, V.: Finding clusters of different sizes, shapes, and densities in noisy, high dimensional data. In: Proceedings of the 3rd SIAM International Conference on Data Mining, vol. 112, pp. 47–58 (2003)
11. Böhm, C., Plant, C., Shao, J., Yang, Q.: Clustering by synchronization. In: Proceedings of the 16th ACM SIGKDD International Conference on Knowledge Discovery and Data Mining, pp. 583–592 (2010)
12. Goebl, S., He, X., Plant, C., Böhm, C.: Finding the optimal subspace for clustering. In: IEEE International Conference on Data Mining, pp. 130–139 (2014)
13. Dasgupta, A., Raftery, A.E.: Detecting features in spatial point processes with clutter via model-based clustering. J. Am. Stat. Assoc. Theory Methods **93**(441), 294–302 (1998)
14. Wong, W.K., Moore, A.: Efficient algorithms for non-parametric clustering with clutter. In: Proceedings of the 34th Interface Symposium, vol. 34, pp. 541–553 (2002)
15. Cuevas, A., Febrero, M., Fraiman, R.: Estimating the number of clusters. Can. J. Stat. **28**(2), 367–382 (2000)
16. Li, J., Huang, X., Selke, C., Yong, J.: A fast algorithm for finding correlation clusters in noise data. In: Zhou, Z.-H., Li, H., Yang, Q. (eds.) PAKDD 2007. LNCS, vol. 4426, pp. 639–647. Springer, Heidelberg (2007). doi:10.1007/978-3-540-71701-0_68
17. Maurus, S., Plant, C.: Skinny-dip: clustering in a sea of noise. In: Proceedings of the 22nd International Conference on Knowledge Discovery and Data Mining, pp. 1055–1064 (2016)
18. Hartigan, J.A., Hartigan, P.M.: The dip test of unimodality. Ann. Stat. **13**(1), 70–84 (1985)
19. Strehl, A., Ghosh, J.: Cluster ensembles-a knowledge reuse framework for combining multiple partitions. J. Mach. Learn. Res. **3**, 583–617 (2002)
20. Vinh, N.X., Epps, J., Bailey, J.: Information theoretic measures for clusterings comparison: is a correction for chance necessary? In: Proceedings of the 26th Annual International Conference on Machine Learning, pp. 1073–1080 (2009)
21. Guha, S., Rastogi, R., Shim, K.: CURE: an efficient clustering algorithm for large databases. ACM SIGMOD Rec. Int. Conf. Manag. Data **27**(2), 73–84 (1998)
22. Chaoji, V., Al Hasan, M., Salem, S., Zaki, M.J.: SPARCL: efficient and effective shape-based clustering. In: IEEE International Conference on Data Mining, pp. 93–102 (2008)

Evolving Transferable Artificial Neural Networks for Gameplay Tasks via NEAT with Phased Searching

Will Hardwick-Smith, Yiming Peng[(✉)], Gang Chen, Yi Mei,
and Mengjie Zhang

School of Engineering and Computer Science,
Victoria University of Wellington, Wellington, New Zealand
whardwicksmith@gmail.com, {yiming.peng,gang.chen,yi.mei,
mengjie.zhang}@ecs.vuw.ac.nz
http://ecs.victoria.ac.nz/Groups/ECRG/

Abstract. NeuroEvolution of Augmenting Topologies (NEAT) has been successfully applied to intelligent gameplay. To further improve its effectiveness, a key technique is to reuse the knowledge learned from source gameplay tasks to boost performance on target gameplay tasks. We consider this as a Transfer Learning (TL) problem. However, Artificial Neural Networks (ANNs) evolved by NEAT are usually unnecessarily complicated, which may affect their transferability. To address this issue, we will investigate in this paper the capability of *Phased Searching* (PS) methods for controlling ANNs' complexity while maintaining their effectiveness. By doing so, we can obtain more transferable ANNs. Furthermore, we will propose a new Power-Law Ranking Probability based PS (PLPS) method to more effectively control the randomness during the simplification phase. Several recent PS methods as well as our PLPS have been evaluated on four carefully-designed TL experiments. Results show clearly that NEAT can evolve more transferable and structurally simple ANNs with the help of PS methods, in particular PLPS.

Keywords: Transfer learning · Intelligent gameplay · Mario AI · Artificial Neural Networks · NEAT · Phased searching · Power-law

1 Introduction

With well-defined rules, easily controllable environments and clear success criteria, computer games have been increasingly considered favorable for Artificial Intelligence (AI) research [2,10,11]. Among all the different AI technologies, *Artificial Neural Networks* (ANNs) are popular choices for establishing the intelligent game playing strategies since they are highly adaptive on nonlinear problems [10]. Moreover, with the capability of learning the ANN's weights and its topology simultaneously, NeuroEvolution of Augmenting Topologies [14] (NEAT) has shown great potential in successfully playing a wide range of games, such as

© Springer International Publishing AG 2017
W. Peng et al. (Eds.): AI 2017, LNAI 10400, pp. 39–51, 2017.
DOI: 10.1007/978-3-319-63004-5_4

Checkers [2], Car Racing [1], Othello [11], Ms. Pacman [12], Atari Games [5], etc. However, many of these NEAT-based approaches for gameplay require the agent to be trained from scratch for every newly encountered gameplay task, potentially affecting the efficiency and effectiveness of these approaches [20].

As a major solution to the above issue, *Transfer Learning* (TL) is capable of obtaining a solution from a *source* task and transferring the solution to improve learning on a *target* task [9,13]. It is assumed that the source task is previously known and the target task presents related but unseen problems to be encountered in the future. In line with this idea, the usefulness of applying TL to NEAT for intelligent game playing has been fruitfully explored in the literature [17,18,20].

Different from existing works, we focus on a new context of TL in this research. Specifically, both the source and target tasks are assumed known to us. However, it may not be wise to directly tackle the target task as it is more challenging than the source task. A better strategy based on TL is to first identify a solution to the source task by using NEAT, which is subsequently transferred to build a new solution that can perform the target task effectively. For example, the source task could be utilized to teach a NEAT agent to avoid enemies in a computer game. Afterwards the agent can continue to learn how to quickly reach its target while accruing more credits on its way in the target task. Clearly if NEAT can reliably learn transferable ANNs, it is highly likely for difficult gameplay tasks to be conquered effectively and efficiently.

One major hurdle of our TL approach lies in the fact that NEAT is designed to increasingly complexify the topology of evolved ANNs. The learned ANN can be highly complicated and strongly tied to irrelevant features of the source task and hence may not be of any real use in the target task. In fact, our empirical study shows that, without controlling their complexity, ANNs evolved by NEAT from the source target may actually hinder effective learning in the target task. To address this technical problem, we will investigate the *Phased Searching* (PS) [3] techniques that can constantly simplify evolved ANNs while maintaining NEAT's performance at a good level. We believe that, by doing so, the resulting ANNs will be more transferable. To the best of our knowledge, few studies have ever considered PS for learning transferable ANNs in NEAT. Rather than following simple PS methods in [3], in order to further enhance the transferability of ANNs, a new power-law driven PS (PLPS) technique will also be proposed in this paper.

Goals: Motivated by the importance of enhancing TL in NEAT, we aim to develop a new PS based NEAT transfer learning algorithm (PLPS-NEAT-TL) capable of evolving effective and simple ANNs that are transferable for intelligent gameplay. Armed with the new algorithm, we aim to pursue two main research objectives.

- Design a new PS method for evolving transferable (effective and simple) ANNs on various source tasks through NEAT.
- Examine the effectiveness of ANNs evolved by PLPS-NEAT-TL algorithm on various target gameplay tasks.

2   Background

In this section, we firstly review NEAT algorithm. Next, we introduces the application of NEAT for TL to intelligent gameplay. Lastly, we discuss various PS methods for NEAT, which are capable of simplifying evolved ANNs.

2.1   NEAT

NEAT and its variations have been studied for their abilities to play various games such as Ms. Pacman [12], Robot Soccer [19], and collections of Atari 2600 games [4,5]. It is proposed by Stanley and Miikkulainen [15] to discover effective ANNs for solving some given problem. In addition to its capability of tunning the network's weights, NEAT is also armed with a powerful weapon of adjusting the network's topology. To achieve this, it searches possible network topologies by starting from a population of minimal architectures and then incrementally adding and modifying neural components (links and neurons).

2.2   NEAT for Transfer Learning

Transfer learning is a popular direction for intelligent gameplay research that has been studied in many works [9,13,17,20]. Although NEAT shows a great success in intelligent gameplay, only a limited number of studies considered NEAT for transfer learning. Two related works are proposed in [17,20]. These works successfully combined NEAT and TL to improve learning effectiveness on a soccer simulation game. However, as discussed in Sect. 1, they shared a different TL context from our work. We believe that NEAT for TL is an important research topic deserving substantial investigation.

2.3   Phased Searching for NEAT

The original NEAT is designed to increasingly complexify the ANNs during evolution process. As reported in a few works [3,16], this may result in unnecessarily complicated solutions which can be vulnerable to over-fitting to one specific task [16]. Hence, the chance for them to be transfered to another task will be compromised.

To address this issue, a key technique called *Phased Searching* (PS) has been proposed by Green [3] and later extended by Tan et al. [16]. Both works observed that PS can evolve substantially simplified ANNs (measured by the number of connections and neurons) with good performance. This suggests that PS tends to find ANN solutions that are minimal while still preserving structure that is necessary for achieving a high performance that rivals that of regular NEAT. These properties makes phased searching ideal for finding ANN solutions that are transferable.

Another similar work attempts to address the issues is called *Blended Search* (BS) proposed by James and Tucker [6], which can be viewed as a special case of PS methods. BS blends complexifying and simplifying mutations in evolution process which results in finding higher performing ANNs than original NEAT for XOR and tic-tac-toe problems [6].

However, existing PS methods rely on a pure random selection strategy for removing links and hidden neurons of evolved ANNs. Such uncontrollable randomness might affect the transferability of solutions. This question is further investigated experimentally in this research. Motivated by this understanding, we attempt to develop a new PS with easily controllable randomness for evolving transferable ANNs.

3   Methodology

In this section, we present a new PS based NEAT algorithm for TL (PLPS-NEAT-TL) to effectively evolve ANNs for intelligent gameplay. Firstly, we give an overall design of the algorithm. Next, we depict the principle of the new PS method based on a power-law ranking probability to effectively control randomness in ANN simplification phase.

3.1   Overall Design

PLPS-NEAT-TL consists of two learning stages, namely *source task learning* (STL) and *target task learning* (TTL), which are bridged by TL. Figure 1 illustrates the blueprint of the learning algorithm. As seen in the figure, for STL, we rely the learning on NEAT with a power-law ranking probability based PS method (PLPS) so as to simplify the increasingly complexified topologies evolved by NEAT. By doing so, we can obtain reasonably simpler ANNs at the end of STL. A similar algorithmic description for STL can be found in [16]. Subsequently, TL is conducted where the best solution obtained from STL is used as transferable knowledge to initialize NEAT (without using any PS methods) for TTL.

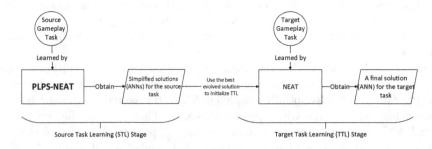

Fig. 1. An overall design of the PLPS-NEAT-TL algorithm.

Algorithm 1. Power-Law Ranking Probability based Phased Searching

---

Require: the population with original individuals P, the population size p, the link removal mutation rate m_l, the neuron removal mutation rate m_n
Ensure: the population with structurally simplified individuals P'
1: **function** POWER_LAW_PHASED_SEARCH(P)
2:    **for** k = 1,2,..., p **do**
3:        $N \leftarrow P[k]$
4:        $G \leftarrow$ SORT(ALL_GENES(N))
5:        **for all** $g \in G$ **do**
6:            **if** IS_LINK(g) **then**
7:                $\Phi_g = $ RANK$(g)^{-1}$
8:            **end if**
9:            **if** IS_HIDDEN_NEURON(g) **then**
10:               $\Phi_g = $ RANK(LINKS$(g))^{-1}$
11:           **end if**
12:       **end for**
13:       **if** RANDOM() $< m_l$ **then**
14:           $l \leftarrow$ SELECT_BY_PROBABILITY(g, G, Φ_g)
15:           $N' \leftarrow$ REMOVE_LINK_MUTATION(l, N)   ▷ Remove the link gene [3]
16:       **end if**
17:       **if** RANDOM() $< m_n$ **then**
18:           $n \leftarrow$ SELECT_BY_PROBABILITY(g, G, Φ_g)
19:           $N' \leftarrow$ REMOVE_NEURON_MUTATION(n, N')   ▷ Remove the neuron gene [3]
20:       **end if**
21:       $P' \leftarrow P' \cup \{N'\}$
22:    **end for**
23:    **return** P'
24: **end function**

3.2   Power-Law Ranking Probability Based Phased Searching

In this work, we develop a new PS method for NEAT to evolve structurally simpler and potentially transferable ANNs. Our new PS method is designed to be able to control randomness in ANN simplification phase, which differentiates from existing PS methods whose randomness is purely uncontrollable. For doing so, we define *removal probability* for each gene (including both links and hidden neurons) based on some ranking of the gene.

This ranking is dependent on the type of the gene. For a link gene, we consider the ranking according to the link's absolute weight value. Because a link's weight with a small absolute value (e.g., close to 0) can be considered little contributing to the learning effectiveness, hence such links can be removed without causing much side-effects to the ANN. Additionally, we rank neuron genes based on the number of links connected to each neuron gene. This is straightforward as a neuron of an ANN with more connections indicates that the ANN has more dependencies on the neuron.

Hence, we can determine the remove probability by considering that it follows a power-law relation with respect to the ranking of each gene. The power-law relation can be expressed as,

$$\Phi_g = \begin{cases} \texttt{RANK}(|\omega_g|)^{-1} & , \text{ if } \texttt{IS\_LINK}(g) \\ \texttt{RANK}(\texttt{LINKS}(g))^{-1} & , \text{ if } \texttt{IS\_HIDDEN\_NEURON}(g) \end{cases} \tag{1}$$

where Φ_g denotes the removal probability for any gene g (NOTE: $\sum_{i=1}^{\texttt{NUMBER\_OF\_GENES}}$ $\Phi_{g_i} = 1$), $\texttt{RANK}(\omega_g)$ extracts the ranking of the link gene g based on its absolute weight value ω_g, and $\texttt{RANK}(\texttt{LINKS}(g))$ returns the ranking of the neuron gene g according to the number of links connected to g, i.e., $\texttt{LINKS}(g)$.

We present an algorithmic description of PLPS in Algorithm 1[1]. Note that, we follow the same functional design for link removal mutation and neuron removal mutation operators presented in [16]. In the simplification phase, these two mutation operations will be conducted sequentially based on the link mutation rate m_l and the neuron mutation rate m_n respectively.

4   Experimental Design

In this section, we firstly present a widely-used game benchmark environment, i.e., Mario AI Benchmark, for evaluating the PLPS-NEAT-TL algorithm. Subsequently, we describe a general experiment setup as well as depict four TL experimental designs.

4.1   Mario AI Benchmark

Mario AI Benchmark (MIB) is a widely-recognized challenging environment for testing intelligent gameplay algorithms [7]. The various challenges of MIB serves as a good testbed for clearly distinguishing the learning ability of any intelligent gameplay algorithm. Additionally, MIB is highly flexible as most of its game properties (e.g., game level, difficulty, time limit, gaming objectives, etc.,) are adjustable. This flexibility makes the implementation of both source and target gameplay tasks straightforward. Hence, we consider MIB ideal for designing our TL experiments.

Environment Representation. In our experiments, the environment representation (a.k.a, feature) is defined as a sensor grid where each grid cell represents the occupancy of a small region of the screen as proposed in [7]. Originally in [7], the representation uses continuous values for each cell, which may make the learning slow and ineffective [8]. To mitigate this affection, as seen in Fig. 2, we simplify the representation where each cell is represented by one scalar: 0 for nothing, 1 for an environmental feature (like walls), and -1 for an enemy.

---

[1] All source code and detailed parameter settings can be found in https://github.com/willhs/NEAT-Mario.

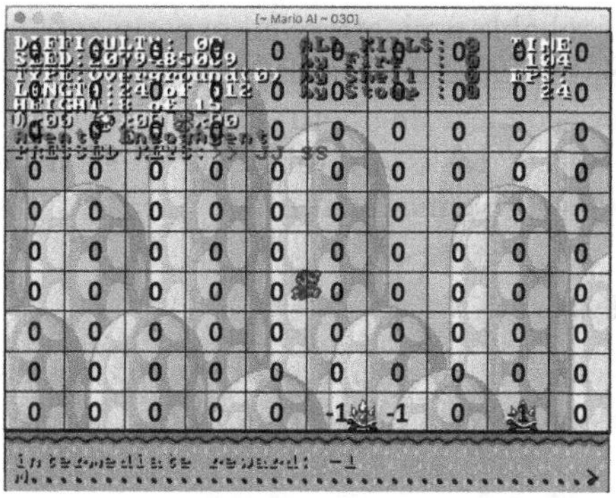

Fig. 2. The environment representation of Mario AI Benchmark.

Action Representation. In MIB, available actions are defined as: *right* (move Mario to the right), *left*, *down* (duck), *jump*, and *speed* (when held makes movements to the left or right further). These actions can be executed in parallel; for instance, the right and jump action can be executed together to jump to the right. Additionally, these available actions are represented as *timed-actions*. This means that the five actions can be executed over a period of time measured by a length of frames. In other words, if an action (or two actions in parallel) is chosen at one frame, it (or they) will be continuously carried out for several subsequent frames. The reason of doing so is to cope with situations as Mario needs to jump higher when the jump action must be held for consecutive frames.

4.2 Experimental Setup

In the following TL experiments, we compare the transferability and complexity of ANNs evolved by different algorithms. These algorithms include original NEAT (NEAT), NEAT with Blended Searching (BS-NEAT), NEAT with Green's Phased Searching (GPS-NEAT), NEAT with Tan's Phased Searching (TPS-NEAT) and NEAT with Power-Law Ranking Probability based Phased Searching (PLPS-NEAT). They are used independently to learn on the source tasks, then the learned ANNs are transfered to original NEAT for learning on the target tasks. In addition, we also apply original NEAT to learning on the target tasks only for all experiments as a baseline for demonstrate the effectiveness of TL.

To evaluate transferability and complexity of ANNs evolved by each algorithm, we define two measurements respectively. Transferability is measured by the final learning performance (fitness value) of the best ANN obtained by an algorithm on a target task. Besides, we measure complexity by counting the total number of links and neurons of the best ANNs in STL phase. We focus on transferable and simplified ANNs, thus the complexity only needs to be gauged in STL phase.

For the purpose of reliable evaluation, all experiments have been conducted over 30 trials. For each trial, the fitness value for one algorithm is averaged over 10 unique game instances on learning both source and target tasks. Additionally, seeds for source and target tasks are different to ensure that the knowledge transferred cannot be level-specific nuances.

4.3   Experimental Design

In this research, we carefully design four TL experiments on MIB in order to assess the transferability as well as complexity of evolved ANNs of each algorithm.

Experiment 1: Speed-Enemies. For this experiment, the source task is designed as that the player must travel as fast as possible to the right while navigating hilly terrain randomly generated for each task instance. Score is determined by the distance traveled by Mario (measured in game tiles) minus the time taken in seconds. The target task is designed similar to the source task but with the addition of Goomba enemies. If the player touches a Goomba (with the exception of jumping on its head) Mario dies and score is taken from that point. The objective of the target task is that the player must travel fast and avoid Goombas.

Experiment 2: Speed-Coins. In the source task of this experiment, the player must travel as far to the right as fast as possible in a flat landscape while avoiding enemies (Goombas). Afterwards in the target task a new objective of collecting coins is added. Touching a coin will give the player a boost in score of the equivalent of traveling 5 game tiles. The positions of enemies and coins are randomly generated for each unique task. The optimal results can be achieved when the solutions capable of balancing three conflicting objectives: running to the end of the level as fast as possible, avoiding Goombas, and collecting coins.

Experiment 3: Dist-Kills. In the source task, the player is scored by the distance traveled through hilly terrain occupied by Goombas. The target task differs by offering additional points for each Goomba killed by the player (by stomping on them). This is another example of a transfer learning task where an additional objective is introduced, making it more difficult to obtain an optimal score.

Experiment 4: Goombas-Winged Goombas. In the experiment, the player is scored by their progression through a level with hilly terrain and Goombas (the same as the source task in Sect. 4.3) in the source task. Slightly different form the source task, regular Goombas are replaced with Winged Goombas in the target task. The challenge of the target task is that Winged Goombas can jump as high as Mario and may collide with the player in midair resulting in a death. Thus the objective is to achieve a higher score in a more difficult task.

5   Results and Discussion

In this section, the experimental results obtained from the four experiments are presented and analyzed separately. The section ends with a discussion on transferability and complexity of ANNs evolved by different testing algorithms.

5.1   Results on Speed-Enemies Experiment

In the Speed-Enemies experiment, we find that NEAT with PLPS can evolve more effective (higher fitness value shown in Fig. 3(a) and (b)) and less complex ANNs (smaller number of links and neurons illustrated in Fig. 3(c)) than other candidate algorithms. In STL phase, learning performance of NEAT with PS methods are competitive to that of the original NEAT shown in Fig. 3(a). In TTL phase, observably competitive performance of PLPS-NEAT+NEAT against other algorithms can be evidenced in Fig. 3(b). Moreover, PLPS-NEAT+NEAT yields p-values of 1.2214×10^{-3}, 0.0041 and 0.0342 while the performance of it is compared to that of Nothing+NEAT, NEAT+NEAT and BPS-NEAT+NEAT respectively. Nevertheless, the statistical significance cannot be supported between PLPS-NEAT+NEAT and TPS-NEAT+NEAT(or GPS-NEAT+NEAT) with p-value 0.4447 (or 0.1660). Lastly, Fig. 3(c) clearly illustrates that the complexity of evolved ANNs by NEAT with PS methods are managed to lower levels compared to that of original NEAT.

5.2   Results on Speed-Coins Experiment

While being performed in Speed-Coins experiment, PLPS-NEAT exhibits higher learning performance meanwhile results in structurally simplified ANNs. As seen in Fig. 4(a) and (b), in terms of learning performance, PLPS-NEAT not only observably outperforms all other algorithms either in STL or TTL phase, but also is confirmed statistically better. For example, in TTL phase, the p-values

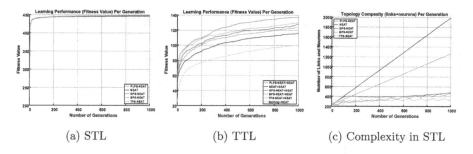

    (a) STL   (b) TTL   (c) Complexity in STL

Fig. 3. The comparison of transferability and complexity of ANNs (averaged over 30 trails) obtained by different algorithms on the Speed-Enemies experiment: (a) displays the averaged learning performances on STL (y-axis in scale [200,450]), (b) displays the averaged learning performances on TTL (y-axis in scale [20,140]), and (c) displays the averaged total numbers of links and neurons for the best ANNs obtained from STL.

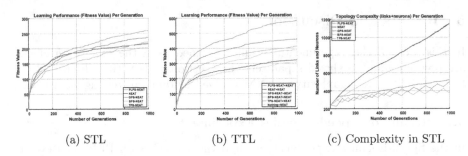

(a) STL   (b) TTL   (c) Complexity in STL

Fig. 4. The comparison of transferability and complexity of ANNs (averaged over 30 trails) obtained by different algorithms on the Speed-Coins experiment: (a) displays the averaged learning performances on STL (y-axis in scale [0,300]), (b) displays the averaged learning performances on TTL (y-axis in scale [0,600]), and (c) displays the averaged total numbers of links and neurons for the best ANNs obtained from STL.

are 9.1103×10^{-6} (Nothing+NEAT), 1.8500×10^{-5} (NEAT+NEAT), 0.0102 (GPS-NEAT+NEAT), 0.0015 (BPS-NEAT+NEAT), and 0.0076 (TPS-NEAT+NEAT). In addition, the complexity of final ANNs obtained by NEAT with PS methods is effectively controlled as shown in Fig. 4(c).

5.3   Results on Dist-Kills Experiment

Results on the Dist-Kills experiment also evidently show that PLPS-NEAT is capable of producing simpler ANNs to learn both source and target tasks effectively in the TL context. In Fig. 5(a) and (b), PLPS-NEAT is observed to be more effective among all candidate algorithms. To verify this observation in TTL phase, we perform pair-wised T-tests in-between PLPS-NEAT against all other algorithms. Statistical results reject the null hypothesis with p-values 1.3132×10^{-7} (Nothing+NEAT), 8.1118×10^{-6} (NEAT+NEAT),

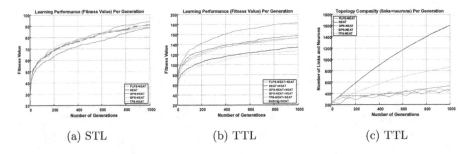

(a) STL   (b) TTL   (c) TTL

Fig. 5. The comparison of transferability and complexity of ANNs (averaged over 30 trails) obtained by different algorithms on the Dist-Kills experiment: (a) displays the averaged learning performances on STL (y-axis in scale [20,100]), (b) displays the averaged learning performances on TTL (y-axis in scale [20,200]), and (c) displays the averaged total numbers of links and neurons for the best ANNs obtained from STL.

0.0094 (GPS-NEAT+NEAT), 0.0426 (BPS-NEAT+NEAT) and 0.0322 (TPS-NEAT). Figure 5(c) also shows that PLPS is able to well control the complexity of its evolved ANNs.

5.4   Results on Goombas-Winged Goombas Experiment

Similar to the previous three experiments, results of the Goombas-Winged Goombas experiment give evidences of that PLPS-NEAT effectively learns to search ANNs with simple topology in this TL scenario. Clearly, PLPS-NEAT exhibits a leading performance among all testing algorithms in the STL stage as shown in Fig. 6(a). Moreover, Fig. 6(b) also shows that PLPS-NEAT+NEAT conducts a more effective TTL than other algorithms. Statistical tests provide a confirmation of the significance where the p-values are 0.0381, 0.0181, 0.0475, 0.0032 and 0.0297 corresponding to Nothing+NEAT, NEAT+NEAT, GPS-NEAT+NEAT, BPS-NEAT+NEAT and TPS-NEAT+NEAT respectively. Meanwhile, Fig. 6(c) also indicates that PLPS-NEAT as well as other PS methods based NEAT algorithm manage to suppress the topology bloat of evolved ANNs.

5.5   Discussion on Transferability and Complexity

In this research, we have achieved the research goal by successfully developing PLPS-NEAT-TL algorithm which can evolve transferable and simple ANNs on source tasks and later apply to target tasks improve TTL effectiveness.

First of all, PLPS-NEAT can evolve transferable ANNs, which can be verified from two aspects. First, experiments results on source tasks clearly reflect that PLPS-NEAT is effective in terms of the learning performance. Second, while perform PLPS-NEAT+NEAT on target tasks, we can also find that it is competitively effective in comparison to all other testing algorithms.

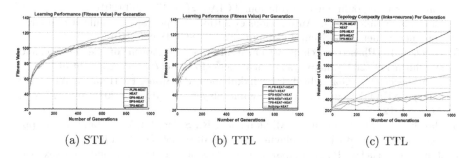

(a) STL   (b) TTL   (c) TTL

Fig. 6. The comparison of transferability and complexity of ANNs (averaged over 30 trails) obtained by different algorithms on the Goombas-Winged Goombas experiment: (a) displays the averaged learning performances on STL (y-axis in scale [20,140]), (b) displays the averaged learning performances on TTL (y-axis in scale [20,140]), and (c) displays the averaged total numbers of links and neurons for the best ANNs obtained from STL.

Secondly, the PLPS-NEAT-TL is capable of controlling the complexity in a reasonably low level. However, for experiment Speed-Enemies and Speed coins, a lower complexity but lower effectiveness has been obtained by TPS-NEAT algorithm compared to PLPS-NEAT-TL algorithm. This can be explained as that, during the simplification process, the pure randomness of TPS-NEAT may delete some important genes resulting in the performance worse than that of PLPS-NEAT-TL. Thus, it is useful to control the randomness during simplification phase for NEAT.

6   Conclusions

This paper explored the transferability of ANNs evolved by NEAT for intelligent gameplay, and further investigated the usefulness of PS. Motivated by the belief that simpler and effective ANNs are more transferable, we focused on NEAT with PS for TL. In line with this, we proposed a PLPS method with power-law ranking probability to effectively control the selection randomness during simplification phase. Experimental evidences showed that the PS methods are capable of improving the transferability of ANNs obtained from NEAT. Specifically, our proposed PLPS method outperformed NEAT and other PS based methods across all our TL experiments. Besides, we also found that the complexity of evolved ANNs can be effectively controlled. The size of ANNs consistently stayed at a low level while the performance was continuously improved. This work provides possibilities of applying PS and similar methods to other TL tasks. The advantages of using Power-Law distribution to control the PS methods should also be investigated in more depth.

References

1. Cardamone, L., Loiacono, D., Lanzi, P.L.: Learning to drive in the open racing car simulator using online neuroevolution. TCIAG **2**(3), 176–190 (2010)
2. Gauci, J., Stanley, K.O.: Autonomous evolution of topographic regularities in artificial neural networks. Neural Comput. **22**(7), 1860–1898 (2010)
3. Green, C.D.: Phased searching with neat: alternating between complexification and simplification (2004). http://sharpneat.sourceforge.net/phasedsearch.html
4. Hausknecht, M., Khandelwal, P., Miikkulainen, R., Stone, P.: HyperNEAT-GGP: a HyperNEAT-based Atari general game player. In: GECCO 2012, pp. 217–224. ACM (2012)
5. Hausknecht, M., Lehman, J., Miikkulainen, R., Stone, P.: A neuroevolution approach to general atari game playing. TCIAG **6**(4), 355–366 (2014)
6. James, D., Tucker, P.: A comparative analysis of simplification and complexification in the evolution of neural network topologies. In: GECCO 2004 (2004)
7. Karakovskiy, S., Togelius, J.: The mario ai benchmark and competitions. TCIAG **4**(1), 55–67 (2012)
8. Kotsiantis, S., Kanellopoulos, D.: Discretization techniques : a recent survey. TCSE **32**(1), 47–58 (2006)

9. Kuhlmann, G., Stone, P.: Graph-based domain mapping for transfer learning in general games. In: Kok, J.N., Koronacki, J., Mantaras, R.L., Matwin, S., Mladenič, D., Skowron, A. (eds.) ECML 2007. LNCS (LNAI), vol. 4701, pp. 188–200. Springer, Heidelberg (2007). doi:10.1007/978-3-540-74958-5_20. (Chap. 20)
10. Mandziuk, J.: Knowledge-Free and Learning-Based Methods in Intelligent Game Playing. Springer, Heidelberg (2010)
11. Moriarty, D.E., Miikkulainen, R.: Discovering complex othello strategies through evolutionary neural networks. Connect. Sci. **7**(3), 195–210 (1995)
12. Schrum, J., Miikkulainen, R.: Solving multiple isolated, interleaved, and blended tasks through modular neuroevolution. ECJ **24**(3), 459–490 (2016)
13. Sharma, M., Holmes, M.P., Santamaría, J.C., Irani, A., Isbell Jr., C.L., Ram, A.: Transfer learning in real-time strategy games using hybrid CBR/RL. In: IJCAI, vol. 7, pp. 1041–1046 (2007)
14. Stanley, K.O.: Efficient reinforcement learning through evolving neural network topologies. In: GECCO 2002. Citeseer (2002)
15. Stanley, K.O., Miikkulainen, R.: Evolving neural networks through augmenting topologies. Evol. Comput. **10**(2), 99–127 (2002)
16. Tan, M., Pu, J., Zheng, B.: Optimization of network topology in computer-aided detection schemes using phased searching with neat in a time-scaled framework. Cancer Inf. **13**(Suppl. 1), 17 (2014)
17. Taylor, M.E., Stone, P.: Behavior transfer for value-function-based reinforcement learning. In: AAMAS, p. 53 (2005)
18. Taylor, M.E., Stone, P.: Transfer learning for reinforcement learning domains: a survey. JMLR **10**(Jul), 1633–1685 (2009)
19. Taylor, M.E., Whiteson, S., Stone, P.: Temporal difference and policy search methods for reinforcement learning: an empirical comparison. In: NAAI, vol. 22, p. 1675. AAAI Press/MIT Press, Menlo Park/Cambridge/London (1999, 2007)
20. Taylor, M.E., Whiteson, S., Stone, P.: Transfer via inter-task mappings in policy search reinforcement learning. In: AAMAS, p. 37. ACM (2007)

Multiple Kernel Learning with One-Level Optimization of Radius and Margin

Shinichi Yamada[✉] and Kourosh Neshatian

Department of Computer Science and Software Engineering,
University of Canterbury, Christchurch, New Zealand
shinichi.yamada@pg.canterbury.ac.nz

Abstract. Generalization error rates of support vector machines are closely related to the ratio of radius of sphere which includes all the data and the margin between the separating hyperplane and the data. There are already several attempts to formulate the multiple kernel learning of SVMs using the ratio rather than only the margin. Our approach is to combine the well known formulations of SVMs and SVDDs. The proposed model is a closed system and always reaches the global optimal solutions.

Keywords: Support vector machines · Support vector data descriptions · Multiple kernel learning · Generalized convex functions

1 Introduction

In (Vapnik [18]), it was shown that the generalization error rates for linear hyperplane models are closely related to the ratio of the radius of enclosing spheres of data and the margin. Later this theorem was extended to nonlinear (kernel-based) hyperplane models (Bartlett and Shawe-Taylor [1]). In this article we propose the combination of standard formulations of support vector machines (SVMs) and support vector data descriptions (SVDDs) for multiple kernel learning (MKL) to directly minimize the ratio of radius and margin, which we call the SVM-SVDD models. The way in which we combine SVM and SVDD guarantees finding the optimal coefficients of kernels without imposing additional constraints such as normalization of kernels or ℓ_p-norm of the coefficients of kernels.

Several authors clearly stated the importance of the ratio of radius and margin and applied it to MKL (Do et al. [4,5]) (Liu et al. [10,11]). In (Gai et al. [6]), the authors firstly proposed the application of the combination of SVMs and SVDDs to multiple kernel learning and formulated a bi-level optimization problem. The present article takes the latter SVM-SVDD approach and improves it in several ways. Firstly we show that the proposed model can be formulated as a standard one-level optimization problem. Then we compute the dual optimal objective values and prove the existence of global optimal solutions.

© Springer International Publishing AG 2017
W. Peng et al. (Eds.): AI 2017, LNAI 10400, pp. 52–63, 2017.
DOI: 10.1007/978-3-319-63004-5_5

Lastly we conduct experiments to show the good prediction accuracy of the proposed method by comparing the performance with the state-of-art ℓ_p-norm MKL methods.

2   Background

In this section we provide a brief review of generalized convex functions and multiple kernel learning (MKL) formulation of SVMs and SVDDs.

2.1   Dual Forms of Generalized Convex Functions

In this paper we consider the following form of optimization problems:

$$P: \quad \min_{\mathbf{x}} \ f(\mathbf{x}) \tag{1}$$
$$\text{s.t. } g_i(\mathbf{x}) \leq 0, \quad i = 1, \ldots, m$$

where $f(\mathbf{x})$ and $g_i(\mathbf{x})$s are called the objective function and constraint functions, respectively.

If $f(\mathbf{x})$ is pseudoconvex and $g_1(\mathbf{x}), \ldots, g_m(\mathbf{x})$ are quasiconvex and if a constraint qualification such as a Slater's weak constraint qualification is satisfied, then the KKT conditions

$$g_i(\mathbf{x}) \leq 0, \quad i = 1, \ldots, m \tag{2}$$
$$\lambda_i g_i(\mathbf{x}) = 0, \quad i = 1, \ldots, m \tag{3}$$
$$\lambda_i \geq 0, \quad i = 1, \ldots, m \tag{4}$$
$$\nabla \left(f(\mathbf{x}) + \sum_{i=1}^{m} \lambda_i g_i(\mathbf{x}) \right) = 0 \tag{5}$$

are necessary and sufficient for optimality (Mangasarian [12]).

For generalized convex functions, two types of dual forms are commonly used (Mond and Weir [14]).

Wolfe Dual: For the optimization problem P in (1), the Wolfe dual is written as:

$$WD: \quad \max_{\mathbf{u}} \ f(\mathbf{u}) + \sum_{i=1}^{m} \lambda_i g_i(\mathbf{u})$$
$$\text{s.t. } \nabla f(\mathbf{u}) + \nabla \sum_{i=1}^{m} \lambda_i g_i(\mathbf{u}) = 0 \tag{6}$$
$$\lambda_i \geq 0, \quad i = 1, \ldots, m.$$

Proposition 1 *(Bector et al. [2], Mond [13]). If $f + \sum_{i=1}^{m} \lambda_i g_i (\lambda_i \geq 0)$ is pseudoconvex, the weak duality and the strong duality hold for the Wolfe dual.*

Mond-Weir Dual: For the optimization problem P in (1), the Mond-Weir dual is defined as:

$$MWD: \quad \max_{\mathbf{u}} \ f(\mathbf{u})$$

$$\text{s.t.} \ \nabla f(\mathbf{u}) + \nabla \sum_{i=1}^{m} \lambda_i g_i(\mathbf{u}) = 0 \tag{7}$$

$$\sum_{i=1}^{m} \lambda_i g_i(\mathbf{u}) \geq 0$$

$$\lambda_i \geq 0, \quad i = 1, \ldots, m.$$

Proposition 2 *(Mond and Weir [14]). If f is pseudoconvex and $\sum_{i=1}^{m} \lambda_i g_i (\lambda_i \geq 0)$ is quasiconvex, the weak duality and the strong duality hold for the Mond-Weir dual.*

Furthermore, the combination of those two dualities is also valid. Let $M = \{1, \ldots, m\}$ and S be a subset of M. If $f + \sum_{i \in S} \lambda_i g_i (\lambda_i \geq 0)$ is pseudoconvex and $\sum_{i \in M \setminus S} \lambda_i g_i (\lambda_i \geq 0)$ is quasiconvex, the weak duality and the strong duality hold for the following dual form (Mond and Weir [14]).

Combination of Wolfe and Mond-Weir dual:

$$W - MWD: \quad \max_{\mathbf{u}} \ f(\mathbf{u}) + \sum_{i \in S} \lambda_i g_i(\mathbf{u})$$

$$\text{s.t.} \ \nabla f(\mathbf{u}) + \nabla \sum_{i=1}^{m} \lambda_i g_i(\mathbf{u}) = 0 \tag{8}$$

$$\sum_{i \in M \setminus S} \lambda_i g_i(\mathbf{u}) \geq 0$$

$$\lambda_i \geq 0, \quad i = 1, \ldots, m.$$

2.2 MKL Formulation for SVMs

Now we turn to the review of the formulation of multiple kernel learning (MKL) for SVMs and SVDDs. For a given set of data:

$$(\mathbf{x}_1, y_1), (\mathbf{x}_2, y_2), \ldots, (\mathbf{x}_n, y_n) \quad \mathbf{x} \in \mathbb{R}^d, \quad y \in Y = \{-1, 1\},$$

the MKL optimization problem for SVMs is formulated as follows:

$$\min_{\hat{\mathbf{w}}, b, \boldsymbol{\xi}, \boldsymbol{\theta} : \boldsymbol{\theta} \geq 0} \sum_{k=1}^{m} \frac{\|\hat{\mathbf{w}}_k\|^2}{\theta_k} + C \sum_{i=1}^{n} \xi_i$$

$$\text{s.t.} \ y_i \Big(\sum_{k=1}^{m} \langle \hat{\mathbf{w}}_k, \Phi_k(\mathbf{x}_i) \rangle + b \Big) \geq 1 - \xi_i, \quad i = 1, \ldots, n \tag{9}$$

$$\xi_i \geq 0, \quad i = 1, \ldots, n$$

where $\Phi(\mathbf{x}_i)$ are nonlinear feature maps which map the input data $\mathbf{x} \in \mathbb{R}^d$ into a Hilbert space H (Kloft et al. [9]).

Here we consider a slightly general optimization problem:

$$\min_{\hat{w},b,\boldsymbol{\xi},\boldsymbol{\theta}:\boldsymbol{\theta} \geq 0} \kappa \sum_{k=1}^{m} \frac{\|\hat{\mathbf{w}}_k\|^2}{\theta_k} + C \sum_{i=1}^{n} \xi_i$$

$$\text{s.t. } y_i(\sum_{k=1}^{m} \langle \hat{\mathbf{w}}_k, \Phi_k(\mathbf{x}_i) \rangle + b) \geq 1 - \xi_i, \quad i = 1, \ldots, n \quad (10)$$

$$\xi_i \geq 0, \quad i = 1, \ldots, n$$

with a positive constant κ.

The Wolfe dual of (10) is derived as:

$$\min_{\boldsymbol{\theta}:\boldsymbol{\theta} \geq 0} \max_{\boldsymbol{\alpha}} \sum_{i=1}^{n} \alpha_i - \frac{1}{4\kappa} (\boldsymbol{\alpha} \circ \mathbf{y})^T K_\theta (\boldsymbol{\alpha} \circ \mathbf{y})$$

$$\text{s.t. } \sum_{i=1}^{n} \alpha_i y_i = 0 \quad (11)$$

$$0 \leq \alpha_i \leq C, \quad i = 1, \ldots, n$$

where $\boldsymbol{\alpha} \circ \mathbf{y}$ is an element-wise product between a vector $\boldsymbol{\alpha}$ and a vector $\mathbf{y}$. $K_\theta = \sum_{k=1}^{m} \theta_k K_k$ and K_k are kernel matrices which are inner products of $\Phi_k(\mathbf{x})$:

$$K_{k,ij} = \langle \Phi_k(\mathbf{x_i}), \Phi_k(\mathbf{x_j}) \rangle, \quad i, j = 1, \ldots, n$$

(Kloft et al. [9]).

2.3   MKL Formulation for SVDDs

In (Tax and Duin [17]), Support Vector Data Descriptions (SVDDs) were introduced as one-class support vector machines for detecting outliers. In this paper we need only "hard-margin" SVDDs and we consider the following MKL optimization problem for SVDDs with a positive constant κ:

$$\min_{R,\hat{\mathbf{a}},\boldsymbol{\theta}:\boldsymbol{\theta} \geq 0} \kappa R^2$$

$$\text{s.t. } \sum_{k=1}^{m} \theta_k \|\Phi_k(\mathbf{x_i})\|^2 - 2 \sum_{k=1}^{m} \langle \Phi_k(\mathbf{x_i}), \hat{\mathbf{a}}_k \rangle + \sum_{k=1}^{m} \frac{\|\hat{\mathbf{a}}_k\|^2}{\theta_k} \leq R^2, \ i = 1, \ldots, n$$

$$(12)$$

where $\mathbf{a}$ and R are center and radius of a sphere which contains $\Phi(\mathbf{x_i})$ (Kloft et al. [8]).

The Lagrangian L is written as:

$$L(R, \hat{\mathbf{a}}, \boldsymbol{\beta}, \boldsymbol{\theta} : \boldsymbol{\theta} \geq 0) = \kappa R^2 +$$

$$\sum_{i=1}^{n} \beta_i \left(\sum_{k=1}^{m} \theta_k \|\Phi_k(\mathbf{x_i})\|^2 - 2 \sum_{k=1}^{m} \langle \Phi_k(\mathbf{x_i}), \hat{\mathbf{a}}_k \rangle + \sum_{k=1}^{m} \frac{\|\hat{\mathbf{a}}_k\|^2}{\theta_k} - R^2 \right) \quad (13)$$

where $\boldsymbol{\beta} \geq 0$ are Lagrange multipliers.

Setting the partial derivatives to zero we obtain the following equations:

$$\frac{\partial L}{\partial R} = 0 \Rightarrow \kappa - \sum_{i=1}^{n} \beta_i = 0 \tag{14}$$

$$\frac{\partial L}{\partial \hat{\mathbf{a}}_k} = 0 \Rightarrow -\sum_{i=1}^{n} \beta_i \Phi_k(\mathbf{x_i}) + \frac{\hat{\mathbf{a}}_k}{\theta_k} \sum_{i=1}^{n} \beta_i = 0 \tag{15}$$

Setting $\tilde{\beta}_i = \frac{\beta_i}{\sum_{i=1}^{n} \beta_i}$ and substituting those values into L, the Wolfe dual of (12) for a fixed θ is computed as:

$$\min_{\boldsymbol{\theta}:\boldsymbol{\theta} \geq 0} \max_{\tilde{\boldsymbol{\beta}}} \ \kappa \left[\sum_{i=1}^{n} \tilde{\beta}_i K_{\theta,ii} - \tilde{\boldsymbol{\beta}}^T K_\theta \tilde{\boldsymbol{\beta}} \right]$$

$$\text{s.t.} \ \sum_{i=1}^{n} \tilde{\beta}_i = 1 \tag{16}$$

$$0 \leq \tilde{\beta}_i, \quad i = 1, \ldots, n.$$

Lemma 1. *For the optimization problem (12), the optimal R^2 is derived as:*

$$R^2 = K_{\theta,ii} - 2K_{\theta,i.}\tilde{\boldsymbol{\beta}} + \tilde{\boldsymbol{\beta}}^T K_\theta \tilde{\boldsymbol{\beta}}$$

for the instances $\mathbf{x}_i$ with $\tilde{\beta}_i > 0$ and the optimal R^2 does not change for any values of κ.

The optimal R^2 is derived as in (Tax and Duin [17]). The latter part of the claim is obvious, because for monotone increasing functions $\psi(\mathbf{x})$,

$$\text{argmin}_{\mathbf{x} \in X} \ \psi(\mathbf{x}) = \text{argmin}_{\mathbf{x} \in X} \ \kappa\psi(\mathbf{x})$$

for any $\kappa > 0$. It is an important property for our model and we show it as a lemma.

3   The Proposed SVM-SVDD Models

In this section we formulate SVM-SVDD models and examine their properties.

3.1   Formulation of SVM-SVDD Models

Combining those two optimization problems (10) and (12), we formulate the MKL optimization problem for SVM-SVDD models:

$$\min_{\boldsymbol{\theta}:\boldsymbol{\theta}\geq 0,\hat{\mathbf{w}},b,R,\hat{\mathbf{a}},\boldsymbol{\xi}} \sum_{k=1}^{m} \frac{\|\hat{\mathbf{w}}_k\|^2}{\theta_k} R^2 + C \sum_{i=1}^{n} \xi_i$$

$$\text{s.t. } y_i(\sum_{k=1}^{m} \langle \hat{\mathbf{w}}_k, \Phi_k(\mathbf{x}_i) \rangle + b) \geq 1 - \xi_i, \qquad i = 1, \ldots, n \qquad (17)$$

$$\xi_i \geq 0, \quad i = 1, \ldots, n.$$

$$\sum_{k=1}^{m} \theta_k \|\Phi_k(\mathbf{x}_i)\|^2 - 2\sum_{k=1}^{m} \langle \Phi_k(\mathbf{x}_i), \hat{\mathbf{a}}_k \rangle + \sum_{k=1}^{m} \frac{\|\hat{\mathbf{a}}_k\|^2}{\theta_k} \leq R^2, i = 1, \ldots, n$$

We assume that $\sum_{k=1}^{m} \frac{\|\hat{\mathbf{w}}_k\|^2}{\theta_k} > 0$ and $R^2 > 0$ and use the convention that $\frac{t}{0} = 0$ if $t = 0$ and ∞ otherwise (Kloft et al. [9]).

As proved in (Gai et al. [6]), this model has an important invariance property for scaling of kernels.

Lemma 2 *(Gai et al. [6]). Multiplying kernel K_θ by a positive constant $\pi > 0$ does not change the optimal value of the objective function in (17).*

3.2 Learning Algorithms

Since the feasible regions for $(\hat{\mathbf{w}}, b, \boldsymbol{\xi})$, $(R, \hat{\mathbf{a}})$ and $(\boldsymbol{\theta})$ are completely different, we apply Gauss-Seidel block coordinate descent methods to solve the optimization problem (17).

Step 1: optimization for $(R, \hat{\mathbf{a}})$ for fixed $\boldsymbol{\theta}$ and $(\hat{\mathbf{w}}, b, \boldsymbol{\xi})$: From Lemma 1, for fixed $\boldsymbol{\theta}$ and $\hat{\mathbf{w}}$ the optimal R and $\hat{\mathbf{a}}$ in (17) can be solved using the optimization problem (16) with $\kappa = 1$.

Step 2: optimization for $(\hat{\mathbf{w}}, b, \boldsymbol{\xi})$ for fixed $\boldsymbol{\theta}$ and $(R, \hat{\mathbf{a}})$: For fixed $\boldsymbol{\theta}$ and $(R, \hat{\mathbf{a}})$, the optimal $\hat{\mathbf{w}}$ and b can be obtained using the optimization problem (11) with $\kappa = R^2$.

Step 3: optimization for $\boldsymbol{\theta}$ for fixed $(\hat{\mathbf{w}}, b, \boldsymbol{\xi})$ and $(R, \hat{\mathbf{a}})$: The Lagrangian L of (17) is:

$$L(\boldsymbol{\theta} : \boldsymbol{\theta} \geq 0, \hat{\mathbf{w}}, b, \boldsymbol{\xi}, \boldsymbol{\alpha}, \boldsymbol{\lambda}, R, \hat{\mathbf{a}}, \boldsymbol{\beta})$$

$$= \sum_{k=1}^{m} \frac{\|\hat{\mathbf{w}}_k\|^2}{\theta_k} R^2 + C \sum_{i=1}^{n} \xi_i$$

$$- \sum_{i=1}^{n} \alpha_i \left[y_i \left(\sum_{k=1}^{m} \langle \hat{\mathbf{w}}_k, \Phi_k(\mathbf{x}_i) \rangle + b \right) - 1 + \xi_i \right] - \sum_{i=1}^{n} \lambda_i \xi_i \qquad (18)$$

$$+ \sum_{k=1}^{m} \frac{\|\hat{\mathbf{w}}_k\|^2}{\theta_k} \left[\sum_{i=1}^{n} \tilde{\beta}_i \left(\sum_{k=1}^{m} \theta_k \|\Phi_k(\mathbf{x}_i)\|^2 - 2\sum_{k=1}^{m} \langle \Phi_k(\mathbf{x}_i), \hat{\mathbf{a}}_k \rangle + \sum_{k=1}^{m} \frac{\|\hat{\mathbf{a}}_k\|^2}{\theta_k} - R^2 \right) \right]$$

where $\tilde{\beta}_i = \frac{\beta_i}{\sum_{i=1}^{n} \beta_i}$.

In order to derive the optimal $\boldsymbol{\theta}$ we solve $\frac{\partial L}{\partial \theta_l} = 0$, which can be done by Newton methods or methods of nonlinear equations (Nocedal and Wright [15]). However the Hessian has terms of $\frac{1}{\theta_k^3}$. Since many θ_k approach to 0, they make the computation quite unstable. Conjugate gradient methods and Quasi-Newton methods which do not use the second derivative information do not work well in terms of speed and stability. Therefore we use the following approximate solution.

Let the Lagrangian (18) to be:

$$
L(\boldsymbol{\theta} : \boldsymbol{\theta} \geq 0, \hat{\mathbf{w}}, b, \boldsymbol{\xi}, \boldsymbol{\alpha}, \boldsymbol{\lambda}, R, \hat{\mathbf{a}}, \boldsymbol{\beta})
$$
$$
= \sum_{k=1}^{m} \frac{\|\hat{\mathbf{w}}_k\|^2}{\theta_k} R^2 + C \sum_{i=1}^{n} \xi_i
$$
$$
- \sum_{i=1}^{n} \alpha_i \left[y_i \left(\sum_{k=1}^{m} \langle \hat{\mathbf{w}}_k, \Phi_k(\mathbf{x}_i) \rangle + b \right) - 1 + \xi_i \right] - \sum_{i=1}^{n} \lambda_i \xi_i
$$
$$
+ \sum_{k=1}^{m} \frac{\|\hat{\mathbf{w}}_k\|^2}{\ddot{\theta}_k} \left[\sum_{i=1}^{n} \tilde{\beta}_i \left(\sum_{k=1}^{m} \theta_k \langle \Phi_k(\mathbf{x}_i), \Phi_k(\mathbf{x}_i) \rangle - 2 \sum_{k=1}^{m} \langle \Phi_k(\mathbf{x}_i), \hat{\mathbf{a}}_k \rangle + \sum_{k=1}^{m} \frac{\|\hat{\mathbf{a}}_k\|^2}{\theta_k} - R^2 \right) \right]
$$

where $\ddot{\theta}_k$ is the θ_k of the previous iteration. If we use this approximation we can solve θ_k analytically.

$$
\frac{\partial L}{\partial \theta_l} = 0 \Rightarrow -\frac{\|\hat{\mathbf{w}}_l\|^2 R^2}{\theta_l^2} + \sum_{k=1}^{m} \frac{\|\hat{\mathbf{w}}_k\|^2}{\ddot{\theta}_k} \left(\sum_{i=1}^{n} \tilde{\beta}_i \langle \Phi_l(\mathbf{x}_i), \Phi_l(\mathbf{x}_i) \rangle - \frac{\|\hat{\mathbf{a}}_l\|^2}{\theta_l^2} \right) = 0
$$
$$
\Rightarrow \theta_l = \sqrt{\frac{\|\hat{\mathbf{w}}_l\|^2 R^2 + \sum_{k=1}^{m} \frac{\|\hat{\mathbf{w}}_k\|^2}{\ddot{\theta}_k} \|\hat{\mathbf{a}}_l\|^2}{\sum_{k=1}^{m} \frac{\|\hat{\mathbf{w}}_k\|^2}{\ddot{\theta}_k} \sum_{i=1}^{n} \tilde{\beta}_i \|\Phi_l(\mathbf{x}_i)\|^2}}
\tag{19}
$$

In summary the optimization problem (17) can be solved by block coordinate descent methods as follows:

Algorithm 1. *Block coordinate descent methods:*

- *input:* feasible $\boldsymbol{\alpha}$, $\boldsymbol{\beta}$, $\boldsymbol{\theta}$
- *while:* optimality conditions are not satisfied *do*
    - *Step 1:* Compute $\boldsymbol{\beta}$ according to (12)
    - *Step 2:* Compute $\boldsymbol{\alpha}$ according to (10)
    - *Step 3:* Compute $\boldsymbol{\theta}$ according to (19)
- *end*

3.3   Convergence Properties

In this section we derive dual objective values of the problem (17). For that purpose we use the dual form of $W - MWD$ in (8). At first we derive the dual form for a fixed $\boldsymbol{\theta}$. In the notation in (8) we put the constraints of the SVM parts into S and the constraint of the SVDD part into $M \setminus S$.

$$S : \begin{cases} y_i(\sum_{k=1}^m \langle \hat{\mathbf{w}}_k, \Phi_k(\mathbf{x}_i) \rangle + b) \geq 1 - \xi_i, & i = 1, \ldots, n \\ \xi_i \geq 0, & i = 1, \ldots, n \end{cases}$$

$$M \setminus S : \sum_{k=1}^m \theta_k \|\Phi_k(\mathbf{x_i})\|^2 - 2 \sum_{k=1}^m \langle \Phi_k(\mathbf{x_i}), \hat{\mathbf{a}}_k \rangle + \sum_{k=1}^m \frac{\|\hat{\mathbf{a}}_k\|^2}{\theta_k} \leq R^2, \, i = 1, \ldots, n$$

For a fixed $\boldsymbol{\theta}$, $W - MWD$ in (8) is derived as:

$$\max_{\boldsymbol{\alpha}, \boldsymbol{\beta}} \sum_{i=1}^n \alpha_i - \frac{1}{4R^2} (\boldsymbol{\alpha} \circ \mathbf{y})^T K_\theta (\boldsymbol{\alpha} \circ \mathbf{y})$$

$$\text{s.t.} \sum_{i=1}^n \alpha_i y_i = 0, \quad 0 \leq \alpha_i \leq C, \quad i = 1, \ldots, n \qquad (20)$$

$$\sum_{i=1}^n \tilde{\beta}_i = 1, \quad 0 \leq \tilde{\beta}_i, \quad i = 1, \ldots, n.$$

$$\sum_{i=1}^n \tilde{\beta}_i K_{\theta,ii} - \tilde{\boldsymbol{\beta}}^T K_\theta \tilde{\boldsymbol{\beta}} - R^2 \geq 0.$$

Now we consider the dual problem as a function of $\boldsymbol{\theta}$:

$$F(\boldsymbol{\theta}) = \sum_{i=1}^n \alpha_i - \frac{1}{4R^2(\boldsymbol{\theta})} (\boldsymbol{\alpha} \circ \mathbf{y})^T K_\theta (\boldsymbol{\alpha} \circ \mathbf{y})$$

$$G(\boldsymbol{\theta}) = \sum_{i=1}^n \tilde{\beta}_i K_{\theta,ii} - \tilde{\boldsymbol{\beta}}^T K_\theta \tilde{\boldsymbol{\beta}} - R^2(\boldsymbol{\theta})$$

where

$$R^2(\boldsymbol{\theta}) = \text{mean}_{\tilde{\beta}_i > 0} \left(K_{\theta,ii} - 2\tilde{\boldsymbol{\beta}}^T K_{\theta,i.} + \tilde{\boldsymbol{\beta}}^T K_\theta \tilde{\boldsymbol{\beta}} \right).$$

Since we are assuming $R^2 > 0$, $\boldsymbol{\theta} \neq 0$ (some elements of $\boldsymbol{\theta}$ are positive). From Lemma 2, scaling of $\boldsymbol{\theta}$ (kernels) does not affect the solution. Therefore we add a constraint of $\sum_{k=1}^m \theta_k = 1$ and solve the following optimization problem for a fixed $\boldsymbol{\alpha}$ and $\boldsymbol{\beta}$:

$$\min_{\boldsymbol{\theta}} \sum_{i=1}^n \alpha_i - \frac{1}{4R^2(\boldsymbol{\theta})} (\boldsymbol{\alpha} \circ \mathbf{y})^T K_\theta (\boldsymbol{\alpha} \circ \mathbf{y})$$

$$\text{s.t.} \sum_{k=1}^m \theta_k = 1 \qquad (21)$$

$$\theta_k \geq 0, \quad k = 1, \ldots, m$$

$$\sum_{i=1}^n \tilde{\beta}_i K_{\theta,ii} - \tilde{\boldsymbol{\beta}}^T K_\theta \tilde{\boldsymbol{\beta}} - R^2(\boldsymbol{\theta}) \leq 0$$

where
$$R^2(\boldsymbol{\theta}) = \text{mean}_{\tilde{\beta}_i > 0} \left(K_{\theta,ii} - 2\tilde{\boldsymbol{\beta}}^T K_{\theta,i\cdot} + \tilde{\boldsymbol{\beta}}^T K_\theta \tilde{\boldsymbol{\beta}} \right).$$

Note that in the last inequality $G(\boldsymbol{\theta}) \leq 0$ (not $G(\boldsymbol{\theta}) \geq 0$), because $\tilde{\beta}_i \geq 0$ and $g_i(\mathbf{x}) \leq 0$, $i = 1, \ldots, m$ in the optimization problem P in (1). $\frac{1}{4R^2}(\boldsymbol{\alpha} \circ \mathbf{y})^T K_\theta (\boldsymbol{\alpha} \circ \mathbf{y})$ is of the form of a homogeneous linear fractional problem $\frac{\mathbf{a}^T \boldsymbol{\theta}}{\mathbf{b}^T \boldsymbol{\theta}}$, which clearly shows scaling of $\boldsymbol{\theta}$ does not affect the optimal value of the solution. Substituting $\sum_{k=1}^{m} \theta_k = 1$, it becomes of the form of a linear fractional programming problem $\frac{\mathbf{c}^T \boldsymbol{\theta} + \alpha}{\mathbf{d}^T \boldsymbol{\theta} + \beta}$. Since it is both pseudoconvex and pseudoconcave (Cambini and Martein [3]), a local minimum is the global optimal solution. Linear fractional programming problems are transformed to linear programming problems and can be solved with standard linear problem solvers (Uddin et al. [16]).

By substituting $\boldsymbol{\theta}$ into (21), we obtain a dual objective value of (17). From the weak duality it guarantees that the optimal solutions in (17) are bounded from below. We can use the dual objective values to compute the duality gap as a stopping criteria.

Now we consider the convergence of our algorithm in the previous section. We use the following results about the Gauss-Seidel block coordinate descent methods:

Proposition 3 *(Grippo and Sciandrone [7]). Suppose that $f(\mathbf{x})$ is pseudoconvex on X, If the sequence $\{\mathbf{x}^k\}$ generated by the Gauss-Seidel block coordinate methods has limit points $\bar{\mathbf{x}} = \lim_k \mathbf{x}^k$, then every limit point $\bar{\mathbf{x}}$ of $\{\mathbf{x}^k\}$ is a global optimal point of $f(\mathbf{x})$.*

The next theorem establishes convergence of the proposed algorithm. The proof of the theorem is directly derived from the proposition:

Theorem 1. *The Gauss-Seidel block coordinate descent method in Algorithm 1 converges to the global optimal solutions in (17).*

Proof. The optimization problems of Step 1 and Step 2 in Algorithm 1 are solved on the compact domain $\{0 \leq \alpha_i \leq C, i = 1, \ldots, n\}$ and $\{\sum_{i=1}^{n} \tilde{\beta}_i = 1, 0 \leq \tilde{\beta}_i, i = 1, \ldots, n\}$, respectively. For Step 3, the domain of θ_k can be restricted to $\{\sum_{k=1}^{m} \theta_k = 1, 0 \leq \theta_k, k = 1, \ldots, m\}$ without changing the optimal solutions from Lemma 2. Therefore, the sequence $\{\mathbf{x}^k\}$ generated by the block coordinate methods has limiting points on the compact sets, which are the global optimal solutions from Proposition 3.

4   Experimental Results

The purpose of the experiments is to demonstrate capability of the proposed method compared with the state-of-art ℓ_p-norm MKL methods ($p \geq 1$). We use datasets with various levels of sparsity. The datasets are the same as those in (Kloft et al. [9]) which are synthesized as follows. The input data $\mathbf{x}$ have 50 features $(\mathbf{x}_i = (x_{i,1}, \ldots, x_{i,50}))$. Each feature $x_{i,k}$ is generated from the independent Gaussian distribution with the equal variance 1 and the mean $1.75\theta_k$ for the label 1 and $-1.75\theta_k$ for the label -1 and the θ_k has the value of $\{1, 0\}$.

In the most sparse data only one θ_k is set to 1 and the rest are set to 0; in other words, only one feature has discrimination power and the rest are noise. There are a total of six data sets. In the least sparse data set, all 50 θ_ks are set to 1; that is, all the features are relevant. When more than one feature are relevant, all of them are required to achieve the maximum prediction. The ratio of noisy features for the six data sets are $\{0, 0.44, 0.66, 0.82, 0.92, 0.98\}$.

We train the model using the training datasets of 50 instances. We construct a set of kernels for all features and for each single feature. For each of those kernels we prepare a set of Gaussian kernels with different width parameters $\sigma^2 \in \{2^{-10}, 2^{-9}, \ldots, 2^{10}\}$. In total, we use a linear combination of 51 (features) $\times$ 21 (width parameters) = 1071 kernels. The regularization parameter $C \in \{2^{-10}, 2^{-9}, \ldots, 2^{10}\}$ is tuned by the validation datasets of 5,000 instances. We simply choose the value of C with the highest accuracy on the validation data. Finally we evaluate the prediction accuracy of the proposed method by the test datasets of 5,000 instances and compare the results with those of the ℓ_p-norm methods with $p \in \{1, 2, 4, 8, 16\}$. Those numbers are chosen this way so that the results are comparable with the original paper. We repeat the experiments 100 times for each dataset.

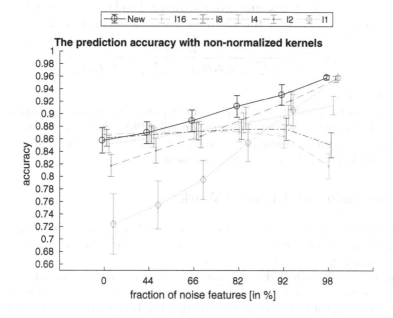

Fig. 1. The prediction accuracy on the non-normalized test datasets

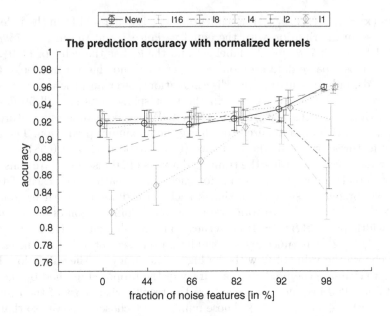

Fig. 2. The prediction accuracy on the normalized test datasets

In the experiments we examine both normalized and non-normalized kernels. The former is normalized by the multiplicative normalization method:

$$k(x, x') \Rightarrow \frac{k(x, x')}{\frac{1}{n} \sum_{i=1}^{n} k(x_i, x_i) - \frac{1}{n^2} \sum_{i,j=1}^{n} k(x_i, x_j)} \quad (22)$$

(Kloft et al. [9]).

Figure 1 is the prediction accuracy on the non-normalized test datasets and Fig. 2 is the prediction accuracy on the normalized test datasets. The new solutions have comparable prediction accuracy to ℓ_1-norm methods for sparse data and are much more robust for non-sparse data.

5   Conclusion and Future Work

The combination of SVM and SVDD can be formulated as a one-level optimization problem. We proved that it is a closed system and has a global optimal solution that is guaranteed to be reached.

The proposed method directly minimizes the ratio of radius and margin, which is the key term in the generalization error rates of support vector machines. However our primal objective of constructing the better MKL method has not been completed. Empirical results indicate that p in ℓ_p-norm method which adjusts the sparsity of solutions is also an important parameter. Therefore the reincorporation of the adjusting parameter into the model is the next target of our research.

References

1. Bartlett, P., Shawe-Taylor, J.: Generalization performance of support vector machines and other pattern classifiers. In: Advances in Kernel Methods, pp. 43–54. MIT Press, Cambridge (1999)
2. Bector, M.K., Bector, C.R., Klassen, J.E.: Duality for a nonlinear programming problem. Util. Math. **11**, 87–99 (1977)
3. Cambini, A., Martein, L.: Generalized Convexity and Optimization, 1st edn. Springer, Heidelberg (2009)
4. Do, H., Kalousis, A.: Convex formulations of radius-margin based support vector machines. In: Proceedings of the 30th International Conference on Machine Learning, Cycle 1. JMLR Proceedings, vol. 28, pp. 169–177. JMLR.org (2013)
5. Do, H., Kalousis, A., Woznica, A., Hilario, M.: Margin and radius based multiple kernel learning. In: Buntine, W., Grobelnik, M., Mladenić, D., Shawe-Taylor, J. (eds.) ECML PKDD 2009. LNCS, vol. 5781, pp. 330–343. Springer, Heidelberg (2009). doi:10.1007/978-3-642-04180-8_39
6. Gai, K., Chen, G., Zhang, C.: Learning kernels with radiuses of minimum enclosing balls. In: Proceedings of the 23rd International Conference on Neural Information Processing Systems, NIPS 2010, pp. 649–657. Curran Associates Inc., USA (2010)
7. Grippo, L., Sciandrone, M.: On the convergence of the block nonlinear gauss-seidel method under convex constraints. Oper. Res. Lett. **26**(3), 127–136 (2000)
8. Kloft, M., Brefeld, U., Düessel, P., Gehl, C., Laskov, P.: Automatic feature selection for anomaly detection. In: Proceedings of the 1st ACM Workshop on Workshop on AISec, AISec 2008, pp. 71–76. ACM, New York (2008)
9. Kloft, M., Brefeld, U., Sonnenburg, S., Zien, A.: lp-norm multiple kernel learning. J. Mach. Learn. Res. **12**, 953–997 (2011)
10. Liu, X., Wang, L., Yin, J., Zhu, E., Zhang, J.: An efficient approach to integrating radius information into multiple kernel learning. IEEE Trans. Cybern. **43**(2), 557–569 (2013)
11. Liu, X., Yin, J., Long, J.: On radius-incorporated multiple kernel learning. In: Torra, V., Narukawa, Y., Endo, Y. (eds.) MDAI 2014. LNCS, vol. 8825, pp. 227–240. Springer, Cham (2014). doi:10.1007/978-3-319-12054-6_20
12. Mangasarian, O.L.: Nonlinear Programming (1969)
13. Mond, B.: Mond-weir duality. In: Pearce, C., Hunt, E. (eds.) Optimization, pp. 157–165 (2009)
14. Mond, B., Weir, T.: Generalized concavity and duality. In: Schaible, S., Ziemba, W.T. (eds.) Generalized Concavity in Optimization and Economics, pp. 263–279. Academic Press (1981)
15. Nocedal, J., Wright, S.J.: Numerical Optimization. Springer, New York (1999)
16. Uddin, M., Saha, S., Hossain, M., Mondal, R.: A new approach of solving linear fractional programming problem (LFP) by using computer algorithm. Open J. Optim. **4**, 74–86 (2015)
17. Tax, D.M.J., Duin, R.P.W.: Support vector data description. Mach. Learn. **54**(1), 45–66 (2004)
18. Vapnik, V.N.: Statistical Learning Theory, 1st edn. Wiley, Hoboken (1998)

A Deterministic Actor-Critic Approach to Stochastic Reinforcements

Yemi Okesanjo[(✉)] and Victor Kofia

University of Toronto, Toronto, ON M5T 1N4, Canada
{o.okesanjo,victor.kofia}@mail.utoronto.ca

Abstract. Learning optimal policies under stochastic rewards presents a challenge for well-known reinforcement learning algorithms such as Q-learning. Q-learning has been shown to suffer from a positive bias that inhibits it from learning under inconsistent rewards. Actor-critic methods however do not suffer from such bias but may also fail to acquire the optimal policy under rewards of high variance. We propose the use of a reward shaping function in order to minimize the variance within stochastic rewards. By reformulating Q-learning as a deterministic actor-critic, we show that the use of such reward shaping function improves the acquisition of optimal policies under stochastic reinforcements.

Keywords: Actor-critic · Gumbel-Max · Moving median · Reward shaping · Double-Q · Q-learning · Stochastic reinforcements · Reinforcement learning

1 Introduction

Teaching agents how to act under uncertainty is one of the pursuits of artificial intelligence. In reinforcement learning, agents learn how to act from the rewards they receive when exploring an unknown environment [25]. The environment can be deterministic, in which case an agent is certain to enter another state because of an action or receive a particular reward for said action. The environment can also be stochastic, in which case entering another state because of an action becomes probable - as are the rewards. There are many sources of stochasticity in an environment such as the underlying functions governing state transitions and rewards or the policy of an agent. In this paper, we focus on the case where the underlying reward function is the source of stochasticity.

Stochastic rewards can be problematic for well known reinforcement learning algorithms such as Q-learning [25]. Q-learning belongs to a class of temporal difference (TD) algorithms that improve an agent's policy once the next state and reward are observed [22]. Due to lack of information about future rewards, Q-learning assigns higher policy values (Q-values) to actions that appear better at the moment. This introduces a bias that is pronounced under environments

---

Y. Okesanjo—Code at https://github.com/ev0/Dac-mdp.

W. Peng et al. (Eds.): AI 2017, LNAI 10400, pp. 64–75, 2017.
DOI: 10.1007/978-3-319-63004-5_6

with inconsistent or high-variance rewards [9]. In such environments, it can fail to acquire the optimal policy.

There have been several approaches to mitigate the effects of stochastic rewards on Q-learning. These approaches either combine double estimators in order to get unbiased policy values [10], regularize the policy values themselves [6] or interpret the stochasticity as noise to be filtered [15]. Of these approaches, the use of double estimators has been the most effective. In the double estimator approach, each estimator updates its policy using Q-values from the other estimator. This makes the policy values unbiased and reduces the effect an inconsistent reward has on a single estimator.

It is well known that actor-critic algorithms do not suffer from the bias present in Q-learning [3,19] as they improve their policy differently. Using a deterministic actor-critic, we extend this notion to the estimation of Q-values. However under stochastic rewards of high variance, actor-critic methods are still susceptible to sub-optimal policies. We reduce this variance in the rewards by using a shaping function. Reward shaping functions are functions that guide an agent towards better policies by adding more information about a task to the given rewards [16]. In order to reduce the variance in the given rewards, we scale such rewards using a moving median function. The moving median function maintains a fixed-sized buffer of recently observed rewards and at each point in time, returns the median of the rewards within the buffer. This presents a clearer and more consistent form of reinforcement for many agents. We demonstrate that with this kind of shaping function, deterministic actor-critic methods can acquire optimal policies under stochastic rewards.

Our contributions are a deterministic actor-critic for Q-value estimation and a moving-median reward shaping function, which we term *smoothing* function, that extends the temporal difference update. The rest of this paper is organized as follows: Sect. 2 briefly discusses the background knowledge concerning our work. Section 3 presents our proposed method, Incremental Deterministic Smoothed Actor-Critic (Idsac). Section 4 discusses methods related to our work. Section 5 discusses experimental results obtained on environments with stochastic rewards. Finally, Sect. 6 contains our conclusion and a discussion on future work.

2   Preliminaries

Consider an underlying Markov decision process (MDP) with a set of discrete states, S, and actions, A. At each time step, t, an agent takes an action, a_t, when in a state, s_t. The action is taken according to a policy, π, which is a function over S and A. Upon taking a_t, the agent transitions into the next state, s_{t+1}, and is given an immediate reward, r_{t+1}, that is drawn from a reward function with distribution, $p(r_{t+1}|s_t, a_t)$. Under this formulation, the agent's goal is to acquire the optimal policy, π^*, which maximizes the expected cumulative rewards given by the MDP. For any policy, this problem is represented by the objective

$$J^{\pi} = \mathbb{E}[\sum_{t=0}^{\infty} \gamma^t r_{t+1} | s_t, \pi] = \mathbb{E}[Q^{\pi}(s_t, a_t) | s_t, \pi] \tag{1}$$

where $\gamma \in (0,1]$ is a discount factor for future rewards and $Q^{\pi}(s,a)$, known as the action-value, is the expected cumulative rewards gotten for taking an action in a state according to the policy.

2.1 Reward Shaping

The reward, r_{t+1}, represents prior knowledge of a given task. Additional knowledge can be added to it so that an agent acquires the optimal policy faster. Suppose an MDP is expressed as $M = \langle S, A, T, R \rangle$, where T and R are the underlying state transition and reward functions. A change to r_{t+1} also changes R such that we have a new function, R', that can be expressed as

$$R'(s_t, a_t, s_{t+1}) = R(s_t, a_t, s_{t+1}) + F(s_t, a_t, s_{t+1}) \tag{2}$$

where $F(s_t, a_t, s_{t+1})$ is known as the reward-shaping function [16]. F can also represent an arbitrary transformation, in which case we have

$$R'(s_t, a_t, s_{t+1}) = F(r_{t+1}, s_t, a_t, s_{t+1}) \tag{3}$$

where $r_{t+1} = R(s_t, a_t, s_{t+1})$. Here the reward-shaping function scales the reward by a fixed positive value [16]. Using R' results in a different MDP, $M' = \langle S, A, T, R' \rangle$. To ensure that any optimal policy acquired under M' is also optimal under M, F must be potential-based such that for some function, Φ,

$$F(s_t, a_t, s_{t+1}) = \gamma\Phi(s_{t+1}) - \Phi(s_t) \tag{4}$$

2.2 Actor-Critic Algorithms

In order to maximize the objective, J^{π}, the policy can be represented by a density function, $\pi_{\theta} : S \times A \mapsto (0,1)$. J^{π} is then maximized by taking the log-likelihood gradient

$$\nabla_{\theta}J^{\pi}(\theta) = \mathbb{E}[Q^{\pi}(s_t, a_t)\nabla_{\theta}\log\pi_{\theta}(a_t|s_t)|s_t, \pi] \tag{5}$$

The gradient above suffers from a high variance [18] that is reduced by subtracting a baseline, $b_v(s_t)$. Now in addition to $Q^{\pi}(s_t, a_t)$, we define a state value, $V^{\pi}(s_t)$, that represents the expected cumulative reward gotten in a state. This is written as, $V^{\pi}(s_t) = [Q^{\pi}(s_t, a_t)|\pi]$ and (5) becomes

$$\nabla_{\theta}J^{\pi}(\theta) = \mathbb{E}[(V^{\pi}(s_t) - b_v(s_t))\nabla_{\theta}\log\pi_{\theta}(a_t|s_t)|s_t, \pi] \tag{6}$$

The above is maximized when the baseline is equals to the value of the state. However the state value is unknown. We bootstrap it using $V^{\pi}(s_t) = \mathbb{E}[r_{t+1}|s_t, a_t] - \gamma b_v(s_{t+1})$ such that

$$\nabla_{\theta}J^{\pi}(\theta) = \mathbb{E}[\delta_t\nabla_{\theta}\log\pi_{\theta}(a_t|s_t)|s_{t+1}, s_t, \pi] \tag{7}$$

where $\delta_t = \mathbb{E}[r_{t+1}|s_t, a_t] + \gamma b_v(s_{t+1}) - b_v(s_t)$, is the TD error [23]. In practice, the immediate reward, r_{t+1}, is used in place of $\mathbb{E}[r_{t+1}|s_t, a_t]$ as it is unknown. The actor-critic framework essentially comprises of two functions: $b_v(s)$, the critic and $\pi_\theta(a|s)$, the actor. Actions are selected from $\pi_\theta(a|s)$ and their value, with regards to the next state, is evaluated by $b_v(s)$.

2.3 Bias Maximization

Algorithms such as Q-learning utilize a deterministic policy $a_t = \mu(s)$ that is always taken in a state. In order to select the action, discrete deterministic policies often employ a greedy maximization over the set of actions in a state [20]. For Q-learning, this is $\mu_\theta(s) = \arg\max_a Q_\theta(s, a)$. We can learn the optimal Q-values by minimizing the squared TD error [22] such that

$$\nabla_\theta J^\mu(\theta) = (Q^\mu(s_t, a_t) - Q_\theta(s_t, a_t))\nabla_\theta Q_\theta(s_t, a_t) \tag{8}$$

where the TD error, $\delta_t = Q^\mu(s_t, a_t) - Q_\theta(s_t, a_t)$. But bootstrapping the true action-value requires a max operator which results in biased updates. Note that

$$Q^\mu(s_t, a_t) = \arg\max_{a_{t+1}} \mathbb{E}[r_{t+1} + \gamma Q^\mu(s_{t+1}, a_{t+1})|s_{t+1}, s_t] \tag{9}$$

where the max is returned after taking expectation over many samples [9].

Nevertheless, a_{t+1} can be chosen after each sample so as to estimate Q^μ. After many samples, the expectation becomes $\mathbb{E}[r_{t+1} + \gamma \arg\max Q^\mu(s_{t+1}, a_{t+1})]$ and by Jensen's inequality,

$$\mathbb{E}[\arg\max_{a_{t+1}} Q_\theta(s_{t+1}, a_{t+1})] \geq \arg\max_{a_{t+1}} \mathbb{E}[Q_\theta(s_{t+1}, a_{t+1})] \tag{10}$$

which results in Q-values that are higher than they ought to be.

This does not always hinder the acquisition of optimal policies because for many tasks, the rewards are deterministic such that $r_{t+1} = \mathbb{E}[r_{t+1}|s_t, a_t]$. Problems arise when the rewards are stochastic, as $r_{t+1} \sim p(r_{t+1}|s_t, a_t)$ can either increase or decrease the Q-value of an action such that a^*, the true optimal action, is not selected. As a form of bias, the action with the highest Q-value is selected and in the long run, it leads to sub-optimal policies.

3 Incremental Deterministic Smoothed Actor Critic

3.1 Deterministic Actor-Critic

The maximization bias can be circumvented by using the on-line TD(0) update of the actor-critic framework which does not depend on the value of the next action. This way, a policy can be updated without using the max operator. The TD error, δ_t, obtained through this method is considered an unbiased estimate of an action's advantage [3, 19].

However in order to utilize δ_t for a deterministic policy, we re-parametrize the stochastic policy for the actor-critic framework such that $\pi_\theta(a_t|s_t) = \mu_\theta + \epsilon$, where $\mu_\theta(s)$ is a deterministic policy [20]. Using the Gumbel-Max trick [5,17],

$$\pi_\theta(a|s) = \mu_\theta(s,\epsilon) = \arg\max_a \frac{\theta_a^\top \phi(s)}{\tau} + \epsilon_a, \quad \epsilon_a \sim \text{Gumbel}(0,1) \tag{11}$$

where τ is the policy temperature and ϵ_a is a standard Gumbel noise. The temperature can be annealed to increase the determinism of the policy [12] but in this paper we induce determinism by applying the noise according to an e-greedy schedule.

The above policy does not estimate anything in particular unlike in Q-learning where the policy estimates the expected cumulative rewards. Here the policy terms are important only when compared against that of other actions in a state. We refer to this as the deterministic actor-critic (Dac). Its update is expressed as

$$\theta_a = \theta_a + \delta \nabla_\theta \mu_{\theta_a}(s) \tag{12}$$

where $\nabla_\theta \mu_{\theta_a}(s)$ is the policy gradient. To estimate the expected cumulative rewards, note that

$$Q^\mu(s,a) = A^\mu(s,a) + V^\mu(s) \tag{13}$$

where $A^\mu(s,a)$ represents the advantage value of an action [2]. It can also be represented using $A_\theta(s,a) = \mu_{\theta_a}(s)$. Since the TD errors obtained using $b_v(s_t)$ are unbiased estimates of the advantage, we learn the policy by minimizing its squared distance from δ_t such that

$$\theta_a = \theta_a + (\delta - A_\theta(s_t, a_t)) \nabla_\theta \mu_{\theta_a}(s) \tag{14}$$

In our experiments, we find that this policy update results in a better performance than that of (12). The advantage function has been noted by [7] as resulting in a better performance than Q-learning because it does include a state value estimate and for stochastic policies, it has been reported by [3] as following the natural gradient which is the steepest descent direction in the policy parameter space. While [3] involves a stochastic policy, we utilize a deterministic policy and as such refer to the actor using update (14) as the Incremental deterministic actor-critic (Idac).

3.2   Smoothing Function

Although the Idac estimates the Q-values without suffering from the maximization bias, it can still fail under stochastic rewards. If the rewards are spurious and have a high variance, they can prevent it from acquiring the optimal policy.

We reduce this variance in the rewards by using a reward shaping function, $G(r_{t+1}, s_t, a_t, s_{t+1})$, which we refer to as a *smoothing* function. Any shaping function can be used as a smoothing function, as long as the output reward, r'_{t+1}, has lesser variance than the input rewards. Even with less variance, applying a shaping function to Q-learning can still cause it to acquire sub-optimal policies due to the maximization bias.

In this paper, we use a moving median for the smoothing function. The moving median is widely used in computer vision and signal processing to reduce variance and remove noise from signals because of its robustness to outliers. We implement it by using a buffer of size $L = 2N + 1$ that contains the most recent $2N$ rewards for each observed transition pair (s, a, s'). Upon receiving a reward, r_{t+1}, for a transition, it is added to the buffer and the median of the rewards for said transition is returned. If r_{t+1} is deterministic, it is returned. Otherwise if it is stochastic and differs greatly from the observed rewards of a transition, it is adjusted to fit the range of reward values. We refer to the Idac that uses a smoothing function as the Incremental deterministic smoothed actor-critic (Idsac).

Algorithm 1. Incremental deterministic smoothed actor-critic (Idsac)

1: Initialize parameters θ and v.
2: Initialize step sizes $\alpha, \beta \in (0, 1)$.
3: **for** $t \in T$ **do**
4:     Choose action, $a_t = \mu_\theta(s_t) + \epsilon$, $\epsilon \sim \text{Gumebl}(0, 1)$.
5:     Observe the next state, s_{t+1}, and reward, r_{t+1}.
6:     $\delta_t \leftarrow G(r_{t+1}, s_t, a_t, s_{t+1}) + \gamma b_v(s_{t+1}) - b_v(s_t)$
7:     $v \leftarrow v + \beta \delta_t \nabla_v b_v$
8:     $\theta \leftarrow \theta + \alpha(\delta_t - A(s_t, a_t))\nabla_\theta \mu_{\theta_i}(s)$
9:     $s_t \leftarrow s_{t+1}$
10: **return**

3.3   Convergence

We now prove that the Idsac converges to the optimal policy for an MDP. The proof follows from that of [14] for stochastic actor-critic algorithms. There the TD error is only used in the critic update [3]. Nevertheless, we follow the same ideas but for a deterministic policy under tabular representation.

To prove convergence in an MDP, M, we first prove that the actor and the critic converge under the transformed MDP M'. Convergence in M' then extends to M if the smoothing function is potential-based [16]. Both the actor and critic are updated at different time steps, α and β, which we account for by requiring that the actor appear stationary to the critic during the critic's update. This means that, $\alpha/\beta \to 0$ [14]. The critic is updated using on-line TD(0) and so we refer the reader to the convergence proof of TD(λ) in [11] where the substitution for λ can be made. To prove that the actor converges, we use the following lemma from [21].

Lemma 1. *Consider a stochastic process (ζ_t, Δ_t, F_t), where $\zeta_t, \Delta_t, F_t : X \to \mathbb{R}$ satisfy the equation*

$$\Delta_{t+1}(x_t) = (1 - \zeta_t(x_t))\Delta_t(x_t) + \zeta_t(x_t)F_t(x_t),$$

for $x_t \in X$ and $t \in \{0, 1, 2, ...\}$. Let P_t be a sequence of increasing σ-fields such that ζ_0 and δ_0 are P_0-measurable and ζ_t, Δ_t and F_{t-1} are P_t-measurable, $t \geq 1$. Assume that: (1) The set X is finite. (2) $\zeta_t(x_t) \in [0, 1], \sum_t \zeta_t(x_t) = \infty, \sum_t (\zeta_t(x_t))^2 < \infty$ w.p.1 and $\forall x \neq x_t : \zeta_t(x_t) = 0$. (3) $\|\mathbb{E}[F_t | P_t]\| \leq \kappa \|\Delta_t\| + c_t$, where $\kappa \in [0, 1)$ and c_t converges to 0 w.p.1. (4) $Var\{F_t(x_t) | P_t\} \leq K(1 + \kappa \|\Delta_t\|)^2$, where K is some constant.

Let $\|.\|$ denote a maximum norm. Then Δ_t converges to zero with probability one.

To use the above lemma, we show that as a stochastic process, the actor satisfies all the conditions listed above. Now consider the following

Theorem 1. *In an ergodic MDP, M, the actor as defined by (12) will converge to the optimal policy as long as the conditions below are fulfilled:*
(1) The MDP is finite i.e. $|S \times A| < \infty$. (2) $\alpha_t(x_t) \in [0, 1], \sum_t \alpha_t(x_t) = \infty$, $\sum_t (\alpha_t(x_t))^2 < \infty$ w.p.1 and $\forall x \neq x_t : \alpha_t(x_t) = 0$. (3) $\alpha_t(x_t) / \beta_t(x_t) \to 0$. (4) $R'_{sa} = R_{sa} + \gamma \Phi(s') - \Phi(s)$. (5) $\gamma \in [0, 1)$. (6) $Var\{R^{s'}_{sa}\} < \infty$.

Proof. For the actor under M', the following apply. The first two conditions of Lemma 1 are satisfied by the first three assumptions of the theorem. The fourth condition follows from the sixth assumption [9]. To satisfy the third condition, note that we can express the actor update as

$$A_{t+1}(s_t, a_t) = (1 - \alpha_t(s_t, a_t)) A_t(s_t, a_t) + \alpha_t(s_t, a_t) \delta_t(s_t, a_t)$$

and we relate it with Lemma 1 by subtracting the optimal value, $A^*(s, a)$, from both sides. This means that $\Delta_t(s_t, a_t) = A_t(s_t, a_t) - A^*_t(s_t, a_t)$ and we have

$$\Delta_{t+1}(s_t, a_t) = (1 - \alpha_t(s_t, a_t)) \Delta_t(s_t, a_t) + \alpha_t(s_t, a_t) (\delta_t(s_t, a_t) - A^*_t(s_t, a_t))$$

where $F_t(s_t, a_t) = \delta_t(s_t, a_t) - A^*_t(s_t, a_t)$

$$= R' + \gamma V(s_{t+1}) - (V(s_t) + A^*_t(s_t, a_t))$$

$$\leq R' + \gamma V(s_{t+1}) - Q^*_t(s_t, a_t) = F^Q_t(s_t, a_t)$$

It is well-known that $\|\mathbb{E}\{F^Q_t(s_t, a_t) | P_t\}\| \leq \gamma \|\Delta_t\|$ s.t $\mathbb{E}\{F^Q_t(s_t, a_t) | P_t\}$ is a contraction mapping under maximum norm [9,21]. Hence $\|\mathbb{E}[F_t(s_t, a_t) | P_t]\| \leq \gamma \|\Delta_t\|$, with $\kappa = \gamma$ and $c_t = 0$. Since the conditions for the lemma are satisfied, the actor process converges under M'. From the fourth assumption of our theorem, the optimal policy of the actor is optimal under M [16]. Hence the actor converges under M.

4   Related Work

The Idac and Idsac both belong to the family of advantage algorithms proposed by [2]. This family of algorithms estimate the advantage value and have been noted as performing better than Q-learning because of its scaling problem [8]. Not all algorithms in this class are as effective as the Idac under stochastic rewards. The advantage learning algorithm [7] also suffers from a positive bias as it uses the max operator in the same way as Q-learning. The advantage updating algorithm [2] on the other hand does not seem to and so we compare its performance with the Idac in our experiments.

Stochastic rewards have been studied under the context of noisy reinforcements by [15]. There the rewards are filtered using a simple moving average. However this method is very susceptible to outliers and non-Gaussian noise where it performs worse. Our work can be seen as an extension to a wider class of filters that are more robust to such noise.

The high variance from stochastic reinforcements was used by [9] to highlight the problem of using a single estimator to calculate the Q-values. Combining two estimators in the form of a Double-Q algorithm was shown to reduce this variance. As discussed earlier, Double-Q is very effective under stochastic rewards. However it is rather slow due to the manner in which the estimators are updated. By comparison, Idsac converges to the optimal policy faster.

Average targeted DQN is also another attempt at variance reduction for Q-learning. In order to reduce the variance in deep Q-networks (DQN), [1] proposed replacing the target network in the DQN with one averaged over a given time period. At various intervals, the parameters for a target network are stored in a buffer. At each time step, the weighted average of the networks within the buffer is then used to estimate the TD error.

5   Experimental Results

We compare the effectiveness of both Idsac and Dac in learning optimal policies alongside algorithms such as Double-Q, Advantage Updating, Q-learning and smoothed Q-learning. Our experiments evaluate these algorithms under games of chance where the rewards are stochastic and the bias maximization problem has been studied [9].

5.1   French Roulette

French roulette is a classic casino game in which bets are placed against the outcome of a spinning wheel. The wheel is typically marked with a sequence of numbers between 0–36. As the wheel spins, a dealer rolls a ball unto it. Before doing so, players place bets on which number the ball will fall on once the wheel stops spinning. If a bet wins, a player receives his/her initial wager and the payout for the bet. Otherwise the wager is lost.

There are many kinds of bets. These include *straight* bets where a player bets on a single number; *dozen* bets where a player bets on either the first (1–12), second (13–24) or third (25–36) dozens; *odd* bets where the player bets on odd numbers etc. We represent a bet as an action. For example, a *single* bet on say 17 is an action, as is either of the *dozen* bets. In total we use 155 actions [13].

Assume an agent wagers $1 on each betting round. There is a single state and each action returns to it. In addition, there is an action that stops play and terminates the episode. No reward is given for this action. Suppose a bet covers k numbers on the wheel. The reward for winning the bet is $r_{t+1} = \frac{36}{k} - 1$. Despite this, it is expected that repeating any bet will result in a long term loss for an agent because the probability of winning the bet is less than the probability of losing it [9]. Hence the optimal policy is to terminate the episode.

5.2   Chuck-a-Luck

Chuck-a-luck is a similar game of chance in which a player bets on the outcome of three rolled dice. The dice are housed in a cage that is rotated by the dealer in each betting round. Here five kinds of bets can be made: *single, any triple, high, low* and *field* bets [4]. Without loss of generality, we only use the first four.

Single bets are placed on a certain number appearing in a given round. If the number in question appears on one die, the player receives a payout of $1. If it appears on two dice, $2 is received. If it appears on all three dice, $10 is received. A larger payout of $30 is received for an *any triple* bet in which any number appears on all three dice. The *high* and *low* bets have a smaller payout of $1 each. For *high* bets, the sum of the three dice must be greater than 10, with the exclusion of the higher triples: $\{4, 4, 4\}, \{5, 5, 5\}$ and $\{6, 6, 6\}$. Similarly, for *low* bets, the sum must be less than 11 with the exclusion of the lower triples.

The MDP for this problem is also a recurrent single state with each action representing a bet. Again it is expected that in the long term, each bet results in a loss [24] and as such the optimal action is to terminate the episode. An example of this can be seen by comparing the rewards for a *single* bet with the expected reward, $\mathbb{E}[r_{t+1}] = -\$0.0463$.

In the above problems, the learning parameters and test procedure for the algorithms are similar to those used in [9]. They are: $\gamma = 0.95, \epsilon = 0.1, \alpha = 1/n(s, a) = 1/$no. of visits to (s, a) and $1/n(s) = 1/$no. of visits to (s). Each agent was trained on a problem for $100,000$ steps, after which the optimal policy was tested. This was repeated over 10 trials and the average results are discussed in the following section.

5.3   Results

The graph below shows the percentage of trials in which the aforementioned algorithms acquire the optimal policy for Chuck-a-luck. Only Double-Q and Idsac acquire the optimal policy in all trials. The Idac and Dac algorithms perform better than the remaining algorithms but still fail to acquire the optimal policy in some trials (Fig. 1).

From the graph above, we see that the smoothing function improves both the Idac and Q-learning algorithms as their smoothed counterparts: Idsac and Q-learning solve for the optimal policy in significantly more trials. The training graph below shows the average value of each bet against the value of the optimal action for each algorithm (Fig. 2).

We observe that the bias present in Q-learning causes it to value the bets higher than the optimal action, whereas our algorithm Idsac assigns a lower value

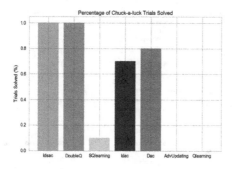

Fig. 1. Percentage of trails solved for chuck-a-luck.

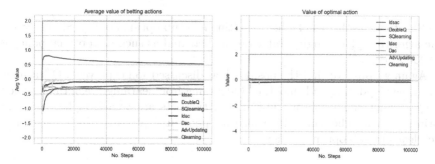

Fig. 2. Average value of bets vs value of the optimal action in chuck-a-luck.

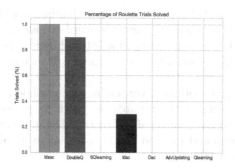

Fig. 3. Percentage of trails solved for french roulette.

to the bets. This bias results in both Q-learning and smoothed Q-learning not acquiring the optimal policy for Chuck-a-luck. Similarly, Advantage Updating values the bets slightly higher than the optimal action. This is likely due to its use of a max operator in updating and normalizing the advantage values. Hence it also fails to acquire the optimal policy (Fig. 3).

In roulette, Idsac effectively acquires the optimal policy as does the Double-Q algorithm [9]. The smoothing function in Idsac causes it to consistently assign lower values to roulette bets whereas the variance in the payouts sometimes cause

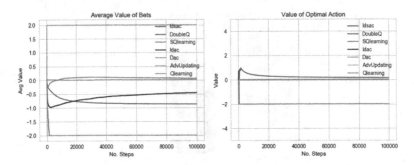

Fig. 4. Average value of bets vs value of the optimal action in french roulette.

the Idac to value the bets higher, resulting in a sub-optimal policy. Similarly, the Dac algorithm places higher value on the bets and as such the optimal policy is not found (Fig. 4).

Again we observe that the positive bias discussed so far prevents Q-learning, Advantage Updating and smoothed Q-learning from learning the optimal policy. In Q-learning and smoothed Q-learning, the bets are valued higher than the optimal action. The same thing also happens in Advantage Updating and as such leads to sub-optimal policies.

6   Conclusion

So far, we have proposed the use of a reward shaping function as a means of reducing the variance in stochastic rewards. We have also proved and demonstrated that reformulating Q-learning as a deterministic actor-critic avoids the problem of bias maximization and improves the use of such reward shaping function.

A direction for future work involves scaling this method to more challenging real world problems in which the rewards are much more uncertain and inconsistent. When the proposed smoothing function is represented by a function approximator, our proposed method has a potential to obtain optimal behavioural policies for artificial agents.

Acknowledgements. The authors would like to thank Prof. Guerzhoy for the helpful guidance and discussions.

References

1. Anschel, O., Baram, N., Shimkin, N.: Deep reinforcement learning with average target DQN (2016). https://arxiv.org/abs/1611.01929v2. Accessed Mar 2017
2. Baird, L.: Reinforcement learning in continuous time: advantage updating. In: IEEE International Conference on Neural Networks, pp. 2448–2453 (1994)
3. Bhatnagar, S., Sutton, R., Ghavamzadeh, M., Lee, M.: Incremental natural actor-critic algorithms. Neural Inform. Process. Syst. **20**, 105–112 (2007)

4. Casino-To-Go: Rules and playing guide: Chuck-a-luck (2007). http://www. casino-to-go.co.uk/downloads/Chuck-A-Luck%20Rules%20and%20Guide.pdf. Accessed Mar 2017
5. Chen, Y., Ghahramani, Z.: Scalable discrete sampling as a multi-armed bandit problem. In: 33rd International Conference on Machine Learning (2016)
6. Fox, R., Pakman, A., Tishby, N.: Taming the noise in reinforcement learning via soft updates. In: 32nd Conference on Uncertainty in AI (2016)
7. Harmon, M., Baird, L.: Residual advantage learning applied to a differential game. In: International Conference on Neural Networks (1996)
8. Harmon, M., Harmon, S.: Reinforcement learning: a tutorial (1997)
9. Hasselt, H.: Double q-learning. In: Neural Information Processing Systems, vol. 23 (2010)
10. Hasselt, H., Guez, A., Silver, D.: Deep reinforcement learning with double q-learning. In: AAAI (2016)
11. Jaakkola, T., Jordan, M., Singh, S.: On the convergence of stochastic iterative dynamic programming algorithms. In: Neural Information Processing Systems, vol. 7 (1994)
12. Jang, E., Gu, S., Poole, B.: Categorical reparametrization with gumbel-softmax. In: International Conference on Learning Representations (2016)
13. Kavouras, I.: How to play roulette: Rules, odds & payouts. http://www.roulette30. com/2014/04/how-to-play-roulette-beginners-guide.html. Accessed Mar 2017
14. Konda, V., Tsitsiklis, J.: Actor-critic algorithms. Neural Inform. Process. Syst. **12**, 1008–1014 (1999)
15. Moreno, A., Martin, J., Soria, E., Magdalena, R., Martinez, M.: Noisy reinforcements in reinforcement learning: some case studies based on grid worlds. In: 6th WSEAS International Conference on Applied Computer Science (2006)
16. Ng, A., Harada, Y., Russell, S.: Policy invariance under reward transformations: theory and application to reward shaping. In: 16th International Conference on Machine Learning, pp. 278–287 (1999)
17. Papandreou, G., Yuille, A.: Perturb-and-map random fields: using discrete optimization to learn and sample from energy models. In: International Conference on Computer Vision (2011)
18. Peters, J., Schaal, S.: Policy gradient methods for robotics. In: IEEE International Conference on Intelligent Robotics Systems, pp. 2219–2225 (2006)
19. Silver, D.: Reinforcement learning: policy gradient (2015). http://www0.cs.ucl.ac. uk/staff/D.Silver/web/Teaching_files/pg.pdf. Accessed Mar 2017
20. Silver, D., Lever, G., Heess, N., Degris, T., Wierstra, D., Riedmiller, M.: Deterministic policy gradient algorithms. In: 31st International Conference on Machine Learning (2014)
21. Singh, S., Jaakkola, T., Littman, M.L., Szepesvári, C.: Convergence results for single-step on-policy reinforcement-learning algorithms. Mach. Learn. **38**, 287–308 (2000)
22. Sutton, R., Barto, A.: Reinforcement Learning: An Introduction, chap. 6, pp. 143–145, 2nd edn. The MIT Press, Cambridge (2016)
23. Sutton, R., McAllester, D., Singh, S., Mansour, Y.: Policy gradient methods for reinforcement learning with function approximation. Neural Inform. Process. Syst. **12**, 1057–1063 (2000)
24. Tannenbaum, P.: Mini-Excursion 4: the mathematics of managing risk. In: Excursions in Modern Mathematics, 7 edn. Pearson, London (2010)
25. Watkins, C., Dayan, P.: Q-learning. Machine Learning **8**, 9–44 (1992)

SecMD: Make Machine Learning More Secure Against Adversarial Malware Attacks

Lingwei Chen and Yanfang Ye[✉]

Department of Computer Science and Electrical Engineering,
West Virginia University, Morgantown, WV 26506, USA
lgchen@mix.wvu.edu, yanfang.ye@mail.wvu.edu

Abstract. As machine learning based systems have been successfully deployed for malware detection, the incentive for defeating them increases. In this paper, we explore the security of machine learning in malware detection on the basis of a learning-based classifier. In particular, (1) considering different capabilities of the attackers (i.e., how much knowledge they have regarding feature representation, training set, and learning algorithm), we present a set of corresponding adversarial attacks and implement a general attack model *AdvAttack* to thoroughly assess the adversary behaviors; (2) to effectively counter these evasion attacks, we propose a resilient yet elegant secure-learning paradigm *SecMD* to improve the system security against a wide class of adversarial attacks. Promising experimental results based on the real sample collections from Comodo Cloud Security Center demonstrate the effectiveness of our proposed methods.

Keywords: Secure machine learning · Malware detection · Adversarial attack

1 Introduction

Malware (short for *mal*icious soft*ware*) is software that deliberately fulfills the harmful intent of an attacker, such as viruses, trojans, and ransomware. It has been used as the major weapon by the cyber-criminals to launch a wide range of security attacks (e.g., compromising computers, stealing user's confidential information), which present serious damages and significant financial loss to Internet users. It's reported that up to one billion dollars were stolen in roughly two years from financial institutions worldwide due to malware attacks [13]. In order to combat the malware attacks, systems applying machine learning techniques have been developed for malware detection in recent years [5,7,12,17,28]. In these systems, based on different feature representations, a variety of classification methods are used for model construction to detect malware. Though these techniques offer unparalleled flexibility in malware detection, machine learning itself may open the possibility for an adversary who maliciously "mis-trains" a classifier (e.g., by changing data distribution or feature importance) in the

© Springer International Publishing AG 2017
W. Peng et al. (Eds.): AI 2017, LNAI 10400, pp. 76–89, 2017.
DOI: 10.1007/978-3-319-63004-5_7

detection system. When the learning system is deployed in a real-world environment, it is of a great interest for malware attackers to actively manipulate the data to make the classifier produce minimum true positive (i.e., maximumly misclassifying malware as benign), using some combination of prior knowledge, observation, and experimentation.

Malware attackers and defenders are engaged in a never-ending arms race. At each round, both the attackers and defenders analyze the vulnerabilities of each other, and develop their own optimal strategies to overcome the opponents, which has led to considerable countermeasures of variability and sophistication between them. For example, when signature-based methods [9] prevailed in malware detection, attackers began to use code obfuscation and encryption to evade the detection [14]. Currently, the issues of understanding machine learning security in adversarial settings are starting to be leveraged, from either adversarial or defensive perspectives. Unfortunately, most existing researches for adversarial machine learning [3,6,10,16,18,20,29] are rarely conducted on malware detection. With the popularity of machine learning based detections, such adversaries will sooner or later present. In this paper, with the inputs of Windows Application Programming Interface (API) calls extracted from the Portable Executable (PE) files, we explore the security of machine learning in malware detection on the basis of a learning-based model Valkyrie [28] which has been successfully deployed in real application. The major contributions of our work can be summarized as follows:

- *Providing insights into malware evasion attacks under different scenarios:* The attackers may have different levels of knowledge of the learning system [22]. We define a set of evasion attacks corresponding to the different scenarios, and implement a general attack model *AdvAttack* to thoroughly assess the adversary behaviors.
- *Building a secure-learning model for malware detection against adversarial attacks:* Resting on the learning-based classifier which is degraded by the adversarial malware attacks, we propose a secure-learning model *SecMD* to counter these attacks. In our proposed method, we incorporate adversarial data manipulation into the learning algorithm to formalize the impact of attacks, and enhance the robustness of the classifier using the security regularization terms.
- *Comprehensive experimental study on real sample collections from an anti-malware industry company:* Resting on the real sample sets from Comodo Cloud Security Center, we build a practical solution for malware evasion and detection based on our proposed methods and provide a series of comprehensive experiments to empirically evaluate the performances of these methods.

Note that here we only exploit Windows API calls as a case study for our approaches, but the proposed methods can also be readily applied to other feature representations (e.g., n-grams, dynamic system calls, etc.). The rest of the paper is organized as follows: Sect. 2 defines the problem of machine learning based malware detection. Section 3 presents the adversarial attacks under different scenarios and Sect. 4 describes the implementation of the adversarial attacks.

Section 5 introduces the secure-learning model. Section 6 systematically evaluates the effectiveness of the proposed methods. Section 7 discusses the related work. Finally, Sect. 8 concludes.

2   Machine Learning Based Malware Detection

A malware detection system using machine learning techniques attempts to identify zero-day malware or variants of known malware through building a classification model based on the labeled training sample set and predefined feature representations. Based on the collected PE files, without loss of generality, in this paper, we extract Windows API calls as the features to represent the file samples, since they can effectively reflect the behaviors of program codes (e.g., the API "GetFileType" in "KERNEL32.DLL" can be used to retrieve the file type of the specified file) [26].

Resting on the extracted API calls, we denote our dataset D to be of the form $D = \{\mathbf{x}_i, y_i\}_{i=1}^n$ of n file samples, where $\mathbf{x}_i$ and y_i is the set of API calls and the class label of file i respectively ($y_i \in \{+1, -1, 0\}$, +1: malicious, −1: benign, and 0: unknown). Let d be the number of all extracted API calls in the dataset D. Each of the PE file can be represented by a binary feature vector:

$$\mathbf{x}_i =< x_{i1}, x_{i2}, x_{i3}, ..., x_{id} >, \tag{1}$$

where $\mathbf{x}_i \in \mathbb{R}^d$, and $x_{ij} = \{0, 1\}$ (i.e., if file i includes API_j, then $x_{ij} = 1$; otherwise, $x_{ij} = 0$).

The malware detection problem can be stated in the form of: $f : \mathcal{X} \to \mathcal{Y}$ which assigns a label $y \in \mathcal{Y}$ (i.e., −1 or +1) to an input file $\mathbf{x} \in \mathcal{X}$ through the learning function f. To illustrate but without loss of generality, we explore the adversarial attacks based on a learning-based classifier Valkyrie [28], which is a linear classification model successfully deployed in the real application, denoted as:

$$\mathbf{f} = \text{sign}(f(\mathbf{X})) = \text{sign}(\mathbf{X}^T \mathbf{w} + \mathbf{h}), \tag{2}$$

where $\mathbf{f}$ is a label vector of file samples to be predicted, each column of matrix $\mathbf{X}$ is the API feature vector of a PE file, $\mathbf{w}$ is the coefficients and $\mathbf{h}$ is the biases. Considering the *prior* labeled information vector $\mathbf{y}$ and Lagrange multiplier $\boldsymbol{\xi}$, the malware detection can be formalized as an optimization problem:

$$\underset{\mathbf{f}, \mathbf{w}, \mathbf{h}; \boldsymbol{\xi}}{\text{argmin}} \ \frac{1}{2}||\mathbf{y} - \mathbf{f}||^2 + \frac{1}{2\beta}\mathbf{w}^T\mathbf{w} + \frac{1}{2\gamma}\mathbf{h}^T\mathbf{h} + \boldsymbol{\xi}^T(\mathbf{f} - \mathbf{X}^T\mathbf{w} - \mathbf{h}), \tag{3}$$

subject to Eq. (2), where β and γ are the regularization parameters. In this classification model, $\frac{1}{2}||\mathbf{y} - \mathbf{f}||^2$ denotes the total loss with respect to all file samples, $\frac{1}{2\beta}\mathbf{w}^T\mathbf{w}$ and $\frac{1}{2\gamma}\mathbf{h}^T\mathbf{h}$ are penalty terms to deal with the overfitting problem in the learning model. Note that Eq. (3) is a typical linear classification model consists of specific loss function and regularization terms. Without loss of generality, the equation can be transformed into different linear models depending on the choices of loss function and regularization terms.

3   Adversarial Attacks

In malware detection, adversaries would like to violate the security context by either (a) allowing malicious files to be misclassified as benign (*integrity attack*) or (b) creating a denial of service in which benign files are incorrectly classified as malicious (*availability attack*). In this paper, we focus on the integrity attack. Considering that the attacker may have different levels of knowledge of the target learning system about [22]: (i) the feature space, (ii) the training sample set, and (iii) the learning algorithm, we characterize the attacker's knowledge in terms of Ψ that encodes the feature space X, the training sample set D, and the classification function f. Accordingly, we present three well-defined evasion attack scenarios to facilitate analysis of the adversary behaviors as below.

Mimicry Attacks. In this scenario, the attackers are assumed to know the feature space and be able to obtain a collection of file samples to imitate the original training dataset, i.e., $\Psi = (X, \hat{D})$. In such attack, the strategy of the attackers is to manipulate a set of features (API calls in our case) to probe the learning system. It's more likely that the attackers may effectively evade the detection if the file samples drawn from surrogate dataset are distributed closely as the training sample set.

Imperfect-Knowledge Attacks. Further than the previous scenario, we assume that both the feature space and the original training sample set can be fully controlled by the attackers, i.e., $\Psi = (X, D)$. Compared with mimicry attacks, the knowledge of the malware and benign files in the original training dataset definitely leverage clearer insight for the attackers to conduct the adversarial attacks to evade the learning system's detection, although they may have no knowledge of the learning algorithm.

Ideal-Knowledge Attacks. This is the worst case where the learning algorithm is also known to the attackers, i.e., $\Psi = (X, D, f)$. When the attackers can perfectly access to the learning system, they can thoroughly investigate the vulnerability of the learning system, and accurately manipulate data to evade the target system with the strongest probability. Since this worst case provides a potential upper bound on the degradation suffered by the learning system under the adversarial attacks, it can be deployed to evaluate the performance of the learning system under other limited scenarios.

4   Implementation of Adversarial Attacks

4.1   Adversarial Cost

Given an original malware sample $\mathbf{x} \in \mathcal{X}^+$, the potential attacks attempt to manipulate it to be detected as benign (i.e., $\mathbf{x}' \in \mathcal{X}^-$), with the minimal adversarial cost. Since the API calls of each file is represented by a binary feature vector, a typical modification can be characterized by the addition or elimination of each binary. Hence the cost of the manipulation, can be encoded by the number of features that are changed from $\mathbf{x}$ to $\mathbf{x}'$:

$$c(\mathbf{x}', \mathbf{x}) = \sum_{i=1}^{d} a_i |x_i' - x_i|. \tag{4}$$

The weight a_i denotes the relative cost of changing a feature. For the attackers, to evade the detection, adding or hiding some API calls in a malware sample does not seem difficult. However, some specific API calls may affect the structure for intrusive functionality, which may be more expensive to be modified. Therefore we view the adversarial cost c practically significant.

For an adversarial attack, the attackers would not modify a malware into a benign file at any cost, but only make it being misclassified as benign with its malicious functionalities. For instance, the attacker will not modify an adware's related API calls to make it lost its malicious functionality automatically displaying or downloading advertisements when victims are online. Accordingly, there is a constraint of the cost for each attack, which is the upper limit of the maximum manipulations that can be made to the original malware $\mathbf{x}$. Therefore, the manipulation function $\mathcal{A}(\mathbf{x})$ can be formulated as

$$\mathcal{A}(\mathbf{x}) = \begin{cases} \mathbf{x}' & \text{sign}(f(\mathbf{x}')) = -1 \text{ and } c(\mathbf{x}', \mathbf{x}) \leq \delta_{max} \\ \mathbf{x} & \text{otherwise} \end{cases}, \tag{5}$$

where the malware sample is manipulated to be misclassified as benign (i.e., negative) only if the adversarial cost is less than or equal to a maximum cost δ_{max}.

Let $\mathbf{f}' = \text{sign}(f(\mathcal{A}(\mathbf{X})))$, then the adversarial attack model can be generally formulated as:

$$\underset{\mathbf{f}'}{\text{argmax}} \; \frac{1}{2} ||\mathbf{y} - \mathbf{f}'||^2, \tag{6}$$

subject to Eqs. (5) and (4). The main idea for an adversarial attack is to maximize the total loss of classification, which means that the more malware samples are misclassified as benign files, the more effective the adversarial attack could be. An ideal adversarial attack modifies a small but optimal portion of features of the malware with minimal adversarial cost, while makes the classifier achieve lowest true positive rate.

4.2 *AdvAttack*: Adversarial Attack Method

To achieve the adversary goal, it's important for the attackers to choose a relevant subset of API calls applied for feature addition and elimination. Therefore, it's worth to investigate the importance of each API call. We analyze a real sample collection of $10,000$ labeled files obtained from Comodo Cloud Security Center, from which $3,503$ API calls are extracted. In this paper, we use Max-Relevance algorithm ($I(x, y)$) [19], which is one of the popular approaches to define dependency of variables and has been successfully applied in malware detection [27], to calculate the relevance score of each API call for the classification of malware and benign file respectively. Figure 1 shows the distribution of API calls' relevance scores for malware and benign files, from which we can see that for those with high relevance scores, some are explicitly relevant to malware, while some have high influence on the classification of benign files. Note that API calls with extremely low relevance scores (about 85% lower than 0.0005) have limited or no contributions in malware detection (e.g., *SetLocal-Time* in *KERNEL32.DLL*), thus they will not be considered for the further investigated adversarial attacks.

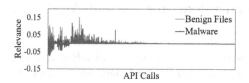

Fig. 1. Relevance score distribution of API calls

More specifically, the different importances of API calls rely on their functionalities. For example, *CreateFileW* in *KERNEL32.DLL* is substantially run by malware to create or copy files to spread malware distribution [2]. Based on the general statistical properties observed, to evade the detection with lower adversarial cost, the attackers may manipulate the API calls by the way of injecting the ones most relevant to benign files while removing the ones with higher relevance scores to malware. To stimulate the attacks, we rank each API call and group them into two sets: $\mathcal{M}$ (i.e., those highly relevant to malware) and $\mathcal{B}$ (i.e., those highly relevant to benign files) in the descent order of $I(x, +1)$ and $I(x, -1)$ respectively.

To evaluate the capability of an adversarial attack, we further define a function $g(\mathcal{A}(\mathbf{X}))$ to represent the accessibility to the learning system by the attack:

$$g(\mathcal{A}(\mathbf{X})) = ||\mathbf{y} - \mathbf{f}'||^2, \tag{7}$$

subject to Eq. (5), which implies the number of malware being misclassified as benign. The underlying idea of our adversarial attack *AdvAttack* is to perform feature manipulations with minimum adversarial cost while maximize the total loss of classification in Eq. (7). Here we adopt the wrapper method [29] which selects optimal features based on the capability of the attack using cross-validation. Specifically, we conduct bi-directional feature selection, that is, forward feature addition performed on $\mathcal{B}$ and backward feature elimination performed on $\mathcal{M}$. At each iteration, an API call will be selected for addition or elimination depending on the fact how it influences the value of $g(\mathcal{A}(\mathbf{X}))$. The adversarial attack $\boldsymbol{\theta} = \{\boldsymbol{\theta}^+, \boldsymbol{\theta}^-\}$ will be drawn from the iterations, where $\boldsymbol{\theta}^+ \in \{0, 1\}^d$ (if API_i is selected for elimination, then $\theta_i^+ = 1$; otherwise, $\theta_i^+ = 0$), and $\boldsymbol{\theta}^- \in \{0,1\}^d$ (if API_i is selected for addition, then $\theta_i^- = 1$; otherwise, $\theta_i^- = 0$). The iterations will end at the point where the adversarial cost reaches to maximum ($\delta_{\max}$), or the features available for addition and elimination are all manipulated.

Here, $\mathcal{M}$ and $\mathcal{B}$ significantly decrease the number of searches, and thereby reduce the computational complexity of the attack. Given $m = \max(|\mathcal{M}|, |\mathcal{B}|)$, $AdvAttack$ requires $O(n_t m(\mu^+ + \mu^-))$ queries, in which n_t is the number of testing malware samples, μ^+ and μ^- are the numbers of selected features for elimination and addition respectively ($\mu^+ \ll d$, $\mu^- \ll d$, $m \ll d$). Note that, this algorithm is applicable in all the scenarios described in Sect. 3.

5 $SecMD$: Secure-learning Model Against Adversarial Attacks

In response to the adversary's strategy, as an adversary-aware learning model, its action space should be practically independent from the knowledge of the attackers. To this end, we provide a systematic security-learning model to formalize the impact of the adversarial attacks and improve the robustness of the learning-based model in malware detection without exhibiting significant evidence of manipulation.

It's recalled that the malware detection can be formalized as Eq. (3). The optimization learning is coherent to two assumptions [21]: (i) data points tend to reserve the initial labels over the classification, and (ii) nearby data points are likely to have the same label. Equation (3) merely utilize the first assumption which may give attackers a good chance to evade it. To ideally formalize the assumptions as security terms in our malware detection problem, it is intuitively to design a pairwise relationship $\mathbf{R} \in \mathbb{R}^{n \times n}$ with respect to the intrinsic property revealed by labeled and unlabeled files [30]. Given our dataset $\{\mathbf{x}_i, y_i\}_{i=1}^n$, we can obtain $\mathbf{R}$ from the file relation graph defined as $G = (V, E)$, where V is file samples $\mathbf{X}$ and E denotes the relations between file samples weighted by $\mathbf{R}$. We employ the Jaccard similarity to measure the weight between two files $\mathbf{x}_i$ and $\mathbf{x}_j$, i.e., $R_{ij} = J(\mathbf{x}_i, \mathbf{x}_j)$. We deem any relationship as weak when $R_{ij} \leq \epsilon$, which will not be considered in our method.

The security terms combined with a fitting constraint and a smoothness constraint over constructed file graph leverages strong robustness of the learning model: (1) every file iteratively spreads its label information to its neighbors until a global stable state is achieved; (2) the transductive learning model enforces the attacker to manipulate more features to change the structure and relationship for evasion. If a larger number of features has to be manipulated to evade detection, it may be infeasible to generate such malware variant. Therefore, in our proposed secure-learning model $SecMD$, we will enhance the classifier by using security regularization terms with a fitting constraint over the adversarial cost and a smoothness constraint through graph regularization.

Fitting Constraint. From the analysis of the adversary problem [3], we can find that the larger the adversarial cost, the more manipulations need to be performed, and the more difficult the attack is. Accordingly, we first define the resilience coefficient of a classifier as:

$$s(\mathbf{x}', \mathbf{x}) = \frac{1}{c(\mathbf{x}', \mathbf{x})}, \tag{8}$$

subject to Eq. (4), which is converse to the adversarial cost. Since the defender may have no knowledge of the adversarial attacks in practice, we approximate the resilience coefficient as $s(\mathbf{x}', \mathbf{x}) = 1/\sum_{i=1}^{d} a_i |x_i' - x_i| = 1/\sum_{i=1}^{d} a_i p_i$ where p_i is the probability of API call x_i being manipulated. We then define a diagonal matrix for the adversary action denoted as $\mathbf{S} \in \mathbb{R}^{n \times n}$, where $S_{ii} = s(\mathbf{x}_i', \mathbf{x}_i)$ and the remaining elements in the matrix are 0. Thus the fitting constraint can be improved with the resilience term as $\frac{1}{2}\mathbf{f}^T \mathbf{S} \mathbf{f}$.

Smoothness Constraint. When the label information converges over the constructed file relation graph, a robust learning model should not change too much between nearby files. Based on the adjacency weight matrix $\mathbf{R}$, graph Laplacian can be defined as $\mathbf{L} = \mathbf{D} - \mathbf{R}$, where $\mathbf{D}$ is the diagonal matrix with $\mathbf{D}_{ii} = \sum_k \mathbf{R}_{ik}$ while the remain elements are 0. Built on the graph regularization in terms of the positive semi-definite Laplacian [25], we can format the smoothness constraint as $\frac{1}{2}\sum_{i,j=1}^{n} R_{ij}(f_i - f_j)^2 = \frac{1}{2}\mathbf{f}^T \mathbf{L} \mathbf{f}$.

To further analyze the effectiveness of the constraints imposed on our secure-learning model, we take insights into their specific functionalities. The fitting constraint is calculated as the sum of the differences between each file before and after classification, and the variations undergoing the potential attacks. Minimizing the local fitting term constrains each file to capture the initial label assignment as much as possible, and smooths the effects of the attack may cause. The smoothness constraint aggregates the dissimilarities between nearby files related with weighted edges. The label information can be essentially split at each file among the edges attached to it before the local changes being computed, which offsets the influence of the local feature manipulations and in turn helps to promote the optimal solution for the local minima in the optimization problem.

Combining the fitting and smoothness constraints as the security regularization terms, our secure-learning model *SecMD* can be formulated as

$$\underset{\mathbf{f},\mathbf{w},\mathbf{h};\boldsymbol{\xi}}{\mathrm{argmin}} \; \frac{1}{2}\|\mathbf{y} - \mathbf{f}\|^2 + \frac{\alpha}{2}\mathbf{f}^T \mathbf{S} \mathbf{f} + \frac{\lambda}{2}\mathbf{f}^T \mathbf{L} \mathbf{f} + \frac{1}{2\beta}\mathbf{w}^T \mathbf{w} + \frac{1}{2\gamma}\mathbf{h}^T \mathbf{h} + \boldsymbol{\xi}^T(\mathbf{f} - \mathbf{X}^T \mathbf{w} - \mathbf{h}), \tag{9}$$

where α and λ are the regularization parameters for the constraints. To solve the problem in Eq. (9), let

$$\mathcal{L}(\mathbf{f}, \mathbf{w}, \mathbf{h}; \boldsymbol{\xi}) = \frac{1}{2}\|\mathbf{y} - \mathbf{f}\|^2 + \frac{\alpha}{2}\mathbf{f}^T \mathbf{S} \mathbf{f} + \frac{\lambda}{2}\mathbf{f}^T \mathbf{L} \mathbf{f} + \frac{1}{2\beta}\mathbf{w}^T \mathbf{w} + \frac{1}{2\gamma}\mathbf{h}^T \mathbf{h} + \boldsymbol{\xi}^T(\mathbf{f} - \mathbf{X}^T \mathbf{w} - \mathbf{h}). \tag{10}$$

Based on the substitution and derivation from $\frac{\partial \mathcal{L}}{\partial \mathbf{w}} = 0$, $\frac{\partial \mathcal{L}}{\partial \mathbf{h}} = 0$, $\frac{\partial \mathcal{L}}{\partial \boldsymbol{\xi}} = 0$, $\frac{\partial \mathcal{L}}{\partial \mathbf{f}} = 0$, we can get the final security-learning problem as:

$$(\mathbf{I} + \lambda \mathbf{L} + (\beta \mathbf{X}^T \mathbf{X} + \gamma \mathbf{I})^{-1})\mathbf{f} = (\mathbf{I} - \frac{\alpha}{2}\mathbf{S})\mathbf{y}. \tag{11}$$

Since the size of $\mathbf{X}$ is $d \times n$, the computational complexity in terms of time for Eq. (11) is $O(n^3)$. If $d < n$, we can also follow Woodbury identity [24] to transform Eqs. (11) and (12) whose corresponding computational complexity in time is $O(d^3)$.

$$(\mathbf{I} + \gamma^{-1}\mathbf{I} - \gamma^{-1}\mathbf{X}^T(\gamma\beta^{-1}\mathbf{I} + \mathbf{X}\mathbf{X}^T)^{-1}\mathbf{X} + \lambda\mathbf{L})\mathbf{f} = (\mathbf{I} - \frac{\alpha}{2}\mathbf{S})\mathbf{y}. \qquad (12)$$

To solve the above secure-learning in Eq. (11) (or Eq. (12)), conjugate gradient descent method can be applied through some amount of iterations. The convergence rate depends on the choice of the initial gradient step size and the condition number of the matrix in Eq. (11) (or Eq. (12)).

6   Experimental Results and Analysis

In this section, we present three sets of experiments to empirically validate the proposed methods. The real sample collection obtained from Comodo Cloud Security Center contains $10,000$ file samples with $3,503$ extracted API calls, where $4,444$ are malware, $4,556$ are benign files, and $1,000$ are unknown (with the analysis by the anti-malware experts of Comodo Security Lab, 556 of them are labeled as malware and 444 of them are benign). In our experiments, those $9,000$ file samples are used for training, while the $1,000$ unknown files are used for testing. Since not all of the API calls will contribute to the classification as analyzed in Sect. 4.2, those API calls whose relevance scores are lower than the empirical threshold (i.e., 0.0005 in our application) will be excluded for feature manipulations. Therefore, $|\mathcal{M}| = 810$, $|\mathcal{B}| = 1,183$, and all the file samples can be represented as binary feature vectors with 1,993-dimensions.

As described in Sect. 4.1, the cost of the adversary is encoded by the weighted manipulated API calls. Considering different weights for API calls (e.g., the ones that can be easily manipulated are with lower weights; vise versa), we optimize the weight for each feature by applying its normalized relevance score for the classification ($a \in [0,1]$). According to the Cumulative Distribution Function (CDF) for the number of API calls the file samples include, we exploit the average number of API calls that each file possesses, which is 109, to define the maximum manipulation cost $\delta_{\max}$. We run our evaluation of the proposed evasion attacks with $\delta_{\max}$ varies in $\{5\%, 10\%, 15\%, 20\%, 50\%\}$ of 109, which is $\{5, 11, 16, 22, 55\}$.

6.1   Comparisons of *AdvAttack* and Other Attacks

We first compare our proposed adversarial attack *AdvAttack* with other attack methods using different feature manipulation approaches including: (1) only manipulating API calls from $\mathcal{B}$ for addition; (2) only manipulating API calls from $\mathcal{M}$ for elimination; (3) sequentially selecting $(1/2 \times \delta_{\max})$ API calls from $\mathcal{B}$ for addition and $(1/2 \times \delta_{\max})$ API calls from $\mathcal{M}$ for elimination; (4) simulating anonymous attack by randomly manipulating API calls for addition and elimination.

The experimental results shown in Fig. 2 illustrate that the attack performances vary when using different feature manipulation methods with certain adversarial costs $\delta_{\max}$: (1) the manipulation of only feature elimination performs worst with lowest false negative rate (*FNR*, i.e., the percentage of malware misclassified as benign); (2) the manipulation which sequentially selecting features for addition and elimination performs better than the methods only using feature addition or elimination, and the anonymous attack, due to its bi-directional feature manipulation over $\mathcal{B}$ and $\mathcal{M}$; (3) *AdvAttack* can greatly improve the *FNR* to 0.7086 while degrade the accuracy of the classifier to 58.50%, when $\delta_{\max} = 22$; the attackers can achieve ideal attack using *AdvAttack* (i.e., *FNR* almost reaches to 1, which means almost malware samples are misclassified), when $\delta_{\max} = 55$. Due to its well-crafted attack strategy, *AdvAttack* outperforms other adversarial attack methods with different feature manipulation approaches.

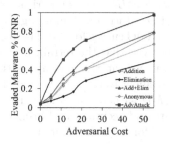 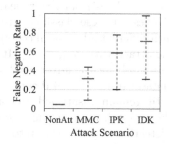

Fig. 2. Comparisons of different attacks   **Fig. 3.** *AdvAttack* under different scenarios (Color figure online)

6.2 Evaluation of *AdvAttack* under Different Scenarios

We further implement and evaluate our proposed attack *AdvAttack* under different scenarios described in Sect. 3: (1) In mimicry (MMC) attack ($\Psi = (X, \hat{D})$), the attackers are assumed to know the feature space and be able to obtain a file collection to imitate the original training dataset. In our experiment, we randomly select 1,000 file samples (500 benign and 500 malicious) from the 9,000 training set as our mimic dataset and exploit commonly used linear SVM as the surrogate classifier to train these 1,000 mimic file samples. (2) In imperfect-knowledge (IPK) attack ($\Psi = (X, D)$), we assume that both the feature space and the original training sample set can be fully controlled by the attackers. Therefore, we perform the IPK attack conformably as MMC attack where the only difference is that we apply 9,000 samples to train SVM. (3) In Ideal-knowledge (IDK) attack ($\Psi = (X, D, f)$), the attackers can perfectly access to the classifier system. The previous experiments of *AdvAttack* are conducted based on such assumption. To be comparable, *AdvAttack* is applied to all these scenarios resting on the same cost settings. The experimental results are shown in Fig. 3, in which red bar denotes the *FNR* of the classifier before attack (NonAtt) and different attacks with the adversarial cost $\delta_{max} = 22$. The *FNR* values float up or down depending on the knowledge the attackers have and the adversarial cost. The experimental results demonstrate that the available knowledge for the attackers significantly contributes to the performance of the attack. With perfect knowledge, the IDK attack can well evade the detection (e.g., 70.86% of the testing malware samples are misclassified as benign when $\delta_{max} = 22$).

6.3   Evaluation of *SecMD* Against Adversarial Attacks

In response to well-crafted attacks, we'd like to assess the effectiveness of *SecMD*. We use *AdvAttack* to taint the malware in the testing sample set, and validate the classification performance in different ways: (1) the baseline before attack (NonAtt) with detection accuracy of 95.70%; (2) the classifier under attack (UnderAtt); (3) the classifier retrained using the updated training dataset (i.e., $\mathbf{x} + \boldsymbol{\theta}$) (Retrained); (4) our secure-learning model *SecMD*. The comparisons of the effectiveness of these classifiers are shown in Fig. 4 (accuracy values against attacks with different adversarial costs) and Fig. 5 (ROC curves for the classifiers against the attack with $\delta_{max} = 22$). It can be observed that the retrained classifier ideally applying the adversarial attack $\boldsymbol{\theta}$ to transform the malware in the training dataset from $\mathbf{x}$ to $\mathbf{x} + \boldsymbol{\theta}$ can somehow be resilient to the attacks, but the accuracy still remain unsatisfied. In contrast, *SecMD* without any knowledge of the attacks, can well improve the true positive rate and accuracy, and bring the malware detection system back up to the desired performance level, approaching the detection results before the attack. It may also be interesting to know how robust that our learning system can combat the anonymous attacks. We conduct the anonymous attack by randomly selecting the features for addition or elimination, which does not exploit any knowledge of the target system. Under the anonymous attack, *SecMD* also has zero knowledge of what the attack is. Even in such case, *SecMD* can still improve the detection accuracy from 75.50% to 93.60%. Based on these properties, *SecMD* can be a resilient solution in malware detection when the attackers know completely, partially, or do not have any information of the learning system.

We also examine the ability of detecting the tainted malware using *SecMD* in comparison with the popular anti-malware scanners such as Kaspersky, McAfee, and Symantec through VirusTotal[1]. *SecMD* can effectively sustain the true positive rate to 0.9406, while the highest true positive rate for Kaspersky, McAfee, and Symantec can only reach 0.5180. As for the efficiency, *SecMD* performs well in detection efficiency: it just takes about 0.2 s for each unknown sample prediction including feature extraction. This enables our system to be a promising practical solution for resilient malware detection in real industrial application.

---

[1] https://www.virustotal.com/.

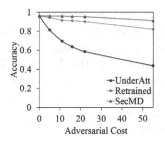
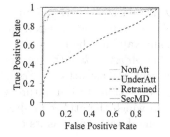

Fig. 4. Accuracies of different models   **Fig. 5.** Comparisons of ROC curves

7 Related Work

In some cyber security domains, such as spam email detection, there are ample evidences that show adversaries can actively modify their behaviors to avoid detection. [4] presented the interaction between the learner and the data generator as a static game, and explored the adversarial conditions and properties to find the equilibrial prediction model. [29] took gradient steps to find the closest evasion point $\mathbf{x}'$ to the malicious sample $\mathbf{x}$. [11] developed a new approach to learn the behavioral model of a bounded rational attacker by observing how the attacker responded to three defender strategies. To adjust the issues of adversarial attacks, increasing research efforts have been devoted to the security of machine learning. [15] investigated a feature reweighting technique to improve the performance and robustness of standard classifiers.

[8] explored randomization to generalize learning model by randomly choosing dataset or features, and estimated some parameters that fit the data best. [23] modeled the adversary action as it controlling a vector $\boldsymbol{\alpha}$ to modify the training dataset $\mathbf{x}$, and transformed the classifier into a convex optimization problem.

However, most of these works investigated the security of machine learning in the domains of spam email detection or intrusion detection either set unbounded rationale to play optimal strategies, or make strong assumptions about the structure of the data [11]. Different from the existing works, in this paper, we explore the security of machine learning in malware detection in the sense that we take the further step in developing the theory and approaches to learn the behavioral models for both attackers and defenders under generic settings.

8 Conclusion and Future Work

In this paper, we explore the security of machine learning in malware detection to understand the interactions between malware attackers and defenders. Considering different capabilities of the attackers, we implement a general attack model *AdvAttack* under three scenarios to conduct the adversarial attacks by manipulating an optimal portion of the features. Accordingly, a secure-learning model

SecMD, regularized by the security terms, is presented against these attacks. Three sets of experiments based on the real sample collections are conducted to empirically validate the proposed approaches. The experimental results demonstrate that *AdvAttack* with reasonable cost can greatly evade the detection. To stay resilient against attacks, *SecMD* can be a robust and practical solution in malware detection. In our future work, we will further explore the poisoning attacks in which the attackers alter the training precess through influence over the training data, as well as its corresponding resilient detection.

Acknowledgments. The authors would also like to thank the anti-malware experts of Comodo Security Lab for the data collection, as well as the helpful discussions and supports. This work is supported by the U.S. National Science Foundation under grant CNS-1618629 and WVU Senate Grants for Research and Scholarship (R-16-043).

References

1. Bailey, M., Oberheide, J., Andersen, J., Mao, Z.M., Jahanian, F., Nazario, J.: Automated classification and analysis of internet malware. In: Kruegel, C., Lippmann, R., Clark, A. (eds.) RAID 2007. LNCS, vol. 4637, pp. 178–197. Springer, Heidelberg (2007). doi:10.1007/978-3-540-74320-0_10
2. Baldangombo, U., Jambaljav, N., Horng, S.-J.: A static malware detection system using data mining methods. CoRR J. **1308**(2831) (2013)
3. Biggio, B., Corona, I., Maiorca, D., Nelson, B., Šrndić, N., Laskov, P., Giacinto, G., Roli, F.: Evasion attacks against machine learning at test time. In: Blockeel, H., Kersting, K., Nijssen, S., Železný, F. (eds.) ECML PKDD 2013. LNCS, vol. 8190, pp. 387–402. Springer, Heidelberg (2013). doi:10.1007/978-3-642-40994-3_25
4. Bruckner, M., Kanzow, C., Scheffer, T.: Static prediction games for adversarial learning problems. J. Mach. Learn. Res. **13**(1), 2617–2654 (2012)
5. Chen, L., Hardy, W., Ye, Y., Li, T.: Analyzing file-to-file relation network in malware detection. In: Wang, J., Cellary, W., Wang, D., Wang, H., Chen, S.-C., Li, T., Zhang, Y. (eds.) WISE 2015. LNCS, vol. 9418, pp. 415–430. Springer, Cham (2015). doi:10.1007/978-3-319-26190-4_28
6. Dalvi, N., Domingos, P., Sanghai, S.M., Verma, D.: Adversarial classification. In: KDD 2004 (2004)
7. Das, S., Liu, Y., Zhang, W., Chandramohan, M.: Semantics-based online malware detection: towards efficient real-time protection against malware. IEEE Trans. Inf. Forensics Secur. **11**(2), 289–302 (2016)
8. Debarr, D., Sun, H., Wechsler, H.: Adversarial spam detection using the randomized hough transform-support vector machine. In: ICMLA 2013, pp. 299–304 (2013)
9. Filiol, E., Jacob, G., Liard, M.: Evaluation methodology and theoretical model for antiviral behavioural detection strategies. J. Comput. Virol. **3**(1), 23–37 (2007)
10. Goodfellow, I.J., Shlens, J., Szegedy, C.: Explaining and harnessing adversarial examples. In: ICLR 2015 (2015)
11. Haghtalab, N., Fang, F., Nguyen, T.H., Sinha, A., Procaccia, A.D., Tambe, M.: Three strategies to success: learning adversary models in security games. In: IJCAI 2016 (2016)
12. Hardy, W., Chen, L., Hou, S., Ye, Y., Li, X.: DL4MD: a deep learning framework for intelligent malware detection. In: DMIN 2016, pp. 61–67 (2016)

13. KasperskyLab.: The great bank robbery (2015). http://www.kaspersky.com/abo ut/news/virus/2015/Carbanak-cybergang-steals-1-bn-USD-from-100-financial-ins titutions-worldwide
14. Kolbitsch, C., Kirda, E., Kruegel, C.: The power of procrastination: detection and mitigation of execution-stalling malicious code. In: CCS 2011, pp. 285–296 (2011)
15. Kolcz, A., Teo, C.H.: Feature weighting for improved classifier robustness. In: CEAS 2009 (2009)
16. Li, B., Vorobeychik, Y., Chen, X.: A general retraining framework for adversarial classification. In: NIPS (2016)
17. Nissim, N., Moskovitch, R., Rokach, L., Elovici, Y.: Novel active learning methods for enhanced PC malware detection in windows OS. Expert Syst. Appl. **41**(13), 5843–5857 (2014)
18. Papernot, N., McDaniel, P., Wu, X., Jha, S., Swami, A.: Distillation as a defense to adversarial perturbations against deep neural networks. In: IEEE Symposium on Security and Privacy (SP), pp. 582–597 (2016)
19. Peng, H., Long, F., Ding, C.: Feature selection based on mutual information: Criteria of max-dependency, max-relevance, and min-redundancy. IEEE Trans. Pattern Anal. Mach. Intell. **27**(8) (2005)
20. Roli, F., Biggio, B., Fumera, G.: Pattern recognition systems under attack. In: Ruiz-Shulcloper, J., Sanniti di Baja, G. (eds.) CIARP 2013. LNCS, vol. 8258, pp. 1–8. Springer, Heidelberg (2013). doi:10.1007/978-3-642-41822-8_1
21. Santos, I., Nieves, J., Bringas, P.G.: Semi-supervised learning for unknown malware detection. In: International Symposium on Distributed Computing and Artificial Intelligence, pp. 415–422 (2011)
22. Šrndic, N., Laskov, P.: Practical evasion of a learning-based classifier: a case study. In: SP 2014, pp. 197–211 (2014)
23. Wang, F., Liu, W., Chawla, S.: On sparse feature attacks in adversarial learning. In: ICDM 2014 (2014)
24. Woodbury, M.A.: Inverting modified matrices. Memorandum report. 42, Statistical Research Group, Princeton University, Princeton, NJ (1950)
25. Yang, P., Zhao, P.: A min-max optimization framework for online graph classification. In: CIKM 2015 (2015)
26. Ye, Y., Wang, D., Li, T., Ye, D., Jiang, Q.: An intelligent pe-malware detection system based on association mining. J. Comput. Virol. **4**(4), 323–334 (2008)
27. Ye, Y., Li, T., Jiang, Q., Han, Z., Wan, L.: Intelligent file scoring system for malware detection from the gray list. In: KDD 2009, pp. 1385–1394 (2009)
28. Ye, Y., Li, T., Zhu, S., Zhuang, W., Tas, E., Gupta, U., Abdulhayoglu, M.: Combining file content and file relations for cloud based malware detection. In: KDD 2011, pp. 222–230 (2011)
29. Zhang, F., Chan, P.P.K., Biggio, B., Yeung, D.S., Roli, F.: Adversarial feature selection against evasion attacks. IEEE Trans. Cybern. **46**(3), 766–777 (2015)
30. Zhou, D., Bousquet, O., Lal, T.N., Weston, J., Scholkopf, B.: Learning with local and global consistency. Adv. Neural Inform. Process. Syst. **16**, 321–328 (2004)

Optimization

Enhanced Pareto Interpolation Method to Aid Decision Making for Discontinuous Pareto Optimal Fronts

Kalyan Shankar Bhattacharjee[✉], Hemant Kumar Singh, and Tapabrata Ray

School of Engineering and Information Technology,
University of New South Wales, Canberra, Australia
k.bhattacharjee@student.adfa.edu.au, {h.singh,t.ray}@adfa.edu.au

Abstract. Multi-criteria decision making is of interest in several domains such as engineering, finance and logistics. It aims to address the key challenges of search for optimal solutions and decision making in the presence of multiple conflicting design objectives/criteria. The decision making aspect can be particularly challenging when there are *too few* Pareto optimal solutions available as this severely limits the understanding of the nature of the Pareto optimal front (POF) and subsequently affects the confidence on the choice of solutions. This problem is studied in this paper, wherein a decision maker is presented with a few outcomes and the aim is to identify *regions of interest* for further investigation. To address the problem, the contemporary approaches attempt to generate POF approximation through linear interpolation of a given set of (a few) Pareto optimal outcomes. While the process helps in gaining an understanding of the POF, it ignores the possibility of discontinuities or voids in the POF. In this study, we investigate two measures to alleviate this difficulty. First is to make use of infeasible solutions obtained during the search, *along with* the Pareto outcomes while constructing the interpolations. Second is to use proximity to a set of uniform reference directions to determine potential discontinuities. Consequently, the proposed approach enables approximation of both continuous and discontinuous POF more accurately. Additionally, a set of interpolated outcomes along uniformly distributed reference directions are presented to the decision maker. The errors in the given interpolations are also estimated in order to further aid decision making by establishing confidence on predictions. We illustrate the performance of the approach using four problems spanning different types of fronts, such as mixed (convex/concave), degenerate, and disconnected.

Keywords: Pareto front approximation · Linear interpolation · Infeasibility · Decision making

1 Introduction

Optimization and decision making in presence of multiple conflicting criteria is relevant to several domains, including engineering, management, logistics,

© Springer International Publishing AG 2017
W. Peng et al. (Eds.): AI 2017, LNAI 10400, pp. 93–105, 2017.
DOI: 10.1007/978-3-319-63004-5_8

finance, etc. The optimum solution to a multi-objective optimization (MOO) problem comprises a set of solutions (designs) representing the best trade-off in the outcome space, referred to as the Pareto optimal front (POF). The first aspect, i.e., obtaining the POF, is typically handled using multi-objective evolutionary algorithms (MOEAs) [6] which are a popular choice due their capability of searching for global optimum and handling highly non-linear/black-box functions. The second key aspect relates to supporting mechanisms for decision making, i.e., means to identify solution(s) of interest from the POF for real-life implementation.

Decision making is particularly challenging when there are too many or too few Pareto/non-dominated outcomes available. In the former case, the challenge is to device appropriate quantitative metrics based on which the final design(s) are selected [4]. In the latter case the challenge is to gain an understanding of the Pareto front using a few available sparse solutions to make a reasonable decision [3,9]. This paper focuses on the second scenario, where a decision maker is presented with a few outcomes and the aim is to identify regions of interest to aid decision making and interactive optimization. An existing approach towards achieving this is Pareto front interpolation, which involves building an approximate POF using interpolation techniques of different order (e.g. linear/quadratic) [3,9,12]. One of the notable methods is the PAINT (PAreto INTerpolation) algorithm presented in [9,10], in which the interpolations are represented using simplexes. Similar principles are used in two other recent methods, namely Pareto Linear Interpolation (PLI) [3] and PROjection based Pareto interpolation (PROP) [14]. However, the above methods do not consider the possibility of discontinuities in the POF. To the authors' knowledge, the only attempt towards this is a variation of PAINT algorithm known as PAINT-SiCon [8]. In PAINT-SiCon, both objective and decision spaces are approximated in order to detect potential discontinuities. Thus, the input set for PAINT-SiCon includes both decision variables as well as outcome values.

This study extends the PLI method developed by the authors earlier [3]. The method aims to deliver a comprehensive set of piecewise linearly interpolated approximation for both continuous and discontinuous POF more accurately. Unlike PAINT-SiCon, the proposed approach does not use design variable information of the given Pareto outcomes as an input. Instead, it utilizes the infeasible solutions obtained during the evolutionary search (if available), and a set of uniformly distributed reference directions to identify potential discontinuous regions in the POF.

2   Preliminaries

We first briefly recap the fundamentals of the PAINT [9] and PLI methods [3], both of which use simplexes to generate piecewise linear interpolations. A *simplex* (in $\mathbb{R}^n$) is a special case of a convex polytope[1], namely one with exactly $n + 1$

---

[1] Note that in previous works, polytopes has also been used to refer to simplex directly, since only convex polytopes are involved in the process.

extremal points (the convex hull of $n+1$ points in general position, that is to say they do not lie in a $n-1$ dimensional affine subspace). Throughout this paper, the term n-simplex will be used to denote a simplex with $n+1$ vertices.

2.1 PAINT

To construct the approximation using N given Pareto outcomes in M dimensions, PAINT starts by generating a set of candidate simplexes, and then uses certain rules to eliminate undesirable ones. The remaining set of simplexes form the final, inherently non-dominated approximation.

The initial set of simplexes is generated through *Delaunay triangulation*. For the given Pareto optimal outcomes of an M-objective problem, it creates a set of polyhedrons with $(M+1)$ vertices (e.g. tetrahedron for a 3-objective problem), which are thus M-simplexes. Each of these simplexes are then further recursively broken down into simplexes of lower degree (e.g. tetrahedron (3-simplex) is divided into the constituting faces (2-simplexes), which are in turn divided into the constituting edges (1-simplexes), and so on). The resulting set of $\{M, (M-1), (M-2) \ldots 0\}$–simplexes form the initial simplex set.

Subsequently, certain simplexes are eliminated using three rules[2]: (R1.1) *point-simplex dominance*, i.e., a given Pareto outcome dominates or is dominated by a simplex, (R1.2) *self dominance*, i.e., an point in a simplex dominates another, and (R2) *simplex-simplex dominance* a point on one simplex dominates a point on another simplex. The simplexes that survive the above eliminations form the final approximation.

2.2 PLI

The PLI method was developed by the authors in [3]. The approach differs from PAINT in one fundamental aspect: it aims to generate a *comprehensive* linear interpolation instead of *inherently non-dominated* interpolation set obtained by PAINT. Thus PLI aims to deliver all possible simplexes on which no point dominates or is dominated by the given Pareto outcomes. However, there may exist an interpolated point on one of the simplexes which dominates another interpolated point in another simplex. The reason behind retaining such simplexes is that since both the points are interpolated, none of them is guaranteed to be optimal, and hence such an elimination may result in removal of a potentially useful region for a decision maker. Instead of Delaunay Triangulation, PLI generates the initial set through constructing all possible unique simplexes with number of vertices M, $M-1$, through to 1, where M is the number of objectives. Subsequently, it uses rule R1.1 to eliminate the undesirable simplexes. It further offers a set of well distributed set of interpolated outcomes along a diverse set of reference directions, and quantifies error measures associated with them.

As discussed in Sect. 1, both the above methods rely only on the given Pareto optimal outcomes to construct the piecewise linear interpolations. In the absence

---

[2] In [10], the first two rules R1.1 and R1.2 are covered as a single rule R1.

of any other information, this results in a continuous approximation, even in the regions where the POF may have a discontinuity. In order to eliminate the interpolation that are in regions with discontinuity, in this study we propose to use the infeasible solutions that are obtained as the part of the search during the interpolation process. Furthermore, we also consider a set of uniformly distributed reference directions and eliminate simplexes along those that are not associated (nearest to) any of the Pareto optimal outcomes.

3   Proposed Approach

The eventual goal of solving a multi-objective problem is to obtain a well spread set of feasible solutions on the POF. If the problem is constrained, it is evident that some of the solutions evaluated during the search could be infeasible. Such solutions are typically dealt with using some form of ranking and selection. Even though the infeasible solutions are not part of the final POF, they can be utilized to improve the search, as investigated in a number of studies [13]. In this paper, we propose that the use of such infeasible solutions can then be further extended to aid decision making for disconnected POFs. Therefore, the proposed algorithm starts from not only a set of (feasible) Pareto outcomes, but also, if available, some infeasible solutions obtained during the search of these Pareto outcomes (which are otherwise ignored in the interpolation methods discussed so far). Furthermore, we also eliminate some of the simplexes by observing the proximity of the given Pareto optimal solutions to a set of uniformly distributed reference directions. Thus, the method can deal with more generic types (continuous and discontinuous) of POF compared to PLI [3] and hence is referred to here as PLI_G. The pseudo-code of PLI_G is given in Algorithm 1, followed by description of its key components.

Algorithm 1. Proposed PLI_G algorithm

Require: PF_0 (Given set of Pareto optimal outcomes along with (if available) infeasible outcomes), $|W|$ (Number of reference directions).

1: $PF \leftarrow$ all non-dominated (feasible+infeasible) outcomes in PF_0
2: **Create simplexes:** all possible unique $M-1$, $M-2$,...,0−simplexes having every vertex as a subset of the given PF.
3: **Apply elimination rules:** point-simplex dominance rule, infeasible exclusion and reference direction based deletion rule to eliminate certain simplexes.
4: **Generate** $|W|$ uniform reference directions using systematic sampling [5].
5: **Identify** points of intersection between each reference direction and all survived simplexes.
6: **Compute** error metrics along each reference direction.

3.1   Identify Non-dominated Outcomes

The first step in the proposed approach is to identify infeasible solutions that will be used during the interpolation. These are identified as the ones which are non-dominated with respect to the given Pareto outcomes in the objective space. The process is schematically shown in Fig. 1(a). The infeasible points shown in red are either unattainable (since they dominate the given Pareto outcomes) or not relevant to the shape/nature of Pareto front since they are dominated by one of the Pareto outcomes; and hence discarded. The infeasible outcomes shown in blue on the other hand are non-dominated with respect to the given Pareto outcomes, and hence indicate a possibility of a discontinuity in the POF. Therefore, these points are retained for the subsequent interpolation. Thus, after this step, all outcomes in the resulting set (denoted as PF) are non-dominated; some feasible and others infeasible.

3.2   Create Simplexes

Given the set (PF) containing N outcomes (including feasible and infeasible), all possible unique $k-$simplexes ($k = 0, 1, \ldots M - 1$) constructed, by selecting the $k + 1$ outcomes from PF. Hence, the number of $k - simplexes$ would be $\binom{N}{k+1}$. The resulting set, denoted here by TP, will thus contain a total of $\sum_{k=1}^{m} \binom{N}{k}$ simplexes.

3.3   Apply Elimination Rules

Once the set of simplexes TP is constructed, we apply the following three elimination rules in order to remove undesirable simplexes from it:

Point-Simplex Dominance: To begin with, we apply the *point-simplex* dominance rule as done in [3]. A simplex is eliminated if any point in the simplex dominates or is dominated by a point of the given PF. The application of the above rule results in a first set of surviving simplexes (TP_{s1}).

Eliminate Infeasible Simplexes: Next, if any of the survived simplexes in TP_{s1} contains infeasible outcome(s), it is eliminated. In order to determine whether an infeasible outcome is contained within any of the simplexes, a linear programming (LP) presented in Eq. 1 is solved. In the equation, the jth objective of an infeasible outcome is denoted as $I_j (\forall\ j = 1, \ldots, M)$ and a $(k-1) - simplex$ defined using vertices $v_1, \ldots, v_k$.

$$
\text{Find} \quad \alpha_i \atop {\scriptstyle i=1,\ldots,k}
$$

$$
\text{such that} \sum_{i=1}^{k} \alpha_i = 1; \quad \left(\sum_{i=1}^{k} \alpha_i v_i \right)_j = I_j, \ \forall\ j = 1, \ldots, M; \tag{1}
$$

$$
\text{where } \alpha_i \in [0, 1], \ \forall\ i = 1, \ldots, k
$$

The above problem is solved for each infeasible outcome against each survived simplex in TP_{s1}; executed in parallel for minimal run-time. The simplex is eliminated if there exists a feasible solution of the above LP (implying that the simplex contains an infeasible outcome). The elimination process results in a second set of surviving simplexes denoted as TP_{s2}.

Simplexes Along "Empty" Reference Directions: In the next stage a structured set of W reference points is generated spanning a hyperplane with unit intercepts in each objective axis (obtained by normalizing each objective between 0 and 1). This systematic sampling method is known as Normal Boundary Intersection (NBI) [5] and it is used in most current decomposition based evolutionary algorithms [1] for generating uniformly distributed reference vectors. It generates $|W|$ points on the hyperplane with a uniform spacing of $\delta = 1/s$ for a given number of objectives M with s unique sampling locations along each objective axis. The total number of reference points $|W| = \binom{M+s-1}{s}$. The idea behind generating this structured set of points is to create reference direction vectors by joining them to the Ideal point (origin in the scaled space) which is termed as W^I, as shown in Fig. 1(b). Similarly, W^N is considered as the set of reference directions originating from the Nadir point (Fig. 1(c)). The total number of reference direction is taken as close as possible to $|PF|$, i.e., $|W^I| + |W^N| \approx |PF|$ in this study.

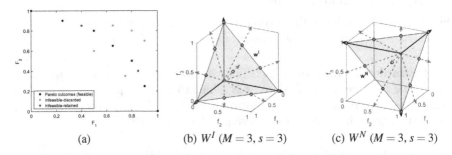

(a)   (b) W^I ($M = 3, s = 3$)   (c) W^N ($M = 3, s = 3$)

Fig. 1. (a) Identification of infeasible solutions used for interpolation (b,c) structured set of reference directions originating from Ideal and Nadir points, respectively.

After constructing the above set of reference directions, the perpendicular distances (referred to as d_2 in most decomposition based algorithms [1]) from each Pareto optimal outcome to all reference directions (both W^I and W^N) in the scaled objective space are computed. For each Pareto optimal outcome, based on minimum d_2, the closest reference directions from both W^I and W^N are identified. This process may result in some unassigned reference directions. Once the unassigned reference directions are identified, any simplex which has an intersection with these reference directions (using Eq. 2) are deleted. Since these unassigned directions were not close to any of the given Pareto outcomes, it may indicate a potential void in the Pareto outcome space along that direction. Such a void could be a manifestation of discontinuities in the front (for example, due to constraints, e.g. C2DTLZ2) or degeneracy in the front (e.g. Viennet), both of which are illustrated later in the paper. This elimination process will result in a third and final set of surviving simplexes TP_{s3}.

$$
\begin{aligned}
&\text{Find} \quad \alpha_i, \ \beta \\
&\qquad {\scriptstyle i=1,\ldots,k} \\
&\text{such that } \sum_{i=1}^{k} \alpha_i = 1; \ \left(\sum_{i=1}^{k} \alpha_i v_i \right)_j = (\mathbf{w}\beta)_j, \ \forall \, j = 1, \ldots, M \qquad (2) \\
&\text{where } \alpha_i \in [0,1], \ \forall \, i = 1, \ldots, k; \beta \in (0, \infty),
\end{aligned}
$$

Note that in some cases, infeasible solutions may not be available, or the problem may have discontinuous regions but no constraints. The proposed method can be applied in such cases as well, since it incorporates elimination based on both infeasible solutions and reference directions. In Sect. 4, we consider both types of cases, i.e., those where some infeasible solutions are available, and those where they are not.

3.4 Identify Interpolations Along Uniform Reference Directions

Once the final set of surviving simplexes TP_{s3} is obtained, a uniformly spread set of interpolated outcomes in TP_{s3} is identified to offer diverse additional choices to the DM. To achieve this, a structured set W reference points is generated using NBI method. A good multi-objective approximation would contain a representative solution along (or close to) each of these uniformly distributed directions. This concept is used in some of the prominent contemporary *many-objective* optimization algorithms [1].

Once the reference directions are constructed, in order to determine the point of intersection between each reference direction and the surviving simplexes (TP_{s3}), the vertices of the simplexes are first normalized with respect to the Ideal and Nadir points. Thereafter, the problem formulated in Eq. 2 is solved for each direction against each simplex (executed in parallel for minimal run-time). A feasible solution to the above LP corresponds to one interpolated outcome in TP_{s3} for a direction. It is important to highlight that there may be more than one interpolated points along a given reference direction for problems with three or more objectives.

3.5 Estimate Errors

Since the additional outcomes are generated using interpolation of the given Pareto optimal outcomes, they are not guaranteed to be Pareto optimal for the original problem, even though they are non-dominated with the given Pareto outcomes. Therefore, it is important to quantify errors associated with the interpolated outcomes, as this information is useful for determining confidence on these outcomes during decision making. Two metrics are considered in this study to quantify the merit: dominance measure and nearest neighbor distance. Note that both of them are calculated in normalized (between 0 and 1) objective space to avoid any bias due to range of values in different objectives.

1. *Dominance measure:* Given an interpolated point (after the linear approximation has been constructed) this metric determines the minimum amount required to be subtracted from it to dominate or added to it to be dominated by a Pareto optimal outcome in the given set. In this paper, positive dominance measure (Fig. 2(a)) is quantified as the minimum value when added to any one of the objectives of an outcome, it will be dominated by at least one of given Pareto outcomes. On the other hand, negative dominance measure (Fig. 2(b)) of an outcome is the minimum value to be subtracted in any one of the objectives in order to dominate at least one given Pareto outcome. For more details, please refer to [3].
2. *Nearest neighbor distance:* To provide further insights for better decision making, we propose a second metric, termed as the *nearest neighbor distance*. It measures the shortest Euclidean distance of an interpolated outcome along a reference direction to its nearest Pareto outcome, as shown in Fig. 2(c). A large value of this metric would suggest low confidence in existence of a solution along that direction, since the nearest Pareto outcomes are far away from it.

Overall, the above two metrics determine the quality of the interpolated outcomes along any direction, which is useful when these outcomes are used for further evolutionary search and decision making.

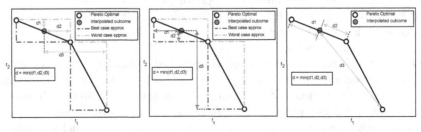

(a) Positive dominance error (b) Negative dominance error (c) Nearest neighbor distance

Fig. 2. Error metrics

4   Numerical Experiments

We study the performance of PLI_G using one bi-objective and three tri-objective test problems. The number of reference directions used for determining additional outcomes is set to 300 for bi-objective problem and 990 for all the tri-objective problems. The number of reference directions determines the resolution of the obtained points on the interpolated Pareto front. The given set of outcomes for all the problems are available for download at [2]. Table 1 shows a summary of results (size of initial set, number of initial and survived simplexes, number of interpolated solutions and reference directions having intersections) for all the problems. The observations for individual problems are discussed below.

Table 1. Summary of results for all problems*

Problem	$|P_f|, |IO_{ND}|, |IO_D|$	$|1 - simplexes|$	$|1 - simplexes^S|$	$|2 - simplexes|$	$|2 - simplexes^S|$	$|IS|(|W|)$	$|UI|(|W|)$
TNK	37,0,0	666	34	0	0	192(300)	192(300)
DTLZ2mod	28,14,7	861	89	11480	88	1958(990)	862(990)
Viennet2	50,0,0	1225	103	19600	93	807(990)	188(990)
C2DTLZ2	34,28,5	1891	135	37820	161	2096(990)	562(990)

*Note: $|P_f|$ = Number of (feasible) Pareto optimal outcomes, $|IO_{ND}|$ = number of non-dominated infeasible outcomes, $|IO_D|$ = number of dominating/dominated infeasible outcomes, $k - simplexes^S$ = Number of final survived $k - simplexes$, $|IS|$ = Total number of interpolated solutions obtained along $|W|$ reference directions, $|UI|$ = Number of unique $|W|$ reference directions having intersections.

TNK: We start with a bi-objective constrained problem involving both convex and non-convex parts. The DM is provided with only 37 Pareto optimal outcomes and no infeasible outcomes. For this problem, all the initial simplexes are shown in Fig. 3(a). The *PF* corresponding to the final set of survived simplexes is presented in Fig. 3(b). The representative Pareto front (in light blue background) and the set of interpolated outcomes along 300 uniformly distributed reference directions are presented in Fig. 3(c). The estimated errors are shown in Figs. 3(d)–(f). *Please note that the same conventions regarding sub-figures (a–f) are used in the subsequent examples, and hence the descriptions are not repeated for the sake of brevity.* As seen, the discontinuity in the front is captured using the proposed approach. Based on Table 1 some reference direction did not have any intersections with the survived simplexes due to the discontinuity. The remaining reference directions had unique intersections.

DTLZ2mod: Next we present the results on three objective DTLZ2 problem [7], which is modified to have a hole in the middle of the POF by imposing an additional constraint. The POF is non-convex and the DM is provided with 28 Pareto optimal outcomes and 21 infeasible outcomes, of which 14 end up being non-dominated with the Pareto optimal outcomes. The set of interpolated outcomes along 990 uniformly distributed directions are presented in Fig. 4(c). The error estimates are shown in Fig. 4(d)–(f). One can notice the hole due to infeasibility exclusion in Fig. 4(b). As shown in Table 1, multiple intersections exist along a number of reference directions, while there are no intersections along the directions passing through the hole.

If the infeasible solutions were not considered (as done in the existing PLI approach [3]), approximation (simplexes) obtained will be as shown in Fig. 5(a),

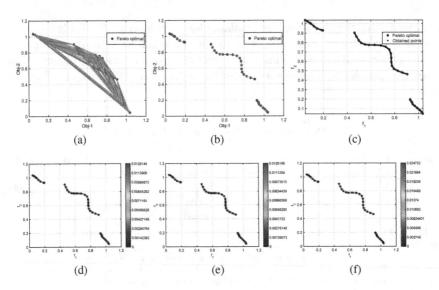

Fig. 3. Results obtained for TNK problem: (a) Set of initial simplexes (b) Survived Simplexes (c) Interpolated outcomes (d) Negative dominance measure (e) Positive dominance measure (f) Nearest neighbor distance

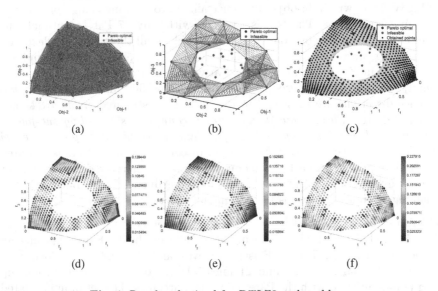

Fig. 4. Results obtained for DTLZ2mod problem

with corresponding obtained points shown in Fig. 5(b). One can note that the approximation is unable to detect the hole and consequently suggesting points in the infeasible region. The example clearly illustrates the utility of the proposed enhancement in discarding the undesirable solutions.

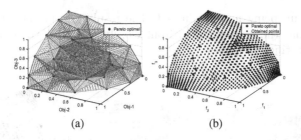

(a)   (b)

Fig. 5. Approximation without considering the infeasible solutions for DTLZ2mod problem

Viennet2: Next we illustrate the performance of the proposed approach on a problem with a degenerate front, the three objective Viennet2 [15] problem. For this problem the total number of initial Pareto optimal outcomes are 50, and there are no constraints (and hence no infeasible solutions). The interpolated outcomes along every reference directions are shown in Fig. 6(c). Due to the degeneracy in the POF for most part (it is a curve instead of a surface), very few reference directions (188 out of 990) had intersection with the final surviving simplexes. However, a small part of the POF is a surface and some reference directions had multiple intersections with surviving simplexes.

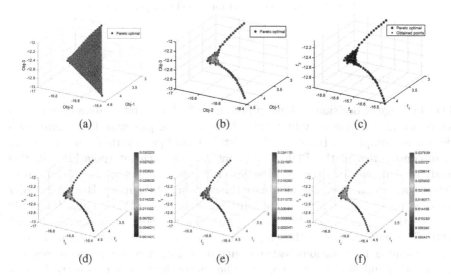

Fig. 6. Results obtained for Viennet2 problem

C2DTLZ2: Lastly, we consider the three objective C2DTLZ2 [11] problem, which contains four disconnected regions in its (non-convex) POF. The DM is provided with 34 Pareto optimal outcomes, and 33 infeasible outcomes out of which 28 end up being non-dominated. The results are presented in Fig. 7. It can be seen that the approximated front closely resembles the true POF with four patches distinctly visible.

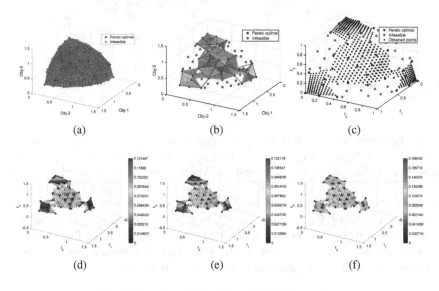

Fig. 7. Results obtained for C2DTLZ2 problem

5   Summary

The challenge of decision making in presence of a few Pareto outcomes has been addressed in contemporary literature through use of piecewise linear interpolations using simplexes. However, the existing techniques overlook the possibility of discontinuities in the POF while constructing such interpolations. In this study we demonstrated the use of infeasible solutions and reference directions to detect such continuities and eliminate the corresponding interpolations, in order to come up with a more accurate representation of the POF. Thus, the study extends the current capability to deal with generic (continuous/discontinuous) POF. The performance of the proposed approach was illustrated on four problems spanning POF various features such as a mix of convex/concave regions, degenerated and disconnected regions. The approach was able to construct piecewise linear interpolations that can closely resemble these features of the true POF, and thus shows a potential as a powerful tool to support decision making.

Acknowledgement. The second author would like to acknowledge the UNSW Special Research Grant 2017.

References

1. Asafuddoula, M., Ray, T., Sarker, R.: A decomposition-based evolutionary algorithm for many objective optimization. IEEE Trans. Evol. Comput. **19**(3), 445–460 (2015)
2. Bhattacharjee, K.S., Singh, H.K., Ray, T.: http://www.mdolab.net/Ray/Research-Data/AI-Polytope-dataset.zip (2017)
3. Bhattacharjee, K.S., Singh, H.K., Ray, T.: An approach to generate comprehensive piecewise linear interpolation of Pareto outcomes to aid decision making. J. Global Optim. **68**, 1–23 (2016)
4. Bhattacharjee, K.S., Singh, H.K., Ray, T.: A study on performance metrics to identify solutions of interest from a trade-off set. In: Ray, T., Sarker, R., Li, X. (eds.) ACALCI 2016. LNCS, vol. 9592, pp. 66–77. Springer, Cham (2016). doi:10.1007/978-3-319-28270-1_6
5. Das, I., Dennis, J.E.: Normal-boundary intersection: a new method for generating pareto optimal points in multicriteria optimization problems. SIAM J. Optim. **8**(3), 631–657 (1998)
6. Deb, K.: Multi-objective Optimization Using Evolutionary Algorithms, vol. 16. Wiley, Hoboken (2001)
7. Deb, K., Thiele, L., Laumanns, M., Zitzler, E.: Scalable multi-objective optimization test problems. In: Proceedings of the IEEE Congress on Evolutionary Computation, pp. 825–830. IEEE, Honolulu (2002)
8. Hartikainen, M., Lovison, A.: PAINT-SiCon: constructing consistent parametric representations of Pareto sets in nonconvex multiobjective optimization. J. Global Optim. **62**(2), 243–261 (2014)
9. Hartikainen, M., Miettinen, K., Wiecek, M.M.: Constructing a Pareto front approximation for decision making. Math. Methods Oper. Res. **73**(2), 209–234 (2011)
10. Hartikainen, M., Miettinen, K., Wiecek, M.M.: PAINT: Pareto front interpolation for nonlinear multiobjective optimization. Comput. Optim. Appl. **52**(3), 845–867 (2012)
11. Li, K., Deb, K., Zhang, Q., Kwong, S.: An evolutionary many-objective optimization algorithm based on dominance and decomposition. IEEE Trans. Evol. Comput. **19**(5), 694–716 (2015)
12. Ruzika, S., Wiecek, M.M.: Approximation methods in multiobjective programming. J. Optim. Theory Appl. **126**(3), 473–501 (2005)
13. Singh, H.K., Alam, K., Ray, T.: Use of infeasible solutions during constrained evolutionary search: a short survey. In: Ray, T., Sarker, R., Li, X. (eds.) ACALCI 2016. LNCS, vol. 9592, pp. 193–205. Springer, Cham (2016). doi:10.1007/978-3-319-28270-1_17
14. Singh, H.K., Bhattacharjee, K.S., Ray, T.: A projection-based approach for constructing piecewise linear pareto front approximations. J. Mech. Des. **138**(9), 091404 (2016)
15. Van Veldhuizen, D.A.: Multiobjective evolutionary algorithms: classifications, analyses, and new innovations. Ph.D. thesis, Air Force Institute of Technology (1999)

Use of a Non-nested Formulation to Improve Search for Bilevel Optimization

Md Monjurul Islam, Hemant Kumar Singh[(✉)], and Tapabrata Ray

School of Engineering and Information Technology, University of New South Wales,
Canberra, Australia
md.islam5@student.adfa.edu.au, {h.singh,t.ray}@adfa.edu.au

Abstract. Bilevel optimization involves searching for the optimum of
an *upper level* problem subject to optimality of a nested *lower level* problem. These are also referred to as the *leader* and *follower* problems, since
the lower level problem is formulated based on the decision variables at
the upper level. Most evolutionary algorithms designed to deal with such
problems operate in a nested mode, which makes them computationally
prohibitive in terms of the number of function evaluations. In the classical literature, one of the common ways of solving the problem has been to
re-formulate it as a single-level problem using optimality measures (such
as Karush-Kuhn-Tucker conditions) for lower level problem as complementary constraint(s). However, the mathematical properties such as lin-
earity/convexity limits their application to more complex or black-box
functions. In this study, we explore a non-nested strategy in the context
of evolutionary algorithm. The constraints of the upper and lower level
problems are considered together at a single-level while optimizing the
upper level objective function. An additional constraint is formulated
based on local exploration around the lower level decision vector, which
reflects an estimate of its optimality. The approach is further enhanced
through the use of periodic local search and selective "re-evaluation" of
promising solutions. The proposed approach is implemented in a commonly used evolutionary algorithm framework and empirical results are
shown for the SMD suite of test problems. A comparison is done with
other established algorithms in the field such as BLEAQ, NBLEA, and
BLMA to demonstrate the potential of the proposed approach.

Keywords: Bilevel optimization · Non-nested formulation · Complementary constraints

1 Introduction and Background

Bilevel optimization involves solving an upper level (UL) optimization problem
subject to the optimality of a nested lower level (LL) problem. The upper and
lower level problems are also referred to as the leader and follower problems,
respectively. Both levels have their associated objective(s), variable(s) and con-
straint(s). Such problems model real-life scenarios where the performance at the

© Springer International Publishing AG 2017
W. Peng et al. (Eds.): AI 2017, LNAI 10400, pp. 106–118, 2017.
DOI: 10.1007/978-3-319-63004-5_9

upper level is meaningful/practical only if the lower level decision variables are optimal (for the lower level problem). A number of practical applications in the field of engineering [14], logistics [22], economics [21] and transportation [16] have an inherent nested structure that is suited to this type of modeling.

Bilevel optimization has been a subject of interest for a few decades. Majority of earlier studies focused on problems involving linear or quadratic functions, solved using exact analytical techniques [23]. The use of metaheuristic methods such as evolutionary algorithms is relatively recent and has gained traction in the last few years owing to the need for tackling more complex and blackbox problems [2,8,19]. Though evolutionary algorithms are well suited to such problems, their shortcoming is that they often require substantial number of function evaluations to obtain a near-optimum solution, which may not always be affordable. For bilevel problems, this is further aggravated by the fact that an optimization routine is needed to evaluate *each* upper level solution [2,20]. Therefore, additional mechanisms are needed to improve the search so that good results could be obtained in fewer function evaluations. Some of the plausible strategies to accomplish this are briefly discussed below.

1.1 Hybridization of Global and Local Search

The idea of using global search methods with classical/local search methods has been explored in a few recent works. Among these, the method presented in [24] used differential evolution (DE) to solve the leader problem, while interior point (IP) method was used for solving the follower problem. Similarly, in [15], DE was used to solve the upper level problem and a gradient search was used for the lower level optimization. Although these schemes led to reduction in the number of function evaluations, there is a considerable likelihood of obtaining a local optimum at the lower level, which in turn would affect the upper level search. To improve on this aspect, a bilevel memetic algorithm (BLMA) that uses global and local searches at both levels during different phases of the search was introduced in [11,12]. Improvements in performance were demonstrated over nested strategies that used only local or global search at each level.

1.2 Use of Approximation Models

For conventional (single-level) optimization problems, it is a common practice to use surrogates/approximation models to guide the search in order to solve a problem with relatively few true function evaluations [6,13]. This methodology is particularly preferred if each true evaluation is computationally expensive. The success of surrogate-assisted evolutionary algorithms for such problems has motivated their extension to bilevel problems, though such developments are relatively few and recent. In [18], a nested evolutionary algorithm was modified such that the lower level problem is first attempted to be modeled as a quadratic programming problem. If the model is built successfully, then a quadratic programming approach is used to solve the (approximate) problem and the solution is accepted as optimal if the true evaluation at the point is close to the approximate optimum. In a subsequent approach [19], the nested search was improved by approximating the optimum lower level variable values as a function of the upper level variables. Again, if a quadratic fit was successful, then the optimum lower level variable values were approximated (using the quadratic model) instead of evaluated (through lower level optimization), saving on significant number of lower level evaluations. The method was extended to include further enhancements using archiving in [17]. Along similar lines, a bilevel differential evolution algorithm was enhanced to include similarity-based surrogate model (SBSM) based on k nearest neighbors in [3]. The choice of using a true evaluation (lower level optimization) or a surrogate model to identify the lower level optimum was determined through a probability β. As the probability of using the surrogate model (β) was increased, it was observed that the performance of the algorithm deteriorated. In a recent work [10], the authors proposed the use of multiple spatially distributed surrogate models to substantially reduce the function evaluations required for lower level optimization.

1.3   Re-formulation to a Single-Level Problem

In the classical literature, a common approach is to re-formulate a bilevel problem into a single-level problem by incorporating the optimality conditions of the lower level in the formulation. The incorporation could be via an unconstrained formulation (e.g. [1]), or through a complementary constraint using Karush-Kuhn-Tucker (KKT) or other optimality conditions (e.g. [5]). The methods are usually computationally efficient, but often require assumptions on the mathematical properties (such as linearity and convexity) of the functions to be applicable or effective. While the re-formulation approach is typical in classical methods, there is scarce literature reporting its use in the context of evolutionary or hybrid methods.

The above discussion forms the motivation for the work presented herein. In this paper, we perform an exploratory study on using non-nested formulation to improve the search within the context of a hybrid algorithm. The main idea is to re-formulate the bilevel problem as a non-nested problem, with an additional constraint that tries to estimate the optimality of a lower level solution within its neighborhood. The inclusion of the constraint is expected to drive the evolutionary search towards near-optimal solutions at the lower level, since the constraint will be satisfied at the optimum. To improve the search further, we incorporate *re-evaluation* and a periodic nested search using selected promising solutions in the proposed algorithm.

The rest of the paper is organized as follows. The problem definition is presented in Sect. 2. Section 3 discusses the re-formulation of the problem and the optimization approach. Numerical experiments are presented in Sect. 4, and the findings of the study are summarized in Sect. 5.

2 Problem Definition

Mathematically, a single-objective bilevel optimization problem with one leader and one follower objective is defined as shown in Eq. 1. The subscript u is used to denote attributes of the upper level problem, whereas the subscript l is used for the lower level problem. The upper objective (real-valued) function is $F_u(\mathbf{x}_u, \mathbf{x}_l)$ and the lower level objective function is $f_l(\mathbf{x}_u, \mathbf{x}_l)$. The vectors $\mathbf{x}_u$ and $\mathbf{x}_l$ denote the upper level variables (in a box domain $\mathbb{X}_u$) and lower level variables (in a box domain $\mathbb{X}_l$) respectively. G and H are the sets of q_u inequality and r_u equality constraints for upper level problem. Similarly, there are q_l inequality constraints in g and r_l equality constraints in h for lower level problem. For a given upper level vector $\mathbf{x}_u$, the evaluation of upper level objective requires the $\mathbf{x}_l$ for the corresponding lower level problem (with $\mathbf{x}_u$ held constant) to be at the optimum. Thus, the upper level objective function is optimized with respect to $\mathbf{x}_u$, while the lower level objective function is optimized with respect to $\mathbf{x}_l$ using a fixed $\mathbf{x}_u$. This relation leads to the nested nature of the bilevel problem.

$$
\begin{aligned}
&\underset{\mathbf{x}_u}{\text{Minimize}} \;\; F_u(\mathbf{x}_u, \mathbf{x}_l), \\
&\text{S.t.} \qquad G_k(\mathbf{x}_u, \mathbf{x}_l) \leq 0, k = 1, \ldots, q_u, \\
&\qquad\qquad H_k(\mathbf{x}_u, \mathbf{x}_l) = 0, k = 1, \ldots, r_u, \\[4pt]
&\underset{\mathbf{x}_l}{\text{Minimize}} \;\; f_l(\mathbf{x}_u, \mathbf{x}_l), \\
&\text{S.t.} \qquad g_k(\mathbf{x}_u, \mathbf{x}_l) \leq 0, k = 1, \ldots, q_l, \\
&\qquad\qquad h_k(\mathbf{x}_u, \mathbf{x}_l) = 0, k = 1, \ldots, r_l, \\
&\text{where } \mathbf{x}_u \in \mathbb{X}_u, \;\; \mathbf{x}_l \in \mathbb{X}_l.
\end{aligned}
\tag{1}
$$

3 Proposed Approach

The first step in the proposed approach is to re-formulate the problem as a non-nested problem. Thereafter, a hybrid (combination of global and local) search is employed to solve it. The re-formulated problem and search strategy are outlined in the following subsections.

3.1 Re-formulation

The re-formulated problem is shown in Eq. 2. Effectively, it becomes a minimization problem of the upper level objective $F_u(\mathbf{X})$, subject to all constraints of upper and lower level problem, along with an additional constraint $G'(\mathbf{X})$. Here, $\mathbf{X}$ refers to a combined decision vector $\{\mathbf{x}_u, \mathbf{x}_l\}$.

$$
\begin{aligned}
&\underset{\mathbf{x}_u, \mathbf{x}_l}{\text{Minimize}} \;\; F_u(\mathbf{X}), \\
&\text{S.t.} \qquad G_k(\mathbf{X}) \leq 0, k = 1, \ldots, q_u, \\
&\qquad\qquad H_k(\mathbf{X}) = 0, k = 1, \ldots, r_u, \\
&\qquad\qquad g_k(\mathbf{X}) \leq 0, k = 1, \ldots, q_l, \\
&\qquad\qquad h_k(\mathbf{X}) = 0, k = 1, \ldots, r_l, \\
&\qquad\qquad G'(\mathbf{X}) \; (= CV_l) = 0.
\end{aligned}
\tag{2}
$$

In order to calculate CV_l, a *local exploration* is performed at the lower level, keeping $\mathbf{x}_u$ fixed. This is done by sampling $2n_l$ lower level decision vectors, where n_l is the number of lower level variables. Out of these, the first n_l vectors are created by adding δ to each of the variables in turn, where δ is a small quantity (used as 10^{-6} in this study). Similarly, the second set is created by subtracting δ from each variable. The collective set of neighborhood solutions is denoted as $\mathbf{x}_{l\delta}$, and its construction is shown in Eq. 3. Once constructed, if any of the solutions in $\mathbf{x}_{l\delta}$ violate any bounds, they are clipped to the boundary value of the decision space. Any copies, if they exist, are removed so that the final $\mathbf{x}_{l\delta}$ contains only unique neighboring solutions. Thereafter, CV_l is calculated as shown in Eq. 4.

$$\mathbf{x}_{l\delta} = \begin{bmatrix} x_{l1} + \delta & x_{l2} & x_{l3} \cdots & x_{lnl} \\ x_{l1} & x_{l2} + \delta & x_{l3} \cdots & x_{lnl} \\ \vdots & \vdots & \vdots \ddots & \vdots \\ x_{l1} & x_{l2} & x_{l3} \cdots x_{lnl} + \delta \end{bmatrix} \cup \begin{bmatrix} x_{l1} - \delta & x_{l2} & x_{l3} \cdots & x_{lnl} \\ x_{l1} & x_{l2} - \delta & x_{l3} \cdots & x_{lnl} \\ \vdots & \vdots & \vdots \ddots & \vdots \\ x_{l1} & x_{l2} & x_{l3} \cdots x_{lnl} - \delta \end{bmatrix} \quad (3)$$

$$CV_l = \begin{cases} 0, \text{ if } \mathbf{x}_l \text{ is infeasible at lower level (i.e., w.r.t } g_k(\mathbf{x}_u, \mathbf{x}_l) \text{ in Eq. 2)} \\ \sum max(f_l(\mathbf{x}_u, \mathbf{x}_l) - f_l(\mathbf{x}_u, \mathbf{x}_{l,j}), 0) \, \forall \text{ feasible } \mathbf{x}_{l,j} \in \mathbf{x}_{l\delta}, \text{ otherwise} \end{cases} \quad (4)$$

The intent behind using the two conditions in Eq. 4 is as follows:

- First case is when the lower level solution $\mathbf{x}_l$ is infeasible. Consequently, the upper level solution $\mathbf{x}_l$ will be invalid, since $\mathbf{x}_l$ is obviously not the optimum solution of the lower level problem. The CV_l is set to 0 in this case and the neighborhood solutions are not evaluated. This is done in order to drive the lower level solutions towards the feasibility first (through satisfaction of original constraints) instead of optimality (through satisfaction of additional constraint).
- Secondly, we look at the cases where $\mathbf{x}_l$ is feasible. In such cases, if the objective function value $f_l(\mathbf{x}_u, \mathbf{x}_l)$ is better than the objective value of all feasible solutions in the neighborhood, then this solution is estimated to be optimal (although locally), and the CV_l is set to 0. However, if there exist better feasible solutions in the vicinity ($\mathbf{x}_{l\delta}$) of $\mathbf{x}_l$, then a penalty is added based on the difference between $f_l(\mathbf{x}_u, \mathbf{x}_l)$ and the objective values at the neighborhood solutions whose f_l value is better (lower). The evolutionary algorithm will try to reduce this value over generations, in the process preferring the solutions which are (at least locally) optimal.

3.2   Algorithm Details

Once the problem has been re-formulated, a hybrid search (named so since it uses both global and local search methods) is conducted in order to solve it. Overall, the evolution of the solutions ($\mathbf{X}$) is driven by an elitist real-valued evolutionary algorithm operating on the formulation presented in Eq. 2. In order to enhance its performance three key components are further incorporated: (a) the concept of *re-evaluation*, (b) periodic use of nested local search, and (c) modified ranking. These key components are discussed individually below, while the overall non-nested bilevel (NNBL) approach is outlined in Algorithm 1.

Algorithm 1. The proposed non-nested bilevel (NNBL) algorithm

---

Require: N: Population size, T: No. of generations
    N_l: Population size for re-evaluation, T_l: No. of generations for re-evaluation
    T_{ls}: Frequency of nested local search
    p_c, p_m, η_c, η_m: Crossover and mutation probabilities and indices
    FE_{ls}: Maximum number of evaluations allowed for each local search
1: Set $gen = 0$
2: Set $Archive_R = \{\}$ {Archive to store all re-evaluated solutions}
3: Initialize pop
4: Evaluate pop (use non-nested formulation, Eq. 2)
5: Rank pop
6: Re-evaluate top solution in pop, update ranks and $Archive_R$
7: **for** $i = 2$ to T **do**
8:    $cpop^i = \text{Evolve}(pop^{i-1})$
9:    Evaluate $cpop^i$ (use non-nested formulation, Eq. 2)
10:   $rpop^i = pop^{i-1} \cup cpop^i$ {Combined parent+child pop}
11:   $rpop^i = \text{Rank}\ (rpop^i)$ {Rank parent + child pop}
12:   $pop^i = \text{Reduce}\ (rpop^i)$
13:   **if** $(i \mod T_{ls}) = 0$ **then**
14:      Call nested local search from the top solution (use original formulation, Eq. 1)
15:      Re-evaluate the solution obtained.
16:   **else**
17:      Re-evaluate the existing top ranked UL solution {If top solution has already been evaluated in the past, pick the next ranked solution (and so on)}
18:   **end if**
19:   Update $Archive_R$
20:   $pop^i = \text{Rank}_{AF}\ (pop^i, Archive_R)$
21:   $pop^i = \text{Reduce}\ (pop^i)$ {Retain the top N solutions}
22:   Update best $\mathbf{x}_u^*, \mathbf{x}_l^*, F_u^*, f_l^*$ as the top-ranked solution in $Archive_R$ based on UL.
23: **end for**
24: Return best $F_u^*, f_l^*, \mathbf{x_u^*}, \mathbf{x_l^*}$ in $Archive_R$ based on UL.

Evolutionary Search: For the top level global search, the widely popular non-dominated sorting genetic algorithm II (NSGA-II) [9] is employed. Since the problems considered here are single-objective, the non-dominated sorting (of the feasible solutions) defaults to sorting of the scalar objective values. The initialization is done using uniform random sampling of N solutions within the variable bounds, where N denotes the population size. During each generation, N offspring are evolved from the current population by using selection, crossover, and mutation operators. For parent selection, binary tournament selection is used. The crossover operation is performed between two selected parents using simulated binary crossover [9], whereas the mutation is performed using polynomial mutation [9]. Thereafter, the offspring are evaluated (Eq. 2), and the combined (parent + child) population is ranked. In order to make the ranking more suited to bilevel problems, a slight modification is introduced in the sorting process. First, the feasible solutions are sorted based on increasing order of the upper level objective value F_u, as done in NSGA-II. However, if two or more solutions have the same upper level function value F_u, then they are further internally ranked in the increasing order of their lower level objective value f_l. This is done to promote solutions with better upper as well as lower level objective values. The infeasible solutions are ranked separately based on their constraint violation (lower the better), and appear below the feasible solutions in the ranked population. Thereafter, the top N solutions are selected as the next generation population.

Re-evaluation: One of the key challenges in bilevel optimization is that an inaccurate lower level optimum may result in a superior upper level objective value compared to the true lower level optimum. This creates a challenge for ranking at the upper level, since it would be difficult to remove such spurious solutions due to their superior upper level objective values. For certain deceptive problems, this property may mislead the upper level search drastically towards a sub-optimal region [12].

While this possibility cannot be eliminated theoretically (since optimality cannot be guaranteed for most cases), we use a stricter check on the highly ranked solution(s) in the population to reduce the possibility of this happening. This is done through a *re-evaluation* step, wherein the top ranked upper level solution undergoes a more extensive lower level search. The search operates on true lower level evaluations, and comprises a global search first, followed by a further local search. This process consumes relatively high number of function evaluations, but since it is done selectively on only the top ranked solutions (instead of on all solutions), the total number of overall evaluations are still significantly low compared to conventional nested evolutionary approaches. In the framework presented here, since the additional constraint violation in the formulation only includes local information, it is all the more necessary to verify that the top ranked solutions are in fact superior for the original bilevel problem.

The evolutionary search during re-evaluation of a solution is performed using NSGA-II *on the lower level problem*. Thereafter, a local search is done (again on the lower level problem) using interior point (IP) algorithm [7], starting from the best solution obtained using NSGA-II. The IP algorithm is used here for doing quick local improvements based on its ability to handle constraints and non-convexity unlike other available local search methods. The implementation of this IP algorithm as available in the `fmincon` package within Matlab 2013b is used in this study. Default parameters for the algorithm (as set in Matlab) are used during optimization.

There may be instances where the top ranked solution in a population has already been evaluated previously. All re-evaluated solutions are tracked through the use of an archive ($Archive_R$). If the top solution in a population identified to be re-evaluated already exists in the archive, then the next best solution in the population is considered for re-evaluation instead (and so on).

Nested Local Search: To further expedite the upper level search, a nested local search is performed after every few generations. During this process, IP is used to improve the objective value at the upper level, while also using the IP for lower level optimization. The top individual from the upper level population is chosen as the starting solution for the upper level search. For each of the lower level searches, the initial lower level solution is identified as follows. From the archive of re-evaluated solutions, the solution closest to the current $\mathbf{x}_u$ is identified. The optimum lower level solution ($\mathbf{x}_l^*$) corresponding to this $\mathbf{x}_u$ is then chosen as the starting point. This method for choosing the starting lower level solution has also been earlier adopted in [11]. It relies on the assumption that two solutions which are close at the upper level are likely to have close lower level optima. The solution obtained through the above nested local search undergoes re-evaluation before being added to the population again. Subsequently, it is also added to the archive of re-evaluated solutions ($Archive_R$).

Ranking: The last key component of the proposed approach is the ranking of solutions. After the EA based ranking (discussed above), the upper level ranking is further enhanced by different treatment of re-evaluated solutions.

The re-evaluated solutions may be considered as the most promising solutions encountered so far during the search. As discussed above, an archive of all such re-evaluated ($Archive_R$) solutions is maintained and continually updated whenever a new solution is re-evaluated. The confidence in the upper level objective values of these solutions is evidently high due the extensive lower level search. Therefore, just before the end of the generation, the final ranking of the solutions involves placing all the solutions of $Archive_R$ ahead of the other solutions. Among the $Archive_R$ solutions, the solutions are ordered according to feasibility first scheme, as discussed above for NSGA-II framework. The remaining solutions (which have not been re-evaluated) retain the order obtained by the original ranking. This process is referred to as Rank$_{AF}$ (i.e., Ranking with $Archive_R$ first) in Algorithm 1. Thereafter, the top N solutions are selected to progress to the next generation.

4   Numerical Experiments

In this section, numerical experiments are presented using NNBL. The experiments and comparisons are done for the SMD benchmark suite of test problems proposed in [20]. SMD suite contains twelve scalable problems, of which the first eight are unconstrained, whereas the rest are constrained problems. We use five variables for each problem, two at the upper and three at the lower level. A comparison is performed with three established approaches, namely NBLEA [20], BLEAQ [19], and BLMA [11]. The comparisons are based on the accuracy, measured using the absolute difference between the obtained optima and true optima, as done in [11]. The parameter settings of these algorithms are outlined below:

1. BLMA [11]: For BLMA, a population size of 50 is used. The upper level is run for a maximum of 5 generations for the unconstrained problems (SMD1-SMD8) and 10 generations for the constrained problems (SMD9-SMD12). For lower level, population size of 50 and 20 generations are used. The switch from global to local search for lower level optimization is done after 4 and 8 generations for two different settings respectively. For IP, a maximum of 250 function evaluations are used for both unconstrained and constrained problems.

2. NBLEA [20]: Nested bilevel evolutionary algorithm (NBLEA) is a nested algorithm which uses an evolutionary algorithm for the upper level and quadratic programming or evolutionary algorithm for the lower level optimization. The implementation available for download at http://bilevel.org is used in this study, with population size 50 and default parameter settings[1].

3. BLEAQ [19]: Bilevel evolutionary algorithm with quadratic approximation (BLEAQ) attempts to reduce the computational cost of a nested evolutionary algorithm by estimating the values of lower level optimum variables instead of explicit search. Based on the truly evaluated solutions during the search, the lower level optimum variables are approximated as a quadratic function of the upper level variables. The implementation available for download at http://bilevel.org is used in this study, with population size 50 and default parameter settings.

For the proposed algorithm NNBL, a population size of $N = 50$ is used. The upper level evolutionary algorithm is run for a maximum of $T = 100$ generations for all problems. The same population size $(N_l = N)$ and number of generations $(T_l = T)$ are also used for the re-evaluation of the best upper level individual for each generation. The probabilities of crossover (p_c) and mutation (p_m) are set to 0.9 and 0.1 respectively, while the corresponding indices (η_c, η_m) are set to 20 and 30 respectively. For IP, similar to BLMA, a maximum of 250 function evaluations are used for each local search.

The comparison between the proposed NNBL, BLMA, NBLEA and BLEAQ is presented in Table 1 (in terms of accuracy) and Table 2 (in terms of function evaluations used[2]). The values shown are median results from 29 independent runs.

---

[1] Please note that the current version of the code has certain modifications from the one used for the study in [20].

[2] Please note that population size and number of variables used in earlier studies [19,20] are different from those in this paper, and hence the difference in reported function evaluations.

Table 1. Comparison of the median accuracy obtained using NNBL, BLMA, NBLEA and BLEAQ on SMD series problems

Prb Name	NNBL		BLMA		NBLEA		BLEAQ	
	UL Acc	LL Acc	UL Acc	LL Acc	UL Acc	LL Acc	UL Acc	LL Acc
SMD1	5.98E−14	3.33E−14	**5.97E−14**	**3.32E−14**	5.03E−06	2.37E−06	1.16E−09	7.13E−10
SMD2	**6.08E−14**	**2.22E−14**	3.63E−14	1.32E−13	3.17E−06	3.43E−06	5.44E−06	5.50E−06
SMD3	4.83E−14	4.36E−14	**4.57E−14**	**3.81E−14**	1.37E−05	8.95E−06	7.55E−06	5.50E−06
SMD4	**6.51E−09**	**8.58E−11**	2.24E−07	2.08E−07	9.29E−06	6.19E−06	1.15E−07	1.86E−06
SMD5	**1.14E−11**	**6.90E−12**	6.58E−10	6.24E−10	4.36E−07	1.79E−07	2.00E−07	2.50E−07
SMD6	**4.76E−14**	**6.59E−14**	4.44E−13	1.70E−13	6.40E−08	1.44E−08	1.34E−07	9.82E−09
SMD7	9.25E−14	1.87E−13	**9.01E−14**	**1.86E−13**	3.69E−06	7.42E−07	5.81E−06	9.23E−06
SMD8	5.51E−04	1.31E−04	2.54E−03	7.69E−04	**4.74E−05**	**1.54E−05**	2.21E−04	5.53E−05
SMD9	**6.84E−14**	**2.72E−14**	1.55E−05	2.58E−05	4.91E−01	7.55E−01	4.22E−06	1.16E−05
SMD10	1.78E−01	1.05E−01	**4.27E−06**	**3.98E−06**	2.47E−02	4.08E−02	1.02E−03	8.55E−04
SMD11	6.30E−01	4.01E−05	7.00E−03	**1.14E−07**	5.99E−03	8.78E−03	**1.28E−03**	2.08E−03
SMD12	1.41E−01	5.69E−02	**3.75E−06**	**6.00E−06**	3.82E−02	7.81E−02	4.56E−02	2.00E−02

Table 2. Comparison of the function evaluations used by NNBL, BLMA, NBLEA and BLEAQ on SMD series problems

Prb Name	NNBL		BLMA		NBLEA		BLEAQ	
	UL FE	LL FE	UL FE	LL FE	UL FE	LL FE	UL FE	LL FE
SMD1	6.82E+02	4.74E+04	4.12E+02	2.75E+05	1.52E+03	9.52E+05	1.19E+03	2.37E+05
SMD2	6.94E+02	4.89E+04	4.24E+02	2.76E+05	1.56E+03	9.63E+05	1.20E+03	4.06E+05
SMD3	6.82E+02	5.01E+04	4.12E+02	2.80E+05	1.56E+03	1.04E+06	1.29E+03	2.83E+05
SMD4	1.47E+03	1.00E+05	5.51E+02	3.05E+05	1.53E+03	8.33E+05	1.31E+03	3.84E+05
SMD5	8.21E+02	7.15E+04	5.52E+02	2.99E+05	3.40E+03	2.22E+06	2.06E+03	8.42E+05
SMD6	6.82E+02	5.21E+04	4.32E+02	2.85E+05	4.06E+03	1.11E+05	4.08E+03	6.04E+03
SMD7	3.52E+03	2.86E+05	4.24E+02	2.73E+05	1.58E+03	9.56E+05	1.27E+03	3.82E+05
SMD8	7.77E+03	5.04E+05	5.52E+02	2.99E+05	4.09E+03	2.85E+06	3.54E+03	1.73E+06
SMD9	6.94E+02	4.90E+04	6.72E+02	4.76E+05	4.24E+03	3.08E+06	1.26E+03	4.03E+05
SMD10	6.19E+03	5.17E+05	5.86E+02	4.58E+05	2.96E+03	2.93E+06	1.92E+03	5.45E+05
SMD11	6.17E+03	5.27E+05	5.95E+02	4.57E+05	3.35E+03	3.10E+06	2.39E+03	4.62E+06
SMD12	6.16E+03	5.23E+05	5.86E+02	4.56E+05	2.99E+03	3.25E+06	1.50E+03	4.79E+05

It is seen that for most of the problems, NNBL obtains very competitive results. For SMD1-SMD5, SMD7, SMD9 it shows better accuracy for both levels with fewer function evaluations compared to NBLEA and BLEAQ. BLMA shows similar accuracy values as NNBL but typically consumes higher number of function evaluations for problems SMD1-SMD7 and SMD9. For SMD8, NNBL showed better accuracy than BLMA but used higher number of function evaluations. In the remaining cases, NNBL is marginally worse in accuracy and computational cost compared to BLMA. The best accuracy values among the compared algorithms are shown in bold for each problem in Table 1. Also to be noted is that for SMD1-SMD7, the differences between the values of NNBL and BLMA are insignificant as both algorithms are extremely close to the true optimum (the accuracy values are nearly zero for these cases).

4.1   Performance Profile

Apart from reporting the performance on individual problems above, we also present a statistical comparison of the performance using *performance profile* [4]. The function $\rho(\tau)$ is the cumulative distribution function for performance measure τ. The τ value effectively represents the factor (ratio) of the performance compared to the best performance. Thus the minimum value for τ is 1 (or 0 if plotted in log scale). In our study, the median accuracy and median function evaluations are used as the performance measures, plotted in $\log_{10}$ scale. The resulting performance profile of the algorithms NNBL, BLMA, NBLEA, BLEAQ are shown in the Fig. 1 considering the twelve problems studied. From the figures, it is clearly seen that for the accuracy values, both NNBL and BLMA lie to the left of NBLEA and BLEAQ, indicating better performance. Among the two (NNBL and BLMA), the performance is comparable with one algorithm outperforming the other for some problems and vice versa. In terms of function evaluations, however, the benefit of the proposed NNBL could be distinctively seen, where the performance profile of NNBL is significantly superior in comparison of the remaining three algorithms. Thus, it can be seen the NNBL is able to achieve competitive results in relatively fewer function evaluations, indicating significant reduction in computational cost.

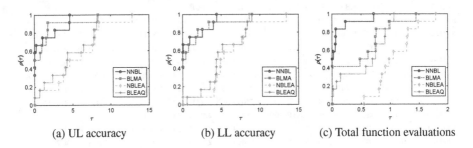

(a) UL accuracy   (b) LL accuracy   (c) Total function evaluations

Fig. 1. Comparison of performance profiles of NBLEA, BLEAQ, BLMA and NNBL

5   Conclusions

Bilevel optimization is a problem of theoretical and practical interest, with a number of unique challenges when compared to traditional single-level optimization problems. While the past efforts in the field were directed towards solving problems with exact methods, recently there has been an increasing interest in developing metaheuristic methods such as evolutionary algorithms, in order to deal with more complex or black-box functions. However, when operated in nested mode, such algorithms may require exorbitant number of function evaluations, which limits their use. In this work, we explored a non-nested formulation in order to reduce the computational expense while solving bilevel problems. The original problem is re-formulated into a conventional single-level problem through use of an additional constraint based on the estimated optimality of a given lower level solution. Comparisons with prominent contemporary algorithms clearly show that the proposed approach is able to achieve the best or competitive results for most of the problems, at a lower computational cost. Thus, the proposed approach shows promise in solving bilevel optimization problems more efficiently, and paves way for more advanced strategies based on non-nested formulations.

Acknowledgments. The second author would like to acknowledge the Early Career Researcher (ECR) grant from the University of New South Wales, Australia.

References

1. Aiyoshi, E., Shimizu, K.: A solution method for the static constrained Stackelberg problem via penalty method. IEEE Trans. Autom. Control **29**(12), 1111–1114 (1984)
2. Angelo, J.S., Krempser, E., Barbosa, H.J.: Differential evolution for bilevel programming. In: IEEE Congress on Evolutionary Computation, pp. 470–477 (2013)
3. Angelo, J.S., Krempser, E., Barbosa, H.J.: Differential evolution assisted by a surrogate model for bilevel programming problems. In: IEEE Congress on Evolutionary Computation, pp. 1784–1791 (2014)
4. Barbosa, H.J., Bernardino, H.S., Barreto, A.: Using performance profiles to analyze the results of the 2006 CEC constrained optimization competition. In: IEEE Congress on Evolutionary Computation, pp. 1–8 (2010)
5. Bard, J.F., Falk, J.E.: An explicit solution to the multi-level programming problem. Comput. Oper. Res. **9**(1), 77–100 (1982)
6. Bhattacharjee, K.S., Singh, H.K., Ray, T.: Multi-objective optimization with multiple spatially distributed surrogates. J. Mech. Des. **138**(9), 091401 (2016)
7. Byrd, R.H., Hribar, M.E., Nocedal, J.: An interior point algorithm for large-scale nonlinear programming. SIAM J. Optim. **9**(4), 877–900 (1999)
8. Colson, B., Marcotte, P., Savard, G.: An overview of bilevel optimization. Ann. Oper. Res. **153**(1), 235–256 (2007)
9. Deb, K., Pratap, A., Agarwal, S., Meyarivan, T.: A fast and elitist multiobjective genetic algorithm: NSGA-II. IEEE Trans. Evol. Comput. **6**(2), 182–197 (2002)
10. Islam, M.M., Singh, H.K., Ray, T.: A surrogate assisted approach for single-objective bilevel optimization. IEEE Trans. Evol. Comput. (2017)
11. Islam, M.M., Singh, H.K., Ray, T.: A memetic algorithm for solving single objective bilevel optimization problems. In: 2015 IEEE Congress on Evolutionary Computation (CEC), pp. 1643–1650. IEEE (2015)
12. Islam, M.M., Singh, H.K., Ray, T., Sinha, A.: An enhanced memetic algorithm for single-objective bilevel optimization problems. Evol. Comput. (2016). doi:10.1162/EVCO_a_00198
13. Jin, Y.: A comprehensive survey of fitness approximation in evolutionary computation. Soft. Comput. **9**(1), 3–12 (2005)
14. Kirjner-Neto, C., Polak, E., Der Kiureghian, A.: An outer approximations approach to reliability-based optimal design of structures. J. Optim. Theory Appl. **98**(1), 1–16 (1998)

15. Koh, A.: A metaheuristic framework for bi-level programming problems with multi-disciplinary applications. In: Talbi, E.-G. (ed.) Metaheuristics for Bi-level Optimization, vol. 482, pp. 153–187. Springer, Heidelberg (2013)

16. Migdalas, A.: Bilevel programming in traffic planning: models, methods and challenge. J. Global Optim. 7(4), 381–405 (1995)

17. Sinha, A., Malo, P., Deb, K.: An improved bilevel evolutionary algorithm based on quadratic approximations. In: IEEE Congress on Evolutionary Computation, pp. 1870–1877 (2014)

18. Sinha, A., Malo, P., Deb, K.: Nested bilevel evolutionary algorithm (N-BLEA) code and user guide. http://www.bilevel.org

19. Sinha, A., Malo, P., Deb, K.: Efficient evolutionary algorithm for single-objective bilevel optimization. arXiv preprint (2013). arXiv:1303.3901

20. Sinha, A., Malo, P., Deb, K.: Test problem construction for single-objective bilevel optimization. Evol. Comput. 22(3), 439–477 (2014)

21. Sinha, A., Malo, P., Frantsev, A., Deb, K.: Multi-objective Stackelberg game between a regulating authority and a mining company: a case study in environmental economics. In: IEEE Congress on Evolutionary Computation, pp. 478–485 (2013)

22. Sun, H., Gao, Z., Wu, J.: A bi-level programming model and solution algorithm for the location of logistics distribution centers. Appl. Math. Model. 32(4), 610–616 (2008)

23. Vicente, L.N., Calamai, P.H.: Bilevel and multilevel programming: a bibliography review. J. Global Optim. 5(3), 291–306 (1994)

24. Zhu, X., Yu, Q., Wang, X.: A hybrid differential evolution algorithm for solving nonlinear bilevel programming with linear constraints. IEEE International Conference on Cognitive Informatics, pp. 126–131 (2006)

Let's Consider Two Objectives When Estimating Hand Postures

Shahrzad Saremi, Seyedali Mirjalili$^{(\boxtimes)}$, Andrew Lewis,
and Alan Wee-Chung Liew

School of Information and Communication Technology, Griffith University, Brisbane,
QLD 4111, Australia
{shahrzad.saremi,seyedali.mirjalili}@griffithuni.edu.au,
{a.lewis,a.liew}@griffith.edu.au

Abstract. Hand posture estimation is an important step in hand gesture detection. It refers to the process of modeling hand in computer to accurately represent the actual hand obtained from an acquisition device. In the literature, several objective functions (mostly based on silhouette or point cloud) have been used to formulate and solve the problem of hand posture estimation as a minimisation problem using stochastic or deterministic algorithms. The main challenge is that the objective function is computationally expensive. In the case of using point clouds, decreasing the number of points results in a better computational cost, but it decreases the accuracy of hand posture estimation. We argue in this paper that hand posture estimation is a bi-objective problem with two conflicting objectives: minimising the error versus minimising the number of points in the point cloud. As an early effort, this paper first formulates hand posture estimation as a bi-objective optimisation problem and then approximates its true Pareto optimal front with an improved Multi-Objective Particle Swarm Optimisation (MOPSO) algorithm. The proposed algorithm is used to determine the Pareto optimal front for 16 hand postures and compared with the original MOPSO. The results proved that the objectives are in conflict and the improved MOPSO outperforms the original algorithm when solving this problem.

Keywords: Hand posture estimation · Mulit-Objective Particle Swarm Optimisation · Multi-objective optimisation · MOPSO

1 Introduction

Most of the current vision-based hand gesture detection techniques have common phases: detecting hand gestures, tracking the motion of hand, and recognition of gestures. In the detection phase, the shape of hand is detected and segmented. The segmentation [1,2] removes unimportant elements of the image taken from the camera(s) and extracts the desired parts of hand(s). Due to the cheap cost of depth cameras these days, the first phase is substantially less challenging than before. After obtaining the visual picture of hands from either RGB or depth

© Springer International Publishing AG 2017
W. Peng et al. (Eds.): AI 2017, LNAI 10400, pp. 119–130, 2017.
DOI: 10.1007/978-3-319-63004-5_10

camera, the hands are also represented in this phase. The representation of hands are mostly done by 3D models [3] or appearance-based techniques [4].

Tracking is the second phase in vision-based gesture recognition, in which the motion of hands is continuously detected and identified. In this phase, the deformation of hands and trajectory/velocity of movement are important factors to track. In the systems that utilise 3D model of hands and involves occlusion, this phase also deals with the prediction of hand movement and estimation of features that become invisible to the camera. Popular methods are template methods [5], particle filtering [6], and optimal estimation [7].

The last phase of hand gesture recognition is the recognition of gestures. This phase interprets the combination of pose, position, and motion of hands. This interpretation can be done based on static or dynamic models created in the previous phases. Both types of gestures can be detected by employing classifiers.

2   Vision-Based Hand Pose Estimation

One of the main operations when detecting hand gestures is hand modeling, in which a model of the hand is created in a computer using the data acquired from RGB or depth camera. Although raw data can be extracted from the image, processing such data, which are mostly of high dimension, is computationally expensive. With a model in the computer, these drawbacks can be alleviated.

In the hand modelling, the main step is to estimate the hand pose in the computer. This refers to the process of finding an accurate pose using the hand model in the computer. According to Barsonum [8] and Taylor *et al.* [9], *"finding an optimal pose of hand (hand pose estimation) in the computer is still an open research question"* due similarity between fingers, agility of hands, self-similarities of fingers, and speed of changing poses.

There are two types of hand gestures: static versus dynamic. Consequently, we have two main classes of methods for hand gesture recognition: static hand gesture recognition and dynamic hand gestures recognition. In static hand gesture recognition, there is no movement. Therefore, the classification is done based on the shape of the hand model in the hand modelling phase. In dynamic hand gesture recognition, both hand pose and motion should be considered. This means that in dynamic hand gesture recognition, we still need to do static hand gesture detection. But this should be done for each frame of the dynamic gesture and must be accompanied with the features of movement. The sequence of postures in the gesture has been modelled with Finite State Machine, Hidden Markov Model, and so on. Therefore, hand pose estimation is a key to success in recognising both static and dynamic gestures.

In the literature, there are several approaches for hand pose estimation, dividing in three main classes: model-based fitting [7], template methods [5], and hybrid model and template [10]. In model-based fitting (generative) methods, a 2D or 3D model of hand is employed to represent the actual hand in the computer. Some of the popular models are motion-based models, deformable models, colour-based models [11], skeleton models, volumetric models, geometric models, and kinematic models [4]. In template-matching (discriminative) methods neural networks (NNs) are popular methods. In such approaches, a large dataset of hand postures and/or motion is built first. The main objective is to use the image itself (without any model) to recognise the gesture. Popular methods are deep convolutional neutral networks [4,12] and random forest methods [13]. Other similar works that use NNs to recognise hand poses or gestures can be found in [14,15]. In hybrid methods, model-based and template-based are mostly used sequentially. Each of the above-mentioned techniques have their own advantages and drawbacks summarised in Table 1.

Table 1. Advantages and disadvantages of model-based fittings methods versus template-matching methods

Generative methods		Discriminative methods	
Advantage	Drawback	Advantage	Drawback
1. Flexibly predict complex poses	1. Finding the optimal shape of model is computationally very expensive	1. Speed is fast	1. Less flexibility to predict complex poses
2. Can be used in both discrete and continuous poses	2. Sensitive to initialisation	2. Not sensitive to initialisation	2. Only able to only estimate discrete poses
3. Able to consider previous pose	3. Not accurate for differing hand sizes (sensitive to hand scale)	3. Accurate for different hand sizes	3. Does not consider the previous pose
4. Adaptable to new scenarios			4. Difficult to adapt to new scenarios

This table shows that template-matching methods benefit from high speed and accuracy for different hand sizes. Also, the initial pose of hand (hand pose obtained in the previous frame) does not impact the performance of the pose estimator. However, the main drawback is the lack of flexibility to estimate complex poses. In other words, such template-based methods are limited to the poses in the database. In addition, template-based methods do not consider the previous pose and are only able to estimate discrete poses.

Conversely, generative methods are very flexible in estimating complex hand poses. Also, they mostly consider the previous poses and the initial pose to estimate the new pose to reduce the computational time. They can also be used in estimating both discrete and continuous poses. However, the main challenge in such methods is that generating the optimal shape for the hand is computationally expensive. Another difficulty is the sensitivity to the initial pose and recovering from an incorrect pose estimated in the previous frame. This paper, for the first time, tackles the high computational cost of hand posture estimation from a multi-objective perspective to maximise accuracy and minimise the computational cost simultaneously. The current deterministic methods simplify the objective function, which changes the search space and results in less accurate estimation. On the other hand, stochastic methods are all used considering one objective, so they cannot address the conflicting objectives in the hand posture estimation problem.

3   Hand Pose Estimation Considering Two Objectives

This section first presents the two objectives used in this paper. The objectives are then employed to formulate hand posture estimation as a bi-objective minimisation problem.

3.1   Objective Functions

The most reliable objective functions in the literature are calculated using depth images. To mathematically model and implement such objective functions, the first step is to create the 3D point cloud. For obtaining a 3D point cloud to be used in hand pose estimation, we have to use the raw depth data or depth image. Raw depth data normally requires the details of the hardware (camera calibration, focal focus, etc.) to accurately find the corresponding 3D point for each pixel. This makes them more difficult to use compared to depth images. For the sake of simplicity, this work only uses depth images. In order to extract a hand from a depth image, one needs the range value along the x axis. Different datasets have different range due to the technical set up.

As an example, depth images and 3D point clouds of four standard data set are drawn in Fig. 1. In the first dataset, the main issue is the existence of ground truth of the hand skeleton in the depth image. As may be seen in Fig. 1, skeletons cause gaps in the point cloud. This is not a major issue since we have to down sample the point cloud anyway.

The first two data sets can be considered as synthetic datasets. Synthetic data is mostly used in the literature since the ground truth of real images is difficult to obtain. In fact, the current works approximate the ground truth and use it in the comparison when using real images. Also, the noise has been removed, while in real images there are always errors. This is the reason why researchers normally use synthetic data in quantitative comparison and real data in qualitative comparison. In the literature there are also datasets that show noisy images. Outliers are undesired 3D points in the point cloud, which might negatively impact the hand posture estimation and should be considered to avoid its consequences.

No matter if there is an outlier in the point cloud or not, they are the best tools to calculate the discrepancy of a 3D hand model with the hand obtained from a camera. At the moment, the majority of objective functions utilise point clouds. However, some researchers also use the segmented image of the hand.

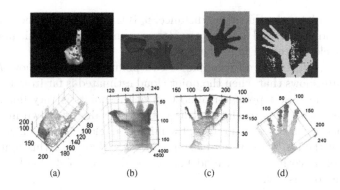

Fig. 1. Three poses selected from MSRA [16] (a), FingerPoint [10] (b), ICVL [17] (c), and Teaser datasets (d) [16] and created point clouds

This means that they first get the projection of a 3D model of a surface and calculate the discrepancy between the projection and the segmented hand.

The point cloud generated from the depth image is the reference. After obtaining the reference point cloud, the next step is to create the point cloud using the 3D model. This should be done by uniform sampling on the surface of the 3D model. As an example, Fig. 2(a) is given which shows 200 random points on the surface of the 3D hand model.

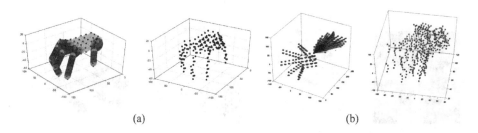

Fig. 2. (a) Point cloud generated from the 3D model proposed in this paper, (b) The process of calculating the objective function. The distance between the closest point in point clouds (left: $f = 1.9592e + 04$ (average: 97.9612), right: $1.8164e + 03$ (average: 9.0820))

In the objective function, the distance between each of the points in the point cloud generated from 3D model and depth image is calculated. The sum of all the distances should be minimised to find an accurate estimation of hand pose. Therefore, the objective function is defined as follows:

$$E(\boldsymbol{p}) = \frac{\sum_{i=1}^{n} d(p_i - q_i)}{n} \tag{1}$$

where $d()$ calculates the Euclidean distance, p_i is the ith point in the point cloud of the 3D hand model, and q_i shows the closest point in the synthetic point cloud or the point cloud created from the depth image.

Figure 2(b) illustrates an example of two points clouds and how E works. The left figure shows that when the point cloud estimated is far from the desired point cloud, the closest point for almost all of the points is very limited (even one in some cases). This results in a high objective value as shown in Fig. 2(b). As the points become closer, however, the number of closest points increases and consequently the objective value becomes smaller. Note that this figure shows the results of a synthetic hand model since the desired point cloud is obtained from a 3D model as well.

To show how the objective function works for real data, Fig. 3 is given. This figure shows that in order to calculate the objective value of a given hand model, the depth image should be first taken and used to create a point cloud. Since there is normally an extremely large number of points (one point for every pixel) in the point cloud, we have to down-sample it. Figure 3 shows that with an appropriate percentage of down-sampling, the shape of the hand remains intact. The next step is to create the 3D models and point cloud estimated. With these two point clouds, the distance between each pair of closest points can be easily calculated. This is where the problem starts; reducing the number of points (n) in the reference point cloud decrease the computational cost. However, it also increases the error (E) rate and gives a less accurate representation of the actual hand model.

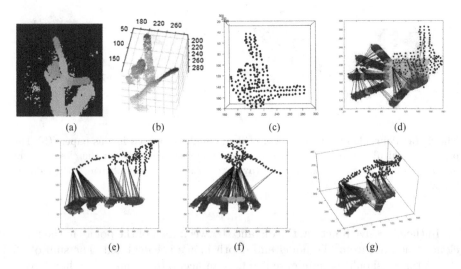

(a)   (b)   (c)   (d)

(e)   (f)   (g)

Fig. 3. The process of calculating the objective function for a real hand posture. (a) depth image obtained from a depth camera, (b) point cloud created, (c) down-sampled points cloud to have only 200 points, (d) X-Y view of hand model and point clouts, (e) X-Z view, (f) Y-Z view, and (g) 3D view.

3.2   Multi-objective Formulation of the Problem

The problem of estimating hand model can be formulated as a bi-objective problem to minimise the discrepancy and minimise the number of points in the point cloud. These two objectives are in conflict, meaning that reducing the number of points will increase the discrepancy and error rate. In order to get a better estimation, we need a large number of points in the point cloud. As discussed in the literature review of this paper, addressing these two objectives simultaneously has not been investigated in the literature. Therefore, this section formulates the problem as a multi-objective problem and the next section solves it with a multi-objective algorithm.

According to the definition of multi-objective optimisation, there is no single solution for such problems. For a problem with a single objective, there is one global optimum since there is one criterion. For instance, hand pose estimation considering discrepancy will result in one hand model with minimum discrepancy. However, there is more than one solution when considering multiple objectives. The set of all the optimal solutions (non-dominated solutions) is called the Pareto optimal set and their corresponding projection in the objective space is called Pareto optimal front. The problem of hand posture estimation can be formulated as a bi-objective minimisation problem as follows:

$$Minimise : E(\boldsymbol{p}) \tag{2}$$
$$Minimise : n \tag{3}$$

where n is the number of points and $\boldsymbol{p}$ includes 26 variables defining the number of points on the hand shape (1), the angle of each joint depending on the number of DoF (20), location of wrist in the search space (3), and the orientation of the hand (3).

Figure 4 shows the main 26 parameters of $\boldsymbol{p}$ and the hand skeleton with 36 DoF employed in this paper.

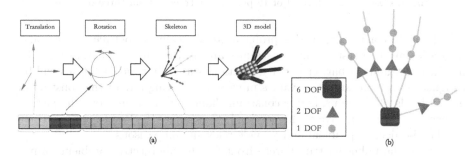

Fig. 4. (a) The variable vector and its components defining the final position, orientation, and shape of the 3D model, (b) Hand model with 26 DoF

4   Results

In order to approximate the true Pareto optimal solutions for the bi-objective problem formulated in the preceding section, Multi-Objective Particle Swarm Optimisation (MOPSO) [18] algorithm is improved. This is because it was observed that MOPSO considers all the variables similarly and re-initialising the particles will change the variables for the global position and orientation as well. Also, this algorithm may get trapped in local Pareto optimal fronts, especially for fingers, and there is a need to suddenly move them.

In the Improved MOPSO (IMOPSO), particles are randomly re-initialised around randomly selected archive members every two iterations. The main point here is that the 'worst' (dominated) solutions in the population are re-initialised around the best solutions (non-dominated) with the hope of improvement. Since we observed MOPSO is good at finding optimal values for the translation and rotation, the initialisation is applied for the skeleton parameters only (pink blocks in Fig. 4).

To test the performance of the IMOPSO algorithm, a total of 16 postures are employed from three standard datasets [10, 19, 20]. The datasets and postures are shown in Fig. 5.

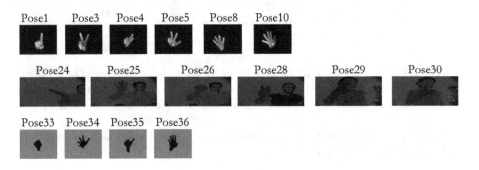

Fig. 5. Case studies: a total of 16 postures extracted from three datasets

The main constraints in this problem are the collision between fingers and fingers/palm. The rest of the constraints are on the range of parameters. To handle constraints, a barrier penalty function is used, in which solutions will be assigned with large objective values in case of violating any of the constraints at any levels. Although a better constraint handling might improve the performance, the main objective of this section is to estimate the Pareto optimal front for the bi-objective problem and provide relevant comparisons.

Due to the unknown true Pareto front for the bi-objective problem formulated in this work, the results are collected and presented qualitatively only. The best Pareto optimal fronts during 30 runs are illustrated in Fig. 6. Note that 60 particles are employed over 300 iterations to estimate the Pareto optimal fronts. The dimension of each particle is 26: three variables for defining translation, three for rotation, and 20 for the skeleton. It is interesting that the Pareto

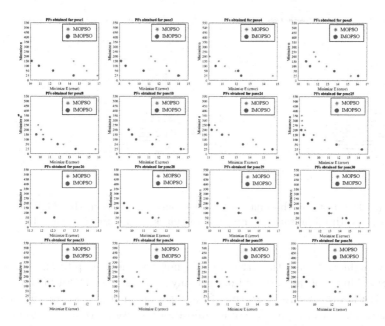

Fig. 6. Comparison of MOPSO and IMOPSO for the postures in the all datasets

optimal fronts obtained by IMOPSO dominate those obtained by MOPSO. The trade-offs between point number and error rate can be seen in these figures. A good decision may be to pick one of the solutions in the middle of the front, but further discussion in this area is out of the scope of this work.

Overall, the figures show that IMOPSO is able to dominate the MOPSO algorithm on most of the case studies—the Pareto optima front obtained by IMOPSO completely dominates that of MOPSO (e.g. pose1, pose8, pose25, etc.). In the rest of the test cases, a large portion MOPSO's front is dominated by that of IMOPSO. This behaviour can clearly be seen in the pose8, pose35, etc. case studies which result in having one of a maximum of two solutions that are non-dominated with respect to each other. Some of the solutions obtained by MOPSO occasionally dominate one of the solutions obtained by IMOPSO, but these results show that proposed random component generally is beneficial for MOPSO for the problem of hand posture estimation.

In the previous experiment the range of the number of points in the point cloud was [25,550]. It was observed that further increasing the number of points does not necessarily decrease the error rate. To show this in detail, Fig. 7(a) is given, in which the number of points in the point cloud could be varied up to 2000.

It may be seen that once the number of points goes above 500 the solution becomes dominated completely. It is also interesting that the search history becomes sparse as well. This figure shows that increasing the number of points extracted from the 3D hand model does not necessarily decrease the error rate. After 500 points, the error becomes greater, which might be similar to over-fitting in Neural Networks. With more points the optimisation algorithm might gravitate towards the regions with higher density.

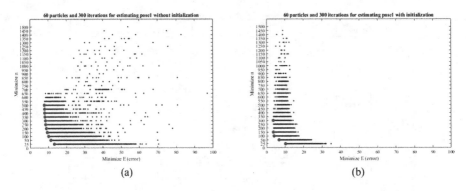

(a)   (b)

Fig. 7. (a) IMOPSO on the first posture without initialisation, (b) IMOPSO on the first posture with initialisation. Note that the black points are the search history.

One might say that the error rate is not very low despite the success of IMOPSO. This is because we did not use any initialisation. IMOPSO starts estimating the hand posture every time from a set of random postures. To see how good the results will be in case of an initialisation, we start with a good initial point for the first posture and re-do the experiment. The results are depicted in Fig. 7(b). This figure evidently shows that the error becomes significantly better, and the same pattern can be observed when increasing the number of points.

Finally, to investigate how much better the IMOPSO with initial pose is compared to IMOPSO without initial pose, Fig. 8 is provided. It can be seen that the Pareto optimal front obtained when there is a good initial pose

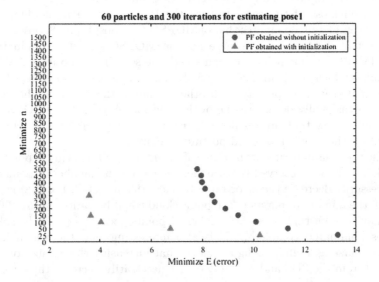

Fig. 8. PF obtained by IMOPSO with and without initialisation

completely dominates the Pareto optimal front without an initial pose. It is worth mentininge that the shape of Parato optimal fronts estimated in this section show that the objectives are in conflict and justify the use of a multi-objective optimisation algorithm for this problem.

5 Conclusion

This paper formulated the problem of estimating hand posture as a bi-objective problem for the first time in the literature. The main motivation was to minimise the error and number of points in the point cloud simultaneously. After formulating the problem, an improved MOPSO was employ to approximate the true Pareto optimal front. In the IMOPSO algorithm, dominated particles were randomly initialised around randomly selected solutions in the archive. The changes were only applied to the skeleton details of 3D hand model and not translation or rotation since it was observed that changing such parameters dramatically reduces the quality of solutions most of the time. To test the performance of IMOPSO, a number of postures extracted from three standard datasets was used. The results demonstrated the merits of this algorithm in determining the true Pareto optimal front. The paper also considered investigation of the search history and impacts of a good initial pose for the optimiser. Another finding was that increasing the number of points in the point cloud does not necessarily decrease error and a good range is [200,500]. The results also proved that hand posture estimation is a bi-objective problem with two conflicting objectives.

For future work, it would be interesting to visualise the parallel coordinates and analyse the results further to find the relations between the parameters and objectives. The impact of different constraint handling techniques on the performance of IMOPSO or MOPSO when solving this problem is also worth investigation.

References

1. Coogan, T., Awad, G., Han, J., Sutherland, A.: Real time hand gesture recognition including hand segmentation and tracking. In: Bebis, G., et al. (eds.) ISVC 2006. LNCS, vol. 4291, pp. 495–504. Springer, Heidelberg (2006). doi:10.1007/11919476_50

2. Singhai, S., Satsangi, C.: Hand segmentation for hand gesture recognition. In: Workshop on Interactive Multimedia on Mobile and Portable Devices, vol. 1, pp. 48–52 (2014)

3. Lee, J., Kunii, T.L.: Model-based analysis of hand posture. IEEE Comput. Graph. Appl. 15(5), 77–86 (1995)

4. Bourke, A.K., Obrien, J.V., Lyons, G.M.: Evaluation of a threshold-based tri-axial accelerometer fall detection algorithm. Gait Posture 26(2), 194–199 (2007)

5. Darrell, T.J., Essa, I.A., Pentland, A.P.: Task-specific gesture analysis in real-time using interpolated views. IEEE Trans. Pattern Anal. Mach. Intell. 18(12), 1236–1242 (1996)

6. Isard, M., Blake, A.: Condensation conditional density propagation for visual tracking. Int. J. Comput. Vis. **29**(1), 5–28 (1998)

7. Argyros, A.A., Lourakis, M.I.A.: Binocular hand tracking and reconstruction based on 2D shape matching. In: 18th International Conference on Pattern Recognition, ICPR 2006, vol. 1, pp. 207–210. IEEE (2006)

8. Barsoum, E.: Articulated hand pose estimation review. arXiv preprint arXiv:1604.06195 (2016)

9. Taylor, J., Bordeaux, L., Cashman, T., Corish, B., Keskin, C., Sharp, T., Soto, E., Sweeney, D., Valentin, J., Luff, B., et al.: Efficient and precise interactive hand tracking through joint, continuous optimization of pose and correspondences. ACM Trans. Graph. (TOG) **35**(4), 143 (2016)

10. Sharp, T., Keskin, C., Robertson, D., Taylor, J., Shotton, J., Kim, D., Rhemann, C., Leichter, I., Vinnikov, A., Wei, Y., et al.: Accurate, robust, and flexible real-time hand tracking. In: Proceedings of the 33rd Annual ACM Conference on Human Factors in Computing Systems, pp. 3633–3642. ACM (2015)

11. Rautaray, S.S., Agrawal, A.: Vision based hand gesture recognition for human computer interaction: a survey. Artif. Intell. Rev. **43**(1), 1–54 (2015)

12. Ji, S., Wei, X., Yang, M., Kai, Y.: 3D convolutional neural networks for human action recognition. IEEE Trans. Pattern Anal. Mach. Intell. **35**(1), 221–231 (2013)

13. Fanelli, G., Gall, J., Van Gool, L.: Real time head pose estimation with random regression forests. In: 2011 IEEE Conference on Computer Vision and Pattern Recognition (CVPR), pp. 617–624. IEEE (2011)

14. Kopinski, T., Gepperth, A., Handmann, U.: A simple technique for improving multi-class classification with neural networks. In: Proceedings, p. 469. Presses universitaires de Louvain (2015)

15. Sato, Y., Saito, M., Koike, H.: Real-time input of 3D pose and gestures of a user's hand and its applications for HCI. In: Proceedings of 2001 IEEE Virtual Reality, pp. 79–86. IEEE (2001)

16. Tang, D., Yu, T.-H., Kim, T.-K.: Real-time articulated hand pose estimation using semi-supervised transductive regression forests. In: Proceedings of the IEEE International Conference on Computer Vision, pp. 3224–3231 (2013)

17. Sun, X., Wei, Y., Liang, S., Tang, X., Sun, J.: Cascaded hand pose regression. In: Proceedings of the IEEE Conference on Computer Vision and Pattern Recognition, pp. 824–832 (2015)

18. Coello, C.A.C., Pulido, G.T., Lechuga, M.S.: Handling multiple objectives with particle swarm optimization. IEEE Trans. Evol. Comput. **8**(3), 256–279 (2004)

19. Ge, L., Liang, H., Yuan, J., Thalmann, D.: Robust 3D hand pose estimation in single depth images: from single-view CNN to multi-view CNNs. In: Proceedings of the IEEE Conference on Computer Vision and Pattern Recognition, pp. 3593–3601 (2016)

20. Tompson, J., Stein, M., Lecun, Y., Perlin, K.: Real-time continuous pose recovery of human hands using convolutional networks. ACM Trans. Graph. (ToG) **33**(5), 169 (2014)

Scaling up Local Search for Minimum Vertex Cover in Large Graphs by Parallel Kernelization

Wanru Gao[1(✉)], Tobias Friedrich[1,2], Timo Kötzing[2], and Frank Neumann[1]

[1] School of Computer Science, The University of Adelaide, Adelaide, Australia
wanru.gao@adelaide.edu.au
[2] Hasso Plattner Institute, Potsdam, Germany

Abstract. We investigate how well-performing local search algorithms for small or medium size instances can be scaled up to perform well for large inputs. We introduce a parallel kernelization technique that is motivated by the assumption that graphs in medium to large scale are composed of components which are on their own easy for state-of-the-art solvers but when hidden in large graphs are hard to solve. To show the effectiveness of our kernelization technique, we consider the well-known minimum vertex cover problem and two state-of-the-art solvers called NuMVC and FastVC. Our kernelization approach reduces an existing large problem instance significantly and produces better quality results on a wide range of benchmark instances and real world graphs.

Keywords: Vertex cover · Local search algorithms

1 Introduction

Local search algorithms belong to the most successful approaches for many combinatorial optimization problems [1,8]. The general problem of local search approaches is that they can be trapped in local optima. Since often these approaches include a random initialization or random components, running an algorithm several times on a given instance might help with finding a global optimum. However, if the probability of getting stuck in a local optimum is high, then even repeated runs might not help to evade local optima.

In this paper, we present a new approach for scaling up existing high-performing local search solvers in order to perform well on large graphs. Our approach builds on the assumption that large graphs are composed of different (hidden) substructures. Substructures are often found in large social network graphs as social networks usually consist of (loosely connected) sub-communities. In large graphs, the issue of local optima might occur in the different substructures of the given problem instance; having a large number of these substructures where an algorithm even just fails with a small probability might make it very hard for local search approaches to obtain the optimal solution. We present a simple parallel kernelization approach that builds on theoretical investigations regarding substructures on large graphs.

© Springer International Publishing AG 2017
W. Peng et al. (Eds.): AI 2017, LNAI 10400, pp. 131–143, 2017.
DOI: 10.1007/978-3-319-63004-5_11

Kernelization approaches have been shown to be very effective for designing algorithms which have a good performance guarantee [7]. Recently, a technique of incorporating kernelization in evolutionary algorithms is proposed to the NP-hard independent set problem [10]. The key idea of this approach is to pre-process a given instance by making optimal decisions on easy parts of the given input such that the overall problem instance is reduced. There are several kernelization techniques available for the minimum vertex cover problem which perform well if the number of vertices in an optimal solution is small. However, the applicability to difficult instances which are usually dense graphs is limited as the pre-processing does not significantly reduce the problem instance size. As proposed by [15], identifying the 'backbone' solution component and then making use of this information is beneficial for the local search algorithm.

We present a new way of reducing the problem instance size by parallel kernelization (note that this is not a kernelization in the theoretical sense). In Sect. 2 we present theoretical investigations which assume that small substructures can be solved effectively by a local search heuristic; we then turn these observations into a parallel kernelization technique. The approach uses existing local search solvers to deal with large graphs. The key idea is to do μ parallel runs of such a solver and reduce the given instance by fixing components that have been selected in all μ runs and reducing the instance afterwards. The resulting *reduced* instance is then solved by an additional run of the local search solver and the combined result is returned as the final solution.

We consider the NP-hard minimum vertex cover (MVC) problem to illustrate the effectiveness of our approach. Popular local search approaches for tackling MVC include PLS [11], NuMVC [6], TwMVC [5], COVER [12] and FastVC [4]. Recently a branch-and-reduce algorithm for MVC is proposed [2]. Although this exact algorithm gets stuck in solving some well-known benchmark problems, it has shown good performance in dealing with sparse real world graphs.

The MVC algorithms are usually evaluated on standard benchmarks and (in more recent years on) large real world graphs. We take NuMVC and FastVC as the baseline local search solvers for our new kernelization approach. These two algorithms belong to the best-performing approaches for MVC. Our experimental results show that our new kernelization technique does not do any harm on instances where NuMVC and FastVC are already performing well while improving results on graphs containing benchmark instances as connected components.

The outline of the paper is as follows. In Sect. 2, we present the theoretical motivation for our parallel kernelization technique that is based on the assumption that large graphs are composed of substructures. Section 3 outlines the resulting local search approach with parallel kernelization for the vertex cover problem. We evaluate the performance of our new approach on two state-of-the-art MVC solvers in Sects. 4 and 5 on combinations of classical benchmark instances and large real world graphs. Finally, we finish with some concluding remarks.

2   Substructures in Large Graphs

Large graphs originating for example from social networks consist of a large number of vertices and edges. Our approach builds on the assumption that these graphs are composed of different substructures which on their own and at a small scale would not be hard to handle by current local search approaches. This is for example the case for social networks which are composed of different communities. The difficulty arises through the composition of substructures which are not known to the algorithm and which are hard to extract from the given instances.

We would like to illustrate the problem by the following simple observations. Assume that you are running some (randomly initialized) local search algorithm on an instance that consists of different subparts s_i, $1 \leq i \leq k$, where each part s_i has the probability p_i of failing to obtain that optimal sub-solution independently of the other components. Then the probability of obtaining the optimal solution is

$$\prod_{i=1}^{k}(1 - p_i).$$

Even if there is only a constant probability $p' = \min_{i=1}^{k} p_i$, $0 < p' < 1$ of failing in each of the k components, the probability that the local search algorithm would solve the overall instance would be exponentially small in k, meaning, we only succeed with probability

$$\prod_{i=1}^{k}(1 - p_i) \leq \prod_{i=1}^{k}(1 - p') = (1 - p')^k \approx e^{-p' \cdot k}. \tag{1}$$

In our kernelization, we run μ instances of the same local search algorithm (randomly initialized). After some time t_1 for each of these runs, we stop the algorithm. After all μ solutions are computed, we *freeze* the setting for all those components which are set the same way in all μ runs; then we run the local search algorithm on the *reduced instances* with the frozen components removed.

Consider a component s_i again where the probability of failing is p_i. The probability that a run obtains the optimal solution for this component is $(1 - p_i)$ and the probability that μ random runs identify an optimal solution is $(1 - p_i)^\mu$. As long as the failure probability p_i is only a small constant and μ is not large, this term is still a constant that is sufficiently large, which shows that the kernelization will likely be successful as well. Let $|s_i|$ be the size of component s_i. Furthermore, we assume that the whole instance s is composed of the k subcomponents and we have $|s| = \sum_{i=1}^{k} |s_i|$.

The expected decrease in size of the original problem consisting of the components s_i is given by

$$\sum_{i=1}^{k}(1 - p_i)^\mu |s_i|$$

Algorithm 1. Local Search with Parallel Kernelization

---

1 Initialize P with μ solutions after μ different independent runs of MVC solver with cutoff time t_1.
2 Let set V_a be the set of vertices which are selected by all solutions in P.
3 Construct an instance I with vertices $v \notin V_a$ and edges which are not adjacent to any vertex in V_a.
4 Run MVC solver on instance I with cutoff time t_2 to get a minimum vertex cover V_s.
5 Construct the final solution $V = V_a \cup V_s$.

Assuming $\hat{p} = \max_{i=1}^{k} p_i$, then we get

$$\sum_{i=1}^{k}(1 - p_i)^{\mu}|s_i| \geq (1 - \hat{p})^{\mu}\sum_{i=1}^{k}|s_i| = (1 - \hat{p})^{\mu} \cdot |s|, \tag{2}$$

which reduces the whole instance by a fraction of at least $(1 - \hat{p})^{\mu}$.

We now consider the probability that one of the different components has not achieved an optimal sub-solution in at least one of the μ runs. In such a case our algorithm could potentially reduce the instance and fix vertices of that component which do not belong to an optimal solution. In this case, the kernelization step would fail and prevent us from obtaining the overall optimal solution. Consider component s_i. The probability that all μ runs do not obtain the optimal sub solution for this component is p_i^{μ}. The probability that at least one of them obtains the optimal sub-solution is therefore at least

$$1 - p_i^{\mu}$$

and the probability that all components have at least one run where the optimal sub-solution is obtained is therefore at least

$$\prod_{i=1}^{k}(1 - p_i^{\mu}) \geq (1 - \hat{p}^{\mu})^k \approx e^{-\hat{p}^{\mu} \cdot k}. \tag{3}$$

As an example, assume that the probability of the original approach failing on each subcomponent is 10%, $\mu = 3$, and $k = 50$. Then the expected reduction according to Eq. 2 is $(1 - 0.1)^3 \cdot |s| = 0.729 \cdot |s|$, that is, the resulting instance has only 27.1% of the original number of vertices. The probability of not failing in the reduction step according to Eq. 3 is $(1 - 0.1^3)^k = 0.999^k$ whereas the probability of a single run of the original approach not failing in at least one component according to Eq. 1 is $(1 - 0.1)^k = 0.9^k$. For $k = 50$ we get a probability of not failing in the kernelization step of $0.999^{50} \approx 0.95$ and a probability of not failing in the original algorithm of $0.9^{50} \approx 0.005$.

The user can control μ, and from our calculations we observe a trade-off between reducing the number of vertices and the probability of fixing the wrong vertices in at least one of these components, depending on μ.

3 Parallel Kernelization for Minimum Vertex Cover

We now show how to use the ideas discussed in the previous section in an algorithmic sense. As mentioned previously, our approach assumes that there is already a good local search solver for the given problem P for small to medium size instances. Our goal is to use parallel kernelization to make it work for large instances. While we taking the well-known NP-hard minimum vertex cover problem as an example problem, we expect that our approach is applicable to a wide range of other problems as well.

The minimum vertex cover (MVC) problem can be defined as follows. Given an undirected graph $G = (V, E)$ where V denotes the set of vertices and E denotes the set of edges, the goal is to find a smallest subset $C \subseteq V$ such that for all edge $e \in E$ there is at least one endpoint included in C.

The main idea is to kernelize the vertex set and form a smaller instance for the MVC solver to solve. Firstly the MVC solver is run μ times on the given graph $G = (V, E)$ with a cutoff time t_1 for each run to achieve a set of μ solutions. The vertices which are selected in all μ solutions, are added to a separate set V_a and the edges that are covered by the vertices of V_a are removed from the edge set. The new instance $G' = (V', E')$ is formed by the vertices that are not selected in all μ solutions and the edge set after deletion, meaning, we have $V' = V \setminus V_a$ and $E' = E \setminus \{e \in E \mid e \cap V_a \neq \emptyset\}$. The MVC solver is run on the new instance G' to obtain a minimum vertex cover V_s. The overall solution for the original graph G is

$$VC = V_a \cup V_s$$

and consists of the set of vertices which are selected in all μ initial solutions and the minimum vertex cover achieved by the MVC solver running on the new instance G'. It should be noted that it is crucial that the cutoff time t_1 allows the μ runs to have obtained at least nearly locally optimal solutions. A detailed description of our approach is given in Algorithm 1.

For our experimental investigations we use NuMVC [6] and FastVC [4] as the MVC solvers. Both algorithms are based on the idea of iteratively solving the deterministic problem from MVC.

NuMVC is one of the best performing local search approaches for MVC and has an advantage over TwMVC [5] in that it does not require parameter tuning for different types of benchmark instances. The authors introduce techniques to select the vertices for exchange in two separate stages, which enable the local search in a wider neighbourhood. The NuMVC algorithm keeps track of the exchange in order to avoid reversing behavior. These two techniques make NuMVC perform well in dealing with most MVC benchmark problems.

FastVC is a fast local search algorithm designed for dealing with large MVC problems. It involves some relaxation in selecting the candidate vertices for exchange, which accelerate the search process. It has performed well in some large real world graphs.

In the following sections, we discuss our experiments carried out with Algorithm 1 compared with the single run of the MVC solver; the total time budget that both approaches can use is the same.

All of the experiments are executed on a machine with 48-core Authenti-cAMD 2.80 GHz CPU and 128 GByte RAM; note that the program uses only a single core. The memory consumption depends on the instance size and the MVC solver. The runtime will benefit from multi-threading and other parallel execution techniques.

4   Experimental Results from NuMVC with Parallel Kernelization

The implementation of NuMVC is open-source and implemented in C++. We compiled the source code with g++ with '−O2' option. The parameter set-ting follows what is reported in [6]. We take NuMVC as the MVC solver in Algorithm 1 The new approach to solve MVC is referred to as NuMVC-PK, since it is strongly based on the original NuMVC program.

Each experiment on a certain instance for each algorithm is executed 10 times in order to gather statistics. The cutoff time for the first run in NuMVC-PK is set based on initial experimental investigations on the different classes of instances considered. Based on our theoretical investigations carried out in

Table 1. This table contains instances that have been tested on, which are generated by duplicating one existing hard instance in BHOSLIB and DIMACS benchmark. The instance name contains the name of original instance and the number of copies. The cutoff time of single NuMVC is set to $3,000$ s. The parameters for NuMVC-PK are set to $\mu = 5$, $t_1 = 500$ and $t_2 = 500$. The average time for NuMVC to find the local optima is reported in column t_{avg}. The p-value is labelled as NA if the results from the 10 independent runs of the two algorithms are the same.

Instance				NuMVC-PK				NuMVC			Comparison			
Name	OPT	$|V|$	$|E|$	$|V'|$	$|E'|$	VC_{min}	VC_{avg}	VC_{min}	VC_{avg}	t_{avg}	Δ	Δ'	p-value	
frb40-19-1_10	7,200	7,600	413,140	576.0	1469.1	7,200	7,200.0±0	7,200	7,200.0±0	294.10	0	0.0	NA	no diff.
frb40-19-2_10	7,200	7,600	412,630	1,538.7	12,595.2	7,202	7,203.6±1.174	7,204	7,206.2±0.919	1,498.15	2	2.6	0.0005	better
frb40-19-3_10	7,200	7,600	410,950	1,201.8	7,466.7	7,200	7,200.3±0.483	7,200	7,201.9±0.994	1,645.52	0	1.6	0.0015	better
frb40-19-4_10	7,200	7,600	416,050	1,369.5	10,071.3	7,200	7,201.7±0.949	7,201	7,203.2±1.135	1,853.66	1	1.5	0.0083	better
frb40-19-5_10	7,200	7,600	416,190	1,599.5	13,801.8	7,203	7,205.5±1.269	7,205	7,206.7±1.252	1,438.47	2	1.2	0.0669	no diff.
frb45-21-1_10	9,000	9,450	591,860	1,722.6	14,822.9	9,000	9,001.6±0.966	9,001	9,002.1±0.994	1,929.33	1	0.5	0.3215	no diff.
frb45-21-2_10	9,000	9,450	586,240	1,808.0	16,134.1	9,002	9,003.5±1.269	9,002	9,003.9±0.994	2,050.30	0	0.4	0.5058	no diff.
frb45-21-3_10	9,000	9,450	582,450	1,875.2	17,610.1	9,004	9,007.0±1.247	9,006	9,007.1±0.738	1,936.15	2	0.1	0.8390	no diff.
frb45-21-4_10	9,000	9,450	585,490	1,735.1	14,302.0	9,001	9,003.1±1.197	9,004	9,004.5±0.707	1,606.35	3	1.4	0.0085	better
frb45-21-5_10	9,000	9,450	585,790	1,843.3	17,119.2	9,002	9,004.7±1.767	9,003	9,005.4±1.897	1,889.51	1	0.7	0.4900	no diff.
frb50-23-1_10	11,000	11,500	800,720	2,127.5	20,889.9	11,006	11,008.9±1.729	11,009	11,010.8±1.033	2,124.59	3	1.9	0.0164	better
frb50-23-2_10	11,000	11,500	808,510	2,079.4	19,760.5	11,009	11,011.0±1.414	11,010	11,011.8±1.033	2,035.62	1	0.8	0.1301	no diff.
frb50-23-3_10	11,000	11,500	810,680	2,133.2	21,310.8	11,010	11,011.5±1.269	11,010	11,012.6±1.075	1,795.17	0	1.1	0.0512	no diff.
frb50-23-4_10	11,000	11,500	802,580	2,116.1	20,679.4	11,003	11,005.6±1.506	11,004	11,006.3±1.252	2,219.85	1	0.7	0.2963	no diff.
frb50-23-5_10	11,000	11,500	800,350	2,097.7	20,008.5	11,006	11,007.7±1.337	11,009	11,010.2±0.632	1,885.96	3	2.5	0.0002	better
brock800_2_10	7,760	8,000	1,114,340	930.2	11,653.2	7,790	7,779.0±0	7,790	7,790.0±0	205.93	0	0.0	NA	no diff.
brock800_2_20	15,520	16,000	2,228,680	1,850.3	23,019.0	15,580	15,580.0±0	15,580	15,580.0±0	1,219.59	0	0.0	NA	no diff.
brock800_2_30	23,280	24,000	3,343,020	2,822.9	35,894.6	23,370	23,371.0±0.667	23,370	23,370.7±0.823	2,349.51	0	-0.3	0.3486	no diff.
brock800_4_10	7,740	8,000	1,119,570	888.0	10,866.5	7,790	7,790.0±0	7,790	7,790.0±0	285.43	0	0.0	NA	no diff.
brock800_4_20	15,480	16,000	2,239,140	1,842.5	23,371.4	15,580	15,580.0±0	15,580	15,580.2±0.422	1,880.70	0	0.2	0.1675	no diff.
brock800_4_30	23,220	24,000	3,358,710	2,836.8	36,873.8	23,372	23,374.0±0.943	23,372	23,373.7±1.767	2,248.83	0	-0.3	0.4157	no diff.
C1000.9_10	9,320	10,000	494,210	2,603.0	24,603.4	9,321	9,323.3±1.252	9,323	9,324.9±1.101	1,345.04	2	1.6	0.0111	better
C2000.5_10	19,840	20,000	9,991,640	739.1	10,880.3	19,842	19,843.9±0.876	19,840	19,840.0±0	1,003.06	-2	-3.9	0.0001	worse
C2000.9_10	19,200	20,000	1,994,680	3,339.6	42,224.1	19,239	19,243.8±2.394	19,232	19,239.6±3.471	1,664.31	-3	-4.2	0.0030	worse

Sect. 2, it is important that each of the μ runs obtains at least a nearly locally optimal solution for the given problem. This implies that a too small cutoff time t_1 might have detrimental effects.

Table 2. Experimental results on instances from some instances in *DIMACS10* benchmark set. The cutoff time of the single NuMVC run is set to $1,000$ s. The parameters for NuMVC-PK are set to $\mu = 3$, $t_1 = 200$ and $t_2 = 400$.

	Instance				NuMVC-PK		NuMVC		Comparison			
Name	$|V|$	$|E|$	$|V'|$	$|E'|$	VC_{min}	VC_{avg}	VC_{min}	VC_{avg}	Δ	Δ'	p-value	
dimacs10-citationCiteseer	268,495	1,156,647	47,588.5	35,638.2	118,175	118,188.2±8.817	118,329	118,345.5±13.640	154	157.3	0.0002	better
dimacs10-coAuthorsCiteseer	227,320	814,134	63,325.5	37,318.9	129,193	129,193.1±0.316	129,193	129,195.1±1.197	0	2.0	0.0005	better
dimacs10-cs4	22,499	43,858	12,607.1	18,548.6	13,376	13,379.7±2.869	13,364	13,380.6±6.703	-12	0.9	0.2383	no diff.
dimacs10-cti	16,840	48,232	14,788.0	41,176.5	8,752	8,782.4±26.082	8,752	8,774.9±14.813	0	-7.5	0.6478	no diff.
dimacs10-delaunay-n15	32,768	98,274	9,991.4	11,339.9	22,460	22,464.4±4.033	22,460	22,463.1±2.025	0	-1.3	0.6185	no diff.
dimacs10-delaunay-n16	65,536	196,575	24,120.0	28,304.3	44,995	45,007.7±6.430	45,045	45,070.4±19.115	50	62.7	0.0002	better
dimacs10-delaunay-n17	131,072	393,176	53,422.6	65,915.5	90,356	90,373.1±12.306	90,639	90,677.8±23.522	283	304.7	0.0002	better
dimacs10-delaunay-n18	262,144	786,396	92,241.1	83,516.9	183,791	183,876.3±48.413	181,481	181,541.4±32.695	-2,310	-2,334.9	0.0000	worse
dimacs10-delaunay-n19	524,288	1,572,823	183,692.3	166,235.6	367,552	367,662.8±48.385	370,869	371,033.8±119.084	3,317	3,371.0	0.0002	better
dimacs10-fe-body	45,087	163,734	12,001.0	13,040.01	31,361	31,364.6±3.062	31,346	31,348.0±1.633	-15	-16.6	0.0002	better
dimacs10-fe-rotor	99,617	662,431	36,987.1	73,892.5	78,058	78,193.5±77.739	78,171	78,272.5±59.642	113	79.0	0.0211	better
dimacs10-fe-tooth	78,136	452,591	7,298.1	5,461.8	50,347	50,347.8±0.789	50,346	50,348.0±0.943	-1	0.2	0.4933	no diff.

4.1   DIMACS and BHOSLIB Benchmarks

There are some well-known MVC benchmarks which have been used to evaluate the performance of different MVC solvers. Two of the benchmarks are the *DIMACS* and the *BHOSLIB* benchmark sets.

The *BHOSLIB* (Benchmarks with Hidden Optimum Solutions) problems are generated from translating the binary Boolean Satisfiability problems randomly generated based on the model RB [14]. These instances have been proven to be hard to solve, both theoretically and practically. The *DIMACS* benchmark is a set of challenge problems which comes from the Second *DIMACS* Implementation Challenge for Maximum Clique, Graph Coloring and Satisfiability [9]. The original Max Clique problems are converted to complement graphs to serve as MVC problems.

With the same overall time budget, both NuMVC and NuMVC-PK have good success rate for most of the instances.

4.2   Multiple Copies of the Well-Known Benchmark Problems

Most *BHOSLIB* instances and *DIMACS* instances can be solved with good success rates by NuMVC [6]. We propose some simple combinations of these existing benchmarks as new test cases. These will serve as very simple first test cases for our kernelization method. The new instances are composed of several sub-graphs and large in size of both vertices and edges. In particular, we construct a new instance by considering independent copies of an existing instance. Each single copy is easy to be solved by the MVC solver with a high success rate, while the combined instance is much harder to solve.

Table 3. Experimental results on instances from some real world graphs about social networks, collaboration networks and websites. The cutoff time of the single NuMVC run is set to $1,000\,s$. The parameters for NuMVC-PK are set to $\mu = 3$, $t_1 = 300$ and $t_2 = 100$. The p-value is labelled as NA if the results from the 10 independent runs of the two algorithms are the same.

Name	Instance				NuMVC-PK		NuMVC		Comparison			
	$|V|$	$|E|$	$|V'|$	$|E'|$	VC_{min}	VC_{avg}	VC_{min}	VC_{avg}	Δ	Δ'	p-value	
soc-BlogCatalog	88,784	2,093,195	6,071.8	3,871.1	20,752	20,752.0±0	20,752	20,753.0±0.816	0	1.0	0.0021	better
soc-brightkite	56,739	212,945	9,717.3	6,157.2	21,190	21,190.0±0	21,194	21,196.7±2.003	4	6.7	0.0001	better
soc-buzznet	101,163	2,763,066	9,104.1	6,328.5	30,614	30,615.5±1.080	30,614	30,614.4±0.516	0	-1.1	0.0182	worse
soc-delicious	536,108	1,365,961	29,325.7	40,112.0	85,477	85,494.0±13.275	85,553	85,587.6±19.744	76	93.6	0.0002	better
soc-digg	770,799	5,907,132	24,412.2	15,814.8	103,239	103,240.7±0.823	103,297	103,323.4±10.793	58	82.7	0.0001	better
soc-douban	154,908	327,162	304.2	153.5	8,685	8,685.0±0	8,685	8,685.0±0	0	0.0	NA	no diff.
soc-epinions	26,588	100,120	4,730.8	2,864.2	9,757	9,757.0±0	9,757	9,757.0±0	0	0.0	NA	no diff.
soc-flickr	513,969	3,190,452	62,566.8	44,148.2	153,277	153,283.2±3.676	153,346	153,353.7±5.438	69	70.5	0.0002	better
soc-flixster	2,523,386	7,918,801	4,123.2	2,283.0	96,317	96,330.1±14.083	96,318	96,321.5±1.900	1	-8.6	1	no diff.
soc-FourSquare	639,014	3,214,986	10,305.2	7,374.8	90,110	90,111.8±1.398	90,131	90,136.9±3.635	21	25.1	0.0002	better
soc-gowalla	196,591	950,327	39,962.5	27,978.6	84,252	84,260.3±6.237	84,309	84,332.0±10.176	57	71.7	0.0002	better
soc-lastfm	1,191,805	4,519,330	3,738.3	2,149.1	78,688	78,689.2±1.033	78,694	78,696.2±2.098	6	7.0	0.0002	better
soc-LiveMocha	104,103	2,193,083	12,452.3	9,062.6	43,428	43,432.1±3.178	43,437	43,440.7±3.889	9	8.6	0.0003	better
soc-slashdot	70,068	358,647	11,063.8	6,839.8	22,373	22,373.0±0	22,376	22,379.1±1.912	3	6.1	0.0001	better
soc-twitter-follows	404,719	713,319	42.0	21.0	2,323	2,323.0±0	2,323	2,323.0±0	0	0.0	NA	no diff.
soc-youtube	495,957	1,936,748	65,727.2	42,496.9	146,469	146,500.9±16.093	146,453	146,469.3±8.667	-16	-31.6	0.0006	worse
soc-youtube-snap	1,134,890	2,987,624	160,650.9	88,012.0	277,828	277,857.6±21.752	278,542	278,603.7±31.049	714	746.1	0.0002	better
ca-citeseer	227,320	814,134	68,049	41,230	129,193	129,193.0±0	129,194	129,194.8±0.919	1	1.8	0.0001	better
ca-coauthors-dblp	540,486	15,245,729	93,319	69,523	472,250	472,257.3±5.832	472,324	472,334.8±7.540	74	77.5	0.0002	better
ca-dblp-2010	226,413	716,460	65,615	39,019	121,969	121,969.5±0.527	121,971	121,974.4±1.955	2	4.9	0.0001	better
ca-dblp-2012	317,080	1,049,866	78,406	43,526	164,951	164,953.2±1.687	164,956	164,958.2±2.486	5	5.0	0.0005	better
ca-MathSciNet	332,689	820,644	78,800	48,359	139,955	139,958.7±2.163	139,981	139,988.1±4.175	26	29.4	0.0002	better
web-arabic-2005	163,598	1,747,269	26,120	19,511	114,444	114,448.1±2.759	114,468	114,475.3±3.529	24	27.2	0.0002	better
web-baidu-baike-related	415,641	3,284,387	67,615	74,066	143,581	143,629.8±26.318	144,155	144,190.2±19.424	574	560.4	0.0002	better
web-google-dir	875,713	5,105,039	117,405	95,026	347,783	347,795.6±12.842	347,771	347,826.4±55.674	-12	30.8	0.1403	no diff.
web-it-2004	509,338	7,178,413	71,247	64,798	415,017	415,043.3±21.505	414,861	414,895.6±14.447	-156	-147.7	0.0002	worse
web-sk-2005	121,422	334,419	35,409	26,361	58,179	58,181.9±2.424	58,201	58,206.4±3.718	22	24.5	0.0002	better

Some examples of these kinds of instances are given in Table 1. The original instances are selected from the *BHOSLIB* benchmark set or the *DIMACS* benchmarks. The last number in the instance name after the underscore denotes the number of copies of the given instance indicated by the first part of the instance name. Although the original instances can be solved by NuMVC in reasonable time, it takes much longer time for NuMVC to solve the multiplicated new instances. NuMVC may get trapped at local optima, which are far away from the global optima in search space. Table 1 shows the comparison between results from NuMVC-PK and single run of NuMVC. The basic information about the instances is included in Table 1 in the column Instance. The OPT column lists the optimal (or minimum known) vertex cover size. The numbers in the $|V|$ and $|E|$ columns are the numbers of vertices and edges in the corresponding instances. NuMVC-PK is executed with parameters $\mu = 5$, $t_1 = 500$ and $t_2 = 500$, which means 5 independent runs of NuMVC to get initial solutions after $500\,s$ and then the original instance is processed based on the information gathered from the five solutions to generate a new instance. As the last step, NuMVC is run for another $500\,s$ on the newly generated instance to achieve the final solution. The information of the generated reduced instance is listed in columns $|V'|$ and $|E'|$, where the average number of non-isolated vertices and edges of the new instance are listed. NuMVC is executed for $3,000\,s$ to be compared to NuMVC-PK, which had the same time budget. We report the average time for NuMVC to find the best solution in each run in the column t_{avg}.

The size difference between the minimum vertex cover and the average value found by the two approaches is reported in the column of Δ and Δ' respectively. We used the Wilcoxon unpaired signed-rank test on the solutions from different runs of the algorithms for a given instance; the p-value is listed in Table 1. The difference is evaluated based on a significance level of 0.05.

Since *BHOSLIB* and *DIMACS* benchmarks are hard MVC problems, making sure all sub-graphs to be solved to optimality is hard for a single run of NuMVC, which easily gets trapped in some local optimum. On the other hand, NuMVC-PK shrinks the large instances and takes a fresh start on the reduced instance, thereby improving the performance of the local search.

From the results we see that NuMVC-PK is able to reduce the instance size. For the duplicated *BHOSLIB* and *DIMACS* instances, after 5 runs of NuMVC, the NuMVC-PK generates new instances which keep only 1% to 3% of the edges and 8% to 20% of the vertices. Unlike NuMVC, which usually makes no improvement after 2,000 s, NuMVC-PK finds the global optimum for 4 instances where NuMVC ends up with local optima after 3,000 s in all 10 runs. The parallel kernelization mechanism significantly improves the performance of single run of NuMVC in 7 of the instances.

4.3 Real World Graphs

Now we turn our attention to comparing NuMVC-PK with NuMVC on large real world graphs as given by [13]. All of these selected graphs are undirected, unweighted and with a large number of vertices and edges. In contrast to the benchmark sets considered in Sect. 4.2, the global optima of these instances are unknown. The graphs examined are taken from the social network, collaboration network and web link (Miscellaneous) network packages. Some samples are also selected from the *DIMACS10* data sets which come from the 10th *DIMCAS* implementation challenge [3]. The graphs have a number of vertices in the range of 15,000 to 2,600,00 and a number of edges in the range of 40,000 to 16,000,000.

The experimental results are summarized in Tables 2 and 3. Just as in Table 1, the columns of $|V|$ and $|E|$ provide the brief information of the graphs (number of vertices and edges, respectively). The categories NuMVC-PK and NuMVC give the comparison between NuMVC-PK and single run of NuMVC. Since the large real world graphs are not designed to be as hard as the combined *BHOSLIB* instances, we use $\mu = 3$ to get the initial solution set. The minimum vertex cover found and the average number of minimum vertex cover in the ten independent runs is reported in the table. The standard deviation for each instance is also included to show the stability of the algorithms. NuMVC is run for 1,000 s, corresponding to the total budget of NuMVC-PK. Some easy instances which can be easily solved by single run of NuMVC in short run time are omitted from the table since both algorithms have a 100% success rate.

For the real world graphs in social networks, collaboration networks and web link networks packages, NuMVC-PK reduces the instances size by more than 90% in the number of vertices and 70% in the number of edges. The size of the instance is one of the main factors that affect the performance of the MVC solvers for the real world graphs. The instances after shrinking have less than 200,000 vertices and 100,000 edges. For graphs in *dImacs10* package, the generated instances maintain around 20% vertices and 40% edges in most cases.

Regarding Tables 2 and 3, we make the following observations.

- NuMVC-PK finds smaller minimum vertex cover in the ten independent runs than NuMVC in 26 out of the 39 graphs.
- There are 4 graphs for which NuMVC-PK is not able to return a better solution than NuMVC. These graphs have the property that they are hard or large instances so local optima are not reached within time t_1 or even 1,000 s.
- There are 10 graphs where NuMVC-PK finds a minimum vertex cover smaller by more than 50 than NuMVC.

For some large instances, the initialization process of NuMVC is very time consuming. Enough time should be given for NuMVC to get initial solutions at least near the local optima. For the same time limit, longer single initial runs are more beneficial than shorter initial runs and longer runs after the freezing phase. Therefore, a combination of larger t_1 and smaller t_2 may result in a better solution for these instances.

Table 4. Experimental results on instances from some real world graphs about social networks. The cutoff time of the single FastVC run is set to 1,000 s. The parameters for FastVC-PK are set to $\mu = 3$, $t_1 = 200$ and $t_2 = 400$. The p-value is labelled as NA if the results from the 10 independent runs of the two algorithms are the same.

Name	Instance		FastVC-PK				FastVC			Comparison		
	$|V|$	$|E|$	$|V'|$	$|E'|$	$VC_{\min}$	VC_{avg}	$VC_{\min}$	VC_{avg}	Δ	Δ'	p-value	
soc-BlogCatalog	88,784	2,093,195	6,128.0	3,952.0	20,752	20,752.0±0	20,752	20,752.0±0	0	0.0	NA	no diff.
soc-brightkite	56,739	212,945	9,673.3	6,167.4	21,190	21,190.0±0	21,190	21,190.1±0.316	0	0.1	0.3681	no diff.
soc-buzznet	101,163	2,763,066	9,014.2	6,200.0	30,625	30,625.4±0.516	30,625	30,625.4±0.516	0	0.0	1	no diff.
soc-delicious	536,108	1,365,961	23,939.2	23,483.8	86,121	86,139.5±19.363	86,215	86,230.8±15.303	94	91.3	0.0002	better
soc-digg	770,799	5,907,132	23,165.2	14,455.8	103,244	103,244.4±0.516	103,244	103,244.7±0.483	0	0.3	0.2039	no diff.
soc-douban	154,908	327,162	297.6	152.1	8,685	8,685.0±0	8,685	8,685.0±0	0	0.0	NA	no diff.
soc-epinions	26,588	100,120	4,841.7	3,032.7	9,757	9,757.1±0.316	9,757	9,757.6±0.966	0	0.5	0.2328	no diff.
soc-flickr	513,969	3,190,452	64,695.7	40,410.1	153,271	153,271.0±0	153,271	153,271.0±0	0	0.0	NA	no diff.
soc-flixster	2,523,386	7,918,801	3,807.5	2,068.8	96,317	96,317.0±0	96,317	96,317.0±0	0	0.0	NA	no diff.
soc-FourSquare	639,014	3,214,986	9,306.2	6,177.9	90,108	90,109.0±0.471	90,108	90,108.8±0.422	0	-0.2	0.3566	no diff.

5   Experimental Results from FastVC with Parallel Kernelization

Like NuMVC, FastVC is also open-source and implemented in C++. The original code in version 2015.11 is compiled with g++ and '−O2' option. We use the parameters as reported in [4]. Following the same terminology used for NuMVC, we refer to the new algorithm with FastVC as the MVC solver in Algorithm 1 as FastVC-PK.

Table 5. This table contains instances that have been tested on, which are generated by duplicating one existing hard instance in BHOSLIB benchmark. The instance name contains the name of original instance and the number of copies. The cutoff time of single FastVC is set to $3,000\,s$. The parameters for FastVC-PK are set to $\mu = 5$, $t_1 = 500$ and $t_2 = 500$. The average time for FastVC to find the local optima is reported in column t_{avg}.

Name	Instance			FastVC-PK			FastVC			Comparison		
	OPT	$|V|$	$|E|$	$|V'|$	$|E'|$	VC_{min}	VC_{avg}	VC_{min}	VC_{avg}	t_{avg}	Δ Δ' p-value	
frb40-19-1_10	7,200	7,600	413,140	1,523.6	11,972.5	7,208	7,212.0±3.091	7,213	7,217.2±2.098	537.57	5 5.2 0.0014	better
frb40-19-2_10	7,200	7,600	412,630	1,620.7	13,962.8	7,218	7,219.5±1.581	7,218	7,221.1±1.663	264.05	0 1.6 0.0507	no diff.
frb40-19-3_10	7,200	7,600	410,950	1,526.7	12,369.6	7,209	7,212.1±1.853	7,213	7,216.4±2.066	612.91	4 4.3 0.0006	better
frb40-19-4_10	7,200	7,600	416,050	1,590.0	13,536.9	7,217	7,219.8±1.549	7,221	7,222.6±1.075	236.07	4 2.8 0.0009	better
frb40-19-5_10	7,200	7,600	416,190	1,583.7	13,234.2	7,214	7,217.6±2.221	7,219	7,221.0±1.054	593.26	5 3.4 0.0005	better
frb45-21-1_10	9,000	9,450	591,860	1,833.4	16,832.7	9,015	9,023.8±4.341	9,024	9,026.6±2.011	872.19	9 2.8 0.0795	better
frb45-21-2_10	9,000	9,450	586,240	1,839.6	16,771.4	9,019	9,025.2±3.327	9,019	9,026.9±3.071	785.91	0 1.7 0.2151	no diff.
frb45-21-3_10	9,000	9,450	582,450	1,857.5	17,019.8	9,023	9,026.8±2.394	9,028	9,030.4±1.430	119.15	5 3.6 0.0029	better
frb45-21-4_10	9,000	9,450	585,490	1,825.9	16,049.0	9,019	9,022.9±3.281	9,024	9,025.9±1.524	459.29	5 3.0 0.0399	better
frb45-21-5_10	9,000	9,450	585,790	1,855.7	17,270.0	9,021	9,024.6±2.413	9,025	9,027.2±1.619	530.08	4 2.6 0.0198	better
frb50-23-1_10	11,000	11,500	800,720	2,068.0	19,489.4	11,029	11,034.9±3.542	11,032	11,036.9±2.378	434.04	3 2.0 0.2995	no diff.
frb50-23-2_10	11,000	11,500	808,510	2,061.0	19,335.2	11,033	11,035.1±1.912	11,032	11,035.9±2.025	842.49	-1 0.8 0.3555	no diff.
frb50-23-3_10	11,000	11,500	810,680	2,133.2	21,310.8	11,033	11,035.6±1.955	11,034	11,036.9±1.449	170.23	1 1.3 0.1532	no diff.
frb50-23-4_10	11,000	11,500	802,580	2,073.7	19,727.2	11,028	11,032.8±3.765	11,030	11,034.6±2.319	648.05	2 1.8 0.2538	no diff.
frb50-23-5_10	11,000	11,500	800,350	2,061.3	19,186.2	11,024	11,030.8±2.658	11,032	11,035.1±1.912	143.89	8 4.3 0.0008	better
brock800_2_10	7,760	8,000	1,114,340	915.3	11,355.5	7,793	7,797.1±2.923	7,799	7,802.0±1.247	866.12	6 4.9 0.0019	better
brock800_2_20	15,520	16,000	2,228,680	1,818.7	22,420.9	15,593	15,598.1±3.178	15,607	15,608.9±1.370	747.21	14 10.8 0.0002	better
brock800_2_30	23,280	24,000	3,343,020	2,728.7	33,696.8	23,398	23,404.7±4.572	23,413	23,418.6±4.222	187.10	15 13.9 0.0002	better
brock800_4_10	7,740	8,000	1,119,570	915.4	11,470.7	7,797	7,799.3±2.003	7,799	7,803.5±1.900	920.42	2 4.2 0.0017	better
brock800_4_20	15,480	16,000	2,239,140	1,813.4	22,549.1	15,598	15,604.6±3.627	15,608	15,612.4±2.503	1,015.30	10 7.8 0.0002	better
brock800_4_30	23,220	24,000	3,358,710	2,715.4	33,832.3	23,399	23,408.4±7.777	23,419	23,422.0±1.414	948.31	20 13.6 0.0006	better
C1000.9_10	9,320	10,000	494,210	2,507.6	22,457.3	9,324	9,329.6±2.459	9,328	9,331.1±1.853	920.80	4 1.5 0.1513	no diff.
C2000.5_10	19,840	20,000	9,991,640	690.0	9,468.4	19,848	19,851.7±2.003	19,857	19,858.6±1.350	745.16	9 6.9 0.0002	better
C2000.9_10	19,200	20,000	1,994,680	3,268.6	40,788.3	19,266	19,272.4±4.006	19,269	19,275.6±4.326	386.93	3 3.2 0.1195	no diff.

Both FastVC and FastVC-PK are tested on each certain instance for 10 times in order to gather statistics. The cutoff time for the initial runs in FastVC-PK is set based on initial experimental investigations on the different classes of instances considered as FastVC. This step is important so that each of the μ runs should obtain at least a nearly locally optimal solution for the given problem according to the theoretical analysis in Sect. 2.

Similar to NuMVC, the integration of parallel kernelization into FastVC keeps the good performance of the original algorithm in solving *BHOSLIB* and *DIMACS* benchmarks. Some of the experimental results are reported in Table 4. Then we turn to test FastVC and FastVC-PK with the multiple copies of the benchmark problems. The results are presented in Table 5. The layout of the table follows the same rules of the tables in the previous section.

According to the statistics in Table 5, we can make the following observations:

- Among the 24 instances, FastVC-PK significantly improves the solution quality of FastVC in 16 instances.
- In the 8 graphs where both algorithms obtain similar solutions, there are 5 instances where FastVC-PK finds the minimum vertex cover in the 10 runs and the average solution size found by FastVC-PK is smaller than that from FastVC in 7 instances.

– There are 21 graphs where FastVC-PK finds a minimum vertex cover smaller than that from FastVC.

From the experimental results, we find that the instances generated after parallel kernelization have around 20% of the non-isolated nodes and less than 3% of the edges in the original graphs. In most instances shown in the table, FastVC gets stuck in some local optima after running for less than 1,000 s and after that there is no improvement until the time limit is reached.

The graphs constructed from several independent copies of the existing instances are denser than the real world graphs. A single run of FastVC performs good in solving the real world graphs. Experiments are conducted on FastVC and FastVC-PK on these kinds of graphs as well. Since FastVC-PK is already able to find good solutions in a short time for most real world graphs from the benchmark set, both approaches obtain similar results for the sparse real world graphs. The parallel kernelization mechanism only improves FastVC in a few instances. The experimental results from some example testcases are shown in Table 4.

6   Conclusions

We have presented a new approach on scaling up local search algorithms for large graphs. Our approach builds on the theoretical assumption that large graphs are composed of different substructures which are on their own not hard to be optimized. Our approach is based on parallel kernelization and reduces the given graph by making μ parallel randomized runs of the given local search and fixing components that have been chosen in all μ runs. The resulting instance is then tackled by an additional run of the local search approach. Considering the Vertex Cover problem and the state-of-the-art local search solver NuMVC and FastVC, we have shown that our parallel kernelization technique is able to reduce standard benchmark graphs and large real world graphs to about 10–20% of their initial sizes. Our approach outperforms the baseline local search algorithm NuMVC and FastVC in most test cases.

The parallel kernelization approach presented in this paper can be applied to a wide range of combinatorial optimization problems for which well performing local search solvers are available. We plan to investigate the application to other problems such as Maximum Clique and Maximum Independent Set in the future.

References

1. Aarts, E., Lenstra, J.K. (eds.): Local Search in Combinatorial Optimization. Discrete Mathematics and Optimization. Wiley, Chichester (1997)
2. Akiba, T., Iwata, Y.: Branch-and-reduce exponential/FPT algorithms in practice: a case study of vertex cover. Theor. Comput. Sci. **609**, 211–225 (2016)
3. Bader, D.A., Meyerhenke, H., Sanders, P., Schulz, C., Kappes, A., Wagner, D.: Benchmarking for Graph Clustering and Partitioning. In: Alhajj, R., Rokne, J. (eds.) Encyclopedia of Social Network Analysis and Mining, pp. 73–82. Springer, New York (2014)

4. Cai, S.: Balance between complexity and quality: local search for minimum vertex cover in massive graphs. In: Proceedings of the Twenty-Fourth International Joint Conference on Artificial Intelligence, IJCAI 2015, Buenos Aires, Argentina, 25–31 July 2015, pp. 747–753 (2015)
5. Cai, S., Lin, J., Su, K.: Two weighting local search for minimum vertex cover. In: Proceedings of the Twenty-Ninth AAAI Conference on Artificial Intelligence, pp. 1107–1113 (2015)
6. Cai, S., Su, K., Sattar, A.: Two new local search strategies for minimum vertex cover. In: Proceedings of the Twenty-Sixth AAAI Conference on Artificial Intelligence (2012)
7. Downey, R.G., Fellows, M.R.: Fundamentals of Parameterized Complexity. TCS. Springer, London (2013)
8. Hoos, H.H., Stützle, T.: Stochastic Local Search: Foundations and Applications. Elsevier, San Francisco (2005)
9. Johnson, D.J., Trick, M.A. (eds.): Cliques, Coloring, and Satisfiability: Second DIMACS Implementation Challenge, Workshop, 11–13 October 1993. American Mathematical Society, Boston (1996)
10. Lamm, S., Sanders, P., Schulz, C., Strash, D., Werneck, R.F.: Finding near-optimal independent sets at scale. In: Proceedings of the Eighteenth Workshop on Algorithm Engineering and Experiments, ALENEX 2016, Arlington, Virginia, USA, 10 January 2016, pp. 138–150 (2016)
11. Pullan, W.: Phased local search for the maximum clique problem. J. Comb. Optim. **12**(3), 303–323 (2006)
12. Richter, S., Helmert, M., Gretton, C.: A stochastic local search approach to vertex cover. In: Hertzberg, J., Beetz, M., Englert, R. (eds.) KI 2007. LNCS (LNAI), vol. 4667, pp. 412–426. Springer, Heidelberg (2007). doi:10.1007/978-3-540-74565-5_31
13. Rossi, R.A., Ahmed, N.K.: The network data repository with interactive graph analytics and visualization. In: AAAI, pp. 4292–4293 (2015). http://networkrepository.com
14. Xu, K., Boussemart, F., Hemery, F., Lecoutre, C.: A simple model to generate hard satisfiable instances. In: Proceedings of the Nineteenth International Joint Conference on Artificial Intelligence, IJCAI 2005, pp. 337–342 (2005)
15. Zhang, W., Rangan, A., Looks, M.: Backbone guided local search for maximum satisfiability. In: Proceedings of the Eighteenth International Joint Conference on Artificial Intelligence, IJCAI 2003, pp. 1179–1186 (2003)

An Integer Linear Programming Model for Binary Knapsack Problem with Dependent Item Values

Davoud Mougouei[✉], David M.W. Powers, and Asghar Moeini

School of Computer Science, Engineering, and Mathematics, Flinders University,
Adelaide, Australia
d.mougouei@gmail.com

Abstract. *Binary Knapsack Problem* (BKP) is to select a subset of items with the highest value while keeping the size within the capacity of the knapsack. This paper presents an *Integer Linear Programming* (ILP) model for a variation of BKP where the value of an item may depend on presence or absence of other items in the knapsack. Strengths of such *Value-Related Dependencies* are assumed to be imprecise and hard to specify. To capture this imprecision, we have proposed modeling value-related dependencies using fuzzy graphs and their algebraic structure. We have demonstrated through simulations that our proposed ILP model is scalable to large number of items.

Keywords: Binary knapsack problem · Integer linear programming · Dependency · Value · Fuzzy graph

1 Problem Definition

The classical binary knapsack problem (BKP) [6] is concerned with finding an optimal subset of items with the highest value while respecting the capacity of the knapsack. However, it is common in real-world problems that the value of a knapsack item positively or negatively depends on selection of other items due to the value-related dependencies among those items. In other words, the value of an item is not known until the decision is made about other items.

Among the many applications of this problem, is the release planning problem [11,14]: given a set of n features with independent known costs, compute a subset of features with the highest value with a given budget. In practice, it is often the case that the value of a feature is influenced by selecting or ignoring other features [14]. This motivates us to formulate a binary knapsack problem in which sizes (costs) of items are known with certainty while values are dependent random variables. We refer to this problem as the *Binary Knapsack Problem with Dependent Item Values* (BKP-DIV).

There have been a few attempts to capture the uncertainty associated with the values of knapsack items in the literature [3,5,18,20]. Nonetheless, such works have mainly assumed that values of items are independent [3,5].

© Springer International Publishing AG 2017
W. Peng et al. (Eds.): AI 2017, LNAI 10400, pp. 144–154, 2017.
DOI: 10.1007/978-3-319-63004-5_12

Such models referred to as the *Stochastic Knapsack Problem* (SBKP) [5] models aim to maximize the expected value of a selected subset of items to account for uncertainty of the values as given in (1). In this equation, x_i is a decision variable specifying whether an item e_i is selected ($x_i = 1$) or not ($x_i = 0$). Moreover, v_i and $E(v_i)$ denote the value of an item e_i and the expected value of e_i respectively. Also, capacity of the knapsack is denoted by C while s_i denotes the size of an item e_i. The expected value of the selected subset of items is written as the summation of the expected values of the selected items in (1).

$$\text{Maximize } \sum_{i=1}^{n} x_i E(v_i) \tag{1}$$

$$\text{Subject to } \sum_{i=1}^{n} x_i s_i \leq C \tag{2}$$

$$x_i \in \{0,1\} \qquad i = 1, ..., n \tag{3}$$

One may consider formulating value-related dependencies in terms of covariances of values of items. In that case, a similar approach to Markowitz' *Modern Portfolio Theory* (MPT) [9,17] can be taken as given by (4)–(7), to achieve a target expected value with a given capacity (C) while minimizing the variance of the value of the selected items referred to as the *Risk*. This is equivalent to minimizing the summation of covariances of values of selected items. It is clear that $\forall i = j, \sigma_{i,j} = \sigma_i^2$ where $\sigma_{i,j}$ and σ_i^2 denote covariance of items e_i and e_j, and variance of e_i respectively.

$$\text{Minimize } \sigma^2 \left(\sum_{i=1}^{n} x_i v_i \right) = \sum_{i=1}^{n} \sum_{j=1}^{n} x_i x_j \sigma_{i,j} \tag{4}$$

$$\text{Subject to } \sum_{i=1}^{n} x_i E(v_i) \geq V \tag{5}$$

$$\sum_{i=1}^{n} x_i s_i \leq C \tag{6}$$

$$x_i \in \{0,1\} \qquad i = 1, ..., n \tag{7}$$

Nonetheless, the integer programming model (4)–(7) in its present form is not scalable to problems of large sizes. The reason is that the objective function (1) is a quadratic function.

Solving optimization models with quadratic objective functions (constraints) however, is more difficult than solving linear optimization problems. The model (4)–(7) nevertheless, can be linearized through adding constraints (11)–(13) and introducing an auxiliary decision variable y_{ij} which is set to 1 when both items e_i and e_j are selected ($x_i = x_j = 1$) and 0 otherwise. The linearized model is given in (8)–(14). However, there are two major problems with (4)–(7) and (8)–(14) as follows.

$$\text{Minimize} \sum_{i=1}^{n} \sum_{j=1}^{n} y_{ij} \sigma_{i,j} \tag{8}$$

$$\text{Subject to} \sum_{i=1}^{n} x_i E(v_i) \geq V \tag{9}$$

$$\sum_{i=1}^{n} x_i s_i \leq C \tag{10}$$

$$y_{ij} \leq x_i \tag{11}$$

$$y_{ij} \leq x_j \tag{12}$$

$$y_{ij} \geq x_i + x_j - 1 \tag{13}$$

$$x_i, y_{ij} \in \{0,1\} \qquad i = 1, ..., n \tag{14}$$

First, covariance is a measure of correlation and does not capture causality. As such, the direction of value-related dependencies cannot be captured by covariance. For instance, consider items e_1 and e_2 where e_2 positively influences the value of e_1 but selection of e_1 has no influence on the value of e_2 whatsoever. This logic can not be captured by covariance. In other words, by using covariance one is assuming that all value-related dependencies are bidirectional and the strengths of dependencies in either directions are equal. Such assumption, however, may not hold in real world problems.

Second, covariance can only capture linear correlations among values of items. In other words, relying on covariance results in missing non-linear dependencies even if they are of significant strengths.

To address these issues, we propose an integer linear programming model that (a) captures direction of value-related dependencies, (b) does not assume linearity of value-related dependencies, (c) considers imprecision of strengths of value-related dependencies by using algebraic structure of fuzzy graphs, and (d) can be solved efficiently even for large number of knapsack items. We have employed fuzzy graphs and their algebraic structure for modeling value-related dependencies and reasoning about strengths and qualities (positive or negative) of those dependencies.

2   Modeling Value-Related Dependencies

Fuzzy logic in general and fuzzy graphs in particular have demonstrated to properly capture imprecision of real world problems [10, 14, 15]. Hence, we have used algebraic structure of fuzzy graphs for capturing the imprecision associated with strengths of value-related dependencies. We have specially modified the classical definition of fuzzy graphs in order to consider not only the strengths but also the qualities (positive or negative) of value-related dependencies (Definition 1).

Definition 1. *Value Dependency Graph* (VDG). A VDG is a signed directed fuzzy graph [21] $G = (E, \sigma, \rho)$ in which a non-empty set of items $E : \{e_1, ..., e_n\}$ constitute the graph nodes. Also, the qualitative function $\sigma : E \times E \rightarrow \{+, -, \pm\}$

and the membership function $\rho : E \times E \rightarrow [0,1]$ denote qualities and strengths of explicit value-related dependencies receptively. As such, a pair of items (e_i, e_j) with $\rho_{i,j} \neq 0$ and $\sigma_{i,j} \neq \pm$ denotes an explicit value-related dependency from e_i to e_j. It is clear that we have $\rho_{i,j} = 0$ if the value of an item e_i is not explicitly influenced by selecting or ignoring e_j. In such cases we have $\sigma_{i,j} = \pm$ where $\pm$ denotes the quality of (e_i, e_j) is non-specified.

For instance, in the VDG $G = (E, \sigma, \rho)$ of Fig. 1 with $R = \{e_1, e_2, e_3, e_4\}$, $\sigma(e_1, e_2) = +$ and $\rho_{1,2} = 0.4$ state that selection of item e_2 has an explicit positive influence on the value of item e_1 and the strength of this influence is roughly 0.4.

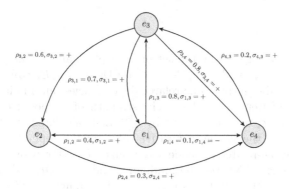

Fig. 1. A sample value dependency graph.

Definition 2. *Value-Related Dependencies.* A value-related dependency in a VDG $G = (E, \sigma, \rho)$ is defined as a sequence of items $d_i : \big(e(1), ..., e(k)\big)$ such that for each $e(j)$ in d_i, $2 \leq j \leq k$, we have $\rho_{j-1,j} \neq 0$. A consecutive pair $\big(e(j-1), e(j)\big)$ specifies an explicit value-related dependency (directed edge) from the item $e(j-1)$ to $e(j)$ in the VDG.

The strength of a value-related dependency $d_i : \big(e(1), ..., e(k)\big)$ is calculated by (15). That is, the strength of a value-related dependency equals to the strength of the weakest of all the $k-1$ explicit value-related dependencies along the path. $\wedge$ denotes fuzzy AND operator that is taking minimum over operands. The quality of a value-related dependency $d_i : \big(e(1), ..., e(k)\big)$ on the other hand, is calculated through employing qualitative sequential inference [4,8,22] as given by (16) and Table 1. Quantitative serial inferences in Table 1 are discussed by Wellman and Derthick [22] and De Kleer and Brown [4]. Also, Kusiak and Wang [8] has explained the details of employing them in constraint negotiation.

$$\forall d_i : \big(e(1), ..., e(k)\big), \quad \rho(d_i) = \bigwedge_{j=2}^{k} \rho_{j-1,j} \tag{15}$$

$$\forall d_i : (e(1), ..., e(k)), \quad \sigma(d_i) = \prod_{j=2}^{k} \sigma_{j-1,j} \tag{16}$$

Table 1. Qualitative serial inference in VDGs.

$\sigma(e(j-1), e(j), e(j+1))$		$\sigma_{j,j+1}$		
		+	−	±
$\sigma_{j-1,j}$	+	+	−	±
	−	−	+	±
	±	±	±	±

Let $D = \{d_1, d_2, ..., d_m\}$ be the set of all explicit and implicit value-related dependencies from $e_i \in E$ to $e_j \in E$ in a VDG $G = (E, \sigma, \rho)$. As explained earlier, positive and negative value-related dependencies can simultaneously exist between a pair of items e_i and e_j. The strength of all positive value-related dependencies from e_i to e_j is denoted by $\rho_{i,j}^{+\infty}$ and calculated by (17), that is to find the strength of the strongest positive value-related dependency [16] among all the positive value-related dependencies from e_i to e_j. Fuzzy operators $\wedge$ and $\vee$ denote Zadeh's fuzzy AND (taking minimum) and fuzzy OR (taking maximum) operations respectively [12]. In a similar way, the strength of all negative value-related dependencies from e_i to e_j is denoted by $\rho_{i,j}^{-\infty}$ and calculated by (18).

$$\rho_{i,j}^{+\infty} = \bigvee_{\substack{d_m \in D \\ \sigma(d_m)=+}} \rho(d_m) \tag{17}$$

$$\rho_{i,j}^{-\infty} = \bigvee_{\substack{d_m \in D \\ \sigma(d_m)=-}} \rho(d_m) \tag{18}$$

$$I_{i,j} = \rho_{i,j}^{+\infty} - \rho_{i,j}^{-\infty} \tag{19}$$

The overall strength of all positive and negative value-related dependencies from e_i to e_j is referred to as the *Overall Influence* of e_j on the value of e_i and denoted by $I_{i,j}$. As given by (19), $I_{i,j} \in [-1, 1]$ is calculated by subtracting the strength of all negative value-related dependencies ($\rho_{i,j}^{-\infty}$) from the strength of all positive value-related dependencies ($\rho_{i,j}^{+\infty}$). $I_{i,j} > 0$ states that e_j will ultimately influence the value of e_i in a positive way whereas $I_{i,j} < 0$ indicates that the ultimate influence of e_j on e_i is negative.

Example 1. Consider the set of all value-related dependencies from an item e_1 to e_4: $D = \{d_1 = (e_1, e_2, e_4), d_2 = (e_1, e_3, e_4), d_3 = (e_1, e_4)\}$ in the VDG of Fig. 1. Using (16) qualities of value-related dependencies in D are calculated as follows. $\sigma(d_1) = \Pi(+, +) = +$, $\sigma(d_2) = \Pi(+, +) = +$, and $\sigma(d_3) = \Pi(-) = -$. Also strengths of value-related dependencies in D are calculated by (15) as: $\rho(d_1) = \wedge(\rho_{1,2}, \rho_{2,4}) = min(0.4, 0.3) = 0.3$, $\rho(d_2) = \wedge(\rho_{1,3}, \rho_{3,4}) = min(0.8, 0.8) = 0.8$, $\rho(d_3) = 0.1$. Using (17) we have: $\rho_{1,4}^{+\infty} = \vee(\rho(d_1), \rho(d_2)) = max(0.3, 0.8) = 0.8$. Also, using (18) we have $\rho_{1,4}^{-\infty} = \rho(d_3) = 0.1$. Therefore, we have $I_{1,4} = \rho_{1,4}^{+\infty} - \rho_{1,4}^{-\infty} = 0.7$. $I_{1,4} = 0.7 > 0$ indicates that positive influence of e_4 on the value of e_1 prevails. Table 2 lists overall influences of items in VDG of Fig. 1 on the values of each other.

Table 2. Overall influences for VDG of Fig. 1.

$I_{i,j} = \rho_{i,j}^{+\infty} - \rho_{i,j}^{-\infty}$	e_1	e_2	e_3	e_4
e_1	$0.0 - 0.0 = 0.0$	$0.6 - 0.1 = 0.5$	$0.8 - 0.1 = 0.7$	$0.8 - 0.1 = 0.7$
e_2	$0.2 - 0.0 = 0.2$	$0.0 - 0.0 = 0.0$	$0.2 - 0.0 = 0.2$	$0.3 - 0.0 = 0.3$
e_3	$0.7 - 0.1 = 0.6$	$0.6 - 0.1 = 0.5$	$0.0 - 0.0 = 0.0$	$0.8 - 0.1 = 0.7$
e_4	$0.2 - 0.0 = 0.2$	$0.2 - 0.0 = 0.2$	$0.2 - 0.0 = 0.2$	$0.0 - 0.0 = 0.0$

Definition 3. *Value Dependency Level (VDL) and Negative Value Dependency Level (NVDL).* Let $G = (R, \sigma, \rho)$ be a VDG with $E = \{e_1, ..., e_n\}$, k be the total number of explicit value-related dependencies in G, and m be the total number of negative explicit value-related dependencies in G. Then, VDL and NVDL of G are derived by (20) and (21) respectively. For the special case of $k = 0$, we define $NVDL = 0$.

$$VDL(G) = \frac{k}{{}^nP_2} = \frac{k}{n(n-1)} \tag{20}$$

$$NVDL(G) = \frac{m}{k} \tag{21}$$

Example 2. Consider the value-related dependency graph G of Fig. 1 for which we have $n = 4$, $k = 8$, and $m = 1$. $VDL(G)$ is derived by (20) as: $VDL(G) = \frac{8}{4 \times 3} = \frac{8}{12} \approx 0.67$. Also we have from Eq. (21), $NVDL(G) = \frac{1}{8} = 0.125$.

3   The Integer Linear Programming Model

The extent to which the value of an item e_i is influenced by ignoring positive value-related dependencies and/or selecting negative value-related dependencies of e_i, is referred to as the penalty of e_i and denoted by p_i. p_i is calculated by taking supremum over the overall influences of all ignored positive dependencies and selected negative dependencies of e_i as given by (22)–(23). In these equations, n denotes the total number of items ($E : \{e_1, ..., e_n\}$) and x_j specifies whether an item e_j is selected ($x_j = 1$) or not ($x_j = 0$).

$$p_i = \bigvee_{j=1}^{n} \left(\frac{x_j(|I_{i,j}| - I_{i,j}) + (1 - x_j)(|I_{i,j}| + I_{i,j})}{2} \right) =$$

$$\bigvee_{j=1}^{n} \left(\frac{|I_{i,j}| + (1 - 2x_j)I_{i,j}}{2} \right) \quad i = 1, ..., n \tag{22}$$

$$x_j \in \{0, 1\} \qquad\qquad j = 1, ..., n \tag{23}$$

Equations (24)–(28) give our proposed integer programming model where x_i is a selection variable denoting whether an item $e_i \in E : \{e_1, ..., e_n\}$ is selected ($x_i = 1$) or not ($x_i = 0$). Also, s_i and v_i denote size and value of an item e_i respectively while C specifies the capacity of the knapsack. Moreover, p_i denotes the penalty of an item e_i which is the extent to which ignoring positive value-related dependencies and/or selecting negative value-related dependencies of e_i influence the value of e_i.

$$\text{Maximize} \sum_{i=1}^{n} x_i(1 - p_i)v_i \tag{24}$$

$$\text{Subject to} \sum_{i=1}^{n} x_i s_i \leq C \tag{25}$$

$$p_i \geq \left(\frac{|I_{i,j}| + (1 - 2x_j)I_{i,j}}{2} \right), \qquad i \neq j = 1, ..., n \tag{26}$$

$$x_i \in \{0, 1\} \qquad\qquad i = 1, ..., n \tag{27}$$

$$0 \leq p_i \leq 1 \qquad\qquad i = 1, ..., n \tag{28}$$

For an item e_i, p_i is a function of x_j and $I_{i,j}$: $p_i = f(x_j, I_{i,j})$. Hence, the objective function (24) can be expressed as $\sum_{i=1}^{n} x_i v_i - f(x_j, I_{i,j})x_i v_i$ with a quadratic expression [2] $exp = f(x_j, I_{i,j})x_i v_i$ which shows the integer programming model (24)–(28) is a non-linear model. On the other hand, the optimization problem (24)–(28) is to maximize a concave objective function over linear constraints which makes the problem a convex optimization problem [1].

Convex optimization problems are known to be solvable [1]. However, for problems of large sizes, integer linear programming (ILP) models are preferred [1] as they are known to be solvable more efficiently due to the advances in solving ILP models [7] and availability of efficient tools such as ILOG CPLEX. This, motivates us to develop an ILP version of the model as given by (29)–(37).

$$\text{Maximize} \sum_{i=1}^{n} x_i v_i - y_i v_i \tag{29}$$

$$\text{Subject to} \sum_{i=1}^{n} s_i x_i \leq C \tag{30}$$

$$p_i \geq \left(\frac{|I_{i,j}| + (1 - 2x_j)I_{i,j}}{2} \right) \qquad\qquad i \neq j = 1, ..., n \qquad (31)$$

$$-g_i \leq x_i \leq g_i \qquad\qquad i = 1, ..., n \qquad (32)$$

$$1 - (1 - g_i) \leq x_i \leq 1 + (1 - g_i) \qquad\qquad i = 1, ..., n \qquad (33)$$

$$-g_i \leq y_i \leq g_i \qquad\qquad i = 1, ..., n \qquad (34)$$

$$-(1 - g_i) \leq (y_i - p_i) \leq (1 - g_i) \qquad\qquad i = 1, ..., n \qquad (35)$$

$$x_i, y_i, g_i \in \{0, 1\} \qquad\qquad i = 1, ..., n \qquad (36)$$

$$0 \leq p_i \leq 1 \qquad\qquad i = 1, ..., n \qquad (37)$$

Hence, we have converted (24) to its corresponding linear form by substituting the non-linear expression $x_i p_i$ with the linear expression y_i. On the other hand, we are expecting either $a : (x_i = 0, y_i = 0)$, or $b : (x_i = 1, y_i = p_i)$ to occur. In order to capture the relation between p_i and y_i in a linear form, we have introduced an auxiliary variable $g_i = \{0, 1\}$ and (32)–(36) are added to the original model. As such, we have either $(g_i = 0) \rightarrow a$, or $(g_i = 1) \rightarrow b$. The resulting model as given by (29)–(37) is an integer linear model.

It is also worth mentioning that the (expected) value of an item is determined by how frequently that item is selected. On this basis, value-related dependencies among items can be formulated in terms of their selection frequency i.e. *selection preferences*. Selection preferences for an item, may be influenced by preferences for other items. Based on this logic, value-related dependencies among items can be inferred from causal relations [19] among preferences for those items. For instance, when preferences for an item e_j positively influences preferences for an item e_i, this implies a value-related dependency from e_i to e_j with $\rho_{i,j} \neq 0$ and $\sigma_{i,j} = +$. As such, strengths of casual relations among items can be used to estimate the strengths and qualities of value-related dependencies [13].

4   Scalability

To demonstrate scalability of the proposed ILP model for solving the Binary Knapsack Problem with Dependent Item Values (BKP-DIV), experiments were carried out for various numbers of items (Fig. 2(a)), knapsack capacities (Fig. 2(b)), value dependency levels (Fig. 2(c)), and negative value dependency levels (Fig. 2(d)). Uniformly distributed random numbers in $[-1,1]$ were generated to simulate the strengths of value-related dependencies and their qualities. Also, random numbers in $[0,20]$ where generated to simulate values and sizes of items. Callable library ILOG CPLEX was used to implement our proposed ILP model.

Figure 2 provides plots of our results. Each plot has a linear y-axis, and a linear x-axis where y-axis shows the runtime and the x-axis gives the number of knapsack items (Fig. 2(a)), percentages of knapsack capacities (Fig. 2(b)), value dependency levels (Fig. 2(c)), and negative value dependency levels (Fig. 2(d)).

Our simulations were repeated for various number of knapsack items ($N \in \{0, 1, ..., 1500\}, \%C = 50, VDL = NVDL = 0.1$) and it was observed (Fig. 2(a))

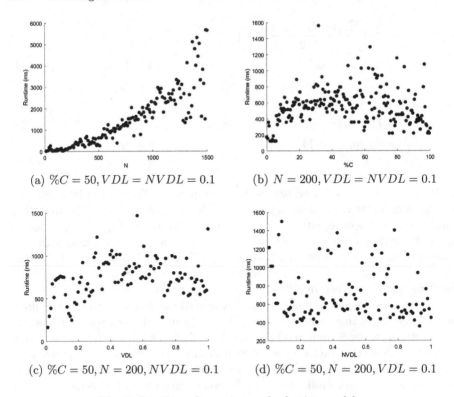

(a) $\%C = 50, VDL = NVDL = 0.1$ (b) $N = 200, VDL = NVDL = 0.1$

(c) $\%C = 50, N = 200, NVDL = 0.1$ (d) $\%C = 50, N = 200, VDL = 0.1$

Fig. 2. Runtime of experimented selection models

that runtime of the model almost monotonically increased when the size of the knapsack was increased.

Our simulation results for various percentages of knapsack capacities ($\%C = \{0, 1, ..., 100\}, N = 200, VDL = NVDL = 0.1$) however, showed (Fig. 2(b)) that the model runs slightly faster in the presence of relatively small ($\%C \leq 20$) or large capacities ($\%C \geq 90$). This is due to the fact that there are less feasible solutions available when the capacity of the knapsack is small. As such, the solution space will be reduced and a decision can be made faster. On the other hand, when sufficient budget is available, only few infeasible solutions (size exceeds the capability) can exist and therefore, it will be easier for the selection model to make a decision as to whether or not ignore an item.

In a similar way, we repeated the simulations for various levels of value dependencies ($VDL \in \{0, 0.01, ..., 1\}, \%C = 50, N = 200, NVDL = 0.1$) and it was observed (Fig. 2(c)) that increasing the level of value dependencies has arbitrary impact of relatively small magnitude on the runtime in most places in Fig. 2(c).

We further, observed that the runtime of the model was arbitrarily influenced by the level of negative value-related dependencies ($\%NVDL$) where the simulations were carried out for $N = 200, \%C = 50, VDL = 0.1, \%NVDL = \{0, 0.01, ..., 1\}$. This arbitrarily influence, however, was relatively small.

5   Conclusions and Future Work

In this paper we presented an integer linear programming (ILP) model for solving a variation of the binary knapsack problem referred to as the Binary Knapsack Problem with Dependent Item Values (BKP-DIV) where values of the knapsack items may depend on presence or absence of other items in the knapsack. The strengths of such dependencies (value-related dependencies) are assumed to be imprecise and hard to specify. To capture this imprecision, we used algebraic structure of fuzzy graphs. We demonstrated through simulations that the proposed ILP model is scalable to BKP-DIV with large number of items.

The work can be extended in several directions. One is to apply the proposed ILP model to real world instances of the BKP-DIV. In doing so, we are currently developing a framework based on our proposed ILP model. Automated identification of value-related dependencies and their characteristics would be another way to extend the present work. Such extension would enhance the practicality of our proposed ILP model. We will, in this regard, explore various data mining techniques and measures of casual strength to improve accuracy of estimating the qualities and strengths of value-related dependencies.

References

1. Boyd, S., Vandenberghe, L.: Convex Optimization. Cambridge University Press, Cambridge (2004)
2. Burkard, R.E.: Quadratic assignment problems. Eur. J. Oper. Res. **15**(3), 283–289 (1984)
3. Carraway, R.L., Schmidt, R.L., Weatherford, L.R.: An algorithm for maximizing target achievement in the stochastic knapsack problem with normal returns. Naval Res. Logist. (NRL) **40**(2), 161–173 (1993)
4. De Kleer, J., Brown, J.S.: A qualitative physics based on confluences. Artif. Intell. **24**(1), 7–83 (1984)
5. Henig, M.I.: Risk criteria in a stochastic knapsack problem. Oper. Res. **38**(5), 820–825 (1990)
6. Kellerer, H., Pferschy, U., Pisinger, D.: Knapsack Problems. Springer, Heidelberg (2004)
7. Kivijärvi, H., Korhonen, P., Wallenius, J.: Operations research and its practice in finland. Interfaces **16**(4), 53–59 (1986)
8. Kusiak, A., Wang, J.: Dependency analysis in constraint negotiation. IEEE Trans. Syst. Man Cybern. **25**(9), 1301–1313 (1995)
9. Markowitz, H.M.: Foundations of portfolio theory. J. Financ. **46**(2), 469–477 (1991)
10. Mordeson, J.N., Nair, P.S.: Applications of fuzzy graphs. In: Mordeson, J.N., Nair, P.S. (eds.) Fuzzy Graphs and Fuzzy Hypergraphs. Studies in Fuzziness and Soft Computing, vol. 46, pp. 83–133. PhysicaVerlag HD, Heidelberg (2000). doi:10.1007/978-3-7908-1854-3_3
11. Mougouei, D.: Factoring requirement dependencies in software requirement selection using graphs and integer programming. In: Proceedings of the 31st IEEE/ACM International Conference on Automated Software Engineering, pp. 884–887. ACM (2016)

12. Mougouei, D., Nurhayati, W.: A fuzzy-based technique for describing security requirements of intrusion tolerant systems. Int. J. Softw. Eng. Appl. **7**(2), 99–112 (2013)
13. Mougouei, D., Powers, D.: Dependency-aware software release planning through mining user preferences. arXiv preprint arXiv:1702.05592 (2017)
14. Mougouei, D., Powers, D.M.W., Moeini, A.: Dependency-aware software release planning. In: Proceedings of the 39th International Conference on Software Engineering Companion, ICSE-C 2017, pp. 198–200. IEEE Press, Piscataway (2017)
15. Mougouei, D., Rahman, W.N.W.A., Almasi, M.M.: Measuring security of web services in requirement engineering phase. Int. J. Cyber-Secur. Digit. Forensics (IJCSDF) **1**(2), 89–98 (2012)
16. Rosenfeld, A.: Fuzzy graphs. Fuzzy Sets Appl. **77**, 95 (1975)
17. Sharpe, W.F.: Portfolio Theory and Capital Markets. McGraw-Hill College, New York (1970)
18. Sniedovich, M.: Preference order stochastic knapsack problems: methodological issues. J. Oper. Res. Soc. **31**(11), 1025–1032 (1980)
19. Sprenger, J.: Foundations for a probabilistic theory of causal strength (2016)
20. Steinberg, E., Parks, M.: A preference order dynamic program for a knapsack problem with stochastic rewards. J. Oper. Res. Soc. **30**(2), 141–147 (1979)
21. Wasserman, S., Faust, K.: Social Network Analysis: Methods and Applications, vol. 8. Cambridge University Press, Cambridge (1994)
22. Wellman, M.P., Derthick, M.: Formulation of Tradeoffs in Planning Under Uncertainty. Pitman, London (1990)

Swarm Intelligence and Evolutionary Computing

A 'Breadcrumbs' Model for Controlling an Intrinsically Motivated Swarm Using a Handheld Device

Sarah Jean Bowley[(⊠)] and Kathryn Merrick

School of Engineering and Information Technology,
University of New South Wales Canberra, Canberra, Australia
s.bowley@student.adfa.edu.au, k.merrick@adfa.edu.au

Abstract. This paper presents a model for controlling an intrinsically motivated swarm, designed for use on a handheld device. We map touch-screen gestures to a set of 'breadcrumbs' that can be placed to influence the behaviour of the swarm. We describe a prototype system implementing the breadcrumbs model. Then we evaluate the prototype by examining how members of the swarm respond to each breadcrumb. Our results characterize the behaviour of the intrinsically motivated swarm in response to each type of 'breadcrumb' and discuss the implications for swarms of different types of robots.

Keywords: Boids · Swarm · Motivated division of labor · Breadcrumbs · Human-swarm interaction

1 Introduction

Future built environments or 'Smart Worlds' will incorporate large numbers of mobile and immobile robots. These heterogeneous robot swarms will be able to assist humans with complex tasks. However, the promised ubiquity of such swarms raises the questions of (1) how humans will interact with large numbers of robots and (2) how robot swarms will proactively support human goals. This paper addresses the first question by designing a protocol for humans to interact with artificial swarms. This paper focuses specifically on interaction through small, handheld devices, such as a mobile phone or tablet, which are already part of our everyday lives. Another key innovation of this paper is the focus on an intrinsically motivated swarm [1] where different robots may have different motivations and may respond differently to a given command as a result. This permits autonomous division of labour in the swarm, but makes human interaction with the swarm potentially more difficult.

The remainder of this paper is organised as follows: Sect. 2 presents a brief review of the literature related to robot swarms and human-swarm interaction (HSI) and provides background of the swarm algorithms, including the intrinsically motivated approach, used in this paper. Section 3 introduces our 'breadcrumbs' model for human interaction with swarms and describes our prototype touch screen application implementing this model. The model and application is evaluated in Sect. 4. We conclude and consider directions for future work in Sect. 5.

© Springer International Publishing AG 2017
W. Peng et al. (Eds.): AI 2017, LNAI 10400, pp. 157–168, 2017.
DOI: 10.1007/978-3-319-63004-5_13

2 Literature Review

This section reviews literature in two areas: human swarm interaction (Sect. 2.1) and swarm algorithms (Sect. 2.2). This provides the background necessary for the model presented in Sect. 3.

2.1 Human Swarm Interaction

A recent survey identifies HSI as an emerging research direction [2] in robotics and swarm intelligence. This field has been supported by advances in technology permitting robots of reduced size and cost. This permits systems comprised of large numbers of robots to collaborate autonomously. However, human interaction with large numbers of robots is a task of high cognitive complexity. This requires the development of novel interaction protocols to ease this burden. Kolling et al. [2] identify three challenging aspects of such interfaces: (1) managing cognitive complexity, (2) swarm state estimation and visualization and (3) control methods (how to convey operator intent to the swarm). The research in this paper falls in the third of these categories. The novel focus of this work is to consider control methods for HIS with an intrinsically motivated swarm [1].

Kolling et al. [2] further categorize existing control methods for swarms as (1) algorithms and behaviour selection, (2) control via parameter setting, (3) environmental influence and (4) leader selection. In this paper, we are particularly concerned with HSI via handheld devices such as mobile phones or tablets. These items are ubiquitous in our modern lives, with 'apps' a key way of interacting with banks, shops, and even ordering transportation. This paper proposes a model for HSI, designed to meet the challenges of a small screen and to make use of touch screen technology. We take an approach that falls in the category of 'environmental influence' through a 'breadcrumbs' metaphor. We find this approach appropriate because touch screen technology naturally lends itself to environmental influence through touch.

Existing approaches to environmental influence for HSI include influencing the swarm by injecting pheromone information to nearby robots [3], using digital pheromone fields [4] and using simulated beacons that can be placed by an operator and signal to nearby robots [5]. Different types of beacons include 'stop', 'come', 'rendezvous', 'deploy', 'random', 'heading' and 'leave' beacons. An alternative beacon-like model has been used for swarms of drones dropped from jets [6]. This model uses multiple beacons as attractors and directional indicators. In contrast to existing work, our 'breadcrumbs' approach is specifically designed for small, touch-screen platforms, with small numbers of beacons able to influence large numbers of agents. This paper presents the computational model for our approach. The next section presents the background formalisms for this approach.

2.2 Algorithms for Robot Swarms

A range of algorithms has been proposed for robot swarms [7]. Tan and Zheng [7] characterize these algorithms as being decentralized, autonomous and able to cope with great variation in population size. They are further characterized by local sensing and communication. Depending on the algorithms used, a range of swarm behaviours have been identified [8]. These include (1) spatial organization behaviours such as aggregation, dispersion, pattern formation, chain formation and self-assembly; (2) navigation behaviours such as foraging, exploration, and collective transport; and (3) decision-making behaviours such as task allocation and consensus achievement.

A simple swarm model that we adapt in this paper is Reynold's boids model [9]. This model uses three rules for (1) Cohesion: move towards the average position (centre of mass) of local flockmates; (2) Separation: move to avoid crowding local flockmates; and (3) Alignment: match orientation and velocity of local flockmates. With these rules alone, we can achieve a number of behaviours of the swarm, including grouping and ordering of agents. With the addition of more complex rules, such as obstacle avoidance and goal seeking, different and more complex behaviours can be achieved.

Formally, we can describe the boids model as follows: For each agent A^j at any time t it will have a corresponding position vector, x_t^j and a velocity vector, v_t^j. At each step of time, the velocity of the agent is updated using the following equation:

$$v_{t+1}^j = W_d v_t^j + W_c c_t^j + W_a a_t^j + W_s s_t^j \tag{1}$$

c_t^j is a vector towards the average position (cohesion) of local agents within a certain range; a_t^j represents the average direction (alignment) of local agents within a certain range; and s_t^j is a vector away from the average position (separation) of local agents within a certain range. W_c, W_a and W_s are the relative magnitude of the corresponding force and W_d is the perceived importance of the agent's existing velocity. From this, an agent's new position is updated:

$$x_{t+1}^j = x_t^j + v_{t+1}^j \tag{2}$$

As noted above many calculations or decisions are based on agents within a certain range of a particular agent A^j. These neighbors are defined in a subset N^j of agents within the range R; such that:

$$N^j = \{A^k | A^k \neq A^j \wedge dist(A^k, A^j) < R\}. \tag{3}$$

Noting that $dist(A^k, A^j) < R$ refers to the Euclidean distance between the particular agent A^j and its neighbor A^k is less than the set range.

An intrinsically motivated extension of the boids model assigns each boid an optimally motivating incentive (OMI), [1]. The OMI stipulates an incentive value that an agent finds maximally motivating. Motivation for a goal G with incentive $I(G)$ is calculated as:

$$M^j(G) = I^{max} - |I(G) - \Omega^j| \tag{4}$$

where I^{max} is the maximum available incentive recognized by the agent. Each agent can construct a set $\mathbf{G}_t^j$ of motivating goals within a range R_m according to:

$$\mathbf{G}_t^j = \{G^i | dist(g_t^i, x_t^j) < R_m \wedge M^j(G) > M\} \tag{5}$$

Where g_t^i is the position of goal G^i and M is a threshold motivation for inclusion in the an agent's set of goals. Equation (1) is modified to include a force in the direction of each motivating goal as follows:

$$v_{t+1}^j = W_d v_t^j + W_c c_t^j + W_a a_t^j + W_s s_t^j + W_m \sum_i (g_t^i - x_t^j) \tag{6}$$

In this paper, we use this idea to form the basis of division of labour among sub-groups in the swarm, without requiring the human to explicitly form the sub-groups.

3   The 'Breadcrumbs' Model for Human-Swarm Interaction

A range of basic gestures have been developed for touch screen technologies [10]. These include 'touch down' (touching the screen), 'touch up' (removing the finger from the screen), 'drag/swipe' (touch down followed by movement and then touch up), 'flick' (a fast drag/swipe) and 'pinch' (bringing the fingers together while touching the screen) gestures, as well as scope for free-form gestures. In this paper we have mapped a series of different 'breadcrumbs' (which we think of as beacons for a touch screen) to the touch up, touch down and flick gestures.

3.1   Model

Table 1 introduces the breadcrumbs, the model for the force they produce, and their corresponding gestures. For a given agent A^j at time t their effect can be explained in terms of different ranges and vectors of direction will need to be calculated for each breadcrumb type. The breadcrumb with position C_t^j, will apply these forces on the agents within the given range.

Table 1. Breadcrumbs for human-swarm interaction via a touch screen.

Breadcrumb name/type	Force	Gesture to place the crumb
Attractor (T_t^j)	$T_t^j = C_t^j - x_t^j$	Touch down
Recall (R_t^j)	$R_t^j = C_t^j - x_t^j$	Touch down
Obstacle (O_t^j)	$O_t^j = x_t^j - C_t^j$	Touch down
Direction indicator (D_t^j)	$\vec{D}_t \ j = \vec{C}_t \ j - x_t^j$ & $\vec{C}_t \ j = P_d^j - P_u^j$	Flick
Speed multiplier (M_t^j)	$V_{t+1}^j = V_{t+1}^j \times M_t^j$ & $M_t^j = x_t^j - C_t^j$	Touch down
Speed divisor (S_t^j)	$V_t^j = V_{t+1}^j \times S_t^j$ & $S_t^j = x_t^j - C_t^j$	Touch down
Circle (L_t^j)	$L_t^j = C_t^j - x_t^j$ & $\vec{L}_t \ j = \vec{C}_t \ j - x_t^j$ $L_t^j = x_t^j - C_t^j$	Touch down

The Attractor Breadcrumb is based on the ant behaviours of swarming, goal orientation and division of labour. It acts as an attractor for boids with an OMI matching that of the crumb. Implementation is through the application of an attractive (cohesion) force within a set radius. The T_t^j vector represents the force of attraction as calculated by the position of the crumb minus the boid's position (if within a specified radius of influence) multiplied by a factor.

The Obstacle Breadcrumb is based on the principle of self-preservation and danger avoidance. The Obstacle breadcrumb is designed to provide obstacle avoidance control to the user. This crumb acts as a repulsion point, based on the rule of separation. Unlike the Attractor, here the vector O_t^j is calculated through boid's position minus the crumbs position. This reversal results in a vector pointing outward from the breadcrumbs position which is then multiplied by a set factor. Dependant on the level of repulsion required the factor can be adjusted, which in conjunction the radius of influence can create a clear obstacle of repulsion or allows minimal movement within its radius.

The Recall Breadcrumb is an attractor that is effective regardless of the motivation of the boids. The Recall breadcrumb provides environment-wide attraction to the group; developed as an extension to the Attractor crumb. The essence of this breadcrumb is for swarm wide control in emergency or end of exercise situations. Here the computation of the R_t^j is identical to the Attractor however the factor of multiplication and the area of influence is exponentially increased.

The Direction Breadcrumb is based on the concept of ant behaviour for travel. It is implemented on the touch-up with the direction controlled by the relative difference in the location of the touch-down and touch-up (a flick). As such, this crumb enables behaviour to direct the flow of the swarm similar to how pheromones are used to specify paths. It is implemented using a variation of the alignment rule. Computation of the breadcrumb vector D_t^j uses the same formula to the Attractor breadcrumb to allow movement of agents through the radius of influence and prevent a obstacle behaviour occurring. However, this uses a very small multiplication factor; additionally a vector is summed with this $\overrightarrow{C_t^j}$ with direction calculated by the difference in the touch up/down locations.

The Circle Breadcrumb incorporates aspects of the attractor, obstacle and direction crumbs using all three boid rules. There is an associated attraction to create recruitment and repulse to set an inner radius for circular motion. As seen in ant behaviour to surround a food source this crumb extends the swarming goal orientation to provide this ability. Further by using the alignment rule the direction of rotation can be controlled. The breadcrumbs for direction, speed control and circle are more useful for control in a small area, with a number of practical applications drawn from natural and artificial systems.

The Divider and Multiplier Breadcrumb affect the maximum speed of the boids within a defined radius by decreasing/increasing the final velocity vector sum for each boid respectively. Although mostly unseen, ants vary speed dependent on the strength of the pheromones setting the path and the locality of a goal. Ideally large movements are reduced close to a food source or colony while movements are very quick in transit. This crumb uses this concept such that the relative effect of these crumbs is dependent on the distance of the boid from the crumb; developed for swarm logistical control.

3.2   Prototype and Simulation

An operational interface was developed in Java using Android Studio to create an App for Android smart phones. Simple layout design establishes a method of selection and execution that is fluid and intuitive with minimal disruption to swarm behaviour.

Figure 1 shows four screen shots of the swarm responding to four of the crumbs presented in Table 1. The orange dots are the breadcrumbs with radii of 100 pixels (or 350 pixels in the Recall breadcrumb case). The red dots are the agents (or boids). Further, the arrows show the effect of the breadcrumb on the velocity and behaviour of the boids.

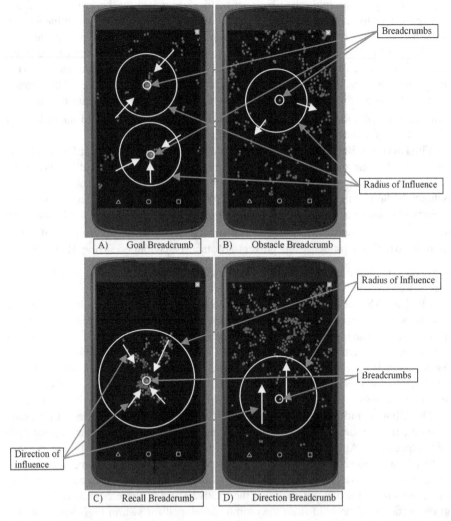

Fig. 1. Effect of different breadcrumbs: (a) attractor (b) obstacle (c) recall (d) direction (Color figure online)

This model and prototype is designed to enable control of multiple robots. Connection of these robots could be achieved over a number of channels (Wi-Fi, Bluetooth, etc.). Depending on the type of robot, the mapping between the physical world and the simulation will differ. For example, small robots such as Lego Mindstorms robots operate effectively over Bluetooth with a maximum speed of 0.5 km/hr [11]. The screen on the touch screen device could reasonable represent a room in the case of such robots. For robots with a higher maximum speed, the screen could reasonably represent an area the size of football field, although the accuracy of touch control may be reduced. We do not focus on these issues further in this paper, but instead evaluate how our model influences the characteristic behaviour of boids in the next section.

4   Experiments

The aim of the experiments in this section is to characterize the behaviour of a swarm in response to each of the breadcrumbs presented in Sect. 3. The following sections present our experimental method and results.

4.1   Method

Our prototype was tested in a series of experiments outlined in Table 2. Simulations were conducted over a 1,000 time-steps to best demonstrate the desired swarming behaviour. The results are averaged over ten simulations to give a greater level of accuracy of the boids' behaviour as a whole and are displayed in the appropriate figure.

Experiment 1: The Attractor breadcrumb, shown in Fig. 1(a), is designed to provide localised goal orientation and swarming control to the group, this experiment is developed to empirically demonstrate a grouping behaviour is observed. Data collected for this crumb was conducted as the percentage of the boids within concentric radii compared to those in the 300-pixel radius.

Experiment 2: Extending from experiment 1, we test the effect of the Recall breadcrumb to affect the entire swarm. Shown in Fig. 1(c) the attractive force acts over a larger area resulting in greater recruitment. Data collected for this crumb was the percentage of the boids within concentric radii compared to those in the 300-pixel radius. As such it is expected that the percentage will increase overtime with the inner radii increasing slower than the outer as more boids are attracted. However, since the force and area of effect is significantly increased it is expected to have a more immediate compared to the Goal crumb.

Experiment 3: This experiment aims to demonstrate an obstacle avoidance behaviour with the application of a repulsive (separation) force within a set radius, as shown in Fig. 1(b). Data collected for this crumb was the percentage of the boids within concentric radii compared to those in the 300-pixel radius. This radial force is expected to

Table 2. Experiment summary

Expt	Description/Experimental aim	Experimental conditions	Measurements
1	Attrractor breadcrumb: goal orientation and swarming	200 boids; fixed location of crumb; no obstacles	Time taken Percentage within radius
2	Recall breadcrumb: goal orientation and swarming	200 boids; fixed location of crumb; no obstacles	Time taken Percentage within radius
3	Obstacle breadcrumb: obstacle avoidance	200 boids; fixed location of crumb; no obstacles	Time taken Percentage within radius
4	Direction breadcrumb: boid alignment	200 boids; crumb direction set as up $(x < 0)$; fixed location of crumb; no obstacles	Time taken Percentage with alignment matching direction crumb
5	Circle breadcrumb: swarming and goal orientation.	300 boids; radius of circle = 250 pixels. Fixed location of crumb; No obstacles	Time lapse pictures at $t = 0, 10, 50,$ and 100
6	Goal breadcrumb: motivated goal orientation and swarming	300 boids; 2 crumbs with different incentives; fixed location of crumbs; no obstacles	Time taken Percentage within radius with matching incentive

have a repetitive behaviour as boids are continuously moving within the area of influence and then subsequently repelled.

Experiment 4: The Direction Breadcrumb is designed to provide boid alignment within a selected area essentially indicating a path for the boids to follow. As shown in Fig. 1(d) the behaviour of boids is to match the orientation directed by the placed breadcrumb. Empirical results were computed based upon the percentage of boids within concentric radii with a movement/alignment matching the selection (with some variance).

Experiment 5: Swarming and goal orientation is combined through the Circle Breadcrumb to provide more complex behaviour. This experiment aims to demonstrate the recreation of circular swarming as seen ants. Data is collated about relative location and behaviour of boids over time through using a time-lapse comparison.

Experiment 6: This experiment aims to demonstrate division of labour can be achieved by introducing motivation to the boids. Utilising two goal breadcrumbs with differing incentives, we expect the boids will swarm to the goal that most closely matches their own OMI. For the simulations and experiments conducted within this paper we allocated the crumb characteristics within the code rather than on the hand-held device interface.

4.2 Results

The Attractor Breadcrumb. As seen in the screen shot of Fig. 1(a), boids are attracted to the breadcrumb once within its sphere of influence. Figure 2(a) shows the empirical results of the observed behaviour; where as expected the percentage gradually increased overtime with the inner radii increasing slower than the outer as more boids are attracted. Statistically over the course of ten simulations on average 95% of all boids were within the inner radius of 75 pixels after 1,000 time-steps. The orientation and swarming toward a directed goal is essential to all swarm scenarios.

The Recall Breadcrumb. As an extension of the goal breadcrumb in an effort to provide speedy interaction within the swarm was the next tested. Figure 2(b) shows that the Recall Breadcrumb has an immediate impact when compared to the Attractor crumb. Total recruitment of the boids occurred in 129 time steps for the Recall breadcrumb.

The Obstacle Breadcrumb. Experimental analysis the radius was set to 150 pixels, which explains the variable nature of the data at a radius of 200 pixels as shown in the below Fig. 2(c). Here again the data was averaged over ten simulations. For an obstacle crumb, no more than 40% of boids within a range of 300 pixels will be within 200

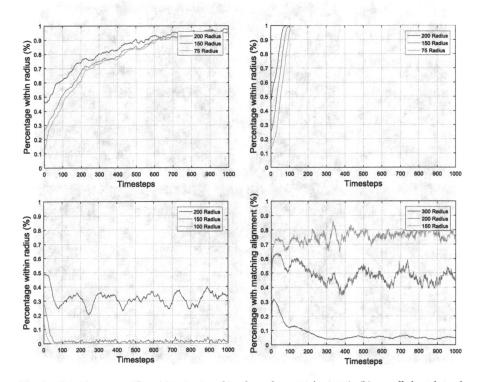

Fig. 2. Experiment results: (a) attractor breadcrumb: experiment 1 (b) recall breadcrumb experiment 2 (c) obstacle breadcrumb experiment 3 (d) direction breadcrumb experiment 4

pixels of that crumb. Importantly for the mentioned situations the challenge is raised as to whether this control is automated or user defined. Arguments exist for both implementations; however, in the instance for handheld device control, regardless of the implementation method centralized data collection (system server) would be required for transmission of information to all users/controllers.

The Direction Breadcrumb defines specified swarm traffic flow. As seen from the results in Fig. 2(d) as the boid comes closer within the area of effect of the direction the percentage of boids with alignment matching the crumb increases. Hence, the Direction breadcrumb performs as expected, directing the boids in the selected direction.

The latter experiments specifically for the circle and motivation division of labor exist for the implicit purpose of practical robot control. The applications vary from crowd modelling to transport control. These breadcrumbs rather than implicitly achieve a single goal are designed for the application or direction around multiple tasks, either indicating or directing.

The Circle Breadcrumb. Figure 3 demonstrates a time-lapse of this breadcrumb displaying the gradual circular behaviour of the boids. Notably the force of attraction is minimal at the x-y axis creating a 'star' like shape; this is particularly evident at times $t = 40, 60, 80 \& 100$.

Fig. 3. Time lapse of circle breadcrumb for times (a) t = 0, (b) t = 20, (c) t = 40, (d) t = 60, (e) t = 80, (f) t = 100, (g) t = 200, (h) t = 300

Motivated Division of Labor. Figures 4(a) and (b) show the gradual recruitment behaviour as seen from Expt 1. When considered together, this results in a divergent behaviour with boids of a set motivation attracted the goal with the same motivation while the others were unaffected. As such the results behaviour displays a divided approach to goal orientation as expected from the motivated implementation. Importantly the agents of differing motivation whilst unaffected by the goal breadcrumbs still pass through the radius, the decreasing percentage is attributed to the simultaneous testing with two breadcrumbs. When using a single breadcrumb of set motivation the percentage of gents of other motivations is much higher dependent upon the level of crowding within the system.

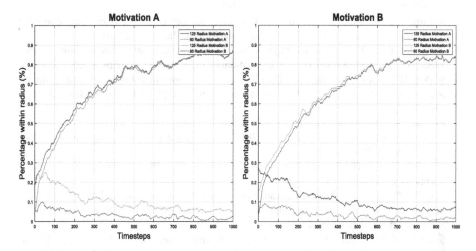

Fig. 4. (left) Attractor breadcrumb with motivation A (right) Attractor breadcrumb with Motivation B

This swarm control through parameter setting and environmental influence are two of the pillars of the HSI model discussed by Kolling et al. [2]. The algorithms and inherent and emergent behaviours evident in this testing creates a varied scope for practical testing. Our approaches answers many of the questions posed by Kolling et al. [2], and has potential for further extension.

5   Conclusion and Future Work

In conclusion, this paper has explored a model for HSI using a touch screen device. Two user-interface models were presented for application to handheld devices and discussed with considerations made for screen size and situation awareness. We have demonstrated and evaluated the behaviour boids in response to six breadcrumbs for mapping swarm behaviours to gestures on a handheld device, with promising results supporting swarm mechanics.

Our future work will extend upon the ideas and models proposed here, importantly a practical approach to controlling intrinsically motivated swarms. Consideration will be in two directions: (1) studies of human effectiveness using the interface to complete set tasks and (2) extension of the simulation to connect to physical robots. This will raise the challenges of (1) translation of behavioural architypes to situational applications and (2) swarm state visualization and situation estimation.

References

1. Merrick, K.: Computational Models of Motivation for Game-Playing Agents. Springer, Heidelberg (2016). doi:10.1007/978-3-319-33459-2
2. Kolling, A., Walker, P., Chakraborty, N., Sycara, K., Lewis, M.: Human interaction with robot swarms: a survey. IEEE Trans. Hum.-Mach. Syst. **46**, 9–26 (2016)
3. Daily, M., Cho, Y., Martin, K., Payton, D.: World embedded interfaces for human-robot interaction. In: 36th Annual Hawaii International Conference on Systems Science (2002)
4. Walter, B., Sannier, A., Reiners, D., Oliver, J.: UAV swarm control: calculating digital pheromone fields with the GPU. J. Def. Model. Simul.: Appl. Methodol. Technol. **3**, 167–176 (2006)
5. Kolling, A., Nunnally, S., Lewis, M.: Towards human control of robot swarms. In: Proceedings of the 17th Annual ACM/IEEE International Conference on Human Robot Interaction, pp. 89–96 (2012)
6. Condliffe, J.: A 100-Drone Swarm, Dropped from Jets, Plans Its Own Moves. MIT Technology Review, 10 January 2017
7. Tan, Y., Zheng, Z.-Y.: Research advance in swarm robotics. Def. Technol. **9**, 18–39 (2013)
8. Bonabeau, E., Dorigo, M., Theraulaz, G.: Swarm Intelligence: From Natural to Artificial Systems. Oxford University Press, New York (1999)
9. Reynolds, C.W.: Flocks, herds, and schools: a distributed behavior model. Comput. Graph. **21**(4), 21–34 (1987). ACM SIGGRAPH 1987 Conference Proceedings, Anaheim, California
10. Embedded_Interactions_Lab: Touch Screen Gestures (2017)
11. Watanabe, R., Knuth, K., Benedettelli, D.: NXT motor internals. In: Lego - Philohome (2008)

Genetic Programming for Multi-objective Test Data Generation in Search Based Software Testing

Jiatong Huo[1], Bing Xue[1(✉)], Lin Shang[2], and Mengjie Zhang[1]

[1] Victoria University of Wellington, PO Box 600, Wellington 6140, New Zealand
huojiat@myvuw.ac.nz, {Bing.Xue,Mengjie.Zhang}@ecs.vuw.ac.nz
[2] State Key Laboratory of Novel Software Technology,
Nanjing University, Nanjing, China
shanglin@nju.edu.cn

Abstract. Software testing is an indispensable part in software development to ensure the quality of products. Multi-objective test data generation is a sub-area of search-based software testing, which focuses on automatically generating test data to form high quality test suites. Due to the limited data representation and the lack of specific multi-objective optimization methods, existing approaches have drawbacks in dealing with real-world programs. This paper presents a new approach to multi-objective test data generation problems using genetic programming (GP), while two genetic algorithm (GA) based approaches are also implemented for comparison purposes. Furthermore, three multi-objective optimization frameworks are used and compared to examine the performance of the GP-based methods. Experiments have been conducted on two types of test data generation problems: integer and double. Each consists of 160 benchmark programs with different degrees of nesting. The results suggest that the new GP approaches perform much better than the two GA-based approaches, and a random search baseline algorithm.

Keywords: Software testing · Automatic test data generation · Genetic programming · Multi-objective optimization

1 Introduction

A typical software development process consists of four phases: specification, designing, coding and testing, where software testing is an indispensable part to ensure the quality of software products [17]. Traditionally, software products are tested by executing groups of typical test cases selected by test engineers manually for specific test objectives. However, the performance of testing is highly depended on the ability and experience of test engineers. This makes the testing tasks difficult to manage. Furthermore, the labour intensive nature leads software testing to a high cost process. It is estimated that approximately half of

© Springer International Publishing AG 2017
W. Peng et al. (Eds.): AI 2017, LNAI 10400, pp. 169–181, 2017.
DOI: 10.1007/978-3-319-63004-5_14

the project budget is spent on testing [9]. This explains the increasing interests in automatic software testing in both academia and software industry [5].

Search-based software testing is the main sub-area of search-based Software Engineering (SBSE) concerned with automatic software testing [1,8]. SBSE is used to generate test data, prioritize test cases, minimize test suites, optimize software test oracles, reduce human labour cost, verify software models, test service-orientated architectures, construct test suites for interaction testing, and validate real-time properties. Given the fact that test data is the fundamental of almost all software testing processes, search-based test data generation continues to be the major research area with an increasing amount of research.

Search-based test data generation successfully implements automatic test data generation using search techniques, for example, Genetic Algorithms (GAs), Genetic Programming (GP), and Hill Climbing (HC) [15]. In addition to a reduction of oracle cost, search-based test data generation also improves the quality of test suites because of the sufficient search for possible solutions. Currently, the majority of existing approaches focus on single-objective test data generation with a focus on only one objective (e.g. branch coverage which is the degree to which the source code of a program is tested by a particular test suite) while comparatively little study on multi-objective (e.g. considering branch coverage, execution time and memory consumption simultaneously) test data generation [9]. Unfortunately, real-world testing problems are complicated with multiple conflicting objectives and are unlikely to be captured by a single objective.

Among the relatively small amount of multi-objective test data generation research, evolutionary multi-objective optimization (EMO) is the main approach because multiple solutions can be obtained in a single run due to the population based search in evolutionary computation. However, there is not much research on designing specific EMO methods for multi-objective test data generation. Furthermore, as one of the most popular evolutionary algorithms, GAs have been widely used in search-based test data generation. However, binary encoded representation in GAs is not capable of generating complicated test data and many non-functional objectives are difficult to deal with. More effective and specific multi-objective optimization methods can be used to improve the accuracy and efficiency. GP is such an method that is potentially more powerful in dealing with complicated data because of the flexible representation, but this has not been investigated.

Goals: This paper aims to develop a GP based multi-objective test data generator using EMO with the purpose of improving the overall performance and contributing to search-based test data generation. To achieve this goal, we will develop a GP based multi-objective test data generation approach. Due to the flexible representation, this approach is expected to solve more complicated test data generation problems than existing ones. We will investigate the performance of the proposed GP approach by comparing it with other successful evolutionary test data generation approaches.

2   Background

2.1   Search-Based Test Data Generation

In search-based test data generation, the problem is modeled as a numerical function optimization problem and some heuristic is used to solve it. The techniques typically rely on the provision of "guidance", i.e. objectives, to the search process via feedback from program executions. Search-based test data generation for functional testing generally employs a search and optimization technique with the aim of causing assertions at one or more points in the program to be satisfied. There has been a growing interest in such techniques. More and more applications of these techniques to software testing can be seen in recent years. To evaluate the applicability of such approaches many tools have been developed in the past, e.g. TESTGEN [16], Kalman filter-based approach [2] and prioritized pairwise approach [5].

Software testing has multiple objectives, which are branch coverage, memory consumption, time consumption, CPU consumption, etc. Due to the fact that many of the objectives are conflicting to each other, trade-offs should be considered in order to produce desirable test suits. Additionally, a considerable amount of budget can be saved if test data can be generated automatically. However, software testing is a complicated process with different kinds of testing and a variety of objectives. The most popular technique to test programs consists of executing the program with a set of test data. Test engineers select a set of configurations for the Program Under Test (PUT), called test suite, and check the PUT behavior with them. To avoid execute the PUT with all the possible configurations, which is infeasible in practice, the program can be tested with a representative set of test data [5,6]. Therefore, automatic test data generation aims to generate an adequate set of test data in an automatic way to test a program, thus preventing engineers from the task of selecting an adequate set of test data to test the PUT. Therefore, another objective is the minimization of the cost, which can be achieved by minimizing the test suite sizes. So, the software testing problem can be defined:

Let P be a program, B_p denotes its full set of branches and $BranchExec_p(C)$ denotes the set of branches covered in P by the execution of a given set of test data, C. The branch coverage of the test suite C is represented by $BrCov_p(C)$, which is the ratio between the traversed branches in the executions of the program P with C as the set of test data and $|B_p|$ representing the total number of branches of the program, i.e., $BrCov_p(C) = \frac{|BranchExec_p(C)|}{|B_p|}$. The adequacy criterion of branch coverage states that a test suite C for a program P is "adequate" when $BrCov_p(C) = 1$. However, it is not always possible to reach such a perfect coverage, and in case of reaching it, the cost to test the entire program may be unaffordable. Consequently, a balance between coverage and the cost to achieve such a perfect coverage, and in case of reaching it, the cost to test the entire program can be unaffordable. Since the cost of the testing phase depends on the test suites size (the number of test cases in a test suite), minimizing the test suite size, denoted with $|C|$, should be another goal. However, the majority of existing approaches are single objective with a focus on branch coverage [9], and ignore the test suite size.

2.2 Related Work

In the research area of test data generation, the majority research focuses on single-objective test data generation with the aim of achieving an optimal solution on a particular objective. Only a few research papers focus on multi-objective test date generation.

Lakhotia et al. [11] implement and compare two multi-objective approaches for test data generation - Pareto GA and weighted GA. In addition to the objective of branch coverage, they also use the memory consumption as the second objective. However, the limitation is that it is difficult to choose the weights for each objective. Pinto et al. [14] propose two new solution representation for solving multi-objective test data generation problems. In order to have a flexible representation, they use an array list to represent an individual rather than a binary string in GA. Each item in the array list is one single test data. Different types of solutions can be explored in the problem search space with this representation. In order to adapt to more complex testing problems such as object-oriented programs, another representation is proposed. Ghiduk et al. [7] propose a GA-based multi-objective test data generator to automatically generate test data for data-flow coverage criteria.

Oster and Saglietti [13] propose a novel approach to object-oriented test data generation problems. This approach is fully automatic and it can be used in any Java programs without any restriction. This approach focuses on maximizing branch coverage and minimizing the sizes of test suites which are the most popular and useful objectives in test date generation problem. The experimental results show that the approach adopting evolutionary computation methods performs significantly better than the random testing approach.

3 Proposed Approach

In this section, a GP-based approach is proposed to generate software test data, and two GA-based approaches, GA-B and GA-R, are also investigated for comparisons. GP [10] is an evolutionary approach to generating computer programs, commonly represented by a tree, for solving a given problem. A typical GP representation is a tree-like structure, where a function set including a number of operators are used to form the internal nodes of the tree, and a terminal set including variables of the problems and random numbers are used to form the leave nodes of the tree. GP consists of a population of trees, where each individual/tree represents a candidate solution for the target problem. A general GP evolutionary process starts with a random initial population, and the population of individuals are evaluated based on the fitness function, and updated by applying selection, mutation, crossover and reproduction operators. The evolutionary process stops when a predefined stopping criterion is met. Therefore, in the rest

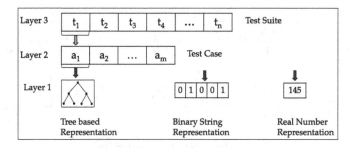

Fig. 1. Three-layer data representation

of the section, we will discuss the representation, the crossover and the mutation operators, the objectives, and the evolutionary multi-objective frameworks.

3.1 Representations

A typical program in a software can contain one or more arguments, several branches and many statements. The test suite for this program contains a set of configurations, each of which is a set of arguments with particular values. The size of a test suite is the number of configurations. The branch coverage is the total proportion of branches executed after executing all the configurations in the test suite.

To represent the data structure in the test data generation problems, this paper adopts a three-layer data representation for each GP individual, as shown in Fig. 1. Different from the traditional single tree based GP, there are multiple trees in each individual. The first layer is a typical GP tree in the GP approach. The terminal sets and function sets are configured regarding the arguments type. The second layer is a set of GP trees. Each tree represents an argument of the PUT and the length is fixed according to the PUT, e.g. for a PUT with three arguments, the length of the second layer is three. Each set of trees in this layer is a single test case. The third layer represents the entire test suite, where its length is unfixed because it is the test suite size, i.e. one of the objectives. This length may change after each crossover and mutation operation.

For comparison purposes, two GA based approaches are also developed in this paper. One approach represents the solutions using a binary strings, which is named GA-B. The other represents the solutions using real numbers, which is named GA-R. These two approaches adopt the same three-layer representation. However, in the first layer, GA-B approach uses binary strings while GA-R approach uses real numbers.

3.2 Crossover

The crossover operation plays an important role in the GP approach. Due to the data presentation structure, this paper adopts a modified crossover operation.

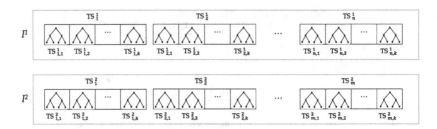

Fig. 2. The selected two individuals

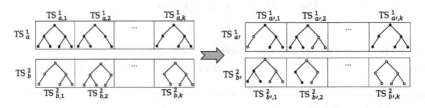

Fig. 3. The crossover operator

Before crossover, two individuals are selected by a selection operation, in this work, a tournament selection scheme is used. Let the selected individuals be I^1 and I^2. I^1 and I^2 may have different lengths, that is, I^1 and I^2 may have different numbers of test cases. Figure 2 shows an example of the structure of I^1 and I^2, where n is the length of individual I^1, m is the length of individual I^2, k is the number of arguments of PUT, and $TS^1_{2,k}$ can be read as the kth tree (for the kth argument of the PUT) of the second test case in parent I^1.

After selecting the individuals as the two parents, I^1 and I^2, we randomly select a tree set TS^1_a from parent I^1 and a tree set TS^2_b from parent I^1. Then we apply the crossover operation to the two tree sets. In detail, for each tree $TS^1_{a,i}$, $c = 1,2 \cdots k$, do crossover operation with the tree $TS^2_{b,i}$. That is, the crossover operation is applied to the GP trees in the same position of the two selected tree sets. For the two GP trees under the crossover operation, we randomly select a node form each of $TS^1_{a,i}$ and $TS^2_{a,i}$, where the probability of selecting a function node type is q_f and that of a terminal node type is q_t, $q_f + q_t = 1$. After selecting one node from each of the two GP trees, we swap the subtrees rooted at the selected nodes. Then we repeat the whole step s times, where s is the length of the shorter individual. Figure 3 shows an example of the crossover operation, where the crossover operation is applied on the second and third trees in both TS^1_a and TS^2_b.

A detailed description of the modified crossover operation is given as follows:

Step (1) Randomly select t (tournament size) individuals from the population using the tournament selection;

Step (2) Select the best two individuals (I^1 and I^2) from the tournament for the crossover operation;

Step (3) Randomly select two tree sets (TS_a^1 and TS_b^2) from I^1 and I^2;

Step (4) Select trees from the same position of TS_a^1 and TS_b^2 as $TS_{a,i}^1$ and $TS_{b,i}^2$;

Step (5) Choose a node type: a function node type is chosen with probability q_f and a terminal node type is selected with probability q_t. Randomly select a node for the chosen type from each of the trees $TS_{a,i}^1$ and $TS_{b,i}^2$.

Step (6) Swap the subtrees rooted at the selected nodes of $TS_{a,i}^1$ and $TS_{b,i}^2$.

Step (7) Repeat Step 3 to Step 6 s times, where s is the length of the shorter individual.

This crossover operation has some interesting aspects. First, we apply crossover operation to individuals with different length. Second, only trees in the same position in a tree set (test case) are applied crossover operation. As a result, programs with different types of arguments can also be handled with this GP approach.

For the GA-B approach, the crossover operation is a modified one-point crossover. It randomly selects two parents and applies the one-point crossover operation on the selected test data using similar strategy to the GP approach. However, because of the nature of real number encoded approaches, GA-R approach does not apply classical crossover operations on individuals.

3.3   Mutation

Mutation operation is also important for test data generation problem. In this process, we change the length of the selected individuals. The mutation operator adds new test cases to the individuals with probability P_{add} (Mutation-Add), deletes one test case with probability P_{delete} (Mutation-Delete) and keeps the individual unchanged with the probability $P_{unchanged}$ (Mutation-Unchanged). $P_{add} + P_{delete} + P_{unchanged} = 1$. Thought this operation, new test cases can be added in to the individuals and the length of them can be changed after each mutation operation.

The GA-B and GA-R approaches adopt the same mutation operation as the GP approach.

3.4   Two Objectives

In this work, we deal with the multi-objective test data generation problems with two conflicting objectives of maximizing the branch coverage and minimizing the test suite size.

3.5   Multi-objective Frameworks

GP was originally proposed as a single objective approach. Recently many different evolutionary multi-objective optimization methods have been proposed. As the first work of using GP for multi-objective test data generation, we would like to introduce popular evolutionary multi-objective search mechanisms to the GP approaches, which are

- Non-dominated Sorting Genetic Algorithms II (NSGAII), introduced by Deb et al. [3]
- The Strength Pareto Evolutionary Algorithm (SPEA2) is a multi-objective evolutionary algorithm proposed by Zitler et al. [18].
- Multi-Objective Cellular Genetic Algorithm (MOCell), proposed by Nebro et al. [12], is a cellular genetic algorithm which is new but performs better than NSGA-II in some situations [5,12].

The details of NSGAII, SPEA2, and MOCell are not presented here and readers are referred to the corresponding literature. The overall structure of the proposed GP-based multi-objective test data generations will follow the basic structure of these three multi-objective approaches by using the new representation, crossover, mutation and objectives described above.

4   Experiment Configuration

4.1   Benchmark

Ferrer et al. [4] developed a benchmark generator for software testers aiming to provide standard benchmark of programs to be used for comparing test data generators. This generator is designed to automatically generate programs with all branches reachable on the basis of certain features defined by the users. As a result, it is capable of generating significantly different programs in order to comprehensively compare different multi-objective test data generators. The current version of this benchmark generator can only generate programs with integer inputs, so that we propose to adopt more programs with double inputs.

The experiments used 160 Java programs with integer input and 160 Java programs with double input as the benchmarks to evaluate the performance of the proposed multi-objective methods. These programs cover four nesting degrees on the basis of the numbers of branches.

4.2   Parameter Settings

Using the three representations (i.e. GP with tree based encoding, GAs with binary encoding and GAs with real-value encoding) and the three multi-objective frameworks (i.e. NSGAII, SPEA2 and MOCell), nine different methods are investigated in this paper, which are denoted as NSGP, SGP, MCGP, NSGAB, SPGAB, MCGAB, NSGAR, SGAR, and MCGAR.

In the three GP based methods, each individual is encoded as a tree based three-layer structure. The population size is 200 and the maximum number of generations is 100, that is, 20000 evaluations in total. Binary tournament selection, the modified crossover and mutation operators described in the previous section are applied, where the mutation operation adds new test cases with the probability of 0.2, deletes one test case with the probability of 0.6 and keeps the individual unchanged with the probability of 0.2. The function set consists of addition, subtraction, multiplication and protected division. The terminal set consists of random real numbers. The max tree depth is 5.

In the six GA based methods, the total number of evaluations is also 20000, but the population size is 20 [11,14]. Binary tournament selection, the modified crossover and mutation operators are also applied in the GA based methods with the same setting as in the GP methods. In the GA-R methods, the range of random number is from −32768 to 32767 which is a commonly used range of integers. In the GA-B methods, each number is encoded as an 8-bit string regard to the input ranges of the benchmarks.

For the purpose of evaluating the evolutionary approaches, a random multi-objective test data generation approach is implemented as a baseline approach. This approach randomly produces test suites for the input Java programs. The final result of this approach is a set of all the non-dominated solutions found. The total number of solutions generated by the random methods is 20000, which is the same as the total number of evaluations in the evolutionary multi-objective methods.

All the methods have been conducted for 50 independent runs on each benchmark program. Hypervolume (HV), a commonly used multi-objective performance indicator, is used to compare the performance of different algorithms, where the best solutions achieve by all the methods are used as reference points.

5   Results and Discussions

5.1   Integer Problems

Since it is extremely hard to present the results of the nine algorithms on 160 benchmark programs, we summarized the results into two tables. Table 1 shows that on different nesting degrees, the number of times that one algorithm has the best median HV value (median of the 50 runs) among the nine algorithms. The total number is greater than 160 because there may exist two or multiple algorithms have the same best HV value on a benchmark program. Since the branch coverage is more important than the size of the test suits, we also presents the comparisons between the nine algorithms in terms of the median branch coverage results, which are shown in Table 2.

According to Table 1, overall, the MCGP achieved the best HV values or the best solutions in 88 out of the 160 benchmark programs, i.e. better than the other eight methods. The second best algorithm is NSGP, which obtained the best solutions in 55 cases. NSGAR, SPGARand SPGARo btained the best solutions only in a small number of cases. The random search baseline algorithm did not obtain any best solution in the 160 benchmark problems. Such patterns can be observed from the benchmarks with all the four different nesting degrees.

Comparing the three different multi-objective frameworks, MOCell provides a better searching mechanism for automated test data generation problems, evidenced by the superior performance of MCGP. SPEA2 performed the worst, where only SPGAR achieved the best solution in 4 cases. In terms of the representation, the proposed GP representation achieved the best solutions in 143

Table 1. Summary of the integer results

Approaches	Nesting Degree				
	1	2	3	4	Total
NSGP	15	12	17	11	55
NSGAB	0	0	0	0	0
NSGAR	0	0	0	1	1
SPGP	0	0	0	0	0
SPGAB	0	0	0	0	0
SPGAR	1	1	1	1	4
MCGP	21	24	20	23	88
MCGAB	0	0	0	0	0
MCGAR	2	4	2	2	10
Random	0	0	0	0	0

Table 2. Summary of the integer results according to branch coverage

Approaches	Nesting degree				
	1	2	3	4	Total
NSGP	31	27	26	27	111
NSGAB	0	0	0	0	0
NSGAR	0	1	0	0	1
SPGP	12	11	11	5	39
SPGAB	0	0	0	0	0
SPGAR	1	1	0	0	2
MCGP	25	26	18	21	90
MCGAB	1	1	0	0	2
MCGAR	0	0	0	0	0
Random	0	0	0	0	0

out of the 160 benchmark programs, which is much better than the integer and double representations. The reasons might be that the tree structure is more flexible and the three-level structure is rich for producing good solutions. The binary encoding does not perform better than the real-value encoding, which might be due to that each integer number is encoded by 8 bits, leading to a higher dimension in the binary encoding than in the real-value encoding. All the three encoding schemes achieved better performance than random search.

Furthermore, according to Table 2, the three GP methods achieved the best branch coverage on almost all the benchmark problems. One reason might be that the GP approach has a larger search space that it has the potential to find test cases covering more branches. Additionally, all the GA-B, GA-R and GP approaches perform much better than the random search approach.

5.2   Double Problems

Table 3 shows that on different nesting degrees in double benchmark problems, the number of times that one algorithm has the best median HV value (median of the 50 runs) among the nine algorithms. The sum of the numbers is greater than 160 because there may exist two or more algorithms have the same best HV value on a benchmark program. Since the branch coverage is more important than the test suits size, we also presents the comparisons between the nine algorithms in terms of the median branch coverage results, which are shown in Table 4.

According to Table 3, the NSGP and MCGP methods achieved the best HV values or the best solutions on almost all the benchmark problems. Only in 3 cases, SPGP achieved the best or the same best solutions compared with

Table 3. Summary of the double results

Approaches	Nesting degree				
	1	2	3	4	Total
NSGP	26	18	20	19	83
NSGAB	0	0	0	0	0
NSGAR	0	0	0	0	0
SPGP	2	0	1	0	3
SPGAB	0	0	0	0	0
SPGAR	0	0	0	0	0
MCGP	15	22	20	21	78
MCGAB	0	0	0	0	0
MCGAR	0	0	0	0	0
Random	0	0	0	0	0

Table 4. Summary of the double results according to branch coverage

Approaches	Nesting degree				
	1	2	3	4	Total
NSGP	30	26	27	26	109
NSGAB	0	0	0	0	0
NSGAR	0	1	0	0	1
SPGP	12	12	11	4	39
SPGAB	0	0	0	0	0
SPGAR	1	1	0	0	2
MCGP	26	26	17	23	92
MCGAB	1	1	0	0	2
MCGAR	0	0	0	0	0
Random	0	0	0	0	0

NSGP and MCGP. All of them achieved better performance than the random search method. Comparing the three multi-objective frameworks, both NSGAII and MOCell performed better than SPEA2. Furthermore, the GP methods with the tree-based representation achieved the best solutions on all the benchmark problems. Furthermore, according to Table 4, the three GP methods achieved the best branch coverages on almost all the benchmark problems, which may be due to the same reasons described above.

6   Conclusions and Future Work

This paper presents a new approach to multi-objective test data generation using GP, where a new representation, and corresponding crossover and mutation operators were proposed to generate test suites with the objectives of maximizing the branch coverage and minimizing the test suite size. Three multi-objective optimization frameworks (NSGAII, SPEA2 and MOCell) are used to investigate the potential of GP based multi-objective test data generation approaches. Two different kinds of benchmark programs are adopted to examine the performance of the new approaches. A random search approach and two GA-based methods are implemented as baselines for comparison. The results suggest that the new GP approaches perform the best on the two types of benchmark programs.

This is a preliminary work, but can show the ability of the flexible three-based representation in GP for multi-objective software testing data generation. In the future, we would like to work on handling multi-objective test data generation problem involving tree-based GP techniques. This paper only involves three of the software testing objectives, branch coverage, test suite size and execution time. More objectives can be involved and analyzed in the further work such as CPU consumption, memory consumption, path coverage, instruction coverage, line coverage etc. In addition, more complex problems can be handled by extending the tree-based GP approach. For example, dealing with classes and lists may also be interesting for handling the increasing number of object-oriented programs.

References

1. Afzal, W., Torkar, R., Feldt, R.: A systematic review of search-based testing for non-functional system properties. Inf. Softw. Technol. **51**(6), 957–976 (2009)
2. Aleti, A., Grunske, L.: Test data generation with a kalman filter-based adaptive genetic algorithm. J. Syst. Softw. **103**, 343–352 (2015)
3. Deb, K., Pratap, A., Agarwal, S., Meyarivan, T.: A fast and elitist multiobjective genetic algorithm: NSGA-II. IEEE Trans. Evol. Comput. **6**(2), 182–197 (2002)
4. Ferrer, J., Chicano, F., Alba, E.: Benchmark generator for software testers. In: Iliadis, L., Maglogiannis, I., Papadopoulos, H. (eds.) AIAI/EANN - 2011. IAICT, vol. 364, pp. 378–388. Springer, Heidelberg (2011). doi:10.1007/978-3-642-23960-1_45
5. Ferrer, J., Chicano, F., Alba, E.: Evolutionary algorithms for the multi-objective test data generation problem. Softw.: Pract. Exp. **42**(11), 1331–1362 (2012)

6. Galler, S.J., Aichernig, B.K.: Survey on test data generation tools. Int. J. Softw. Tools Technol. Transfer **16**(6), 727–751 (2014)
7. Ghiduk, A.S., Harrold, M.J., Girgis, M.R.: Using genetic algorithms to aid test-data generation for data-flow coverage. In: 14th Asia-Pacific Software Engineering Conference, APSEC 2007, pp. 41–48. IEEE (2007)
8. Harman, M., Jia, Y., Langdon, W.B.: Strong higher order mutation-based test data generation. In: Proceedings of the 19th ACM SIGSOFT Symposium and the 13th European Conference on Foundations of Software Engineering, pp. 212–222. ACM (2011)
9. Harman, M., Jia, Y., Zhang, Y.: Achievements, open problems and challenges for search based software testing. In: IEEE 8th International Conference on Software Testing, Verification and Validation (ICST), pp. 1–12. IEEE (2015)
10. Koza, J.R.: Introduction to genetic programming tutorial: from the basics to human-competitive results. In: Proceedings of the 12th Annual Conference Companion on Genetic and Evolutionary Computation, pp. 2137–2262. ACM (2010)
11. Lakhotia, K., Harman, M., McMinn, P.: A multi-objective approach to search-based test data generation. In: Proceedings of the 9th Annual Conference on Genetic and Evolutionary Computation, pp. 1098–1105. ACM (2007)
12. Nebro, A.J., Durillo, J.J., Luna, F., Dorronsoro, B., Alba, E.: Mocell: a cellular genetic algorithm for multiobjective optimization. Int. J. Intell. Syst. **24**(7), 726–746 (2009)
13. Oster, N., Saglietti, F.: Automatic test data generation by multi-objective optimisation. In: Górski, J. (ed.) SAFECOMP 2006. LNCS, vol. 4166, pp. 426–438. Springer, Heidelberg (2006). doi:10.1007/11875567_32
14. Pinto, G.H., Vergilio, S.R.: A multi-objective genetic algorithm to test data generation. In: 2010 22nd IEEE International Conference on Tools with Artificial Intelligence (ICTAI), vol. 1, pp. 129–134. IEEE (2010)
15. Sahin, O., Akay, B.: Comparisons of metaheuristic algorithms and fitness functions on software test data generation. Appl. Soft Comput. **49**, 1202–1214 (2016)
16. Tracey, N.J.: A search-based automated test-data generation framework for safety-critical software. Ph.D. thesis, Citeseer (2000)
17. Wang, Z., Tang, K., Yao, X.: Multi-objective approaches to optimal testing resource allocation in modular software systems. IEEE Trans. Reliab. **59**(3), 563–575 (2010)
18. Zitzler, E., Laumanns, M., Thiele, L., Zitzler, E., Zitzler, E., Thiele, L., Thiele, L.: SPEA2: improving the strength Pareto evolutionary algorithm (2001)

Class Dependent Multiple Feature Construction Using Genetic Programming for High-Dimensional Data

Binh Tran, Bing Xue$^{(\boxtimes)}$, and Mengjie Zhang

School of Engineering and Computer Science, Victoria University of Wellington,
PO Box 600, Wellington 6140, New Zealand
{binh.tran,bing.xue,mengjie.zhang}@ecs.vuw.ac.nz

Abstract. Genetic Programming (GP) has shown promise in feature construction where high-level features are formed by combining original features using predefined functions or operators. Multiple feature construction methods have been proposed for high-dimensional data with thousands of features. Results of these methods show that several constructed features can maintain or even improve the discriminating ability of the original feature set. However, some particular features may have better ability than other features to distinguish instances of one class from other classes. Therefore, it may be more difficult to construct a better discriminating feature when combing features that are relevant to different classes. In this study, we propose a new GP-based feature construction method called CDFC that constructs multiple features, each of which focuses on distinguishing one class from other classes. We propose a new representation for class-dependent feature construction and a new fitness function to better evaluate the constructed feature set. Results on eight datasets with varying difficulties showed that the features constructed by CDFC can improve the discriminating ability of thousands of original features in most cases. Results also showed that CFDC is more effective and efficient than the hybrid MGPFC method which was shown to have better performance than standard GP to feature construction.

Keywords: Genetic programming · Class-dependent · Feature construction · Feature selection · Classification · High-dimensional data

1 Introduction

More and more high-dimensional data appears in machine learning especially in classification thanks to the advances in data collection technologies [15]. With thousands of features, these datasets bring challenges to learning algorithms not only because of the curse of dimensionality but also the existence of many irrelevant and redundant features. Therefore, dimensionality reduction is an essential step in preprocessing these datasets. By eliminating irrelevant and redundant features, feature selection is a popular technique for this purpose. In addition to

© Springer International Publishing AG 2017
W. Peng et al. (Eds.): AI 2017, LNAI 10400, pp. 182–194, 2017.
DOI: 10.1007/978-3-319-63004-5_15

feature selection, feature construction is also promising in reducing the number of features by creating a smaller number of high-level features from the original ones while maintaining or even improving the discriminating ability of the data.

Feature construction methods can be categorised into wrapper, filter, or embedded based on how a learning algorithm is involved in the feature construction process [6]. Wrapper methods use a learning algorithm to evaluate the goodness of the constructed features, while a measure based on data characteristics is used in filter methods. Therefore, filters are usually faster than wrappers while wrappers usually acquire higher classification accuracy than filters. In order to synthesise strengths of both approaches, combination of filter and wrapper (or hybrid) has been proposed in [11] as well. Different from wrappers and filters, embedded methods construct features during the process of learning a model.

Compared to feature selection, feature construction is more challenging due to its large search space. Feature construction has to choose informative features from 2^N possible combinations of N features and appropriate operators to combine them. Because of the high complexity, feature construction methods need a global and powerful search technique to generate better high-level features.

Genetic programming (GP) [7] is an evolutionary computation technique which can automatically evolve good solutions or models from a population of potential ones. Using a predefined fitness function, individuals are evaluated and selected to evolve new solutions using crossover or mutation. The process of evaluation-selection-evolution will be continued until a stopping criterion is met. Then GP returns the fittest individual found so far as the best solution. GP has shown promise for feature construction in general [10,12] as well as in high-dimensional data [1,12]. The most popular representation of constructed features in GP is tree with internal nodes being operators (e.g. $+$, $-$, etc.) and terminal nodes being original features.

GP has been proposed for multiple feature construction for high-dimensional data using either single-tree [1] or multiple-tree [11] representation. Results of these methods have shown that GP is promising in feature construction. However, some particular features may have better ability than other features to distinguish instances of one class from other classes [13]. For example, a feature may be good at distinguishing samples of class A from those of class B, C and D, but may not be good at differentiating samples of class B from those of C and D. Therefore, it may be more difficult to construct a better discriminating feature when combing features that are relevant to different classes. In this study, we propose a new multiple feature construction method that takes into account class-dependency in selecting features for feature construction.

Goals

This study proposes a class-dependent feature construction (CDFC) method using GP for high-dimensional data. CDFC constructs a small number of new high-level features, each of which focuses on distinguishing one class from other classes. The small set of constructed features is expected to improve the classification performance of common learning algorithms including k-Nearest Neighbour

(KNN), Naive Bayes (NB) and Decision Tree (DT). Performance of the CDFC constructed features will be tested and compared with the original feature set and those constructed by the hybrid MGPFC method [11]. Since [11] has shown a better performance achieved by MGPFC over standard GP, we do not compare CDFC with standard GP to save space in this paper. Specifically, we will investigate the following research objectives:

- How to construct class-dependent features;
- Whether the class-dependent constructed features achieve better classification accuracy than the original full feature set and those constructed by MGPFC;
- Whether the features selected by CDFC have better discriminating features than those selected by MGPFC; and
- Whether CDFC is faster than MGPFC.

2   Related Work

GP has been used to solve different tasks such as classification [6], feature selection [9], and feature construction [10]. Here we only review the prior work related to GP for feature construction. Readers are referred to [6,14] for broader and more comprehensive reviews.

GP has been proposed to construct multiple features using different strategies. In [8], each individual comprised of $2m$ trees representing m new features and m hidden features where m is the desired number of constructed features. Hidden features are good features which are kept out of the evolutionary process to avoid loosing them. The results showed that constructed features improved the DT performance on five out of six datasets. Cooperative coevolutionary GP was also proposed to construct m new features in [3] using m populations. Another approach is to run a single-tree GP method multiple times [10] to construct multiple features, each for one class. Experiments on datasets with small numbers of features showed promising results. However, this approach required to run GP as many times as the number of constructed features, which may be inefficient especially for high-dimensional data.

For high-dimensional data, Ahmed et al. [1] proposed to use a single-tree GP representation to construct multiple features from all possible subtrees of the best individual. Two fitness functions were proposed to create two feature construction methods; one uses classification accuracy of random forest (RF), and the other uses entropy gain of RF and the p-value of an ANOVA test on the selected features. Results showed that the latter had better generalisation ability with a smaller number of features than the former. However, the features constructed in this way may be redundant since one subtree can be a multiplication of a constant with its subtree, generating two correlated features from these subtrees. This may explain why their performance is inferior to the combination of the constructed feature from the root and the selected features in terminal nodes as demonstrated in [12]. Multiple-tree GP was proposed in [11] to construct as many features as required based on a user-defined ratio. Using a hybrid approach of filter and wrapper in evaluating the constructed features, the proposed method obtained a better results than [12].

In summary, with a very flexible representation and a global search technique, GP has shown its high potential in feature construction. However, constructing features from class-dependent features which could potentially further improve the performance has not been investigated.

3   The Proposed Method CDFC

3.1   Representation

The aim of this study is to construct multiple features, each of which focuses on discriminating one class from the others. Furthermore, constructing only one feature per class may not be enough to represent complex problems. Therefore, CDFC allows to construct multiple features for one class depending on a user given ratio r which can be 1, 2, 3, etc. The number of constructed features m is equal to r multiplied by the number of classes. For example, with a given ratio $r = 2$, CDFC will construct $m = 4$ features for a binary-class problem, and $m = 6$ features for a problem with 3 classes. Each GP individual has m trees, each of which corresponds to one constructed feature of a class. Figure 1 shows an example of a GP individual with $r = 1$ for a three-class problem.

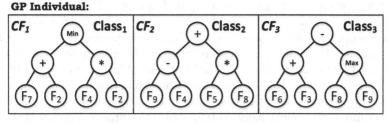

⇨ **1. Constructed feature set:**   CF$_1$, CF$_2$, CF$_3$
- CF$_1$ = Min ((F$_7$ + F$_2$), (F$_4$ * F$_2$))
- CF$_2$ = (F$_9$ - F$_4$) + (F$_5$ * F$_8$)
- CF$_3$ = (F$_6$ + F$_3$) - Max (F$_8$, F$_9$))

⇨ **2. Selected feature set:**   **F$_2$, F$_3$, F$_4$, F$_5$, F$_6$, F$_7$, F$_8$, F$_9$**

Fig. 1. Representation of a GP individual and the generated feature sets.

3.2   Class-Dependent Terminal Sets

Since one constructed feature aims at discriminating instances of a class (c) from instances of other classes, it should be constructed based on features that are relevant to class c. In other words, constructed features of different classes should select different sets of features. Therefore, different trees in an individual will have different terminal sets, each of which comprises of features that are relevant to the focused class only. Since one feature may be important to different classes, there may be overlap between different terminal sets.

A feature f is relevant to class c if its values appeared in class c are significantly different from its values in other classes. In CDFC, t-Test is used to measure how relevant a feature f is to class c. First of all, values of f will be divided into two groups, one comprises values belonging to class c and one from other classes. Then, the relevant measure $Rel_{f,c}$ is calculated based on Eq. (1). $Rel_{f,c}$ is set to 0 if two groups are not significantly different (i.e. p-value ≥ 0.05). Otherwise, it is equal to the absolute of t-value divided by p-value. Therefore, the larger the value of $Rel_{f,c}$, the more relevant the feature f to class c.

$$Rel_{f,c} = \begin{cases} 0, & \text{if p-value} \geq 0.05 \\ \dfrac{|\textbf{t-value}(f_{class=c}, f_{class \neq c})|}{\textbf{p-value}}, & \text{otherwise} \end{cases} \tag{1}$$

For each class c, features are ranked by its $Rel_{f,c}$ values. Then half of the top-ranked features will be used to form the terminal set of class c. By doing so, we not only eliminate irrelevant features but also narrow the search space so that the searching process will be more efficient.

3.3 A New Fitness Function

To evaluate an individual, its m constructed features are used to transform the training set into a new training set with m features. The discriminating ability of the transformed dataset indicates how good the constructed features are. While a wrapper measure based on a learning algorithm can improve its classification accuracy, the constructed features may not be general for other learning algorithms. Furthermore, the computational cost of wrappers is usually high. Therefore, in this study, we propose a new fitness function using two filter measures that are simple and fast to calculate, and can provide a good indicator for data discriminating ability. Equation (2) shows the fitness function that maximises two measures combined using a weight α. Individual size is used as a pressure for small-tree preference when two individuals have the same measure values.

$$Fitness = \alpha \cdot AvgIG + (1 - \alpha) \cdot Distance - 10^{-7} \cdot indSize \tag{2}$$

The first measure is the average information gain (IG) of the constructed features which is calculated based on Eq. (3) where f_{max} is the best feature with the highest IG among m constructed features. The f_{max}'s IG is added to bias toward those candidates that have f_{max} with higher IG. IG of feature f is calculated based on unconditional and conditional entropy H as in Eq. (4). Finally, $AvgIG$ is divided by the best IG to scale it to the range of [0,1].

$$AvgIG = \frac{\displaystyle\sum_{i=1}^{m} IG(f_i, class) + IG(f_{max}, class)}{(m+1)(\log_2 nbr\_classes)} \tag{3}$$

$$IG(f, class) = H(class) - H(class|f) \tag{4}$$

Although IG is a good measure for feature relevancy, it can only evaluate features individually. Therefore, it can not show how good the whole set of constructed features in discriminating instances of different classes. Therefore, we combine IG with distance measure to overcome this limitation. In CDFC, we use the *Distance* measure [2] as shown in Eq. (5) to maximise the distance of instances *between* class (D_b) and minimise the distance of instances *within* the same class (D_w). Therefore, the larger the *Distance* value, the better the feature set. As a result, the proposed fitness function is a maximisation function where α defines the weight of the IG measure.

D_b is approximated by the average distance between an instance and its nearest miss which is the nearest instance of other classes. D_w is approximated by the average distance between an instance and its farthest hit which is of the same class. Let S be the training set, they are computed based on Eqs. (6 and 7).

$$Distance = \frac{1}{1 + e^{-5(D_b - D_w)}} \tag{5}$$

$$D_b = \frac{1}{|S|} \sum_{i=1}^{|S|} \min_{\{j|j \neq i, class(V_i) \neq class(V_j)\}} Dis(V_i, V_j) \tag{6}$$

$$D_w = \frac{1}{|S|} \sum_{i=1}^{|S|} \max_{\{j|j \neq i, class(V_i) = class(V_j)\}} Dis(V_i, V_j) \tag{7}$$

where $Dis(V_i, V_j)$ is an approximate distance between two vectors V_i and V_j. In this study, we use Czekanowski distance [4] which is calculated based on the shared portion between two vectors as shown in Eq. (8). Its value is bounded in the interval [0,1] where 1 is the best case showing two dissimilar vectors.

$$Czekanowski(V_i, V_j) = 1 - \frac{2\sum_{d=1}^{m} \min(V_{id}, V_{jd})}{\sum_{d=1}^{m} (V_{id} + V_{jd})} \tag{8}$$

3.4 The Overall System

Figure 2 shows the overall system of CDFC. Based on the training set, CDFC forms different terminal sets for different classes using the relevance measure in Eq. (1). These terminal sets are then input to GP for class-dependent feature construction. The best individual is used to generate the constructed and selected feature sets as described in Fig. 1. The training and test sets will be transformed based on these feature sets and used to evaluate the performance of CDFC.

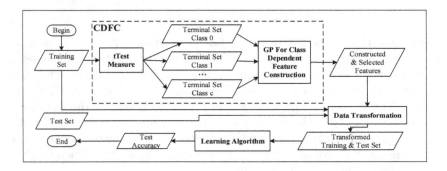

Fig. 2. CDFC overall system.

4   Experiment Design

Datasets. To test the performance of CDFC, eight gene datasets[1] with thousands to tens of thousands of features are used in the experiments. As shown in Table 1, the number of instances of these datasets are much smaller than the numbers of features, which makes these problems challenging due to the curse of dimensionality. On top of that, they are more challenging due to the unbalanced class distribution as shown in the last column of the table.

Table 1. Datasets

Dataset	#Features	#Ins.	#Class	Class 1	Class 2	Class 3	Class 4
Colon	2,000	62	2	35%	65%	-	-
DLBCL	5,469	77	2	25%	75%	-	-
Leukemia	7,129	72	2	35%	65%	-	-
CNS	7,129	60	2	35%	65%	-	-
Prostate	10,509	102	2	50%	50%	-	-
Ovarian	15,154	253	2	36%	64%	-	-
Leukemia1	5,327	72	3	13%	35%	53%	-
SRBCT	2,308	83	4	13%	22%	30%	34%

Another challenge when working with gene expression data is the existence of noise generated during microarray experiments involving reverse transcription, hybridisation of the samples, etc. Therefore, in this study, data is pre-processed before entering the feature construction process using a simple discretisation method suggested in [5] and used in [11,12]. Each feature is first standardised to have zero mean and unit variance. Then its values are discretised into −1, 0

---

[1] These datasets are publicly available at http://www.gems-system.org, and http://csse.szu.edu.cn/staff/zhuzx/Datasets.html.

and 1 representing three states which are the under-expression, the baseline and the over-expression of gene. Values that are in $[-0.5, 0.5]$ will belong to state 0. Values that are smaller than -0.5 or larger than 0.5 will belong to state -1 or 1, respectively.

Experiment Configuration and Parameter Settings. Due to the small number of instances in each dataset, 10-fold cross validation (10F-CV) is used to generate training and test set for evaluating CDFC performance. As GP is a stochastic algorithm, 30 independent runs of CDFC with 30 different random seeds are applied on each training set. Average of 300 results (30×10) are used in comparisons to eliminate statistical variations. Performance of the constructed and selected feature sets generated by CDFC is compared with the original feature set and those created by MGPFC using the average test accuracy of KNN, NB and DT.

Table 2. GP and parameter settings

Function set	$+, -, \times, max, if$	Generations	50
Population size	#features x β	Crossover rate	0.8
Initial population	Ramped half-and half	Mutation rate	0.2
Maximum tree depth	8	Elitism size	1
Selection method	Tournament method	Tournament size	7
CF_Ratio r	2	Fitness weighting α	0.8

Table 2 describes the parameter settings of GP. CDFC uses the same settings as MGPFC. The function set comprises of 3 arithmetic operators $(+, -, \times)$, max function which returns the maximum values from the two inputs and if function which returns the second argument if the first argument is positive and returns the third argument otherwise. No constant values are used in terminal set for simplicity. The population size is set proportional to the dimensionality of the problem using a coefficient β which is set to 3 for Colon dataset and to 2 for others due to memory limit.

5   Results and Analysis

5.1   Performance of the Constructed Features

Table 3 shows the average test accuracy of KNN, NB and DT using constructed features obtained from 30 independent runs of CDFC compared with "Full" (i.e. using the original feature set) and MGPFC [11]. For each learning algorithm, the best (B), the mean and standard deviation (M ± Std) results are displayed. The best result among the three compared methods on each dataset is highlighted. In

Table 3. Results of the constructed features

Dataset	Method	#F	B-KNN	M ± Std-KNN	S_1	B-NB	M ± Std-NB	S_2	B-DT	M ± Std-DT	S_3
Colon (62)	Full	2000	74.28		−	72.62		−	74.29		−
	MGPFC	4	85.47	72.48 ± 5.95	−	85.48	71.10 ± 6.32	−	85.48	71.42 ± 5.82	−
	CDFC	4	88.81	**82.09 ± 3.16**		90.47	**83.89 ± 2.75**		87.38	**77.68 ± 4.35**	
DLBCL (77)	Full	5469	84.46		−	81.96		−	80.89		−
	MGPFC	4	97.32	89.50 ± 3.23	−	97.32	89.01 ± 3.55	−	94.82	87.47 ± 4.34	−
	CDFC	4	98.75	**95.76 ± 2.10**		98.75	**95.28 ± 2.24**		95.00	**90.31 ± 3.27**	
Leuk (72)	Full	7129	88.57		−	91.96		−	91.61		+
	MGPFC	4	95.89	92.71 ± 1.89	−	95.89	92.45 ± 1.88	−	95.89	90.99 ± 2.76	=
	CDFC	4	98.57	**94.80 ± 1.73**		97.32	**93.92 ± 1.49**		94.46	90.19 ± 2.46	
CNS (60)	Full	7129	56.67		−	58.33		−	50.00		−
	MGPFC	4	71.67	58.00 ± 8.27	−	71.67	58.67 ± 7.88	−	78.33	58.00 ± 8.93	=
	CDFC	4	71.67	**65.39 ± 4.03**		71.67	**65.94 ± 3.44**		68.34	**61.00 ± 5.39**	
Prostate (102)	Full	10509	81.55		−	60.55		−	86.18		−
	MGPFC	4	92.18	86.44 ± 3.08	−	92.18	85.89 ± 2.73	−	91.27	85.29 ± 3.04	−
	CDFC	4	95.18	**92.43 ± 1.75**		96.09	**92.41 ± 1.52**		94.09	**88.30 ± 2.52**	
Ovarian (253)	Full	15154	91.28		−	90.05		−	98.41		−
	MGPFC	4	100.00	99.23 ± 0.40	−	100.00	99.23 ± 0.52	−	99.60	98.82 ± 0.50	=
	CDFC	4	100.00	**99.79 ± 0.31**		100.00	**99.59 ± 0.32**		99.60	**98.86 ± 0.56**	
Leuk1 (72)	Full	5327	88.57		−	88.75		−	94.46		+
	MGPFC	6	95.89	89.53 ± 3.25	−	95.89	91.55 ± 2.70	=	95.89	91.53 ± 2.07	+
	CDFC	6	95.89	**92.87 ± 1.86**		95.89	**92.49 ± 2.03**		94.46	88.79 ± 3.41	
SRBCT (83)	Full	2308	80.83		−	97.50		+	72.36		−
	MGPFC	8	95.14	87.80 ± 3.74	−	94.03	87.69 ± 3.87	−	91.39	83.10 ± 4.45	−
	CDFC	8	100.00	**95.91 ± 1.74**		100.00	94.87 ± 2.51		93.89	**87.84 ± 3.01**	

addition, the Wilcoxon significance test is applied on the results with 5% significance level. Its results for KNN, NB and DT are displayed in column S_1, S_2, and S_3, respectively. "+" or "−" indicates that the corresponding method is significantly better or worse than the proposed method CDFC. "=" means they have similar performance. In other worse, the more "−", the better the proposed method.

CDFC Versus Full. All the "−"s appeared in column S_1 of Table 3 show that the constructed features help KNN achieve significantly higher accuracy than using full feature sets on all the eight datasets. The highest improvement is on SRBCT dataset with 15% on average and 20% in the best case, reaching 100% accuracy. The modest improvement is still 4% on average and 10% in the best case on Leukemia. The results show that the discriminating ability of the constructed features is much higher than the original all features although the number of constructed features is negligible to the original dimensionality.

For NB, the features constructed by CDFC also obtain better performance than Full on almost all datasets. For example, using the 4 constructed features on Prostate dataset, NB achieves 32% higher accuracy than using the whole 10,509 features. Similarly on Colon and CNS, the improvement is 11% and 14% on average with 18% and 17% in the best case, respectively. Only on SRBCT, CDFC has about 2.6% lower accuracy than Full. However, the best accuracy achieved by CDFC is 100% which is 2.5% higher than the Full accuracy.

Compared to using Full, DT using features constructed by CDFC also has significantly better performance on six datasets. An improvement of at least 10% on average accuracy is achieved on three datasets, namely SRBCT, CNS and DLBCL, with the best accuracy improved from 15% to 21%. CDFC obtains about 1% and 6% lower average accuracy than Full on Leukemia and Leukemia1. However, their best results are higher and equal to Full, respectively.

In general, over 24 comparisons with Full using the three learning algorithms on 8 datasets, CDFC wins 21 and loses 3 in terms of average accuracy. However, in term of the best accuracy, CDFC outperforms Full in all 24 cases except for the NB result on SRBCT. Results showed that CDFC can construct a very small number of features with high discrimination and generalised well to the three learning algorithms in most cases.

CDFC Versus MGPFC. As shown in Table 3, although both methods construct the same number of features, KNN using features constructed by CDFC achieves significantly better performance than using those of MGPFC on all datasets. The highest improvement of 10% on average is found on Colon which MGPFC failed to maintain its Full accuracy. The results show that using terminal sets comprising of features that are relevant to a specific class, CDFC achieves much better results than MGPFC, allowing it to obtain the best KNN accuracy on all datasets.

Similarly, NB using features constructed by CDFC achieves better accuracy on 7 datasets than using those constructed by MGPFC. Among these datasets, CDFC further improves the performance of MGPFC from 6% to 12% on 5 datasets. Only on Leukemia1, CDFC obtains a similar accuracy as MGPFC.

For DT, features constructed by CDFC obtain significantly better performance than those of MGPFC on four datasets, namely Colon, DLBCL, Prostate and SRBCT with a further improvement of 3% to 6%. Among the other five datasets, CDFC has similar performance as MGPFC on four and worse on one.

In summary, features constructed by CDFC have significantly better performance than those constructed by MGPFC on 19 cases, similar on 4 and worse on 1. Note that results of CDFC on almost all datasets have smaller standard deviation than MGPFC despite of the learning algorithms being used. This indicates that by constraining the terminal sets to class relevant features, the performance of CDFC is better and more stable than MGPFC.

5.2   Performance of the Selected Features

To further investigate CDFC's performance, we also compared the performance of CDFC selected features with those selected by MGPFC. Figure 3 shows the differences in performance of KNN, NB and DT when using features selected by the two methods. The larger the difference, the better the performance of CDFC. If the difference is significantly different, a "*" is displayed above the corresponding bar.

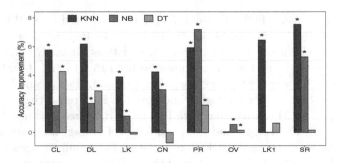

Fig. 3. Improvement of CDFC over MGPFC using the selected features (in colour).

As can be seen from Fig. 3, KNN combined with CDFC has significantly higher accuracy than with MGPFC on seven datasets. Among the three learning algorithms, KNN also has the largest improvements on six out of the eight datasets. NB has better performance on 6 datasets and similar on the remaining two. Similar pattern is seen in DT. Although the DT accuracy on CNS degrades 0.72%, the difference is not significant.

In general, over the 24 comparisons, CDFC selected features have significantly better performance than MGPFC on 17 cases and perform similar to MGPFC on the remaining 7 cases. The results indicate that by forming terminal sets with class-relevant features, thus narrowing the GP search space, CDFC can select more relevant features. These features are then used to construct features leading to further improvement in some datasets, e.g. from less than 2% to more than 12% for NB on the Colon dataset as shown in Table 3.

Another component contributing to CDFC superior performance is the new fitness function. Although both methods use the same distance measure described in Sect. 3.3, they also use an additional different measure in their fitness functions. While CDFC uses average IG, MGPFC uses average accuracy of DT. Although IG is the base measure of DT, the two fitness functions behave differently, leading to a significant improvement in the performance of CDFC. Using average IG, CDFC tries to maximise IG of all constructed features. On the other hand, using DT accuracy, MGPFC searches toward those set of constructed features that can produce better DT classifiers which may not use all constructed features. As a result, MGPFC fitness does not reveal the goodness of the whole set of constructed features.

In summary, performance of the three learning algorithms showed that the constructed and selected features by CDFC have better discriminating ability than MGPFC. The results also demonstrate the effectiveness of the proposed strategy in CDFC. In the next section, we will investigate how efficient CDFC is compared to MGPFC.

5.3   Computation Time

Figure 4 shows the average running time to complete a single run for MGPFC and CDFC. Compared with MGPFC running time, CDFC only takes less than one third in 4 out of 8 datasets, less than half in 3 datasets, and more than half in the largest dataset, Ovarian.

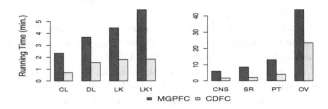

Fig. 4. Computation time of CDFC versus MGPFC (in colour).

Note that both methods have the same population size and maximum generations. In other words, they have the same number of evaluations. However, CDFC running time is much shorter than MGPFC in all datasets. The main reason behind this reduction is the computation time of the fitness evaluations. While the CDFC fitness function comprises of two filter measures, distance and IG, MGPFC combines distance with a wrapper measure. This again confirms the efficiency of filter measures.

6   Conclusion

The goal of this work is to propose a class-dependent feature construction method (CDFC) that can produce a smaller number of high-level features which can improve the performance of common learning algorithms on high-dimensional data. The goal was achieved by creating different terminal sets for constructing different class-dependent features. t-Test is used as a relevance measure to rank features in the context of a given class. A new fitness function is also proposed to better evaluate a set of constructed features based on two filter measures.

Performances of the CDFC constructed and selected features are compared with those on the original set and those generated by MGPFC using KNN, NB and DT. Results on the eight high-dimensional datasets show that CDFC is not only more effective in almost all cases but also more efficient than MGPFC in all cases. The proposed strategies in CDFC demonstrate that by forming the GP terminal set with class-relevant features and a good fitness function, the proposed filter method can achieve better performance than a hybrid approach.

In CDFC, the fitness function combines two filter measures using a fix weight. Furthermore, the number of top-ranked features used to form terminal sets for each class is also predefined. A dynamic weight and an automatic adjustment of the terminal sets based on the performance of the constructed features can be investigated to further improve the CDFC performance. Finally, our future work also includes more analysis to provide more insights on the proposed method.

References

1. Ahmed, S., Zhang, M., Peng, L.: A new GP-based wrapper feature construction approach to classification and biomarker identification. In: IEEE Congress on Evolutionary Computation, pp. 2756–2763 (2014)
2. Al-Sahaf, H., Al-Sahaf, A., Xue, B., Johnston, M., Zhang, M.: Automatically evolving rotation-invariant texture image descriptors by genetic programming. IEEE Trans. Evol. Comput. **21**(1), 83–101 (2016)
3. Bhanu, B., Krawiec, K.: Coevolutionary construction of features for transformation of representation in machine learning. In: Proceedings of Genetic and Evolutionary Computation Conference, pp. 249–254. Press (2002)
4. Cha, S.H.: Comprehensive survey on distance/similarity measures between probability density functions. Int. J. Math. Models Methods Appl. Sci. **1**, 300 (2007)
5. Ding, C., Peng, H.: Minimum redundancy feature selection from microarray gene expression data. J. Bioinform. Comput. Biol. **3**(02), 185–205 (2005)
6. Espejo, P., Ventura, S., Herrera, F.: A survey on the application of genetic programming to classification. IEEE Trans. Syst. Man Cybern. Part C Appl. Rev. **40**(2), 121–144 (2010)
7. Koza, J.R.: Genetic Programming: On the Programming of Computers by Means of Natural Selection. MIT Press, Cambridge (1992)
8. Krawiec, K.: Genetic programming-based construction of features for machine learning and knowledge discovery tasks. Genet. Program. Evol. Mach. **3**, 329–343 (2002)
9. Nag, K., Pal, N.: A multiobjective genetic programming-based ensemble for simultaneous feature selection and classification. IEEE Trans. Cybern. **46**(2), 499–510 (2016)
10. Neshatian, K., Zhang, M., Andreae, P.: A filter approach to multiple feature construction for symbolic learning classifiers using genetic programming. IEEE Trans. Evol. Comput. **16**(5), 645–661 (2012)
11. Tran, B., Zhang, M., Xue, B.: Multiple feature construction in classification on high-dimensional data using GP. In: 2016 IEEE Symposium Series on Computational Intelligence (SSCI), pp. 1–8 (2016)
12. Tran, B., Xue, B., Zhang, M.: Genetic programming for feature construction and selection in classification on high-dimensional data. Memetic Comput. **8**(1), 3–15 (2015)
13. Wang, L,, Zhou, N., Chu, F.: A general wrapper approach to selection of class-dependent features. IEEE Trans. Neural Netw. **19**(7), 1267–1278 (2008)
14. Xue, B., Zhang, M., Browne, W.N., Yao, X.: A survey on evolutionary computation approaches to feature selection. IEEE Trans. Evol. Comput. **20**(4), 606–626 (2016)
15. Zhang, J., Wang, S., Chen, L., Gallinari, P.: Multiple Bayesian discriminant functions for high-dimensional massive data classification. Data Mining Knowl. Discovery **31**(2), 1–37 (2016)

Comprehensive Quality-Aware Automated Semantic Web Service Composition

Chen Wang[1]([⊠]), Hui Ma[1], Aaron Chen[1], and Sven Hartmann[2]

[1] School of Engineering and Computer Science, Victoria University of Wellington,
Wellington, New Zealand
{chen.wang,hui.ma,aaron.chen}@ecs.vuw.ac.nz
[2] Department of Informatics, Clausthal University of Technology,
Clausthal-Zellerfeld, Germany
sven.hartmann@tu-clausthal.de

Abstract. Web service composition has been a prevailing research direction in recent years. There are two major challenges faced by researchers, semantic matchmaking and Quality of Service (QoS) optimisation. Semantic matchmaking aims to discover interoperable web services that can interact with each other by their resources described semantically. QoS optimisation aims to optimise the non-functional requirements of service users, such as minimum cost and maximum reliability. To meet the requirements of service users, both semantic matchmaking quality and QoS should be considered simultaneously. Most existing works on web service composition, however, focus only on one of these two aspects. Therefore, we propose a comprehensive quality model that takes both semantic matchmaking quality and QoS into account with the aim of achieving a more desirable balance of both sides. Further, we develop a PSO-based service composition approach with explicit support for the proposed comprehensive quality model. We also conduct experiments to explore the effectiveness of our PSO-based approach and the desirable balance achieved by using our comprehensive quality model.

Keywords: Web service composition · Semantic web services · QoS optimisation · Semantic matchmaking · Evolutionary computation

1 Introduction

Web service composition aims to loosely couple a set of web services to provide a value-added composite service that accommodates complex functional and non-functional requirements of service users. Two most notable challenges for web service composition are ensuring interoperability of services and achieving Quality of Service (QoS) optimisation [5]. *Interoperability* of web services presents challenge in syntactic and semantic dimensions. The syntactic dimension is covered by the XML-based technologies, such as *WSDL*, *SOAP*. The semantic dimension enables a better collaboration through ontology-based semantics, such

© Springer International Publishing AG 2017
W. Peng et al. (Eds.): AI 2017, LNAI 10400, pp. 195–207, 2017.
DOI: 10.1007/978-3-319-63004-5_16

as OWL-S, WSML, and SAWSDL [12]. *Semantic web services composition* is distinguished from the syntactic service composition, as the resources of semantic web services are described semantically to enable a better interoperability for chaining web services. Another challenge is related to QoS optimisation. This challenge gives birth to *QoS-aware service composition* that aims to find composition solutions with optimised QoS.

Existing works on service composition focus mainly on addressing only one challenge above. In these works, huge efforts have been devoted to QoS-aware web service compositions assuming a pre-defined abstract workflow is given. This is generally considered as a *semi-automated web service composition*. Generating composition plans automatically in discovering and selecting suitable web services is a NP-hard problem [10]. In the past few years, many approaches [6,8,14,19–21] to QoS-aware web service composition employ Evolutionary Computation (EC) techniques to automatically generate composition solutions. Genetic Programming (GP) based approaches produce promising results, but often require repairing or penalising the solutions [8,21], which restrict their searching space. Particle Swarm Optimisation (PSO) based approaches are therefore proposed to avoid producing invalid solutions to effectively search for near-optimal solutions [19]. All these works have enabled an *automatic web service composition*, but do not optimise QoS and quality of semantic matchmaking simultaneously to achieve a desirable balance on both sides.

The overall goal of this paper is to *develop a PSO-based approach to comprehensive quality-aware automated semantic web service composition that simultaneously optimises both QoS and semantic matchmaking quality*. Particularly, this paper extends existing works on QoS-aware service composition by considering jointly optimising the both quality aspects, which is proposed as a comprehensive quality model. We will achieve three objectives in this work:

1. To propose a comprehensive quality model that addresses QoS and semantic matchmaking quality simultaneously with a desirable balance on both sides.
2. To propose a PSO-based service composition approach using the proposed comprehensive quality model. To do that, we aim to find a service candidate queue that can be decoded into a service composition with near-optimal comprehensive quality.
3. To address the effectiveness of our PSO-based approach and a desirable balance achieved using our comprehensive quality model, we first compare our PSO-based approach with one recent GP-based approach [8] using our proposed quality model, and then compare our proposed quality model with one widely used QoS model using our proposed PSO-based approach.

2   Related Work

While web service composition has attracted much research over the last decade, most efforts focus on either semantic web service composition [1,3,9] or QoS-aware web service composition [6,8,14,19–21]. Only very few works address both semantic matchmaking quality and QoS for web service composition problems. To the best of our knowledge, [4, 7, 13] reported about first attempts that consider both aspects together.

Semantic web service composition [1, 3, 9] captures semantic descriptions of the parameters of web services using some kind of logic (i.e., description logic) to ensure the interoperability of web services. In these approaches, the goal is often to minimise the number of services or the size of a graph representation for a web service composition to obtain optimised composition solutions. However, these approaches do not guarantee an optimised QoS of service compositions.

QoS-aware web service composition, on the other side, has been studied using classical optimisation techniques or EC techniques for finding near-optimised solutions. [14] proposes a local optimisation and enumeration method, where a small number of promising candidates related to each task are considered by local selection, and composition solutions are enumerated to reach the near optimal QoS. EC techniques are widely used to automatically generate solutions with optimal QoS. [6] employs a modified Genetic Algorithm (GA) using a binary string as an individual, which demands to be decoded into composition solutions. [21] uses GP for finding near-optimal solutions that are reached by penalising infeasible solutions using a fitness function. A hybrid approach employing a greedy search and GP is introduced in [8] to generate functionally correct tree-based representations, which are transformed from graph-based representations. [20] introduces a promising graph-evolutionary approach to eliminate the transformation process. [19] proposes an indirect PSO-based approach, where a service queue is used as an indirect representation that is decoded into a directed acyclic graph. However, these QoS-aware approaches [6, 8, 14, 19–21] do not consider the semantic matchmaking quality of service compositions.

Only a few works [4, 7, 13] consider both semantic matchmaking quality and QoS simultaneously. [7] proposes a semi-automated web service composition using GA to encode a given abstract service workflow, where the evaluation of semantic matchmaking quality requires a complete and formal definition of ontology using description logic. Another GA-based approach [4] utilise the structure of process description languages to encode pre-stored cases-based workflows, where workable services are composed to complete this workflow. An automated immune-inspired web service composition approach [13] employs a clonal selection algorithm to proliferate decoded planning graphs, but this approach is only evaluated with some simple cases.

In summary, despite a large number of approaches for semantic web service composition and QoS-aware service composition approaches, there is a lack of a fully automated semantic service composition approach to optimise semantic matchmaking quality and QoS simultaneously.

3   Problem Description and Comprehensive Quality Model

Our goal is to develop a PSO-based approach for automatically generating good service compositions. Often, many different service compositions can meet a user request but differ significantly in terms of QoS and semantic matchmaking quality. For example, in the classical travel planning context, some component service must be employed to obtain a travel map. Suppose that two services can be considered for this purpose. One service S can provide a street map at a price of 6.72. The other service S' can provide a tourist map at a price of 16.87. Because in our context a tourist map is more desirable than a street map, S' clearly enjoys better semantic matchmaking quality than S but will have negative impact on the QoS of the service composition (i.e., the price is much higher). One can easily imagine that similar challenges frequently occur when looking for service compositions. Hence, a good balance between QoS and semantic matchmaking quality is called for. We therefore propose a *comprehensive quality model* in considering semantic matchmaking quality and QoS simultaneously.

We consider a *semantic web service* (*service*, for short) as a tuple $S = (I_S, O_S, QoS_S)$ where I_S is a set of service inputs consumed by S, O_S is a set of service outputs produced by S, and $QoS_S = \{t_S, c_S, r_S, a_S\}$ is a set of non-functional attributes of S. The inputs in I_S and outputs in O_S are parameters modelled through concepts in a domain-specific ontology $\mathcal{O}$. The attributes t_S, c_S, r_S, a_S refer to the response time, cost, reliability, and availability of service S, respectively. These four QoS attributes are most commonly used [22].

A *service repository* $\mathcal{SR}$ is a finite collection of services with a common ontology $\mathcal{O}$. A *service request* (also called *composition task*) over $\mathcal{SR}$ is a tuple $T = (I_T, O_T)$ where I_T is a set of task inputs, and O_T is a set of task outputs. The inputs in I_T and outputs in O_T are parameters that are related to concepts in the ontology $\mathcal{O}$.

A service composition is commonly represented as a *directed acyclic graph* (DAG). Its nodes correspond to the services in the composition. Two services S and S' are connected by an edge e if some outputs of S service serve as inputs for S'. Apparently, such outputs and inputs must semantically match to ensure the correct execution of the service composition. The mechanism to compose services relies on the semantic descriptions of inputs and outputs, which enables inputs of services to be matched by outputs of other services. The following *matchmaking types* are often used to describe the level of a match [11]: For concepts a, b in $\mathcal{O}$ the *matchmaking* returns *exact* if a and b are equivalent ($a \equiv b$), *plugin* if a is a sub-concept of b ($a \sqsubseteq b$), *subsume* if a is a super-concept of b ($a \sqsupseteq b$), and *fail* if none of previous matchmaking types is returned.

In this paper we are only interested in robust compositions where only *exact* and *plugin* matches are considered, see [7]. As argued in [7] *plugin* matches are less preferable than *exact* matches due to the overheads associated with data processing. We suggest to consider the semantic similarity of concepts when comparing different *plugin* matches. For concepts a, b in $\mathcal{O}$ the *semantic similarity* $sim(a, b)$ is calculated based on an edge counting method in a taxonomy like WorldNet or Ontology using Eq. (1) [15]. This method has the advantages of simple calculation and good performance [15]. In Eq. (1), N_a, N_b and N_c measure the distances from concept a, concept b, and the closest common ancestor c of a and b to the top concept of the ontology $\mathcal{O}$, respectively.

$$sim(a,b) = \frac{2N_c \cdot e^{-\lambda L/D}}{N_a + N_b} \tag{1}$$

For our purposes, λ can be set to 0 as we do not measure the similarities of neighbourhood concepts, the matching type not considered in this paper.

Given a service request $T = (I_T, O_T)$, we represent a service composition solution for T with services $S_1, \ldots, S_n$ by a weighted DAG, $WG = (V, E)$ with node set $V = \{Start, S_1, S_2, \ldots, S_n, End\}$ and edge set $E = \{e_1, e_2, \ldots e_m\}$. $Start$ and End are two special services defined as $Start = (\emptyset, I_T, \emptyset)$ and $End = (O_T, \emptyset, \emptyset)$ that account for the input and output requirements given by the request. Each edge e from a service S to a service S' means that service S produces an output $a \in O_S$ that is matched (exact or plugin) to an input $b \in I_{S'}$ to be consumed by service S' in the composition. Based on the matchmaking type ($type_e$), the semantic similarity (sim_e) of edge e can be defined as follow:

$$type_e = \begin{cases} 1 & \text{if } a \equiv b \,(exact \text{ match}) \\ p & \text{if } a \sqsubseteq b \,(plugin \text{ match}) \end{cases}, \quad sim_e = sim(a,b) = \frac{2N_c}{N_a + N_b}$$

with a suitable parameter $p, 0 < p < 1$. p is determined by user's preference, see Sect. 5. However, if more than one pair of matched output and input exist from service S to service S', $type_e$ and sim_e will take on their average values.

The semantic matchmaking quality of the service composition can be obtained by aggregating $type_e$ and sim_e, respectively, over all edges in E as follow:

$$MT = \prod_{j=1}^{m} type_{e_j}, \qquad SIM = \frac{1}{m} \sum_{j=1}^{m} sim_{e_j}$$

The QoS of the service composition can be obtained by aggregating the QoS values of the participating services [8]. For a service composition with services $S_1, S_2, \ldots S_n$ we obtain the reliability $R = \prod_{k=1}^{n} r_{S_k}$, the availability $A = \prod_{k=1}^{n} a_{S_k}$, the cost $C = \sum_{k=1}^{n} c_{S_k}$, and the response time T is the time of the most time-consuming path in the composition, i.e., assuming h is the number of path,

$$T = MAX\{\sum_{k=1}^{\ell_j} t_{S_k} | j \in \{1, \ldots, h\}, \text{ and } \ell_j \text{ is the number of nodes in a path } P_j\}$$

When multiple quality criteria are involved into decision making, then the overall fitness of a solution can be defined as a weighted sum of the individual criteria in Eq. (2) that the preference of each quality criterion is provided by users.

$$Fitness = w_1\hat{MT} + w_2\hat{SIM} + w_3\hat{A} + w_4\hat{R} + w_5(1 - \hat{T}) + w_6(1 - \hat{C}) \tag{2}$$

with $\sum_{k=1}^{6} w_k = 1$. We call this objective function the comprehensive quality model for service composition. The weights can be adjusted according to users' preferences. $\hat{MT}$, $\hat{SIM}$, $\hat{A}$, $\hat{R}$, $\hat{T}$, and $\hat{C}$ are normalised values calculated within the range from 0 to 1 using Eq. (3). To simplify the presentation we also use the notation $(Q_1, Q_2, Q_3, Q_4, Q_5, Q_6) = (MT, SIM, A, R, T, C)$. Q_1 and Q_2 have minimum value 0 and maximum value 1. The minimum and maximum value of Q_3, Q_4, Q_5, and Q_6 are calculated across all task-related candidates in the service repository $\mathcal{SR}$ using the greedy search in [8,18].

$$\hat{Q}_k = \begin{cases} \frac{Q_k - Q_{k,min}}{Q_{k,max} - Q_{k,min}} & \text{if } k = 1, \ldots, 4 \text{ and } Q_{k,max} - Q_{k,min} \neq 0, \\ \frac{Q_{k,max} - Q_k}{Q_{k,max} - Q_{k,min}} & \text{if } k = 5, 6 \text{ and } Q_{k,max} - Q_{k,min} \neq 0, \\ 1 & \text{otherwise.} \end{cases} \quad (3)$$

To solve the composition task satisfactorily our goal is to maximize the objective function in Eq. (2).

4   PSO-Based Approach to Comprehensive Quality-Aware Automated Semantic Web Service Composition

4.1   An Overview of Our PSO-Based Approach

As PSO has shown promise in solving combinatorial optimisation problems, we propose a PSO-based approach to comprehensive quality-aware automated semantic web service composition. Figure 1 shows an overview of our approach consisting of four steps:

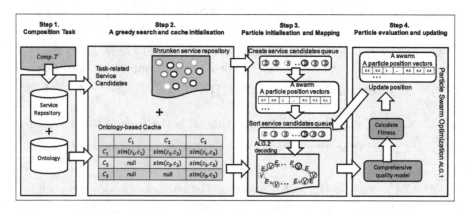

Fig. 1. An overview of our PSO-based approach to comprehensive quality-aware automated semantic web service composition.

Step 1: The composition process is triggered by a composition task, which is clearly defined in Sect. 3.

Step 2: The composition task is used to discover all task-related service candidates using a greedy search algorithm adopted from [8], which contributes to a shrunken service repository. This greedy search algorithm keeps adding outputs of the invoked services as available outputs (initialised with I_T), and these available outputs are used to discover task-related services from a service repository and updated with the outputs of these discovered services. This operation is repeated until no service is satisfied by the available outputs. During the greedy search, an ontology-based cache (*cache*) is initialised, which stores the concept similarities of matched inputs and outputs of task-related candidates. This *cache* is also used to discover services by checking whether *null* is returned by given two output-related and input-related concepts.

Step 3 and Step 4: These two steps follow the standard PSO steps [16] except for some differences in particles mapping and decoding processes. In particular, these two differences are related to sorting a created service queue using service-to-index mapping for a particle' position vectors and evaluating the fitness of a particle after decoding this service queue into a WG respectively. Those differences are further addressed in Algorithms 1 and 2 in Sect. 4.2.

4.2   The Algorithms for Our PSO-Based Approach

The overall algorithm investigated here is made up of a PSO-based web service composition technique (Algorithm 1) and a WG creating technique from a service queue (Algorithm 2). In Algorithm 1, the steps 4, 5, 6 and 7 are different from those of standard PSO: In step 4, the size of task-related service candidates generated by a greedy search determines the size of each particle's position. Each service candidate in a created service candidates queue is mapped to an index of a particles position vectors, where each vector has a weight value between 0.0 and 1.0. In step 5, service candidates in the queue are sorted according to their corresponding weight values in descending order. In step 6, this sorted queue is

---

Algorithm 1. Steps of PSO-based service composition technique [19]

1: Randomly initialise each particle in the swarm;
2: **while** *max. iterations not met* **do**
3:     **foreach** *particle in the swarm* **do**
4:         Create a service candidates queue and map service candidates to a particle's position vectors;
5:         Sort the service queue by position vectors' weights;
6:         Use Algorithm 2 to create a WG from the service queue;
7:         Calculate the WG fitness value;
8:         **if** *fitness value better than pBest* **then**
9:             | Assign current fitness as new *pBest*;
10:        **else**
11:            | Keep previous *pBest*;
12:     Assign best particle's *pBest* value to *gBest*, if better than *gBest*;
13:     Calculate the velocity of each particle;
14:     Update the position of each particle;

---

used as one of the inputs of the forward decoding Algorithm 2 to create a WG. In step 7, the fitness value of the created WG is the fitness value of the particle calculated by the comprehensive model discussed in Sect. 3.

Algorithm 2 is a forward graph building algorithm extended from [2]. This algorithm takes one input, a sorted service queue from step 5 of Algorithm 1. Note that different service queues may lead to different WGs. In addition. I_T, O_T and $cache$ are also taken as the inputs. Firstly, $Start$ and End are added to V of WG as an initialisation, and $OutputSet$ is also created with I_T. The following steps are repeated until O_T can be satisfied by $Outputset$ or the service queue is $null$. If all the inputs I_S of the first popped S from $queue$ can be satisfied by provided outputs from $OutputSet$, this S is added to V and its outputs are added to $OutputSet$, and S is removed from $queue$. Otherwise, the second popped S from $queue$ is considered for these operations. Meanwhile, e is created with $type_e$ and sim_e if S is added, and calculated using information provided from $cache$. This forward graph building technique could lead to more services and edges connected to the WG, these redundancies should be removed before WG is returned.

Algorithm 2. Create a WG from a sorted service queue

    Input : I_T, O_T, $queue$, $cache$
    Output: WG
1: $WG = (V, E)$;
2: $V \leftarrow \{Start, End\}$;
3: $OutputSet \leftarrow \{I_T\}$;
4: **while** O_T *not satisfied by OutputSet* **do**
5:      **foreach** S *in queue* **do**
6:         **if** I_S *satisfied by OutputSet* **then**
7:            insert S into V;
8:            adjoin O_S to $OutputSet$;
9:            $queue$.remove S;
10:           $e \leftarrow$ calculate $type_e$, sim_e using $cache$;
11:           insert e into E;

12: remove *dangling nodes* and *edges* from WG;
13: **return** WG;

---

5   Experiment Study

In this section, we employ a quantitative evaluation approach with a benchmark dataset used in [8,18], which is an augmented version of Web Service Challenge 2009 (WSC09) including QoS attributes. Two objectives of this evaluation are to: (1) evaluate the effectiveness of our PSO-based approach, see comparison test in Sect. 5.1. (2) evaluate the effectiveness of our proposed comprehensive quality model to achieve a desirable balance on semantic matchmaking quality and QoS, see comparison test in Sect. 5.2.

The parameters for the PSO are chosen from the settings from [16], In particular, PSO population size is 30 with 100 generations. We run 30 times independently for each dataset. We configure the weights of fitness function to properly balance semantic matchmaking quality and QoS. Therefore, w_1 and w_2 are set equally to 0.25, and w_3, w_4, w_5, w_6 are all set to 0.125. The p of $type_e$ is set to 0.75 (*plugin* match) according to [7]. In general, weight settings and parameter p are decided according to users' preferences.

5.1   GP-Based vs. PSO-Based Approach

To evaluate the effectiveness of our proposed PSO-based approach, we compare our PSO-based method with one recent GP-based approach [8] using our proposed comprehensive quality model. We extend this GP-based approach by measuring the semantic matchmaking quality between parent nodes and children nodes. To make a fair comparison, we use the same number of evaluations (3000 times) for these two approach. We set the parameters of that GP-based approach as 30 individuals and 100 generations, which is considered to be proper settings referring to [17].

The first column of Table 1 shows five tasks from WSC09. The second and third column of Table 1 show the original service repository size and the shrunk service repository size after the greedy search respectively regarding the five tasks. This greedy search helps reducing the original repository size significantly, which contributes to a reduced searching space. The fourth and fifth column of Table 1 show the mean fitness values of 30 independent runs accomplished by two methods. We employ independent-samples T tests to test the significant differences in mean fitness value. The results show that the PSO-based approach outperforms the existing GP-based approach in most cases except Task 3. Note that all p-values are consistently smaller than 0.01. Using our PSO-based approach, small changes to sorted queues (particles in PSO) could lead to big changes to the composition solutions. This enables the PSO-based approach to escape from local optima more easily than the GP-based approach.

Table 1. Mean fitness values for comparing GP-based approach

WSC09	Original $\mathcal{SR}$	Shrunken $\mathcal{SR}$	PSO-based approach	GP-based approach
Task 1	572	80	0.5592 ± 0.0128 ↑	0.5207 ± 0.0208
Task 2	4129	140	0.4701 ± 0.0011 ↑	0.4597 ± 0.0029
Task 3	8138	153	0.5504 ± 0.0128	0.5679 ± 0.0234 ↑
Task 4	8301	330	0.4690 ± 0.0017 ↑	0.4317 ± 0.0097
Task 5	15211	237	0.4694 ± 0.0008 ↑	0.2452 ± 0.0369

5.2 Comprehensive Quality Model vs. QoS Model

Recently, a QoS Model, $Fitness = w_1\hat{A} + w_2\hat{R} + w_3(1 - \hat{T}) + w_4(1 - \hat{C})$, where $\sum_{i=1}^{4} w_i = 1$, is widely used for QoS-aware web service composition [8,19,20]. To show the effectiveness of our proposed comprehensive quality model, we compare the best solutions found by this QoS model and our comprehensive model using our PSO-based approach. We record and compare the mean values of both SM ($SM = 0.5\hat{MT} + 0.5\hat{SIM}$) and QoS($QoS = 0.25\hat{A} + 0.25\hat{R} + 0.25(1 - \hat{T}) + 0.25(1 - \hat{C})$) of best solutions over 30 independent runs. To make the comparison informative, all these recorded values have been normalised from 0 to 1, and compared using independent-samples T tests, see Table 2. Note that p-values are consistently smaller than 0.001 in the results indicating significant differences in performance.

In Table 2, the mean values of QoS using QoS model are significantly higher than those using comprehensive quality model for Tasks 2, 3, 4 and 5. However, the mean value of SM using the comprehensive quality model are significantly higher than those using the QoS model, while a slight trade-off in QoS are observed in all tasks. In addition, our comprehensive model achieves a consistently higher comprehensive quality in terms of a combination of SM and QoS, which is significantly better in Tasks 1, 2, 3 and 4.

Table 2. Mean values of SM, QoS and sum of SM and QoS for QoS model and comprehensive quality model using PSO-based approach

WSC09		QoS model	Comprehensive quality model
Task1	SM	0.5373 ± 0.0267	0.5580 ± 0.0094 ↑
	QoS	0.5574 ± 0.0156	0.5604 ± 0.0164
	$SM + QoS$	1.0947 ± 0.0423	1.1184 ± 0.0258 ↑
Task2	SM	0.4549 ± 0.0033	0.4630 ± 0.0042 ↑
	QoS	0.4800 ± 0.0012 ↑	0.4772 ± 0.0025
	$SM + QoS$	0.9349 ± 0.0045	0.9402 ± 0.0067 ↑
Task3	SM	0.5538 ± 0.0082	0.6093 ± 0.0054 ↑
	QoS	0.4940 ± 0.0013 ↑	0.4913 ± 0.0009
	$SM + QoS$	1.0478 ± 0.0095	1.1006 ± 0.0063 ↑
Task4	SM	0.4398 ± 0.0037	0.4604 ± 0.0000 ↑
	QoS	0.4845 ± 0.0010 ↑	0.4734 ± 0.0044
	$SM + QoS$	0.9243 ± 0.0047	0.9338 ± 0.0044 ↑
Task5	SM	0.4580 ± 0.0065	0.4639 ± 0.0013 ↑
	QoS	0.4764 ± 0.0005 ↑	0.4750 ± 0.0007
	$SM + QoS$	0.9344 ± 0.0070	0.9389 ± 0.0020

5.3   Further Discussion

To analyse the effectiveness of achieving a good comprehensive quality at the expense of slightly reduced QoS, we demonstrate two best solutions produced using Task 3 as an example. Figure 2 (1) and (2) show two weighted DAGs, WG_1 and WG_2, which have been obtained as the best service compositions solutions based on the QoS model and on the comprehensive quality model, respectively. Both WGs have exactly the same service workflow structure, but some service vertices and edges denoted in red are different. To better understand these differences, we list the overall semantic matchmaking quality SM, overall QoS and semantic matchmaking quality sm_{e_n} associated to these different edges in WG_1 and WG_2. (Note: $sm_{e_n} = 0.5type_{e_n} + 0.5sim_{e_n}$), where ΔQ reveals the gain (positive ΔQ) or a loss (negative ΔQ) of the listed qualities for our comprehensive quality model. Therefore, we achieve a comprehensive quality gain (+0.1433), a result of a gain in semantic matchmaking quality (+0.1467) and a loss in QoS (−0.0034). To understand the improvement of semantic matchmaking quality from these numbers, we pick up e_4 that is associated with the smallest ΔQ. The e_4 of WG_1 and WG_2 has two different source nodes, $Ser1640238160$ and $Ser947554374$, and two the same End nodes. $Ser1640238160$ and $Ser947554374$ are services with output parameters $Inst582785907$ and $Inst795998200$ corresponds to two concepts $Con2037585750$ and $Con103314376$ respectively in the given ontology shown in Fig. 2 (4). As $Inst658772240$ is a required parameter of End, and related to concept

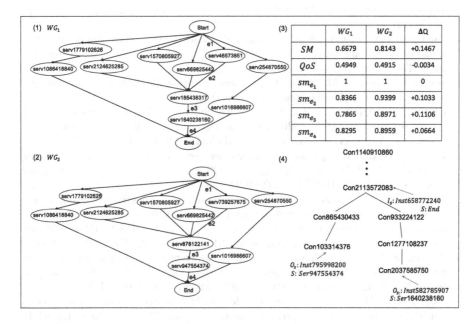

Fig. 2. An example for the comparison of the best solutions obtained based on the QoS model and on the comprehensive quality model for Task 3.

$Con2113572083$, $Inst795998200$ is closer to the required output $Inst658772240$ than $Inst582785907$. Therefore, $Ser947554374$ is selected with a better semantic matchmaking quality compared to $Ser1640238160$.

6   Conclusion

In this work, we propose an effective PSO-based approach to comprehensive quality-aware semantic web service composition, which also has shown promise in achieving a better comprehensive quality in terms of a combination of semantic matchmaking quality and QoS compared to existing works. Future works can investigate multi-objective EC techniques to produce a set of composition solutions for the situations when the quality preference is not known.

Acknowledgments. This research is supported by the Marsden fund council from Government funding, administered by the Royal Society of New Zealand.

References

1. Bansal, S., Bansal, A., Gupta, G., Blake, M.B.: Generalized semantic web service composition. Serv. Oriented Comput. Appl. **10**(2), 111–133 (2016)
2. Blum, A.L., Furst, M.L.: Fast planning through planning graph analysis. Artif. Intell. **90**(1), 281–300 (1997)
3. Boustil, A., Maamri, R., Sahnoun, Z.: A semantic selection approach for composite web services using OWL-DL and rules. Serv. Oriented Comput. Appl. **8**(3), 221–238 (2014)
4. FanJiang, Y.Y., Syu, Y.: Semantic-based automatic service composition with functional and non-functional requirements in design time: a genetic algorithm approach. Inf. Softw. Technol. **56**(3), 352–373 (2014)
5. Fensel, D., Facca, F.M., Simperl, E., Toma, I.: Semantic Web Services. Springer Science & Business Media, Heidelberg (2011)
6. Gupta, I.K., Kumar, J., Rai, P.: Optimization to quality-of-service-driven web service composition using modified genetic algorithm. In: 2015 International Conference on Computer, Communication and Control (IC4), pp. 1–6. IEEE (2015)
7. Lécué, F.: Optimizing QoS-aware semantic web service composition. In: Bernstein, A., et al. (eds.) ISWC 2009. LNCS, vol. 5823, pp. 375–391. Springer, Heidelberg (2009). doi:10.1007/978-3-642-04930-9_24
8. Ma, H., Wang, A., Zhang, M.: A hybrid approach using genetic programming and greedy search for QoS-aware web service composition. In: Hameurlain, A., Küng, J., Wagner, R., Decker, H., Lhotska, L., Link, S. (eds.) TLDKS XVIII. LNCS, vol. 8980, pp. 180–205. Springer, Heidelberg (2015). doi:10.1007/978-3-662-46485-4_7
9. Rodriguez-Mier, P., Pedrinaci, C., Lama, M., Mucientes, M.: An integrated semantic web service discovery and composition framework. IEEE Trans. Serv. Comput. **9**(4), 537–550 (2016). doi:10.1109/TSC.2015.2402679. ISSN 1939-1374
10. Moghaddam, M., Davis, J.G.: Service selection in web service composition: a comparative review of existing approaches. In: Bouguettaya, A., Sheng, Q.Z., Daniel, F. (eds.) Web Services Foundations, pp. 321–346. Springer, Heidelberg (2014). doi:10.1007/978-1-4614-7518-7_13

11. Paolucci, M., Kawamura, T., Payne, T.R., Sycara, K.: Semantic matching of web services capabilities. In: Horrocks, I., Hendler, J. (eds.) ISWC 2002. LNCS, vol. 2342, pp. 333–347. Springer, Heidelberg (2002). doi:10.1007/3-540-48005-6_26
12. Petrie, C.J.: Web Service Composition. Springer, Heidelberg (2016)
13. Pop, C.B., Chifu, V.R., Salomie, I., Dinsoreanu, M.: Immune-inspired method for selecting the optimal solution in web service composition. In: Lacroix, Z. (ed.) RED 2009. LNCS, vol. 6162, pp. 1–17. Springer, Heidelberg (2009). doi:10.1007/978-3-642-14415-8_1
14. Qi, L., Tang, Y., Dou, W., Chen, J.: Combining local optimization and enumeration for QoS-aware web service composition. In: 2010 IEEE International Conference on Web Services (ICWS), pp. 34–41. IEEE (2010)
15. Shet, K., Acharya, U.D., et al.: A new similarity measure for taxonomy based on edge counting. arXiv preprint arXiv:1211.4709 (2012)
16. Shi, Y., et al.: Particle swarm optimization: developments, applications and resources. In: Proceedings of the 2001 Congress on Evolutionary Computation, vol. 1, pp. 81–86. IEEE (2001)
17. da Silva, A.S., Ma, H., Zhang, M.: A GP approach to QoS-aware web service composition including conditional constraints. In: 2015 IEEE Congress on Evolutionary Computation (CEC), pp. 2113–2120. IEEE (2015)
18. da Silva, A.S., Ma, H., Zhang, M.: Genetic programming for QoS-aware web service composition and selection. Soft Comput. **20**(10), 3851–3867 (2016). doi:10.1007/s00500-016-2096-z. ISSN 1433-7479
19. Sawczuk da Silva, A., Mei, Y., Ma, H., Zhang, M.: Particle swarm optimisation with sequence-like indirect representation for web service composition. In: Chicano, F., Hu, B., García-Sánchez, P. (eds.) EvoCOP 2016. LNCS, vol. 9595, pp. 202–218. Springer, Cham (2016). doi:10.1007/978-3-319-30698-8_14
20. da Silva, A., Ma, H., Zhang, M.: GraphEvol: a graph evolution technique for web service composition. In: Chen, Q., Hameurlain, A., Toumani, F., Wagner, R., Decker, H. (eds.) DEXA 2015. LNCS, vol. 9262, pp. 134–142. Springer International Publishing, Heidelberg (2015). doi:10.1007/978-3-319-22852-5_12
21. Yu, Y., Ma, H., Zhang, M.: An adaptive genetic programming approach to QoS-aware web services composition. In: 2013 IEEE Congress on Evolutionary Computation, pp. 1740–1747. IEEE (2013)
22. Zeng, L., Benatallah, B., Dumas, M., Kalagnanam, J., Sheng, Q.Z.: Quality driven web services composition. In: Proceedings of the 12th International Conference on World Wide Web, pp. 411–421. ACM (2003)

Monthly Rainfall Categorization Based on Optimized Features and Neural Network

Ali Haidar[✉] and Brijesh Verma

Center for Intelligent Systems, Central Queensland University, Sydney, Australia
{a.haidar, b.verma}@cqu.edu.au

Abstract. Rainfall is a complex process that result from different atmospheric interactions. Rainfall forecasting is highly effective for various industries including the sugarcane industry. In this study, we propose a neural network based approach for classifying monthly rainfall. Rainfall classification is defined as determining the category of rainfall amount based on a certain threshold. Five distinct locations were selected to perform the study: Innisfail, Planecreek, Bingera, Maryborough in Queensland, Australia and Yamba in New South Wales, Australia. Multiple local and global climate indices have been linked to formation of rain. Hence, different local and global climate indices are proposed as possible predictors of rain. A Particle Swarm Optimization (PSO) algorithm was incorporated to select best features for each month in each location. An average accuracy of 87.65% was recorded with the proposed approach over the five selected locations. The developed models were compared against other neural network models where all features were used as input features. An average difference of 25.00%, 23.89%, 24.02%, 20.00%, 20.59% was recorded for Innisfail, Planecreek, Bingera, Maryborough and Yamba respectively. The analysis of statistical results suggests that the artificial neural networks can be used as a promising alternative approach for rainfall categorization over multiple weather zones and over Australia. In addition, selection of input features should be carefully considered when designing rainfall forecasting models.

Keywords: Artificial neural networks · Rainfall prediction · Particle swarm optimization

1 Introduction

Weather forecasting represents a field where the state of an atmospheric variable is determined over a specific location and for a selected duration. Different types of predicting models have been established and tested for forecasting weather variables as temperature, humidity and rainfall. Rainfall is a natural phenomenon that is a result of complex meteorological interactions. Rainfall forecasting is essential for different life aspects including daily activities, agriculture, transportation, etc. Therefore, predictions should be reasonably accurate, have economic impact and communicated well to users in order be considered valuable [1].

Climate variability affects different agricultural sectors in Australia including wheat, cotton, beef environments, and sugar. In fact, for decades, Australia has been

© Springer International Publishing AG 2017
W. Peng et al. (Eds.): AI 2017, LNAI 10400, pp. 208–220, 2017.
DOI: 10.1007/978-3-319-63004-5_17

considered one of the largest global suppliers of raw sugar. During a typical sugarcane season, multiple processes are usually followed: plantation, irrigation, fertilization, and harvest. In addition, various operations are required to maintain a profitable season such as transportation, mills maintenance, etc. Importantly, certain decisions should be considered in earlier durations to ensure profitable season, and these decisions are affected by rainfall amounts to be encountered through parts of the season. Hence, multiple forecasting methods are considered essential and helpful for the sugarcane industry.

The current official rainfall forecasts running in Australia are released by Bureau of Meteorology (BOM) and are based on General Circulation Models (GCMs). Predictive Ocean Atmosphere Model for Australia (POAMA) is the current model that is used to release weekly, seasonal to inter-annual rainfall outlooks. POAMA is applied to forecast different variables including temperature and rainfall. POAMA doesn't predict the actual amount of rainfall to be encountered over a specific location. Instead, it gives a probability value that represents the chance of exceeding a specific threshold, usually average. GCMs have shown low accuracy at some occasions. For seasonal rainfall predictions, forecasts are usually released for multiple months as a probability of exceeding a certain value (usually average) or as a chance of rainfall. Furthermore, these forecasts are given to users over large spatial distributions (≥ 50 km grids).

An alternative approach that took considerable attention over the last two decades is based on neural networks. Artificial neural networks are computer based algorithms that mimic the biological brain. It consists of multiple computational elements called neurons that process information. These neurons imitate the biological brain neurons. Usually, biological neurons are distributed over multiple layers, where each set is responsible for certain sub tasks of the original task. Similarly, artificial neurons are distributed over multiple layers, each responsible to perform certain functionalities. Three layers are typically created when developing a neural network: input, hidden and output layers. The input layer takes features to be given to network, hidden layer processes information, while output layer returns output values (classifications, predictions).

Neural networks require data to perform. The selection of input features is mandatory for good performance. Since rainfall is considered as the final stage of multiple local and global exchanges, different climate indices are investigated in this study to create the input features dataset. A climate index is a numerical value that represents a situation in the oceans or over landscape.

Neural networks have been widely deployed in forecasting rainfall for different ranges and periods. A generalized regression neural network was used to predict annual rainfall amount for Zhengzhou, China [2]. Nagahamulla et al. used ANN to predict monsoon season rainfall in India [3]. Narvekar and Fargose developed a back propagation neural network to forecast daily rainfall and sky conditions [4]. The forecasts were mapped to multiple classes after being released by the network as numerical values. Furthermore, Mekanik et al. applied ANN and multiple regression analysis to estimate spring precipitation in Victoria, Australia, where large global climate indices were used as predictors for precipitation amounts [5]. Abhishek et al. developed a study to compare multiple neural networks with different characteristics: number of neurons, hidden layers and transfer functions to forecast maximum and minimum temperatures for 365 days a year [6]. Nagahamulla et al. developed an ensemble of neural network that consisted of different topologies to predict daily rainfall values for Colombo, Srilanka [7]. The ensemble model was generated using weighted average fusion method and revealed better accuracy than single networks.

Neural network accuracy varies based on selection of multiple elements including topology, number of layers, number of neurons in hidden layer, input features, etc. Using all possible features may not reveal the best performance. Therefore, there is a need to apply feature selection to get the best input features that would reveal the highest accuracy. Evolutionary algorithms including genetic algorithm and particle swarm optimization can be applied to select a subset from all possible variables which would reveal best performance. These algorithms have been deployed in various forecasting applications. Kishtawal et al. applied a genetic algorithm to find the best parameters for an equation used for forecasting summer rainfall in India [8]. Haidar and Verma applied a genetic algorithm for selecting best input features for forecasting monthly rainfall in Bingera, Australia (actual amounts of rainfall were predicted) [9]. Nasseri et al. used a genetic algorithm to optimize a neural network that was used to forecast short term rainfall for Paramatta catchment, Australia [10].

Particle swarm optimization is an evolutionary algorithm inspired by social behavior as bird flocks [11]. It consists of multiple elements called particles that traverse the search space to find the best global solution. Each particle is represented by position and velocity, where particles move toward the best solution. Particle action is impacted by its local best and by the best global solution in the search space. This algorithm does not make any assumption about the problem being optimized (meta-heuristic). It is incorporated in this study to select input features that would reveal highest accuracy for monthly rainfall categorization.

Rainfall forecasting models can be deployed to forecast for diverse periods including hourly, daily, monthly, annually, etc. These models reveal different types of information including: actual amount of rainfall, chance of rainfall, or probability of rainfall based on a certain threshold (exceeding a value). Each of these models has its own effectiveness for prediction.

The aim of this study is to investigate the ability of neural networks with PSO optimization in generating accurate classification for rainfall phenomena. PSO was deployed to select the best features for categorizing monthly rainfall. Section 2 gives a brief description about possible climate input features. Section 3 describes the proposed methodology. Section 4 shows experimental results and comparative analysis. Finally, a conclusion is drawn in Sect. 5.

2 Climate Indices

Climate indices have different impacts on rainfall variability across Australia having El Nino Southern Oscillation (ENSO) as the first source of weather variability [12]. ENSO affects Eastern and Northeastern areas of Australia [13]. Difference in sea surface temperatures between zones in oceans is considered as a leading source for seasonal climate predictability.

Rainfall forecasting relies on climate features. Different forecasting applications were based on large scale climate indices [14]. Although some climate indices are considered rainfall influencers over Australia as Madden Jullian Oscillation (MJO) and winds, recorded values are considered insufficient. Therefore, these values were discarded when generating input features dataset. The selected global climate indices are briefly described in the following section:

2.1 Southern Oscillation Index (SOI)

SOI measures the difference in surface air pressure between Darwin and Tahiti. A high positive value of SOI represents a La Nina event while a high negative value represents El Nino event. La Nina events are associated with cooling events while El Nino events are associated with warming events. It was noticed that SOI values were the highest recorded amounts ever in October and December 2010, and February and March 2011. Floods occurred in specific locations in Australia between September 2010 and March 2011 [15]. Australia wettest 24 months was recorded between April 2010 and March 2012 [15].

2.2 Nino Values (Nino 1.2, Nino 3.0, Nino 3.4, Nino 4.0)

Nino values are used to monitor tropical pacific area. Each index represents sea surface temperature in a specific region: Nino1.2 (0°–10°S, 90°W–80°W), Nino3.0 (5°N–5°S, 150°W–90°W), Nino3.4 (5°N–5°S, 170°W–120°W), Nino4.0 (5°N–5°S, 160°E–150°W).

2.3 Inter-decadal Pacific Oscillation (IPO)

IPO is oceanographic/meteorological phenomenon that is seen around pacific basin. It affects rainfall and temperature over different districts including Australia [16]. IPO covers the whole pacific basin and is linked to decadal weather variability over some of its parts. Salinger et al. claimed that IPO controls decadal rainfall trends [17]. Studies showed that IPO influences Australian rainfall [18].

2.4 Indian Ocean Dipole (IOD)

IOD is a coupled ocean and atmospheric phenomenon that affects rainfall variability across its surrounding regions including Australia. Dipole Mode Index (DMI) is used to measure IOD which is defined as the SST difference in the tropical Indian ocean between the western equatorial Indian Ocean (50°E–70°E and 10°S–10°N) and the south eastern equatorial Indian Ocean (90°E–110°E and 10°S–0°N) [13].

2.5   Tripole Index for Inter-decadal Pacific Oscillation (TPI)

TPI is the difference between the Sea Surface Temperature Average (SSTA) averaged over the central equatorial Pacific and the average of SSTA in the Northwest and Southwest Pacific [18]. It is a robust description for the Inter decadal pacific oscillation. Regions used to calculate TPI: region 1 (25°N–45°N, 140°E–145°W), region 2 (10°S–10°N, 170°E–90°W) and region 3 (50°S–15°S, 150°E–160°W).

2.6   North Pacific Index (NPI)

NPI is an area-weighted sea level pressure over the region 30°S–65°N, 160°E–140°W. NPI is used to measure decadal variations connected to ENSO events. There have been links between NPI and precipitation along southern pacific region, where wetter conditions were associated with positive NPI values [19].

2.7   North Atlantic Oscillation Index (NAO)

NAO is a climate phenomenon in the North Atlantic Ocean. It is originally described as the normalized pressure difference between Iceland and Azores High. It was then extended by using data from Gibraltar and composite sites in south-western Iceland. It is considered as a significant element in the global climate system [20]. This index is the farthest in position to Australia compared to previously mentioned indices.

2.8   Sunspots

Monthly mean sunspots are the sum of the daily observed sun spots over the length of month. The aim of using these values is to incorporate a sunlight variable since sun is considered as a key driver in rainfall ecosystem.

2.9   Pacific Decadal Oscillation (PDO)

PDO is defined as: "the leading empirical orthogonal function for North Pacific sea surface temperature monthly averaged anomalies" [21]. This index is considered long term as it can stay in the same state for 20–30 years. PDO is recognized as an aggregation of multiple physical procedures [22]. There have been links to its effect on ENSO phases (El-Nino, La-Nina), and since ENSO is considered the first driver for climate variability, PDO was included as possible forecaster.

3   Proposed Approach

The proposed approach is based on selecting climate features for predicting rainfall categories. The selection is based on PSO algorithm and the classifications are based on an artificial neural network. The proposed approach is shown in Fig. 1.

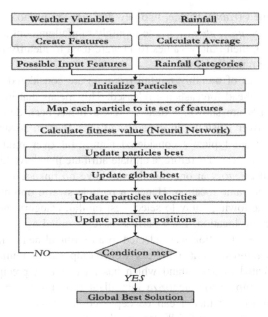

Fig. 1. Proposed approach.

Rainfall classification is described as rainfall categorization into different ranges. In this study, rainfall amounts were categorized into values lower or higher than monthly average. Official rainfall forecasts are generated based on large spatial areas (≥ 50 km grid), while in the following method we target monthly rainfall for a specific location.

Rainfall values are mapped into categories based on each dataset average. These values were mapped into binary classes to represent neural network target as shown in the following equation:

$$C(x) = \begin{cases} [0\,1], & x < z \\ [1\,0], & x \geq z \end{cases} \tag{1}$$

where $z = \frac{\sum_{i=1}^{n} x_i}{n}$, n is the sum of instances in the dataset (training/validation), C is the mapping function of numerical values to classes.

Neural network input plays a key role in determining the overall accuracy, especially in rainfall prediction problems. All the climate indices listed in Sect. 2 are intended to be used as possible predictors for classifying monthly rainfall over selected locations. Developed models learn from previous historical features, and link these indices to classifying rainfall categories. Rainfall lagged values, which are the previous amounts of rainfall up to one year were incorporated in an attempt to enhance rainfall categorization. 12 features were created for each target value from previous monthly rainfall observations starting from observation in the preceding month up to one year.

Furthermore, the first lagged monthly rainfall value ($rain_{t-1}$) and same month value in previous year ($rain_{t-12}$) are considered the most significant against the other 10 for a rainfall value at time t ($rain_t$). Hence, two new features are proposed following those two lagged values ($plag_{t-1}$, $plag_{t-12}$). The monthly rainfall amount average for all the years was calculated, then binary values (0,1) were used to identify the occurrence of higher than average rainfall or not.

Since recent values of monthly rainfall ($rain_{t-1}$) are considered as possible input features, one-month ahead forecasts are released. This means that in the beginning of each month, forecasts are shown. Extensive research has been deployed to identify rainfall influencers over Australia in general and over Eastern Australia particularly. The climate indices are typically considered significant over multiple locations at different periods of the year. Therefore, a climate attribute may have high correlation in determining rainfall category at one month, and have no linkage to categorization at another month in the same location. Hence, a particle swarm optimization algorithm was utilized in the following study to select best rainfall category predictors for each month in each specific location. Each particle is represented as a collection of input features, and the fitness function was selected to an artificial neural network.

In previous literatures, climate indices were compared to rainfall amounts and correlations are created to understand which has an effect on precipitation. We use climate variables at time t to categorize rainfall at time t + 1, where if reasonable accuracy was recorded the model can be deployed for rainfall categorization. The following equation represents rainfall classification with all available features:

$$y_t = f\left(\begin{array}{c} rain_{t-1}, rain_{t-2}, \ldots, rain_{t-12}, plag_{t-1}, plag_{t-12} \\ , input^1_{t-12}, input^2_{t-12}, input^3_{t-12}, \ldots, input^n_{t-12} \end{array}\right) \tag{2}$$

where y_t is rain range at time t, $rain_{t-z}$ is a lagged value for rainfall at time t where $1 \leq z \leq 12$, $plag_{t-1}$ and $plag_{t-12}$ are the proposed new features, $input^i_t$ is a climate variable value at time t, $1 \leq i \leq n$, n is the number of available climate variables, f is the trained neural network model.

4   Data Collection

Five locations were selected to perform this study: Innisfail, Planecreek, Bingera, Maryborough in Queensland and Yamba in New South Wales. The main reason behind this selection is the closeness to sugarcane paddocks and mills. Selected locations are shown in Fig. 2. Various climate indices were investigated on their ability to be included as predictors. The selected climate variables varied between local and global indices. Monthly mean maximum temperature, monthly mean minimum temperature, the two proposed features and lagged monthly values were local while the rest were global variables.

Monthly rainfall values, monthly mean maximum temperature, monthly mean minimum temperature and SOI were collected from Bureau of Meteorology Australia (BOM). Nino1.2, Nino3.0, Nino3.4, Nino 4.0, NPI, NAO, DMI and PDO were gathered from KNMI climate explorer, a web service that contains multiple weather indices. IPO was taken from climate of the 20th century website, while TPI was taken

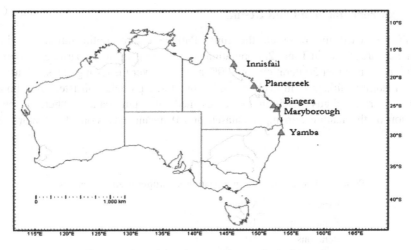

Fig. 2. Selected locations used to perform the study.

from Earth System Research Laboratory (ESRL). Sunspots were taken from Solar Influences Data Analysis Center (SIDC). In total, 28 features were used as possible input features.

5   Experiments and Comparative Analysis

5.1   Pre-processing

Dataset for each location was modified so that it had the same start and finish time. Dataset durations are shown in Table 1, where last column represents annual average for all recorded years. Then, each dataset collected for each location was divided into 12 datasets, each representing one month. Neural networks usually perform better with smaller scales. Therefore, each weather variable was normalized to values between 0 and 1. Rainfall ranges were created based on monthly overall averages over the training/validation dataset. Two ranges were initiated: below or higher than average ([0 1], [1 0]).

Table 1. Datasets created for each location.

Location	Start	Finish	Annual average (BOM)
Innisfail	Jan-1908	Dec-2015	3553.0 mm
Planecreek	Jan-1909	Dec-2015	1762.3 mm
Bingera	Jan-1901	Dec-2015	1024.5 mm
Maryborough	Jan-1909	Dec-2015	1138.2 mm
Yamba	Jan-1899	Dec-2015	1463.7 mm

5.2   Experimental Setup and Results

Matlab was used to create all the runs. Particle swarm optimization algorithm parameters are shown in Table 2. Population size was selected to 10 particles. Stopping conditions were either 50 iterations or 100% accuracy over the testing dataset. Particles were randomly initialized in each monthly run. Each particle consisted of a binary number with 28 digits. Each index represented an input feature, where 1 meant inclusion of the feature into input dataset, and 0 meant exclusion of a feature into dataset.

Table 2. Particle swarm optimization algorithm used parameters.

Parameter	Value
Population	10
Iterations	50
Fitness function	Three-layered feed forward network
Scalar value	Accuracy error over test dataset

The selected objective function for particle swarm optimization algorithm which is the intended model consisted of three-layered feed forward neural network having scaled-conjugate back propagation as the training algorithm, 13 neurons in the hidden layer, hyperbolic tangent as the transfer function over the hidden layer and softmax as transfer function over output layer. The trained model that showed the lowest error in each month in each location was saved. The scalar value of the objective function was the accuracy error. Hence, particles traverse the search space to find the possible combination of input features that would reveal lowest error over the testing dataset.

Each dataset was divided into 70% training, 15% validation and remaining 15% for testing. Usually to measure classification accuracy, cross validation is applied. With cross validation, the dataset is partitioned into subsets where each subset is used as a testing dataset for once. Due to the nature of the problem specified here, and the linkage between dataset instances, the latest 15% of each dataset instances were taken for measuring the accuracy of the proposed model over each month. The testing datasets size varied between each location since different historical values were recorded.

The proposed approach was applied 60 times (once for each month in each location). The calculated accuracies for each month are shown in Table 3. Categorization accuracy varied between 70.59% as the lowest in December-Yamba and 100% accuracy as the highest in multiple months (July-Innisfail, August-Innisfail, September-Innisfail, January-Bingera, May-Maryborough). Innisfail held the highest annual average and the highest accuracy average with 91.15% through all months, followed by Bingera, Planecreek, Yamba and then Maryborough. An overall average of 87.89% accuracy have been recorded over the 60 months in the selected locations. Similar performance was obtained for Planecreek months even if different features were used.

Table 3. Categorization accuracy obtained for each month in each selected location using the proposed approach.

Location	Innisfail	Planecreek	Bingera	Maryborough	Yamba
January	87.5	86.67	**100**	86.67	88.24
February	93.75	86.67	94.12	86.67	82.35
March	93.75	93.33	88.24	86.67	88.24
April	93.75	86.67	88.24	93.33	82.35
May	87.5	86.67	94.12	**100**	82.35
June	87.5	86.67	76.47	80	94.12
July	**100**	86.67	94.12	93.33	94.12
August	**100**	86.67	88.24	80	88.24
September	**100**	86.67	94.12	86.67	88.24
October	75	86.67	82.35	73.33	88.24
November	87.5	86.67	82.35	80	94.12
December	87.5	93.33	76.47	80	70.59
Average	91.15	87.78	88.24	85.56	86.77

The datasets consisted of 28 possible input features: rainfall lagged values, two proposed new features, maximum and minimum temperatures, climate indices. The selected features using particle swarm optimization for each month varied between 7 and 19. The highest feature used was Nino3.0, which was selected in 66.67% of the months (40 times). The highest features used in Innisfail were Nino3.0 and plag-12 (9 months), Planecreek Nino3.0 (10 months), Bingera Nino3.0 and rain-3 (9 months), Maryborough plag-1, DMI and sunspots (9 months), while in Yamba DMI and rain-12 were used for 9 months. It was noticed that Nino 3.0 was used as possible predictor in all February classifications. The two created features that were proposed were selected in 58.33% and 56.67% of all the runs. The variations in the selected features for each month implies that feature selection is essential in forecasting monthly rainfall ranges.

5.3 Comparative Analysis

The developed approach was compared to another neural network that uses all weather variables as possible features. No feature selection was incorporated in the second approach. Same specifications were given to the neural network as the selected objective function in the deployed PSO algorithm. For each month, the network was trained multiple times and the best accuracy was recorded. Categorization accuracies of the comparison model are shown in Table 4. Using all features revealed accuracies that varied between 43.75% as the lowest in June-Innisfail and 88.24% as the highest in September-Bingera.

The differences between the two approaches and their accuracies are shown in Table 5. The proposed approach that applied feature selection revealed better accuracy in all months. An average differences of 25%, 23.89%, 24.02%, 20%, 20.59% were obtained for Innisfail, Planecreek, Bingera, Maryborough and Yamba respectively. This demonstrates the ability of feature selection in increasing rainfall classification

Table 4. Categorization accuracy obtained using a comparison approach (all features).

Location	Innisfail	Planecreek	Bingera	Maryborough	Yamba
January	62.50	73.33	88.24	66.67	58.82
February	68.75	60.00	64.71	53.33	58.82
March	68.75	73.33	52.94	53.33	58.82
April	75.00	60.00	64.71	73.33	76.47
May	81.25	66.67	76.47	73.33	58.82
June	43.75	60.00	52.94	73.33	52.94
July	62.50	53.33	64.71	86.67	88.24
August	68.75	60.00	64.71	60.00	70.59
September	75.00	66.67	88.24	66.67	82.35
October	62.50	66.67	52.94	53.33	64.71
November	62.50	66.67	47.06	60.00	70.59
December	62.50	60.00	52.94	66.67	52.94
Average	66.15	63.89	64.22	65.56	66.18

Table 5. Categorization accuracy difference between the two approaches.

Location	Innisfail	Planecreek	Bingera	Maryborough	Yamba
January	25.00	13.33	11.77	20.00	29.41
February	25.00	26.67	29.41	33.33	23.53
March	25.00	20.00	35.29	33.33	29.41
April	18.75	26.67	23.53	20.00	5.88
May	6.25	20.00	17.65	26.67	23.53
June	43.75	26.67	23.53	6.67	41.18
July	37.50	33.33	29.41	6.67	5.88
August	31.25	26.67	23.53	20.00	17.65
September	25.00	20.00	5.88	20.00	5.88
October	12.50	20.00	29.41	20.00	23.53
November	25.00	20.00	35.29	20.00	23.53
December	25.00	33.33	23.53	13.33	17.65
Average	25.00	23.89	24.02	20.00	20.59

accuracy. It was noticed that the highest difference between accuracies was recorded in locations with lowest annual averages. The use of features should be carefully considered since it is not always guaranteed that its inclusion will enhance the performance. Furthermore, neural networks are considered promising for revealing rainfall classifications (categorizations) if they are well-designed.

6 Conclusion

An artificial neural network based approach was investigated in this paper to classify rainfall patterns. A particle swarm optimization algorithm was incorporated to select features that would expose the highest accuracy for monthly rainfall. Results are promising and represent an alternative for current official rainfall forecasts. The approach is beneficial in terms of selecting accurately the timing and location of rainfall categories (below/higher than average). An overall accuracy of 87.89% was obtained for 5 locations in different weather zones along Eastern Australia. The proposed model showed higher accuracy when compared to another neural network where all features were used as predictors. In future research, new climate indices are to be incorporated and new optimization techniques are to be investigated. In addition, different network parameters of the network will be investigated and compared to enhance categorization.

References

1. McIntosh, P., Carberry, P., Stafford Smith, M., Cullen, B., Ash, A.: Constraints and opportunities in applying seasonal climate forecasts in agriculture [paper in special issue: climate predictions for better agricultural risk management. Holger, M. (ed.)]. Aust. J. Agric. Res. **58**, 952–965 (2007)
2. Zhi-liang, W., Hui-hua, S.: Rainfall prediction using generalized regression neural network: case study Zhengzhou. In: 2010 International Conference on Computational and Information Sciences (ICCIS), pp. 1265–1268 (2010)
3. Nagahamulla, H., Ratnayake, U., Ratnaweera, A.: Monsoon rainfall forecasting in Sri Lanka using artificial neural networks. In: 2011 6th International Conference on Industrial and Information Systems, pp. 305–309 (2011)
4. Narvekar, M., Fargose, P.: Daily weather forecasting using artificial neural network. Int. J. Comput. Appl. **121**, 9–13 (2015)
5. Mekanik, F., Imteaz, M.A., Gato-Trinidad, S., Elmahdi, A.: Multiple regression and artificial neural network for long-term rainfall forecasting using large scale climate modes. J. Hydrol. **503**, 11–21 (2013)
6. Abhishek, K., Singh, M.P., Ghosh, S., Anand, A.: Weather forecasting model using artificial neural network. Procedia Technol. **4**, 311–318 (2012)
7. Nagahamulla, H., Ratnayake, U. Ratnaweera, A.: An ensemble of artificial neural networks in rainfall forecasting. In: 2012 International Conference on Advances in ICT for Emerging Regions (ICTer), pp. 176–181 (2012)
8. Kishtawal, C.M., Basu, S., Patadia, F., Thapliyal, P.K.: Forecasting summer rainfall over india using genetic algorithm. Geophys. Res. Lett. **30**, 1–5 (2003)
9. Haidar, A., Verma, B.: A genetic algorithm based feature selection approach for rainfall forecasting in sugarcane areas. In: 2016 IEEE Symposium Series on Computational Intelligence (SSCI), pp. 1–8 (2016)
10. Nasseri, M., Asghari, K., Abedini, M.J.: Optimized scenario for rainfall forecasting using genetic algorithm coupled with artificial neural network. Expert Syst. Appl. **35**, 1415–1421 (2008)
11. Sumathi, S., Surekha, P.: Computational Intelligence Paradigms: Theory and Applications Using Matlab. CRC Press, Boca Raton (2010)
12. Pui, A., Sharma, A., Santoso, A., Westra, S.: Impact of the El Niño-Southern oscillation, indian ocean dipole, and southern annular mode on daily to subdaily rainfall characteristics in East Australia. Mon. Weather Rev. **140**, 1665–1682 (2012)
13. Risbey, J.S., Pook, M.J., McIntosh, P.C., Wheeler, M.C., Hendon, H.H.: On the remote drivers of rainfall variability in Australia. Mon. Weather Rev. **137**, 3233–3253 (2009)

14. Mekanik, F., Imteaz, M.A., Talei, A.: Seasonal rainfall forecasting by adaptive network-based fuzzy inference system (Anfis) using large scale climate signals. Clim. Dyn. **46**, 3097–3111 (2016)

15. Australian Bureau of Meteorology: Record-Breaking La Nina Events: An Analysis of the La Nina Life Cycle and the Impacts and Significance of 2010–11 and 2011–12 La Nina Events in Australia. Bureau of Meteorology, Melbourne (2012)

16. Dong, B., Dai, A.: The influence of the interdecadal pacific oscillation on temperature and precipitation over the globe. Clim. Dyn. **45**, 2667–2681 (2015)

17. Salinger, M.J., Renwick, J.A., Mullan, A.B.: Interdecadal pacific oscillation and south pacific climate. Int. J. Climatol. **21**, 1705–1721 (2001)

18. Henley, B.J., Gergis, J., Karoly, D.J., Power, S., Kennedy, J., Folland, C.K.: A Tripole index for the interdecadal pacific oscillation. Clim. Dyn. **45**, 3077–3090 (2015)

19. Kenyon, J., Hegerl, G.C.: Influence of modes of climate variability on global precipitation extremes. J. Clim. **23**, 6248–6262 (2010)

20. Jones, P.D., Jonsson, T., Wheeler, D.: Extension to the North Atlantic oscillation using early instrumental pressure observations from Gibraltar and South-West Iceland. Int. J. Climatol. **17**, 1433–1450 (1997)

21. Schneider, N., Cornuelle, B.D.: The forcing of the pacific decadal oscillation*. J. Clim. **18**, 4355–4373 (2005)

22. Newman, M., Alexander, M.A., Ault, T.R., Cobb, K.M., Deser, C., Di Lorenzo, E., Mantua, N.J., Miller, A.J., Minobe, S., Nakamura, H., Schneider, N., Vimont, D.J., Phillips, A.S., Scott, J.D., Smith, C.A.: The pacific decadal oscillation. Revisited J. Clim. **29**, 4399–4427 (2016)

Preliminary Study on Solving Coal Processing and Blending Problems Using Lexicographic Ordering

Sven Schellenberg[1,3,4(✉)], Xiaodong Li[1,3,4], and Zbigniew Michalewicz[2,3,4]

[1] School of Science (Computer Science and IT), RMIT University, Melbourne,
Australia
{sven.schellenberg,xiaodong.li}@rmit.edu.au
[2] Complexica, Adelaide, Australia
zm@complexica.com
[3] Institute of Computer Science, Polish Academy of Sciences, Warsaw, Poland
[4] Polish-Japanese Academy of Information Technology, Warsaw, Poland

Abstract. Despite its known shortcomings, penalty function approaches are among the most commonly used constraint handling methods in the field of evolutionary computation. In this paper, we argue that some of the techniques used to alleviate these shortfalls (namely scaling and normalisation) cannot avoid undesired search biases. Instead, we introduce the notion of desired search biases to effectively solve problems with a large number of competing constraints. The methods using this notion are based on dominance comparison by lexicographic ordering of objectives. For the real-world problem we use, two of the methods outperform the best performing penalty function approach by finding feasible solutions repeatedly.

Keywords: Evolutionary algorithm · Constraints · Lexicographic ordering

1 Introduction

The ability to handle constraints is widely recognised as an important feature for any optimisation algorithm, in particular when addressing real-world problems. In contrast to mathematical programming techniques which lend themselves to handle constraints naturally (as part of their problem formulation), evolutionary algorithms do not explicitly prescribe a specific constraint handling method. As such many constraint handling techniques have been proposed in the field of evolutionary computation [1,8,9]. The most commonly used method in evolutionary algorithms (EA) is the penalty function approach [2]. This approach transforms the constrained problem into an unconstrained optimisation problem by augmenting the objective function by a penalty term. While easy to use, this method has a number of downsides; most prominently mentioned: the appropriate choice of the penalty factor(s). Less mentioned is its inability to search

W. Peng et al. (Eds.): AI 2017, LNAI 10400, pp. 221–233, 2017.
DOI: 10.1007/978-3-319-63004-5_18

the fitness landscape unbiases which is partly, but not entirely, related to the choice of penalty parameters. We argue that even with a priori knowledge of a penalty factor (which is unrealistic for solving many real-world problems), the innate structure of many problems will most-likely introduce *undesired* search biases which (a) the algorithm designer may be unaware of and/or (b) lead to suboptimal solutions.

To avoid undesired search biases, we present a class of methods that use constraint priorities resulting in *desired* search biases. This makes the optimisation process more predictable, and also allows an algorithm designer (or user) to specify the relative priority of constraints.

The prioritisation method, or lexicographic ordering (LO), is not new, but very few publications exist. One reason may be that LO techniques are considered a multi-objective evolutionary algorithm (MOEA) technique according to some MOEA surveys [2,7], and the prevalent focus in this field on finding pareto-optimal solutions for which uneven exploration is unfavourable [2]. In this paper we show how LO can be used for solving single-objective optimisation problems, but since constraints are expressed as multiple objectives, this method is not limited to single-objective problems.

We devise four LO methods which we compare against a penalty function method with four different parameter settings (assuming one of them is the best-tuned setting). To gather preliminary results, we test the methods on a real-world problem from the problem class presented in [12]. The Coal Processing and Blending Problem (CPBP) is a multi-component nonlinear supply chain optimisation problem for which various decisions have to be made simultaneously across components. It exhibits a sizable number of constraints. The LO methods perform equal or better to the best penalty-based (parameter) method. For brevity in this paper, a simplified problem instance is considered which provides preliminary results and valuable insights into the mechanisms of the methods.

With our work, we add to the scant body of research for LO methods to handle constraints in EAs. In addition, we support an earlier study [6] that found random constraint ordering beneficial and propose a LO method that re-orders constraints based on their state. Constraint-handling is a vital aspect in optimising real-world problems and a prioritisation method can resolve issues of other approaches. With this study, we gain insights into fitness evaluations using LO-based dominance and promote this technique as it can be used as drop-in replacement where penalty functions are used.

This paper is structured as follows: In the next section we provide background information on the constraint-handling methods used. Section 3 introduces the real-world problem we use to test the constraint-handling methods on, followed by a description of the methods and other details of the algorithm in Sect. 4. A description of the experimental setup is given in Sect. 5 and the results are presented and discussed in Sect. 6 before concluding this paper in Sect. 7.

2   Constraint Handling Methods

This sections briefly reviews and critiques some EA constraint handling techniques focussing on methods that incorporate measures of constraint violation into the search process. For a more complete survey on constraint handling techniques in EA, the interested reader is referred to [1,8,10].

2.1   Constraint Value Functions

Constrained optimisation problems can be usually expressed in a form of a non-linear programming problem:

$$\text{Optimise } f(\vec{x})$$
$$\text{subject to } g_j(\vec{x}) \leq 0, j = 1, ..., J \text{ and } h_k(\vec{x}) = 0, k = 1, ..., K \tag{1}$$

where $f(\vec{x})$ is the objective function, $g_j(\vec{x})$ and $h_k(\vec{x})$ represent inequality and equality constraints. Equality constraints can be transformed into inequality constraints [3], so in the remainder of this text we do not differentiate between them.

Since EAs do not have a specific, "built-in" way of handling constraints, many techniques have emerged. Some of these, such as penalty-based or bi/multi-objective methods, quantify the level of constraint violation by defining functions that measure the distance to a constraint boundary for each constraint (other measures exist such as calculating the effort of repair or the number of constraint violations, but these are generally considered not favourable [4,11]). We refer to them as *constraint value* (CV) functions.

Different ways exist to derive a CV function from an equality or inequality constraint. For instance, given $g_j(\vec{x}) \geq a_j$, we derive a constraint value function which measures the degree of violation as:

$$CV_j(\vec{x}) = -max(g_j(\vec{x}) - a_j, 0) \tag{2}$$

Assuming that $g_j(\vec{x}) - a_j$ is non-negative when g_j is not violated, $CV_j(\vec{x})$ will be zero. Conversely, if violated, $CV_j(\vec{x})$ takes on a negative value representing the level of violation. This value can have any scale and does not need to be normalised. The only assumption is that if two solutions are compared, the one with lower[1] CV_j value violates constraint g_i more; an assumption that should be met in most if not all cases (monotonicity).

2.2   Penalty Function Approach

Using penalty functions to handle constraints is the most common technique to handle constraints in EAs. The method converts the constrained optimisation

---

[1] This also works for minimisation problems, but in this paper and unless otherwise stated we assume *optimisation* means maximisation of the fitness (and objective/CV) function.

problem into an unconstrained problem by adding a (negative) penalty function to the original objective function to be minimised (maximised). One way of using a penalty function approach is to use the penalty function as measure of distance to the constraint boundaries [4], much like the constraint value function does. A penalty function can be composed of many CV functions, for instance by summation.

$$fitness = f(\vec{x}) + \sum_{j=1}^{J} CV_j(\vec{x}) \tag{3}$$

Due to different scales and units of measurements of constraints and objective, the CV terms are mostly non-commensurable [1]. When summing them, undesired and unnoticed search biases are introduced. For instance, constraints whose CV functions map the level of constraint violation to relatively low numerical values (compared to other CVs) have less of a chance to be satisfied, because other constraints, with higher magnitude constraint values, dominate them. The numerical range of a CV function, however, may not reflect a constraint's importance in the problem domain. Objective function values can have a similar effect making constraints insignificant (or the other way around objective functions being dominated by constraint function values).

To resolve the problem of incommensurability, penalty factors are used that scale CV functions among each other and also in relation to the objective function. This can be one penalty factor p as in Eq. 4 or a separate p_j for each constraint value function CV_j.

$$fitness = f(\vec{x}) + p * \sum_{j=1}^{J} CV_j(\vec{x}) \tag{4}$$

The problem with this approach is that the search is very sensitive to the choice of penalty factor(s) and the search space is distorted [5] as a surrogate model is effectively created by this penalty function transformation.

To maintain an unbiased search (unbiased by problem parameters) some researchers resort to normalising CV values [5]. However, this assumes a priori knowledge of the constraint violation value ranges to balance the numerical ranges with the objective function. This may be an adequate assumption for test functions, but for many real-world optimisation problems this assumption does not hold.

In addition to normalisation, another problem is mostly ignored which is the distribution of CV function values. For instance, assuming normalisation was possible, imagine two constraint value functions $CV_1(\vec{x})$ and $CV_2(\vec{x})$ which map $\vec{x}$ to a range of $[-1, 0]$ (-1... max. constraint violation, 0... no constraint violation). Suppose further, the constraint value functions are non-linear and for random samples of solutions the probability of obtaining CV_1 values close to -1 is higher than for CV_2. In such a scenario when evaluating and selecting individuals, the search process would focus on "fixing" CV_1 more than CV_2. However, this preference (or bias) may not be justified from a problem domain point of view (i.e. by stating CV_1 is more important than CV_2).

As a result, the search is biased towards resolving CV_1 (most likely without the algorithm designer noticing). Static penalty function-based approaches with or without normalisable constraints have thus the tendency to bias the search undesirably.

Other penalty function approaches exist which dynamically adjust penalty factors (dynamic penalties, annealing penalties, adaptive penalties, co-evolved penalties, death penalties), but they also suffer from sensitivity of parameter selection or other problems such as numerical overflows or require a feasible seed solution [1].

2.3 Lexicographic Ordering

To avoid *undesired* search biases, we introduce the notion of *desired* search biases. Instead of leaving this part of the search uncontrolled (and subject to problem parameters), we argue that it is beneficial to be in control, aware and actively influence search biases. This would also allow to express relative importance of constraints (sometimes referred to as *soft* and *hard*-constraints [2]).

A penalty-based equivalent to express such bias by prioritisation of constraints could be achieved by defining penalty factors (Eq. 4) such that each penalty term $(p_j * CV_j(\vec{x}))$ is much smaller than a less important penalty term. However, defining such a "cascade" of penalty factors may be non-trivial. Firstly an approximate range of CV_j needs to be known a priori to create an appropriate p_j value, and secondly, with increasing number of constraints (and thus higher total penalty value $\sum p_j * CV_j(\vec{x})$), the fitness evaluation function may encounter practical numerical issues (overflow of penalty function or floating point representation problems stemming from inaccuracy for large p_j, so that $p_j * CV_j(\vec{x}) + \epsilon = p_j * CV_j(\vec{x})$).

To avoid these kind of issues and reliance on penalty factors, we employ a lexicographic ordering method of constraints and objective to establish dominance among individuals. Instead of scalarising the decision variable vector $\vec{x}$ with a penalty-based fitness function (Eq. 4), the fitness of an individual is expressed as sequence or vector:

$$fitness = \langle CV_1(\vec{x}), CV_2(\vec{x}), ..., CV_J(\vec{x}), f(\vec{x}) \rangle \tag{5}$$

When comparing two individuals a and b with $fitness^a$ and $fitness^b$, each element of the two vectors with index j is compared element-wise starting at $j = 1$, the most important constraint.

Table 1 shows a list of 5 already ranked individuals (lower rank value, better individual). Individual #1 is better than #2 ($fitness^{\#1} \succ^{lex} fitness^{\#2}$), because the most important constraint value CV_1 is better (assuming maximisation). Any subsequent constraint values and the objective function value are ignored (and may not even be calculated for efficiency reasons). In case of a tie, as for individual #2 to #5 at CV_1, the next lower prioritised constraint (CV_2) is used to compare and resolve the tie. Consequently, a ranking of individuals in a population is established that does not rely on penalty parameters, numerical

Table 1. Example ranked population based on constraint values and objective value.

#	Rank	CV_1	CV_2	CV_3	$f(x)$
1	1	0	−0.2	−1000	21
2	2	−0.1	0	−500	50
3	3	−0.1	−0.3	−200	21
4	4	−0.1	−0.4	−1000	10
5	4	−0.1	−0.4	−1000	10

range, normalisation of constraint values and assumptions about the shape of the constraint value functions (except monotonicity).

One of the earliest applications of LO is described by Fourman [6]. The author applies a GA to a chip layout compacting problem; rectangles (electrical components) of fixed sizes are placed on a surface with the constraint not to overlap. The objective is to minimise the required space. The selection favours individuals with fewer constraint violations. If two solutions with equal number of violations are compared, the one with the better smaller area wins. The author experiments with different evaluation functions. Unable to find a penalty function which does not exploit trade-offs in undesired ways, he settles with a LO method that randomly orders constraints; surprisingly this performs best.

3   Problem Description

To test our proposed EA constraint-handling methods, we choose an industry problem from the vast group of supply chain optimisation problems: the Coal Processing and Blending Problem (CPBP), [12]. The problem extends the classical blending problem by allowing non-linear objective functions, constraints and an additional component which is a processing plant. Given a mining schedule with material excavation activities (containing mining date, amount of material, projected qualities, projected quality changes and yields when processed under different processing options), and static constraints such as processing capacity, product production targets and quality specifications, the aim is to find a feasible solution that maximises the obtained profit when selling all produced products.

Products are defined by a quality specification which stipulates feasible ranges for quality attributes. An important quality attribute for the coal industry is 'ash' as it impacts on the slacking behaviour of the coal in the reactor during combustion (lower ash is concentration is better). Calorific value (CVK) is another important property which determines the amount of chemical energy present. Generally speaking, high-energy products achieve higher profits. Both attributes are improved when coal is processed or washed. Figure 1 shows the shift and concentration of these two quality attributes when material is bypassed (no further processing) or washed. Vertical dashed lines indicate the quality specification of product P1. Both qualities are affected positively by processing, but a lot of material is also shifted beyond the upper bound for CVK which makes it difficult to find a feasible blend for product P1. Other quality attributes such as moisture are worsening due to the 'washing' process. In addition, processing reduces the obtained mass by a yield factor, which has negative impacts on the obtained (bulk) product profit.

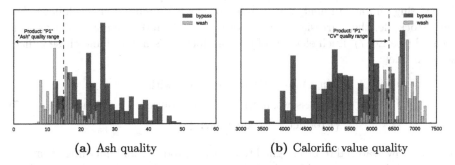

(a) Ash quality   (b) Calorific value quality

Fig. 1. Tonnage-weighted distribution of raw material qualities for two exemplary quality attributes (scenario J1). Quality specification ranges shown for Product P1.

In this paper, we use a simplified version of the actual model of the real-world problem omitting features such as rule-based routing to product stockpiles, nonlinear blending constraints (in order to use a LP formulation of the problem and the simplex method to verify results), and only one time period to reduce runtime and focus on constraint handling techniques.

The scenario is labelled J1 (we intend to publish results for more instances in future). The blend that needs to be produced (product 'P1') has to honour the quality ranges ($\Phi = [\lambda, \mu]$) for $\Phi_{ts} = [0, 0.80]$, $\Phi_{ash} = [0, 14.83]$, $\Phi_{vm} = [30.69, 35.76]$, $\Phi_{moisture} = [0, 13.46]$ and $\Phi_{cvk} = [5950, 6392.48]$. The price function, which is derived from sales contracts and an input of the problem instance, is given in Eq. 6, with symbols ω_k (product quality of attribute $k \in \{ts, ash, vm, moisture, cvk\}$), blend tonnage b, raw tonnage r and bypass ratio α (b, α, r, ω_k are functions of the decision vector $\vec{x}$, see [12] for their definitions). For brevity, we simplified the profit function which makes it appear somewhat arbitrary, but in its expanded form individual cost components as well as penalty and bonus terms are recognisable (see [12] for more information on profit functions). Scenario J1 has unlimited processing capacity and does not define a minimal production target for P1. The mine schedule can be obtained from the authors.

$$f(\vec{x}) = profit = 0.5 * \alpha * b - 0.42 * \alpha * r - 4.8 * \alpha$$
$$+ 0.008432 * b * \omega_{cvk} - 11.5145 * b - 5.38 * r \qquad (6)$$

4   The Algorithm

In this section, we describe the EA that is used to solve the CPBP. We provide details about the representation of the problem, operators, the evaluation of individuals and other design decisions of the algorithm. More details on the algorithm can be found in [12].

4.1   Representation and Operators

The solution to the optimisation problem is a blend plan. The decision variables (processing and assignment) are encoded by the EA's individuals as follows. For each stockpile, the Cartesian product of processing and assignment decisions is created (see Eq. 7). Each element of this product set is indexed and these indices serve as allele.

$$P \times A = \{\, (p, a) \mid p \in P \text{ and } a \in A \,\}, \text{ with}$$
$$P = \{\text{bypass}, \text{wash option 1}, \text{wash option 2}, \ldots\} \text{ and} \qquad (7)$$
$$A = \{\text{Product 1}, \text{Product 2}, \ldots\}$$

To allow raw material to be assigned to multiple products and handling of smaller raw material portions, each stockpile is split into evenly sized chunks. The *chunk size* is a parameter which needs to be set. It controls the resolution at which material can be assigned to products and thus the problem size of this combinatorial problem. Each gene encodes (p, a)-decisions of one of these chunks.

To allow more control over operator selection, a steady-state EA rather than the generational EA from [12] was employed. Three different types of operators are used: mutation ($p_m = 1/$ chromosome_length), single-point crossover and a variable-size neighbourhood search operator.

The neighbourhood search is worth explaining as it incorporates an effective local search mechanisms. Given a parent, this operator randomly selects d genes to perturbe and creates s random offsprings that differ in allele to their parent. A higher value for the neighbourhood distance d allows for more radical changes which makes this operator configuration more exploratory.

4.2   Fitness Evaluation and Selection

The same deterministic selection scheme is used as in [12]. We found that it provides strong search pressure while avoiding genetic drift from superior individuals which could be experienced when using other selection methods such as tournament or roulette wheel selection due to duplication of those dominating individuals. Once the randomly selected operator is applied for the generation, the spawned offspring(s) is/are inserted into the parent population, sorted according to the fitness function and the bottom part of individuals outside the fixed population size are discarded.

The fitness function for the penalty-based approaches is straight-forward according to Eq. 4. The constraint value function for product quality specification is given in Eq. 8 (processing is unlimited which makes this constraint inactive, production targets are also inactive). It is derived from Eq. 2 and sums up the distance to the lower and upper quality range for a quality attribute q of product p (zero if inside the range, i.e. satisfied).

$$CV_{quality} = -\sum_{\substack{p\in Products, \\ q\in Quality_p}} \left\{ \max(0, \lambda_{p,q} - \omega_{p,q}) + \max(0, \omega_{p,q} - \mu_{p,q}) \right\} \quad (8)$$

In addition to the penalty function methods, we devise four methods that are based on lexicographic ordering of constraint and objective values: LSagg, LSsep, LRnd and LAT. These methods differ in the prioritisation and the definition of CV functions. While LSagg and LSsep use static orders of constraint value functions, LRnd and LAT change the prioritisation of constraints dynamically.

Generally speaking, the priorities are $\langle CV_{quality}, profit \rangle$. Method LSagg uses exactly this order and the CV function and profit function in Eqs. 8 and 6. This means the population is driven towards $CV_{quality}$-feasible solutions first and only if feasible (or stagnant), the algorithm maximises the profit function within the bounds of already achieved constraint satisfaction.

LSsep works similarly, but differs in the definition of constraint value functions. Instead of calculating a composite score of $CV_{quality}$ across all products this method considers each term inside the sum separately. We arbitrarily define the static order of quality constraints, but keep them grouped together. The rationale for this method is that unlike LSagg, the EA has the opportunity to clearly discern constraints and focus on optimising each quality constraint violation in a more targetted manner. However, this leaves the weak point of having to decide on priorities among seemingly equally important constraints (e.g. Should $CV_{P1,Ash}$ be prioritised over $CV_{P1,Moisture}$?).

To address this shortcoming, the last two methods LRnd and LAT allow the definition of same-priority constraints within a group. The order of constraints within a group is altered by the method whenever stagnation of search is detected (i.e. no new best solution for a number of generations). While LRnd randomly re-orders the grouped constraints, LAT applies a heuristic of only moving those constraints that are currently active to the top of the priorities. Those that are satisfied are kept in the same order. Active constraints are randomly ordered at the top of the priority list. During the search, previously inactive constraints (at lower priorities) could become active again which would include them in the set of constraint candidates to "bubble up" to the top of the priority list when search stagnation is detected next. Our aim is to avoid that the search converges to a local optimum with constraints still being active. Ensuring different order of constraints would allow constraint boundaries to be entered from different sides of the search space and possible deadlock scenarios to be alleviated (from a fitness landscape point of view, a scenario may exist in which constraint CV_2 has to be resolved before CV_1, but CV_1 is higher prioritised than CV_2).

While LSsep and LSagg implement the desired search bias by taking user-defined priorities into account, for methods LRnd and LAT the desired search bias is controlled by the algorithm by re-ordering constraint priorities based on the state of constraints of incumbent solutions.

5   Experimental Setup

We optimise a CPB problem scenario using eight methods. These methods only differ in particular evaluation parameters and can be classified as penalty function and LO approach. For the penalty function approach four penalty weights $p \in \{10^4, 10^7, 10^{10}, 10^{13}\}$; each is considered a separate 'method' (Pen1e4, Pen1e7, Pen1e10, Pen1e13). Some prior estimation of constraint value ranges and trial runs showed that at least one of the penalty weights should perform competitively.

The four LO methods are described in Sect. 4.2. The priority orders are $\langle CV_{quality}, profit \rangle$ for LSagg with $CV_{quality} = \langle CV_{quality}^{P1,ash}, ..., CV_{quality}^{P1,vm} \rangle$ for LSsep, LRnd and LAT. The stagnation detection threshold was set to 100 iterations.

All methods use the same set of five operators: mutation, crossover and three variants of the neighbourhood search operator (with $s = 10$ and $d \in \{1, 2, 3\}$). The population size is 30 individuals and each individual is randomly initialised. The random initialisation inevitably creates infeasible solutions given. Each method was run 30 times and the means and standard deviations of $CV_{quality}$ and $profit$ were calculated. $CV_{quality}$ is combined in Table 2 to allow for easier comparison of methods, but these were not necessarily the drivers of the optimisation process (LSsep, LRnd and LAT use the individual terms as CV function instead of the sum).

To determine which method performs best, the methods are sorted lexicographically using the same order of constraints/objective (i.e. $\langle CV_{quality}, CV_{profit} \rangle$) used to optimise the scenario. Due to the stochastic nature of the optimisation algorithms and thus the results, the presented mean statistics are not necessarily indicative of the relative method performance. Friedman and Mann-Whitney U tests are used to find and group same-performing methods.

6   Results and Discussion

Table 2 shows the results with each method ordered and grouped from best (top) to worst. Method LRnd produces the best results. It is able to turn randomly initialised and infeasible individuals into feasible solutions for all 30 runs ($\sigma(CV_{quality}) = 0$). Slightly worse with respect to feasibility is the LAT method which produces 29 feasible and 1 (marginally) infeasible solution. The better mean profit value of LAT is statistically not significant. Figure 2 shows the convergence of the composite quality constraints value. LRnd and LAT's $CV_{quality}$ oscillates much more than those for the other methods. This behaviour is due to the randomisation of quality constraint priorities during the search.

Orders of magnitude worse is the performance of the remaining methods for finding feasible solutions. The group of methods Pen1e10, LSagg and Pen1e13 perform statistically the same with respect to the aggregated quality constraint violation. Pen1e10 and Pen1e13 can be considered death penalties. They perform similarly to lexicographic ordering when using the aggregated CV-function. This

Table 2. Exp. results (σ).

Method	$CV_{quality}$	$profit$
LRnd	0.0 (0)	2.45e+7 (2.12e+6)
LAT	−2.0e−5 (1.1e−4)	2.51e+7 (1.99e+6)
Pen1e10	−5.0e−3 (2.4e−3)	3.03e+7 (2.27e+6)
LSagg	−5.3e−3 (2.3e−3)	2.95e+7 (2.33e+6)
Pen1e13	−5.3e−3 (2.4e−3)	2.86e+7 (1.70e+6)
LSsep	−6.5e−3 (1.7e−3)	2.94e+7 (1.92e+6)
Pen1e7	−2.4e−1 (0)	7.11e+7 (0)
Pen1e4	−3.9e−1 (0)	7.14e+7 (0)

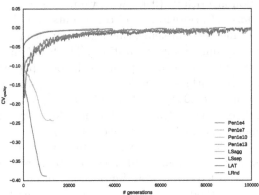

Fig. 2. Mean convergence of $CV_{quality}$.

makes sense because using a death penalty is essentially assigning highest priority to the penalty term, which is exactly what LSagg does; with the benefit of not choosing a penalty parameter).

The next worse performing group contains only LSsep. Its performance is limited by the arbitrary definition of constraint value function priorities; the algorithm is unable to satisfy the ash-quality constraint because it has converged to a higher-prioritised feasible solution for other conflicting quality attributes (CVK value and VM). A different order prioritising ash over the attributes would result in an ash-feasible solution (possibly violating other quality constraints). The difficulty lies in devising a scheme that can reprioritise constraints to escape local optima, which this method is incapable of.

Methods Pen1e4 and Pen1e7 perform worst. Their penalty factors are too low which lets them converge to infeasible solutions trading-off quality vs. profit (Fig. 2 shows that their $CV_{quality}$ scores decrease towards less feasible).

Since most of the methods cannot achieve feasibility, a comparison of objective values (profit) is irrelevant. From this simple scenario, we see that two of the LO methods LRnd and LAT perform very well for finding feasible solutions. However, when comparing the mean profits of LRnd ($24.5\,k$) and LAT ($25.1\,k$) with a lower bound obtained by a (simplified) LP formulation of the problem ($35.8\,k$), it is clear that potential for future improvements exist. The LP formulation assumes a dramatically simplified problem which is only applicable for this test scenario, but not over the range of CPB problems that we attempt to solve.

7   Conclusion

We have argued that penalty function based fitness evaluation has shortcomings beyond the already known penalty factor sensitivity and identified a undesired search bias behaviour. Since search biases are not necessarily harmful for optimisation algorithms (if known), we introduced the notion of desired search biases in form of prioritisation of constraints and objectives by lexicographic ordering. Four methods implementing lexicographic ordering were trialled against different penalty function configurations. The 'random ordering' and 'active top' method were both found to outperform the best performing penalty function configuration. Algorithms using lexicographic ordering dominance can get stuck at local optima (see LSsep), but when changing priorities can escape those local optima and converge to feasible solutions. However, lower-order constraints/objectives' quality may suffer (in our case profit).

While these results are preliminary and from a single problem instance, they are very encouraging and show the two more sophisticated lexicographic ordering methods have potential. Since they can be used without additional parameters, these methods should be considered as candidates for handling constraints in cases where penalty functions would have been chosen as they allow for a controlled desired search bias that is not dependent on numerical values of the problem specification.

Future work on more complex problem instances has to provide more evidence to confirm our findings. Also, more investigation into innovative priority schemes is required.

References

1. Coello, C.A.C.: Theoretical and numerical constraint-handling techniques used with evolutionary algorithms: a survey of the state of the art. Comput. Methods Appl. Mech. Eng. **191**(11), 1245–1287 (2002)
2. Coello, C.C., Lamont, G.B., Van Veldhuizen, D.A.: Evolutionary Algorithms for Solving Multi-objective Problems. Springer Science & Business Media, Heidelberg (2007)
3. Cormen, T.H.: Introduction to Algorithms. MIT press, Cambridge (2009)
4. Dasgupta, D., Michalewicz, Z.: Evolutionary algorithms in engineering applications. Int. J. Evol. Optim. **1**, 93–94 (1999)
5. Deb, K.: Optimization for Engineering Design: Algorithms and Examples. PHI Learning Pvt. Ltd., New Delhi (2012)
6. Fourman, M.P.: Compaction of symbolic layout using genetic algorithms. In: Proceedings of the 1st International Conference on Genetic Algorithms, pp. 141–153. L. Erlbaum Associates Inc. (1985)
7. Mezura-Montes, E., Coello, C.A.C.: A survey of constraint-handling techniques based on evolutionary multiobjective optimization. In: Workshop Paper at PPSN (2006)
8. Mezura-Montes, E., Coello, C.A.C.: Constraint-handling in nature-inspired numerical optimization: past, present and future. Swarm Evol. Comput. **1**(4), 173–194 (2011)
9. Michalewicz, Z.: A survey of constraint handling techniques in evolutionary computation methods. Evol. Program. **4**, 135–155 (1995)
10. Michalewicz, Z., Schoenauer, M.: Evolutionary algorithms for constrained parameter optimization problems. Evol. Comput. **4**(1), 1–32 (1996)

11. Richardson, J.T., Palmer, M.R., Liepins, G.E., Hilliard, M.: Some guidelines for genetic algorithms with penalty functions. In: Proceedings of the Third International Conference on Genetic Algorithms, pp. 191–197. Morgan Kaufmann Publishers Inc., San Francisco (1989)

12. Schellenberg, S., Li, X., Michalewicz, Z.: Benchmarks for the coal processing and blending problem. In: Proceedings of the 2016 Annual Conference on Genetic and Evolutionary Computation (2016)

Text Mining and Linguistic Analysis

Random Set to Interpret Topic Models in Terms of Ontology Concepts

Md Abul Bashar[(✉)] and Yuefeng Li

Electrical Engineering and Computer Science School,
Queensland University of Technology (QUT), Brisbane 4001, Australia
{m1.bashar,y2.li}@qut.edu.au
https://www.qut.edu.au

Abstract. Topic modelling is a popular technique in text mining. However, discovered topic models are difficult to interpret due to incoherence and lack of background context. Many applications require an accurate interpretation of topic models so that both users and machines can use them effectively. Taking the advantage of random set and a domain ontology, this research can interpret the topic models. The interpretation is evaluated by comparing it with different baseline models on two standard datasets. The results show that the performance of the interpretation is significantly better than baseline models.

Keywords: Random set · Topic model · Topic annotation · Topic interpretation · LDA

1 Introduction

Topic modelling, aimed to identify the subject matter of a collection of documents, is defined as a multinomial distribution over terms (words) in a corpus [2]. It has become a popular technique in text mining because of its broad range of applications such as human exploration [6], information retrieval [34], word sense disambiguation [4], machine translation [21], multi-document summarisation [11], etc.

In spite of popularity, topic modelling is ineffective to represent natural language semantics [12]. Topics are generated solely based on term distributions without any grounded *semantics* [27]. As a result, users (i.e. humans) cannot interpret extracted topic models easily, especially when the users are not familiar with the source corpus. There is a recent trend to label topic models so that both users and machines can interpret them effectively, which is required by many applications [19]. Labelling is useful for both machines and users to draw better inference and exploration. For example, topic labelling benefits users who need to analysis and understand document collections, and it benefits search engines that need to find the linkage between a group of words and their inherent topics [13]. Furthermore, many applications need to link text documents to

© Springer International Publishing AG 2017
W. Peng et al. (Eds.): AI 2017, LNAI 10400, pp. 237–249, 2017.
DOI: 10.1007/978-3-319-63004-5_19

an external knowledge base, which benefits to visualisation, knowledge discovery, information retrieval, and classification [13]. In recent years, topic model interpretation is attracting increased attention [13].

Some works [1,2,10] use topic top terms, based on distributions, as the labels; but it is not satisfactory [19]. For example, a person who is not medical science literate would not easily understand the topic models discovered from a medical science corpus using the top words such as *dopamine, cortisol, vasodilator*, etc. Besides, many ideas in topics can better be expressed with multi-word labels [15]. Others [20,32] use more meaningful labels generated manually, but manually generated labels are expensive, time-consuming and subjective. Also, manual generation of labels reduces the domain of applications. For instance, online tasks that require instant generation labels for topic models will not work in this strategy [19]. Therefore, for a satisfactory interpretation of topics in real world applications, automatic generation of meaningful labels is required. However, existing automatic label generation techniques [7,13,15,19] generate too many labels where many of them are not relevant. As a result, their performance in real world applications is poor (experimentally shown in Evaluation section).

In this paper, we propose a model called TIPO (Topic Interpretation by Personalising Ontology) to automatically interpret topic models. The interpretation has two goals: (a) it gives the meanings of topic models in terms of concepts in a domain ontology and (b) provides a new method for generating and extracting features from an ontology for better describing relevant information.

The interpretation produces a concept network that has a set of nodes and connections, where each node corresponds to a concept, and each connection corresponds to a semantic relation (e.g. Is-a, Related-to, Part-of). This concept network provides human understandable knowledge for describing the meaning of the discovered topic models. It gives the user an exploratory view and a visualisation of the topic models. Besides, the semantic relations of concepts help the user to make a further inference, such as generalising concepts or investigating how concepts are semantically related to each other.

TIPO has two steps: (a) labels the discovered topic models with concepts from a domain ontology and (b) construct the concept network using the identified concepts labels and their semantic relations. The research question is how to label the topic models with concepts. The leading idea of labelling is to map the topic models to the concepts in a domain ontology. Then, the set of concepts that are mapped with topic models is used as the labels. Even though current literature has many techniques to automatically label a set of terms, most of the techniques (e.g. [5,25,26,31]) assume that the terms in a term set are *independent* and map each term *individually* (i.e. in isolation) to concepts. In essence, a topic model is a set of terms that frequently co-occur in a text or corpus. A technique that maps each term individually cannot consider the influence of other terms that co-occur with this term.

For instance, if there is a topic model *Java Machine Language Virtual*, the technique will map the term *Java* to both the concepts *Java Coffee* and *Java Language* with the same importance, without considering the co-occurrence of

Language with *Java*. However, the co-occurrence of terms can help in understanding the discovered knowledge. For example, as *Java* frequently co-occur with *Language*, we can easily conclude that the discovered knowledge is about *Java Language* instead of *Java Coffee*. To the best of our knowledge, there are no techniques that address the very specific problem of how to map a set of *co-occurring* terms to the concepts in a domain ontology.

More importantly, each term in a co-occurring term set (i.e. a topic model) can be mapped to many concepts. Therefore, all the terms in a set of topic models will be mapped to a large number of concepts, resulting in information overload. This means, the research issue in mapping is how to incorporate the influence of co-occurring terms and minimise the information overload and mismatch problem.

To address the research issue, we propose to use random set theory [9,14]. The proposed technique incorporates the influence of co-occurring terms when mapping. Besides, it categorises candidate concepts into two groups—strongly relevant concepts and weakly relevant concepts—based on their relevance to the co-occurring term sets, which allows the system to minimise the information overload problem to a large extent.

This paper makes both theoretical and practical contributions. The major contributions are: (a) it provides a theoretical method based on random set to effectively label topic models and (b) it proposes an effective way to interpret topic models.

2 Related Work

The works in [13,19] propose to label topic models in terms of n-grams and phrases that are extracted from a corpus. They assume that extracted n-grams and phrases are semantically meaningful, therefore should express the topic themes. However, in many experiments, it has been observed that automatically extracted phrases and n-grams are not semantically meaningful especially for more than 2-g [19]. Lau et al. [16] propose to find the best term of a topic and use it as the label. Single terms are too general, and therefore cannot accurately capture the themes of a topic [15,19].

Hulpus et al. [13] and Lau et al. [15] propose to map topic models to concepts for semantic meaning. Other researchers (e.g. [7]) propose to model documents by mapping them to concepts. The proposed techniques of these researchers potentially map a huge number of concepts, where many of them are not relevant to the topic models. These nonrelevant concepts can misinterpret the topic models and their appearance can make the labels ineffective for practical use.

3 Basic Definitions

The proposed model TIPO and the corresponding experiments of this paper are designed from a user's perspective. In this section, we describe the basic definitions that are important to understanding the model. This research assumes that a document d is a bag of words. Let us assume that a user has a collection D^+ of documents that are relevant to a specific topic of interest. The user wants to analyse the topic by using the topic models discovered from the document collection (this needs to achieve the first interpretation goal: meanings of topic models in terms of ontology concepts) and want to collect documents from the Web that are relevant to these topic models (this needs to achieve the second interpretation goal: a method for generating and extracting features from ontology for better describing relevant information).

Latent Dirichlet Allocation. Let $D^+ = \{d_1, d_2, ..., d_M\}$ be the collection of M documents that are relevant to a given topic (*topic model* and *topic* are different). Let $D_t = \{t_1, t_2, ..., t_V\}$ be the set of unique terms in the document collection D^+, where V is the size of the vocabulary.

The idea behind LDA is that observed terms in each document are generated by a document-specific mixture of corpus-wide hidden topics [2]. The number of hidden topics are assumed to be fixed to T. A topic z_j is represented as a multinomial probability distribution over the V terms as $p(t_i|z_j)$, where $1 \leq j \leq T$ and $\sum_i^V p(t_i|z_j) = 1$. A document d is represented as probabilistic mixture of topics as $p(z_j|d)$. Therefore, the probability distribution of ith term in a document d can be modelled as a mixer over topics: $p(t_i|d) = \sum_{j=1}^T p(t_i|z_j)p(z_j|d)$. Here the only observable variable is $p(t_i|d)$. The other two variables $p(t_i|z_j)$ and $p(z_j|d)$ are hidden. In this paper, the widely used statistical estimation technique of Gibbs sampling is used for learning the hidden variables. In this research, we want to interpret topic models in terms of concepts in a domain ontology. The domain ontology and the concept are formally defined as follow.

Definition 1 (Domain Ontology). *A domain ontology is a pair $\langle E, R \rangle$, where E is a finite set of concepts in a knowledge domain, and R is a set of triplet $\langle c_1, c_2, r \rangle$, where c_1 and c_2 are two concepts and r is their semantic relation.*

Definition 2 (Concept). *A concept c consists of a set of attributes and represents an idea or object. Each concept is described with a human-understandable label s, where $s = \{t_1, t_2, ..., t_n\}$ is a set of semantically related terms. Each term $t \in s$ represents an attribute of the concept c.*

4   Topic Model Interpretation

This paper proposes to interpret a set of topic models by generating a representative concept network for them. A concept network includes a set of concepts as nodes and their semantic relations as connections. The concept network represents the knowledge in the discovered topic models. This kind of network is the foundation of human cognition [30] and supposed to assist in understanding the topic models. A concept network is useful to understand and analyse the represented information. Its visualisation (e.g. as a graph) can help the user to visually see the represented information. They can easily investigate how concepts are semantically related to each other. As a result, they can make inference about the concepts or can generalise the concepts to understand the presented information from a higher level view.

A domain ontology is represented as an acyclic directed graph, where concepts are vertices, and semantic relations are edges. After the discovered topic models are labelled, an algorithm similar to the minimum spanning tree is run on the domain ontology to connect the labels. The resultant sub-graph is the concept network of the interpretation.

As we said, the leading idea of labelling is to map the topic models to the concepts in a domain ontology. To address the mapping problem, we propose to use random set theory [9,14]. In mathematics and artificial intelligence, the random set is used as a rigorous mechanism for modelling observed phenomena that are sets rather than precise points. As the semantic relationships between topic models and concepts are set valued observation, the random set is an effective tool for the semantic analysis. Use of random set for labelling topic models is discussed in the following subsection.

4.1   Random Set for Topic Labelling

For simplicity, a concept c in a domain ontology is a human-defined set of semantically related terms that together express a human-understandable idea or object. The terms in a concept c are $\{t_1, t_2, ..., t_n\}$. A domain ontology consists of a set of concepts and their semantic relations. Let the evidence space E be the set of all the concepts in the domain ontology, and $\Omega = \{t | t \in c \,\&\, c \in E\}$ be the term vocabulary.

As we mentioned, each concept can be described by a set of terms; therefore, there is a set-valued mapping $\Gamma : E \to 2^{\Omega} - \{\emptyset\}$ such that $\Gamma(c) \subseteq \Omega$ for all $c \in E$. If there is a probability distribution Ψ defined on the evidence space E, then the pair (Ψ, Γ) is called a random set [9,14].

As [28] argued that the main link between a text and an ontology is terms. In this research, the link between ontology and text is set up by discovered topic models. Let Z be a set of discovered topic models. We actually observed topic models first. So, we need to consider the inverse mappings of Γ to decide a suitable distribution Ψ on E.

Let (Ψ, Γ) be a random set, we can have the following three inverse mappings based on the discovered topic models: Γ^{-1^-}, Γ^{-1^+}, $\Gamma^{-1^\odot}$: $2^{\Omega} \to 2^E$.

$$\Gamma^{-1^-}(z) = \{c \in E | \Gamma(c) \neq \emptyset \text{ and } \Gamma(c) \subseteq z\},$$
$$\Gamma^{-1^+}(z) = \{c \in E | \Gamma(c) \cap z \neq \emptyset\}, \text{and}$$
$$\Gamma^{-1^\odot}(z) = \Gamma^{-1^+}(z) - \Gamma^{-1^-}(z)$$

are called the inner coarsening, outer coarsening and boundary region of z, respectively, for all topic models z, where we assume $z \subseteq \Omega$.

In essence, the inner coarsening, outer coarsening and boundary region of z discuss the relationship between the topic model and the concepts, and Γ^{-1^-}

takes co-occurrence of terms in account. For our running example of co-occurring term set *Java Machine Language Virtual*, Γ^{-1^-} will put the concept *Java Coffee* into boundary region and the concept *Java Language* into inner coarsening. Apparently, the mapping reflects the influence of terms that co-occur with each other. Another advantage of using random set is that the belief function, the plausibility function and the mass function for a topic model can easily be obtained from it, which is useful in artificial intelligence and other application areas.

As there is a many-to-many relation between concepts and topic models, a set of topic models together, rather than an individual topic model, should be mapped to the concepts. This is important because, in practice, rather than a single topic model, we use the whole set of topic models to understand the main theme of a document. Therefore, the union of inner coarsenings, outer coarsenings and boundary regions are required for finding relevant concepts: $C^e = \bigcup_{z \in M} \Gamma^{-1^-}(z)$, $C^* = \bigcup_{z \in M} \Gamma^{-1^+}(z)$, $C^p = C^* - C^e$.

The concepts in C^e come from the inner coarsening. As a result, they can represent the knowledge of topic models precisely, and we call them *strongly relevant* concepts. On the other hand, the concepts in C^p come from the boundary region. As a result, they may incorporate some noise, and we call them *weakly relevant* concepts. We use all the strongly relevant concepts and the top weakly relevant concepts as the labels of the set Z of topic models.

To calculate a concept's probability distribution Ψ for selecting top weakly relevant concepts, we design a function $rel(c)$. For a given topic set Z, $rel(c)$ estimates the relevance score for a concept c (see Eq. 1).

$$rel(c) = \frac{|c \cap z_i|}{|c|}$$
$$where, \ z_i \in \arg\max_{z \in Z}(|c \cap z|) \tag{1}$$

Probability distribution $\Psi(c_1)$ is proportional to $rel(c_1)$, and it can be calculated as $\Psi(c_1) = \frac{rel(c_1)}{\sum_{c \in E}(rel(c))}$, where c_1 is a given concept. Weakly relevant concepts are sorted descending order using $\Psi(c)$ value and top $k' = |Z| \times \theta - |C^e|$ of them are selected, where θ is an experimental parameter.

5   Evaluation

The hypothesis of this research is that the concept network generated by our proposed model TIPO can effectively interpret discovered topic models. Our model should help to improve retrieval effectiveness compared with the discovered topic models, other extracted features and other labelling models. As concept and ontology evaluation is always a difficult problem, we apply some well-known information filtering measurements to do the validation. In the following subsections, we discuss data collection, baseline models, experimental design, evaluation measures, experimental setting and experimental results.

5.1 Data Collection

Two standard datasets—RCV1 of TREC-10/2001 filtering track [23] and a large knowledge base LCSH [37]—are used in this research. The first dataset RCV1 has a number of topics; we call these TREC-topics to avoid confusion with topics in topic modelling. Each TREC-topic has a manual specification of information needs written by linguists and has a set of documents. In the first 50 TREC-topics, that are used in this research, the set D^+ of relevant documents are manually selected by users. We extract topic models and train all the baseline models using D^+. The second dataset, LCSH [37], is used as the domain ontology. It contains 491,250 subject headings (concepts) and their named semantic relations. Pre-processing is applied to all the datasets via meta-data and stopwords removing as well as stemming. Porter's suffix-stripping algorithm is used for the stemming.

5.2 Baseline Models

To provide a comprehensive evaluation of our proposed model, we have selected 10 baseline models in this paper.

- *LDA-word* [2,8]: it uses the term frequency to represent topic relevance and association of terms with different topics to represent user interest.
- *TNG* [33]: it is n-Gram based topic model.
- *LDA-based-concept* [7]: it uses statistical LDA technique for annotating text documents with concepts. It treats concepts as topics with constraint $t_i \notin c_j \Rightarrow p(t_i|c_j) = 0$.
- *POM* [25]: it is one of the most recent work that maps document keywords to the standard ontology (LCSH).
- *Pattern Deploying Model (PDM)* [35]: it provides a way to effectively use the text-patterns in the information filtering.
- *FCP* [8]: frequent closed patterns extracted from documents are used to represent user interest.
- *Master Pattern (MP)* [36]: it is a profile-based technique for summarising a collection of frequent closed patterns, using only K representatives. It is popularly used in data mining communities for effective utilisation of patterns.
- *n-Gram* [8]: it uses n-Grams extracted from documents to represent user interest, where n is empirically set to 3.
- *BM25* [22]: is one of the term based state-of-the models for representing documents and thereby user interest.
- *Support Vector Machine (SVM)* [24]: It is considered effective for text filtering and categorisation. We adopt the rank-based SVM[1].
- *Title-based (TB)*: Each TREC topic of RCV1 dataset is enclosed with a specific name (title) for grouping relevant documents. These names were given by domain experts and highly summarised based on their knowledge and past experiences. Therefore, from a human point of view, they can be considered

---

[1] http://svmlight.joachims.org.

as the best representatives of the concepts in TREC-topics. We use RCV1 TREC-topic names as the golden standard for our generated concepts. The frequency of each term in a name is used as the term's weight.

5.3 Experimental Design

In this research, we use the Information Filtering system to evaluate the interpretation. In the TREC Filtering Track [23], when testing a system, the user's information needs are assumed to be stable, and a stream of unknown documents (from the testing dataset) is brought into the system. For each new document, the system has to decide whether the document is relevant to the user's information needs [23].

In this paper, we use the interpretation to predict whether a new document brought into the system is relevant to the subject matters of the topic models. If the use of interpretation can predict the relevance, we believe, it indicates that the interpretation can effectively represent the subject matters of the topic model set. It is a data-driven evaluation of concepts in a real application as suggested by [3]. In the context of machine readability of the Web in the future, this kind of evaluation is appropriate [3].

To prove the hypothesis, a series of experiments have been conducted on the standard dataset RCV1, as in TREC [23]. Because all the baseline models assign a weight to each term selected in the training phase, we estimate a weight for each term in the concepts. The weight is estimated from a set of relevant statistics (described below) calculated from the corpus and the ontology. We use the mapped concepts (i.e. labels) and the estimated term weight as a query (Q) submitted to an information filtering system. A similar approach is applied for the baseline models. If the results of information filtering measures are improved significantly, compared with the baseline models, we can claim that our proposed model, TIPO, effectively interprets the discovered topic models.

Relevant Statistics. In this research, we found the following five relevant statistics that are useful to estimate weights of terms in concepts. This subsection briefly discusses them.

Document Level Statistics: Statistic in this level is relative term frequency, and it is calculated as $f_r(t) = \frac{f(t)}{\sum_{d \in D+} |terms(d)|}$, where $terms(d)$ returns all the terms in the document d.

Topic Level Statistics: In topic modelling (specifically LDA), a document in a corpus is represented by a probabilistic mixture of latent topics [2]. This probabilistic mixture represents a document's focus into the topic. The full semantic theme of a topic is represented by its corresponding multinomial distribution over terms [19]. Therefore, the amount of topical interest that a term contains can be roughly estimated using these two distributions as $w_z(t) = \sum_{j=1}^{T} p(z_j|d) \times p(t|z_j)$. In the case of multiple documents, the average is taken.

Inter-Topic Level Statistics: From the experimental results, Mao et al. [18] concluded that inter-topic relations are useful for improving the accuracy of topic interpretation. To utilise the term overlapping between topics, the frequency distribution of topics to the term t is calculated as $w_\vartheta(t) = \frac{|\{z|t \in z, z \in Z\}|}{|Z|}$.

Ontology Level Statistics: If a term appears in many concepts in the standard ontology, the term is general. The specificity of a term is inversely related to the frequency of concepts in the standard ontology that contains this term [17]. On the other hand, in the semantic structure, the frequency of strongly relevant concepts that contain a given term indicates the term's closeness to the main theme of the interpretation. The ontological significance $spe_o(t) = \frac{|\{c|t \in c, c \in C^e\}|}{|\{c|t \in c, c \in E\}|}$ of a term is estimated using these two frequencies.

Mapping Level Statistics: A given term t can appear in many concepts, and each concept can be related to many topic models. The mapping level statistic $i(t)$ of a term t estimates the relevance of the term t to the set of concepts C in terms of their (concepts) relevance to the topic model set Z. The average relevance of c, taken over all z where $rel(c) > 0$, is called the support $(sup'(c))$ of the concept c. Term support for each term in a given concept c is $tsup(c) = \frac{sup'(c)}{|c|}$. The $i(t)$ of a given term t is the average of term supports, taken over all c. However, as discussed in Sect. 4.1, the strongly relevant and weakly relevant concepts are not the same important to the subject matters. In essence, we have three cases: $case_1$ is when the term t appears in both strongly relevant concepts and weakly relevant concepts, $case_2$ is when it appears in only strongly relevant concepts and $case_3$ is when it appears in only weakly relevant concepts. In $case_1$, we devide $i(t)$ by a factor of 2 because t appears in both category.

Based on the above five statistics, we estimate a single weight for each term in the concepts. The weight can be viewed as a summary of the above five statistics. We estimate the term weight using the following Eq. 2.

$$w(t) = \begin{cases} w_z(t) \times \alpha_1 + \beta_1 \times i(t) \times w_c(t) & if\ case_1 \\ w_z(t) \times \alpha_2 + \beta_2 \times i(t) \times w_c(t) & if\ case_2 \\ w_z(t) & if\ case_3 \end{cases}$$

$$w_c(t) = \begin{cases} spe_o(t) \times f_r(t) & if\ case_1 \\ spe_o(t) \times f_r(t) \times w_\vartheta(t) & if\ case_2. \end{cases} \tag{2}$$

Here, α_1, α_2, β_1, and β_2 are experimental coefficients.

There are a few terms in topic models that have no corresponding matched (strongly relevant or weekly relevant) subject-heading in LCSH. These terms are removed from topic models before applying random set. We assume that these are new concepts created by the author of the text. As these concepts are newly created for expressing the author's view in that document, they are useful and specific to the corpus. Therefore, after the random set is applied, these unmatched terms in topic models are added as new concepts to the labels. We weight these terms using equation $w(t) = w_z(t)$.

5.4   Evaluation Measures

Our proposed hypothesis of the model TIPO is evaluated by different means. Especially, five widely used measures of the information filtering track that are based on relevance judgement. In the relevance judgement, there is a collection of documents and every document is known to be either relevant or irrelevant to the topic. The measures include the Mean Average Precision (MAP), the average precision of the top 20 returned documents (Top–20), the F_{score} measure (F_1), the break-even point (BP), and the interpolated precision averages at 11 standard recall levels (11-$point$).

5.5   Experimental Settings

In this paper, for all LDA-based topic models, the parameters are set as follows: the number of iterations of Gibbs sampling is 1000, the hyper-parameters of the LDA are $\alpha = 50/V$ and $\beta = 0.01$. These parameter values were used and justified in [29]. For extracting frequent closed patterns, the minimum support is sensitive to a given data set. For the RCV1 data set, using trial-and-error, the best value for this experimental coefficient was found to be 0.2. The best values for other experimental coefficients were also determined on the trial-and-error basis in RCV1. The best value for β was found to be 0.2 for generating master patterns; in the topic labelling by random set, the best value for θ was found to be 3.0; and for weighting the terms of the concepts mapped by the TIPO, the best value for α_1, β_1, α_2 and β_2 were found to be 2.1, 55, 1.5 and 56, respectively, in the experiment.

5.6   Experimental Results

Based on the information filtering performance, evaluation results of interpretations are shown in Table 1 and Fig. 1. The results are the average of all 50 TREC topics in RCV1. The table and figure also show the results of the 10 baseline models. The $change\%$ in Table 1 means the percentage change of our proposed TIPO model over the best results of baseline models. An improvement greater than 5% is considered significant.

Table 1 shows that the information filtering performance of our proposed model TIPO is significantly better than the best results of the baseline models. It improved the performance significantly 5.839% (11.180% max and 4.345% min) on average for all four measures. The amount of improvement is significant for all the individual measures too, except for the F_1 (in this case 4.345% improved). The most important measure of information filtering is MAP. The model improved the MAP performance significantly 6.629%. The 11-$point$ results in Fig. 1 shows that the performance is consistently better than baseline models. Based on these results, we can claim that our proposed model TIPO can effectively interpret discovered topic models. This means the obtained results support our hypothesis.

Table 1. Evaluation results

	Top–20	BP	MAP	F_1
TIPO	**0.537**	**0.458**	**0.473**	**0.459**
LDA-word	0.483	0.428	0.444	0.439
PDM	0.473	0.417	0.438	0.436
TB	0.461	0.402	0.413	0.426
POM	0.458	0.400	0.411	0.419
SVM	0.447	0.409	0.408	0.421
BM25	0.434	0.339	0.401	0.410
MP	0.426	0.392	0.393	0.409
TNG	0.446	0.367	0.374	0.388
n-Gram	0.401	0.342	0.361	0.386
FCP	0.428	0.346	0.361	0.385
LDA-based-concept	0.335	0.329	0.326	0.352
change%	**11.180**	**7.043**	**6.629**	**4.345**

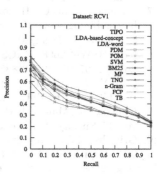

Fig. 1. 11-Point results

6   Conclusions

This paper presents a model to automatically interpret topic models in terms of concepts in a domain ontology. The effectiveness of the interpretation is evident by the experimental results. The interpretation uses a network of concepts and their semantic relations, which provides human understandable knowledge for describing the meaning of the discovered topic models. Its significance is in the process of exploring topic models and selecting relevant features from an ontology for better describing relevant information.

Acknowledgment. This research was partially supported by Grant DP140103157 from the Australian Research Council (ARC Discovery Project).

References

1. Blei, D., Lafferty, J.: Correlated topic models. Adv. Neural Inform. Process. Syst. **18**, 147 (2006)
2. Blei, D.M., Ng, A.Y., Jordan, M.I.: Latent dirichlet allocation. J. Mach. Learn. Res. **3**, 993–1022 (2003)
3. Brewster, C., Alani, H., Dasmahapatra, S., Wilks, Y.: Data driven ontology evaluation. In: International Conference on Language Resources and Evaluation (LREC 2004) (2004)
4. Brody, S., Lapata, M.: Bayesian word sense induction. In: Proceedings of the 12th Conference of the European Chapter of the Association for Computational Linguistics, pp. 103–111. Association for Computational Linguistics (2009)
5. Calegari, S., Pasi, G.: Personal ontologies: generation of user profiles based on the yago ontology. Inform. Process. Manag. **49**(3), 640–658 (2013)

6. Chaney, A.J.-B., Blei, D.M.: Visualizing topic models. In: ICWSM (2012)
7. Chemudugunta, C., Holloway, A., Smyth, P., Steyvers, M.: Modeling documents by combining semantic concepts with unsupervised statistical learning. In: Sheth, A., Staab, S., Dean, M., Paolucci, M., Maynard, D., Finin, T., Thirunarayan, K. (eds.) ISWC 2008. LNCS, vol. 5318, pp. 229–244. Springer, Heidelberg (2008). doi:10.1007/978-3-540-88564-1_15
8. Gao, Y., Xu, Y., Li, Y.: Pattern-based topics for document modelling in information filtering. IEEE Trans. Knowl. Data Eng. **27**(6), 1629–1642 (2015)
9. Goutsias, J., Mahler, R.P., Nguyen, H.T.: Random Sets: Theory and Applications, vol. 97. Springer Science & Business Media, New York (2012)
10. Griffiths, T.L., Steyvers, M.: Finding scientific topics. Proc. Nat. Acad. Sci. **101**(suppl 1), 5228–5235 (2004)
11. Haghighi, A., Vanderwende, L.: Exploring content models for multi-document summarization. In: Proceedings of Human Language Technologies: The 2009 Annual Conference of the North American Chapter of the Association for Computational Linguistics, pp. 362–370. Association for Computational Linguistics (2009)
12. Hu, Z., Luo, G., Sachan, M., Xing, E., Nie, Z.: Grounding topic models with knowledge bases. In: Proceedings of the 24th International Joint Conference on Artificial Intelligence (2016)
13. Hulpus, I., Hayes, C., Karnstedt, M., Greene, D.: Unsupervised graph-based topic labelling using DBpedia. In: Proceedings of the Sixth ACM International Conference on Web Search and Data Mining, pp. 465–474. ACM (2013)
14. Kruse, R., Schwecke, E., Heinsohn, J.: Uncertainty and Vagueness in Knowledge Based Systems. Springer, New York (1991)
15. Lau, J.H., Grieser, K., Newman, D., Baldwin, T.: Automatic labelling of topic models. In: Proceedings of the 49th Annual Meeting of the Association for Computational Linguistics: Human Language Technologies, vol. 1, pp. 1536–1545. Association for Computational Linguistics (2011)
16. Lau, J.H., Newman, D., Karimi, S., Baldwin, T.: Best topic word selection for topic labelling. In: Proceedings of the 23rd International Conference on Computational Linguistics: Posters, pp. 605–613. Association for Computational Linguistics (2010)
17. Li, Y., Algarni, A., Albathan, M., Shen, Y., Bijaksana, M.A.: Relevance feature discovery for text mining. IEEE Trans. Knowl. Data Eng. **27**(6), 1656–1669 (2015)
18. Mao, X.-L., Ming, Z.-Y., Zha, Z.-J., Chua, T.-S., Yan, H., Li, X.: Automatic labeling hierarchical topics. In: Proceedings of the 21st ACM International Conference on Information and Knowledge Management, pp. 2383–2386. ACM (2012)
19. Mei, Q., Shen, X., Zhai, C.: Automatic labeling of multinomial topic models. In: Proceedings of the 13th ACM SIGKDD International Conference on Knowledge Discovery and Data Mining, pp. 490–499. ACM (2007)
20. Mei, Q., Zhai, C.: A mixture model for contextual text mining. In: Proceedings of the 12th ACM SIGKDD International Conference on Knowledge Discovery and Data Mining, pp. 649–655. ACM (2006)
21. Mimno, D., Wallach, H.M., Naradowsky, J., Smith, D.A., McCallum, A.: Polylingual topic models. In: Proceedings of the 2009 Conference on Empirical Methods in Natural Language Processing, vol. 2, pp. 880–889. Association for Computational Linguistics (2009)
22. Robertson, S., Zaragoza, H., Taylor, M.: Simple BM25 extension to multiple weighted fields. In: Proceedings of the Thirteenth ACM International Conference on Information and Knowledge Management, pp. 42–49. ACM (2004)
23. Robertson, S.E., Soboroff, I.: The TREC 2002 filtering track report. In: TREC, vol. 2002, p. 5 (2002)

24. Sebastiani, F.: Machine learning in automated text categorization. ACM Comput. Surv. (CSUR) **34**(1), 1–47 (2002)
25. Shen, Y., Li, Y., Xu, Y.: Adopting relevance feature to learn personalized ontologies. In: Thielscher, M., Zhang, D. (eds.) AI 2012. LNCS, vol. 7691, pp. 457–468. Springer, Heidelberg (2012). doi:10.1007/978-3-642-35101-3_39
26. Sieg, A., Mobasher, B., Burke, R.: Web search personalization with ontological user profiles. In: Proceedings of the Sixteenth ACM Conference on Information and Knowledge Management, pp. 525–534. ACM (2007)
27. Song, Y., Wang, H., Wang, Z., Li, H., Chen, W.: Short text conceptualization using a probabilistic knowledgebase. In: Proceedings of the Twenty-Second International Joint Conference on Artificial Intelligence, vol. 3, pp. 2330–2336. AAAI Press (2011)
28. Spasic, I., Ananiadou, S., McNaught, J., Kumar, A.: Text mining and ontologies in biomedicine: making sense of raw text. Brief. Bioinform. **6**(3), 239–251 (2005)
29. Steyvers, M., Griffiths, T.: Probabilistic topic models. Handb. Latent Semant. Anal. **427**(7), 424–440 (2007)
30. Sun, X., Xiao, Y., Wang, H., Wang, W.: On conceptual labeling of a bag of words. In: Proceedings of the 24th International Conference on Artificial Intelligence, pp. 1326–1332. AAAI Press (2015)
31. Tran, T., Cimiano, P., Rudolph, S., Studer, R.: Ontology-based interpretation of keywords for semantic search. In: Aberer, K., Choi, K.-S., Noy, N., Allemang, D., Lee, K.-I., Nixon, L., Golbeck, J., Mika, P., Maynard, D., Mizoguchi, R., Schreiber, G., Cudré-Mauroux, P. (eds.) ASWC/ISWC -2007. LNCS, vol. 4825, pp. 523–536. Springer, Heidelberg (2007). doi:10.1007/978-3-540-76298-0_38
32. Wang, X., McCallum, A.: Topics over time: a non-markov continuous-time model of topical trends. In: Proceedings of the 12th ACM SIGKDD International Conference on Knowledge Discovery and Data Mining, pp. 424–433. ACM (2006)
33. Wang, X., McCallum, A., Wei. X.: Topical n-grams: phrase and topic discovery, with an application to information retrieval. In: Seventh IEEE International Conference on Data Mining, ICDM 2007, pp. 697–702. IEEE (2007)
34. Wei, X., Croft, W.B.: LDA-based document models for ad-hoc retrieval. In: Proceedings of the 29th Annual International ACM SIGIR Conference on Research and Development in Information Retrieval, pp. 178–185. ACM (2006)
35. Wu, S.-T., Li, Y., Xu, Y.: Deploying approaches for pattern refinement in text mining. In: Sixth International Conference on Data Mining, ICDM 2006, pp. 1157–1161. IEEE (2006)
36. Yan, X., Cheng, H., Han, J., Xin, D.: Summarizing itemset patterns: a profile-based approach. In: Proceedings of the Eleventh ACM SIGKDD International Conference on Knowledge Discovery in Data Mining, pp. 314–323. ACM (2005)
37. Yi, K., Chan, L.M.: Linking folksonomy to library of congress subject headings: an exploratory study. J. Document. **65**(6), 872–900 (2009)

Improving Authorship Attribution in Twitter Through Topic-Based Sampling

Luoxi Pan[1]([⊠]), Iqbal Gondal[2], and Robert Layton[2]

[1] Monash University, Melbourne, Australia
lpan0003@student.monash.edu
[2] Internet Commerce Security Laboratory, Federation University Australia,
Ballarat, Australia
iqbal.gondal@federation.edu.au,
robertlayton@gmail.com

Abstract. Aliases are used as a means of anonymity on the Internet in environments such as IRC (internet relay chat), forums and micro-blogging websites such as Twitter. While there are genuine reasons for the use of aliases, such as journalists operating in politically oppressive countries, they are increasingly being used by cybercriminals and extremist organisations. In recent years, we have seen increased research on authorship attribution of Twitter messages, including authorship analysis of aliases. Previous studies have shown that anti-aliasing of randomly generated sub-aliases yields high accuracies when linking the sub-aliases, but become much less accurate when topic-based sub-aliases are used. N-gram methods have previously been demonstrated to perform better than other methods in this situation. This paper investigates the effect of topic-based sampling on authorship attribution accuracy for the popular micro-blogging website Twitter. Features are extracted using character n-grams, which accurately capture differences in authorship style. These features are analysed using support vector machines using a one-versus-all classifier. The predictive performance of the algorithm is then evaluated using two different sampling methodologies - authors that were sampled through a context-sensitive topic-based search and authors that were sampled randomly. Topic-based sampling of authors is found to produce more accurate authorship predictions. This paper presents several theories as to why this might be the case.

Keywords: Authorship attribution · Twitter authorship · Linguistic analysis

1 Introduction

The idea that we can determine the author of an unknown or disputed piece of writing can be traced back to the 19th century, from studies such as the one by Mendenhall [1] on the plays of Shakespeare. When it comes to communicating with others, we have moved from hand written letters to short messages on our phones and in our emails. Micro-blogging platforms such as Twitter have become increasingly popular in recent years, with a record 500 million tweets being sent every day. Twitter is special because its users are only allowed a maximum of 140 characters per message (called "tweets"). This introduces new challenges.

© Springer International Publishing AG 2017
W. Peng et al. (Eds.): AI 2017, LNAI 10400, pp. 250–261, 2017.
DOI: 10.1007/978-3-319-63004-5_20

Previous research into short text authorship on platforms such as Twitter have tended to assess prediction accuracy based on messages gathered from randomly sampled users. This method of data collection isn't necessarily reflected in its real-world application, especially if we are required to apply authorship analysis to users filtered by topic. This is particularly relevant for law enforcement agencies that wish to profile potential suspects that are known to frequent or discuss certain topics on the Internet. Cybercriminals are known to spread malicious software on social networks such as Twitter using shortened URLs. Even low click rates and low social connectivity can lead to the infection of many users [2]. Cybercriminals are likely to target trending topics for optimal malware propagation across Twitter [3].

1.1 Research Questions

This paper investigates a topic-based sampling approach for authorship attribution, with two key research objectives to consider.

1. How effective is the use of character n-grams in conjunction with a support vector machine classifier in predicting authorship for authors sampled on topic, versus authors that are randomly sampled?
2. Are there any differences in the use of language between the two groups of authors?

Authors that are non-randomly sampled are expected to be closer in authorship style, particularly if they are sampled based on topic. Less diverse authorship styles are expected to result in lower prediction accuracies, compared to more diverse authorship styles that are discovered with random sampling of authors. This assumption then leads to following contributions:

- Investigation that prediction algorithms can lose accuracy when run on non-randomly sampled authors due to less diverse authorship styles. By investigating the linguistic differences between author groups, we may discover contributing factors behind differences in prediction accuracy. Our author group sampled on topic will form a list of authors that talk about the Python programming language.
- Conduct a study to validate or invalidate that Python users (i.e. users that tweet about the programming language) on average have a smaller vocabulary set compared to the control group, since they discuss a more linguistically narrow topic of discussion (i.e. computer programming).

1.2 Previous Work

Outside of authorship attribution, Twitter has been used to predict criminal incidents [4], the stock market [5, 6], elections results [7], and flu epidemics [8, 9]. In a survey of Twitter election prediction studies, Gayo-Avello [10] concludes that previous studies made assumptions that do not hold up under scrutiny: Twitter use is not representative of the population; not all Twitter users comment on a particular topic; and a large amount of tweets come from untrustworthy sources. We reason that authorship attribution makes less assumptions and does not rely on the trustworthiness of the actual content – in fact it contributes to establishing the identities of users. Accurate attribution of authorship has become very important due to the extensive use of microblogging channels (such as Twitter) by criminals to plan criminal activities. Billions of tweets are posted on online, so it is critical to investigate techniques used to predict the identity of authors even with unknown aliases.

Layton et al. [11] first investigated the problem of Twitter authorship attribution by using local n-gram methods on randomly sampled authors as part of a Source Code Authorship Profile (SCAP) methodology. The SCAP methodology was shown to be very accurate for predicting the author of a single tweet, with an accuracy of over 70% for a (n-gram) value of 3. It was demonstrated empirically that 120 tweets were an important threshold for establishing an author's profile, with additional tweets offering a small but insignificant increase in accuracy. This result is important for this study because it offers a rule of thumb for the number of tweets that need to be gathered per author. Lastly, it was demonstrated that a large amount of accuracy is lost (up to 27%) when information regarding whom the user is conversing with is removed (the @replies in a tweet), compared to a smaller loss of accuracy of 1% when hash-tags are removed. These results influenced the decision to avoid pre-processing of Twitter messages for this study.

In a later study, Layton et al. [12] investigated a subset of the authorship problem by looking at alias matching using topic-based sub-aliases rather than randomly generated sub-aliases. It was argued that random sub-aliases were not conducive to real world applications as the use of multiple aliases is likely to coincide with different topics. These sub-aliases were created through topic modelling, which involved the use of clustering. The use of topic-based sub-aliasing resulted in significantly reduced prediction accuracies compared to random sub-aliasing. It was thus shown that the use of randomisation was a contributing factor to the high prediction accuracies of previous studies. This assertion influenced this study's assumption of randomisation (from random sampling) as a contributor to higher prediction accuracies. However, it is important to make the distinction between randomly generated sub-aliases (which are generated from existing authors) and authors which are randomly sampled.

On the selection of features, Kanaris et al. [13] in a comparative study tested the effectiveness of character n-grams versus word n-grams in the context of anti-spam filtering. The application of anti-spam filtering is another type of text classification problem. The study was based on two publicly available corpora to assess the effectiveness of n-grams (Ling-Spam and SpamAssassin). The experiment used ten-fold cross validation in conjunction with a support vector machine classifier. Character n-grams that appeared at least three times made it to the feature set. From the results, Kanaris et al. [13] demonstrated that character n-grams were more effective than word n-grams, and that short n-grams (n = 3) produced the best models. This influenced the decision to use short character n-grams (n = 3) for this study.

In contrast to the first two studies, Bhargava et al. [14] used a more traditional, stylometric approach by analysing lexical features such as total number of words per tweet, word frequency, lexical diversity, etc. A wide-ranging feature set was constructed using these lexical markers and analysed predictions accuracies for different sets of features included. The results demonstrate that removing lexical features from tweets results in lower prediction accuracy, as does increasing the number of candidate authors. We apply these stylometric principles in the analysis of our findings for this paper.

The remaining paper is organised as follows. Section 2 gives details of the methodology, while Sect. 3 gives a brief description of the classification and experimental strategy. Section 4 presents the results of the study and in the end, conclusions are provided.

2 Character n-Grams for Topic-Based Authorship Attribution

A character n-gram is simply a contiguous sequence of characters. For example, if we consider the sentence fragment "hugo, the brown fox", the character tri-grams (i.e. an n-gram that is a sequence of three characters) would be: |hug|, |ugo|, |go_|, |o,_|, |,_o|, etc. The advantages of character n-grams is that it captures the subtleties of writing style, from the author's use of capitalisation and punctuation to context sensitive information [15].

In a traditional bag of words model, each piece of text is represented as a set of words, where each word occurs a certain number of times. With a bag of character n-grams model, n-grams are used in place of words.

Each message may be represented as a vector of length $<x_1, x_2, x_3, \ldots, x_N>$, where N refers to the total number of n-grams extracted. Each x_i then refers to the frequency of an occurrence of n-gram g_i from a corresponding list of n-grams of length $N < g_1, g_2, g_3, \ldots, g_n >$ [7].

2.1 Naïve Bayes Classification for Data Set Selection

Messages were gathered using the Twitter API through a Python wrapper. Tweets were filtered at the API level to include only English language tweets, in addition to retweets being filtered out. This was to guarantee that messages originated from the actual author rather than as a retweet of another author's message. Figure 1 describes the overall workflow starting from data gathering to measuring model performance.

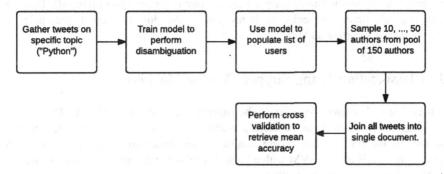

Fig. 1. High level workflow from data gathering to prediction

Topic-Based Group

This first group of authors were gathered from Twitter by searching for tweets containing the word "python". To ensure a consistency of topic and context, messages were disambiguated so that only tweets that referred to Python (the programming language) were selected, rather than "python" (the family of snakes and/or other uses). The disambiguation process used a Naïve Bayes model to compute the probability of a given message belonging to the given class. Firstly, features were extracted using Python's NLTK (Natural Language Toolkit) library, extracting word counts from tweets and transforming them into a vector matrix. Secondly, the Naïve Bayes classifier was trained by manually classifying each collected tweet, which required answering the question, "is this tweet talking about Python (the programming language)?" This in turn produced the training set for the classifier.

Tweets were filtered for English only by specifying English as the language within the Twitter API query. Unfortunately, this was only partially successful due to how Twitter classifies the language of a tweet. Languages other than English were subsequently included, though most of the lexical analysis in later sections were performed on English only tweets by counting words that contained only basic ASCII characters.

2.2 Control Group

The control group was randomly sampled by searching tweets that contained the word "the", since it is the most commonly used English word overall as demonstrated from studies of the Oxford English Corpus [16]. Layton et al. [11] also advocated the use of function words (of which "the" was one of many) for randomly sampling authors. This approach allows us to sample very easily and quickly a list of random Twitter authors.

Because of the nature of this study, it is very likely that bias is introduced using topic-based sampling. By sampling authors on topic, there are going to be authors left out of the sample. In this study, the Python group in theory excludes all individuals that do not talk about the Python programming language. Therefore, this means that this group of authors are not representative of the population. Any constant differences that arise from the comparison of author groups are likely to be due to systematic bias.

In this study, we are intentionally introducing bias to empirically assess prediction accuracy on authors that are generated through topic searches. The application of such an approach allows for immediate profiling of authors (or persons of interest). Thus, the first research objective seeks to investigate authorship prediction accuracies of non-randomly sampled authors.

3 Classification Using Support Vector Machines

Our choice of learning algorithm is the support vector machine (SVM). In text classification problems such as authorship attribution, there are many features in comparison to the training set, where feature vector dimensions can easily be in the thousands. In this case, a SVM with a linear kernel is highly recommended, for reasons to be explained later in the section.

There are several properties of SVMs that make it suitable as a learning algorithm. Firstly, they are effective in handling high dimensional spaces [17]. SVMs have also been demonstrated to avoid the problems of overfitting even when there are several thousand features in use [18], however its performance is diminished when there is the existence of class imbalances. For our data set, there is no class imbalance problem because each class (each author) has an equal number of examples (tweets).

The cost function is as follows [19]:

$$\min_{\theta} C \sum_{i=1}^{m} \left[y^{(i)} cost_1 \left(\theta^T x^{(i)} \right) + (1 - y) cost_1 \left(\theta^T x^{(i)} \right) \right] + \frac{1}{2} \sum_{i=1}^{n} \theta_j^2 \qquad (1)$$

The cost function represents what we want to minimise (theta), given a hypothesis (y = 1; y = 0).

We can parameterise the above cost function as $CA + B$, where:

A is the training data set term:

$$\sum_{i=1}^{m} \left[y^{(i)} cost_1 \left(\theta^T x^{(i)} \right) + (1 - y) cost_1 \left(\theta^T x^{(i)} \right) \right] \qquad (2)$$

C is the relative weight of A compared to B.

B is the regularisation term:

$$\frac{1}{2} \sum_{i=1}^{n} \theta_j^2 \qquad (3)$$

The parameter C controls the trade-off between how well we want to fit the training set versus how much we want to keep the parameters small. If C is very large, then it is going to be more sensitive to outliers as it attempts to fit the data well. A large C is more prone to overfitting, while a small C is more prone to underfitting. The selection of a value for C is accomplished using a grid search. However, before we discuss the parameters in more detail, SVMs are often implemented with what is known as the "kernel trick".

SVMs can be adapted as complex non-linear classifiers using kernels. Kernels are essentially similarity functions that measures how similar a training example is to a set of landmark points. These landmark points are chosen by taking the training data, and for each training example, place a landmark point at the same location. This means we end up with m landmarks, where m is the number of training examples. From these similarity functions (which can use a variety of functions such as Gaussian kernel functions) we compute our feature vector $f \in \mathbb{R}^{m+1}$, given a new training example. As a result, our cost function is now [19]:

$$\min_{\theta} C \sum_{i=1}^{m} \left[y^{(i)} cost_1 \left(\theta^T f^{(i)} \right) + (1 - y) cost_1 \left(\theta^T f^{(i)} \right) \right] + \frac{1}{2} \sum_{i=1}^{m} \theta_j^2 \qquad (4)$$

We are now solving the minimisation problem using f as the feature vector instead of x, and m (the number of features) now equals n (the number of training examples).

The selection of SVM parameters, such as C and the kernel, is accomplished using a grid search, which searches a parameter space for the best cross validation score. This is necessary because these parameters are not directly learnt during the training process.

For this study, the parameter space that the grid search iterates through is as follows:

'C': [1, 10], kernel: 'linear' (i.e. no kernel).
'C': [1, 10], kernel: 'rbf' (i.e. radial basis function, a type of Gaussian kernel function).

In this study, we have many features relative to the number of training examples (n is easily over 10,000 n-grams vs. 120 tweets per author in our training set). Therefore, using a linear kernel is usually sufficient. This is because the minimisation problem is much easier to solve for a linear kernel, and mapping to a higher dimensional space brings no performance gains when the number of features is large [20]. Thus, it is likely that the grid search selects the linear kernel rather than the Gaussian kernel.

Cross validation, in conjunction with the SVM classifier, is used to calculate the mean prediction accuracy. Accuracy is measured using the F1 score, which can be interpreted as the weighted average between precision and recall.

$$F_1 = \frac{2 * (precision * recall)}{precision + recall} \tag{5}$$

Cross validation is a technique used to avoid the problem of overfitting, when assessing the performance of an estimator. Overfitting occurs when the training and test sets are mixed together. This in turn produces a model that performs very well on data it has already seen, but poorly on newly introduced data. Each author set, ranging from 10 authors to 50 authors (in intervals of 10), is sampled and cross validated from the complete set of authors a total of 30 times. The mean accuracy is then calculated and plotted in the graph below.

4   Results

4.1   Prediction Accuracies

Violin plots can represent the distribution of accuracies across several levels of categorical variables (i.e. number of authors sampled). These plots can feature a kernel density estimation of the underlying distribution. Figure 2 is a comparison of prediction accuracies between the control and Python author groups. On the y-axis, we have the prediction accuracies (F1 scores) with the white pips representing the mean accuracy. On the x-axis, we have the number of authors included in the candidate author pool during cross validation.

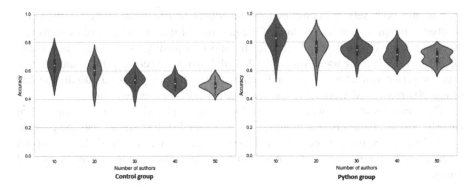

Fig. 2. Comparison of prediction accuracies across groups. The SVM prediction accuracies are higher for the Python group compared to the control group across all author set sizes.

4.2 Lexical Analysis

An analysis of the vocabulary used for both author groups revealed a non-linear increase in the number of unique words used for each author group. This unique set is calculated by taking the N most used words for each group, then eliminating the words that appeared in both groups.

$$\{python_{unique}\} = \{top\ N\ python\} - \{top\ N\ control\} \tag{6}$$

$$\{control_{unique}\} = \{top\ N\ control\} - \{top\ N\ python\} \tag{7}$$

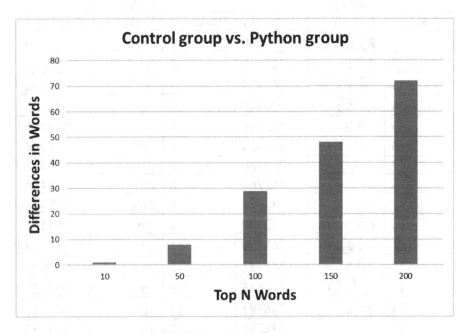

Fig. 3. Vocabulary divergence

Because both sets are composed of the top N words, both sets have the same number of unique elements, because of the negation of the conjunction of two sets (De Morgan's law). Figure 3 reveals that for the most frequently used words, such as the top 10 or top 50 most used words, the low difference reflects that there are only so many waysto construct a sentence in English. However, as we expand into the top 150 or top 200 most used words, we can see a larger difference developing.

The mean vocabulary was calculated by counting all unique words composed of entirely ASCII characters. Each author set was sampled 1000 times and the average vocabulary size was calculated. Table 1 reveals that authors in the Python group on average used a larger range of words in their tweets when compared to the control group.

Table 1. Mean vocabulary size

Sample authors	Mean vocabulary (control)	Mean vocabulary (Python)
10	2681	3181
20	4513	5414
30	6056	7188
40	7390	8776
50	8623	10187

Table 2. Most frequently occurring n-grams for the control and the Python group

	Control			Python	
Rank	N-gram	Frequency	Rank	N-gram	Frequency
1	😂😂😂	769440	1	… h	983686
2	😍 h	767539	2	't '	982678
3	😭😭😭	766725	3	's	982648
4	😭😭	766645	4	' h	982343
5	😭 h	766310	5	– a	980979
6	h	760604	6	zzy	971944
7	… h	753860	7	zza	971443
8	't	752768	8	zy	970485
9	's	752715	9	zwe	969491
10	💯 h	742340	10	zur	968551
11	😂😂	741929	11	zu	968103
12	😭 h	741731	12	zoo	964955
13	💧💧💧	736845	13	zon	964925
14	💀 h	736581	14	zni	964217
15	're	728796	15	zma	963355

In Table 2, Tri-grams were extracted and then sorted to produce a list of the 15 most frequently occurring n-grams across both author groups. Analysis of the most frequently occurring n-grams revealed that the control group featured frequent usage of emojis, whereas the Python group tended to use expressions composed of ASCII characters. Emojis are symbols used by users on the Internet to express emotions within a message. Twitter parses ASCII characters typed in by the users into special Unicode characters that form an expression such as '☺', which is composed of the individual characters ':' and ')'.

5 Conclusion

Firstly, character n-grams used in conjunction with SVMs were very effective for predicting authorship for the Python group. However, the results revealed that prediction accuracies for the control group were lower across every set of sampled authors. This result challenges the hypothesis that random sampling leads to a group of authors with more heterogeneous authorship styles. This expectation was predicated on the assumption that the Python group would feature more linguistically homogenous authors. To the contrary, it has been demonstrated that sampling authors based on topic can yield higher prediction accuracies. Higher accuracies are due to the sampling of a more linguistically diverse set of authors than is representative of the overall population.

Secondly, the differences that may have influenced this systematic difference in prediction accuracy can be explained by differences between the data sets. To start with, authors that tweet about Python programming may reflect a more diverse demographic than previously thought. There may be differences in experience levels and education that isn't reflected in the control group. van Baayen et al. [21] discovered that differences in an author's level of training and background need not be large for distinct authorship styles to emerge.

Furthermore, analysis of the linguistic differences between author groups revealed a larger vocabulary set for the Python author group when compared to the control group, which highlights that users that tweet about programming do not use restricted vocabulary as compared to a randomly sampled group of authors. When it came to features, it is evident that the most frequently occurring n-grams revealed that emojis were frequently used by the control group. This possibly explains to an extent that the control group was more linguistically homogenous, since the usage of emojis are not likely to contribute to diverse authorship styles when they are frequently used by many authors, and therefore potentially contribute to lower prediction accuracies.

6 Future Work

In this research, it was demonstrated that using topic-based sampling of Twitter users resulted in higher accuracies compared to users that were randomly sampled. It would be of interest to explore whether other search terms yield similarly high prediction accuracies to see if this result generalises when more topic-based groups are involved.

The authors hypothesise that the diverse authorship styles found in discussions of the python programming language may be reflective of differences in educational levels and expertise among users. These differences may not be present to the same extent in users sampled on a more common search term such as "music", which is a more universal topic of discussion compared to Python. Furthermore, levels of specificity within topic-based groups may also play a role. Comparisons between prediction accuracies of groups sampled from a more general search term such as "music", versus a more specific term such as "The Beatles".

References

1. Mendenhall, T.C.: The characteristic curves of composition. Sci. 237–249 (1887)
2. Sanzgiri, A., Joyce, J., Upadhyaya, S.: The early (tweet-ing) bird spreads the worm: an assessment of Twitter for malware propagation. Procedia Comput. Sci. **10**, 705–712 (2012)
3. Sanzgiri, A., Hughes, A., Upadhyaya, S.: Analysis of malware propagation in Twitter. In: 2013 IEEE 32nd International Symposium on Reliable Distributed Systems (SRDS). IEEE (2013)
4. Wang, X., Gerber, M.S., Brown, D.E.: Automatic crime prediction using events extracted from twitter posts. In: Yang, S.J., Greenberg, A.M., Endsley, M. (eds.) SBP 2012. LNCS, vol. 7227, pp. 231–238. Springer, Heidelberg (2012). doi:10.1007/978-3-642-29047-3_28
5. Bollen, J., Mao, H., Zeng, X.: Twitter mood predicts the stock market. J. Comput. Sci. **2**(1), 1–8 (2011)
6. Si, J., et al.: Exploiting topic based Twitter sentiment for stock prediction. ACL **2013**(2), 24–29 (2013)
7. Sang, E.T.K., Bos, J.: Predicting the 2011 dutch senate election results with Twitter. In: Proceedings of the Workshop on Semantic Analysis in Social Media. Association for Computational Linguistics (2012)
8. Achrekar, H., et al.: Predicting flu trends using twitter data. In: 2011 IEEE Conference on Computer Communications Workshops (INFOCOM WKSHPS). IEEE (2011)
9. Ritterman, J., Osborne, M. Klein, E.: Using prediction markets and Twitter to predict a swine flu pandemic. In: 1st International Workshop on Mining Social Media (2009). http://homepages.inf.ed.ac.uk/miles/papers/swine09.pdf. Accessed 26 Aug 2015
10. Gayo-Avello, D.: "I wanted to predict elections with Twitter and all i got was this Lousy paper"–a balanced survey on election prediction using Twitter Data (2012). arXiv preprint arXiv:1204.6441
11. Layton, R., Watters, P., Dazeley, R.: Authorship attribution for Twitter in 140 characters or less. In: 2010 Second Cybercrime and Trustworthy Computing Workshop (CTC). IEEE (2010)
12. Layton, R., Watters, P.A., Dazeley, R.: Authorship analysis of aliases: does topic influence accuracy? Nat. Lang. Eng. **21**(04), 497–518 (2015)
13. Kanaris, I., et al.: Words versus character n-grams for anti-spam filtering. Int. J. Artif. Intell. Tools **16**(06), 1047–1067 (2007)
14. Bhargava, M., Mehndiratta, P., Asawa, K.: Stylometric analysis for authorship attribution on Twitter. In: Bhatnagar, V., Srinivasa, S. (eds.) BDA 2013. LNCS, vol. 8302, pp. 37–47. Springer, Cham (2013). doi:10.1007/978-3-319-03689-2_3
15. Stamatatos, E.: A survey of modern authorship attribution methods. J. Am. Soc. Inform. Sci. Technol. **60**(3), 538–556 (2009)

16. Oxford: The Oxford English Corpus: Facts about the language (2015). http://www. oxforddictionaries.com/words/the-oec-facts-about-the-language. Accessed 2015

17. Kanaris, I., Kanaris, K., Stamatatos, E.: Spam detection using character n-grams. In: Antoniou, G., Potamias, G., Spyropoulos, C., Plexousakis, D. (eds.) SETN 2006. LNCS, vol. 3955, pp. 95–104. Springer, Heidelberg (2006). doi:10.1007/11752912_12

18. Stamatatos, E.: Author identification: using text sampling to handle the class imbalance problem. Inf. Process. Manag. **44**(2), 790–799 (2008)

19. Ng, A.: Support vector machines. CS229 Lecture notes **1**(3), 1–3 (2000)

20. Hsu, C.-W., Chang, C.-C., Lin, C.-J.: A practical guide to support vector classification (2003)

21. van Baayen, H., et al.: An experiment in authorship attribution. In: 6th JADT (2002)

Textual Emotion Classification: An Interoperability Study on Cross-Genre Data Sets

Bahadorreza Ofoghi[1(✉)] and Karin Verspoor[1,2]

[1] School of Computing and Information Systems, The University of Melbourne, Melbourne, VIC, Australia
bahadorreza.ofoghi@unimelb.edu.au
[2] Health and Biomedical Informatics Centre, The University of Melbourne, Melbourne, VIC, Australia

Abstract. This paper describes the application and analysis of a previously developed textual emotion classification system (READ-BioMed-EC) on a different data set in the same language with different textual properties. The classifier makes use of a number of lexicon-based and text-based features. The data set originally used to develop this classifier consisted of English-language Twitter microblogs with mentions of Ebola disease. The data was manually labelled with one of six emotion classes, plus sarcasm, news-related, or neutral. In this new work, we applied the READ-BioMed-EC emotion classifier without retraining to an independently collected set of Web blog posts, also annotated with emotion classes, to understand how well the Twitter-trained disease-focused emotion classifier might generalise to an entirely different collection of open-domain sentences. The results of our study show that direct cross-genre application of the classifier does not achieve meaningful results, but when re-trained on the open-domain data set, the READ-BioMed-EC system outperforms the previously published results. The study has implications for cross-genre applicability of emotion classifiers, demonstrating that emotion is expressed differently in different text types.

Keywords: Emotion classification · Lexicon-based · Cross-genre

1 Introduction

Sentiment analysis and classification has been an active research area in natural language processing since the early 2000's [12,26]. Most early sentiment analysis studies focused on the two main polarity classes of "positive" and "negative" [18]. More recently, however, the advances in machine learning and its applications in natural language processing have resulted in the emergence of more sophisticated procedures that aim to identify the emotions behind text.

Finding the emotions expressed in text can be seen as part of the multimodal Human Emotion Recognition process which plays a role in modern Human Computer Interaction (HCI) systems [7]. Textual emotion classification has a broad

© Springer International Publishing AG 2017
W. Peng et al. (Eds.): AI 2017, LNAI 10400, pp. 262–273, 2017.
DOI: 10.1007/978-3-319-63004-5_21

range of applications including public health and surveillance to provide complementary types of evidence when monitoring and detecting traumatic events, such as disease outbreaks, as they occur. The We Feel Project [15] validates the use of Twitter microblogs to measure people's mental health and moods with the aim of utilising social media posts to understand the prevalence and drivers of emotions over a population in real time. The project introduces influenza tracking and public emergencies such as bushfire as possible applications of the online system. The recent study by Ofoghi et al. [16] is an example of an application in public health, exploring the use of emotions as expressed in social media microblogs to detect Ebola outbreaks in specific geographic areas. VisieFee [23] is another system that couples text analytics and emotion-based visualization to explore and extract information from a collection of social media posts.

In this work, we focus on emotion classification from text as a stand-alone component that may have an impact on any of the above applications. We believe this component can only play a significant role in HCI systems or surveillance mechanisms if the classification performance is robust to variation in the syntactical, lexical, and structural characteristics of textual data, i.e., single grammatical sentences, multi-sentence blogs, or larger text excerpts. Therefore, we examine the performance of a recently developed emotion classification system, namely our READ-BioMed-EC system [16], trained with Twitter microblogs, to understand how the classification performance of this system is affected by heterogeneity of monolingual, cross-genre textual data sets. We will demonstrate that there is a strong genre dependency in the performance of the classifier.

The rest of the paper is organised as follows. First, a brief review of existing textual emotion classification systems will be provided. This is followed by the description of the READ-BioMed emotion classifier that we have based our experiments on. Then, two data sets will be introduced: (i) the development and training tweet set used to develop the READ-BioMed-EC system, and (ii) the second benchmark data set used to evaluate the generalised emotion classification performance of the READ-BioMed-EC classifier. This section is followed by the evaluation results of the READ-BioMed-EC emotion classifier against another external classifier that has been trained and evaluated with the second data set. Some discussions and concluding remarks will be given to summarise the findings of the paper.

2   Related Work: Emotion Classification in Text

Emotion detection from textual data has been previously tackled using various rule-based [13], unsupervised [1], and supervised approaches [2,25]. Aman and Szpakowicz [4] utilised corpus-based unigrams, emotion-related words extracted from Roget's thesaurus, and features derived from WordNet-Affect to train a supervised emotion classifier. They employed an emotion inventory developed by Ekman [8], plus a no-emotion class in their work. Wang et al. [24] utilised an overlapping emotion inventory and similar features. They found improvements in tweet emotion classification through consideration of the sentiment of words (positive or negative) as features.

Li et al. [10] approached sentence-level emotion classification as factor graph inference through modelling emotion label and context dependence and achieved improvements over some existing state-of-the-art emotion classifiers. In another work, Li and Xu [11] identified emotions in Chinese microblog posts using complementary knowledge from external fields such as sociology. They implemented a rule-base to extract emotion-related information from text and then used a supervised learner system to classify text into emotion categories.

In the same context of microblog post emotion classification, Schulz et al. [19] made use of Naïve Bayes and SVM classifiers to detect emotions in the text of Twitter posts. They evaluated their emotion detection procedure in the context of situational awareness and crisis management and found that using the fine-grained emotion classes it is possible to retrieve more related users posts that can be utilised for emergency management scenarios. Balabantaray et al. [5] used multi-class SVM kernels with a mix of syntactic and lexical features, including some extracted using WordNet Affect [22], to develop a classifier for Twitter posts. Wen and Wan [26] also studied emotion classification of multiple-sentence microblogs using data mining-based class sequential rules for the different sentences in a micorblog and the SVM classifier. On a test set of 10,000 Chinese microblogs, they achieved an overall F-measure of 0.42. The SVM classifier was also used in [9] to identify the emotions expressed in text using emotional words in WordNet-Affect and the polarity of terms from other external data sets.

To the best of our knowledge, all of the above studies focused on the analysis of emotion or sentiment classification in single domains (i.e., including one genre of text) without any cross-genre evaluation.

3   READ-BioMed-EC Emotion Classifier

The READ-BioMed-EC emotion classifier was first developed in a previous work in the context of syndromic surveillance [16]. The main idea of this work was to use the shift in general public moods and emotions as an indication of the occurrence of nearby traumatic events such as disease outbreaks. The case study given in that work had a focus on whether the distribution of different emotions in tweets can be utilised to signal Ebola outbreaks or the arrival of suspected Ebola in a particular region of the world. The classifier was also utilised in the context of Adverse Drug Reaction classification in Twitter microblogs [17].

The READ-BioMed-EC classifier has the capability to assign an emotion class label to a given tweet from the set of emotion classes including Ekman's six basic emotions [8], i.e., "anger", "disgust", "happiness", "sadness", "surprise", and "fear" as well as three *attitudinal* classes "sarcasm", "news-related", and "criticism". The classifier is an ensemble of a set of binary classifiers for each of the nine classes. The binary classifiers are all based on Naïve Bayes classification, implemented in MALLET toolkit [14]. Several different types of syntactical and lexical features were utilised in the READ-BioMed-EC emotion classifier including:

- The standard bag-of-words features,
- The terms from a vocabulary consisting of 431 emotion-related words and phrases as well as news agency names,
- A list of 68 emoticons,
- Punctuations, i.e., question and exclamation marks,
- Coarse-grained text sentiment determined by the Stanford Sentiment Analyzer, i.e., negative, neutral, or positive [20], and
- A lexicon-based similarity score calculated using an in-built lexicon-based classifier.

The lexicon-based classifier is an unsupervised system that makes use of the same above-mentioned vocabulary and the (binary) vector space model to represent the emotion classes as well as the text of tweets. It then calculates the similarity measure of the text of a given tweet and each of the nine classes. These class similarity measures were used as one of the feature types in the READ-BioMed-EC Naïve Bayes emotion classifier.

Since the lexicon-based sub-classifier of READ-BioMed-EC provides a stand-alone functionality, we were able to use it in separate experiments and evaluate its direct applicability as well.

4   Data Sets

Two different data sets were considered in this study. The first data set contains the Twitter microblogs originally used to develop the READ-BioMed-EC emotion classifier in our prior work [16]. The second data set includes a set of sentences derived from Web blogs that were utilised by Aman and Szpakowicz [3,4] to develop a separate textual emotion classifier. We refer to this data set as AS-WB. In this work, we evaluated the performance of the READ-BioMed-EC classifier on the AS-WB data.

4.1   Tweet Set for READ-BioMed-EC Classifier

A total of 4,405 tweets containing the term "Ebola" were used to develop the READ-BioMed-EC emotion classifier. These tweets were retrieved using the Twitter API in March 2015 and were all pre-processed in a few steps to normalise URLs, email addresses, mentions, and hash tags to specific strings "url", "emailAddress", "atSign", and "hashTag", respectively. Since the focus of the work was on Ebola disease outbreak monitoring and detection, mentions of "#Ebola" were retained and converted to "ebola". The "RT" tags as well as redundant tweets were also removed from the tweet set.

Amazon's Mechanical Turk [6] was used to label the tweets with one of the nine aforementioned emotion and attitudinal classes. No inter-rater agreement analysis was conducted on this data set to measure the quality of the labeling task carried out by the numerous human workers of Mechanical Turk. The labelled tweet set was then pre-processed before being used by the classifier with tokenization, lowercasing of tokens, removal of stop-words, and lemmatization. More details about this data set can be found in [16].

4.2   Web Blog Data Set (AS-WB)

This data set was first prepared and used for emotion annotation and classification by Aman and Szpakowicz [3,4]. A number of Web blog posts were used to create this data set containing individual sentences tagged with an emotion class from the set of Ekman's six basic emotions. In cases where none or a mixture of the six emotions were expressed in the sentence, "no emotion" and "mixed emotion" labels were used, respectively.

To extract the emotion-expressing sentences, the authors prepared a list of seed words for the six basic emotions. Then, they retrieved 173 Web blog posts containing those seed words. The blog posts (4,090 sentences) were labelled by two judges, with one label assigned per sentence. The highest Kappa agreement of annotators was 0.79 for the sentences labelled with the emotion class "fear" while the lowest agreement was 0.43 for the "mixed emotion" class.

5   Evaluation of the READ-BioMed-EC Classifier

5.1   Experiments

We employed the READ-BioMed-EC emotion classifier on the (previously unseen) AS-WB data set. First, we set a baseline classification method, which assigns the most commonly occurring emotion in the blog data set. Then, two experiments were conducted: first, testing the best-performing READ-BioMed-EC classification system as reported in [16] on the complete AS-WB sentence data set, and second, training and testing the READ-BioMed-EC classifier with AS-WB in a cross-validation setting.

Baseline AS-WB Classifier. In the version of the AS-WB data set that was made available to us, we did not find any sentence labelled as "mixed emotion". The total number of sentences provided was 4,090 sentences, slightly less than what was described in [3]. There were 536 "happiness", 173 "sadness", 179 "anger", 172 "disgust", 115 "surprise", 115 "fear", and 2800 "no emotion" sentences in this data set.

The naïve baseline classification system, therefore, classified every sentence as "no emotion" since this class had the largest number of sentences assigned to it. The results of the evaluation of the baseline system are summarised in Table 1.

Cross-Genre Analysis. In this first experiment, the best READ-BioMed-EC classification system introduced in [16] was utilised on the AS-WB data set described in Sect. 4.2. The best READ-BioMed-EC emotion classifier identified in our prior work consists of an ensemble of binary Naïve Bayes classifiers (one classifier per emotion class) that uses the bag-of-words features as well as Stanford sentiment features on lemmatised text.

Table 1. The classification performances on the AS-WB data set. Note: READ-BioMed-EC* = The best performing READ-BioMed-EC with bag-of-words features and Stanford sentiments (lemmatised text) trained on Twitter microblogs, Prec. = Precision, Rec. = Recall, F1 = F1-measure, Hap. = Happiness, Surp. = Surprise, NE = No Emotion, and M. avg. = MACRO average.

Method	Metric	Hap.	Sadness	Anger	Disgust	Surp.	Fear	NE	M. avg.
majority class baseline	Prec.	0	0	0	0	0	0	0.68	0.10
	Rec.	0	0	0	0	0	0	1.00	0.14
	F1	0	0	0	0	0	0	0.81	0.12
READ-BioMed-EC*	Prec.	0.33	0	0.02	0.01	0.04	0.01	0.68	0.16
	Rec.	0.01	0	0.01	0.01	0.09	0.01	0.86	0.14
	F1	0.01	0	0.01	0.01	0.06	0.01	0.76	0.12

This classification system was trained on the entire tweet set described in Sect. 4.1 and tested on all of the sentences in the AS-WB Web blog data set. Table 1 summarises the results of applying this classifier on the blog sentences.

Aman and Szpakowicz [3,4] used a combination of emotion terms in WordNet-Affect, emotion-related semantic categories in the General Inquirer [21], emoticons, punctuations, and Roget's Thesaurus feature to classify these Web blog sentences. Using a 10-fold cross-validation analysis with a SVM classifier, they achieved several category-level results with different feature sets. Their best results for each class are summarised in Table 2. As shown in Table 1, the READ-BioMed-EC emotion classifier, without being trained or developed for the blog sentences data set, did not perform as well as the classifier developed in [4]. At the same time, the macro average performance of the READ-BioMed-EC classifier is lower than that of the baseline system summarised in Table 1.

Table 2. The classification performances on the AS-WB Web blog data set. Note: AS* = Aman and Szpakowicz's individually selected best published performances, LB = Lexicon-Based sub-classifier (tokens lemmatised and lowercased), Prec. = Precision, Rec. = Recall, F1 = F1-measure, Hap. = Happiness, NE = No Emotion, and M. avg. = MACRO average.

Method	Metric	Hap.	Sadness	Anger	Disgust	Surprise	Fear	NE	M. avg.
AS* [3,4]	Prec.	0.84	0.62	0.65	0.77	0.81	0.89	0.59	0.74
	Rec.	0.71	0.42	0.44	0.49	0.41	0.51	0.63	0.51
	F1	0.75	0.45	0.52	0.57	0.52	0.65	0.61	0.58
Lexicon-based (LB)	Prec.	0.49	0.48	0.46	0.47	0.46	0.48	0.66	0.50
	Rec.	0.97	0.91	0.84	0.89	0.86	0.94	0.90	0.90
	F1	0.65	0.62	0.59	0.62	0.60	0.64	0.76	0.64

Table 3. The best READ-BioMed-EC classifier's performance on the AS-WB data based on 10-fold cross-validation

Emotion class	Prec.	Rec.	F1
Happiness	0.81	0.81	0.81
Sadness	0.72	0.70	0.70
Anger	0.75	0.75	0.75
Disgust	0.74	0.72	0.71
Surprise	0.75	0.76	0.75
Fear	0.74	0.74	0.73
No emotion	0.78	0.75	0.76
MACRO avg.	*0.76*	*0.75*	*0.74*

Table 4. The READ-BioMed-EC classifier's overall MACRO avg. performance on the AS-WB data set using 10-fold cross-validation. The text of the blog sentences were lemmatised using Stanford lemmatiser. Note: bow = bag-of-words, LB = Lexicon-based, and +all = +LB similarity +emoticon + punctuation since the LB similarity includes emotion vocabulary.

Feature set	Prec.	Rec.	F1
bow	0.70	0.68	0.67
+LB similarity	0.72	0.70	0.69
+emotion vocabulary	0.71	0.70	0.69
+emoticon	0.70	0.69	0.68
+punctuation	0.71	0.69	0.68
+all	**0.73**	**0.71**	**0.70**

More importantly, similar to the baseline classifier, the best READ-BioMed-EC classifier has low F1 scores for most of the classes (except for the "no emotion" class) and overall. This motivated the next experiments to find how the READ-BioMed-EC classifier will perform once trained on the blog data set.

We then applied the lexicon-based sub-classifier of READ-BioMed-EC emotion classifier to the same sentences of the AS-WB Web blog data set. The results are summarised in Table 2. In this case, the lexicon-based classifier, that required no training, outperformed the classifier developed in [4] for the same data set, in terms of overall F-measure, although the precision remained low. We noted that the results obtained with the lexicon-based sub-classifier of READ-BioMed-EC on the AS-WB data are higher than those of the same sub-classifier initially reported on the tweet data set in [16].

Within-Genre Cross-Validation Analysis. In the second experiment, the READ-BioMed-EC emotion classifier was taken to be trained with the AS-WB Web blog data set and be tested on the same data set. First, the best performing structure of the READ-BioMed-EC classifier (as described above) was used and a 10-fold cross-validation analysis was carried out.

The READ-BioMed-EC emotion classifier, when trained with the AS-WB data set, outperformed the classification method developed by Aman and Szpakowicz [3] on the same data set in terms of precision, recall, and F-measure on the entire set of sentences.

Compared with the classification performance in the first experiment, where the READ-BioMed-EC classifier was only trained with the tweet set, the cross-validation analysis showed large improvements in terms of precision, recall, and

F-measure (see *MACRO avg.* rows in Tables 1 and 3). The cross-validation results of the READ-BioMed-EC classifier are also higher than those of its lexicon-based sub-classifier in terms of F-measure.

The next experiment we carried out with the READ-BioMed-EC emotion classifier was to run this classifier with the different feature sets described in [16] on the AS-WB data set to find how this classifier will perform with those different settings. We, therefore, performed the same 10-fold cross-validation analyses of the READ-BioMed-EC classifier on the AS-WB sentence set. The results are summarised in Table 4.

As shown in Table 4, the READ-BioMed-EC classifier, trained with the blog data set in this experiment, achieved similar performances with the different feature sets applied on lemmatised blog sentences. This similarity in performance is two-fold:

i. The best classification performance was achieved with identical feature sets across the two data sets (the READ-BoMed-EC tweet set and the AS-WB data set), specifically, the bag-of-words model in conjunction with Stanford sentiment features, and
ii. The classification performance of the READ-BioMed-EC classifier with other feature sets (see Sect. 3 for details) were consistently similar across the two data sets, all roughly 0.70 in terms of F1-measure.

Compared with the classifier developed by Aman and Szpakowicz [3] for the same data set, the performance of the READ-BioMed-EC classifier with the feature sets in Table 4 are all higher with respect to recall and F-measure. In other words, the performance of the previous classifier on the AS-WB data set falls short of the performance of the READ-BioMed-EC emotion classifier. This is the case even when the READ-BioMed-EC classifier is not performing its best.

In a final experiment, we merged the tweet set and the AS-WB sentences into a single data set and performed a 10-fold cross-validation analysis using the best READ-BioMed-EC classifier settings. We found that the class-level and macro average classification performance of the emotion classifier is very similar to those obtained with the same classifier on either the AS-WB Web blog data set or the tweet set alone (detailed results not reported).

6   Discussion

From the series of experiments we carried out with the two data sets, i.e., the tweet set and the AS-WB Web blog sentences, it can be seen that the cross-genre performance of the READ-BioMed-EC emotion classifier does not reach reasonable levels in terms of F-measure. However, the READ-BioMed-EC classifier, when set up with its best-performing feature set and trained with AS-WB, outperforms a published emotion classifier previously developed with the AS-WB data set. This suggests that the READ-BioMed-EC emotion classifier can be trained and be effectively employed as a major component not only for its main application of syndromic surveillance but also for other similar application domains. Our finding of similar performance levels and patterns of the READ-BioMed-EC emotion classifier when applied to the two data sets alone as well as merged reconfirms the consistency and applicability of this classifier for identifying human emotions in different types of texts, when sufficient training data is available.

We were interested to understand what textual and/or semantic characteristics may contribute to the above finding with respect to the READ-BioMed-EC classifier's low cross-genre performance for textual emotion classification. For this, we analysed the two data sets in terms of some descriptive token-level and sentiment-level statistics. The sentiment-level analysis was conducted specifically as a result of the best-performing READ-BioMed-EC classifier's feature set containing the Stanford sentiments. The tweet set was first pre-processed in the way described in Sect. 4.1. The results of the descriptive analysis of the two data sets are shown in Table 5.

The two data sets, according to Table 5, share some similar characteristics. First, the total number of tweets is close to the total number of blog sentences and, the total numbers of tokens in the two data sets seem close which results in similar-length overall vocabularies and vector space models. Second, the average number of tokens per tweet (14.14) is not much different from that of the sentences in the blog data set (13.40), which, on average, results in similar-length non-zero term vectors for the two data sets. However, the numbers of texts with very small or very large lengths varies widely between the two data sets, 2 cf. 205 and 3,522 cf. 2,276 texts for single-token and 10+ token texts, respectively. This is also indicated by the different standard deviations of word counts per text in the two data sets (5.20 vs. 10.65 for the tweet set and AS-WB, respectively).

The distinguishably different numbers of single-token texts in the two data sets, i.e., only 2 tweets versus 205 sentences, can potentially result in different levels of classification performance. Classification of single-token texts such as "Burn!", "Ha!", or "anyway." (taken from the AS-WB data set) may not be a trivial machine learning task especially if the tokens appear in many other sentences. The larger number of single-token texts will make the blog sentences more challenging to classify, yet the READ-BioMed-EC classifier can be trained and perform consistently across the two data sets.

In terms of the sentiments of the texts, the two data sets have some similar traits. The distribution of the different texts tagged with positive, neutral, and negative sentiments is similar, i.e., the negative sentiment represents the largest numbers of texts and the positive sentiment has the lowest frequency. However, although the total number of texts is quite similar (4,405 and 4,090 for the tweet set and the blog sentences, respectively), the number of texts with the positive sentiment is much less in the tweet set, accounting for 241 tweets versus 792 blog sentences. This may be due to the class distributions in the two data sets as well. Although this may not be true for every case, the texts tagged with a positive emotion label (such as "happiness" and "surprise") are expected to have been classified with a positive sentiment.

Table 5. The descriptive statistics of the two data sets used for emotion classification using the READ-BioMed-EC classifier. A text is a tweet in the Tweet set or a sentence in AS-WB data set, respectively. Note: Avg. = Average, Sdv. = Standard deviation, pos. = positive, neut. = neutral, neg. = negative.

Data set	#Texts	#Tokens	Avg./Sdv. $[\frac{tokens}{text}]$	#Texts with		#Sentiments		
				1 token	10+ tokens	pos.	neut.	neg.
Tweet set	4,405	62,299	14.14/5.20	2	3,522	241	1,052	3,112
AS-WB	4,090	54,815	13.40/10.65	205	2,276	792	1,201	2,097

From the previous work on the READ-BioMed-EC emotion classifier [16], we know that only 61 tweets were labelled with "happiness" and 67 with "surprise" (in total, ∼3% of the data set) while the rest of the 4,405 tweets were labelled with the other attitudinal or negative classes. On the other hand, in the AS-WB data set, there are 536 sentences tagged with "happiness" and 115 with "surprise", in total, accounting for ∼16% of the entire data set of 4,090 sentences. The two data sets in this study therefore have quite different proportions of positive sentiments and class distributions overall.

Although READ-BioMed-EC's machine learning-based classification performance did not reach high levels in the cross-genre evaluations, the lexicon-based sub-classifier performed well on the blog sentence set. The lexicon-based classifier does not required any training data set and yet it performed well cross-genre on two data sets with specific differences outlined above. This indicates that lexicon/rule-based emotion classifiers are robust to genre change, and may be preferred for cross-domain analyses where no training data is available.

7   Conclusion

In this work, we employed a previously developed textual emotion classifier, called READ-BioMed-EC emotion classifier, on a previously unseen data set to assess the interoperability of this emotion classifier with new contexts. The READ-BioMed-EC classifier was developed based on a data set of human-labeled Ebola disease related Twitter microblogs, while here we tested it on an independent data set of open-domain Web blog posts. The two data sets shared some similar textual characteristics while differing on some other more semantic features such as the distribution of overall sentiments.

When evaluating on the Web blog data set, we found that re-training the READ-BioMed-EC classifier with the new data set outperformed the previously developed classifier which had been specifically trained and tested on that data. More importantly, our evaluation results demonstrate that the READ-BioMed-EC classifier performs consistently after re-training across the two separate data sets. The consistency holds for both the relative benefit of different features for the emotion classification task, as well as the class-level and overall macro average classification performance.

We plan to further evaluate the READ-BioMed-EC classifier with other textual data sets with more distinctive textual and semantic features. The main aim will be to understand what textual characteristics can be utilised to develop a more interoperable emotion classifier for text of different genres. The results of our experiments with the lexicon-based sub-classifier of READ-BioMed-EC, which relies on a static lexicon of emotion-related terms, indicate that lexicon-based approaches are a robust approach to cross-genre data sets without re-training. In future work, we plan to explore strategies that emphasise expansion of the lexicon with words that are robust across genres.

Acknowledgments. We thank Saima Aman and Stan Szpakowicz for sharing their Web blog data set with us for the purpose of this study.

References

1. Agrawal, A., An, A.: Unsupervised emotion detection from text using semantic and syntactic relations. In: Proceedings of the 2012 IEEE/WIC/ACM International Joint Conferences on Web Intelligence and Intelligent Agent Technology, vol. 01, pp. 346–353 (2012)
2. Alm, C.O., Roth, D., Sproat, R.: Emotions from text: machine learning for text-based emotion prediction. In: Proceedings of the Conference on Human Language Technology and Empirical Methods in Natural Language Processing, HLT 2005, pp. 579–586. Association for Computational Linguistics, Stroudsburg, PA, USA (2005). http://dx.doi.org/10.3115/1220575.1220648
3. Aman, S., Szpakowicz, S.: Identifying expressions of emotion in text. In: Matoušek, V., Mautner, P. (eds.) TSD 2007. LNCS, vol. 4629, pp. 196–205. Springer, Heidelberg (2007). doi:10.1007/978-3-540-74628-7_27
4. Aman, S., Szpakowicz, S.: Using roget's thesaurus for fine-grained emotion recognition. In: Proceedings of the Third International Joint Conference on Natural Language Processing, pp. 296–302 (2008)
5. Balabantaray, R., Mohammad, M., Sharma, N.: Multi-class Twitter emotion classification: a new approach. Int. J. Appl. Inform. Syst. **4**, 48–53 (2012)
6. Buhrmester, M., Kwang, T., Gosling, S.D.: Amazon's Mechanical Turk: a new source of inexpensive, yet high-quality, data? Perspect. Psychol. Sci. **6**(1), 3–5 (2011)
7. Danisman, T., Alpkocak, A.: Feeler: emotion classification of text using vector space model. In: Proceedings of the AISB 2008 Convention, Communication, Interaction and Social Intelligence, Scotland (2008)
8. Ekman, P.: Universals and cultural differences in facial expression of emotion. In: Nebraska Symposium on Motivation, Lincoln, Nebraska, pp. 207–283 (1972)
9. Jain, M.C., Kulkarni, V.: TexEmo: conveying emotion from text - the study. Int. J. Comput. Appl. **86**, 43–50 (2014)
10. Li, S., Huang, L., Wang, R., Zhou, G.: Sentence-level emotion classification with label and context dependence. In: Proceedings of the 53rd Annual Meeting of the Association for Computational Linguistics and the 7th International Joint Conference on Natural Language Processing, pp. 1045–1053 (2015)
11. Li, W., Xu, H.: Text-based emotion classification using emotion cause extraction. Expert Syst. Appl. **41**, 1742–1749 (2014)

12. Liu, B.: Sentiment Analysis and Opinion Mining, Synthesis Lectures on Human Language Technologies. Morgan & Claypool Publishers, San Rafael (2012)
13. Masum, S.A., Prendinger, H., Ishizuka, M.: Emotion sensitive news agent: an approach towards user centric emotion sensing from the news. In: Proceedings of the International Conference on Web Intelligence, IEEE/WIC/ACM, pp. 614–620 (2007)
14. McCallum, A.K.: MALLET: A Machine Learning for Language Toolkit (2002). http://mallet.cs.umass.edu
15. Milne, D., Paris, C., Christensen, H., Batterham, P., O'Dea, B.: We feel: taking the emotional pulse of the world. In: Proceedings of the 19th Triennial Congress of the International Ergonomics Association, Melbourne, Australia (2015)
16. Ofoghi, B., Mann, M., Verspoor, K.: Towards early discovery of salient health threats: a social media emotion classification technique. In: Proceedings of Pacific Symposium on Biocomputing (PSB), Hawaii, US, pp. 504–515 (2016)
17. Ofoghi, B., Siddiqui, S., Verspoor, K.: READ-BioMed-SS: adverse drug reaction classification of microblogs using emotional and conceptual enrichment. In: Proceedings of the Social Media Mining Shared Task Workshop at the Pacific Symposium on Biocomputing, Hawaii, US (2016)
18. Pang, B., Lee, L., Vaithyanathan, S.: Thumbs up?: Sentiment classification using machine learning techniques. In: Proceedings of the ACL 2002 Conference on Empirical Methods in Natural Language Processing, Philadelphia, PA, US, vol. 10, pp. 79–86 (2002)
19. Schulz, A., Thanh, T.D., Paulheim, H., Schweizer, I.: A fine-grained sentiment analysis approach for detecting crisis related microposts. In: Geldermann, J., Muller, T., Fortier, S., Comes, F. (eds.) Proceedings of the 10th International Conference on Information Systems for Crisis Response and Management, pp. 846–851 (2013)
20. Socher, R., Perelygin, A., Wu, J.Y., Chuang, J., Manning, C.D., Ng, A.Y., Potts, C.: Recursive deep models for semantic compositionality over a sentiment Treebank. In: Proceedings of the Conference on Empirical Methods in Natural Language Processing (EMNLP 2013), Seattle, USA (2013)
21. Stone, P.J., Dunphy, D.C., Smith, M.S., Ogilvie, D.M.: The general inquirer: a computer approach to content analysis. Am. J. Sociol. **73**(5), 634–635 (1968)
22. Valitutti, R.: WordNet-Affect: an affective extension of WordNet. In: Proceedings of the 4th International Conference on Language Resources and Evaluation, pp. 1083–1086 (2004)
23. Wan, S., Paris, C.: Understanding public emotional reactions on Twitter. In: Proceedings of the Ninth International AAAI Conference on Web and Social Media, Oxford, UK (2015)
24. Wang, W., Chen, L., Thirunarayan, K., Sheth, A.P.: Harnessing Twitter "big data" for automatic emotion identification. In: Proceedings of the International Conference on Privacy, Security, Risk and Trust and the 2012 International Confernece on Social Computing (SocialCom), Amsterdam, pp. 587–592 (2012)
25. Wang, X., Zheng, Q.: Text emotion classification research based on improved latent semantic analysis algorithm. In: Proceedings of the 2nd International Conference on Computer Science and Electronics Engineering, pp. 210–213 (2013)
26. Wen, S., Wan, X.: Emotion classification in microblog texts using class sequential rules. In: Proceedings of the Twenty-Eighth AAAI Conference on Artificial Intelligence, Quebec City, Canada, pp. 187–193 (2014)

Integrating LDA with Clustering Technique for Relevance Feature Selection

Abdullah Semran Alharbi[1,2(✉)] ⓘ, Yuefeng Li[1] ⓘ, and Yue Xu[1] ⓘ

[1] School of EECS, Queensland University of Technology, Brisbane, QLD, Australia
asaharbi@uqu.edu.sa, {y2.li,yue.xu}@qut.edu.au
[2] Department of CS, Umm Al-Qura University, Makkah, Saudi Arabia

Abstract. Selecting features from documents that describe user information needs is challenging due to the nature of text, where redundancy, synonymy, polysemy, noise and high dimensionality are common problems. The assumption that clustered documents describe only one topic can be too simple knowing that most long documents discuss multiple topics. LDA-based models show significant improvement over the cluster-based in information retrieval (IR). However, the integration of both techniques for feature selection (FS) is still limited. In this paper, we propose an innovative and effective cluster- and LDA-based model for relevance FS. The model also integrates a new extended random set theory to generalise the LDA local weights for document terms. It can assign a more discriminative weight to terms based on their appearance in LDA topics and the clustered documents. The experimental results, based on the RCV1 dataset and TREC topics for information filtering (IF), show that our model significantly outperforms eight state-of-the-art baseline models in five standard performance measures.

Keywords: Feature selection · Term weighting · LDA · Extended random set · Intra- Inter-cluster features · Information filtering

1 Introduction

Selecting relevant terms from a documents collection is important for IR, IF [10], text classification and clustering [1]. The core and critical part of any text FS method is the *weighting function*. It assigns a numerical value to each feature, which specifies how informative the feature is to the user's information needs [2]. Clustering is widely used in gaining understanding from unlabelled data and facilitates the discovering of knowledge from documents [32]. For many years, document clustering has been used in retrieval systems to organise documents around subjects or themes, and cluster-based language models show significant improvement against the standard document-based models [19]. However, the effectiveness of document clustering in IF and FS for relevance is still limited.

Latent Dirichlet Allocation (LDA) [5] is a probabilistic topic modelling algorithm that can reduce the dimensionality of text to a set of manageable topics [10]. LDA represents documents by a specified number of topics, where each

W. Peng et al. (Eds.): AI 2017, LNAI 10400, pp. 274–286, 2017.
DOI: 10.1007/978-3-319-63004-5_22

topic is a set of semantically related terms. Thus, it is capable of clustering related words[1] in documents set, which can reduce the impact of common problems like polysemy, synonymy and information overload [1]. However, in reality, LDA treats topics as multinomial distributions over words and documents as a probabilistic mixture on a pre-defined number of hidden topics. LDA calculates a term probability (a.k.a. weight) based on the term local document-topics distributions and the global term-topics assignment. Therefore, in a set of similar documents, a specific term might receive a different weight in each individual document even though this term is semantically identical across all documents. Such approach does not accurately reflect on the semantic meaning and usefulness of this term to the entire user's information needs. It badly influences the performance of LDA for FS as it is difficult to know which weight to assign to the intended term. The average weight? The highest? The lowest? The aggregated? Several experiments in various studies confirm that the local weighting approach of the LDA is ineffective for relevant FS [10].

Given a collection that describe user information needs, the terms global statistics such as the document frequency (df) reveal the discriminatory power of terms [16]. However, in IR, selecting terms based on global weighting schemes did not show better retrieval performance [20], because global statistics cannot describe the local importance of terms [22]. In a document cluster, features with higher document frequency are more important [35]. From the LDA's perspective, it is challenging and still uncertain on how to use LDA's local term weighting function in the global context due to the complex relationships between terms and many entities that represent the entire collection. For example, a term might appear in multiple LDA topics and each topic may also cover many documents or paragraphs that contain the same term. Therefore, the hard question this research tries to answer is: how do we combine the global term weight and the LDA's local weight together for a better global term weighting scheme?

The aim of this research is to develop a cluster-, LDA- and extended random set-based model[2] for relevance FS. By clustering similar long documents, we can limit the impact of frequent subjects in the collection during LDA topic extraction. Therefore, subjects that are less frequent will not be overshadowed by the other highly frequent ones. Furthermore, at the clustering stage, each cluster will be considered as a set of semantically related group of words that address one superficial subject also they tend to be highly correlated and highly redundant [7]. Thus, by splitting the long documents paragraphs, we could implicitly exploit the relationships between terms that are in a similar context [14]. At the second stage, by applying LDA on each cluster paragraphs, we can generate topical distributions that reflect the similarity of cluster documents. Further, LDA can be used to relax the one subject assumption in a cluster as long documents exhibit multiple topics. Therefore, the integration of the two techniques can lead to better documents representation. Therefore, *two major contributions*

---

[1] In this paper, terms, words, keywords or unigrams are used interchangeably.

[2] We will refer to the proposed model from now on as **CBTM-ERS**, a **C**luster-**B**ased **T**opic **M**odel using **E**xtended **R**andom **S**et.

have been made in this paper to the fields of text FS and IF: **(a)** A new theoretical model based on multiple extended random sets (ERS) [24] to represent and interpret the complex relationships between long documents, their paragraphs, LDA topics and all terms in a cluster where a probability function describes each relationship; **(b)** A new and effective term weighting formula that assigns a more discriminately accurate weight to topical terms that represent their importance to the user's information needs. The formula generalises the LDA's local term weight to a global one using the proposed ERS theory and then combines it with another global weight (the df) to answer the previous question in the last paragraph. To test the effectiveness of our model, we conducted substantial experiments on the RCV1 dataset and the TREC topics for filtering track. The results show that our model significantly outperforms all used state-of-the-art baseline models for IF despite the type of text features they use (terms, phrases, patterns, topics or even a different combination of them).

2   Related Works

In the literature, there is a significant amount of work that extends and improves LDA to suit different needs, including text FS [33,36]. Document clustering, on the other hand, is also extensively used for many purposes including FS [7,9,35]. However, to the best of our knowledge, our work is the first attempt to integrate document clustering, LDA and to extend random sets to generalise the local LDA's term weight for more relevant terms selection. Relevance is a fundamental concept in both IR and IF. IR is mainly concerned with the document's relevance to a query about a specific subject. However, IF discusses the document's relevance to user's information needs [18]. In relevance discovery, FS is a method that selects a subset of features that are relevant to user's information needs and it removes those that are irrelevant, redundant and noisy. Existing FS methods adopt different type of text features such as terms [16], phrases (n-grams) [2], patterns [18], topics [5,11] or combinations of them for better performance [10,18,34].

The most efficient FS methods for relevance are the ones that are developed based on weighting function, which is the core and critical part of the selection algorithm [18]. Using LDA words probability to represent the relevance of these words is still limited and does not show encouraging results [10] including similar topic-based models such as the pLSA [11]. For better performance, Gao et al. [10] integrated pattern mining techniques into topic models to discover discriminative features. Apart from being effective, such work can be expensive and susceptible to the features-loss problem. The ERS can measure uncertainties, and it is proven to be effective in describing complex relationships between different entities and interprets them by a probability function [17]. Thus, the ERS-based model is used to weight closed sequential patterns more accurately and, thus, facilitates the discovery of specific ones as appears in Albathan et al. study [3]. However, selecting the most useful patterns is challenging due to the large number of patterns generated from relevant documents using various minimum supports (min_sup), and may also lead to feature-loss. To avoid such a problem, our approach ranks features based on their importance and does not exclude any terms from relevant documents before the weighting process takes place.

3   Background Overview

Given a collection of long documents D that describes user's information needs, the proposed CBTM-ERS requires D to be statically organised into groups (a.k.a. clusters) based on some similarity (a.k.a. distance) measures using a clustering algorithm. A cluster C_r in this paper is a subset of relevant long documents that share a similar subject. Therefore, $cluster(D) = \{C_1, C_2, \ldots, C_S\}$ such that $C_r = \{d_i : i \leq n, d_i \in D\}$, where $n = |D|$, S is the total number of clusters of D and $C_r \subseteq D$. Also in CBTM-ERS, a cluster C_r can be seen as a new relevant document set.

3.1   Document Clustering

Clustering D is the first stage in CBTM-ERS, and the bisecting k-means (BKM) algorithm [30] is used for this task. BKM is a partitional clustering technique, and it is accepted among researchers in clustering large documents collection due to its effectiveness and the low computational overheads [4, 28, 32]. BKM groups similar documents together in a cluster by maximising the intra-cluster similarity between documents and minimising it between inter-cluster (maximise the inter-cluster distance). First, BKM requires the pairwise document similarity to be calculated using some distance measures. CBTM-ERS uses the cosine similarity [12] as the distance measure to be used by the BKM algorithm. It is the most widely used similarity measure, and it shows effective results with BKM [30]. BKM also requires the number of cluster k to be specified beforehand. However, it is challenging to specify accurately the optimal number of clusters [8, 13]. Thus, we do not assume that the number of clusters is optimal, and the trial-error approach is used in our experiment.

3.2   Latent Dirichlet Allocation (LDA)

For each cluster C_r, CBTM-ERS uses LDA to reduce the dimensionality of the subset of relevant documents (paragraphs in our case) to a set of manageable topics Z, and V is the number of topics. Each document is assumed to have multiple latent topics [10]. LDA defines each topic $z_j \in Z$ as a multinomial probability distribution over all terms in C_r as $p(t_i \mid z_j)$ in which Ω represents all terms in C_r, $t_i \in \Omega$ and $1 \leq j \leq V$ such that $\sum_i^{|\Omega|} p(t_i \mid z_j) = 1$. LDA also represents an individual document d (a paragraph in our case) as a probabilistic mixture of topics as $p(z_j \mid d)$. As a result, and based on the number of latent topics, the probability (local weight) of term t_i in document d can be calculated as $p(t_i|d) = \sum_{j=1}^{V} p(t_i \mid z_j) p(z_j \mid d)$. Finally, all hidden variables, $p(t_i \mid z_j)$ and $p(z_j \mid d)$, are statistically estimated by the Gibbs sampling algorithm [31].

4   The Proposed Model

The proposed CBTM-ERS (Fig. 1) deals with the local weight problem of document terms that is assigned by the LDA probability function (described in Sect. 3.2). At a cluster level, CBTM-ERS explores all possible relationships between different entities that influence the term weighting process. The targeting entities are documents, paragraphs, topics, and terms. The possible relationships between these entities are complex (a set of one-to-many relationships). For example, a document can have many paragraphs; a paragraph can have multiple topics; a topic can have many terms. Inversely, a topic can cover many paragraphs, and a term can appear in many topics.

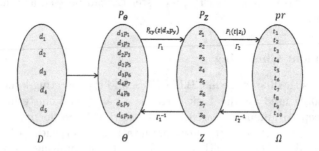

Fig. 1. The proposed CBTM-ERS model

4.1   Extended Random Sets (ERS)

A random set is a random object that has values, which are subsets that are taken from some space [24]. Let Z and Ω be finite sets. Z is also called the evidence space. We propose $\Gamma : Z \to 2^{\Omega}$ as a set-valued mapping from Z onto Ω to generalise the local weight of term t in document d that is estimated by the LDA. P is a probability function defined on Z, and, in this case, the pair (P, Γ) is called a random set [15]. By extending Γ to an extended set-valued mapping [17] $\xi :: Z \to 2^{\Omega \times [0,1]}$ which satisfies $\sum_{(t,p) \in \xi(z)} p = 1$ for each $z \in Z$, where Z is a set of topics (or evidences) and Ω is a set of terms (objects) as defined previously.

Let P be a probability function on Z, such that $\sum_{z \in Z} P(z) = 1$. We call (ξ, P) an extended random set. For each $z_i \in Z$, let $P_i(t \,|\, z_i)$ be a conditional probability function on Ω, such that $\Gamma(z_i) = \{t \,|\, t \in \Omega, P_i(t \,|\, z_i) > 0\}$ while the inverse mapping of Γ is defined as $\Gamma^{-1} : \Omega \to 2^Z$; $\Gamma^{-1}(t) = \{z \in Z \,|\, t \in \Gamma(z)\}$. A probability function $pr(t)$ can be decided by the extended Γ on Ω that satisfies $pr :: \Omega \to [0, 1]$ as follows:

$$pr(t) = \sum_{z_i \in \Gamma^{-1}(t)} (P(z_i) \times P_i(t \,|\, z_i)) \tag{1}$$

where $pr(t)$ is the estimated generalised weight of term t at the cluster level, $P(z_i)$ represents the weight of topic z_i, $P_i(t\,|\,z_i)$ is the probability of term t in topic z_i, and Γ^{-1} is a mapping function.

In CBTM-ERS, we proposed four ERSs to describe such complex relationships, where each ERS can be described by a probability function that helps to determine the importance of the main entity in the relationship. The proposed ERS theory is then used to develop a new intra-cluster term weighting scheme to generalise LDA's term probability to a global one that is still descriptive locally and more discriminative when it is combined with the document frequency (df).

The ERS Γ_1 is proposed to describe the relationships between paragraphs and topics using the conditional probability function $P_{xy}(z\,|\,d_xp_y)$ as $\Gamma_1 : \Theta \to 2^{Z \times [0,1]}$; $\Gamma_1(d_xp_y) = \{(z_1, P_{xy}(z_1\,|\,d_xp_y)), \ldots\}$ where Θ is the set of paragraphs in a cluster. Similarly, Γ_2 is also proposed to describe the relationship between topics and terms using the defined conditional probability function $P_i(t|z_i)$ as $\Gamma_2 : Z \to 2^{\Omega \times [0,1]}$; $\Gamma_2(z_i) = \{(t_1, P_i(t_1\,|\,z_i)), \ldots\}$. Based on the inverse mapping specified in Sect. 4.1, two ERSs Γ_1^{-1} and Γ_2^{-1} are proposed. Γ_1^{-1} describes the inverse relationships between topics and paragraphs using the probability function $P_z(z_i)$ such that $\Gamma_1^{-1}(z) = \{d_xp_y\,|\,z \in \Gamma_1(d_xp_y)\}$ while Γ_2^{-1} describes the inverse relationships between terms and topics using the probability function $pr(t)$ such that $\Gamma_2^{-1}(t) = \{z\,|\,t \in \Gamma_2(z)\}$.

4.2   Intra-cluster Terms Weighting

To calculate the generalised term t weight in document d in a specific cluster C_r, we need to calculate two probabilities based on Γ_1^{-1} and Γ_2^{-1}. The first one is the probability of each topic $P_z(z_i)$ in each paragraph of document d and similarly for all documents of C_r in which we assume $P_\Theta(d_xp_y) = \frac{1}{N}$, where N is the total number of paragraphs in C_r as follows:

$$
\begin{aligned}
P_z(z_i) &= \sum_{d_xp_y \in \Gamma_1^{-1}(z_i)} \left(P_\Theta(d_xp_y) \cdot P_{xy}(z_i\,|\,d_xp_y)\right) \\
&= \frac{1}{N} \sum_{d_xp_y \in \Gamma_1^{-1}(z_i)} P_{xy}(z_i\,|\,d_xp_y)
\end{aligned}
\tag{2}
$$

where $P_{xy}(z_i\,|\,d_xp_y)$ is estimated by LDA, d_xp_y refers to paragraph y in document x. Γ_1^{-1} is a mapping function defined previously.

Second, for each topic z_i in Z at the same cluster, we need to calculate the conditional probability of term t given topic z_i, $P_i(t\,|\,z_i)$ (which is estimated by LDA in our case). Thus, the generalised term weight can be calculated using Eq. 1, which can be expanded using Eq. 2 as follows:

$$pr(t) = \sum_{z_i \in \Gamma_2^{-1}(t)} (P_z(z_i) \cdot P_i(t \mid z_i))$$

$$= \sum_{z_i \in \Gamma_2^{-1}(t)} \left[\left(\frac{1}{N} \sum_{d_x p_y \in \Gamma_1^{-1}(z_i)} P_{xy}(z_i \mid d_x p_y) \right) \cdot P_i(t \mid z_i) \right] \qquad (3)$$

$$= \frac{1}{N} \sum_{z_i \in \Gamma_2^{-1}(t)} \left[P_i(t \mid z_i) \cdot \left(\sum_{d_x p_y \in \Gamma_1^{-1}(z_i)} P_{xy}(z_i \mid d_x p_y) \right) \right]$$

The final global term weight at the cluster level is calculated by multiplying the generalised LDA local weight (Eq. 3) by the df as follows:

$$w(t) = pr(t) \times df(t) \qquad (4)$$

4.3   Inter-cluster Terms Weighting

To effectively select the most relevant terms across all clusters, we simply sum up the weights of all identical terms in all clusters using the following formula:

$$Rank(t) = \sum_{t \in C_i} w_i(t) \qquad (5)$$

where $w_i(t)$ is the weight of term t in cluster C_i that is calculated by Eq. 4. Lastly and based on the newly ranked inter-cluster terms, a top-k terms are selected and send as a query to the IF system.

5   Evaluation

To verify CBTM-ERS, we designed two hypotheses. First, CBTM-ERS can generalise the local LDA term weight in each cluster for a better term weighting scheme across all clusters. Second, CBTM-ERS is more effective in selecting relevant features than most state-of-the-art baseline models. To support these two hypotheses, we conducted an experiment and evaluated its performance.

5.1   Dataset

The first 50 collections of the standard *Reuters Corpus Volume 1* (RCV1) dataset is used due to being assessed by domain experts at NIST [29] for TREC[3] filtering track. This number of collections is sufficient and stable for better and reliable experiments [6]. RCV1 is collections of documents where each document is a news story in English published by Reuters. It is one of the most widely used dataset in testing text mining and machine learning models. RCV1 is a large dataset with more than 806,000 documents that cover 100 different subjects. Each collection has been split into training and testing sets, and each set has some relevant and irrelevant documents to the subject they describe.

---

[3] http://trec.nist.gov/.

5.2   Baseline Models

We compared the performance of CBTM-ERS to eight different baseline models. These models are categorised into five groups based on the type of feature they use. The proposed CBTM-ERS is trained only on relevant documents and does not consider irrelevant ones. Therefore, for fair comparison and judgement, we can only select a baseline model that either unsupervised or does not require the use of irrelevant documents.

We selected *Okapi BM25* [26], which is one of the best term-based ranking algorithm. The phrase-based model *n-Grams* is selected. It represents user's information needs as a set of phrases where $n = 3$ as it is the best value reported by Gao et al. [10]. The *Pattern Deploying based on Support* (PDS) [37] is one of the pattern-based models. It can overcome the limitations of pattern frequency and usage. We selected the *Latent Dirichlet Allocation* (LDA) [5] as the most widely used topic modelling algorithm. From the same group we also selected the *Probabilistic Latent Semantic Analysis* (pLSA) [11]; it is similar to the LDA and can deal with the problem of polysemy. Three models were selected from the mix-based category. First, we selected the *Pattern-Based Topic Model* (PBTM-FP) [10] that incorporates topics and frequent patterns *FP* to obtain semantically rich and discriminative representation for information filtering. Secondly, the *PBTM-FCP* [10], which is similar to the PBTM-FP except it uses the frequent closed pattern *FCP* instead. Lastly, we selected the *Topical N-Grams* (TNG) [34] that integrates the topic model with phrases (n-grams) to discover topical phrases that are more discriminative and interpretable.

5.3   Evaluation Measures

The effectiveness of CBTM-ERS is measured based on relevance judgements by five metrics that are well-established and commonly used in the IR and IF communities. These metrics are the *average precision* of the top-20 ranked documents (top-20), *break-even point* (b/p), *mean average precision* (MAP), *F-score* (F_1) measure, and *11-points interpolated average precision* (IAP). For more details about these measures, the reader can refer to Manning et al. [21].

5.4   Experimental Design

We treated CBTM-ERS as a relevance FS model for IF based on the testing system of the TREC filtering track [27]. Therefore, to effectively measure the performance of CBTM-ERS and its baselines, we conducted a series of experiments on the first 50 collections of the standard RCV1 dataset and their TREC relevance judgements that are assessed by domain experts. These experiments have been carried out to prove that our evaluation hypotheses are valid.

For each collection, we use the BKM algorithm to group the relevant long documents into some clusters based on a specified similarity criterion. Then, we train CBTM-ERS on all paragraphs of the subset of D in each cluster by using LDA to extract ten topics, because it is the best number for each collection as it has reported in [10]. Then, CBTM-ERS weights documents' terms, ranks them and uses the top-k features as a query to an IF system. The IF system uses unknown documents (from the testing part of the same collection) to decide their relevance to the user's information needs (relevant or irrelevant). However, specifying the value of k is experimental. If the results of the IF system returned by the five metrics are better than the baseline results, then we can claim that our model is significant and outperforms a baseline model.

5.5   Experimental Settings

We use the CLUTO toolkit to cluster the relevant documents of each collection into hard clusters using its graphical tool (gCLUTO) [25]. We select the repeated bisecting algorithm to be our clustering algorithm. Other parameter settings in the gCLUTO environment are set as follows: the similarity function is set to be the cosine; I2 is the criterion function; 10 for the number of trials; the default values are accepted for the remaining parameters. For the number of clusters k, we apply a trial-error approach. We set it initially to be $k = 2$ and analyse the results (the goodness of clusters based on the measures provided by gCLUTO). Then, we increase k by one until we reach a better result.

The MALLET toolkit [23] is used to implement all LDA-based models except for the pLSA model where we used the Lemur toolkit[4] instead. All topic-based models require some parameters to be set. For the LDA-based models, we set the number of iterations for the Gibbs sampling to be 1000 and for the hyper-parameters to be $\alpha = 50/V$ and $\beta = 0.01$ as they were justified in [31]. We configured the number of iterations for the pLSA to be 1000 (default setting). Lastly, we should mention that the clustering task and the LDA estimation need only to be done once and off-line.

5.6   Experimental Results

Table 1 and Fig. 2 show the evaluation results of CBTM-ERS and the baselines. These results are the average of the 50 collections of the RCV1. The results in Table 1 have been categorised based on the type of feature used by the baseline model and the *improvement%* represents the percentage change in our model's performance compared to the best result of the baseline model (marked in bold if there is more than one baseline model in the category). We consider any improvement that is greater than 5% to be significant.

Table 1 shows that CBTM-ERS outperformed all baseline models for IF in all five measures. Regardless of the type of feature used by the baseline model, CBTM-ERS is significantly better on average by a minimum improvement of 8.3% and 43.4% maximum. Moreover, the 11-*points* result in Fig. 2 illustrates the superiority of CBTM-ERS and confirms the significant improvements that shown in Table 1.

---

[4] https://www.lemurproject.org/.

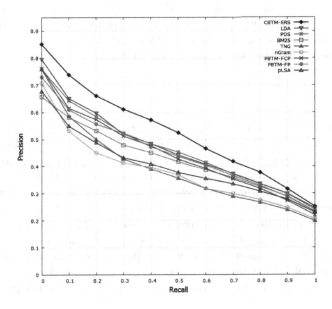

Fig. 2. 11-*points* result of CBTM-ERS in comparison with baselines averaged over the first 50 document collections of the RCV1 dataset.

Table 1. Evaluation results of CBTM-ERS in comparison with the baselines (grouped based on the type of feature used by the model) for all measures averaged over the first 50 document collections of the RCV1 dataset.

Model	Top-20	b/p	MAP	$F_{\beta=1}$	IAP
CBTM-ERS	**0.575**	**0.484**	**0.500**	**0.476**	**0.526**
LDA	**0.492**	**0.414**	**0.442**	**0.437**	**0.468**
pLSA	0.423	0.386	0.379	0.392	0.404
improvement%	**+17.0%**	**+16.9%**	**+13.3%**	**+8.8%**	**+12.3%**
PDS	0.496	0.430	0.444	0.439	0.464
improvement%	**+15.9%**	**+12.4%**	**+12.8%**	**+8.3%**	**+13.3%**
n-Gram	0.401	0.342	0.361	0.386	0.384
improvement%	**+43.4%**	**+41.5%**	**+38.6%**	**+23.3%**	**+37.1%**
BM25	0.445	0.407	0.407	0.414	0.428
improvement%	**+29.2%**	**+18.8%**	**+23.0%**	**+14.9%**	**+22.9%**
PBTM-FCP	**0.489**	**0.420**	0.423	0.422	0.447
PBTM-FP	0.470	0.402	**0.427**	**0.423**	**0.449**
TNG	0.447	0.360	0.372	0.386	0.394
improvement%	**+17.6%**	**+15.2%**	**+17.2%**	**+12.5%**	**+17.1%**

Based on the results, we are confident in claiming that CBTM-ERS can effectively weight terms at a cluster level, and, thus, provide more representative weight for all terms across all clusters. Also, CBTM-ERS is more effective in selecting relevant features to acquire user's information needs.

6   Conclusion

This paper presents CBTM-ERS, an innovative cluster- and LDA-based FS model for relevance discovery. CBTM-ERS extends random sets to generalise the local LDA terms probability at a cluster level. Then, a term weighting scheme is developed to accurately weight topical terms based on their appearance in the LDA topics distributions and relevant documents across all clusters. The calculated weight effectively reflects the relevance of a term to user's information needs and maintains the same semantic meaning of terms across all relevant documents spread in multiple clusters. The proposed model is tested for IF on the standard RCV1 dataset, TREC topics, five different performance metrics and eight state-of-the-art baseline models. The experimental results show that our model achieved significant performance compared to all other models.

References

1. Aggarwal, C.C., Zhai, C.: A survey of text clustering algorithms. In: Aggarwal, C.C., Zhai, C.X. (eds.) Mining Text Data, pp. 77–128. Springer, New York (2012)
2. Albathan, M., Li, Y., Algarni, A.: Enhanced N-gram extraction using relevance feature discovery. In: Cranefield, S., Nayak, A. (eds.) AI 2013. LNCS, vol. 8272, pp. 453–465. Springer, Cham (2013). doi:10.1007/978-3-319-03680-9_46
3. Albathan, M., Li, Y., Xu, Y.: Using extended random set to find specific patterns. In: WI 2014, vol. 2, pp. 30–37. IEEE (2014)
4. Beil, F., Ester, M., Xu, X.: Frequent term-based text clustering. In: KDD 2002, pp. 436–442. ACM (2002)
5. Blei, D.M., Ng, A.Y., Jordan, M.I.: Latent Dirichlet allocation. J. Mach. Learn. Res. **3**, 993–1022 (2003)
6. Buckley, C., Voorhees, E.M.: Evaluating evaluation measure stability. In: SIGIR 2000, pp. 33–40. ACM (2000)
7. Chao, S., Cai, J., Yang, S., Wang, S.: A clustering based feature selection method using feature information distance for text data. In: Huang, D.-S., Bevilacqua, V., Premaratne, P. (eds.) ICIC 2016. LNCS, vol. 9771, pp. 122–132. Springer, Cham (2016). doi:10.1007/978-3-319-42291-6_12
8. Das, S., Abraham, A., Konar, A.: Automatic clustering using an improved differential evolution algorithm. IEEE Trans. Syst. Man Cybern.-Part A: Syst. Hum. **38**(1), 218–237 (2008)
9. Ferreira, C.H., de Medeiros, D.M., Santana, F.: Fcfilter: feature selection based on clustering and genetic algorithms. In: CEC 2016, pp. 2106–2113. IEEE (2016)
10. Gao, Y., Xu, Y., Li, Y.: Pattern-based topics for document modelling in information filtering. IEEE TKDE **27**(6), 1629–1642 (2015)
11. Hofmann, T.: Unsupervised learning by probabilistic latent semantic analysis. Mach. Learn. **42**(1–2), 177–196 (2001)

12. Huang, A.: Similarity measures for text document clustering. In: NZCSRSC 2008, pp. 49–56 (2008)
13. Jain, A.K.: Data clustering: 50 years beyond k-means. Pattern Recogn. Lett. **31**(8), 651–666 (2010)
14. Krikon, E., Kurland, O.: A study of the integration of passage-, document-, and cluster-based information for re-ranking search results. Inf. Retr. **14**(6), 593 (2011)
15. Kruse, R., Schwecke, E., Heinsohn, J.: Uncertainty and Vagueness in Knowledge Based Systems: Numerical Methods. Springer Science & Business Media, Heidelberg (2012)
16. Lan, M., Tan, C.L., Su, J., Lu, Y.: Supervised and traditional term weighting methods for automatic text categorization. IEEE TPAMI **31**(4), 721–735 (2009)
17. Li, Y.: Extended random sets for knowledge discovery in information systems. In: Wang, G., Liu, Q., Yao, Y., Skowron, A. (eds.) RSFDGrC 2003. LNCS (LNAI), vol. 2639, pp. 524–532. Springer, Heidelberg (2003). doi:10.1007/3-540-39205-X_87
18. Li, Y., Algarni, A., Albathan, M., Shen, Y., Bijaksana, M.A.: Relevance feature discovery for text mining. IEEE TKDE **27**(6), 1656–1669 (2015)
19. Liu, X., Croft, W.B.: Cluster-based retrieval using language models. In: SIGIR 2004, pp. 186–193. ACM (2004)
20. Macdonald, C., Ounis, I.: Global statistics in proximity weighting models. In: Web N-Gram Workshop, p. 30. Citeseer (2010)
21. Manning, C.D., Raghavan, P., Schütze, H.: Introduction to Information Retrieval. Cambridge University Press, Cambridge (2008)
22. Maxwell, K.T., Croft, W.B.: Compact query term selection using topically related text. In: SIGIR 2013, pp. 583–592. ACM (2013)
23. McCallum, A.K.: Mallet: A machine learning for language toolkit (2002)
24. Molchanov, I.: Theory of Random Sets. Springer Science & Business Media, London (2006)
25. Rasmussen, M., Karypis, G.: gCLUTO: an interactive clustering, visualization, and analysis system. UMN-CS TR-04 **21**(7) (2004)
26. Robertson, S., Zaragoza, H.: The Probabilistic Relevance Framework: BM25 and Beyond. Now Publishers Inc., Breda (2009)
27. Robertson, S.E., Soboroff, I.: The TREC 2002 filtering track report. In: TREC, vol. 2002, p. 5 (2002)
28. Savaresi, S.M., Boley, D.L.: On the performance of bisecting k-means and PDDP. In: ICDM 2001, pp. 1–14. SIAM (2001)
29. Soboroff, I., Robertson, S.: Building a filtering test collection for TREC 2002. In: SIGIR 2003, pp. 243–250. ACM (2003)
30. Steinbach, M., Karypis, G., Kumar, V., et al.: A comparison of document clustering techniques. In: KDD Workshop on Text Mining, vol. 400, Boston, pp. 525–526 (2000)
31. Steyvers, M., Griffiths, T.: Probabilistic topic models. Handb. Latent Semant. Anal. **427**(7), 424–440 (2007)
32. Tagarelli, A., Karypis, G.: Document clustering: the next frontier. In: Data Clustering: Algorithms and Applications, p. 305. CRC Press (2013)
33. Tasci, S., Gungor, T.: LDA-based keyword selection in text categorization. In: ISCIS 2009, pp. 230–235. IEEE (2009)
34. Wang, X., McCallum, A., Wei, X.: Topical n-grams: phrase and topic discovery, with an application to information retrieval. In: ICDM 2007, pp. 697–702. IEEE (2007)

35. Wu, Q., Ye, Y., Ng, M., Su, H., Huang, J.: Exploiting word cluster information for unsupervised feature selection. In: Zhang, B.-T., Orgun, M.A. (eds.) PRICAI 2010. LNCS (LNAI), vol. 6230, pp. 292–303. Springer, Heidelberg (2010). doi:10.1007/978-3-642-15246-7_28
36. Zhang, Z., Phan, X.H., Horiguchi, S.: An efficient feature selection using hidden topic in text categorization. In: AINAW 2008, pp. 1223–1228. IEEE (2008)
37. Zhong, N., Li, Y., Wu, S.T.: Effective pattern discovery for text mining. IEEE TKDE **24**(1), 30–44 (2012)

Vision and Image

Non Sub-sampled Contourlet Transform Based Feature Extraction Technique for Differentiating Glioma Grades Using MRI Images

Razia Zia[1]($\boxtimes$), Pervez Akhtar[2], Arshad Aziz[1], Maroof Ali Shah[1], and Dur-E-Shahwar Kundi[1]

[1] National University of Science and Technology (PNEC - NUST), H-12, Islamabad, Pakistan
razia.zia@pnec.nust.edu.pk
[2] Hamdard University, Karachi, Pakistan

Abstract. More distinguishable features can greatly improve the performance of any classification system. In this study a feature extraction method using shift and rotation-invariant non-subsampled contourlet transform (NSCT) and isotropic gray level co-occurrence matrix (GLCM) is proposed for the classification of three glioma grades (II, III and IV). The classification is done using support vector machines (SVMs). A dataset of 93 MRI brain tumor images containing three grades of glioma are classified using 10 fold cross validation scheme. The proposed method is also compared with Discrete Wavelet Transform (DWT) approach. The highest accuracy of 83.33% for grade III, sensitivity of 86.95% and specificity of 92.82% achieved in case of grade II.

Keywords: Brain tumors · MRI · Non-subsampled contourlet transform (NSCT) · Gray level co-occurrence matrix (GLCM)

1 Introduction

The field of medical image classification is one of the attention gaining research area in the recent times due to the increasing requirement for an efficient tool that can help doctors in making quick and correct diagnosis. There are more than hundred different types of brain tumors that mainly include primary (arising from supportive tissue of the brain) and secondary tumors (generated outside the brain) [1]. The standard technique for classifying brain tumors is based on visual examination of MRI followed by surgical biopsy or resection. The visual examination means that the radiologist classify tumor by observing the texture uniformity or non-uniformity of tumor region. An appropriate mathematical model based on these visual features of an MRI image can be used for designing a computer assisted diagnosis (CAD) system for brain tumor classification [2–5].

The published studies show that there are mainly two types of research in brain tumor classification [6]. The first one, the researchers are working for detection of tumor and ends with the classification of normal and pathological brain

© Springer International Publishing AG 2017
W. Peng et al. (Eds.): AI 2017, LNAI 10400, pp. 289–300, 2017.
DOI: 10.1007/978-3-319-63004-5_23

[4,7,8]. The second one, the focus is on classification of different types of brain tumors, which ends in multi classification results [3,7,9], in this type of research the work is complex and very few studies have been presented because of complicated geometry of brain tumors. It is very difficult to explain the proper shape, intensity, location and boundary of these tumors hence, the classification task becomes very difficult [5,10].

The main steps of any CAD system include segmentation, feature extraction and classification, either classifying normal and abnormal brains or differentiating different types of tumors. A lot of research work has been done in these three main areas and number of efficient algorithms have been proposed [3]. In this study, the focus is on feature extraction techniques for multi-classification of brain tumor MRI images. An optimum and discriminating feature set also contributes to the improvement of classification results [10]. In previously reported works various feature extraction techniques like minimum noise fraction transform, Gabor features, discriminant analysis, wavelet transform, nonparametric weighted feature extraction, principal component analysis, decision boundary feature extraction, texture features and spectral mixture analysis have been used for classification of MRI brain images [11–13]. The literature review of efficient classification methods for human brain, shows that they have extensively used Discrete Wavelet Transform (DWT) for feature extraction. In [3,13], authors considered DWT for feature extraction of normal and abnormal brain classification. Though, DWT is one of most popular multi-resolution transform in the field of image processing, but it has limitation of directionality and anisotropy. These limitations does not allow it to perform well in capturing smooth contours and directional edges [18]. A new transform known as Contourlet Transform (CT) was introduced by [15] to overcome the limitation of DWT, but this transform has a disadvantage of shift variant. A version of CT known as Non Sub-sampled Contourlet Transform (NSCT) was proposed by [16], which is a shift invariant multi-resolution transform. NSCT has been efficiently used in number of medical image processing applications [14,17,19]. The main motivation of this study is to analyze the performance of NSCT based feature extraction approach for multi-classification problem of three brain tumor types (grade II, III, IV gliomas). Previously, [3,9,20] also worked on classification of grade II, III, and IV gliomas but they used intensity and texture feature for multi-classification.

The remaining paper is organized as follows: Sect. 2 describes the proposed system, in Sect. 3 experimental setup and results are discussed in detail and finally Sect. 4 concludes the work.

2   Proposed Methodology

The block diagram of the proposed system is shown in Fig. 1. It consists of three stages:

1. Segmentation and rectangular cropping of tumor area
2. Feature extraction method
3. Classification.

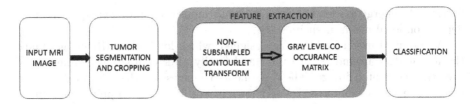

Fig. 1. Block diagram of proposed system

2.1   Segmentation and Rectangular Cropping of Tumor Area

In first stage, the Localized Region Based Active Contour (LRBAC) method is used for segmentation of tumor region [21]. In this semi-automatic method, the tumor region (region of interest (ROI)) in MRI image, is marked by the user [22,23], as shown in Fig. 2(a).

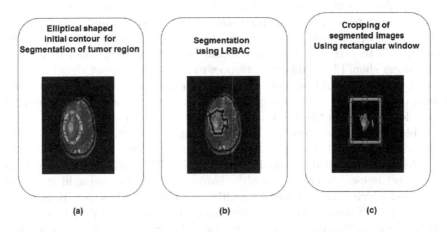

Fig. 2. Segmentation and cropping of tumor region: (a) elliptical shaped initial contour; (b) segmentation using LRBAC; (c) rectangular cropping of tumor region

Let A denotes an image defined on the $\Re$ domain and κ represents an initial closed contour defined by the user around the region of interest. Consider, i and j present a single point in $\Re$ domain. We introduce a circular characteristic function $C(i,j)$ with radius R. In LRBAC method a number of local regions (LR) along the initial contour are inspected separately. The selected contour around region of interest divides these LRs into local interior and local exterior. Characteristic function $C(i,j)$ is used for masking the LRs. Within the radius R this characteristic function $C(i,j)$ will be one and zero otherwise. Local energies are calculated at all points of the contour. In each LR the energy improvement is done by fitting an optimization energy model to each LR [24]. A generic internal energy is used to characterize the native commitment at every point of contour, to a specific energy model. For separation of regions the internal energy functions depend on local mean intensities [21].

A graphical user interface was designed, which loads the MRI image, mark the initial ROI around brain tumor and finally after completing segmentation save the segmented image. These segmented images are then cropped using a rectangular window of fixed size, as shown in Fig. 2(c). The cropping can remove any noise in the segmented image and also the resultant image is smaller in size which makes the classification process faster.

2.2   Feature Extraction Method

In this proposed work, shift and rotational invariant NSCT and GLCM is used for feature extraction of segmented images. In this section, we will briefly review the NSCT and GLCM.

Non Subsample Contourlet Transform. Directionality and anisotropy are the two limitations of wavelet transform. Due to these limitations, wavelet transform does not perform well in representing images containing smooth edges and contours in different directions [15]. Contourlet Transform (CT) was proposed in [15] to overcome these limitations faced by using wavelet transform. A transform should be stable with respect to any shift of input signal in other words transform should be shift invariant. Previous studies shows that Contourlet transform has a problem of shift variant. In this work, Non-subsampled contourlet transform (NSCT) is used because of its shift invariant property.

A block diagram of NSCT is shown in Fig. 3. The NSCT consists of two shift-invariant parts: (1) a Non-subsampled pyramid filter band (NSPFB) and (2) a Non-subsampled directional filter bank (NSDFB) structure. Using double channel non-subsampled 2-D filter banks (NSFB), the pyramid structure is achieved which is responsible for multiscale property. These NSFB are built from low pass filters. Directional filter bank offers directionality. The combination of critically-sampled two-channel fan filter banks and resampling operations are used in directional filter bank. The 2-D frequency plane is divided in directional slices using directional filters. A nonsubsampled DFB (NSDFB) offers shift-invariant directional expansion. The downsamplers and upsamplers are eliminated from directional filter bank for the formation of NSDFB [16].

In this study, the segmented images are transformed in to frequency domain using NSCT at three level of decomposition with 'maxflat' pyramidal filter and 'dmaxflat7' directional filter [16]. Only low-pass sub-band coefficients are used for classification purpose.

Gray Level Co-occurrence Matrix. In statistical texture analysis, the calculation of image texture features, depends on the statistical distribution of a pixel intensity at any given point relative to the remaining pixel intensities of the image. Statistics of first or higher-order can be calculated depending on the number of pixels in each combination [8]. In this study, gray-level co-occurrence

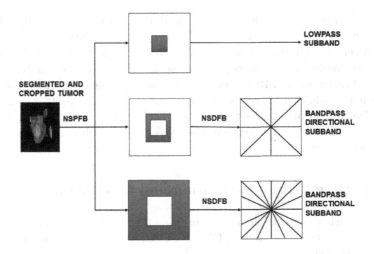

Fig. 3. Nonsubsampled contourlet transform (NSCT)

matrix (GLCM) which corresponds to second-order statistics, is used in the feature extraction step.

If a and b are the intensity of two neighboring pixels in an image then, any element $A(a, b| \triangle m, \triangle n)$ in GLCM matrix is the relative frequency with which two pixels with respective intensities a and b are separated by a pixel distance $(\triangle m, \triangle n)$. The GLCM matrix provides information of how frequently different combinations of gray levels appear in an image or image segment. In this proposed work, the segmented tumor region is first transformed into frequency domain using NSCT then this spectral information is used for the calculation of GLCM matrix to achieve more distinguishable features [25]. GLCM is a popular structural descriptor, combined with NSCT. Usually, GLCM is used to calculate the second-order statistical features like contrast, correlation, energy, and homogeneity. In this work, first we have calculated GLCM in four direction ($0°$, $45°$, $90°$, and $135°$), then average of these GLCMs is taken as feature vector. This method is also known as isotropic GLCM. Elements of isotropic GLCM perform better than second-order statistics [6].

2.3   Classification

SVM has been successfully employed in number of classification works for its generalization ability [7]. SVMs map the input signal or feature vector into a high-dimensional feature space and construct an optimal hyperplane to separate samples from the two classes. Initially they are trained for each class and then tested for the unknown data from any class [26]. In this work, data (known and unknown) is features of three grades of glioma brain tumors. The distinct features of specific class data also contribute in the improvement of classification accuracy.

Classification of three glioma grades is done with the help of three binary SVM classifiers with radial basis function, as it has an ability to map nonlinear data to a very high dimension feature space [14,27]. The final result is based on majority voting from all classifiers. To avoid overfitting of data and estimating the generalization ability, 10-fold cross validation is applied [27]. In ten fold cross validation the whole data set is organized in ten equal subsets. Each subset contain features of nine images, three from each tumor class. Sequentially, one set in each round is used as test data set and the remaining nine sets are used as training data set.

3   Experiment Implementation and Discussion

Proposed method was implemented in MATLAB R2014a on the PC under windows-7 operating system with CPU 2.3 GHz, Core-i5 processor and 4.00 GB of memory (RAM).

3.1   Database

The algorithm was tested using 93 MR brain tumor slices (23 grade II, 45 grade III, and 25 grade IV from dataset of 33 patients) from NCIGT [28] dataset. All the images were 640 × 640, T2-weighted MR brain images in axial plane containing three different glioma brain tumors: grade II, grade III and grade IV gliomas. Each image contain 20 brain slices, slices that contain tumor were considered only. Few images from NCIGT are shown in Fig. 4.

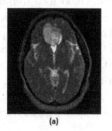 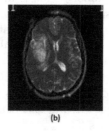 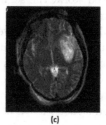

(a)   (b)   (c)

Fig. 4. MR images containing three different glioma grades brain tumours: (a) grade II gliomas; (b) grade III gliomas; (c) grade IV gliomas [28]

3.2   Experimental Setup

Tumor region was segmented using LRBAC method, with maximum of 100 iterations. The segmented images were cropped using a rectangular window (Window size was adjusted according to the largest tumor in the data base) in order to remove noise and to reduce the mathematical complexity of the system, as shown in Fig. 2. The features of cropped and segmented images were calculated using the NSCT coefficients followed by GLCM. Finally, the classification was performed using SVM classifier. The performance of classifier was investigated for the classification of three grades of glioma (II, III and IV). In an other experiment, we used Discrete Wavelet Transform (DWT) for feature extraction in place of NSCT. The performance of DWT approach was compared with the proposed methodology (NSCT approach) in terms of accuracy, sensitivity and specificity.

3.3   Results and Discussion

The confusion matrix for the proposed method is shown in Table 1. The maximum accuracy of 83.33% for grade III, sensitivity of 86.95% and specificity of 92.82% achieved in case of grade II. The classification results achieved using proposed NSCT based feature extraction method was also compared with DWT approach. The confusion matrix for DWT approach is shown in Table 2. The comparison of both approaches in terms of sensitivity, specificity and accuracy is shown in Figs. 5, 6 and 7. It can be observed that the proposed NSCT approach performs much better then the DWT approach. In both approaches, maximum misclassification cases were observed in grade III gliomas.

Table 1. Confusion matrix for proposed NSCT approach.

	Giloma grades predicted		
Ground truth ⇓	Grade II	Grade III	Grade IV
Grade II	20	2	1
Grade III	3	35	7
Grade IV	2	5	18

Table 2. Confusion matrix for DWT approach.

	Giloma grades predicted		
Ground truth ⇓	Grade II	Grade III	Grade IV
Grade II	15	5	3
Grade III	7	30	8
Grade IV	3	6	16

Differentiating between different glioma grade is one of the most difficult tasks. The possible reasons for misclassification of glioma grades is the presence of different histopathologic features in an individual tumor, which makes it very difficult to predict the glioma grade correctly. Brain neoplasms are mostly heterogeneous [29]. It is noticed from the above comparison that using the same classifier, an efficient feature extraction technique can help in discriminating the tumor grade. Increasing the datasets in each class can also improve the accuracy and generalization ability of proposed method.

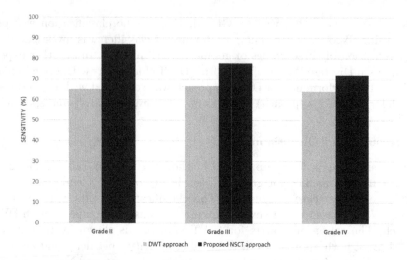

Fig. 5. Comparison in term of sensitivity

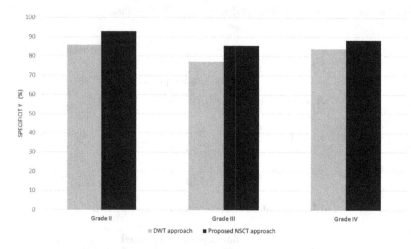

Fig. 6. Comparison in term of specificity

Performance comparison of the proposed method with earlier methods can not be done directly because the data set used is not the standard one. Various studies have used variety of brain tumors types, different sizes and resolution of MRI image data for classification purposes. If compared on the basis of similar type of tumor it is observed that [11] worked on primary neoplasm glioma, meningioma and secondary neoplasm metastatic, [9,29] worked on classification of three grades (II, III, IV) of primary neoplasm glioma and secondary neoplasm metastasis, whereas [3] worked on primary brain tumors, secondary brain tumor (metastasis), as well as normal regions (NR). In current study, three grades of primary glioma tumor (II, III and IV) are classified.

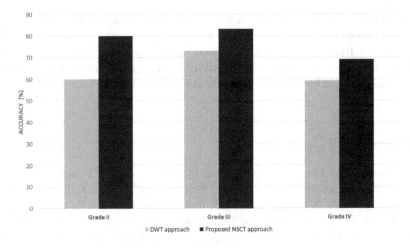

Fig. 7. Comparison in term of individual class accuracy

The comparison with earlier studies in terms of feature extraction methods and type of classification is shown in Table 3. From Table 3 it can be noticed that in previous studies, intensity based features like mean, variance, skewness, and

Table 3. Comparison with earlier studies in terms of feature extraction methods and type of classification

Authors	Features	Type of classification
Georgiadis et al. [11]	Histogram, co-occurrence matrices and run-length matrices	Multi-class (metastases, meningiomas and gliomas)
Zacharaki et al. [9]	Tumor shape, intensity and gabor texture	Multi-class (meningioma, glioma grade (II, III and IV), and metastasis)
Zacharaki et al. [29]	Age, tumor shape and intensity	Multi-class (meningioma glioma (grade II, III and IV), and metastasis)
Sachdeva et al. [3]	Intensity and texture	Multi-class (astrocytoma, glioblastoma, medulloblastoma, meningioma, metastatic, and normal regions)
El-Dahshan et al. [2]	DWT	Binary classification (normal and abnormal)
Cheng et al. [6]	Intensity histogram, GLCM and BoW	Multi-class (meningioma, glioma, and pituitary tumor)
This study	NSCT coefficients and isotropic GLCM	Multi-class (glioma grade II, III and IV)

kurtosis were extensively used. Multi-resolution transforms like various types of wavelet transform and contourlet transform were also employed in number of studies for feature extraction of normal and abnormal brain classification [3, 30, 31]. This study has used NSCT, a time invariant multi-resolution transform and isotropic GLCM for the multi-classification of three brain tumors with better accuracies.

4   Conclusion

In this paper a new feature extraction method based on NSCT and GLCM, was proposed for the classification of three different types of brain tumors (grade II, III and IV gliomas). A dataset of 93 MR images were used for the classification. Segmentation of tumor region was done using a semi-automatic segmentation technique (LRBAC) followed by cropping, in which a small rectangular window of fixed size was used to crop the unwanted area, in order to reduce noise and complex calculations. A level three NSCT and isotropic GLCM were used for feature extraction and SVM for classification. The proposed NSCT based method was compared with DWT based method in terms of accuracy, sensitivity and specificity. The proposed method performed better than DWT approach, in classification of all three glioma grades. The obtained maximum individual classification accuracy, sensitivity and specificity were 83.33%, 86.95% and 92.82% respectively.

References

1. The American Brain Tumor Association. http://www.abta.org/brain-tumor-information/types-of-tumors/
2. El-Dahshan, E.S.A., Mohsen, H.M., Revett, K., Salem, A.B.M.: Computer-aided diagnosis of human brain tumor through MRI: a survey and a new algorithm. Expert Syst. Appl. 41(11), 5526–5545 (2014)
3. Sachdeva, J., Kumar, V., Gupta, I., Khandelwal, N., Ahuja, C.K.: Segmentation, feature extraction, and multiclass brain tumor classification. J. Digit. Imaging 26(6), 1141–1150 (2013)
4. Selvaraj, H., Selvi, S.T., Selvathi, D., Gewali, L.: Brain MRI slices classification using least squares support vector machine. Int. J. Intell. Comput. Med. Sci. Image Process. 1(1), 21–33 (2007)
5. Shanthakumar, P., Ganeshkumar, P.: Performance analysis of classifier for brain tumor detection and diagnosis. Comput. Electr. Eng. 45, 302–311 (2015)
6. Cheng, J., Huang, W., Cao, S., Yang, R., Yang, W., Yun, Z., Feng, Q.: Enhanced performance of brain tumor classification via tumor region augmentation and partition. PloS ONE 10(10), e0140381 (2015)
7. El-Dahshan, E.S.A., Hosny, T., Salem, A.B.M.: Hybrid intelligent techniques for MRI brain images classification. Digit. Signal Process. 20(2), 433–441 (2010)
8. Haralick, R.M., Shanmugam, K.: Textural features for image classification. IEEE Trans. Syst. Man Cybern. 3(6), 610–621 (1973)

9. Zacharaki, E.I., Wang, S., Chawla, S., Soo Yoo, D., Wolf, R., Melhem, E.R., Davatzikos, C.: Classification of brain tumor type and grade using MRI texture and shape in a machine learning scheme. Magn. Reson. Med. **62**(6), 1609–1618 (2009)
10. Bankman, I.: Handbook of Medical Image Processing and Analysis. Academic Press, New York (2008)
11. Georgiadis, P., Cavouras, D., Kalatzis, I., Daskalakis, A., Kagadis, G.C., Sifaki, K., Solomou, E.: Improving brain tumor characterization on MRI by probabilistic neural networks and non-linear transformation of textural features. Comput. Methods Progr. Biomed. **89**(1), 24–32 (2008)
12. Zarandi, M.F., Zarinbal, M., Izadi, M.: Systematic image processing for diagnosing brain tumors: a type-II fuzzy expert system approach. Appl. Soft Comput. **11**(1), 285–294 (2011)
13. Zhang, Y., Dong, Z., Wu, L., Wang, S.: A hybrid method for MRI brain image classification. Expert Syst. Appl. **38**(8), 10049–10053 (2011)
14. Khalighi, S., Tirdad, P., Pak, F., Nunes, U.: Shift and rotation invariant iris feature extraction based on non-subsampled contourlet transform and GLCM. In: ICPRAM (2), pp. 470–475, February 2012
15. Do, M.N., Vetterli, M.: The contourlet transform: an efficient directional multiresolution image representation. IEEE Trans. Image Process. **14**(12), 2091–2106 (2005)
16. Da Cunha, A.L., Zhou, J., Do, M.N.: The nonsubsampled contourlet transform: theory, design, and applications. IEEE Trans. Image Process. **15**(10), 3089–3101 (2006)
17. Jasmine, J.L., Baskaran, S., Govardhan, A.: An automated mass classification system in digital mammograms using contourlet transform and support vector machine. Int. J. Comput. Appl. **31**(9), 54–60 (2011)
18. Khalighi, S., Pak, F., Tirdad, P., Nunes, U.: Iris recognition using robust localization and nonsubsampled contourlet based features. J. Signal Process. Syst. **81**(1), 111–128 (2015)
19. Kazmi, M., Aziz, A., Akhtar, P., Maftun, A., Afaq, W.B.: Medical image denoising based on adaptive thresholding in contourlet domain. In: 2012 5th International Conference on Biomedical Engineering and Informatics (BMEI), pp. 313–318. IEEE Press, October 2012
20. Emblem, K.E., Zoellner, F.G., Tennoe, B., Nedregaard, B., Nome, T., Due Tonnessen, P., Bjornerud, A.: Predictive modeling in glioma grading from MR perfusion images using support vector machines. Magn. Reson. Med. **60**(4), 945–952 (2008)
21. Lankton, S., Tannenbaum, A.: Localizing region-based active contours. IEEE Trans. Image Process. **17**(11), 2029–2039 (2008)
22. Farhi, L., Yusuf, A., Raza, R.H.: Adaptive stochastic segmentation via energy-convergence for brain tumor in MR images. J. Vis. Commun. Image Represent. **46**, 303–311 (2017)
23. Zia, R., Akhter, P., Kazmi, M.: Performance comparison of LRBAC method with DRLSE for the segmentation of tumors in MRI images. Mehran Univ. Res. J. Eng. Technol. **34**, 69–76 (2015)
24. Yezzi, A., Tsai, A., Willsky, A.: A fully global approach to image segmentation via coupled curve evolution equations. J. Vis. Commun. Image Represent. **13**(1–2), 195–216 (2002)
25. Wang, Z.Z., Yong, J.H.: Texture analysis and classification with linear regression model based on wavelet transform. IEEE Trans. Image Process. **17**(8), 1421–1430 (2008)

26. Zhou, J., Chan, K.L., Chong, V.F.H., Krishnan, S.M.: Extraction of brain tumor from MR images using one-class support vector machine. In: 27th Annual International Conference of the Engineering in Medicine and Biology Society. IEEE-EMBS 2005, pp. 6411–6414. IEEE Press, January 2006

27. Bauer, S., Nolte, L.-P., Reyes, M.: Fully automatic segmentation of brain tumor images using support vector machine classification in combination with hierarchical conditional random field regularization. In: Fichtinger, G., Martel, A., Peters, T. (eds.) MICCAI 2011. LNCS, vol. 6893, pp. 354–361. Springer, Heidelberg (2011). doi:10.1007/978-3-642-23626-6_44

28. National Center for Image Guided Therapy. https://central.xnat.org/app/template

29. Zacharaki, E.I., Kanas, V.G., Davatzikos, C.: Investigating machine learning techniques for MRI-based classification of brain neoplasms. Int. J. Comput. Assist. Radiol. Surg. **6**(6), 821–828 (2011)

30. Kharat, K.D., Kulkarni, P.P., Nagori, M.B.: Brain tumor classification using neural network based methods. Int. J. Comput. Sci. Inform. **1**(4), 2231–5292 (2012)

31. Youssef, S.M., Korany, E.A., Salem, R.M.: Contourlet-based feature extraction for computer aided diagnosis of medical patterns. In: 2011 IEEE 11th International Conference on Computer and Information Technology (CIT), pp. 481–486. IEEE Press, August 2011

Large-Scale Automatic Species Identification

Jeff Mo[1]($\boxtimes$), Eibe Frank[1], and Varvara Vetrova[2]

[1] Department of Computer Science, University of Waikato, Hamilton, New Zealand
jeff941027@gmail.com, eibe@cs.waikato.ac.nz
[2] School of Mathematics and Statistics, University of Canterbury,
Christchurch, New Zealand
varvara.vetrova@canterbury.ac.nz

Abstract. The crowd-sourced Naturewatch GBIF dataset is used to obtain a species classification dataset containing approximately 1.2 million photos of nearly 20 thousand different species of biological organisms observed in their natural habitat. We present a general hierarchical species identification system based on deep convolutional neural networks trained on the NatureWatch dataset. The dataset contains images taken under a wide variety of conditions and is heavily imbalanced, with most species associated with only few images. We apply multi-view classification as a way to lend more influence to high frequency details, hierarchical fine-tuning to help with class imbalance and provide regularisation, and automatic specificity control for optimising classification depth. Our system achieves 55.8% accuracy when identifying individual species and around 90% accuracy at an average taxonomy depth of 5.1—equivalent to the taxonomic rank of "family"—when applying automatic specificity control.

Keywords: Species identification · Convolutional neural networks

1 Introduction

Can we use a commodity camera to take a snapshot of an animal or a plant in the wild and identify its species automatically using convolutional neural networks? This is the question we investigate in this paper, based on a large crowd-sourced image dataset[1] provided by iNaturalist.org. The data, annotated by experts and deemed research grade, comprises approximately 1.2 million photographs of more than 20 thousand species observed in their natural habitat. It contains images taken by ordinary people under a wide variety of uncontrolled conditions and is heavily imbalanced. On the other hand, the data poses a hierarchical classification problem, making it possible to abstain from a species-level classification if the classification model is insufficiently confident, returning a classification at a higher level of the taxonomy instead.

---

[1] http://www.gbif.org/dataset/50c9509d-22c7-4a22-a47d-8c48425ef4a7.

© Springer International Publishing AG 2017
W. Peng et al. (Eds.): AI 2017, LNAI 10400, pp. 301–312, 2017.
DOI: 10.1007/978-3-319-63004-5_24

We use a state-of-the-art pre-trained convolutional neural network, the InceptionResnetV2 [10] network trained on the Imagenet [8] data, and fine-tuned it on the Naturewatch data. We introduce two novel techniques—multi-view classification, and hierarchical fine-tuning—along with automatic specificity control for optimising classification depth. Multi-view classification enables the network to retain high frequency details while also increasing representational power, and can be generalised to problems requiring multiple correlated views of an object, while hierarchical fine-tuning helps with class imbalance and provides regularisation.

Our system achieves 55.8% accuracy when identifying species and around 90% accuracy at an average taxonomy depth of 5.1—equivalent to the taxonomic rank of 'family'—when applying automatic specificity control.

Species identification using machine learning is not a new idea and has been attempted before, but in a much more constraint setting on a much smaller scale. We review related work in the next section before presenting our deep-learning-based system in Sect. 3. Section 4 describes how we prepared the data and Sect. 5 presents our results. Section 6 concludes the paper.

2   Related Work

Classification of moths is the subject of [6], based on a dataset containing 774 images across 35 classes. Images are mostly dorsal views of moths on a uniformly coloured background. Prior to classification with a support vector machine, global image statistics, colour histograms, local patch intensity statistics and other features are extracted from each image. The system achieves an accuracy of 85% in 10-fold cross validation.

Colour histogram features are also used for species classification in [7], but in the context of constructing hierarchically structured ensembles of neural networks trained using evolutionary optimisers. The classification hierarchy is traversed from the topmost level (genus) down to the species level to produce labels. If insufficient information is provided to the classifier, traversal is stopped and a less specific label produced. This is similar to the hierarchical approach we present in this paper. The classifier is evaluated on images of orchids.

A different set of features is used in [13], which presents experiments on a dataset of 120 images across seven species. The images are processed by an edge detector and have their contours digitised with the elliptic Fourier transform. A support vector machine classifier is trained on the elliptic Fourier coefficients, yielding a final per-species accuracy ranging from 90% to 98%.

Deep convolutional networks have also been considered for species classification. In [5], a fine-tuned deep convolutional neural network classifier for plant leaves is presented, using a dataset consisting of 2816 images across 44 classes of plant leaves. The system achieves an accuracy of 99.5%, demonstrating the efficacy of convolutional neural networks.

Deep neural networks are also used in [2], which applies a technique similar to HD-CNN [12] over a base network of fine-tuned VGGNets. With 200 k

Fig. 1. A visualization of the two views the network receives

images spread across 277 classes, this method attains an accuracy of 44.6%. As in our work, the images are commodity images taken in various conditions and backgrounds. Along with the relatively large number of classes this is a likely explanation for the relatively low accuracy.

3 Hierarchical Species Classification with Deep Learning

We use a modified version of the InceptionResnetV2 network trained on the Imagenet data as the starting point for our experiments. The modified version of the network has a different architecture than the one described in [10], and makes use of auxiliary classifiers as in [11]. In the following, we describe how we apply multi-view classification, hierarchical knowledge transfer, and automatic specificity control to yield our final system.

3.1 Multi-view Classification

Our multi-view network architecture is inspired by three related works. In [3], two different scales of video frames are used for video classification—one neural network is trained on the entire image region, and another on only the central region. The outputs of the two networks are merged at the "bottleneck" layer and classification is performed from there. In [9], a network composed of multiple views of an object is trained and combined using pooling, with the results being passed to another convolutional neural network for final classification. All views of the object are passed through the same initial network which acts as a feature extractor. Finally, in TreeNets, as presented in [4], the authors demonstrate that branching of networks after a few layers and ensembling the results, instead of branching at input—as for normal ensembles—results in useful sharing of common early-level convolutional filters general to most images, and leads to increased accuracy.

Our multi-view classification technique uses two sections of the input image, both at the same resolution but at different magnification scales, to perform training and classification (Fig. 1). This is important for species identification as both the high frequency details and the overall shape of the image have a significant impact on what the species is. The first five convolution layers of our architecture act as a shared feature extractor for both views. Parameters are shared up to and including the stem block of the architecture, after which the network splits into two, each with its own set of parameters. To allow features from the different input images to correlate with each other, we concatenate the output of the two branches, doubling the depth, and perform a 1×1 convolution with output depth equal to that before concatenation. We then use the rest of the InceptionResnetV2 network's pipeline as normal. See Fig. 2 for the overall network architecture.

One issue with our multi-view technique is that during training time, the region of interest is not known and thus we compromise and take the central region. However, if the object of interest is not within the central region, then this may lead to an unexpected combination of features leading to a possibly misinformed classification. One way of overcoming this obstacle would be to

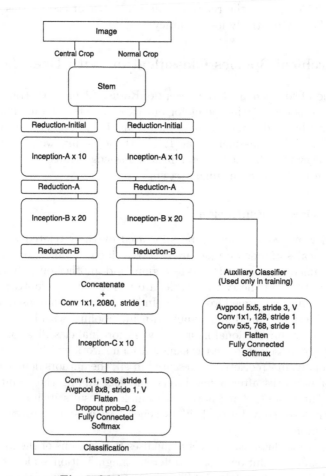

Fig. 2. Multi-view network architecture

use a training set with bounding boxes on objects of interest. Then, during classification, the user could be asked to specify a bounding box for the region of interest.

Network Specific Adjustments. Google's Inception series of networks use an auxiliary classifier [11] as an additional source to optimise for. We keep the auxiliary classifier only on the whole-view branch. Another adjustment we make is that the crop-view branch is not initialized from a pretrained network but randomly, to encourage diversity between the two branch networks. As the layers before and after this branch both have pretrained weights, this branch should quickly adapt [14] to the training data.

3.2 Hierarchical Knowledge Transfer

Overfitting is an acute problem when dealing with very small classes containing few observations. Given the hierarchical nature of our dataset, we combat this problem by translating labels to those of their superclasses, effectively reducing the number of classes and increasing the number of samples per class.[2] This can be applied recursively up the hierarchy until a desired number of samples-per-class is achieved. We then first train against this reduced-complexity problem, progressively increasing the difficulty of the dataset by translating labels down the hierarchy and copying final-layer weights to the corresponding subclasses. This is done recursively until the original problem is recovered.

Formally, let k_d be the number of different classes at depth d, X be the set of input examples, $d_0 \in \{0, \ldots, d_{max} - 1\}$ be the starting depth, and $\mathbf{w}_d$ be the weights of the (currently) final layer of the network, for classifying at depth d. Moreover, let $f: X \times W \to \{1, \ldots, k_d\}$ be the model classifying an example using weights w and $t_d: \{1, \ldots, k_d\} \to \{1, \ldots, k_{d-1}\}$ be the translation function at depth d that maps a label to its parent label.

We optimise f using $\mathbf{w}_{d_0}$ until convergence, then create new weights $\mathbf{w}_{d+1}$, where weights for each class i are set according to $\mathbf{w}_{d+1}^{(i)} = \mathbf{w}_d^{(t_d(i))}$. Finally, to obtain diversity in the weight vectors, we mix in randomization for $\mathbf{w}_{d+1}$ as explained below. We continue this process, incrementing d until $d = d_{max}$.

The aim of this process—through the combined effect of smoother error surfaces due to the simpler problems being initially tackled, and superclass-based weight initialization—is to achieve a strong regularising effect and enhance classification accuracy for under-represented classes. This technique also aids convergence speed as superclasses usually have more distinguishing features between them, helping the network quickly locate the features that actually matter.

Weight Vector Randomization. Here we will derive the expression for mixing weights. We will be using uniform distributions for adding randomness as it was the initialization method used in the base network architecture

---

[2] We can also view this as an extreme form of input augmentation.

InceptionResnetV2. We want to mix the two weights using a user-determined scalar factor $a \in [0, 1]$ while maintaining variance, assuming both already have optimal variance. Let X, Y be independent random variables with equal variances such that $Var[X] = Var[Y]$. For any scaled distribution,

$$Var[kX] = k^2 Var[X]$$

thus to recover the original variance we need to scale X and Y by $\sqrt{a}$ and $\sqrt{1-a}$:

$$Var[\sqrt{a}X + \sqrt{1-a}Y] = aVar[X] + (1-a)Var[Y]$$
$$= Var[X] = Var[Y]$$

Therefore, to maintain the original variance, we mix weights according to:

$$\mathbf{w} = \sqrt{a}\mathbf{w}_0 + \sqrt{1-a}\mathbf{w}_{random}$$

3.3   Automatic Specificity Adjustment

Given the nature of our data it is clear that we will not achieve high accuracy across the full set of species. We can try to avoid presenting misleading information to the user of our system by classifying at higher levels of the hierarchy when necessary. The method presented in [1] classifies the input along a given hierarchy such that maximum information gain is achieved, while maintaining a targeted accuracy. It is based on the observation that classifying at the root node of the hierarchy would result in perfect accuracy, but with zero information gain, while always classifying at a leaf node would maximise information gain, but yield potentially low accuracy. A threshold dictates the cut-off point that is used to determine which level of the hierarchy an input is classified at, such that information gain is maximised while satisfying an accuracy target. The optimal threshold is found using binary search on accuracy values obtained through evaluating the test set against the current threshold. In operation, real data is, of course, different from that in the test set, and thus this method cannot guarantee accuracy given unseen examples.

For our work, we use the absolute depth as the metric instead of information gain, as information gain has little bearing in terms of species classification. We classify at the deepest node that provides an estimated class probability greater or equal to the user-provided confidence threshold. Additionally, we allow one to specify a series of prior nodes to begin search from, instead of always using the hierarchy root, such that users with additional information can improve their classification accuracy and granularity.

To classify at a level higher than leaf level, some method must be employed to produce class probability estimates for those higher level nodes. One method is to climb up the hierarchy from the most likely leaf class but this does not yield a probability; another is to use separate classifiers for each branching point, which is unsuitable for large and computationally complex networks such as InceptionResnetV2. Yet another one is to approximate class probabilities for higher-level nodes as the sums of all probabilities of successor nodes. The last method is what we use in this paper.

Ideally, we would like to classify as close to leaf-level as possible. Using a probability threshold, we can determine the optimal level of the hierarchy to classify at. Formally, let $Children(n)$ be all child nodes under node n. Let $Depth(n)$ be the depth of node n. Let $Probability(n)$ be the probability of a leaf node n. Let $t \in [0, 1]$ be the confidence threshold. Define $NodeProbability(n)$, the probability at node n, as:

$$NodeProbability(n) = \begin{cases} Probability(n) & \text{if n is leaf} \\ \sum_{l \in Children(n)} NodeProbability(l) & \text{otherwise} \end{cases}$$

The goal is the to find

$$\underset{n}{\operatorname{argmax}} \quad Depth(n) + NodeProbability(n)$$

$$\text{subject to} \quad NodeProbability(n) < t$$

An optimal way to find this node is to traverse the tree in a depth-first manner such that depths and probabilities are obtained whenever a node's children have been traversed.

As the test set is not an exact representation of real data, there is little need for having a mathematically guaranteed accuracy in practical scenarios. A probabilistic approximation may serve the purpose whilst taking significantly less time to optimise. Under this assumption, we build on the prior work in [1] in that instead of using full binary search for the best threshold, we use hillclimbing to optimise the threshold parameter with regards to a target accuracy while running the evaluation. With a learning factor that reduces as optimisation proceeds, we can converge to a threshold that nearly maximises specificity while hitting the target accuracy. Hill climbing is effective in this case as an increase in threshold will always lead to an increase in accuracy.

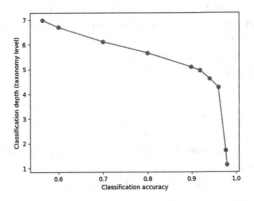

Fig. 3. Classification depth versus target accuracy, for our final model.

One can see in Fig. 3 that there is always a trade-off between target accuracy and classification depth. As we approach a target accuracy of 1, classification depth decreases sharply, as even root level nodes fail to classify to the specified accuracy. A graph like this can be useful in inferring a target accuracy that still provides results at a meaningful depth.

4   Data Preparation

Our image set exhibits a significant number of challenges. The distance from camera, lighting conditions, background, and image quality are very variable. The same species could look drastically different in two given images. Furthermore, species may be at any stage in their lifecycle—for example images labelled as a monarch butterfly may represent this species in egg or butterfly form. The image may not contain the labelled species at all—foot prints, faecal matter, and other identifiable aspects may be present in the image set, which leads to the next point: the expert labelling may be based on more than the image itself, taking into account location, time and the submitted text brief to produce a labelling. The images may also contain more than one species. These issues make it extremely challenging for the classifier to build a robust model. We should also note that our species hierarchy is a taxonomic hierarchy and not necessarily based on visual differences. Behaviour, habitat, and genome sequence are often key differentiators in the taxonomy but cannot necessarily be captured in images. Given a hierarchy corresponding to the visual similarity between the classes, the accuracy of classification would likely improve.

The full dataset consisted of images separated into over 100,000 different species. These images are mostly in JPEG format with resolutions ranging from 0.3 to over eight megapixels. Non-JPEG images were not downloaded for our experiments. Also, during the downloading process, some images could not be retrieved, and some of the species had an unusual taxonomy and were discarded. Many species had fewer than five images under their name, making them unsuitable for training a deep learning type model. Such images were also discarded. Finally, the dataset of usable images consisted of 1,214,141 images across 19,027 classes. The dataset was randomly separated into 2 sets, training and validation, in a 80–20 split. The training set was used for training, while the validation set was used to test and measure classification accuracy. In total, 16,583 species were present in the validation set, instead of the full 19,027 in the training set. As a standard practice to improve accuracy, these selected images underwent random augmentation when training the network, where each image entered into the network was cropped, horizontal-flipped with a random chance, and had its brightness adjusted by $\pm 12.5\%$, contrast adjusted by $\pm 50\%$, hue adjusted by $\pm 20\%$ and saturation adjusted by $\pm 50\%$. Vertical flipping and rotation was not used for augmentation as almost all plant or animals are captured at a certain angle. The augmentation was performed in a stream-wise manner as images were loaded in for training.

5   Experimental Results

The following default parameters originally used for training the InceptionResnetV2 network on the Imagenet dataset [10], were also reused for all experiments in this paper:

– L2 weight decay with $\lambda = 0.00004$
– Batch normalisation with $Decay = 0.9997$, $\epsilon = 0.001$
– Xavier initialization in [10]
– Dropout before final layer with $DropProbability = 0.2$
– Adam optimiser with $\beta_1 = 0.9$, $\beta_2 = 0.999$ and $\epsilon = 1$

Parameter tuning was not performed, to enable a more controlled comparison between the different networks used. Further optimising hyperparameters may lead to an increase in accuracy.

For automatic specificity adjustment, we targeted an accuracy of 90%. We split the validation set into two even parts, with one part not being used to affect the confidence threshold. The average classification depth and accuracy was based solely off the unseen set of 100,000 images. We reused this configuration for all three of our experiments concerning automatic specificity adjustment.

Our first experiment with the large dataset was with a pretrained and unmodified InceptionResnetV2 network. For this experiment, a batch size of 32 was used. We trained for a total of six epochs, using a learning rate of 0.01 for the first three epochs, followed by 0.001 for the next two, and 0.0001 for the final one. A final accuracy of 46.6% was attained. Using automatic specificity adjustment, we achieved an accuracy of 90.0% at an average taxonomy depth of 4.78.

Our second experiment used the modified multi-view InceptionResnetV2 network. For this experiment, a batch size of 16 was used, due to the increased model size, forcing us to reduce batch size to free up enough memory. We trained for a total of four epochs, using a learning rate of 0.1 for the first two epochs, followed by 0.01 for the next one-and-a-half, 0.001 for the next half, and 0.0001 for the final half epoch. A final accuracy of 54.8% was attained, an increase of 9.2% above the state-of-the-art InceptionResnetV2 network. Using automatic specificity adjustment, we achieved an accuracy of 90.0% at an average taxonomy depth of 4.96, which is a 5.6% increase in depth. When testing on the training set, an accuracy of 68.2% was attained—a significant increase over that on the validation set, which shows signs that the network is overfitting.

Our third experiment used the multi-view InceptionResnetV2 network along with the hierarchical knowledge transfer technique. A batch size of 16 was again used. Training was done in two stages—first we trained at the genus level (taxonomy level 6) over one-and-a-half epochs using a learning rate of 0.1. Then we translated and trained at the species level (taxonomy level 7) for three more epochs, using a learning rate of 0.1 for the first epoch, 0.01 for the next one, 0.001 for the next half, and 0.001 for the final half. A final accuracy of 55.8% was attained, an increase of 1.0% above what we achieved with the multi-view InceptionResnetV2 network. Using automatic specificity adjustment, we achieved an accuracy of 90.0% at an average taxonomy depth of 5.09, which is a further 3.3%

increase above the depth in the previous experiment. Interestingly, when tested on the training set, an accuracy of 57.8% was attained. Compared to using the multi-view approach alone, we see that applying hierarchical knowledge transfer reduces the amount of overfitting significantly.

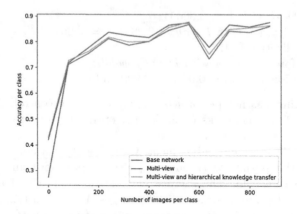

Fig. 4. The differences in accuracy for classes of different sizes, for the three experiments.

In Fig. 4 we can see that multi-view networks provided a large improvement in accuracy for small classes, at the cost of reduced accuracy for larger classes. We speculate that this is due to the improved model being more able to distinguish the small difficult classes, thus no longer sacrificing their accuracy for those of the larger, easier classes. Surprisingly, hierarchical knowledge transfer provided gains across all class sizes. This goes against the initial hypothesis in Sect. 3.2 and means that, at least in this dataset, not only under-represented classes but all classes, benefit from the pretraining and initialization from parameters of superclasses. It is interesting to note from Table 1 that although hierarchical

Table 1. Evaluation results for the three experiments.

Network	Accuracy (validation set)	Accuracy (training set)	Automatic specificity accuracy	Automatic specificity depth
InceptionResnetV2	46.6%	-	90.0%	5.78
InceptionResnetV2 + multi-view	54.8%	68.2%	90.0%	5.96
InceptionResnetV2 + multi-view + hierarchical knowledge transfer	55.8%	57.8%	90.0%	6.09

knowledge transfer gains only 1% improvement in raw accuracy, it delivers 3.3% increased classification depth at the same target accuracy when automatic specificity adjustment is applied, while multi-view learning alone delivered a 9.2% increase in raw accuracy but only a 5.6% increase in classification depth.

6   Conclusions

We investigated the viability of large-scale species identification from commodity images using state-of-the-art image recognition based on a convolutional neural network. The experimental results are highly encouraging, with 55.8% classification accuracy when discriminating between the almost 20,000 individual species in the dataset and 90.0% accuracy at an average taxonomy depth of 5.1 when applying automatic specificity control.

There is potential for the developed system to be used in a diverse range of applications, for example, identifying tree species in autonomous UAV surveys, or classifying harmful pests in one's backyard. However, for more critical applications, the granularity or accuracy may not yet be sufficient. The primary reason for this is that many species in the dataset are represented by very few images.

Two of the methods considered in this paper, hierarchical knowledge transfer and multi-view classification, may warrant investigation in other classification settings as well. Moreover, it would be useful to consider the effect of tuning the parameters for hierarchical knowledge transfer and experimenting with architecture variations for multi-view classification. The latter technique could be generalised to any classification task that requires different views of an object. For each additional view, we can add another column after the initial split point in the network and merge at the concatenation point. These multiple views may stem from different images or from sub-regions of the same image as in this paper. Depending on the similarity of features in these views, the network should be tuned such that an appropriate amount of parameters is shared between views.

Acknowledgements. We would like to acknowledge financial support from the MBIE Endeavour research grant "Biosecure-ID". We would like to thank Dr. Michael Cree for many useful discussions and Dr. Jerry Cooper and Dr. Aaron Wilton as the experts behind NatureWatch for their contribution.

References

1. Deng, J., Krause, J., Berg, A.C., Fei-Fei, L.: Hedging your bets: optimizing accuracy-specificity trade-offs in large scale visual recognition. In: Proceedings of the 2012 IEEE Conference on Computer Vision and Pattern Recognition, pp. 3450–3457. IEEE (2012)
2. Glick, J., Miller, K.: Insect classification with heirarchical deep convolutional neural networks. Final report for convolutional neural networks for visual recognition (CS231N), Stanford University (2016). http://cs231n.stanford.edu/reports/2016/pdfs/283_Report.pdf

3. Karpathy, A., Toderici, G., Shetty, S., Leung, T., Sukthankar, R., Fei-Fei, L.: Large-scale video classification with convolutional neural networks. In: Proceedings of the 2014 IEEE Conference on Computer Vision and Pattern Recognition, pp. 1725–1732. IEEE (2014)

4. Lee, S., Purushwalkam, S., Cogswell, M., Crandall, D., Batra, D.: Why M heads are better than one: training a diverse ensemble of deep networks (2015). arXiv preprint: arXiv:1511.06314

5. Lee, S.H., Chan, C.S., Wilkin, P., Remagnino, P.: Deep-plant: plant identification with convolutional neural networks. In: Proceedings of the 2015 IEEE International Conference on Image Processing, pp. 452–456. IEEE (2015)

6. Mayo, M., Watson, A.T.: Automatic species identification of live moths. Knowl. Based Syst. **20**(2), 195–202 (2007)

7. Pereira, S., Gravendeel, B., Wijntjes, P., Vos, R.: OrchID: a generalized framework for taxonomic classification of images using evolved artificial neural networks (2016). bioRxiv preprint 070904

8. Russakovsky, O., Deng, J., Su, H., Krause, J., Satheesh, S., Ma, S., Huang, Z., Karpathy, A., Khosla, A., Bernstein, M., Berg, A.C., Fei-Fei, L.: Imagenet large scale visual recognition challenge. Int. J. Comput. Vis. **115**(3), 211–252 (2015)

9. Su, H., Maji, S., Kalogerakis, E., Learned-Miller, E.: Multi-view convolutional neural networks for 3D shape recognition. In: Proceedings of the 2015 IEEE International Conference on Computer Vision, pp. 945–953. IEEE (2015)

10. Szegedy, C., Ioffe, S., Vanhoucke, V., Alemi, A.A.: Inception-v4, inception-ResNet and the impact of residual connections on learning. In: Proceedings of the 3rd AAAI Conference on Artificial Intelligence (2017)

11. Szegedy, C., Vanhoucke, V., Ioffe, S., Shlens, J., Wojna, Z.: Rethinking the inception architecture for computer vision. In: Proceedings of the 2016 IEEE Conference on Computer Vision and Pattern Recognition, pp. 2818–2826. IEEE (2016)

12. Yan, Z., Zhang, H., Piramuthu, R., Jagadeesh, V., DeCoste, D., Di, W., Yu, Y.: HD-CNN: hierarchical deep convolutional neural network for large scale visual recognition. In: Proceedings of the 2015 IEEE Conference on Computer Vision and Pattern Recognition, pp. 2740–2748. IEEE (2015)

13. Yang, H.P., Ma, C.S., Wen, H., Zhan, Q.B., Wang, X.L.: A tool for developing an automatic insect identification system based on wing outlines. Sci. Rep. **5**, 12786 (2015)

14. Yosinski, J., Clune, J., Bengio, Y., Lipson, H.: How transferable are features in deep neural networks? In: Advances in Neural Information Processing Systems, vol. 27, pp. 3320–3328. Curran Associates Inc. (2014)

Other Areas in Artificial Intelligence

On the Combination of Argumentation Solvers into Parallel Portfolios

Mauro Vallati[1](✉), Federico Cerutti[2], and Massimiliano Giacomin[3]

[1] University of Huddersfield, Huddersfield, UK
m.vallati@hud.ac.uk
[2] Cardiff University, Cardiff, UK
[3] Università degli Studi di Brescia, Brescia, Italy

Abstract. In the light of the increasing interest in efficient algorithms for solving abstract argumentation problems and the pervasive availability of multicore machines, a natural research issue is to combine existing argumentation solvers into parallel portfolios. In this work, we introduce six methodologies for the automatic configuration of parallel portfolios of argumentation solvers for enumerating the preferred extensions of a given framework. In particular, four methodologies aim at combining solvers in static portfolios, while two methodologies are designed for the dynamic configuration of parallel portfolios. Our empirical results demonstrate that the configuration of parallel portfolios is a fruitful way for exploiting multicore machines, and that the presented approaches outperform the state of the art of parallel argumentation solvers.

Keywords: Argumentation reasoning · Parallel computing · Algorithm selection

1 Introduction

Dung's theory of abstract argumentation [11] is a unifying framework able to encompass a large variety of specific formalisms in the areas of nonmonotonic reasoning, logic programming and computational argumentation. It is based on the notion of argumentation framework (AF), consisting of a set of *arguments* and a binary *attack* relation between them. Arguments can thus be represented by nodes of a directed graph, and attacks by arcs. The nature of arguments is left unspecified: it can be anything from logical statements to informal natural language text. For instance, [21] shows how argumentation can be efficiently used for supporting critical thinking and intelligence analysis in military-sensitive contexts.

Different *argumentation semantics* declare the criteria to determine which arguments emerge as "justified" among conflicting ones, by identifying a number of *extensions*, i.e. sets of arguments that can "survive the conflict together". In [11] four "traditional" semantics were introduced, namely *complete*, *grounded*, *stable*, and *preferred* semantics. For a complete overview of subsequently proposed alternative semantics, the interested reader is referred to [3].

© Springer International Publishing AG 2017
W. Peng et al. (Eds.): AI 2017, LNAI 10400, pp. 315–327, 2017.
DOI: 10.1007/978-3-319-63004-5_25

The main computational problems in abstract argumentation include *decision*—e.g. determine if an argument is in all the extensions prescribed by a semantics—and *construction* problems, and turn out to be computationally intractable for most argumentation semantics [12]. In this paper we focus on the *extension enumeration* problem, i.e. constructing *all* extensions for a given AF: its solution provides complete information about the justification status of arguments and allows for solving the other problems as well.

Nowadays, increases in computational power are mostly achieved through hardware parallelisation. Almost every machine on the market is equipped with a multicore CPU, therefore, parallel solvers are gaining importance in many areas of Artificial Intelligence. However, the manual constructions of parallel solvers is a very challenging task, as it often requires to design specific algorithms, rather than adapting existing sequential ones. One promising approach for exploiting the computational power provided by multicore machines is then to combine solvers into parallel portfolios, which have been recently introduced in areas such as SAT and ASP [1,17]. Notably, while work has been done in the area of sequential portfolios for argumentation [10], there is a lack of approaches aiming at combining solvers into parallel portfolios.

In this work, we consider the automatic construction of static and dynamic portfolios of argumentation solvers for enumerating the preferred extensions of a given AF. In particular, we introduce four methodologies for configuring static portfolios, and two for the dynamic selection of solvers to be executed in parallel. The designed techniques are general, in the sense that they are able to configure portfolios for any given number of available cores—here we focus on the 4-cores case, which correspond to most widely available machines. Our extensive experimental analysis demonstrates that: (i) combining argumentation solvers in parallel portfolios is an effective way for exploiting multiple cores; (ii) static portfolios that execute more solvers on each core are extremely robust; and (iii) the configured parallel portfolios outperform state-of-the-art native parallel argumentation solvers.

2   Dung's Argumentation Framework

An argumentation framework [11] consists of a set of arguments and a binary attack relation between them.

Definition 1. *An* argumentation framework *(AF) is a pair* $\Gamma = \langle \mathcal{A}, \mathcal{R} \rangle$ *where* $\mathcal{A}$ *is a set of arguments and* $\mathcal{R} \subseteq \mathcal{A} \times \mathcal{A}$. *We say that* b attacks a *iff* $\langle b, a \rangle \in \mathcal{R}$, *also denoted as* $b \to a$.

The basic properties of conflict-freeness, acceptability, and admissibility of a set of arguments are fundamental for the definition of argumentation semantics.

Definition 2. *Given an AF* $\Gamma = \langle \mathcal{A}, \mathcal{R} \rangle$:

- *a set* $S \subseteq \mathcal{A}$ *is a* conflict-free *set of* Γ *if* $\nexists\, a, b \in S$ *s.t.* $a \to b$;

- *an argument $a \in \mathcal{A}$ is* acceptable *with respect to a set $S \subseteq \mathcal{A}$ of Γ if $\forall b \in \mathcal{A}$ s.t. $b \rightarrow a$, $\exists\, c \in S$ s.t. $c \rightarrow b$;*
- *a set $S \subseteq \mathcal{A}$ is an* admissible set *of Γ if S is a conflict-free set of Γ and every element of S is acceptable with respect to S of Γ.*

An argumentation semantics σ prescribes for any *AF* Γ a set of *extensions*, denoted as $\mathcal{E}_\sigma(\Gamma)$, namely a set of sets of arguments satisfying the conditions dictated by σ. Here we need to recall the definition of preferred (denoted as PR) semantics only.

Definition 3. *Given an AF $\Gamma = \langle \mathcal{A}, \mathcal{R} \rangle$: a set $S \subseteq \mathcal{A}$ is a* preferred extension *of Γ, i.e. $S \in \mathcal{E}_{PR}(\Gamma)$, iff S is a maximal (w.r.t. set inclusion) admissible set of Γ.*

3   Configuring Parallel Portfolios of Argumentation Solvers

In this section we describe the techniques we designed for combining argumentation solvers into parallel portfolios. Each approach requires as input: (i) the number of cores and the runtime available for the configured portfolio, (ii) a set of basic solvers that given an *AF* return the corresponding set of preferred extensions, (iii) a set of training *AF*s, and (iv) measures of performance of solvers on the training set. Solvers' performance is measured in terms of Penalised Average Runtime (PAR) score. This metric trades off coverage (i.e. the percentage of *AF*s successfully processed by the cutoff time) and runtime for successfully analysed *AF*s: runs that do not solve the given problem get ten times the cutoff time (PAR10), other runs get the actual runtime. The PAR10 score of a solver on a set of *AF*s is the average of the relevant scores.

3.1   Static Parallel Portfolios

The first approach, called *S-Naive*, orders solver according to PAR10 performance achieved on the training instances. Given k available cores, top k solvers are allocated to one core each, and run for all the available runtime.

The second approach for generating static portfolios is called *S-Overall*, and also assigns one solver per core. It starts from an empty portfolio, and iteratively adds the solver—not already included—that maximises the improvement of the PAR10 score of the portfolio. It continues until no more cores are available, or it is not possible to further improve the PAR10 score of the portfolio on the training instances. In the latter case, remaining x cores are allocated to the x solvers with the best PAR10 that are not yet member of the portfolio.

Two other approaches, called *Iterative-Single* and *Iterative-All*, are inspired by the hill-climbing method introduced in [15]. The mentioned approach had to be extended in order to be able to handle multiple parallel cores, and to generate portfolios for minimising the (expected) runtime.

S-Iter-Single configures a different sequential portfolio for each available core. Given a core, this method starts by an empty portfolio, and iteratively either add a new basic solver to the portfolio, or extend the allocated CPU-time of a solver already added to the portfolio, depending on what maximises the decrement of the PAR10 score for the considered sequential portfolio. Once the sequential portfolio for the given core has been configured, the selected solvers are removed from the pool of available solvers, and the process moves to the next core. As it is apparent, the portfolio configured for a given core has no information about the other portfolios, running on the other processing units, or the number of available cores. This approach aims at reducing the complexity of generating a parallel portfolio, and at the same time maximising the diversity of included solvers.

S-Iter-All configures a single general parallel portfolio by considering at the same time all the available cores, and distributing solvers among them. In each step of the configuration process, either the CPU-time allocated to one included solver is increased, or a new solver is added to the portfolio. In the latter case, the solver is scheduled on the core that allows it the earliest start.

3.2 Dynamic Parallel Portfolios

Dynamic portfolios rely on instance features for configuring an instance-specific portfolio. For each AF a vector of features is computed; each feature is a real number that summarises a potentially important aspect of the considered AF. Similar instances should have similar feature vectors, and, on this basis, portfolios are configured using empirical performance models [16].

In this investigation we consider the largest set of features available for AFs [6]. Such set includes 50 features, extracted by exploiting the representation of AFs both as directed (loss-less) or undirected (lossy) graphs. Features are extracted by considering aspects such as the size of graphs, the presence of connected components, the presence of auto-loops, etc. The features extraction process has been parallelised in order to minimise its impact on portfolio performance. Remarkably, as features are extracted by considering two different representations of AFs, their extraction is suitable to be parallelised on two different cores. Following this approach, feature extraction usually requires less than 1 wallclock time second on average.

In this work we propose two techniques, inspired by [10], for generating per-instance parallel portfolios, both based on regression models. Regression models predict the runtime needed by a solver for analysing the considered AF on the basis of the extracted features and on the performance observed on training instances.

The *R-Overall* approach orders the solvers according to the predicted runtime on the given AF, and then allocates one solver per core. While simplistic, this approach aims at reducing the detrimental impact of underestimation mistakes of the predictive model. Instead, the proposed *R-Iterative* technique initially allocates the solvers predicted to be fastest on available processing units. However, each solver is run only for its predicted CPU-time (increased by 10%

for accounting minor underestimation mistakes). If a solver does not success-fully analyse the considered AF in the allocated CPU-time, it is stopped and no longer available to be selected, and the process iterates by selecting a different solver.

4 Experimental Analysis

Our experimental analysis aims to evaluate the fruitfulness of parallel portfo-lios for solving hard argumentation problems, by focusing on the problem of enumerating preferred extensions.

We randomly generated 2,000 AFs based on four different graph models: Barabasi-Albert [2], Erdös-Rényi [13], Watts-Strogatz [23] and graphs featuring a large number of stable extensions (hereinafter StableM).

Erdös-Rényi graphs [13] are generated by randomly selecting attacks between arguments according to a uniform distribution. While Erdös-Rényi was the pre-dominant model used for randomly generated experiments, [5] investigated also other graph structures such as *scale-free* and *small-world* networks. As discussed by Barabasi and Albert [2], a common property of many large networks is that the node connectivities follow a *scale-free* power-law distribution. This is gen-erally the case when: (i) networks expand continuously by the addition of new nodes, and (ii) new nodes attach preferentially to sites that are already well con-nected. Moreover, Watts and Strogatz [23] show that many biological, technolog-ical and social networks are neither completely regular nor completely random, but something in the between. They thus explored simple models of networks that can be tuned through this middle ground: regular networks *rewired* to intro-duce increasing amounts of disorder. These systems can be highly clustered, like regular lattices, yet have small characteristic path lengths, like random graphs, and they are named *small-world* networks by analogy with the small-world phe-nomenon. The AFs have been generated by using AFBenchGen2 [7]. It is wor-thy to emphasise that Watts-Strogatz and Barabasi-Albert produce undirected graphs: in this work, differently from [5], each edge of the undirected graph is then associated with a direction following a probability distribution, that can be provided as input to AFBenchGen. Finally, the fourth set has been generated using the code provided in Probo [8] by the organisers of ICCMA-15 [20].

In order to identify challenging frameworks—i.e., neither trivial nor too com-plex to be successfully analysed in the given CPU-time—AFs for each set have been selected using the protocol introduced in the 2014 edition of the Interna-tional Planning Competition [22]. This protocol lead to the selection of AFs with a number of arguments between 250 and 650, and number of attacks between (approximately) 400 and 180,000.

The set of AFs has been divided into training and testing sets. For each graph model, we randomly selected 200 AFs for training, and the remaining 300 for testing. Therefore, out of the 2,000 AFs generated, 800 have been used for training purposes, while the remaining 1,200 have been used for testing and comparing the performance of trained approaches.

We considered all the 15 solvers that took part in the EE-PR track of ICCMA-15 [20]. For the sake of clarity and conciseness, we removed from the analysis single solvers that did not successfully analyse at least one AF or which were always outperformed by another solver. The interested reader is referred to [19] for detailed descriptions of the solvers. Hereinafter, we will refer to such systems as *basic solvers*, regardless of the approach they exploit for solving argumentation-related problems.

Experiments have been run on a cluster with computing nodes equipped with 2.5 GHz Intel Core 2 Quad Processors, 4 GB of RAM and Linux operating system. A cutoff of 600 wallclock seconds was imposed to compute preferred extensions for each AF. For each solver we recorded the overall result: success (if it solved the considered problem), crashed, timed-out or ran out of memory.

Given the large availability of quad-core processing units, in this work we focus on portfolios configured to run on four cores. Notably, the proposed configuration techniques are general, and can be straightforwardly exploited for configuring portfolios for a different number of cores.

After a set of experiments on a subset of the training instances, the M5-rule technique [14] has been selected for generating the regression models for predicting the expected runtime of solvers.

4.1 Results

Table 1 compares the results of solvers and the proposed parallel portfolio approaches on the testing set of 1,200 AFs. In ICCMA, solvers have been evaluated by considering only coverage (in case of ties the overall runtime on solved instances). Here results are shown in terms of PAR10, coverage and number of time an approach has been the fastest. These results clearly indicate that combining solvers in parallel portfolios is a very fruitful way for reducing the wall-clock time required for successfully analyse an AF. Table 1 also shows the performance of the Virtual Best Solver (VBS). The VBS shows the performance of a (virtual) oracle which always selects the best (fastest) solver for the given framework. The performance gap between the best basic solver and the VBS gives a good indication about the level of complementarity of the considered reasoners.

Remarkably, the performance of the S-Overall and R-Overall approaches are very close to those of the VBS: this is a clear indication that the proposed techniques are able to effectively select and combine the basic solvers. In particular, the per-instance portfolio R-Overall is able to identify the fastest solver, and run it first, in the 95.7% of the cases. It is also interesting to note that iterative approaches, i.e. those that are allowed to run sequentially more than one solver per core, are not able to fruitfully exploit this additional degree of freedom. Our intuition is that the underestimation of the CPU-time needed by basic solvers, due to the fact that training instances are smaller than and/or different from testing ones, is strongly affecting the performance of iterative approaches. On the contrary, overall approaches do not need to consider this aspect, at the cost of a reduced number of solvers that can be run.

Table 1. Performance, in terms of PAR10 and coverage (cov.)—percentage of *AF*s successfully analysed—of the considered *basic solvers* and generated parallel portfolios, for solving the preferred enumeration problem on the complete testing set (All) of 1,200 *AF*s. F.t column indicates the number of times a system has been the fastest among considered. Systems are listed in the order of increasing PAR10.

System	PAR10	Cov.	F.t
VBS	562.9	91.4	1118
S-Overall	569.6	91.3	968
R-Overall	573.6	91.2	1070
S-Iter-All	665.9	89.8	629
R-Iterative	907.3	85.4	911
S-Naive	1013.3	84.3	511
S-Iter-Single	1032.4	84.1	214
Cegartix	1350.4	79.1	229
ArgSemSAT	1916.2	69.1	35
LabSATSolver	2050.3	66.8	9
prefMaxSAT	2057.2	66.8	273
DIAMOND	2417.0	61.0	1
ASPARTIX-D	2728.6	56.1	4
ASPARTIX-V	2772.2	55.2	21
CoQuiAas	3026.4	50.5	78
ASGL	3477.3	43.2	1
Conarg	3696.3	39.3	158
ArgTools	3906.2	35.2	322
Gris	4543.7	24.4	174

In order to shed some light on the configuration of static portfolios, Table 2 shows the CPU-time allocated to each solver by the proposed techniques. Interestingly, the S-Iter-Single approach shows a behaviour that is very different from what can be observed for S-Iter-All. The former opted for including a huge number of solvers, in fact all but one; the latter instead is allocating most of the cores to a single solver each. Unsurprisingly, given the fact that it is by far the best basic solver, all the static approaches are including Cegartix. It is the only solver that is identified by all the techniques as important and worthy to be run. Similarly, we noticed that per-instance portfolios are usually including it. As a side note, given the good performance observed on training instances, the R-Iterative approach tend to allocate to Cegartix a short amount of CPU-time.

When considering the results shown in Tables 1 and 2, the question about the actual importance of Cegartix—or the other considered basic solvers—for a portfolio naturally arises. In other words, what is the added value provided by a solver to a portfolio? For answering this question, thus getting some insights into the state of the art of argumentation solvers for enumerating preferred extensions, we rely on the notion of *state-of-the-art contributors* (SOTA) [18,24]. SOTA assess the contribution of a basic solver by the performance decrease of the VBS when the considered solver is omitted. This method reflects the

Table 2. Solvers included in the portfolios configured by the proposed techniques. ■ indicates that the solver has been selected for running on a core for the maximum available time, otherwise allocated CPU-time seconds are shown.

Solver	S-Naive	S-Overall	S-Iter-All	S-Iter-Single
Cegartix	■	■	570	210
ArgSemSAT	■		■	420
LabSATSolver	■			150
prefMaxSAT	■	■		210
DIAMOND				300
ASPARTIX-D				300
ASPARTIX-V				300
CoQuiAas				150
ASGL				
Conarg			30	30
ArgTools		■	■	150
Gris		■	■	180

added value due to a given solver much more effectively than comparing average performance. This is because, for instance, the SOTA method can identify—and correctly recognise—solvers that may have poor performance on average, but are able to analyse some extremely challenging AFs that would not be analysed by any other basic solver.

Figure 1 presents the top five basic solvers according to their marginal PAR10 contribution—evaluated following the SOTA method previously recalled—to the VBS. For the sake of readability, solvers with low marginal score—i.e, less than 1 PAR10 point—are not shown.

Surprisingly, the largest marginal PAR10 increment is provided by Gris, followed by Cegartix and prefMaxSAT. These results are in apparent contradiction with results shown in Table 1: however, they are explained by the great performance of Gris on Barabasi AFs. It is the only considered basic solver that is able to analyse the vast majority of such frameworks. Similarly, prefMaxSAT does not show outstanding overall performance, but it tends to be fast on some challenging frameworks. It is also interesting to notice the very limited contribution of ArgTools to the VBS. ArgTools is the solver that would have been ranked first according to the number of time it has been the fastest. Yet its contribution is limited because such AFs are quickly addressed also by other solvers.

To assess the generalisation ability of the proposed approaches for static and per-instance portfolios, we exploited the *leave-one-out* methodology. Starting from the original training set composed by 800 AFs, we removed all the frameworks corresponding to one set at a time, and randomly oversampled frameworks from the remaining three sets—in order to have again approximately 800 frameworks for training. The generated portfolios were then tested on the complete testing set of 1,200 frameworks. The results of this analysis are presented in Table 3.

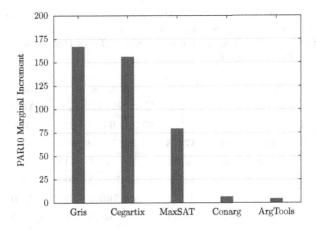

Fig. 1. PAR10 marginal increments, with regard to the VBS, given by the top five solvers that took part in ICCMA 2015. PAR10 of the VBS, including all the available solver, is 562.9.

Static portfolios usually show better generalisation performance; per-instance approaches tend to be more sensitive to the lack of representativeness of the training set, with regards to testing instances. On the one hand, results presented in Table 3 confirm that the performance of static portfolios remain very stable regardless of the used training set, and the S-Overall portfolio is consistently among the best options. On the other hand, per-instance regression-based portfolio R-Overall guarantees very good generalisation. In particular, the predictive model is able to provide accurate runtime predictions even when Barabasi or Erdos frameworks are removed from the training set. This suggests that the exploited features are sufficiently informative for the task of identifying solvers to run in parallel. However, as indicated by the generally poor performance of R-Iterative, predicting the actual runtime is significantly harder.

Comparison with SoA of Parallel Argumentation Reasoning. In order to assess the fruitfulness of exploiting parallel computational units by combining sequential solvers into parallel portfolios, and to better contextualise the performance of the configured portfolios, in this section we compare the generated static and per-instance portfolios with the state of the art of parallel solvers for enumerating preferred extensions: P-SCC-REC [9].

P-SCC-REC is based on the SCC-recursive schema [4]. It recursively decomposes a framework so as to compute semantics labellings (that are in a one-to-one relationship with extensions) on restricted sub-frameworks, in this case strongly-connected components, in order to reduce the computational effort. The labellings computation is then parallelised: each core is dedicated to a single SCC, and results are merged at each recursion layer. Here we consider the P4 version, which exploits four parallel cores.

Table 3. Performance, in terms of PAR10 and coverage (cov.)—percentage of *AF*s successfully analysed—of the systems considered in this study on the complete testing set, when trained on a training set not containing *AF*s of that structure (leave-one-set-out scenario). Best results in bold.

Solver	Barabasi		Erdos		Stable		Watts	
	PAR10	Cov.	PAR10	Cov.	PAR10	Cov.	PAR10	Cov.
R-Iterative	1310.8	78.7	1223.8	80.2	989.4	84.1	835.9	86.8
R-Overall	**823.9**	**87.1**	**574.8**	**91.3**	744.0	88.4	799.2	87.6
S-Iter-All	958.7	85.2	664.1	89.9	957.1	84.8	699.8	89.2
S-Iter-Single	1598.0	74.2	1068.7	83.5	1218.3	80.8	1056.0	83.8
S-Overall	958.6	85.2	664.1	89.9	**569.6**	**91.3**	645.0	**90.1**
S-Naive	1916.2	69.1	1350.4	79.1	1916.2	69.1	1916.2	69.1

It has been shown that P-SCC-REC takes advantage of available parallel cores when the number of SCCs is higher than 40 [9]. In the benchmarks considered in our analysis, this is not usually the case. Therefore, for this comparison we generated 120 *AF*s following the distribution used in [9]. These are extremely large *AF*s, with a number of SCCs between 90 and 150, the number of arguments between 2,700 and 6,000, and considering different uniformly distributed probabilities of attacks, either between arguments or between different SCCs, leading to *AF*s with a number of attacks between approximately 100 thousands and more than 1 million.

Given the extreme size of the *AF*s, we observed that the sequential CPU-time required for extracting features can be significant, between 2 and 250 s. However, the extraction process can be parallelised on the available cores. In this way, we were able to reduce the wall-clock time to one third of the sequential time. In the followings, extraction time is included in the portfolio results.

Table 4. Performance, in terms of PAR10 and coverage (cov.)—percentage of *AF*s successfully analysed—of the generated parallel portfolios and of the parallel solver P-SCC-REC, for solving the preferred enumeration problem on the testing set of 120 *AF*s. Systems are listed in the order of increasing PAR10.

System	PAR10	Cov.
S-Iter-Single	15.8	100.0
R-Overall	21.0	100.0
S-Iter-All	28.6	100.0
S-Naive	29.8	100.0
S-Overall	39.7	100.0
R-Iterative	71.0	99.2
P-SCC-REC	816.8	89.2

Table 4 shows the PAR10 and coverage performance of P-SCC-REC, and of the parallel portfolio approaches. Portfolios have been configured according to the complete training set exploited in the previous analysis. Despite this, results clearly indicate that portfolio-based approaches, either static or per-instance, are able to outperform the state of the art parallel solver P-SCC-REC. The portfolio generated following the R-Iterative approach is the only portfolio-based system that is not able to solve the 100% of the testing frameworks. According to our analysis, this is due to a huge overestimation of the runtime of solvers. The testing AFs are significantly larger than those used for training purposes.

Summary. Results of this extensive experimental analysis support the hypothesis that combining solvers in parallel portfolios is, at the state of the art, the most fruitful way for exploiting multicore machines for abstract argumentation problems. Sequential solvers are able to provide very good performance, due to the higher level of optimisation, and their complementarity allows to combine effectively them in portfolios.

5 Conclusion

In the light of the current trend of increasing computational power through hardware parallelisation, we presented six approaches for configuring parallel portfolios of argumentation solvers for enumerating preferred extensions. We introduced four methodologies for configuring static portfolios, and two techniques for configuring and executing dynamic portfolios.

Our extensive experimental analysis: (i) assessed the marginal increments given by state-of-the-art solvers; (ii) demonstrated that static portfolios tend to generalise better on previously unseen testing AFs; (iii) confirmed that parallel portfolios outperform the state-of-the-art parallel argumentation solver, thus are a fruitful way for exploiting multicore machines.

Future work includes the investigation of techniques for combining solvers in *mixed* portfolios, i.e. partly dynamically and partly statically configured. Given the number of abstract argumentation computational problems, we are also interested in identifying methodologies for generating portfolios of solvers that can solve different problems in parallel, therefore minimising the overall time required to get a complete overview of a given AF.

Acknowledgement. The authors would like to acknowledge the use of the University of Huddersfield Queensgate Grid in carrying out this work.

References

1. Balyo, T., Sanders, P., Sinz, C.: HordeSat: a massively parallel portfolio SAT solver. In: Heule, M., Weaver, S. (eds.) SAT 2015. LNCS, vol. 9340, pp. 156–172. Springer, Cham (2015). doi:10.1007/978-3-319-24318-4_12

2. Barabasi, A., Albert, R.: Emergence of scaling in random networks. Science **286**(5439), 509–512 (1999)
3. Baroni, P., Caminada, M., Giacomin, M.: An introduction to argumentation semantics. Knowl. Eng. Rev. **26**(4), 365–410 (2011)
4. Baroni, P., Giacomin, M., Guida, G.: SCC-recursiveness: a general schema for argumentation semantics. Artif. Intell. **168**(1–2), 165–210 (2005)
5. Bistarelli, S., Rossi, F., Santini, F.: Benchmarking hard problems in random abstract AFs: the stable semantics. In: COMMA 2014, pp. 153–160 (2014)
6. Cerutti, F., Giacomin, M., Vallati, M.: Algorithm selection for preferred extensions enumeration. In: Proceedings of COMMA, pp. 221–232 (2014)
7. Cerutti, F., Giacomin, M., Vallati, M.: Generating structured argumentation frameworks: AFBenchGen2. In: Proceedings of COMMA, pp. 467–468 (2016)
8. Cerutti, F., Oren, N., Strass, H., Thimm, M., Vallati, M.: A benchmark framework for a computational argumentation competition. In: Proceedings of COMMA, pp. 459–460 (2014)
9. Cerutti, F., Tachmazidis, I., Vallati, M., Batsakis, S., Giacomin, M., Antoniou, G.: Exploiting parallelism for hard problems in abstract argumentation. In: Proceedings of AAAI, pp. 1475–1481 (2015)
10. Cerutti, F., Vallati, M., Giacomin, M.: Where are we now? State of the art and future trends of solvers for hard argumentation problems. In: Proceedings of COMMA, pp. 207–218 (2016)
11. Dung, P.M.: On the acceptability of arguments and its fundamental role in non-monotonic reasoning, logic programming, and n-person games. Artif. Intell. **77**(2), 321–357 (1995)
12. Dunne, P.E., Wooldridge, M.: Complexity of abstract argumentation. In: Simari, G., Rahwan, I. (eds.) Argumentation in Artificial Intelligence, pp. 85–104. Springer, Heidelberg (2009). doi:10.1007/978-0-387-98197-0_5
13. Erdös, P., Rényi, A.: On random graphs I. Publ. Math. Debr. **6**, 290–297 (1959)
14. Hall, M., Frank, E., Holmes, G., Pfahringer, B., Reutemann, P., Witten, I.H.: The WEKA data mining software: an update. SIGKDD Explor. **11**(1), 10–18 (2009)
15. Helmert, M., Röger, G., Karpas, E.: Fast downward stone soup: a baseline for building planner portfolios. In: Proceedings of the ICAPS 2011 Workshop of AI Planning and Learning (PAL) (2011)
16. Hutter, F., Xu, L., Hoos, H.H., Leyton-Brown, K.: Algorithm runtime prediction: methods & evaluation. Artif. Intell. **206**, 79–111 (2014)
17. Lindauer, M., Hoos, H., Hutter, F.: From sequential algorithm selection to parallel portfolio selection. In: Dhaenens, C., Jourdan, L., Marmion, M.-E. (eds.) LION 2015. LNCS, vol. 8994, pp. 1–16. Springer, Cham (2015). doi:10.1007/978-3-319-19084-6_1
18. Sutcliffe, G., Suttner, C.: Evaluating general purpose automated theorem proving systems. Artif. Intell. **131**(1), 39–54 (2001)
19. Thimm, M., Villata, S.: System descriptions of the first international competition on computational models of argumentation (ICCMA 2015). arXiv preprint (2015). arXiv:1510.05373
20. Thimm, M., Villata, S., Cerutti, F., Oren, N., Strass, H., Vallati, M.: Summary report of the first international competition on computational models of argumentation. AI Mag. **37**(1), 102–104 (2016)
21. Toniolo, A., Norman, T.J., Etuk, A., Cerutti, F., Ouyang, R.W., Srivastava, M., Oren, N., Dropps, T., Allen, J.A., Sullivan, P.: Agent support to reasoning with different types of evidence in intelligence analysis. In: Proceedings of AAMAS, pp. 781–789 (2015)

22. Vallati, M., Chrpa, L., Grzes, M., McCluskey, T., Roberts, M., Sanner, S.: The 2014 international planning competition: progress and trends. AI Mag. **36**(3), 90–98 (2015)
23. Watts, D.J., Strogatz, S.H.: Collective dynamics of 'small-world' networks. Nature **393**(6684), 440–442 (1998)
24. Xu, L., Hutter, F., Hoos, H., Leyton-Brown, K.: Evaluating component solver contributions to portfolio-based algorithm selectors. In: Cimatti, A., Sebastiani, R. (eds.) SAT 2012. LNCS, vol. 7317, pp. 228–241. Springer, Heidelberg (2012). doi:10.1007/978-3-642-31612-8_18

Exploring the Use of Case-Based Reasoning to Play Eurogames

Michael Woolford and Ian Watson[✉]

Department of Computer Science, University of Auckland,
Auckland, New Zealand
mwool19@aucklanduni.ac.nz, ian@cs.auckland.ac.nz
https://www.cs.auckland.ac.nz/research/gameai/

Abstract. Game AI is a well-established area of research. Classic strategy board games such as Chess and Go have been the subject of AI research for several decades, and more recently modern computer games have come to be seen as a valuable test-bed for AI methods and technologies. Modern board games, in particular those known as German-Style Board Games or Eurogames, are an interesting mid-point between these fields in terms of domain complexity, but AI research in this area is more sparse. This paper discusses the design, development and performance of a game-playing agent, called SCOUT that uses the Case-Based Reasoning methodology as a means to reason and make decisions about game states in the Eurogame Race for the Galaxy. The purpose of this research is to explore the possibilities and limitations of Case-Based Reasoning within the domain of Race for the Galaxy and Eurogames in general.

Keywords: Case-Based reasoning · Game AI

1 Introduction

Historically, the most prominent examples of game AI research have focused on achieving and exceeding human skill levels of performance in classic board games [4, 16, 17], while others have used those games as a test bed for experimenting with specific technologies and methodologies, or within the bounds of various limitations such as avoiding using domain knowledge [5, 15, 18].

Laird and Van Lent [8] argued that despite impressive successes in their specific domains, this research had done little to progress the field towards development of a general human-level AI, and that modern computer games of many different genres, including computer strategy games, provided a superior test bed for human-level AI.

Race for the Galaxy (RftG) falls into a category of modern board games known as Eurogames. These games typically involve more complex rule-sets than traditional card and board games, have mixtures of hidden and open information and deterministic and stochastic elements, and are less abstract. Because of this, they bear more similarities to computer strategy games than do traditional board games. In recent years several agents for playing various Eurogames have been developed [6, 7, 19]. In general the approach to creating these agents has been more in keeping with the approaches taken in classic strategy board game AI systems. In contrast, a key aim of this project is to train

© Springer International Publishing AG 2017
W. Peng et al. (Eds.): AI 2017, LNAI 10400, pp. 328–339, 2017.
DOI: 10.1007/978-3-319-63004-5_26

SCOUT from examples of games played by a human player, using the Case-Based Reasoning (CBR) methodology [2]. Our hope is that if SCOUT can successfully mimic the decisions made by a human player, then it can implicitly gain some of the benefit of the human's strategic reasoning, and demonstrate a style of playing the game that resembles that of the human. Of course the primary goal of playing a game like RftG is to win, so that remains our main focus in terms of results, but we would also like to observe the way in which SCOUT goes about winning, and try to encourage diverse and adaptive play styles. Additionally, where possible we aim to limit our use of RftG domain knowledge in developing the system, with an eye toward exploring methods that could be generalised to other Eurogames.

2 Race for the Galaxy

Race for the Galaxy [9] is a popular Eurogame in which players attempt to build the best empire by constructing a tableau of cards. The game is highly stochastic as the game progresses as cards are randomly drawn from the deck, lending a high degree of variety and unpredictability to gameplay, but player actions are resolved deterministically, resulting in a richly strategic and skillful game. RftG has several expansions which increase the complexity of the game further, and can be played by up to six players. Currently, SCOUT is designed to be played only in a two-player game without expansions.

The rules are significantly more complex than classic board games such as chess; fortunately, it is not necessary for the purposes of this paper to understand how to play the game. A complete description of the game and its rules is available at the publisher's website [14].

2.1 Computer RftG

Multiple computer implementations of RftG have been developed for online play. Currently, the most commonly used game engine is that hosted by the site boardgamearena.com, while our work was done with an offline open-source game engine developed by Jones [7]. In terms of its reasoning processes, SCOUT is designed to function largely independently of the game engine with which it is playing RftG, and could be implemented to work with any game engine. Henceforth we will use "RftG game engine" when referring to this part of the system in general, and "Keldon game engine" when referring to the specific engine used in our implementation. The Keldon AI is sophisticated by the standards of popular game AI and plays the game competently at an intermediate level. It is generally outplayed by a skilled human player but is able to win with favourable draws, and it will regularly beat a novice human player (Fig. 1).

Fig. 1. A game of RftG in progress in the Keldon engine [7], with the human player close to defeating the Keldon AI with a military strategy.

3   SCOUT's Design

This section aims to give an overview of each of the functional elements of the latest version of SCOUT. The next section will detail the specific design choices and developments which lead to this structure.

SCOUT consists of a group of independent modules, each of which handles one aspect of its functionality, along with a multipart case-base. The aim of this approach is to be flexible and to facilitate easy experimentation with, and comparison of, different approaches to developing an AI system for RftG or potentially other Eurogames. This was inspired by Molineaux and Aha's TIELT system for integrating AI systems with RTS games [1, 10].

There are 6 modules in the current iteration of SCOUT:

1. The Head module
2. The Interface module
3. The Case Controller module
4. The Placement Reasoning module
5. The Phase Reasoning module
6. The Payment Reasoning module

In brief, the Head module determines how to process incoming requests from the RftG game engine and facilitates communication between separate modules; The Interface receives game information and decision requests from the game engine and translates them into the specification used by SCOUT; The Case Controller module organises and maintains a registry of the case bases; The Placement, Phase, and Payment modules each reason about the game state and make decisions when a relevant request is made by the game engine.

This model is very flexible, for example: In order to work with a different implementation of RftG, only the Interface module would need to be modified. If we wished to try a completely new reasoning process for card placement, we could swap out the Placement module. Alternatively, if we wish to disable any part of SCOUT's reasoning system and defer back to the Keldon AI, this can be achieved with a simple switch in the Head module. Meanwhile, all other parts of the system function unchanged. This is particularly useful during testing, as it allows us to measure the influence of another part of the system on SCOUT's overall performance in isolation. Modules make requests of one another via the Head but their internal processes are irrelevant to each other, particularly with regards to the reasoning modules. The Case Controller is of course specific to a CBR approach, but the Placement system, for example, could be reworked to classify a game state using a neural network while the Phase module continued to use the CBR system and each would still work in tandem (Fig. 2).

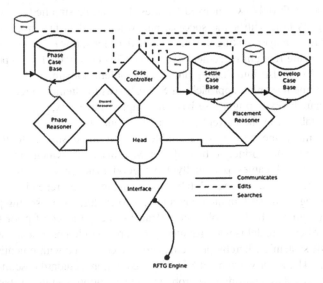

Fig. 2. Visibility between the modules that constitute SCOUT.

4 SCOUT's Development

The basis of SCOUT's reasoning faculties was an initial case-base generated by a human player playing 1,000 games against the Keldon AI. Every game that the human player won (748 games) was stored, and cases were extracted from it. By using these cases, we hoped that SCOUT would be able to take advantage of the human player's superior skill by mimicking their play style. We also experimented with cases generated by running the Keldon AI against itself, in order to generate more cases than a human player could do in a reasonable amount of time.

SCOUT maintains three distinct case-bases that are interrelated but organised independently of one another. These are:

1. The Phase Case Base
2. The Settlement Case Base
3. The Development Case Base

Each case base is used for a particular decision, clearly indicated by its name: The Settlement and Development Case-Bases are used by the Placement Reasoner to make Settle and Develop decisions respectively, and the same case-bases are used by the Payment Reasoner to make Payment decisions, while the Phase Case-Base is used by the Phase Reasoner to make Phase decisions.

4.1   SCOUT Prototype

The initial prototype of SCOUT, programmed in Python, was capable of making placement decisions using a k-nearest neighbour (k-NN) algorithm on a case-base with simplified cases with only two indexed features. Despite its simplicity, it was capable of performing its task with some success, and when used in tandem, with the Keldon AI or a human player making the other game decisions, it was consistently superior to a system making random placement decisions. This encouraged us to proceed with the project and was also illuminating about the problem domain.

In essence, the reasoning approach for SCOUT was to attempt to recreate previous winning tableaux by exploring a case-base of completed tableaux, retrieving those most similar to the tableau in the current problem state, and then choosing to place a card which would make the current state's tableau even more similar to the retrieved tableau. The motivating principle behind this was that cards which are together in a tableau in successful games potentially have good synergy with one another and attempting to recreate a successful tableau is analogous to repeating a successful placement strategy. The system therefore attempts to capture the reasoning process of a human player trying to build a coherent tableau from experience of prior games.

This type of case model is what Richter and Weber would describe as "an extended view of a CBR system", whereby problem states are compared with potential solutions directly [13, p. 41]. Later versions of SCOUT used a more standard case model, where a case is represented as a pairing of a problem and a solution, and the system compares problem states to other problems in the case-base, as opposed to comparing potential solutions.

A major factor in beginning with this approach was that completed game tableaux were able to be exported from a completed game within the Keldon engine by default, and thus we were able to prototype the system before beginning the challenging task of reverse-engineering the Keldon game engine to produce more sophisticated cases.

4.2   Retrieval

The reasoning approach for SCOUT's placement system was essentially to attempt to find the game states from previous successful games most similar to the current game state and adapt the decision made in that case to the current situation. This was a more standard CBR approach than the system used by the prototype. The rationale behind this was that if a case was similar enough to the current state in the relevant features then SCOUT could take advantage of all of the reasoning and planning that the player used to make a decision in the original case.

A k-NN algorithm was used to retrieve cases. Each case in the case-base now represented a specific game state, defined in the same terms as the problem situation, and with a single solution. Deciding what card to place in the current game state essentially became a classification problem, where each of the 95 cards were represented by a class, and cases with a particular card as a solution belonged to the class representing that card. By correctly classifying the problem case, the system determined the best card to place.

As is typical, the algorithm passed through the entire case-base and evaluated the similarity of a case to the problem case by summing the weighted similarities of each indexed case feature. From each of the k best matching cases an appropriate solution for the problem was adapted and added to a multiset of solutions, and finally, a single element of the multiset was randomly selected as the solution. The elements in the multiset were frequently homogeneous because SCOUT's retrieval algorithms were effective in classifying the cases consistently. Therefore the random element was much less pronounced and often completely deterministic, as all retrieved cases yielded the same solution. When the stochastic element did come into effect this was generally heavily biased toward a single good possibility, with an improbable secondary possibility providing some desirable variation.

Indexing

SCOUT processes cases into an internal representation of the case with 23 features, representing a game state, paired with the decision that was made in response to that game state, which constitutes the case's solution. The features are as follow, and are unindexed where not specified:

game id. A non-unique nominal id shared by all cases which were generated within the same game.

case name. A unique nominal id for each case.

game round. An integer representing the game round in which the game state occurs. Indexed with high importance for both decision types.

player chips. An integer representing the number of victory point chips the player possesses.

player hand. A set of nominal ids representing the cards in the player's hand. Indexed with low importance for both decision types.

player hand size. An integer representing the number of cards in the player's hand. Indexed with high importance for Action/Phase Selection decisions.

player military. An integer representing the player's military score. Indexed with high importance for Placement decisions.

player goods. A set of nominal ids representing the player's goods. Indexed with high importance for Action/Phase Selection decisions.

player score. An integer representing the player's total score. Indexed with low importance for both decision types.

player tableau. A set of nominal ids representing the cards in the player's tableau. Indexed with very high importance for both decision types.

player tableau size. An integer representing the number of cards in the player's tableau. Indexed with high importance for both decision types.

opponent chips. An integer representing the number of victory point chips the opponent possesses.

opponent hand size. An integer representing the number of cards in the opponent's hand. Indexed with high importance for Action/Phase Selection decisions.

opponent goods. A set of nominal ids representing the opponent's goods.

opponent military. An integer representing the opponent's military score

opponent score. An integer representing the opponent's total score.

opponent tableau. A set of nominal ids representing the cards in the opponent's tableau. Indexed with moderate importance for Action/Phase Selection decisions.

opponent tableau size. An integer representing the number of cards in the opponent's tableau. Indexed with very low importance for both decision types.

score difference. An integer representing the player's score minus the opponent's total score. Indexed with moderate importance for Action/Phase Selection decisions.

deck. An integer representing the number of cards currently in the deck.

discard. An integer representing the number of cards currently in the discard pile.

pool. An integer representing the number of victory point chips currently available. Indexed with high importance for Action/Phase Selection decisions.

Two of these features, case name and game id, have no meaning within the game and are only used to identify cases, but the remaining features are all potentially indexed features. We judged this number to be too high; especially since player tableau and opponent tableau in particular are highly complex features in themselves. Thus, we aimed to identify which of these features were most relevant to Placement decisions. Reducing the number of features as much as possible was important because k-NN algorithms have a tendency to be sensitive to irrelevant, interacting and noisy features [12] Such identifications could be made with domain expertise, however since we wished to find a method by which this could be done naively, and also which had the potential to expose unexpected patterns, we used statistical analysis on the case-base to identify the most relevant features. For each numeric feature, the distribution of values across the entire case-base was compared to its distribution of values among cases from each class separately, and if these distributions were found to vary significantly across several classes and the general distribution then these features were determined to be of relevance in terms of case similarity. For example, the Development "Contact Specialist" is almost always played when the player has 0 or −1 military score, while across the entire case base cards are played with various military scores.

5   Results and Discussion

5.1   SCOUT's Performance vs. Keldon AI

SCOUT's overall performance does not reach the Keldon AI's level, let alone that of a human player, but it does demonstrate an ability to play reasonably and competitively.

This section will cover the results of many runs of games against the Keldon AI, along with other benchmarks. This will be followed by discussion about SCOUT's strengths and weaknesses as indicated by these results.

For comparison we tested other agents controlling the placement decision: the Keldon AI, a Random agent, and a Human. The Random agent merely selects one of the possible options with equal probability. The purpose of this is to give an indication of the absolute minimum level of performance possible. The Human player is the same whose cases comprise SCOUT's case-base. Contrasting the Random agent, this is intended to give a rough indication of ideal performance.

Each test was comprised of 5,000 games against a player controlled by a pure Keldon AI agent, except for the Human, for which the test was only 1,000 games. The number of games was selected by running the Keldon AI against itself until it reached a stable victory rate. The victory rate includes tied matches, hence the Keldon AI's victory rate against itself being slightly greater than 50% (Table 1).

Table 1. Victory rate of four different agents controlling all strategically significant decisions vs. the Keldon AI agent

Full controlling agent	Victory rate
SCOUT2	30.2%
Keldon AI	51.0%
Random	0.04%
Human	74.8%

The Human's win rate is clearly the best, but the results show the total inability of the Random agent to win a game (barring very exceptional circumstances). This demonstrates the reasoning quality of the controlling agent. This is the most important result, as it clearly indicates that SCOUT, though not as strong as the Keldon AI in overall performance, is capable of playing and winning in a way that a non-reasoning agent cannot.

5.2   Score Distribution

Figure 3 shows the distribution of score ratios across 5,000 games between SCOUT and Keldon AI. Scores are best measured relative to the opponents score, as it is not useful to measure scores in absolute terms across multiple matches. Shorter matches typically have a lower winning score, but they are not necessarily indicative of inferior performance to a higher score from a different match, indeed the opposite is often the case. Within a single match, however, close scores typically give some indication that the performance of the competing players was also close.

Representing the score of a match as $S_i = S_{si}/S_{ki}$ where S_{si} is SCOUT's score in a match and S_{ki} is Keldon AI's score, gives log-normal distribution of scores. These scores show that although SCOUT loses the majority of matches against Keldon AI, it usually achieves a competitive and respectable score. The score ratios have a median of

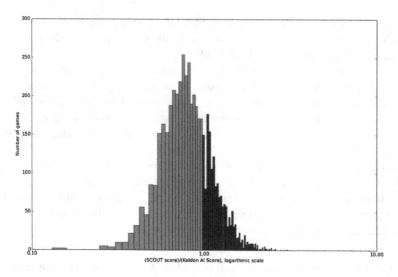

Fig. 3. Distribution of scores from 5000 games between SCOUT and Keldon AI, SCOUT won or drew the game when x >= 1.0 (31.7%). Note that the value of won or drawn games here is slightly higher as it includes those drawn matches that went against SCOUT in the tiebreaker.

0.85, indicating that although reaching a 50% win rate against Keldon AI would mean an 66% increase in win rate; it would take only an 18% increase in SCOUT's scoring to bring it to that level.

5.3   Phase Selection

Comparing the frequency of selected Actions/Phases of SCOUT to the Keldon AI and the human player whose cases trained it, it can be seen that SCOUT's choices follow the same general trend of both other players (Fig. 4). This is evidence of reasonable play compared to the random agent that would have an equal frequency distribution across all actions.

A noticeable feature is that despite our observance that SCOUT follows a Consume-Produce strategy as frequently as possible, it in fact does not select Produce as frequently as either other player. This is likely explained by SCOUT's inability to perfectly manage its producer cards against its consumer cards. We regularly observed it producing many more goods than it could consume at once, and hence over three turns it would call Produce, then Consume, then Consume again, whereas a skilled human player, and to a lesser extent Keldon AI, tend to have more balanced numbers and thus call Produce and Consume on alternate turns.

A more promising observation is that across the first four action types, SCOUT's frequencies are more similar to the human player than to Keldon AI, indicating some success in mimicking the human's play style, at least in terms of selection frequency.

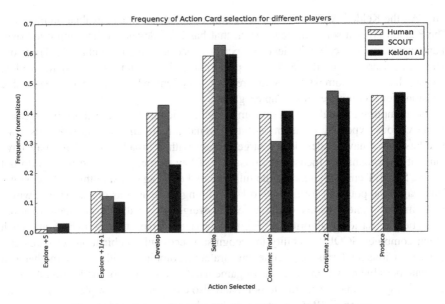

Fig. 4. Frequency of Action Card selection for different agents

5.4 Directly Observed Games

Finally, during development we directly observed and analysed many hundreds of games played between SCOUT and Keldon AI. This section describes results and observations of a random selection of games observed during the 4th era of a run. Game 1 was selected to be observed at random, and the rest are those that occurred in sequence thereafter. It represents better than average performance by SCOUT, which won 50% of these games. These observations are limited by their subjective nature, but they are useful in terms of gaining more insight into SCOUT's performance than simply raw scores and victory rates can provide. The final game states of each of these games as they are exported by the Keldon engine are available online.

Game 1, SCOUT: 26 - Keldon AI: 23 - Won with Consume-Produce strategy against Consume-Produce Strategy. Made a questionable early decision to pass on a good placement, likely triggered by having another good card in hand that SCOUT played two turns later. Both cards could have been placed with correct hand management, however.

6 Future Work and Conclusions

The aim of this research was to explore the use of CBR to play a modern board game, a domain that has received comparatively little attention in game AI research, despite offering many interesting challenges. SCOUT has demonstrated that a system using CBR and very limited domain knowledge can create a feasible agent for playing RftG. As of yet, however, it does not play at the same level as the current standard of

RftG AI, the Keldon AI, which uses more conventional search and evaluation methods. The Keldon AI is a sophisticated system that has been developed and improved over many years, and reaching its level of performance is a high benchmark. Therefore while it is disappointing that SCOUT's performance is not up to this standard, we feel that we have had some success in creating a system which can make reasonable decisions for a complete and complex game.

In attempting to create a system from scratch, which includes the capacity to reason about various types of decision and to evaluate, maintain, and improve its own case-bases, we have undertaken a large project with a broad scope. This may have come at the expense of focused optimisation of key elements. As a result, we do not believe SCOUT currently reaches the full potential of an agent using this methodology. This leaves the potential for future work in refining these aspects of the system, which could include systematically deriving feature weighting, or the development of more sophisticated retrieval algorithms. From a broader perspective, a hybrid approach which combines SCOUT's ability to recognise successful combinations of cards and make decisions in terms of a coherent strategy, combined with a system that can evaluate possible moves in the terms of game itself, such as that of the Keldon AI, may result in a system that is superior to both, and also closer to a human player's reasoning process. Combining CBR with other methodologies is a popular approach to such systems [3, 20]. SCOUT's architecture has the potential to be used as a basis for different AI agents for RftG, as could our fork of Keldon Jones' RftG engine, with the improved modularity of its control system.

While this paper focused on training SCOUT with human players' cases in an attempt to benefit from their reasoning, it may also be interesting to experiment with automatic case elicitation as per Powell's CHEBR system [11], beginning with a small or empty initial case-base. We have demonstrated, however, that a random agent is completely incapable of winning a game of RftG, so a different approach would need to be taken in the early stages of generating the case-base. In particular, an evaluation function that took more into account than the final result would be necessary. The overall performance of SCOUT's learning functionality proved to be limited, but there is potential to adjust its parameters and tweak its deletion policies.

Most importantly, future work that aims to improve upon SCOUT's performance would require access to a much larger case-base of games by skilled human players. This could open up the possibility for using data mining techniques to gain insight into feature weights, and of course give greater coverage in the initial case-bases. A case-base that includes negative cases to indicate potentially poor decisions to SCOUT, may also improve performance [2].

References

1. Aha, D.W., Molineaux, M., Ponsen, M.: Learning to win: case-based plan selection in a real-time strategy game. In: Muñoz-Ávila, H., Ricci, F. (eds.) ICCBR 2005. LNCS, vol. 3620, pp. 5–20. Springer, Heidelberg (2005). doi:10.1007/11536406_4

2. Aamodt, A., Plaza, E.: Case-based reasoning: foundational issues, methodological variations, and system approaches. AI Commun. **7**(1), 39–59 (1994)
3. Auslander, B., Lee-Urban, S., Hogg, C., Muñoz-Avila, H.: Recognizing the enemy: combining reinforcement learning with strategy selection using case-based reasoning. In: Althoff, K.D., Bergmann, R., Minor, M., Hanft, A. (eds.) Advances in Case-Based Reasoning. ECCBR 2008. LNCS, vol. 5239, pp. 59–73. Springer, Heidelberg (2008). doi:10.1007/978-3-540-85502-6_4
4. Campbell, M., Hoane, A.J., Hsu, F.: Deep blue. Artif. intell. **134**(1), 57–83 (2002)
5. Fogel, D.: Blondie24: Playing at the Edge of AI. Morgan Kaufmann, Burlington (2001)
6. Heyden, C.: Implementing a computer player for carcassonne. Master's thesis, Maastricht University (2009)
7. Jones, K.: Race for the Galaxy AI. www.keldon.net/rftg. Accessed 22 Oct 2016
8. Laird, J., Van Lent, M.: Human-level AI's killer application: interactive computer games. AI Mag. **22**(2), 15 (2001)
9. Lehmann, T.: Game Preview: Race for the Galaxy, Boardgame News, 26 September 2008
10. Molineaux, M., Aha, D.W.: TIELT: a testbed for gaming environments. In: AAAI-05, pp. 1690. AAAI Press (2005)
11. Powell, J., Hauff, B., Hastings, J.: Utilizing case-based reasoning and automatic case elicitation to develop a self-taught knowledgeable agent. In: Challenges in Game Artificial Intelligence: Papers from the AAAI Workshop (2004)
12. Reyes, O., Morell, C., Ventura, S.: Evolutionary feature weighting to improve the performance of multi-label lazy algorithms. Integr. Comput.-Aided Eng. **21**(4), 339–354 (2014)
13. Richter, M.M., Weber, R.O.: Case-Based Reasoning. Springer, Heidelberg (2013)
14. Rio Grande Games: Race for the Galaxy. http://riograndegames.com/Game/240-Race-for-the-Galaxy. Accessed 22 Oct 2016
15. Rubin, J., Watson, I.: Investigating the effectiveness of applying case-based reasoning to the game of texas hold'em. In: FLAIRS Conference, pp. 417–422 (2007)
16. Schaeffer, J., Burch, N., Bjornsson, Y., Kishimoto, A., Muller, M., Lake, R., Lu, P., Sutphen, S.: Checkers is solved. Science **317**(5844), 1518–1522 (2007)
17. Silver, D., Huang, A., Maddison, C., Guez, A., Sifre, L., Van den Driessche, G., Schrittwieser, J., Antonoglou, I., Panneershelvam, V., Lanctot, M.: Mastering the game of Go with deep neural networks and tree search. Nature **529**(7587), 484–489 (2016)
18. Sinclair, D.: Using example-based reasoning for selective move generation in two player adversarial games. In: Smyth, B., Cunningham, P. (eds.) Advances in Case-Based Reasoning. EWCBR 1998. LNCS, vol. 1488, pp. 126–135. Springer, Heidelberg (1998). doi:10.1007/BFb0056327
19. Szita, I., Chaslot, G., Spronck, P.: Monte-Carlo tree search in settlers of catan. In: van den Herik, H.J., Spronck, P. (eds.) Advances in Computer Games. ACG 2009. LNCS, vol. 6048, pp. 21–32. Springer, Heidelberg (2010). doi:10.1007/978-3-642-12993-3_3
20. Wender, S., Watson, I.: Combining case-based reasoning and reinforcement learning for unit navigation in real-time strategy game AI. In: Lamontagne, L., Plaza, E. (eds.) Case-Based Reasoning Research and Development. ICCBR. LNCS, vol. 8765, pp. 511–525. Springer, Cham (2014). doi:10.1007/978-3-319-11209-1_36

Min-Max Message Passing and Local Consistency in Constraint Networks

Hong Xu$^{(\boxtimes)}$ (iD), T.K. Satish Kumar, and Sven Koenig

University of Southern California, Los Angeles, CA 90089, USA
hongx@usc.edu, tkskwork@gmail.com, skoenig@usc.edu

Abstract. In this paper, we uncover some relationships between local consistency in constraint networks and message passing akin to belief propagation in probabilistic reasoning. We develop a new message passing algorithm, called the min-max message passing (MMMP) algorithm, for unifying the different notions of local consistency in constraint networks. In particular, we study its connection to arc consistency (AC) and path consistency. We show that AC-3 can be expressed more intuitively in the framework of message passing. We also show that the MMMP algorithm can be modified to enforce path consistency.

Keywords: Message passing · Constraint network · Local consistency

1 Introduction

A *constraint network* (CN)—i.e., a *constraint satisfaction problem* instance—can be defined by a tuple $\langle \mathcal{X}, \mathcal{D}, \mathcal{C} \rangle$, where $\mathcal{X} = \{X_1, X_2, \ldots, X_N\}$ is the set of variables; $\mathcal{D}$, the *domain* of the CN, is a function that maps a variable to its discrete domain $\mathcal{D}(X_i)$; and $\mathcal{C} = \{C_1, C_2, \ldots, C_M\}$ is the set of constraints. Each C_i consists of a subset $S(C_i)$ of $\mathcal{X}$ and a list of allowed assignments of values to these variables chosen from their domains. The task is to solve the CN, i.e., find an assignment of values to all variables in $\mathcal{X}$ such that all constraints are satisfied. A constraint is satisfied iff it allows the assignment. CNs have been used to solve real-world combinatorial problems, such as map coloring and scheduling [7].

Local consistency of CNs is a class of properties over subsets of variables. A CN is said to be K-consistent iff, for any subset of $(K-1)$ variables, any consistent assignment of values to them (i.e., no constraints between them are violated) can be extended to any other variable, i.e., there exists an assignment of a value to this variable that is consistent with the $(K-1)$ variables. Local consistency is enforced by procedures that make implicit constraints explicit in a CN. Node consistency—i.e., 1-consistency—is the property that each value in the domain of a variable satisfies the unary constraint on it. Arc consistency (AC)—i.e., 2-consistency—is the property that each value in the domain of a variable

---

The research at the University of Southern California was supported by NSF under grant numbers 1409987 and 1319966.

W. Peng et al. (Eds.): AI 2017, LNAI 10400, pp. 340–352, 2017.
DOI: 10.1007/978-3-319-63004-5_27

has a consistent extension to any other variable. Path consistency (PC)—i.e., 3-consistency—is the property that each consistent assignment of values to any 2 variables has a consistent extension to any other variable. A CN is said to be strongly K-consistent iff it is k-consistent for all $k \leq K$.

The procedures that enforce local consistency have practical as well as theoretical significance. On the practical side, enforcing local consistency prunes the search space. On the theoretical side, enforcing strong K-consistency solves a CN if K is greater than or equal to the treewidth of the CN [2]. If the constraint graph of a CN with only binary constraints is a tree, then AC ensures backtrack-free search in linear time [2]. Enforcing AC is also known to solve CNs with only max-closed constraints [3]. Similarly, PC is known to ensure global consistency for CNs with only connected row convex constraints [1].

Message passing is a well-known technique for solving many combinatorial problems across a wide range of fields, such as probabilistic reasoning, artificial intelligence, statistical physics, and information theory [5,10]. It is based on local information processing and communication, and avoids an exponential time complexity with respect to the number of variables and constraints. Although a complete theoretical analysis of its convergence and correctness is elusive, it works well in practice on many combinatorial problems such as those that arise in statistical physics, computer vision, error-correcting coding theory, or, more generally, on graphical models such as Bayesian networks and Markov random fields [10]. It has also been used to study problems such as K-satisfiability [6] and weighted constraint satisfaction [8].

Despite the significance of local consistency in constraint processing and message passing in probabilistic reasoning, the connection between them remains understudied. In this paper, we report on the close relationship between them. In light of this connection, we develop a new message passing algorithm, called the min-max message passing (MMMP) algorithm, for solving CNs. We then show how the MMMP algorithm relates to AC and how the AC-3 algorithm can be expressed more intuitively in the framework of message passing. We also show that it can be modified to enforce PC. In general, we show that the framework of message passing unifies the different concepts of local consistency.

2   Applying Message Passing to CNs

In this section, we develop a new message passing algorithm that is analogous to the standard min-sum and max-product message passing algorithms [5]. For simplicity of exposition, we assume that CNs are node-consistent. A CN can then be solved by message passing as follows. Given a CN $\langle \mathcal{X}, \mathcal{D}, \mathcal{C} \rangle$, we reformulate it as computing

$$a^* = \underset{a \in \mathcal{A}(\mathcal{X})}{\arg\min} \left[E(a) \equiv \max_{C_j \in \mathcal{C}} E_{C_j}(a|S(C_j)) \right]. \tag{1}$$

Here, $\mathcal{A}(\mathcal{X}) \equiv \mathcal{D}(X_1) \times \mathcal{D}(X_2) \times \cdots \times \mathcal{D}(X_N)$ is the set of all assignments of values to all variables in $\mathcal{X}$. (For notational convenience, we also define

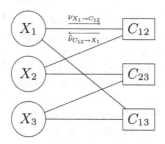

Fig. 1. Illustrates the factor graph of a CN with 3 variables $\{X_1, X_2, X_3\}$ and 3 constraints $\{C_{12}, C_{23}, C_{13}\}$. Here, $X_1, X_2 \in S(C_{12})$, $X_2, X_3 \in S(C_{23})$, and $X_1, X_3 \in S(C_{13})$. The circles represent variable vertices, and the squares represent constraint vertices. $\nu_{X_1 \to C_{12}}$ and $\hat{\nu}_{C_{12} \to X_1}$ are the messages from X_1 to C_{12} and from C_{12} to X_1, respectively. Such a pair of messages annotates each edge (even though not all of them are shown).

$\mathcal{A}(\emptyset) = \{\emptyset\}$.) $a|S(C_j)$ is the projection of assignment a onto the set of variables $S(C_j)$. For α, an assignment of values to variables in $S(C_j)$, $E_{C_j}(\alpha)$ is equal to 0 if is allowed by C_j; otherwise it is equal to 1. Therefore, the CN is solvable if $\min_{a \in \mathcal{A}(\mathcal{X})} E(a) = 0$, and its solution is any assignment a such that $E(a) = 0$; otherwise, it is not solvable. We compute a^* in Eq. (1) using message passing as follows:

1. Construct an undirected bipartite graph G_f (factor graph), where each variable is represented by a vertex (variable vertex) in the first partition and each constraint is represented by a vertex (constraint vertex) in the second partition. (For convenience of exposition, we use "variable vertices" and "constraint vertices" interchangeably with "variables" and "constraints", respectively.) Connect X_i and C_j with an edge $\overline{X_i C_j}$ iff $X_i \in S(C_j)$. Figure 1 illustrates a factor graph.

2. Send messages in both directions along each edge. Messages $\nu_{X_i \to C_j}$ and $\hat{\nu}_{C_j \to X_i}$ are sent along edge $\overline{X_i C_j}$ from X_i to C_j and from C_j to X_i, respectively. Both messages are vectors of 0/1 values and of size $|D(X_i)|$. Formally,

$$\nu_{X_i \to C_j} = \langle \nu_{X_i \to C_j}(X_i = x) \mid x \in \mathcal{D}(X_i) \rangle \tag{2}$$

$$\hat{\nu}_{C_j \to X_i} = \langle \hat{\nu}_{C_j \to X_i}(X_i = x) \mid x \in \mathcal{D}(X_i) \rangle. \tag{3}$$

$\nu_{X_i \to C_j}(X_i = x)$ and $\hat{\nu}_{C_j \to X_i}(X_i = x)$ are called "components $X_i = x$" of $\nu_{X_i \to C_j}$ and $\hat{\nu}_{C_j \to X_i}$, respectively. Figure 1 illustrates the messages.

3. Initialize all messages to 0 and then perform update operations on them (i.e., update messages) iteratively according to

$$\hat{\nu}_{C_j \to X_i}^{(t)}(X_i = x) = \min_{a \in \mathcal{A}(\partial C_j \setminus \{X_i\})} \left[\max \left[E_{C_j}(a \cup \{X_i = x\}), \right. \right.$$

$$\left. \left. \max_{X_k \in \partial C_j \setminus \{X_i\}} \nu_{X_k \to C_j}^{(t-1)}(a|\{X_k\}) \right] \right] \tag{4}$$

$$\nu_{X_i \to C_j}^{(t)}(X_i = x) = \max_{C_k \in \partial X_i \setminus \{C_j\}} \hat{\nu}_{C_k \to X_i}^{(t)}(X_i = x) \tag{5}$$

for a chosen $X_i \in \mathcal{X}$ and $C_j \in \mathcal{C}$, and for all $x \in \mathcal{D}(X_i)$, where ∂X_i and ∂C_j are the sets of adjacent vertices of X_i and C_j in G_f, respectively; the superscript (t) indicates the update operation number; and the max operators yield 0 if they are applied on empty sets. Different from the min-sum message passing algorithm, all summations are replaced by maximizations and no normalization constants are needed since we only care about whether the values of the variables are equal to 0. Repeat this step until convergence, i.e., Eqs. (4) and (5) hold for all $X_i \in \mathcal{X}$, $C_j \in \mathcal{C}$, and $x \in \mathcal{D}(X_i)$.

4. A set of values of all messages is called a *fixed point* iff it satisfies Eqs. (4) and (5) for all $X_i \in \mathcal{X}$, $C_j \in \mathcal{C}$, and $x_i \in \mathcal{D}(X_i)$. Convergence in Step 3 always leads to a fixed point, and all messages at such a fixed point are denoted by the superscript (∞). For each variable $X_i \in \mathcal{X}$, a final assignment of value $x_i \in \mathcal{D}(X_i)$, if it exists, is given such that

$$\max_{C_j \in \partial X_i} \hat{\nu}_{C_j \to X_i}^{(\infty)}(X_i = x_i) = 0. \tag{6}$$

The set $\mathcal{D}_m^F(X_i)$ of values x_i that satisfy Eq. (6) for X_i is called the *message passing domain* of X_i at the fixed point F.

Since the message update rules of Eqs. (4) and (5) involve only operations of minimization and maximization, we name this message passing algorithm the *min-max message passing* (MMMP) algorithm. The MMMP algorithm works analogously to other standard message passing algorithms, such as the min-sum and max-product message passing algorithms [5]. Similar to them, the MMMP algorithm neither specifies the order of the message updates in Step 3, nor provides any guarantee for the correctness of the final assignment.

We now prove that the MMMP algorithm always converges in finite time, even though convergence is not guaranteed for other message passing algorithms, such as the min-sum and max-product message passing algorithms.

Lemma 1. *No component of any message that is equal to 1 is changed to 0 by the MMMP algorithm in any update operation.*

Proof (by induction). This lemma holds trivially for the first update operation, since all components of all messages equal 0 before it.

Assume that the lemma holds for the first t update operations. Consider the $(t+1)^{\text{th}}$ update operation and a component of a message from a constraint vertex to a variable vertex such that $\hat{\nu}_{C_j \to X_i}^{(t)}(X_i = x) = 1$ and $\hat{\nu}_{C_j \to X_i}^{(t+1)}(X_i = x) = 0$. From Eq. (4), $E_{C_j}(a \cup \{X_i = x\})$ does not change. Therefore, there must exist an $X_k \in \partial C_j \setminus \{X_i\}$ and an $x' \in \mathcal{D}(X_k)$ such that $\nu_{X_k \to C_j}(X_k = x')$ changed from 1 to 0 during the first t update operations, which contradicts the induction assumption. A similar contradiction occurs for messages from variable vertices to constraint vertices from Eq. (5). The lemma continues to hold for the first $(t+1)$ update operations. □

Theorem 1. *There exists an order of message update operations such that the running time of the MMMP algorithm is bounded.*

Proof. Let the MMMP algorithm update messages in a sweeping order, i.e., messages are updated in rounds and in each round all messages are updated once. From Lemma 1, the MMMP algorithm terminates after $\mathcal{O}(d \cdot \max_{C_j \in \mathcal{C}} |S(C_j)| \cdot |\mathcal{C}|)$ rounds, where $d = \max_{X_i \in \mathcal{X}} |\mathcal{D}(X_i)|$. This upper bound measures the number of components of all messages.   □

3   Arc Consistency and the MMMP Algorithm

In this section, we study the relationship between AC and the MMMP algorithm. Consider a binary CN $P = \langle \mathcal{X}, \mathcal{D}, \mathcal{C} \rangle$, i.e., a CN with only binary constraints. Without loss of generality, we assume that no two constraints share the same set of variables. Let C_{ij} denote the binary constraint that involves variables X_i and X_j. The factor graph representation of P therefore has two variable vertices X_i and X_j connected to each constraint vertex C_{ij}. X_i is *arc-consistent* with respect to X_j (and C_{ij}) iff for each $x_i \in \mathcal{D}(X_i)$, there exists an $x_j \in \mathcal{D}(X_j)$ such that the assignment $\{X_i = x_i, X_j = x_j\}$ is allowed in C_{ij}. P is arc-consistent iff all variables are arc-consistent with respect to each other [7]. A domain $\mathcal{D}'$ such that $\mathcal{D}'(X) \subseteq \mathcal{D}(X)$ for all $X \in \mathcal{X}$ is called an *AC domain* of P iff the CN $\langle \mathcal{X}, \mathcal{D}', \mathcal{C} \rangle$ is arc-consistent and retains all solutions of P.

Intuitively, a message from a constraint vertex C_{ij} to a variable vertex X_i encodes the AC of X_i with respect to C_{ij}, and the outgoing messages from X_i encode the prevailing values in its domain. Figure 2 illustrates this intuition.

We now formally prove a relationship between AC and the MMMP algorithm.

Theorem 2. *Under the MMMP algorithm, the CN $P' = \langle \mathcal{X}, \mathcal{D}_m^F, \mathcal{C} \rangle$ is arc-consistent for any fixed point F of any binary CN $\langle \mathcal{X}, \mathcal{D}, \mathcal{C} \rangle$.*

Proof (by contradiction). Assume that there exists a fixed point F' such that P' is not arc-consistent, i.e., there exists a constraint C_{ij} such that

$$\exists x_i \in \mathcal{D}_m^{F'}(X_i) : \forall x_j \in \mathcal{D}_m^{F'}(X_j) : \{X_i = x_i, X_j = x_j\} \notin C_{ij}. \qquad (7)$$

Now consider such an x_i.

– By the definition of $E_{C_{ij}}$, from Eq. (7), we have

$$\forall x_j \in \mathcal{D}_m^{F'}(X_j) : E_{C_{ij}}(\{X_i = x_i, X_j = x_j\}) = 1. \qquad (8)$$

– By the definition of $\mathcal{D}_m^{F'}(X_j)$, we have

$$\forall x_j \in \mathcal{D}(X_j) \setminus \mathcal{D}_m^{F'}(X_j) : \max_{C_{jk} \in \partial X_j} \hat{\nu}_{C_{jk} \to X_j}^{(\infty)}(X_j = x_j) = 1. \qquad (9)$$

Here we consider two cases for all $x_j \in \mathcal{D}(X_j) \setminus \mathcal{D}_m^{F'}(X_j)$.

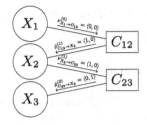

Fig. 2. Illustrates the relationship between AC and the MMMP algorithm. Here, the CN consists of 3 variables $\{X_1, X_2, X_3\}$ and 2 constraints $\{C_{12}, C_{23}\}$. Each variable has a domain of $\{0, 1\}$. C_{12} only allows $\{X_1 = 0, X_2 = 1\}$ and $\{X_1 = 1, X_2 = 1\}$; C_{23} only allows $\{X_2 = 0, X_3 = 1\}$ and $\{X_2 = 1, X_3 = 0\}$. The circles represent variable vertices, and the squares represent constraint vertices. The values of some messages are shown in the figure—the two numbers inside angle brackets are the values of the components 0 and 1, respectively. Both components of the message $\nu_{X_1 \to C_{12}}^{(0)}$ are equal to 0. Hence the message components $\hat{\nu}_{C_{12} \to X_2}^{(1)}(X_2 = 0) = 1$ and $\hat{\nu}_{C_{12} \to X_2}^{(1)}(X_2 = 1) = 0$ indicate the reduced domain $\{1\}$ that makes X_2 arc-consistent with respect to C_{12}. $\nu_{X_2 \to C_{23}}^{(1)}(X_2 = 0) = 1$ and $\nu_{X_2 \to C_{23}}^{(1)}(X_2 = 1) = 0$ indicate that X_2 should only take the value 1 while enforcing the AC of X_3 with respect to C_{23}. $\hat{\nu}_{C_{23} \to X_3}^{(2)}(X_3 = 0) = 0$ and $\hat{\nu}_{C_{23} \to X_3}^{(2)}(X_3 = 1) = 1$ indicate that under such restrictions of X_2, X_3 can only take the value 0 to be arc-consistent with respect to C_{23}.

- x_j satisfies $\exists C_{jk} \in \partial X_j \setminus \{C_{ij}\} : \hat{\nu}_{C_{jk} \to X_j}^{(\infty)}(X_j = x_j) = 1$. From Eq. (5), we have

$$\nu_{X_j \to C_{ij}}^{(\infty)}(X_j = x_j) = 1. \tag{10}$$

- x_j satisfies $\forall C_{jk} \in \partial X_j \setminus \{C_{ij}\} : \hat{\nu}_{C_{jk} \to X_j}^{(\infty)}(X_j = x_j) = 0$. From Eq. (9), this implies $\hat{\nu}_{C_{ij} \to X_j}^{(\infty)}(X_j = x_j) = 1$. By applying Eq. (4) to $\hat{\nu}_{C_{ij} \to X_j}^{(\infty)}(X_j = x_j)$, we have

$$E_{C_{ij}}(\{X_i = x_i, X_j = x_j\}) = 1 \vee \nu_{X_i \to C_{ij}}^{(\infty)}(X_i = x_i) = 1. \tag{11}$$

By applying Eq. (5) on $\nu_{X_i \to C_{ij}}^{(\infty)}(X_i = x_i)$, we have $\nu_{X_i \to C_{ij}}^{(\infty)}(X_i = x_i) = 0$ for the following reasons: (a) if $\partial X_i = \{C_{ij}\}$, then the max operator is applied on an empty set and thus $\nu_{X_i \to C_{ij}}^{(\infty)}(X_i = x_i) = 0$; or (b) otherwise, $\nu_{X_i \to C_{ij}}^{(\infty)}(X_i = x_i) = 1$ implies $x_i \notin D_m^{F'}(X_i)$, which contradicts the assumption. Therefore, in this case, we have

$$E_{C_{ij}}(\{X_i = x_i, X_j = x_j\}) = 1. \tag{12}$$

By applying Eq. (4) to $\hat{\nu}_{C_{ij} \to X_i}^{(\infty)}(X_i = x_i)$ and plugging in Eqs. (8), (10) and (12), we have

$$\hat{\nu}_{C_{ij} \to X_i}^{(\infty)}(X_i = x_i) = 1, \tag{13}$$

which violates Eq. (6) for $X_i = x_i$ and contradicts $x_i \in D_m^{F'}(X_i)$. $\qquad \square$

Theorem 3. *Whenever the MMMP algorithm converges to a fixed point F on a CN P, $\mathcal{D}_m^F$ preserves all solutions of P, i.e., for any solution a, we have $\forall (X_i = x_i) \in a : x_i \in \mathcal{D}_m^F(X_i)$.*

Proof (by induction). From Lemma 1, for a variable vertex X_i, if there exists a component of a message $\hat{\nu}_{C_{ij} \to X_i}(X_i = x_i)$ that changes from 0 to 1 in some update operation, we know that $\mathcal{D}_m^F(X_i)$ does not include x_i; otherwise, $\mathcal{D}_m^F(X_i)$ includes x_i since all messages are initialized to 0. Therefore, we only need to prove that, whenever such a change occurs in the MMMP algorithm, the exclusion of x_i from $\mathcal{D}_m^F(X_i)$ preserves all solutions. We define the message passing domain of X_i after the tth update operation, denoted by $\mathcal{D}_m^{(t)}(X_i)$, as the set of values x_i such that $\max_{C_{ij} \in \partial X_i} \hat{\nu}_{C_{ij} \to X_i}^{(t)}(X_i = x_i) = 0$. Upon convergence, $\mathcal{D}_m^{(t)}(X_i) = \mathcal{D}_m^F(X_i)$.

$\mathcal{D}_m^{(0)}$ preserves all solutions since all messages are initialized to 0. Assume that $\mathcal{D}_m^{(t)}$ preserves all solutions. Consider the $(t+1)^{\text{th}}$ update operation. We only consider the case where $\exists X_i \in \mathcal{X} : \mathcal{D}_m^{(t)}(X_i) \neq \mathcal{D}_m^{(t+1)}(X_i)$; otherwise, there is no solution excluded in this update operation. In this case, there exists a component of a message $\hat{\nu}_{C_{ij} \to X_i}(X_i = x_i)$ that changes from 0 to 1 in this update operation and thus $x_i \notin \mathcal{D}_m^F(X_i)$.

If $\forall x_j \in \mathcal{D}(X_j) : \nu_{X_j \to C_{ij}}^{(t)}(X_j = x_j) = 0$, then $X_i = x_i$ cannot be in any solution, since by applying Eq. (4) to $\hat{\nu}_{C_{ij} \to X_i}^{(t+1)}(X_i = x_i)$ (which equals 1), we have $\forall x_j \in \mathcal{D}(X_j) : E_{C_{ij}}(\{X_i = x_i, X_j = x_j\}) = 1$. Therefore, $\exists x_j \in \mathcal{D}(X_j) : \nu_{X_j \to C_{ij}}^{(t)}(X_j = x_j) = 1$.

If $\exists x_j \in \mathcal{D}_m^{(t)}(X_j) : \nu_{X_j \to C_{ij}}^{(t)}(X_j = x_j) = 1$, from Eq. (5), we have $\partial X_j \setminus \{C_{ij}\} \neq \emptyset$ and $\max_{C_{jk} \in \partial X_j \setminus \{C_{ij}\}} \hat{\nu}_{C_{jk} \to X_j}^{(t)}(X_j = x_j) = 1$, and thus by definition $x_j \notin \mathcal{D}_m^{(t)}(X_j)$, which contradicts the assumption. As a result, we have

$$\forall x_j \in \mathcal{D}_m^{(t)}(X_j) : \nu_{X_j \to C_{ij}}^{(t)}(X_j = x_j) = 0. \tag{14}$$

By applying Eq. (4) to $\hat{\nu}_{C_{ij} \to X_i}^{(t+1)}(X_i = x_i)$, which equals 1, we have

$$\forall x_j \in \mathcal{D}_m^{(t)}(X_j) : \max[E_{C_{ij}}(\{X_i = x_i, X_j = x_j\}), \nu_{X_j \to C_{ij}}^{(t)}(X_j = x_j)] = 1. \tag{15}$$

By plugging Eq. (14) into the equation above, we have $\forall x_j \in \mathcal{D}_m^{(t)}(X_j) : E_{C_{ij}}(\{X_i = x_i, X_j = x_j\}) = 1$. Since $\mathcal{D}_m^{(t)}$ preserves all solutions, $X_i = x_i$ cannot be in any solution of P. □

AC can be enforced on a given CN P by AC algorithms that reduce the domains of variables without losing solutions. Arc Consistency Algorithm #3 (AC-3) is one such algorithm [4]. The graphical representation G of a CN P has vertices that represent variables and undirected edges that connect two variables iff there is a constraint involving them. AC-3 works as follows:

1. Convert G into a directed graph by replacing all edges with two arcs (directed edges) in opposite directions.

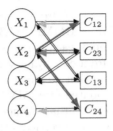

Fig. 3. Illustrates one iteration of Step 3 of MMMP-AC-3. Here, the circles represent variable vertices, and the squares represent constraint vertices. Each arrow represents a message. In this iteration, the message $\hat{\nu}_{C_{23}\to X_2}$ (red) is removed from Q and updated according to Eq. (4). $\nu_{X_2\to C_{12}}$ and $\nu_{X_2\to C_{24}}$ (blue) are updated afterward according to Eq. (5). Assuming that both messages change, the messages $\hat{\nu}_{C_{12}\to X_1}$ and $\hat{\nu}_{C_{24}\to X_4}$ (orange) are inserted into Q. Following the sequence of red, blue, and orange arrows, this iteration intuitively looks like paths expanded from C_{23}. (Colour figure online)

2. Insert all arcs into a queue Q.
3. Remove an arc (X_i, X_j) from Q. Ensure that X_i is arc-consistent with respect to X_j by reducing $\mathcal{D}(X_i)$, if necessary. If $\mathcal{D}(X_i)$ is reduced, insert all arcs incoming to X_i other than (X_j, X_i) into Q. Repeat this step until Q is empty.

AC-3 can be reinterpreted as an MMMP algorithm as follows.

1. Construct the factor graph for CN P.
2. Insert all messages from constraint vertices to variable vertices into a queue Q.
3. Remove a message $\hat{\nu}_{C_{ij}\to X_i}$ from Q. Update it and all messages from X_i to constraint vertices other than C_{ij} according to Eqs. (4) and (5), respectively. If $\nu_{X_i\to C_{ik}}$ changes, insert all messages from C_{ik} to variables other than X_i into Q. Repeat this step until Q is empty. Figure 3 illustrates one such step.
4. Reduce the domain of each variable X_i to its message passing domain.

We call this algorithm *MMMP-AC-3*. Clearly, it is an MMMP algorithm with a particular order of message update operations. Intuitively, the update of a message from a constraint vertex C_{ij} to a variable vertex X_i indicates those domain values of X_i that must be excluded to maintain the AC of X_i with respect to X_j. The update of a message from a variable vertex X_i to a constraint vertex C_{ij} indicates the reduced domain of X_i for the constraint C_{ij}.

Theorem 4. *MMMP-AC-3 terminates in bounded time.*

Proof. In Step 3, each message from a constraint vertex C_{ij} to a variable vertex X_i can be inserted into Q for at most d times, since $\nu_{X_j\to C_{ij}}$ has at most d components and thus (from Lemma 1) can change at most d times. Therefore MMMP-AC-3 has a bounded running time.   □

Lemma 2. *When MMMP-AC-3 terminates, the set of values of all messages is a fixed point.*

Proof. We first prove that no message from a variable vertex to a constraint vertex changes if it is updated after MMMP-AC-3 terminates. This holds since Eq. (5) holds initially and, in Step 3, each message $\nu_{X_i \to C_{ij}}$ is updated immediately after any of the messages from constraint vertices to X_i are updated.

We now prove by contradiction that no message from a constraint vertex to a variable vertex changes if it is updated after MMMP-AC-3 terminates. Assume that there exists a message $\hat{\nu}_{C_{ij} \to X_i}$ that changes if it is updated. Hence, at least one of the messages from variable vertices other than X_i to C_{ij} must have been updated after $\hat{\nu}_{C_{ij} \to X_i}$ was last updated. Therefore, $\hat{\nu}_{C_{ij} \to X_i}$ is in queue Q, which is a contradiction since MMMP-AC-3 would not have terminated then.□

Theorem 5. *MMMP-AC-3 is correct, i.e., it results in an AC domain of P.*

Proof. The theorem immediately follows from Theorems 2 to 4 and Lemma 2.□

4 Strong Path Consistency and Message Passing

In this section, we study the relationship between strong path consistency and message passing. Consider a binary CN $P = \langle \mathcal{X}, \mathcal{D}, \mathcal{C} \rangle$. Once again, we use C_{ij} to denote the binary constraint that involves variables X_i and X_j. X_i and X_j are *path-consistent* with respect to X_k iff, for all values $x_i \in \mathcal{D}(X_i)$ and $x_j \in \mathcal{D}(X_j)$ such that C_{ij} allows $\{X_i = x_i, X_j = x_j\}$, there exists a value $x_k \in \mathcal{D}(X_k)$ such that C_{ik} allows the assignment $\{X_i = x_i, X_k = x_k\}$ and C_{jk} allows the assignment $\{X_j = x_j, X_k = x_k\}$. A binary CN is path-consistent iff every two of its variables are path-consistent with respect to any third variable [7]. A binary CN is *strongly path-consistent* iff it is both arc-consistent and path-consistent.

Generalized message passing allows more than one intersection variable between adjacent vertices. It stems from the Kikuchi approximation of free energy in statistical mechanics [9]. The MMMP algorithm can be modified to a generalized message passing algorithm to enforce strong path consistency (strong PC). We first unify Eqs. (4) and (5) in the MMMP algorithm to

$$\mu^{(t)}_{U_i \to U_j}(S(U_i, U_j) = u_{ij}) = \min_{a \in \mathcal{A}(S(U_i) \setminus S(U_j))} \left[\max \left[E_{U_i}(a \cup \{S(U_i, U_j) = u_{ij}\}), \right. \right.$$
$$\left. \left. \max_{U_k \in \partial U_i \setminus \{U_j\}} \mu^{(t-1)}_{U_k \to U_i}(a \cup \{S(U_i, U_j) = u_{ij}\} | S(U_k, U_i)) \right] \right],$$
(16)

where U_i stands for a vertex in the factor graph; $\mu_{U_i \to U_j}$ is the message sent from U_i to U_j; $S(U_i)$ stands for the scope of U_i, which is defined as

$$S(U_i) = \begin{cases} \{X_i\} & \text{if } U_i \text{ is a variable vertex } X_i, \\ S(C_i) & \text{if } U_i \text{ is a constraint vertex } C_i; \end{cases}$$
(17)

$S(U_i, U_j)$ stands for $S(U_i) \cap S(U_j)$; $S(U_i) = a$ stands for assigning the variables in $S(U_i)$ to a; and E_{U_i} is the potential of U_i, which is defined as

$$E_{U_i}(S(U_i) = a) = \begin{cases} 0 & \text{if } U_i \text{ is a variable vertex } X_i, \\ E_{C_i}(S(C_i) = a) & \text{if } U_i \text{ is a constraint vertex } C_i. \end{cases}$$
(18)

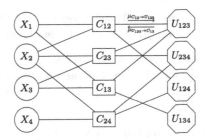

Fig. 4. Illustrates the modified factor graph for the modified MMMP algorithm. The CN consists of 4 Boolean variables $\{X_1, X_2, X_3, X_4\}$ and 4 constraints $\{C_{12}, C_{23}, C_{13}, C_{24}\}$. Here, $S(C_{12}) = \{X_1, X_2\}$, $S(C_{23}) = \{X_2, X_3\}$, $S(C_{13}) = \{X_1, X_3\}$, and $S(C_{24}) = \{X_2, X_4\}$. U_{ijk} is the triplet that represents X_i, X_j, and X_k. The circles, squares, and octagons represent variable vertices, constraint vertices, and triplet vertices, respectively. $\mu_{U_{123} \to C_{12}}$ and $\mu_{C_{12} \to U_{123}}$ are the messages from U_{123} to C_{12} and from C_{12} to U_{123}, respectively. Each of them is a vector of 0/1 values and of size $2 \times 2 = 4$. Such a pair of messages (additional to the messages shown in Fig. 1) annotates each edge that is incident on a triplet vertex (even though not all are shown).

Under this unification, we can enforce strong PC by modifying the MMMP algorithm as follows. After creating the factor graph G_f, we add additional vertices (triplet vertices) with zero potentials that represent all possible combinations of 3 distinct variables, as shown in Fig. 4. A triplet vertex is connected to a constraint vertex C_i iff it includes both variables in $S(C_i)$. In Step 3 of the MMMP algorithm, we replace Eqs. (4) and (5) by Eq. (16). In Step 4 of the MMMP algorithm, we replace Eq. (6) by the generalized equation

$$\max_{U_j \in \partial U_i} \mu_{U_j \to U_i}^{(\infty)} (S(U_i) = u_i | S(U_i, U_j)) = 0. \tag{19}$$

Similar to the MMMP algorithm, we call a set of values of all messages a fixed point iff it satisfies Eq. (16) for all U_i in the modified factor graph. The set $\mathcal{D}_m^F(U_i)$ of values of u_i that satisfy Eq. (19) for each vertex U_i is called the message passing domain of U_i at the fixed point F. The message passing domains of $U_i \in \mathcal{X}$ and $U_i \in \mathcal{C}$ are the assignments of values to each variable and each pair of variables, respectively, that enforce strong PC.

Lemma 3. *No component of any message that is equal to 1 is changed to 0 by the modified MMMP algorithm in any update operation.*

Proof. The proof is similar to that of Lemma 1.   □

Theorem 6. *There exists an order of message update operations such that the running time of the modified MMMP algorithm is bounded.*

Proof. The proof is similar to that of Theorem 1.   □

Theorem 7. *Under the modified MMMP algorithm, the CN $P' = \langle \mathcal{X}, \mathcal{D}_m^F, \mathcal{C} \rangle$ is strongly path-consistent for any fixed point F of any binary CN $\langle \mathcal{X}, \mathcal{D}, \mathcal{C} \rangle$.*

Proof. The proof of AC is similar to that of Theorem 2.

We now prove PC by contradiction. Let the consistent assignment of values to 2 variables $\{X_i = x_i, X_j = x_j\}$ in $\mathcal{D}_m^F(C_{ij})$ violate PC with respect to X_k (but not violate AC) in $\mathcal{D}_m^F$.

- From the PC violation assumption of $\{X_i = x_i, X_j = x_j\}$, we have

$$\forall x_k \in \mathcal{D}_m^F(X_k) : E_{C_{ik}}(\{X_i = x_i, X_k = x_k\}) = 1 \lor E_{C_{jk}}(\{X_j = x_j, X_k = x_k\}) = 1. \tag{20}$$

We use U_{ijk} to denote the triplet vertex that represents X_i, X_j, and X_k. Therefore, for such x_k's, by applying Eq. (16) to $\mu_{C_{ik} \to U_{ijk}}^{(\infty)}(\{X_i = x_i, X_k = x_k\})$ and $\mu_{C_{jk} \to U_{ijk}}^{(\infty)}(\{X_j = x_j, X_k = x_k\})$, we have

$$\forall x_k \in \mathcal{D}_m^F(X_k) :$$
$$\max \left[\mu_{C_{ik} \to U_{ijk}}^{(\infty)}(\{X_i = x_i, X_k = x_k\}), \mu_{C_{jk} \to U_{ijk}}^{(\infty)}(\{X_j = x_j, X_k = x_k\}) \right] = 1. \tag{21}$$

- By definition of the message passing domain of X_k, we have

$$\forall x_k \in \mathcal{D}(X_k) \setminus \mathcal{D}_m^F(X_k) : \max_{C_{ik} \in \partial X_k} \mu_{C_{ik} \to X_k}^{(\infty)}(X_k = x_k) = 1. \tag{22}$$

Then, by applying Eq. (16) to $\mu_{X_k \to C_{ik}}^{(\infty)}(X_k = x_k)$ and $\mu_{X_k \to C_{jk}}^{(\infty)}(X_k = x_k)$, we have

$$\forall x_k \in \mathcal{D}(X_k) \setminus \mathcal{D}_m^F(X_k) : \mu_{X_k \to C_{ik}}^{(\infty)}(X_k = x_k) = 1 \lor \mu_{X_k \to C_{jk}}^{(\infty)}(X_k = x_k) = 1. \tag{23}$$

Then by applying Eq. (16) to $\mu_{C_{ik} \to U_{ijk}}^{(\infty)}(\{X_i = x_i, X_k = x_k\})$ and $\mu_{C_{jk} \to U_{ijk}}^{(\infty)}(\{X_j = x_j, X_k = x_k\})$, we have

$$\forall x_k \in \mathcal{D}(X_k) \setminus \mathcal{D}_m^F(X_k) :$$
$$\max \left[\mu_{C_{ik} \to U_{ijk}}^{(\infty)}(\{X_i = x_i, X_k = x_k\}), \mu_{C_{jk} \to U_{ijk}}^{(\infty)}(\{X_j = x_j, X_k = x_k\}) \right] = 1. \tag{24}$$

Applying Eq. (16) to $\mu_{U_{ijk} \to C_{ij}}^{(\infty)}(\{X_i = x_i, X_j = x_j\})$, we have

$$\mu_{U_{ijk} \to C_{ij}}^{(\infty)}(\{X_i = x_i, X_j = x_j\}) =$$
$$\min_{x_k \in \mathcal{D}(X_k)} \max \left[\mu_{C_{ik} \to U_{ijk}}^{(\infty)}(\{X_i = x_i, X_k = x_k\}), \mu_{C_{jk} \to U_{ijk}}^{(\infty)}(\{X_j = x_j, X_k = x_k\}) \right]. \tag{25}$$

From Eqs. (21) and (24), we have the right-hand side of Eq. (25) equal to 1. This means that $\mu_{U_{ijk} \to C_{ij}}(\{X_i = x_i, X_j = x_j\}) = 1$, which contradicts Eq. (19) for C_{ij}.

Therefore, the modified MMMP algorithm enforces strong PC for P. □

Theorem 8. *Whenever the modified MMMP algorithm converges to a fixed point F on a CN P, D_m^F preserves all solutions of P, i.e., for any solution a, we have $\forall(S(U_i) = u_i) \in a : u_i \in \mathcal{D}_m^F(U_i)$.*

Proof. The proof is similar to that of Theorem 3.

Notes on the Modified MMMP Algorithm

- The running intersection property (RIP) is generally required for message passing algorithms. This property requires that, for any variable X_i, all vertices in G_f that contain it form a unique path. Ensuring the RIP for useful generalized message passing is usually complicated [9]. However, the modified MMMP algorithm does not require it, which is due to Lemma 3. Still, for any variable X_i, all vertices in the modified factor graph that contain it form a connected subgraph. We call this property the *quasi RIP*. Unlike the RIP, ensuring the quasi RIP for the modified MMMP algorithm is easy.
- The modified MMMP algorithm works even if there exist ternary constraints, in which case we simply set the potentials of the corresponding triplet vertices to represent the constraints. Thus, it can also be used to implement "generalized PC" analogous to generalized AC (GAC).
- The modified factor graph is still a bipartite graph—variable vertices and triplet vertices are in one partition, and constraint vertices are in the other partition. MMMP-AC-3 can be extended to enforce PC by treating triplet vertices as variable vertices and following the same order of message update operations[1]. This is equivalent to the Path Consistency Algorithm #2 (PC-2) [4]. The framework of the MMMP algorithm thus unifies AC-3 and PC-2.
- The modified MMMP algorithm can be extended to strong K-consistency by adding vertices that represent larger groups of variables.

5   Conclusions

We presented the MMMP algorithm for solving CNs. We established a relationship between the MMMP algorithm and AC, namely that any fixed point of the MMMP algorithm leads to an AC domain. We then showed that the AC-3 algorithm can be stated as the MMMP algorithm using a particular order of message update operations. We modified the MMMP algorithm to establish a relationship with PC. We showed that the modified MMMP algorithm has benefits that other generalized message passing algorithms do not have.

References

1. van Beek, P., Dechter, R.: On the minimality and global consistency of row-convex constraint networks. J. ACM **42**(3), 543–561 (1995)

---

[1] We note that all messages outgoing from triplet vertices need to be initialized according to Eq. (16) to ensure that Lemma 2 holds.

2. Freuder, E.C.: A sufficient condition for backtrack-free search. J. ACM **29**(1), 24–32 (1982)
3. Jeavons, P.G., Cooper, M.C.: Tractable constraints on ordered domains. Artif. Intell. **79**(2), 327–339 (1995)
4. Mackworth, A.K.: Consistency in networks of relations. Artif. Intell. **8**(1), 99–118 (1977)
5. Mézard, M., Montanari, A.: Information, Physics, and Computation. Oxford University Press, Oxford (2009)
6. Mézard, M., Zecchina, R.: Random k-satisfiability problem: From an analytic solution to an efficient algorithm. Phys. Rev. E **66**(5), 056126 (2002). doi:10.1103/PhysRevE.66.056126
7. Russell, S., Norvig, P.: Artificial Intelligence: A Modern Approach, 3rd edn. Pearson, Upper Saddle River (2009)
8. Xu, H., Satish Kumar, T.K., Koenig, S.: The Nemhauser-Trotter reduction and lifted message passing for the weighted CSP. In: Salvagnin, D., Lombardi, M. (eds.) CPAIOR 2017. LNCS, vol. 10335, pp. 387–402. Springer, Cham (2017). doi:10.1007/978-3-319-59776-8_31
9. Yedidia, J.S., Freeman, W.T., Weiss, Y.: Bethe free energy, Kikuchi approximations, and belief propagation algorithms. Technical report R2001-16, Mitsubishi Electric Research Laboratories (2001)
10. Yedidia, J.S., Freeman, W.T., Weiss, Y.: Understanding belief propagation and its generalizations. Explor. Artif. Intell. New Millenn. **8**, 239–269 (2003)

Deterministic Tournament Selection in Local Search for Maximum Edge Weight Clique on Large Sparse Graphs

Zongjie Ma[1]([⊠]), Yi Fan[1,2], Kaile Su[1], Chengqian Li[3], and Abdul Sattar[1]

[1] Institute for Integrated and Intelligent Systems,
Griffith University, Brisbane, Australia
`zongjie.ma@griffithuni.edu.au`
[2] Department of Computer Science, Jinan University, Guangzhou, China
[3] Department of Computer Science, Sun Yat-sen University, Guangzhou, China

Abstract. The maximum edge weight clique (MEWC) problem is important in both theories and applications. During last decades, there has been much interest in finding optimal or near-optimal solutions to this problem. Many existing heuristics focuses on academic benchmarks of relatively small size. However, very little attention has been paid to solving the MEWC problem in large sparse graphs. In this work, we exploit the so-called deterministic tournament selection (DTS) strategy to improve the local search MEWC algorithms. Experiments conducted on a broad range of large sparse graphs show that our algorithm outperforms state-of-the-art local search algorithms in this benchmark. Moreover it finds better solutions on a list of them.

Keywords: Local search · Maximum edge weight clique · Large sparse graphs

1 Introduction

The rapid growth of the Internet, widespread deployment of sensors and other fields produced huge quantity of massive data sets, which has generated a series of computational challenges to existing algorithms. Hence, new algorithms need to be designed to deal with these data sets. Many data sets can be represented as graphs, and the study of large real-world graphs, also known as complex networks [18], has become an active research agenda over recent decades.

Given a simple undirected graph where edges are weighted, the maximum edge weight clique (MEWC) problem is to find a clique whose total edge weight is maximum. This problem exists in many real applications like [1,2,6,7,14, 15]. However, it is NP-hard and difficult to approximate [11], so improving the algorithms on this problem is of great importance.

Due to the NP-hardness, the research of MEWC problem focuses on developing heuristics to find a "good" clique within reasonable time periods. Up to

© Springer International Publishing AG 2017
W. Peng et al. (Eds.): AI 2017, LNAI 10400, pp. 353–364, 2017.
DOI: 10.1007/978-3-319-63004-5_28

now, there are two types of algorithms for MEWC: complete algorithms *e.g.* [3,12] and incomplete ones *e.g.* [15,17]. In this paper we use local search to find a clique whose weight is as great as possible.

A correlated problem of the MEWC problem is the maximum vertex weight clique (MVWC) problem which asks for a clique with the greatest total vertex weight. Recently this problem attracts much attention in the constraint optimization community like [4,8,10,20,21].

Although there has been great progress in MVWC solving, very little attention is being paid to the MEWC problem. The reason may be that MEWC is more complicated and thus difficult to solve, from the viewpoint of algorithm design. For example in MVWC solving, when computing the upper-bound for a vertex v, we can simply sum up the weights of v's neighbors. However in MEWC, we have to sum up the edge weights among v and its neighbors, which is more complicated. Hence, those bounds which are shown to be useful in MVWC solving may lose their power in MEWC solving. So it is not easy to adopt the strategies in [4,9,13] to solve the MEWC problem.

On the other hand, local search seems to be a simple but effective approach. According to the literature, local search for MVWC usually moves from one clique to another until the cutoff arrives. During the search procedure, it moves to the neighboring clique with the greatest weight by adding, dropping or swapping vertices, according to some tabu criterion. This approach can easily be adopted to solve the MEWC problem. So it seems that for local search, the MVWC problem and the MEWC problem can be solved in very similar ways. Moreover, some well-known strategies like the multi-neighborhood greedy search, the randomized tabu strategy, the strong configuration checking strategy, the deterministic tournament selection and the data structures, can all be adopted to solve the MEWC problem trivially.

In the literature, LSCC[1] is known to be the most prominent local search MVWC solver. It was shown to be effective on both standard and large benchmarks. Our observations find that it can be adapted to solve the MEWC problem in a straightforward way. Similarly, another local search solver LMY-GRS [8], which is powerful for solving the MVWC problem on large sparse graphs, can also be adapted to solve the MEWC problem easily. Therefore, in this paper we adapt them to deal with edge weights, and evaluate them in MEWC solving.

To the best of our knowledge, current local search methods solve the MVWC problem and the MEWC problem in nearly the same way. That is, there are no local search techniques which are specialized for edge weights or vertex weights. Although current techniques can be widely used due to their generality, they may fail to tailor the local search to specific problem structures.

---

[1] In [20], there are LSCC and LSCC+BMS. LSCC is better on DIMACS and BHOSLIB. LSCC+BMS is better on large crafted graphs. For simplicity, we write both versions as LSCC if it is understood from the context or there are no confusions.

1.1   Our Contributions

In this paper we proposed a strategy which is specialized for edge weights. It selects some edges with great weight, and uses their endpoints as the starting point of local search. The intuition is that the search space is huge and we can only visit a very small part of the space within reasonable time periods, so we have to choose some promising parts. More specifically we choose an edge with great weight by the deterministic tournament selections (DTS) [16]. Given a set S and a positive integer k, the DTS heuristic works as follows: *randomly select k elements from S with replacements and then return the best one.* Based on DTS for selecting edges, we develop a new local search solver called LS-DTS[2], which is dedicated to solve the MEWC problem on large sparse graphs.

We conduct experiments on a broad range of large sparse graphs. The experimental results show that our solver LS-DTS significantly outperforms LSCC, LSCC+BMS and LMY-GRS.

2   Preliminaries

Formally the MEWC problem is defined over a graph $G = (V, E, w)$, where $V = \{v_1, \ldots, v_n\}$ is the vertex set, each edge $e \in E$ is a 2-element subset of V and $w : E \mapsto R_{\geq 0}$ is the weighting function on E. A *clique* C is a subset of V s.t. each pair of vertices in C is mutually adjacent. The MEWC problem is to find a clique which maximizes

$$\sum_{v_i, v_j \in C \text{ and } i \neq j} w(\{v_i, v_j\}). \tag{1}$$

Given an edge $e = \{u, v\}$, we say that u and v are neighbors, and u and v are adjacent to each other. Also we use $N(v) = \{u|u \text{ and } v \text{ are neighbors.}\}$ to denote the set of v's neighbors. We use $d_{max}(G)$ to denote the maximum degree of graph G, suppressing G if understood from the context.

2.1   Multi-neighborhood Search

Usually for finding a good clique, the local search moves from one clique to another until the cutoff arrives, then it returns the best clique that has been found. There are three operators: add, swap and drop, which guide the local search to move in the clique space. In [8], two sets S_{add} and S_{swap} were defined as below which ensures that the clique property is preserved.

$$S_{add} = \begin{cases} \{v|v \notin C, v \in N(u) \text{ for all } u \in C\} & \text{if } |C| > 0; \\ \emptyset, \text{otherwise}, \end{cases} \tag{2}$$

---

[2] https://github.com/math6068/LS-DTS.

$$S_{swap} = \begin{cases} \{(u,v) | u \in C, v \notin C, \{u,v\} \notin E, v \in N(w) \text{ for all } w \in C\backslash\{u\}\} & \text{if } |C| > 1; \\ \emptyset, \text{otherwise}, \end{cases}$$

(3)

These definitions have a nice property as below, which make them desirable in solving large sparse graphs.

Proposition 1. $|S_{add}| \leq d_{\max}$, and $|S_{swap}| \leq 2d_{\max}$.

In large sparse graphs d_{max} is always small, so this proposition shows that S_{add} and S_{swap} are always small. Therefore the complexity of best-picking over these two sets are guaranteed to be low.

2.2   Scoring Function

Let S be a set of vertices[3], then we define $w(S)$ as

$$\sum_{v_i, v_j \in S \text{ and } \{v_i, v_j\} \in E} w(\{v_i, v_j\}).$$

(4)

We use $score(v, S)$ to denote the increase of $w(S)$ when v is added into or dropped from S as below

$$score(v, S) = \begin{cases} w(S \cup \{v\}) - w(S) & \text{if } v \notin S; \\ w(S\backslash\{v\}) - w(S) & \text{if } v \in S. \end{cases}$$

(5)

Then we use $score(u, v, S)$ to denote the increase of $w(S)$ when u and v are swapped, that is,

$$score(u, v, S) = w(S\backslash\{u\} \cup \{v\}) - w(S),$$

(6)

where $u \in S$, $v \notin S$ and $\{u, v\} \notin E$.

Notice that the score values may be negative. In our solver we will use the score value to measure the benefits of a local move. For efficiency, we maintain the score values of adding and dropping with the proposition below.

Proposition 2.

1. $score(u, \emptyset) = 0$ for all $u \in V$;
2. $score(v, S\backslash\{w\}) = score(v, S) + w(\{v, w\})$ for all $v \in (N(w) \cap S)$;
3. $score(v, S \cup \{w\}) = score(v, S) - w(\{v, w\})$ for all $v \in (N(w) \cap S)$;
4. $score(v, S\backslash\{w\}) = score(v, S) - w(\{v, w\})$ for all $v \in (N(w)\backslash S)$;
5. $score(v, S \cup \{w\}) = score(v, S) + w(\{v, w\})$ for all $v \in (N(w)\backslash S)$.

Then we compute the score of swapping with the proposition below.

Proposition 3. $score(u, v, S) = score(u, S) + score(v, S)$.

A vertex has two possible states: inside and outside the candidate solution. We use $age(v)$ to denote the number of steps since last time v changed its state.

---

[3] S does not need to be a clique.

2.3   The Strong Configuration Checking Strategy

Recently, [5] proposed a strategy called configuration checking (CC), which exploits the problem structure to reduce cycling in local search. Roughly speaking, for combinatorial problems whose tasks are to find an optimal set of elements, the idea of CC can be described as follows. For an element (such as a vertex), if its local environment remains the same as the last time it was removed out of the candidate set, then it is forbidden to be added back into the candidate set. Typically, the local environment of a vertex refers to the state of its neighboring vertices.

The CC strategy is usually implemented with an array named $confChange$, where $confChange(v) = 1$ means v's local environment has changed since last time it was removed, and $confChange(v) = 0$ otherwise.

Later [20] modified CC into a more restrictive version, which is called Strong Configuration Checking (SCC), to deal with the MVWC problem. The main idea of the SCC strategy is as follows: after a vertex v is dropped from or swapped from C, it can be added back into C only if one of its neighbors is added into C. More specifically the SCC strategy is specified as the following rules.

1. Initially $confChange(v)$ is set to 1 for each vertex v;
2. When v is added, $confChange(n)$ is set to 1 for all $n \in N(v)$;
3. When v is dropped, $confChange(v)$ is set to 0;
4. When $(u, v) \in S_{swap}$ are swapped, $confChange(u)$ is set to 0.

3   DTS for Selecting Edges

Usually the edge weights can vary considerably among each other, so if an edge has a great weight, it is likely to be contained in a good clique. By selecting such an edge, we give higher priority to visit a clique containing it. This provides a promising starting point for the later local search procedure.

In this work we proposed a strategy which is specialized for edge weights. It is based on the well-known deterministic tournament selection which is widely used in genetic algorithms [16]. Given a set S and a positive integer k, the DTS heuristic works as follows: *randomly select k elements from S with replacements and then return the best one.*

We formalize the DTS for selecting edges in Algorithm 1 as below.

The DTS heuristic has some advantages: (1) it is greedy because it approximates the best-picking heuristic well; (2) it provides some diversification in that it chooses an element among some very good ones; (3) the greediness and the randomness can easily be controlled by a parameter.

Actually the parameter k controls the greediness, *i.e.*, a greater k means more greediness while a smaller k means less greediness.

Algorithm 1. DTS

---

    input : an edge set E, a positive integer k
    output: a vertex v

1 $S \leftarrow \emptyset$;
2 $e^* \leftarrow$ a random edge from E;
3 **for** $iteration \leftarrow 2$ **to** k **do**
4     $e \leftarrow$ a random edge from E;
5   **if** $w(e) > w(e^*)$ **then** $e^* \leftarrow e$;;
6 $v \leftarrow$ a random vertex in e^*;
7 **return** v;

---

4 The LS-DTS Algorithm

The top level algorithm of LS-DTS is shown in Algorithm 2, where the `localMove()` procedure is shown in Algorithm 3. For simplicity, in Algorithm 3 we write $score(v)$ in short for $score(v, C)$, and $score(u, v)$ in short for $score(u, v, C)$.

Algorithm 2. LS-DTS

---

    input : A graph $G = (V, E, w_E)$ and the $cutoff$
    output: The best clique that was found

1 $C \leftarrow \emptyset$; $C^* \leftarrow \emptyset$; $step \leftarrow 1$; $confChange(v) \leftarrow 1$ for all $v \in V$;
2 **while** $elapsed\ time < cutoff$ **do** localMove(); ;
3 **return** C^*;

In each local move, LS-DTS selects a neighboring clique with the greatest weight according to the SCC criterion. Every L steps, the search is restarted.

The details of `localMove()` are shown in Algorithm 3. In Algorithm 3, LS-DTS adopts the multi-neighborhood greedy search from MN/TS [21] which is shown between Line 3 and Line 11. In this greedy search procedure, as LSCC, LS-DTS exploits the Strong Configuration Checking (SCC) strategy [19] in place of the randomized tabu strategy in MN/TS. The SCC strategy, which is a dynamic tabu management strategy, exploits local environment information to determine in which condition a forbidden operation will become allowed.

When C becomes an empty clique in Line 1, LS-DTS starts the local search from a vertex return by DTS(). Furthermore, Line 14 ensures that the search will restart every L steps. Anyway, LS-DTS sets L to be 4,000 just as what MN/TS, LSCC and LMY-GRS do.

Lastly we remind readers that we adopted the data structures in LMY-GRS [8] to implement our solver.

5 Experimental Evaluation

In this section, we carry out extensive experiments to evaluate LS-DTS on a wide range of large sparse graphs.

Algorithm 3. LocalMove

1 if $C = \emptyset$ then
2 $\quad \lfloor \; v \leftarrow$ DTS(); add v into C;
3 $v \leftarrow$ a vertex in S_{add} s.t. $confChange(v) = 1$ with the biggest $score(v)$, breaking ties in favor of the oldest one; otherwise $v \leftarrow$ NULL;
4 $(u, u') \leftarrow$ a pair in the S_{swap} s.t. $confChange(u') = 1$ with the biggest $score(u, u')$, breaking ties in favor of the oldest u'; otherwise $(u, u') \leftarrow$ (NULL, NULL);
5 if $v \neq NULL$ then
6 $\quad$ if $(u, u') =$ (NULL, NULL) or $score(v) > score(u, u')$ then $C \leftarrow C \cup \{v\}$; ;
7 $\quad \lfloor$ else $C \leftarrow C \backslash \{u\} \cup \{u'\}$;
8 else
9 $\quad v \leftarrow$ a vertex in C with the biggest $score$, breaking ties in favor of the oldest one;
10 $\quad$ if $(u, u') =$ (NULL, NULL) or $score(v) > score(u, u')$ then $C \leftarrow C \backslash \{v\}$; ;
11 $\quad \lfloor$ else $C \leftarrow C \backslash \{u\} \cup \{u'\}$; ;
12 $step \leftarrow step + 1$;
13 if $w(C) > w(C^*)$ then $C^* \leftarrow C$;
14 ;
15 if $step \bmod L = 0$ then
16 $\quad$ drop all vertices in C;
17 $\quad \lfloor$ $step \leftarrow step + 1$;
18 update $confChange$ array according to SCC rules;
19 if $w(C) > w(C^*)$ then $C^* \leftarrow C$;
20 ;

5.1 The Competitors

So far as we know the most prominent local search solver for the MEWC problem is PLS [17] which extends the Phased Local Search algorithm to MEWC. It solves the MVWC and the MEWC problem in very similar ways.

Considering that there has been great progress in MVWC solving, *e.g.*, the multi-neighborhood greedy search and the strong configuration checking strategy, the approach in [17] falls behind. So in this paper, we adapted two recent local search solvers LSCC[4] and LMY-GRS[5] to solve the MEWC problem, since they represent state-of-the-art.

5.2 Experiment Setup

All the solvers in this work were implemented in C++, and compiled by g++ 4.6.3 with the '-O3' option. The experiments were conducted on a cluster equipped with Intel Xeon E5-2670 v3 2.3 GHz with 32 GB RAM, running CentOS6.

For all the solvers the search depth L was set to 4,000. In LSCC+BMS, the BMS parameter k was set to 100 as is in [20]. For LS-DTS, the DTS parameter k was fixed to 50 for all the experiments[6].

Each solver is executed on each instance with a time limit of 1,000 seconds, with seeds from 1 to 10. For each algorithm on each instance, we report the

---

[4] https://github.com/math6068/MEWC-LSCC-BMP.
[5] https://github.com/math6068/LMY-GRS.
[6] Different values of k are only used to test parameter sensitivity, which will be discussed in Sect. 5.5.

maximum edge weight "w_{max}") and averaged edge weight ("w_{avg}") of the cliques found by the algorithm.

5.3   Details of Benchmarks

We downloaded all 139 instances[7], which were originally online[8], and then transformed to DIMACS graph format.

In many of these large graphs there are millions of vertices and dozens of millions of edges. To obtain the corresponding MEWC instances, we use the same method as in [17]. For the edge $\{i, j\}$, $w(\{u, v\}) = ((i + j) \mod 200) + 1$.

The graphs used in our experiments can be divided into 11 classes: biological networks, collaboration networks, facebook networks, interaction networks, infrastructure networks, amazon recommend networks, retweet networks, scientific computation networks, social networks, technological networks, web link networks. There is also a group of temporal reachability networks, where the graphs are small and the algorithms quickly found the same quality solution on all the graphs. Hence, the result in this group is not reported in our experiment.

5.4   Main Results

The main experimental results are shown in Table 1. From this table we find that,

1. LS-DTS significantly outperforms all other solvers in terms of the solution quality.
2. Compared to LMY-GRS, LS-DTS finds better and worse solutions in 11 and 6 graphs respectively.

Since LS-DTS is based on LMY-GRS, we further compare LS-DTS and LMY-GRS in the following.

Time and Step Improvements. For the 85 instances where LS-DTS and LMY-GRS return both the same w_{max} and w_{avg} values, we compare the averaged time, as well as and the number of steps to locate the respective solutions. From Table 2 we observe that:

1. The time columns show that LS-DTS is faster than LMY-GRS on most of these instances.
2. The step columns illustrate that our *heuristic* is more clever than LMY-GRS on most graphs, in that it needs significantly less steps to locate the solutions.

Further observations show that on each graph in Table 2, LS-DTS found the same quality solution in all runs, so as LMY-GRS. This shows that the two solvers are insensitive to seeds over these graphs.

---

[7] http://lcs.ios.ac.cn/~caisw/Resource/realworld%20graphs.tar.gz.
[8] http://networkrepository.com/networks.php.

Table 1. Experimental results on large sparse graphs where the four algorithms find different w_{max} or w_{avg} values. We bold the better values in shaded cells.

Graph	LSCC $w_{max}(w_{avg})$	LSCC+BMS $w_{max}(w_{avg})$	LMY-GRS $w_{max}(w_{avg})$	LS-DTS $w_{max}(w_{avg})$
ca-citeseer	451135(254584.1)	451135(322432.0)	451135(**451135.0**)	451135(**451135.0**)
ca-coauthors-dblp	5661008(5359200.8)	5661008(5109263.7)	5661008(**5661008.0**)	5661008(**5661008.0**)
ca-dblp-2010	276575(221523.5)	276575(206365.0)	276575(**276575.0**)	276575(**276575.0**)
ca-hollywood-2009	245025624(229025126.6)	245095624(**245095624.0**)	245095624(166832908.6)	245095624(226282461.2)
ca-MathSciNet	32364(20300.9)	25393(18195.9)	32364(**32364.0**)	32364(**32364.0**)
inf-roadNet-CA	597(597.0)	597(597.0)	1050(1050.0)	1050(1050.0)
inf-roadNet-PA	993(993.0)	993(993.0)	1164(1164.0)	1164(1164.0)
inf-road-usa	567(567.0)	567(558.0)	1092(1092.0)	1092(1092.0)
rec-amazon	1686(1531.6)	1686(1566.4)	1866(1866.0)	1866(1866.0)
rt-retweet-crawl	4020(4020.0)	8262(6989.4)	8262(**7413.6**)	8262(6989.4)
sc-ldoor	38990(37260.0)	39570(37846.0)	40610(40610.0)	40610(40610.0)
sc-msdoor	39550(38236.0)	39550(38314.0)	40250(40250.0)	40250(40250.0)
sc-nasasrb	51040(50657.6)	51040(50657.6)	51040(51040.0)	51040(51040.0)
sc-pkustk11	77580(69262.0)	77580(73692.0)	77580(**77580.0**)	77580(**77580.0**)
sc-pkustk13	99915(95501.5)	94080(93468.0)	99915(94393.5)	99915(**96825.0**)
sc-pwtk	51888(50281.2)	51888(50522.8)	51888(**51888.0**)	51888(**51888.0**)
sc-shipsec1	45126(33624.7)	45126(36190.1)	45126(**45126.0**)	45126(**45126.0**)
sc-shipsec5	48576(47223.6)	48576(47335.4)	48576(**48576.0**)	48576(**48576.0**)
soc-digg	123757(94136.7)	123757(102589.9)	123757(111055.5)	123757(**115291.4**)
soc-flixster	47685(**47685.0**)	47685(**47685.0**)	47685(47677.0)	47685(47640.0)
soc-FourSquare	45982(**45982.0**)	45982(**45982.0**)	45982(43121.2)	45982(43539.8)
soc-gowalla	30226(**24149.2**)	22630(22630.0)	22630(22590.0)	30226(23389.6)
soc-lastfm	11266(10412.7)	10047(10047.0)	11266(**10887.3**)	11266(10656.5)
soc-livejournal	81460(28406.8)	81460(32161.4)	2289993(1222371.1)	2289993(**1958073.9**)
soc-orkut	96682(45829.9)	74911(46446.7)	72188(50334.5)	96682(**55740.6**)
soc-pokec	25603(17587.3)	19959(17794.4)	38202(25734.1)	30121(24361.6)
socfb-A-anon	25615(20483.1)	32532(20994.7)	32532(28129.3)	32532(28129.3)
socfb-B-anon	22441(18330.7)	22441(18198.5)	28384(23161.7)	28384(23308.6)
socfb-MIT	54696(**54696.0**)	54696(**54696.0**)	54696(54677.6)	54696(**54696.0**)
socfb-Penn94	93079(**93079.0**)	93079(**93079.0**)	93079(92045.1)	93079(**93079.0**)
socfb-Stanford3	131675(**131675.0**)	131675(**131675.0**)	131675(**131675.0**)	131675(131665.0)
socfb-UF	149419(149419.0)	149419(149419.0)	149419(148600.5)	149419(149419.0)
tech-as-skitter	179915(158512.6)	179915(162907.7)	179915(166687.1)	179915(166687.1)
tech-p2p-gnutella	903(886.5)	903(888.9)	903(903.0)	903(903.0)
web-it-2004	8035767(4233906.9)	9282115(5332859.0)	9308691(9308691.0)	9308691(9308691.0)
web-sk-2005	401124(339784.8)	401124(390852.0)	401124(401124.0)	401124(401124.0)
web-uk-2005	12572200(12559868.4)	12572200(12146305.8)	12572200(12572200.0)	12572200(12572200.0)
web-wikipedia2009	46785(29626.8)	46785(32679.2)	46832(46832.0)	46832(46827.3)

The step columns also show the superiority of our strategy, because the number of steps needed to locate a solution only relies on the strategy. It is irrelevant to the running environment, the data structures as well as the programming techniques.

Robustness. From Tables 1 to 2, among all the 11 classes of graphs,

1. LS-DTS is superior in 7 classes.
2. LMY-GRS is better in 4 classes.

So LS-DTS is more robust than LMY-GRS.

5.5 Parameter Sensitivity

We tested LS-DTS with two different parameter setting for k, *i.e.*, $k = 20$ and $k = 80$. The results are shown in Table 3. We use #win(w_{max}) to denote number

Table 2. Comparative performances on the instances where LMY-GRS and LS-DTS return the same w_{max} and w_{avg} values. We bold the better values in shaded cells.

Graph	time		#step	
	LMY-GRS	LS-DTS	LMY-GRS	LS-DTS
bio-celegans	0.336	0.167	17620.4	8820.5
bio-diseasome	<0.001	<0.001	97.1	94.1
bio-dmela	0.039	0.043	1974.5	2140.1
bio-yeast	<0.001	<0.001	626.5	617
ca-AstroPh	28.262	20.192	404137	347673
ca-citeseer	46.753	4.566	3255350	321791
ca-coauthors-dblp	115.205	75.297	663396	316425
ca-CondMat	9.737	10.588	593689	652068
ca-CSphd	0.001	0.002	1737.4	1760.7
ca-dblp-2010	16.256	5.151	810286	285328
ca-dblp-2012	5.899	2.848	258712	118697
ca-Erdos992	0.001	0.003	108.6	83.6
ca-GrQc	0.01	0.009	1364.8	2545.2
ca-HepPh	0.258	0.139	5611.6	1554
ca-MathSciNet	201.822	201.919	11162200	7602890
ca-netscience	0.036	0.023	30856.3	18025.8
ia-email-EU	0.115	0.119	957.6	587.7
ia-email-univ	0.005	0.002	500.5	484.6
ia-enron-large	24.663	30.129	47745.9	53325.3
ia-enron-only	0.028	0.030	7216.7	8418.7
ia-fb-messages	0.008	0.006	106.3	116
ia-infect-dublin	0.080	0.024	13278.9	3689.5
ia-infect-hyper	0.118	0.208	10035.8	19232
ia-reality	0.005	0.005	274.6	223.2
ia-wiki-Talk	0.729	1.442	1084.9	1406
inf-power	0.010	0.004	2267.5	2035.8
inf-roadNet-CA	3.939	6.724	1912020	2810280
inf-roadNet-PA	1.244	1.234	536135	525639
inf-road-usa	92.853	39.837	26994100	11596300
rec-amazon	0.075	0.111	38215.2	60678.7
rt-retweet	<0.001	<0.001	83.6	121.5
rt-twitter-copen	<0.001	<0.001	74.4	72.8
sc-msdoor	261.813	252.347	31414800	28946000
sc-nasasrb	7.633	8.643	808128	972502
sc-pkustk11	140.514	83.618	10601300	5037680
sc-pwtk	55.054	36.550	5729330	4299690
sc-shipsec1	20.841	17.613	2784070	1876090
sc-shipsec5	78.511	18.981	11293200	2702440
soc-BlogCatalog	120.191	205.804	7770.2	14141.4
soc-brightkite	394.281	143.673	1729650	600864
soc-buzznet	50.438	171.688	3340.5	10203.8
soc-delicious	25.520	35.564	28990.5	38567
soc-dolphins	<0.001	<0.001	19.1	16.5
soc-douban	0.339	0.198	5645.7	2261.5
soc-epinions	53.221	27.777	479236	259627
soc-flickr	55.894	16.425	22618.9	4291.7
soc-karate	<0.001	<0.001	15.6	8.3
soc-LiveMocha	0.381	0.360	198.8	205.5
soc-slashdot	0.277	0.294	529.6	900.4
soc-twitter-follows	5.489	5.323	17262.5	18688.1
soc-wiki-Vote	<0.001	<0.001	105.7	121
soc-youtube	11.455	7.652	5293.5	3680.2
soc-youtube-snap	84.058	132.746	8979.9	12976.7
socfb-A-anon	453.944	347.777	461488	325436
socfb-Berkeley13	189.775	135.750	373326	276905
socfb-CMU	21.011	16.014	69727.4	51317.4
socfb-Duke14	13.409	16.866	38746.7	37527.9
socfb-Indiana	73.643	63.928	235903	149565
socfb-OR	48.231	45.355	207749	223313
socfb-Texas84	116.618	176.882	186177	244536
socfb-uci-uni	86.270	163.999	66388.8	136236
socfb-UCLA	114.036	78.595	337721	209763
socfb-UConn	28.706	15.912	127718	76159.6
socfb-UCSB37	57.321	57.451	266970	183756
socfb-UIllinois	153.354	147.381	554564	455851
socfb-Wisconsin87	96.978	73.474	395674	214891
tech-as-caida2007	0.032	0.040	38.6	47.5
tech-as-skitter	265.709	124.921	52609.7	19752.8
tech-internet-as	0.973	0.393	2436.3	1234.8
tech-p2p-gnutella	0.122	0.102	14829.6	12201.8
tech-RL-caida	3.770	3.461	24900.2	25023.5
tech-routers-rf	0.092	0.071	6860.2	5683.9
tech-WHOIS	2.169	0.962	14634.5	7375.6
web-arabic-2005	0.243	0.179	11523.7	18335.8
web-BerkStan	0.005	0.005	1171.6	1687.4
web-edu	0.050	0.018	3550.7	1119.5
web-google	0.001	0.001	931.1	1307.2
web-indochina-2004	0.130	0.020	9037	1054.3
web-it-2004	12.030	4.754	304937	69621
web-polblogs	<0.001	<0.001	139.9	131.5
web-sk-2005	5.825	0.580	1096210	157384
web-spam	72.264	32.147	776421	328820
web-uk-2005	4.455	2.880	155745	72339.4
web-webbase-2001	7.702	1.248	61332.5	8160
web-wikipedia2009	361.855	362.694	1365900	1174920

of graphs where the new setting finds better w_{max} than the defaulting setting (k=50). Similarly we use #lose(w_{max}), #win(w_{avg}), #lose(w_{avg}) and #draw.

From Table 3 we find that the two variants perform very close to the default solver. That is, our solver is insensitive to the parameter k.

Table 3. Experimental results on different values of k in DTS, compare to the performances when k is set to 50

k	#win(w_{max})	#lose(w_{max})	#win(w_{avg})	#lose(w_{avg})	#draw
20	0	0	7	8	87
80	0	1	6	7	88

6 Conclusions

In this work, we proposed a new algorithm named LS-DTS for the MEWC problem on large sparse graphs. Also we adapted two recent local search solvers LSCC and LMY-GRS to solve the MEWC problem. Experiments on a broad range of large sparse graphs demonstrate the effectiveness of LS-DTS.

As for future works we would like to design more efficient heuristics for the MEWC problem on large sparse graphs and exploit our solver to tackle industrial graphs.

Acknowledgments. This work is supported by ARC Grant No. FT0991785, NSF Grant No. 61463044, NSFC Grant No. 61572234, Grant No. [2014]7421 from the Joint Fund of the NSF of Guizhou province of China.

This research was supported by use of the NeCTAR Research Cloud and by QCIF(http://www.qcif.edu.au). The NeCTAR Research Cloud is a collaborative Australian research platform supported by the National Collaborative Research Infrastructure Strategy.

References

1. Adamczewski, K., Suh, Y., Lee, K.M.: Discrete tabu search for graph matching. In: 2015 IEEE International Conference on Computer Vision, ICCV 2015, Santiago, Chile, 7–13 December 2015, pp. 109–117 (2015)
2. Adluru, N., Yang, X., Latecki, L.J.: Sequential monte carlo for maximum weight subgraphs with application to solving image jigsaw puzzles. Int. J. Comput. Vis. **112**(3), 319–341 (2015)
3. Alidaee, B., Glover, F., Kochenberger, G., Wang, H.: Solving the maximum edge weight clique problem via unconstrained quadratic programming. Eur. J. Oper. Res. **181**(2), 592–597 (2007)
4. Cai, S., Lin, J.: Fast solving maximum weight clique problem in massive graphs. In: Proceedings of 25th International Joint Conference on Artificial Intelligence, IJCAI 2016, New York, NY, USA, 9–15 July 2016, pp. 568–574 (2016)

5. Cai, S., Su, K., Sattar, A.: Local search with edge weighting and configuration checking heuristics for minimum vertex cover. Artif. Intell. **175**(9–10), 1672–1696 (2011)

6. Czajkowska, J., Feinen, C., Grzegorzek, M., Raspe, M., Wickenhöfer, R.: Skeleton graph matching vs. maximum weight cliques aorta registration techniques. Comput. Med. Imaging Graph. Part 2 **46**, 142–152 (2015). Information Technologies in Biomedicine

7. Deng, Z., Todorovic, S., Latecki, L.J.: Unsupervised object region proposals for RGB-D indoor scenes. Comput. Vis. Image Underst. **154**, 127–136 (2017)

8. Fan, Y., Li, C., Ma, Z., Wen, L., Sattar, A., Su, K.: Local search for maximum vertex weight clique on large sparse graphs with efficient data structures. In: Kang, B.H., Bai, Q. (eds.) AI 2016. LNCS (LNAI), vol. 9992, pp. 255–267. Springer, Cham (2016). doi:10.1007/978-3-319-50127-7_21

9. Fang, Z., Li, C., Qiao, K., Feng, X., Xu, K.: Solving maximum weight clique using maximum satisfiability reasoning. In: ECAI 2014–21st European Conference on Artificial Intelligence, 18–22 August 2014, Prague, Czech Republic - Including Prestigious Applications of Intelligent Systems (PAIS 2014), pp. 303–308 (2014)

10. Fang, Z., Li, C., Xu, K.: An exact algorithm based on maxsat reasoning for the maximum weight clique problem. J. Artif. Intell. Res. (JAIR) **55**, 799–833 (2016). http://dx.doi.org/10.1613/jair.4953

11. Feige, U.: Approximating maximum clique by removing subgraphs. SIAM J. Discret. Math. **18**(2), 219–225 (2004)

12. Gouveia, L., Martins, P.: Solving the maximum edge-weight clique problem in sparse graphs with compact formulations. EURO J. Comput. Optim. **3**(1), 1–30 (2015)

13. Jiang, H., Li, C., Manyà, F.: An exact algorithm for the maximum weight clique problem in large graphs. In: Proceedings of 31st AAAI Conference on Artificial Intelligence, 4–9 February 2017, San Francisco, California, USA, pp. 830–838 (2017)

14. Ma, T., Latecki, L.J.: Maximum weight cliques with mutex constraints for video object segmentation. In: 2012 IEEE Conference on Computer Vision and Pattern Recognition, Providence, RI, USA, 16–21 June 2012, pp. 670–677 (2012)

15. Mascia, F., Cilia, E., Brunato, M., Passerini, A.: Predicting structural and functional sites in proteins by searching for maximum-weight cliques. In: Proceedings of 24th AAAI Conference on Artificial Intelligence, AAAI 2010, 11–15 July 2010, Atlanta, Georgia, USA (2010)

16. Miller, B.L., Goldberg, D.E.: Genetic algorithms, tournament selection, and the effects of noise. Complex Syst. **9**(3), 193–212 (1995)

17. Pullan, W.J.: Approximating the maximum vertex/edge weighted clique using local search. J. Heuristics **14**(2), 117–134 (2008)

18. Traud, A.L., Mucha, P.J., Porter, M.A.: Social structure of facebook networks. Phys. A: Stat. Mech. Appl. **391**(16), 4165–4180 (2012)

19. Wang, C., Jonckheere, E., Brun, T.: Differential geometric treewidth estimation in adiabatic quantum computation. Quantum Inf. Process. **15**(10), 3951–3966 (2016)

20. Wang, Y., Cai, S., Yin, M.: Two efficient local search algorithms for maximum weight clique problem. In: Proceedings of 30th AAAI Conference on Artificial Intelligence, 12–17 February 2016, Phoenix, Arizona, USA, pp. 805–811 (2016)

21. Wu, Q., Hao, J., Glover, F.: Multi-neighborhood tabu search for the maximum weight clique problem. Ann. OR **196**(1), 611–634 (2012). http://dx.doi.org/10.1007/s10479-012-1124-3

Robust Lasso Regression with Student-*t* Residuals

Daniel F. Schmidt$^{(\boxtimes)}$ and Enes Makalic

Centre for Epidemiology and Biostatistics, The University of Melbourne, Carlton,
VIC 3053, Australia
{dschmidt,emakalic}@unimelb.edu.au

Abstract. The lasso, introduced by Robert Tibshirani in 1996, has
become one of the most popular techniques for estimating Gaussian linear regression models. An important reason for this popularity is that
the lasso can simultaneously estimate all regression parameters as well
as select important variables, yielding accurate regression models that
are highly interpretable. This paper derives an efficient procedure for fitting robust linear regression models with the lasso in the case where the
residuals are distributed according to a Student-*t* distribution. In contrast to Gaussian lasso regression, the proposed Student-*t* lasso regression
procedure can be applied to data sets which contain large outlying observations. We demonstrate the utility of our Student-*t* lasso regression by
analysing the Boston housing data set.

Keywords: Lasso · Robust regression · Expectation-maximisation
algorithm

1 Introduction

Despite their apparent simplicity, linear regressions remain an important tool
in statistics, machine learning and signal processing. Given a vector of features
$\mathbf{x}_i \in \mathbb{R}^p$, a linear regression models the corresponding target $y_i \in \mathbb{R}$ by

$$y_i = \beta_0 + \mathbf{x}_i'\boldsymbol{\beta} + \varepsilon_i, \quad i = 1, \ldots, n,$$

where $\beta_0 \in \mathbb{R}$ is an intercept, $\boldsymbol{\beta} \in \mathbb{R}^p$ is a vector of regression parameters relating
the features to the target, and ε_i is an unobserved, random disturbance. It is
common to model the disturbance using a normal distribution with a mean of
zero and an unknown variance, and much of the theory of linear regression is
based on this assumption.

In practice, it is usually the case that one has observed the features $\mathbf{X} = (\mathbf{x}_1, \ldots, \mathbf{x}_n)'$ and targets $\mathbf{y} = (y_1, \ldots, y_n)'$, but does not know the values of
the regression coefficients $\boldsymbol{\beta}$, which must instead be estimated from the data.
The principle of least-squares can be used to provide unbiased estimates of $\boldsymbol{\beta}$;
however the resulting coefficient estimates are never exactly zero, even if a feature
is unrelated to the targets. A considerable body of research exists surrounding

© Springer International Publishing AG 2017
W. Peng et al. (Eds.): AI 2017, LNAI 10400, pp. 365–374, 2017.
DOI: 10.1007/978-3-319-63004-5_29

the problem of variable selection; a popular estimator for linear models that can perform variable selection as well as provide estimates for non-zero coefficients is the lasso [10]. The lasso solves the following penalized least-squares problem:

$$\{\hat{\boldsymbol{\beta}}(\gamma), \hat{\beta}_0(\gamma)\} = \arg\min_{\boldsymbol{\beta}} \left\{ \|\mathbf{y} - \mathbf{X}\boldsymbol{\beta} - \beta_0 \mathbf{1}_n\|_2^2 + \gamma \sum_{j=1}^{p} |\beta_j| \right\}, \qquad (1)$$

where $\mathbf{1}_n$ is a column vector of n ones and $\gamma \geq 0$ is a regularisation parameter that controls the sparsity of the solution, i.e., the number of coefficients estimated to be exactly zero. Despite its popularity, the sum-of-squared residuals used by the regular lasso implicitly assumes that the errors (approximately) follow a normal distribution. If the data contains large outlying values, either because certain observations are anomalous, or because of gross errors in the recorded data, the estimates produced by the regular lasso can degrade dramatically. To counter this problem, a number of researchers have combined robust regression techniques, such as quantile regression and Huber estimation, with lasso-style estimators [3,5]. In this paper we instead examine an alternative approach to handling large deviations by treating the errors ε_i as arising from the Student-t distribution which possesses tails heavier than the Gaussian distribution.

1.1 Regression with t-Distributed Errors

A random variable $y_i \sim t_\nu(\mu, \sigma^2)$ is said to follow a Student-t distribution with degrees-of-freedom ν if its probability density is given by

$$p_\nu(y_i \mid \mu, \sigma^2) = \left(\frac{1}{\pi\nu\sigma^2} \right)^{\frac{1}{2}} \left(\frac{\Gamma([\nu+1]/2)}{\Gamma(\nu/2)} \right) \left(1 + \frac{(y_i - \mu)^2}{\nu\sigma^2} \right)^{-\left(\frac{\nu+1}{2}\right)},$$

where μ is a location parameter and σ^2 is a scale parameter. The t-distribution can model data with large outlying values much more effectively than the usual Gaussian distribution, with the value of ν determining the heaviness of the tails of the distribution. For $\nu > 1$, the mean of the distribution is given by μ, and for $\nu > 2$ the variance of the distribution is given by $\sigma^2\nu/(\nu - 2)$; important special cases of ν are $\nu = 1$, which yields the Cauchy distribution, and $\nu = \infty$ which reduces to the usual Gaussian distribution. Fitting a regression model with t-distributed errors using maximum likelihood can be efficiently performed using the expectation-maximisation (EM) algorithm [4].

Surprisingly, there has been little work examining the t-distribution within a lasso framework. Some work has discussed the use of t-distributions in conjunction with the Bayesian lasso (see, for example, [12]), but these are sampling based approaches that do not yield sparse point estimates. A recent paper [2] proposed to estimate graphical models using a multivariate t-likelihood with a lasso-type penalty. Their proposal used the expectation-maximisation (EM) algorithm in conjunction with a coordinate-wise descent algorithm to find the lasso estimates. In contrast, in this paper we use a Bayesian interpretation of the lasso estimates as the posterior mode of a linear regression model with a double-exponential prior distribution over the coefficients β, which we call the t-lasso. This allows us to efficiently solve for the lasso estimates using the expectation-maximisation algorithm [8]. We express the t-lasso by the following Bayesian hierarchy:

$$y_i \,|\, \beta, \beta_0, \sigma^2, \mathbf{x}_i \sim t_\nu(\mathbf{x}_i'\beta + \beta_0, \sigma^2), \qquad i = 1, \ldots, n, \tag{2}$$

$$\beta_j \,|\, \sigma^2, \tau \sim \mathrm{La}(0, 2^{-1/2}\sigma\tau), \qquad j = 1, \ldots, p, \tag{3}$$

$$\beta_0 \sim d\beta_0$$

where $\mathrm{La}(a,b)$ denotes the Laplace distribution with mean a and scale b. The t-lasso is defined as the posterior mode of the hierarchy (2), (3), which can be found by solving

$$\{\hat{\beta}(\tau), \beta_0(\tau)\} = \underset{\beta, \beta_0}{\arg\min} \left\{ -\log p_\nu(\mathbf{y} \,|\, \beta, \beta_0, \sigma^2, \mathbf{X}) + \left(\frac{2}{\tau^2\sigma^2}\right)^{\frac{1}{2}} \sum_{j=1}^{p} |\beta_j| \right\}, \tag{4}$$

where

$$p_\nu(\mathbf{y} \,|\, \beta, \beta_0, \sigma^2, \mathbf{X}) = \prod_{i=1}^{n} p_\nu(y_i \,|\, \mathbf{x}_i'\beta + \beta_0, \sigma^2)$$

is the likelihood function, and hyperparameter τ plays the role of the regularisation parameter γ in the case of the regular lasso, and controls the degree of sparsity of the estimates $\hat{\beta}(\tau)$. In contrast to posterior mean or median estimates obtained by sampling from the posterior distribution of β, maximisation of the posterior distribution can produce sparse estimates. A crucial difference between our t-lasso and the one proposed by Finegold and Drton [2] is that we explicitly condition our lasso penalty on the noise scale parameter σ^2; in the case of the standard Gaussian lasso regression failing to condition the penalty on σ^2 when the objective function is a penalised likelihood, rather than simply a penalised sum of squared residuals, leads to potential problems involving multiple minima in the objective function [7].

2 Finding t-Lasso Estimates Using the EM Algorithm

In our Bayesian lasso hierarchy, the residuals and the regression parameters are modelled using the Student-t and double exponential distributions respectively. Both of these distributions can be represented as exchangable Gaussian variance mixture distributions [11] by introducing appropriate latent variables, which allows us to use expectation-maximisation to efficiently find the posterior mode [8]. Using the scale-mixture representations of the t and Laplace distributions from [4,7] we can rewrite the hierarchy (2), (3) as

$$y_i \,|\, u_i \sim N(\mathbf{x}_i'\beta + \beta_0, \sigma^2/u_i^2), \qquad u_i^2 \sim \chi_\nu^2/\nu, \tag{5}$$

$$\beta_j \,|\, \lambda_j^2 \sim N(0, \lambda_j^2\tau^2\sigma^2), \qquad \lambda_j^2 \sim \mathrm{Exp}(1), \tag{6}$$

where χ_ν^2 denotes a chi-squared random variate with k degrees of freedom, $\mathrm{Exp}(1)$ denotes a standard exponential distribution and $u_1^2, \ldots, u_n^2$ and $\lambda_1^2, \ldots, \lambda_p^2$ are latent variables.

We note that conditional on the latent variables u_i^2 and λ_j^2, the posterior distribution of β and β_0 using the hierarchy (5), (6) is Gaussian, for which maximisation is straightforward. Further, conditional on u_i^2 and λ_j^2, the distribution of the data and the prior distributions of the regression coefficients are conjugate. Maximisation of this conditional posterior distribution with respect to β is therefore equivalent to maximising the likelihood of an appropriately augmented data set. The augmented targets are $\tilde{\mathbf{y}} = (\mathbf{y}', \mathbf{0}_p')'$, and the augmented $\mathbf{X}$ matrix is given by

$$\tilde{\mathbf{X}} = \begin{pmatrix} \mathbf{X} & \mathbf{1}_n \\ \mathbf{I}_p & \mathbf{0}_p \end{pmatrix},$$

where $\mathbf{0}_p$ denotes a column vector of p zeros and $\mathbf{I}_n$ denotes the $n \times n$ identity matrix. This formulation is also convenient as it combines β and β_0 into a single parameter vector $\tilde{\beta}$. Let $\tilde{\theta} = (\tilde{\beta}, \tilde{\sigma}^2)$ denote the parameters of this alternative likelihood. The equivalent "complete data" likelihood, conditional on the latent variables u_i^2 and λ_j^2, up to terms independent of $\tilde{\theta}$ is

$$\left(\frac{n+p}{2}\right) \log(\tilde{\sigma}^2) + \left(\frac{1}{2\tilde{\sigma}^2}\right) \left[\sum_{i=1}^n u_i^2 (y_i - \tilde{\mathbf{x}}_i \tilde{\beta})^2 + \left(\frac{1}{\tau^2}\right) \sum_{j=1}^p \frac{\tilde{\beta}_j^2}{\lambda_j^2} \right]. \tag{7}$$

Conditional on the latent variables, maximisation of (7) with respect to β is a straightforward weighted least squares problem. However, the values of the latent variables are unknown, so the expectation-maximisation algorithm replaces them with their conditional expectations. All the latent variables are conditionally independent, given $\tilde{\beta}$, $\tilde{\beta}_0$ and $\tilde{\sigma}^2$, and the conditional expectations are given by [4,7]

$$\mathbb{E}\left[u_i^2 \mid \tilde{\theta}\right] = w_i(\tilde{\theta}) = \frac{\nu + 1}{\nu + (\tilde{y}_i - \tilde{\mathbf{x}}_i' \tilde{\beta})^2 / \tilde{\sigma}^2}, \qquad i = 1, \ldots, n,$$

$$\left(\frac{1}{\tau^2}\right) \mathbb{E}\left[\lambda_j^{-2} \mid \tilde{\theta}\right] = w_{n+j}(\tilde{\theta}) = \left(\frac{2\tilde{\sigma}^2}{\tau^2 \tilde{\beta}_j^2}\right)^{\frac{1}{2}}. \qquad j = 1, \ldots, p.$$

Let $\tilde{\theta}_{(t)} = (\tilde{\beta}_{(t)}, \tilde{\sigma}_{(t)}^2)$ denote the parameters at iteration t, with some suitable starting values chosen for $t = 1$. The expectation-maximisation algorithm for solving (4) involves iterating the following steps:

$$\mathbf{W}_{(t)} \leftarrow \mathrm{diag}(w_1(\tilde{\theta}_{(t)}), \ldots, w_{n+p}(\tilde{\theta}_{(t)})), \tag{8}$$

$$\tilde{\beta}_{(t+1)} \leftarrow \left(\tilde{\mathbf{X}}' \mathbf{W}_{(t)} \tilde{\mathbf{X}}\right)^{-1} \tilde{\mathbf{X}}' \mathbf{W}_{(t)} \tilde{\mathbf{y}}, \tag{9}$$

$$\tilde{\sigma}_{(t+1)}^2 \leftarrow \left(\frac{1}{n+p}\right) (\tilde{\mathbf{y}} - \tilde{\mathbf{X}} \tilde{\beta}_{(t+1)})' \mathbf{W}_{(t)} (\tilde{\mathbf{y}} - \tilde{\mathbf{X}} \tilde{\beta}_{(t+1)}), \tag{10}$$

until convergence is achieved.

Once the algorithm (8)–(10) has converged to some values of $\tilde{\beta}$ and $\tilde{\sigma}^2$, the lasso estimates for a given regularisation parameter τ are given by

$$\hat{\beta}_j(\tau) = \tilde{\beta}_j, \ j = 1, \ldots, p, \quad \hat{\beta}_0(\tau) = \tilde{\beta}_{p+1}.$$

A quirk of finding the lasso by minimising a negative log-posterior of the form (4) is that the value of the scale parameter $\tilde{\sigma}^2$ produced by the expectation-maximisation algorithm does not maximise the likelihood for the estimates $\hat{\boldsymbol{\beta}}(\tau)$ and $\hat{\beta}_0(\tau)$; instead it maximises the product of the t-likelihood (2) and Laplace prior distributions (3). The regular lasso itself does not provide estimates for σ^2 even in the case of Gaussian noise. To facilitate comparisons between models based on their likelihoods, we do not use $\tilde{\sigma}^2$ as our estimate of the t-distribution scale parameter; instead, we use

$$\hat{\sigma}^2(\tau) = \arg\max_{\sigma^2}\left\{p_\nu(\mathbf{y}\,|\,\sigma^2;\hat{\boldsymbol{\beta}}(\tau),\hat{\beta}_0(\tau),\mathbf{X})\right\},$$

which maximises the likelihood when the regression coefficients are fixed at the t-lasso estimates $\hat{\boldsymbol{\beta}}(\tau)$ and $\hat{\beta}_0(\tau)$.

2.1 Generating Regularisation Paths

The EM algorithm discussed in Sect. 2 gives lasso solutions for the regression coefficients $\hat{\boldsymbol{\beta}}(\tau)$ for a single value of the regularisation parameter τ. By varying τ, the algorithm given by Eqs. (8)–(10) can be used to produce a complete regularisation path for a given data set, from the model in which all the coefficients are zero up to (approximately) the maximum likelihood estimates. In the case of Gaussian lasso regression (1), the minimum and maximum values of the regularisation parameter γ can be obtained in closed form [6].

In the case of our t-lasso regression formulation (4), exact estimates of the minimum and maximum values of the regularisation parameter τ are not easily obtained, as the t-likelihood in the objective function is no longer a simple linear function of the squared residuals. We define the quantity $\tau_{\min}$ as the largest value of τ that leads to the "all zeros" solution $\hat{\boldsymbol{\beta}}(\tau) = \mathbf{0}_p$. For the solution of (4) to be the "all-zeros" solution, the gradient of the objective function evaluated at $\boldsymbol{\beta} = \mathbf{0}_p$ must equal $\mathbf{0}_p$; that is,

$$\mathbf{g} + \left(\frac{2}{\tau^2\sigma^2}\right)^{\frac{1}{2}}\mathbf{v} = \mathbf{0}_p \tag{11}$$

where $v_j \in [-1, 1]$ are sub-derivatives of the absolute value function,

$$\mathbf{g} = -\left(\frac{\nu+1}{\nu\hat{\sigma}^2}\right)\sum_{i=1}^{n}\left[\left(1 + \frac{(y_i - \hat{\beta}_0)^2}{\nu\hat{\sigma}^2}\right)^{-1}(y_i - \hat{\beta}_0)\mathbf{x}_i'\right]$$

is the gradient of the t-regression negative log-likelihood with respect to $\boldsymbol{\beta}$ evaluated at $\boldsymbol{\beta} = \mathbf{0}_p$, and $\hat{\beta}_0$ and $\hat{\sigma}^2$ are the maximum likelihood estimates of β_0 and σ^2, respectively, when $\boldsymbol{\beta} = \mathbf{0}_p$. Solving (11) for τ yields the approximate value

$$\tau_{\min}^2 \approx \frac{2}{\hat{\sigma}^2\,||\mathbf{g}||_\infty^2},$$

where $||\mathbf{g}||_\infty$ denotes the maximum absolute value of the entries of the vector $\mathbf{g}$.

Due to the formulation of the objective function, there is no finite value of τ such that $\hat{\boldsymbol{\beta}}(\tau) = \hat{\boldsymbol{\beta}}_{\mathrm{ML}}$, and in the case that $p \geq n$, the maximum likelihood estimates do not exist. If $p < n$, one can take some sufficiently large value of τ, say $\tau_{\max}$, such that there is little discrepancy between $\hat{\boldsymbol{\beta}}(\tau_{\max})$ and the maximum likelihood estimates. Our implementation uses the heuristic choice

$$\tau_{\max}^2 \approx \frac{2K\,||\hat{\boldsymbol{\beta}}_{\mathrm{ML}}||_1^2}{p^2\hat{\sigma}_{\mathrm{ML}}^2}, \tag{12}$$

where $K > 1$ is a large positive constant, which in our implementation is $K = 100$. The value (12) is obtained by interpreting the penalty function as a negative log-prior distribution for the coefficients $\boldsymbol{\beta}$ and maximising with respect to τ with $\boldsymbol{\beta} = \hat{\boldsymbol{\beta}}_{\mathrm{ML}}$ (see Appendix A); it has the advantage of ensuring that the maximum value adapts to the magnitude of the regression coefficients that would be obtained using maximum likelihood.

Given the minimum and maximum values of the τ, the regularisation path is computed over a logarithmically spaced grid of n_τ values of τ between $\tau_{\min}$ and $\tau_{\max}$; in our implementation, the default choice is $n_\tau = 100$. Values of the negative log-likelihood for $\hat{\boldsymbol{\beta}}(\tau)$ are automatically produced by our implementation and can be used to guide selection of the regularisation parameter τ and the degrees-of-freedom parameter ν.

2.2   Selecting τ and the Degrees-of-freedom ν

In the regular lasso (1), selection of the regularisation parameters is usually performed by minimising either a cross-validation prediction error, or an information criterion such as Akaike's information criterion (AIC) [1] or the Bayesian information criterion (BIC) [9]. The t-lasso also requires a choice of the t-distribution degrees-of-freedom parameter ν, and this can also be selected by cross-validation or an information criteria approach. Generally, the values of τ under consideration are determined by the grid used to produce the regularisation path (see Sect. 2.1). While ν is also a continuous parameter, the nature of the parameter means it is common to examine only a small number of discrete candidates.

To select τ and ν using information criteria we minimise a function of the form

$$\{\hat{\tau}, \hat{\nu}\} = \arg\min_{\tau \in T, \nu \in N} \left\{ -\log p_\nu(\mathbf{y} \mid \hat{\boldsymbol{\beta}}(\tau), \hat{\beta}_0(\tau), \sigma^2(\tau), \mathbf{X}) + \alpha_n ||\hat{\boldsymbol{\beta}}(\tau)||_0 \right\}$$

where T is the grid of n_τ values of τ, N is the set of candidate ν values, $||\boldsymbol{\beta}||_0$ is the number of non-zero elements of the vector $\boldsymbol{\beta}$, and α_n is a suitable penalty term; standard choices are $\alpha_n = 1$ for AIC and $\alpha_n = (1/2)\log n$ for BIC.

Cross-validation works by dividing the data into disjoint training and testing sets, fitting models to the training data and then calculating the prediction errors of the fitted models on the reserved test data. The value of τ which minimises the cross-validation prediction error is then chosen as optimal. The usual prediction error metric used in cross-validation is the mean squared-prediction error. This measure is highly sensitive to the presence of large outlying observations in the testing data, which is exactly the situation we expect when we are using t-regression. In our implementation of t-lasso regression, we choose to minimise the cross-validation estimates of the negative log-likelihood on the testing data. This choice of prediction error explicitly takes into account the heavy tails of the t-distribution and is resistant to large outlying observations when ν is small. For large ν, the negative log-likelihood of the t-distribution is essentially equivalent to the usual mean-squared prediction error. A further advantage of using negative log-likelihood prediction scores is that cross-validation can then also be used to select the degrees-of-freedom ν in addition to the regularisation parameter τ.

3   Real Data Example

We demonstrate the utility of our proposed t-lasso by analysing the Boston housing data set. This data set contains 506 observations ($n = 506$), 13 covariates ($p = 13$) and the target variable is the median value of owner-occupied homes in suburbs of Boston (measured in \$1,000s). Some variables in the data set are strongly positively or negatively correlated; for example, the correlation between the index of accessibility to radial highways and full-value property-tax rate is 0.91 while the correlation between nitric oxides concentration and the weighted distances to five Boston employment centres is -0.77. To estimate the association between the target variable and the 13 covariates, we used Gaussian lasso linear regression and lasso regression with Student-t residuals with degrees-of-freedom $\nu \in \{1, 2, 10, 10000\}$. This set of ν values includes a wide spectrum of distributions ranging from distributions that have light tails (essentially Gaussian for $\nu = 10,000$) to distributions with very heavy tails (Cauchy distribution for $\nu = 1$). An efficient software implementation of our t-lasso, and the scripts required to recreate the analyses in this example are available from the MATLAB Central File Exchange (ID: 63037).

Full regularisation paths for the Gaussian and Student-t regression models where ($\nu = 2$) and ($\nu = 10$) are shown in Fig. 1(a–c). It is clear that the Gaussian regularisation path (Fig. 1(a)) is different from both of the Student-t regression paths for the Boston housing data. In all three regularisation paths, the variable with the largest regression coefficient is nitric oxides concentration (nox). In the Gaussian lasso analysis, the regression coefficient for nox starts at approximately -17 and is shrunk to zero when the penalty parameter $\log \tau^2 \approx -1/2$. In case of the t-lasso for ($\nu = 2$) and ($\nu = 10$), the nox regression coefficients starts at approximately -6.7 and -11.2, and are shrunk to zero at $\log \tau^2 \approx 0$ and $\log \tau^2 \approx -1/2$, respectively. The variable with the second largest regression coefficient is the average number of rooms per dwelling (rm). Interestingly, for the Gaussian lasso path, the regression coefficient for rm starts at around 3.8, and shrinks to zero at $\log \tau^2 \approx -4.5$, while for both t-lasso paths, the rm coefficient is larger, starting at approximately 5.5 and 5.2 for $\nu = 2$ and $\nu = 10$, respectively. When $\nu = 2$, this variable is shrunk more aggressively to zero than when $\nu = 10$.

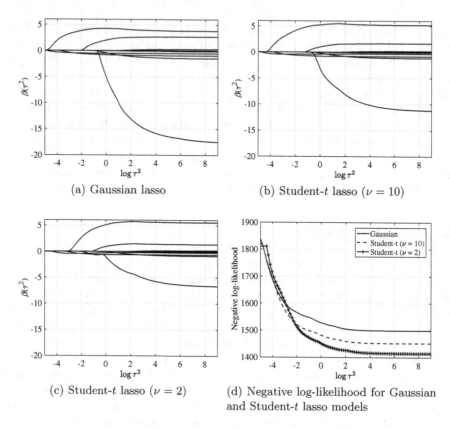

(a) Gaussian lasso

(b) Student-t lasso ($\nu = 10$)

(c) Student-t lasso ($\nu = 2$)

(d) Negative log-likelihood for Gaussian and Student-t lasso models

Fig. 1. Analysis of the Boston housing data using lasso linear regression with Gaussian and Student-t residuals

The negative log-likelihoods for all models in the Gaussian and Student-t regularisation paths are shown in Fig. 1(d). Based solely on the negative log-likelihood, it appears that some form of robust regression, such as the proposed t-lasso regression, is necessary for this data set. The negative log-likelihoods for the two, t-lasso regression models are generally smaller when compared to the negative log-likelihoods of the Gaussian lasso models. To examine this further, we used cross-validation to select one model from each lasso regularisation path as discussed in Sect. 2.2. In the case of Gaussian lasso regression, cross-validation selected a model which included 11 variables with the following two variables omitted: (1) proportion of non-retail business acres per town, and (2) proportion of owner-occupied units built prior to 1940. For Student-t lasso regression, we used cross-validation to select the important variables as well as the estimate of the degrees-of-freedom ν. The model selected by cross-validation for the t-lasso had degrees of freedom $\hat{\nu} = 2$ and included all 13 covariates. The sum of the absolute values of the coefficients was 26.4 and 15.8 for the best Gaussian and $\nu = 2$ model, respectively, which show that the t-lasso has estimated a model with smaller coefficients on average than the Gaussian lasso.

We also conducted a small simulation study to evaluate the predictive performance of the t-lasso and the regular Gaussian lasso on the Boston housing data. We randomly reserved half of the data for training and half for testing, and used cross-validation to select the best Gaussian lasso model, and the best Student-t model, with $\nu \in \{1, 2, 10, 10000\}$ from the training data only. The performance of the selected models was then evaluated by computing the negative log-likelihood of the testing data for both the best t-lasso model and the best Gaussian lasso model. This procedure was repeated one hundred times. In 96 out of the 100 tests, the t-lasso selected $\nu = 2$. The mean negative log-likelihoods attained on the test data were 723.8 and 773.0 for the t-lasso and regular Gaussian lasso respectively, clearly demonstrating the utility of lasso regression with Student-t residuals.

Appendix A

To find an appropriate maximum value $\tau_{\max}$ of τ for producing a regularisation path we use the following heuristic procedure: let $\hat{\beta}_{\mathrm{ML}}$ and $\hat{\sigma}^2_{\mathrm{ML}}$ denote the maximum likelihood estimates for β and σ^2. The negative log-prior probability of the maximum likelihood estimates, under the Laplace prior (3), is given by

$$p\log(\tau) + \left(\frac{\sqrt{2}}{\tau\hat{\sigma}_{\mathrm{ML}}} \right) ||\hat{\beta}_{\mathrm{ML}}||_1 + \mathrm{const},$$

where const denotes terms that do not depend on either τ or $\hat{\beta}_{\mathrm{ML}}$. The value of τ that maximises the prior probability for $\hat{\beta}_{\mathrm{ML}}$ is given by

$$\tilde{\tau} = \frac{\sqrt{2}\,||\hat{\beta}_{\mathrm{ML}}||_1}{p\hat{\sigma}_{\mathrm{ML}}}.$$

We then choose $\tau_{\max} = c\tilde{\tau}$, where $c > 1$ is a constant that controls the distance of the maximum likelihood estimates to the final point on the regularisation path.

References

1. Akaike, H.: A new look at the statistical model identification. IEEE Trans. Autom. Control **19**(6), 716–723 (1974)
2. Finegold, M., Drton, M.: Robust graphical modelling with t-distributions. In: 25th Conference on Uncertainty in Artificial Intelligence (UAI 2009) (2009)
3. Lambert-Lacroix, S.: Robust regression through the Huber's criterion and adaptive lasso penalty. Electron. J. Stat. **5**, 1015–1053 (2011)
4. Lange, K.L., Little, R.J.A., Taylor, J.M.G.: Robust statistical modeling using the t distribution. J. Am. Stat. Assoc. **84**(408), 881–896 (1989)
5. Li, Y., Zhu, J.: l_1-norm quantile regression. J. Comput. Graph. Stat. **17**(1), 1–23 (2008)
6. Osborne, M.R., Presnell, B., Turlach, B.A.: On the LASSO and its dual. J. Comput. Graph. Stat. **9**(2), 319–337 (2000)

7. Park, T., Casella, G.: The Bayesian lasso. J. Am. Stat. Assoc. **103**(482), 681–686 (2008)
8. Polson, N.G., Scott, J.G.: Data augmentation for non-Gaussian regression models using variance-mean mixtures. Biometrika **100**(2), 459–471 (2013)
9. Schwarz, G.: Estimating the dimension of a model. Ann. Stat. **6**(2), 461–464 (1978)
10. Tibshirani, R.: Regression shrinkage and selection via the Lasso. J. Roy. Stat. Soc. (Ser. B) **58**(1), 267–288 (1996)
11. West, M.: On scale mixtures of normal distributions. Biometrika **74**(3), 646–648 (1987)
12. Yi, N., Xu, S.: Bayesian LASSO for quantitative trait loci mapping. Genetics **179**(2), 1045–1055 (2008)

Author Index